D0855920

Marketing
Strategy and Management

The Wiley Series in Marketing

David A. Aaker, Editor

Marketing

Strategy and Management Second Edition

Rom Markin Washington State University, Pullman

1807 1982

John Wiley & Sons New York   Chichester
Brisbane   Toronto   Singapore

Copyedited by Penelope Schmukler
Copyediting Supervised by Deborah Herbert
Production Supervised by Mary E. Halloran
Text and Cover Design by Laura C. Ierardi
Photo Research by Mary Stuart Lang
Photo Editor, Stella Kupferberg
Cover Photograph by Geoffrey Gove

Library of Congress Cataloging in Publication Data:

Markin, Rom J.
Marketing.

(The Wiley series in marketing, ISSN 0273-2955)
Includes bibliographical references and index.
1. Marketing. I. Title. II. Series.

| HF5415.M32385 | 1982 | 658.8 | 81-11463 |
| ISBN 0-471-08522-7 | | | AACR2 |

Printed in the United States of America

10 9 8 7 6 5 4 3 2 1

To Marcia—my last and everlasting duchess

About the Author

Rom J. Markin is Dean of the College of Business and Economics and is a professor of Business Administration in the College of Business and Economics at Washington State University in Pullman, Washington. He has also taught at Indiana University in Bloomington, Indiana and the University of Montana in Missoula, Montana. Dr. Markin has taught graduate and undergraduate courses in general marketing, marketing management, consumer behavior, and retailing management.

A native of Ohio, he received his B.A. degree from Marshall University and his M.B.A. and D.B.A. degrees from Indiana University. He has been a faculty member at WSU since 1961.

Dr. Markin has published extensively in professional and academic journals and frequently contributes papers at meetings of professional and academic societies. His presentations and written articles deal principally with the behavioral implications of marketing, retailing, and consumer behavior. He has also written several books prior to this one. *The Supermarket: An Analysis of Growth, Development and Change; The Psychology of Consumer Behavior; Retailing: Concepts, Institutions and Management; Consumer Behavior: A Cognitive Orientation;* and *Retailing Management.*

Markin is active in several professional organizations including the American Marketing Association and the Association for Consumer Research. He is a member of Beta Gamma Sigma and Phi Kappa Phi and in 1973 was named an Outstanding Educator of America. This awards program honors men and women for their exceptional service, achievements, and leadership in the field of education. Dr Markin is also listed in *Who's Who in the West* and *American Men and Women of Science.*

Preface

This book fuses two essentials in the teaching of college business courses: a stimulating, relevant text and a treatment of subject matter that is consistent with the standards of the professional school of business administration. This second edition emphasizes clarity and ease of understanding and also conveys the sense of excitement and drama that is truly characteristic of marketing today.

We live in a time of change and upheaval. Marketing, because it reflects so vividly the ferment in our economic, political, and cultural environment, is also undergoing many profound changes, and these changes have been woven into the content of this book. The text takes a decidedly managerial stance, but it acknowledges that marketing managers, today and in the years ahead, must be keenly alert to forces such as consumerism, the social responsibilities of business, and social marketing. The emphasis in large measure is on the orthodox structuring of a marketing strategy based on the traditional variables of product planning and development, pricing, channels of distribution, and promotion. However, the discussion also treats in considerable detail new and sometimes disturbing elements—the explosion of international marketing, the growing role and complexity of consumer behavior, the ever-widening need and use of marketing research, and the heightened importance in all endeavors of strategic marketing planning. Two completely new chapters have been added. Most justifiably, an entire chapter is now devoted to market segmentation which, with the chapter on marketing strategy, forms the central planning core of the text. The other chapter deals with the marketing of services, a product category of growing importance and complexity.

The expanded role of marketing in nonprofit organizations is treated extensively in line with their prominent place in modern society. The growing importance of the intensive utilization of energy and its implications for marketing are also highlighted throughout the main body of the text as well as in the concluding chapter. The book covers in depth the major factors, both current and future, that are of concern to contemporary marketers. The discussion is illustrated throughout with numerous real-life examples, problem-related questions, photographs, tables, and graphs, all of which are designed to promote student involvement and learning. Cases at the end of each chapter demonstrate marketing concepts and expose students to managerial problems and issues that demand decision-making skills.

The writing and organization of the text material reflect several deliberate objectives designed to stimulate student interest and readership. For example, descrip-

tive material is broken at several intervals to remind readers of previously stated objectives and to facilitate their attainment. Inserts such as graphics, examples, and incidents from the marketplace are positioned in such a way as to break the reading of straight text material. The book is based on the idea that fun and excitement can be both a part of learning and a means of making learning easier. In this respect, this book is designed, like any good marketing program, "to create a satisfied customer."
To this end, instructors should be aware of these special features:

1. The book is comprehensive and does not sacrifice the treatment of any of the essential topics or concepts of marketing. It accomplishes this with a readable, student-oriented approach in a compact and manageable format.
2. The book is richly illustrated and combines in a single integrated teaching system the latest approaches and techniques for facilitating learning and understanding.
3. The discussion of each chapter is begun with lead-ins and illustrations designed to arouse student interest and to promote readability. The concepts and major issues are vividly demonstrated with examples from the marketing experiences of actual companies and products. Important theoretical concepts are not ignored, but neither is the student given a heavy dose of theory; instead, the ideas are conveyed within a practical context and in a conversational style.
4. The text is part of a comprehensive package, each part of which has been carefully designed and developed to promote the learning and/or teaching of the concepts. A student study guide and instructor's manual are available. Both include a complete package of ideas—projects, self-help examinations, key concepts and terms, chapter summaries and the like—to augment and complement the text materials.
5. The text concludes with an important appendix called *Careers in Marketing: How to Market Your Own Skills.* This appendix details the career paths a person interested in marketing might pursue and, very importantly from the student's perspective, how to locate and land a job.

All of the material in this edition has been thoroughly and critically reviewed as well as extensively class tested. The entire effort has benefited from the comments, reviews, and suggestions of many people.

To the colleagues whose perceptive reviews and helpful suggestions have strengthened and improved the book, I owe special thanks. These include Richard C. Becherer, Wayne State University; Helmut Becker, University of Portland; William Bolen, Georgia Southern College; William Curtis, University of Nebraska; Douglas J. Dalrymple, Indiana University; Donald Dixon, Temple University; E. C. Hackleman, University of Connecticut; Michael D. Hutt, Miami University; Larry A. Johnson, University of Massachusetts; and Mr. Jack R. Kapoor, College of DuPage. The manuscript also benefited from the evaluations of Murray Krieger, Bronx Community College; David Landrum, Central State University, Edmond, Oklahoma; Jerry Olson, Pennsylvania State University; James C. Petersen, California State Polytechnic University; Barbara A. Pletcher, California State University at Sacramento; Ronald Stiff, University of Baltimore; Robert A. Swerdlow, Drake

University; Dharmendra T. Verma, Bentley College; John S. Wright, Georgia State University; Michael d'Amico, University of Akron; James McCullough, University of Arizona; Charles Vanderlip, Menlo College; Al Manduley, Manhattan College; James Maskulka, Gannon College; George Fisk, Syracuse University; William Curtis, University of Nebraska. I extend my sincere thanks to them all.

I am grateful to the Wiley series editor, David Aaker of University of California, Berkeley, for his many helpful suggestions. My deepest debt of gratitude is owed to a former Washington State University colleague, Calvin Duncan, now of the University of Colorado, Boulder, for his generous help in locating materials, numerous suggestions, and unlimited encouragement throughout the project. My thanks also to Chem Narayana of the University of Illinois (Chicago Circle Campus), who assisted me throughout the preparation of the first edition. I am especially grateful for the help of my student assistant, Teresa Bentley, for her activity in coordinating much of the revision effort. Finally, I am grateful to other members of our marketing area group at WSU. Talmadge Anderson (director of the Black Studies Program) and Edna Douglas, Donald Stem, Kenneth Baker, George Hozier, and Kathy Pettit—all are stimulating colleagues who create an atmosphere conducive to professional and personal well-being.

Rom Markin

Contents

Chapter 9   Total Product Strategy   254

Chapter 10   Understanding and Managing Channels of Distribution   286

Chapter 11   Principal Channel Intermediaries: Wholesalers and Retailers   316

Chapter 12   Physical Distribution: Marketing's Other Half   352

Chapter 13   Promotion: Advertising in the Marketing Strategy   381

Chapter 14   Promotion: Personal Selling, Sales Promotion, and Public Relations   415

Chapter 15   Pricing: Basic Considerations   445

Chapter 16   Pricing: Policies and Practices   476

Chapter 17   The Marketing of Services   508

Chapter 1

An Overview of Marketing

A few years ago Charles Lockerby and Scott Dimmick, two Stanford engineering students, after scouting the market for products that were needed but unavailable, devised a small plastic stick with a strip of absorbent material glued to it. Inserted into a potted plant, the strip turns dark green when wet and the word "moist" appears. When the soil dries out, the word fades, telling the indoor gardener that it's time to water the plant again. This simple invention may develop into a million-dollar marketing bonanza.

Moisture Minders sell at three for a dollar. Ortho, a major pesticide manufacturer, has ordered millions of them to market under its own name, Water Reminder. The premium market is also using Lockerby and Dimmick's invention as a giveaway. A business consultant, for example, puts them inside a greeting card with the message, "Don't let your business dry up." One advertisement used to promote Moisture Minders shows a dying plant and asks, "Is your plant a problem drinker?" Lockerby and Dimmick were in their mid-20s when they hit upon the Moisture Minder idea. Actually, what they really hit upon was the conventional notion of marketing—find a need and then fill it!

Contrast the situation of Lockerby and Dimmick, two virtual marketing novices, with that of Polaroid's founder-chairman Edwin Land. Polaroid's 1980 sales volume just missed the magic billion-dollar mark and the firm suffered significant image damage as a result of its ill-fated venture into Polavision in the late 1970s. But in 1980, Polaroid began marketing a faster, brighter film called Time Zero. The film was launched with a national marketing program that included television and newspaper ads in the top 80 markets.

Time Zero was first introduced by Polaroid chief Edwin Land at the company's annual stockholder's meeting in the spring of 1980. The new film offers an image within ten seconds with a full color picture within 90 seconds. Current SX-70 film takes four to five minutes for a finished picture. Land and other Polaroid officials say the new film also produces sharper, brighter colors, through an entirely new chemical method.

What Is Marketing?

Both these stories underscore the importance of marketing. Very often the story of success is the story of marketing. Marketing, in large measure, is finding a need and then filling it successfully by the application of commercial techniques and processes. So, large companies such as Polaroid and unknowns like Lockerby and Dimmick look for market opportunities in order to market products for a profit.

The term "marketing" for most people means a set of business activities. They see marketing as the task of finding and stimulating buyers to consume the firm's output. Most of you could probably identify some of the many marketing activities—product development, pricing, distribution, and communication. And the average person might even recognize that the more progressive firms continuously monitor customers' changing needs and develop new products and services, or modify existing ones, to meet these needs. Even the American Marketing Association accepts this view, defining marketing as "the performance of business activities that directs the flow of goods and services from producer to consumer or user."[1]

An Expanded View of Marketing

Much marketing is carried on by business firms seeking to uncover and stimulate buyer demand in order to sell products for a profit. But to consider marketing only from this point of view is much too limiting.

One of the most striking trends in the United States is the increase in the amount of society's work that is now being performed by organizations other than business firms. More and more nonbusiness organizations are active marketers, seeing that their services are distributed to the people who need them. The United Auto Workers seeks out and organizes industrial workers in need of its bargaining strengths, the Catholic Church strives to reach as many people as possible with its moral and spiritual message, while Washington State University works to attract and hold promising students with its courses of study. Marketing, especially in its more modern and expanded usage, is equally as important in these organizations as it is in such business firms as Procter and Gamble, General Motors, and General Electric. It is certainly true that the art and science of effective marketing management has reached its highest state of development in the business organization, but marketing techniques are now being used throughout a broad spectrum of nonbusiness organizations with great effectiveness.

A Broadened Definition of Marketing

An expanded view of marketing as a set of management activities that can be used by different kinds of organizations calls for an equally expanded definition. A more modern definition of marketing would be *the set of activities by which the demand structure for goods, ideas, and services is managed in order to facilitate the exchange process satisfactorily.* This definition is illustrated in Figure 1-1.

Figure 1-1 The modern marketing process.

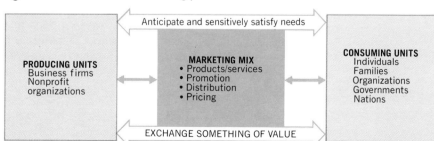

---

[1] American Marketing Association, Committee on Definitions, *Marketing Definitions: A Glossary of Marketing Terms* (Chicago; 1960) p. 15.

The expanded and newer meaning of marketing embraces the idea of sensitively serving and satisfying human needs. From this perspective marketing is a set of activities used by many organizations, both profit and nonprofit. It is used in making products available, but it is also used to provide services as well as to promote the exchange of ideas.

Marketing Is Useful in All Endeavors

Perhaps you can better grasp the notion of the expanded view of marketing by examining Table 1-1.

Table 1-1 consists of four cells,[2] related either to the profit or nonprofit sector, and to a macro or micro level. The profit sector, needless to say, covers organizations or other entities whose stated objectives include the realization of profits; the nonprofit sector covers those whose stated objectives do not include making a profit.

The micro/macro labels describe the level of aggregation. *Micro* refers to the marketing activities of individual units: firms, consumers, or households. *Macro* suggests a higher level of aggregation, usually groups or associations of firms, systems, or consumers.

As we shall see, the exanded view of marketing includes all four cells in the matrix. The more traditional and conservative view of marketing considered only the first cell—marketing by a business firm for profit. In the more modern view, this kind of marketing activity would still be classified in this cell. We would not likely think of a bank, an operator of a private medical clinic, a retirement center, or even a law firm as engaged in marketing. Yet in many respects, in the expanded view of marketing, they are. Consider this example that fits into cell 1-A.

Banking and Modern Marketing

When Thomas R. Wilcox became chief executive officer of the Crocker National Bank, headquartered in San Francisco, his goal was to inject a modern, aggressive marketing orientation into the bank's operations.[3] To achieve this, he reorganized or dismantled most of the bank's internal departments. Two-thirds of the senior executives were replaced by managers strongly geared to marketing. He then had the bank's research department launch a survey of available financial services and consumer demands in his bank's markets. The analysis revealed that the banking service consumers most wanted was free checking accounts, followed by drive-in banking, evening and Saturday banking hours, cash machines, automatic loan arrangements, and free credit cards.

---

[2] Based upon work by Shelby Hunt, "The Nature and Scope of Marketing," *Journal of Marketing* **40** (July 1976), pp. 17–28.

[3] Based on "Crocker's Tom Wilcox: Tough Management for a Stodgy Bank," *Business Week,* August 11, 1975, pp. 38–44.

Table 1-1 The Scope of Marketing

	Micro (A)	Macro (B)
Profit Sector 1	Problems, issues, theories, and research concerning: a. Individual consumer buyer behavior b. How firms determine prices c. How firms determine products d. How firms determine promotion e. How firms determine channels of distribution f. Case studies of marketing practices	Problems, issues, theories, and research concerning: a. Aggregate consumption patterns b. Institutional approach to marketing c. Commodity approach to marketing d. Legal aspects of marketing e. Comparative marketing f. The efficiency of marketing systems g. Whether the poor pay more h. Whether marketing spurs or retards economic development i. Power and conflict relationships in channels of distribution j. Whether marketing functions are universal k. Whether the marketing concept is consistent with consumers' interests
Nonprofit Sector 2	Problems, issues, theories, and research concerning: a. Consumers' purchasing of public goods b. How nonprofit organizations determine prices c. How nonprofit organizations determine products d. How nonprofit organizations determine promotion e. How nonprofit organizations determine channels of distribution f. Case studies of public goods marketing	Problems, issues, theories, and research concerning: a. The institutional framework for public goods b. Whether television advertising influences elections c. Whether public service advertising influences behavior (e.g., "Smokey the Bear") d. Whether existing distribution systems for public goods are efficient e. How public goods are recycled

Source: Adapted from Shelby Hunt, "The Nature and Scope of Marketing," *Journal of Marketing* **40** (July 1976), pp. 17–28.

Crocker's new marketing thrust was soon evident. Interest rates were raised to the legal maximum for passbook savings accounts. The bank stayed open evenings and Saturdays and provided free checking accounts for senior citizens. Cash machines were installed to meet customers' needs for money during nonbanking hours. Two officers were assigned to work solely with corporate clients on investments. Posters of Wilcox, who announced these improved personal services for Crocker customers on local television, were displayed around the bank.

Macro marketing for profit.

LIFE GOT TOUGHER.
WE GOT STRONGER.

Just take a look at those supermarket prices, and you know life seems tougher than ever.

The pressure's on, all right. And it can give you a rotten headache.

But fortunately, there's Extra Strength Excedrin to help fight the pain.

With the two most powerful pain relievers you can buy. And then a third ingredient that may make them both work even harder.

Extra Strength Excedrin.
Nothing you can buy is stronger or works harder on your headache. Absolutely nothing.

Use only as directed. © Bristol-Myers Co. 1981.

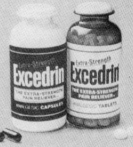

Macro Marketing for Profit

Now consider this application of modern marketing that fits neatly into cell 1-B of Table 1-1. Phil Woosnam is the commissioner of the North American Soccer League. As such, he represents the eighteen teams in the league. Soccer's late success did not come overnight; its promoters have been struggling in the United States for many years. Success has come, however, bringing record crowds and extensive media coverage. This success is directly attributed to a concerted marketing effort to promote the game to fans and sportswriters alike.[4] To popularize the game, members of the North American Soccer League (NASL) realized they would have to make it appeal to a broad audience, not merely to ethnic groups in New York. Each team appointed a marketing director to find out what the fans wanted and then to change their programs accordingly. Soccer players were sent to local high schools to challenge faculty members to volleyball games. Although they did not use their hands in these games, the soccer players usually trounced the teachers. Prizes were offered to fans who correctly guessed how high a soccer ball would bounce after it was dropped from the top of the playing stadium. Fans were urged to have a pregame picnic with their families in the parking lots. The marketing director of each team distributed to all eighteen franchises news of successful promotional ideas—giving free kazoos to fans or printing game schedules on a dry cleaner's garment bags.

To further draw fans, teams charge only $3 to $4 for tickets, on the average, with discounts for children and senior citizens. By contrast, the average National Football League seat costs more than $10.00. Some soccer teams let people in at a flat $10 per carload. Thus, as a result of team cooperation and the marketing effort of the NASL, soccer has become both big business and an increasing source of satisfaction for the lover of spectator sports.

Nonprofit Micro Marketing

Not all firms or organizations using marketing techniques seek to make profits. For example, this illustration belongs in cell 2-A. The Metropolitan Transit Commission (MTC) of Minneapolis–St. Paul, like many public transit systems, is a nonprofit municipal corporation. The fares the transit commission charges are only enough to cover expenses. Often, even these modest goals are not met. Public transportation is offered for the convenience of senior citizens, the poor, and others without cars. It also helps to reduce congestion and pollution. To get car riders to become bus riders, the Metropolitan Transit Commission and its advertising agency, Carmichael-Lynch Advertising, Inc., have hit upon a novel idea: painting buses to look like cars. As part of a new $250,000 marketing drive, MTC has painted a Duesenberg, Volkswagen, and station wagon on the sides of three buses and launched its first local television campaign, promoting the "Greater Metropolitan Car Pool."

---

[4] Based on "The Big Kick Behind Soccer," *Business Week*, September 4, 1977, pp. 94–95.

The campaign marks the second stage of a major marketing effort that began in 1970, when MTC launched a "We're Getting There Program," stressing the addition of new buses, better service, and the general upgrading of what had been a lackluster image. After increasing ridership 13 percent to 15 percent a

Nonprofit micro marketing.

The New York Public Library has been feeding New Yorkers with information and inspiration for over 70 years.

But now it needs help—help to keep its great research libraries open and *free* to everyone.

Surprisingly, the research libraries are not supported by New York City. They rely on contributions from corporations, private citizens, state and federal grants.

With inflation, the cost of everything is way up. Naturally that goes for The Library too. To keep its many services available, it must have your support. Or start cutting back.

If that happens, we'll all be poorer for it.

The New York Public Library is one of the world's great libraries. It can only remain great with your help.

If you give now, the National Endowment for the Humanities will give, too. One dollar for every two you contribute.

For everyone who gives $15.00 or more, we'll mail you a free copy of "Beyond the Lions", a book describing all our services.

Give to The New York Public Library

The New York Public Library

Astor, Lenox and Tilden Foundations

The New York Public Library Box M6
Fifth Avenue & 42nd Street
New York, New York 10018

year since then, says one Carmichael-Lynch staff person, "we felt strong enough to go head on against the main competition—the car."[5]

Nonprofit Macro Marketing

Finally, looking at cell 2-B of the table, consider this last example, which illustrates how marketing techniques are employed by groups of organizations to combat smoking.

There are many groups publicizing the hazards of smoking. GASP (for Group Against Smokers Pollution), ASH (for Action on Smoking and Health), and SHAME (for Society to Humiliate, Aggravate, Mortify and Embarrass Smokers), as well as well-known organizations like the American Cancer Society and the American Heart Association, have had some impressive successes based upon marketing-like campaigns. For example, thirty-one states and scores of cities in the United States have passed laws prohibiting smoking in public places like elevators, hospitals, theaters, and buses. Most of these groups try to persuade smokers to abandon the habit because it is unhealthy. There is widespread support for the cause, but the groups' funds are limited, particularly when measured against the huge advertising resources of the cigarette industry. Basically, the groups' problem is to use their slender funds effectively in persuading smokers and their sympathizers to cut down cigarette consumption. These groups have come up with several ideas for marketing nonsmoking to Americans, including television spots; newspaper, radio and magazine advertising; talk show appearances extolling the virtues of not smoking; books and film-strips showing cancer and heart disease patients; school appearances by medical doctors and other authorities, warning students against smoking; and legal research on company liability for a smoker's loss of health.

What these illustrations all suggest is that modern marketing pervades nearly all organizations. They develop products; promote them; communicate with users; research their markets; distribute, price, and sell their products. The products can be physical like soap or gasoline. Sometimes they are services such as tours, insurance, hair styles, or banking. The "products" marketed are occasionally persons, rock stars, or political candidates. Sometimes it is an organization that is being marketed, the World Hockey League or the American Red Cross. Finally, the product marketed can be an idea. Planned Parenthood is trying to spread the idea of birth control, and the National Council on Automobile Safety markets the idea of safer driving, using seat belts and air bags. So, as you can readily see, the "product" can take many forms, and this is the major reason for broadening the concept of marketing.

Marketers Manage Demand

The broadened definition of marketing given a few pages back describes it as "the set of activities by which the demand structure for goods, ideas and services is managed in order to facilitate the exchange process satisfactorily."

[5] See "Marketing Observer," *Business Week,* January 19, 1974, p. 39.

To manage means to bring about or to take charge of. Today's marketing definition suggests that it is necessary not only to stimulate or increase demand (as in the traditional definition), but also to manage it. The distinction is subtle, but critical. Demand, which reflects consumers' needs and want satisfactions, generates much marketing activity.

Demand problems are one of the major reasons why nonprofit organizations engage in marketing efforts. Colleges are short of students, blood banks must have donors, the Peace Corps and the United States Army need volunteers, and mass transit systems are useless without riders. Of course, most nonprofit organizations also need financial support. Demand problems of organizations vary. Today, profit oriented gas and electric companies have too much demand for the supply they command and therefore are using marketing techniques to manage rather than stimulate demand. They are encouraging users to conserve, to turn down thermostats, and to insulate buildings better.

The Scope of Marketing

Under the expanded notion of marketing, the scope of marketing is unquestionably broad. Often included are such diverse subject areas as consumer behavior, pricing, purchasing, sales management, product management, marketing communications, packaging, channels of distribution, marketing research, social issues in marketing, retailing, wholesaling, international marketing, and physical distribution. The modern marketing approach serves very naturally to describe an important part of all organizational activity. All organizations must develop appropriate products to serve their respective consuming groups and must use modern tools of communication to reach their publics. The business heritage of marketing provides a useful set of concepts as guides.

Marketing Affects Your Life

Marketing may very well be the most significant activity in our society. Your very existence is profoundly affected each day by a wide range of marketing activities. The food you eat, the clothes you wear, the housing that shelters you, and the activities you engage in have all been to some measure affected by marketing activities.

Because it is fundamental in American life, marketing as a discipline should command your careful study and attention. A knowledge of the role and importance of marketing can bring several benefits.

1. *You may choose a career in marketing.* Marketing is an important career opportunity. The study of business is the most widely chosen curriculum major of college and university students in the United States and, within business, marketing is one of the most popular fields. Nearly one out of every three persons employed in this country works in marketing activities. Among the interesting and challenging career paths that may be pursued in marketing are advertising, consumer behavior research, general market research, packaging, transportation, storage, product development, personal

selling, sales management, trade area analysis, wholesaling, and retailing. See Appendix A for a look at marketing careers and how to market yourself.

2. *Regardless of your career field you will likely need to understand marketing.* Most of the other fields within business will require that you work with marketers and understand the marketing process and marketing techniques. Understanding marketing, its institutions, and problems will enable you to do a better job, whether you work in accounting, production, personnel, or operations research. Because of marketing's expanded social role you may also find good use for your marketing skills if you become active in community service organizations.

3. *Marketing can lead to self-improvement.* A knowledge of marketing makes us more informed, better able to cope with the complexities of a dynamic environment. Furthermore, training in this field can improve our performance in one of life's most important roles, namely, as consumers. It can give you a more accurate idea of business firms, consumerism, government regulation, international trade, and even political behavior because much political behavior is rooted in economic and marketing phenomena.

4. *Marketing is a critical part of our economic and cultural heritage.* The major institutions of our society—cultural, political, financial, even religious—base their organization and operation on marketing concepts. Because our culture and economic system are so marketing oriented, one needs to understand the role of marketing in this setting. While rapidly boosting our economy toward the $2 trillion level, marketing contributes to the vitality and stability of the United States and to the welfare of all citizens. Over 12.5 million firms are engaged in marketing activities in the United States. These activities are a potent force in shaping our lives and determining our overall standard of living.

Marketing Costs Money

Marketing activities and the performance of marketing services are not free. As a matter of fact, marketing is often criticized as a wasteful dimension of our culture. Critics of the marketing system will assert that advertising is wasteful, there are too many products and services, style and fashion are overemphasized, and that many products are deliberately designed to become less desirable after a short period of use. This latter practice is often referred to as planned product obsolescence.

To what extent are such criticisms warranted? They have some validity in certain instances, but by and large the overwhelming majority of Americans endorse the system enthusiastically. By their dollar votes, cast in the market place, American consumers reward and reinforce those marketers whose activities generate the goods and services they seek.

The American consumer pays for the performance of marketing services and functions. Slightly more than fifty cents out of each dollar spent by consumers goes to pay for the cost of marketing.

The typical American business firm makes a small percentage of profit on each transaction. Thus, even though marketing costs absorb fifty cents or more out of each dollar the consumer spends, most firms make only a very modest profit after paying the cost of acquiring the merchandise sold and their operating expenses. For example, consider a purchase you might make in a local department store. For each dollar spent:

About $0.60 goes to pay the manufacturer for the goods.
About $0.35 pays for the department store's operating expenses such as wages, heat, light, occupancy costs, and
About $0.05 is left over as profit.

Or suppose you buy your groceries in the local supermarket. For each dollar spent there:

About $0.78 goes to pay manufacturers and suppliers for the goods sold.
About $0.21 pays for operating expenses such as wages, heat, light, occupancy, and
About $0.01 is left over for profit.

Table 1-2 shows the net income as a percentage of sales for the ten largest American retailers for 1979.

Marketing Supports Your Life Style

That total package of goods and services each of us pursues is largely determined by our life styles. Americans, to a great extent are individualists.

Everyone does not like the same thing, nor do we all have the same interests or seek the same goals. There is, in short, a great diversity in the demands

Table 1-2 Net Income as a Percentage of Sales for the Ten Largest U.S. Retailers in 1979

	Percentage	Net Income Rank
Sears Roebuck (Chicago)	4.6	1
Safeway Stores (Oakland)	1.0	8
K-mart (Troy, Michigan)	2.8	2
J. C. Penney (New York)	2.2	3
Kroger (Cincinnati)	0.9	14
Great Atlantic & Pacific Tea Co. (Montvale, N.J.)	N.A.*	49
F. W. Woolworth (New York)	2.7	7
Lucky Stores (Dublin, CA)	1.7	11
Federated Department Stores (Cincinnati)	3.5	4
Montgomery Ward (Chicago)	1.4	18

Source: Fortune, July 14, 1980, pp. 154–55.
*N.A. = not available

made for goods and services and this diversity on the demand side of the consumption equation leads, in turn, to a great diversity on the supply side.

Americans are consumption oriented. We evaluate our economy and market system by how well they fulfill consumers' demands and enable them to pursue their activities. Both the collective and individual life styles of people create the need and desire to consume. For example, the couple who decide to raise a family will be opting for a particular life style that will shape their buying decisions for many years. It costs approximately $90,000 to raise the average baby to adulthood in this country. In round figures, parents spend $3,125 on a child's recreation; $5,000 for medical bills; $8,125 for housing; $8,750 for clothing; $16,250 for food; $17,500 on miscellaneous expenses; and $30,000 on a college education.[6] You can see how and why so many of our expenditures go to pay for marketing activities.

Our life styles, which reflect the sum of our activities, our interests, and our opinions, are supported and fueled by marketing activities.[7] Most of our life styles depend heavily on gratifying our desires through acquiring and using goods.

Leisure—A Spreading Life Style.   As the standard work week shrinks and discretionary income (earnings available for nonessential spending) rises, many of our life styles are geared increasingly to leisure time activities. Tennis, boating, and photography are all growing rapidly in popularity. What are the marketing implications? The answer, in part, is that as we participate more in these activities, they will absorb an increasing proportion of our discretionary income. Personal consumption expenditures for recreation rose from $26.3 billion in 1965 to $95.4 billion in 1980.[8] This increase of nearly $70 billion was spent for children's and adults' toys—motorcycles, boats, televisions, books, games, sporting equipment, and related repair services. People generally want more opportunities for recreation and they are willing to spend more on the necessary gear.

Marketing and Technology

American marketing depends in large measure for its success on our scientific technology. Through science and engineering we devise and produce new products, and American enterprise perceives the possibilities for benefiting consumers with scientific developments and breakthroughs.

Consider, for example, the integrated circuit, which allowed the functional equivalent of 1,000 components and 2,000 transistors to be condensed into

---

[6] Based upon 1980 prices.

[7] For an extended treatment see Douglas K. Hawes, "Leisure and Consumer Behavior," *Journal of The Academy of Marketing Science* **4** (Fall 1979) pp. 391-403.

[8] U.S. Bureau of Economic Analysis, *The National Income and Product Accounts of the United States*, July 1980; and *Survey of Current Business*, July 1980.

Middle America has an outing—leisure is goods oriented.

one silicon chip smaller than a single contact lens. This development was the result of years of research combining electronics, physics, chemistry, and other sciences. The integrated circuit, in turn, has led to a whole series of new first-generation products. Those most familiar to the average consumer are the hand-held digital computer, or calculator, and the digital watch. When such circuits were first produced they cost $20 each to manufacture. Hence, early models of hand-held calculators and digital watches sold for $200 and $500, respectively. Today, because the demand created and stimulated by marketing makes mass production possible, manufacturing costs for some varieties of integrated circuits are as low as five cents each. As a result, the hand-held calculator and the digital watch that formerly only a few could afford can now be purchased by millions of people. Many four-function calculators are today available at $9.95 and digital watches in plastic cases can be had for $6.95.

In many ways, technology and marketing are an example of the chicken-or-the-egg argument. It is difficult to know which comes first. One thing is sure: without marketing to create and then tap markets, many of the benefits of technology would reach only a few. With modern marketing, new products, which are the fruit of technological innovation, can be enjoyed by millions of American consumers.

Marketing's Role in the Exchange Process

Marketing is many things to many people. It is the delivery of a standard of living, an important support of our life styles. It is the buying, promoting, pricing, and selling of products and services. It is moving goods from points of

production to points of consumption. It is storing goods. It is anticipating customer needs and marshalling the resources of organizations to fill those needs. Or to capture all these descriptions of marketing in one definition as we did earlier, marketing is the set of activities by which the demand structure for goods, ideas, and services is managed in order to facilitate the exchange process satisfactorily.

This definition focuses on what marketing is all about. Marketing is a set of human oriented activities purposefully designed to simplify and consummate exchanges. Basically, this means that marketing activities are designed and undertaken to make our lives more comfortable and enjoyable, to help us attain those products and services—from gasoline for our automobiles to a blow-dry hair style—we both need and want in order to achieve the levels of satisfaction promised by our affluent society.

Marketing is an Organized System of Exchange

Another way of underscoring the meaning of marketing is to say that marketing is an organized system of exchange. For example, just imagine trying to buy each of the goods and services you need directly from the profit-oriented individual grower, manufacturer, or supplier who produces it. It would not be easy. To maintain even a modest living standard, you would have to deal with dozens of firms. At your given location, the assortments would likely be limited, and because of the small scale that might be imposed on such direct-selling businesses, prices would probably be high. Marketing institutions such as wholesalers, retailers, advertising agencies, storage and transportation companies, insurance companies, bankers, and others work cooperatively to make it easy for you to obtain a wide variety of goods and services. They collect thousands of different products that they anticipate might match your needs. The cost of gathering, sorting, and taking care of all these products is incorporated into the price of the merchandise, in this way rewarding the firms performing these tasks. Thus, the particular collection of firms or institutions really does constitute an organized system of exchange. Combining the specialized efforts of each participant in the exchange process makes possible a very efficient and relatively low-cost system of exchanges.[9]

Nonprofit organizations use marketing activities and techniques to promote the use of their services by potential clients. For example, a museum attempts to transmit cultural appreciation to the general public. The National Safety Council attempts to promote safer driving, while a police department provides the general public with physical security. Thus, whether it is a profit-seeking firm or a nonprofit organization, marketing consists of the following elements:

- Two or more social units, which may be individuals, groups, organizations, communities, or nations
- At least one of the social units is seeking a specific response from one or more other units
- The attempt to produce the desired responses by creating and offering values to the market.[10]

Suppliers ⇄ Customers

Notice the symbol in the above heading. It conveys a special message about exchanges. The opposing arrows symbolize the interaction and interdependence of customers and marketers. Marketers depend upon customers for the sales that produce profits. Customers look to marketers to supply a desired bundle of goods and services and the psychological satisfaction they bring. This is the exchange basis of marketing and it underscores the notion of transactions. Transactions are exchanges of at least two things of value, usually goods from the standpoint of the marketer and money from the standpoint of the buyer. Transactions presuppose a situation where each party possesses something of value to the other and is capable of communication and delivery. Transactions imply also that each party benefits from the exchange process.

Is Marketing Economics?

Marketing is not economics but it is closely related to economic activities. Marketing is a new discipline, a distinct set of activities separate from, yet a part of, economics. Let's look at the relationships. Economics could very well be called the "mother science" of marketing. What does this mean?

[9] See Richard P. Bagozzi, "Marketing as Exchange," *Journal of Marketing* **39,** no. 4 (October 1975), pp. 32–40.

[10] See Philip Kotler, "A Generic Concept of Marketing," *Journal of Marketing* **36** (April 1972), pp. 46–54.

Economics deals with allocation and exchange processes. It is the science of allocating scarce resources to alternative uses. Because it is so concerned with allocation processes, economics has focused upon the creation and distribution of utilities. Utilities relate to values or things of worth that are presumed to be of value and have worth because they exist in limited amounts. To put it less technically, utilities are the capacity of things to satisfy people's desires. There is a close kinship between economics and marketing. The kind of utility created by economic activity falls into two broad categories: (1) form utility and (2) time, place, possession, and information utility.

Form Utility. Economic activity creating form utility is normally called production. Raw materials, energy, labor, and fabricated parts are combined so that a desired finished item is produced. Through a process sometimes called synergism the total value or utility of the finished product is greater than the sum of the values or utilities of the separate ingredients combined to produce it. A "Big Mac" has more value than its separate components: a quarter-pound of ground beef, a sesame seed bun, pickles, lettuce, and mustard. Both marketing and production are responsible for the creation of form utility. Production is concerned with the actual manufacturing process; marketing, with deciding what goods and services to produce. Figure 1-2 shows that both marketing and production create form utility but marketing alone creates time, place, possession, and information utility.

Time, place, possession and information utilities are created by marketing. The "Big Mac" has increased want-satisfying power or utility when it is made available to you at a time and place you want. It has value to you when it is in your possession and you can eat it; and you may enjoy it more knowing that it has been prepared in a clean, sterile environment and knowing also that the quality of each one you buy will be consistently high. The information provided in the product's promotion may actually increase your satisfaction in using it; that is, as a result of promotion the product's emotional or psychological value is increased as well. "Big Mac" for you may be more than just another hamburger. As we shall learn, people buy things not only for what they can do, but also for what they come to mean.

Figure 1-2 Marketing's role in the creation of total utility.

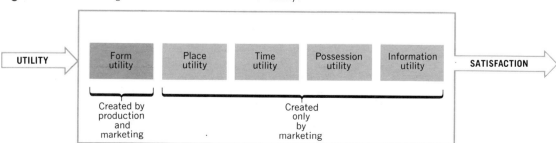

Before proceeding, can you answer these questions:
1. How is marketing related to exchange?
2. How does marketing affect your life style?
3. What utilities are created by marketing? How?

Marketing's Role in Our Economic System

All *cultures,* whether primitive or ultrasophisticated, generate economic systems to deal with these fundamental economic issues:

1. What should be produced?
2. How should it be produced?
3. Who should produce it?
4. How should the rewards of production be distributed among the members of the group?

In a commune these decisions might be made autocratically by a powerful leader, or by democratic vote of the members. In a socialist or communist country, commissars, or government officials chosen for their loyalty and responsiveness to the party and its ideals, make the decisions. In a democratic, market oriented society, all the people, exercising their sovereignty as consumers in the decentralized market places of the country, decide.

What is produced is what the populace in the various market segments of our society demands. How it is produced is determined by questions of efficiency and technology. That is, goods will be produced by means that ensure customer satisfaction at prices buyers are willing to pay. And the rewards are distributed via the profit mechanism among the members of the production-marketing network according to the value added by each.

In such market oriented economies, marketing naturally plays an extremely important role, because its principal purpose is creating satisfied customers. While providing customer satisfaction, marketing activities also smooth the way for accomplishing exchanges. It is these exchanges that constitute the focus of the central questions answered by every economic system.

Beyond Consumption: Demarketing

In the United States there is some indication that the demands for physical goods, especially durables, may be declining relative to other demands. Consumers appear to be opting for more services, more leisure time, and more active recreation. Also, the growing shortages of world resources, energy, clean water and air, and the threat of overcrowding may lead to de-emphasizing the pursuit of buyers, or as one writer calls it, *"demarketing."* There is little doubt that the energy crisis will force an alteration in the role of the marketing man. In some industries, it may alter him out of existence. ...When demand exceeds supply marketing men can be replaced by order takers. The act of selling is unnecessary. There also is no need for advertising, sales promotion, incentives, sweepstakes, trading stamps, free road maps or even windshield cleaning.[11]

[11] Philip Kotler and Sidney Levy, "Demarketing, Yes, Demarketing,"*Harvard Business Review* **49** (November-December 1971), pp. 74–80. Also see Philip Kotler, "Marketing During Periods of Shortage," *Journal of Marketing* **38** (July 1974), pp. 20–29.

America is diversity.

Can this be correct? Perhaps. But marketing in the traditional sense—the search for and stimulation of buyers—is likely to be around for a long time. And sellers will find new ways to serve customers wanting fewer material things but insisting on more leisure, a cleaner atmosphere, and a less stressful environment. Marketing in the expanded view will increase, however, and more and more organizations will use its techniques to facilitate the transactions they want between themselves and the people they aim to serve.

Approaches to the Study of Marketing, or How to Eat an Elephant

Elephants aren't very appetizing to most of us. Our preferences run to roast beef, chicken or lamb chops. But if hunger or good manners forced us to eat an elephant, we would find it to be a most prodigious task. Elephants are too large to eat by oneself, but if one did take on the task, the sensible way to do it would be to cut it up and devour one small piece at a time. Marketing in some respects is like our elephant. It is too large to "eat" at one setting. We need to approach the task one step at a time and carve the "beast" up in segments that our intellectual system can digest.

It is virtually impossible to study marketing without approaching it from a number of different vantage points, or perspectives. Like viewing any topic or object, what we "see" is affected to a great extent by our point of view. Very early, when the first systematic studies of marketing began, they almost always were product or commodity oriented. Today, we still utilize the commodity approach with great success, but this approach is only one of several that are frequently employed.

Early Marketing Approaches

The early (and still acceptable) way of classifying the approaches to the study of marketing is as follows:

- Commodity approach
- Functional approach
- Institutional approach

First, let's discuss these three and then look at the more sophisticated ways that marketing is studied today.

Commodity Approach.   In the commodity approach, marketers study the movement of particular goods from points of production to governmental, industrial, and ultimate consumers. This process and the firms engaged in it must be described for each commodity. After a large number of such studies are completed, marketers usually see generalizations from which they can draw a good picture of the field of marketing. Most commodity studies today, when undertaken, are combined with some one of the other approaches.

Functional Approach.   The functional approach is widely used even today in studying marketing. It is the logical reflection of the "scientific method," which asserts that complex phenomena can best be understood by breaking the whole down into a series of distinct activities, or functions. Marketing is said, in the main, to consist of eight basic functions: buying, selling, transportation, storage, standardization and grading, risk-taking, and providing information.

Buying (or leasing for use) and selling are two critical marketing functions because they are the ones in which title or use rights are transferred. By a careful investigation of how each of these functions is performed, together with an analysis of the costs and problems involved, a comprehensive understanding of marketing can be gained.

The Institutional Approach.   The businesses, agencies, or other groups of individuals who carry out marketing functions and take on a distinct character because of the specialized way they develop and emerge, are called *marketing institutions*. Some, like retailers and wholesalers, are easy to identify and label. Others are not quite so visible in everyday life and thus are not as well known: for example, selling agents, manufacturers' agents, brokers, rack jobbers, and others. The institutional approach examines the way manufacturers, resellers, transportation companies, advertising agencies, and others work together to form a total marketing system.

Modern Marketing Utilizes Additional Approaches

The above approaches are not necessarily outdated. The fact simply is that marketing, especially in the United States and many other Western countries, is so vast, so complex, so sophisticated, and has such a profound impact upon the lives and welfare of people that we need a number of approaches, each geared to a somewhat different task or objective. Although today's vantage points for studying marketing are not altogether different from those used previously, they nonetheless reflect insights and knowledge, as well as sentiments, that are a part of the contemporary scene.

The Systems Approach.   A system is a set of interacting or interdependent groups coordinated to form a unified whole and organized to accomplish a set of goals. The systems approach is based upon the understanding that few activities or processes are unrelated to other activities or processes. It takes a holistic, or unified, view of the study of marketing. As shown in Figure 1-3, it integrates the functional, commodity, institutional, managerial, and social approaches into one comprehensive whole. The systems approach examines marketing linkages, both inside and outside the firm; the changes in the firm's environment; the controls used to correct or modify the behavior of the system; and the means provided for measuring the system's results. In marketing we are concerned with groups of consumers and with the group of individuals who comprise the firm. The systems approach studies the interaction of these

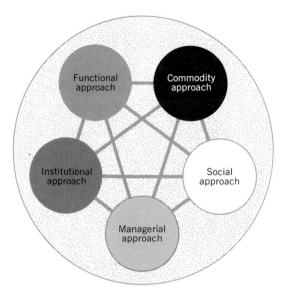

Figure 1-3 The systems approach to marketing.

two groups, and within this framework we analyze information systems, distribution systems, and the processes by which consumers and organizations satisfy their needs.

The Social Approach. In a recent development, marketing, again because of its massive impact upon society, is being studied from a social point of view. Those who take this sociological view insist that marketing recognize its power and behave responsibly. For them marketing is a force and an opportunity to promote clean air and water and decent housing. They advocate using marketing to further such social goals as population control, improved racial tolerance, and better support for education. Marketing, they assert, should promote the good of the public, as well as that of the private, sector. This means that marketing firms must assess not just the profitability of their activities, but their effect on society as well.[12]

The Managerial Approach. The managerial approach is basically firm oriented and stresses the management activity necessary in a complex marketing enterprise. It is perhaps the most popular of all approaches used to study marketing. It reflects the development of the "scientific management approach" and the explosion of knowledge in this field. The managerial approach, therefore, focuses upon the activity of managers and emphasizes the role of decision making and overall strategy in marketing endeavors.

The principal focus of this text is on the managerial approach. However, we shall also take account of the others, particularly the institutional and societal approaches to marketing.

[12] See Gene R. Laczniak, Robert F. Lusch and Patrick E. Murphy, "Social Marketing: Its Ethical Dimensions," *Journal of Marketing* **43** (Spring 1979), pp. 29–36.

Marketing Is Strategic Behavior

Regardless of which approach one follows in studying marketing, it is necessary to consider the strategic nature of marketing activity that permeates nearly all approaches.

The Importance of Strategy.   Strategy is something like a game — a serious game, however, because much is at stake. Basically the prize for the marketing oriented firm is survival and profitability, both of which are functions of customer satisfaction. So, we could conclude then that the firm's ability to produce customer satisfaction depends on its *marketing strategy*.

For example, consider the implications of the following strategic questions facing these companies.

- Should General Electric build energy-efficient appliances, even though they sell for 25 percent more than competitors' products that are not equally energy-efficient?
- Should General Motors build an emission-free automobile, although such a vehicle would cost more than $10,000 and get less than fifteen miles per gallon?
- Should the Canadian government spend large advertising sums urging United States tourists to visit Canadian provinces?
- Should the leading petroleum companies expand their operations into solar energy developments?
- Should major soft drink companies like Coca-Cola and Pepsi Cola continue to promote and expand the market for diet soft drinks when the principal sweetening agent for these products is saccharine? Saccharine usage is likely to be vastly curtailed or prohibited by the Food and Drug Administration because it has been tagged as a cancer producing agent and the prospect of developing alternative sweetening agents appears dim.

Pursuit of a marketing strategy is the continuous process of making such managerial decisions systematically and of anticipating their impact on the firm's future well-being. *Marketing strategy* is a comprehensive plan of action designed to meet the needs of a particular firm operating in a particular environment. Sometimes the environmental factors themselves can be changed; at other times they are unalterable.

The Marketing Mix.   The starting place for effective marketing strategy is with the consumer. Once an organization identifies its consumer group or market segment, it may then begin to direct its activities toward satisfying this group. Though a firm's strategy is made up of many factors, all of its marketing decision making can be classified into four strategy elements:

- Product or merchandise planning
- Marketing channel organization
- Promotion
- Pricing

This total package of elements is called the marketing mix; and the way each of these elements is emphasized makes every firm's marketing strategy unique (see Figure 1-4).

Product Planning. Product planning concerns decisions related to products: merchandise assortments, quality levels, character of product, package design, warranties, brands, new product development, and product life cycle.

Marketing Channels. Channels are the routes goods traverse from manufacturers to ultimate consumers. Channel strategy decisions organize and control marketing institutions through a coordinated arrangement of intermediaries to make successful exchanges easier.

Promotional Strategy. Promotional strategy deals with the blend of personal selling, advertising, and other promotional tools to be employed. In general, it is the combination of publicizing efforts the firm uses to communicate with its market.

Pricing Strategy. Determining pricing strategy is a delicate task. It consists of assessing customer demand and analyzing cost in order to choose a price that will create customer satisfaction and yield a satisfactory level of profit. Profits are the firm's reward for accepting the risks and committing its resources to a business venture. In the nonprofit enterprise, pricing is still an important element in the marketing mix. Pricing in these organizations may mean that the price is set (1) to cover expenses, (2) to charge a reasonable fee based on

Figure 1-4 The elements in the marketing strategy.

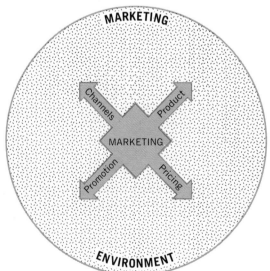

clients' incomes, or (3) to generate sufficient revenues to make up the difference between donations and total expenses.

While these four factors or elements are important individually, their real significance lies in the mix, the unique way they are combined as a careful plan, or strategy, in a dynamic marketing environment.

The Marketing Concept

Many firms are successful, in large measure, because they are not just customer oriented but marketing oriented. It is one thing to proclaim, "The customer is king." But it is another matter altogether to develop, organize, and operate a business entirely from the marketing point of view. This way of conducting an enterprise is rooted in the marketing concept.

History of the Marketing Concept

The first man in the United States to see marketing clearly as the creation of customers, the central function of the business enterprise, and the primary thrust of management was Cyrus H. McCormick (1809–1884). You remember that he established himself in the history books as the inventor of the mechanical harvester. However, he also originated the basic concepts of modern marketing: marketing research and market analysis, market standing or share of market, pricing policies, service salespeople, parts and supply service to customers, and installment credit.[13]

Production Was Preeminent. Even a hundred years ago there were companies, although few in number, whose vision was sufficiently sharp and clear to enable them to recognize the importance of creating customers rather than products. Some knew, like Andrew Carnegie, that a market was to be more valued than a mill. But the overwhelming number of companies then, and to a large extent *even* today, are production oriented, or company oriented, or engineering oriented—rather than customer and marketing oriented. Too frequently the production oriented company is myopic—its vision is shortsighted. Such companies focus upon internal company abilities and traditional manufacturing. Their attitude is "The sales department will have to sell whatever the company produces." Figure 1-5 contrasts the sales and marketing concepts.

Although the marketing concept first emerged in the nineteenth century and was adopted in its early forms by a few farsighted companies, it did not become widespread until the 1950s. As an operating business philosophy it was a systematic and orderly new way of looking at business enterprise from the customer's point of view. The marketing concept said simply: "The firm must take its marching orders from the market; it is our foremost job to produce what the market needs." Marketing became the pivot of the entire business. It

---

[13] See Peter F. Drucker, *Management: Tasks, Responsibilities, Practices* (New York: Harper & Row, 1974), p. 62.

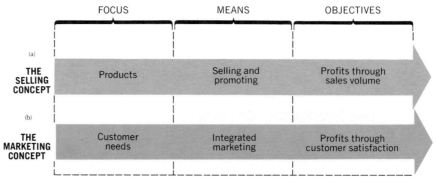

Figure 1-5 The sales and marketing concepts contrasted.
(a) The $ selling concept. (b) The marketing concept.

was the whole business seen from the vantage point of its final result: namely, from the customer's point of view. Therefore, concern and responsibility for marketing came to permeate all areas of the enterprise.

Before proceeding, can you answer these questions:
1. What is a marketing strategy?
2. What are the elements in the marketing mix?
3. What is meant by "the marketing concept"?

Is the Marketing Concept Working?

In many respects the marketing concept is working and working well. Many business organizations have enthusiastically embraced this operating business philosophy; and can point to satisfied customers and generous earnings as evidence of their great success. Yet, in too many firms, management's thinking is not geared toward creating customer satisfaction through modern marketing.

The marketing concept is based upon two fundamental ideas: one old, the other relatively new. The new idea replaces the old notion of "Let the buyer beware" with a new version, "Let the seller take care."* Such sovereignty has given the consumer the power of life and death over business in the marketplace. It has changed the direction and style of operation of many firms so that the consumer is usually well served.

However, the other idea upon which the marketing concept rests is the basis of American enterprise, the notion of profit and profit maximization. The marketing concept asserts that every alternative considered in the decision processes of the profit-seeking firm should be analyzed in terms of its contribution

*From the Latin *caveat emptor* and *caveat venditor,* respectively.

to profit and overhead, and that the alternative making the greatest contribution should be chosen.

The Consumer Is Pivotal.   There is something that bothers many firms about these two notions. Isn't there a flaw in a philosophy that advocates serving the consumer and maximizing profits? Aren't these contradictory statements? They are for some companies and the resultant confusion causes the company much difficulty and leads to an agitated, distressed consumer. For those concerns that have not yet resolved this conflict, the marketing concept is mere lip service. The slavish addiction to profit maximization, unless carefully restrained, converts too quickly to customer exploitation and a production and selling orientation.

The astute firms that truly follow the marketing concept believe that the way to reconcile these apparently conflicting notions is to attain profits as a by-product of supplying what the customer wants. Then the customer is truly the pivotal element in the development of the firm's marketing strategy.

But What about Consumerism?   The marketing concept obviously isn't working perfectly. We read too much about "consumerism" and the "consumer movement" to believe that it is. Every day we hear of false or misleading advertising, "bait and switch sales," products that don't work, and shady practices by business organizations. Again, too many of these stories are true. Many consumers have become militant in their attempts to redress their grievances in the market place. We call this behavior "consumerism" and the collective, organized effort of all those working to promote the objectives of consumerism, "the consumer movement."[14]

Consumerism has been called "the shame of marketing."[15] It certainly proves a lack of sincerity in some businesses and shows that not all consumers are docile, well-satisfied customers. Marketers should pay special attention to these organized, vocal critics whose anger has uncovered a confusion of purpose in American business.

True marketing, as we will learn increasingly throughout our exploration of the subject, starts out with the customers, their demographics, their needs, realities, life styles, and values. This kind of true marketing does not ask, "What do we want to sell?" Or state, "This is what our product or service does." Instead, it asks, "What does the customer want to buy?" And then, "These are the satisfactions the customers have stated they want; these are the customers' values and needs. How can we best fulfill them?"

Summary

Marketing is the set of activities by which the demand structure for goods, ideas, and services is managed in order to facilitate the exchange process satisfactorily. In the past, marketing was looked upon as a set of activities used

[14] See Rom J. Markin, *Consumer Behavior: A Cognitive Orientation* (New York: Macmillan, 1974), especially chapter 2, "Consumerism: Militant Consumer Behavior," pp. 24–50.

[15] Drucker, *Management,* p. 64.

by the business firm almost exclusively to stimulate demand and to search for buyers so as to create profits. The expanded view of marketing sees it as a broad set of activities used by both profit and nonprofit organizations to manage demand and make possible a host of satisfying and rewarding exchanges. Marketing is critically important to individuals and to society in general.

Economics is the "mother science" of marketing. It deals with the allocation of scarce resources to alternative uses and is that branch of the social sciences concerned with the creation of utility. Utility is the want-satisfying power of things. Production activities create form utility, but marketing has an even larger role: the creation of time, place, and information utility. The means by which the major economic questions in our society are answered is the market system, sometimes referred to as free enterprise. The vast, complex marketing system in the United States reflects the complexity and diversity of our economic and social systems.

Marketing, we have learned, is strategic behavior. Marketing organizations must develop comprehensive plans of action, or strategy. The firm's marketing mix contains the major elements of its marketing plan or strategy. Today's astute business organizations have adopted an enlightened operating philosophy, called the marketing concept, that focuses upon the company's need to create satisfied customers. Not all customers in today's market place are satisfied, and some measure of their dissatisfaction can be found in the growing strength of consumerism.

There are a number of approaches to the study of marketing; commodity, institutional, functional, systems, societal, and managerial. Our principal orientation will be managerial, but we shall not neglect the others, especially the institutional and the societal aspects of marketing.

Review Questions

1. How does marketing affect consumers' life styles?

2. Marketing costs about 50 cents for every dollar spent on consumption. Is this cost justified? Why? And to what extent?

3. Many argue that marketing promotes waste and materialism. Do you believe these accusations are well founded? Why?

4. Define marketing. Describe in your own words what you think marketing does.

5. "Marketing is a part of the exchange process." Explain.

6. How does marketing aid and lead to the consummation of exchanges?

7. What is meant by the statement, "Economics is the mother science of marketing"?

8. What utilities are created by marketing?

9. What forces have led to the concept known as demarketing?

10. What is meant by a marketing strategy?

11. What are the elements that constitute the marketing mix?

12. What is the meaning of the marketing concept?

Case 1-1

Charles Hall's Waterbed

Charles Hall is generally credited with inventing the waterbed. It made him neither rich nor famous but it did leave him with some interesting and nostalgic memories about Jello.

Hall was a design student living in San Francisco's Haight-Ashbury district when he came up with the forerunner of the waterbed ten years ago. His invention, actually a vinyl bag filled with 300 pounds of Jello and styrene pellets, was in his words, "interesting but not successful because you needed a forklift to move it." There were other problems. The bag developed a leak and Jello began oozing into the downstairs apartment. Hall decided it had to go. "There was all this goo mixed with styrene beads," he recalls, "I was afraid it would clog the toilet and I just couldn't throw it out. So I ended up taking it out at night in little bags and putting them in garbage cans at the beach."

Hall persevered, substituting water for Jello and adding a frame and heater. An art gallery invited him to show his invention and he responded by coming up with an eight-foot-square waterbed covered in red velvet and dubbed "the Pleasure Pit."

"It was a big hit," he said, "I thought the merits of the waterbed would be seen immediately." It didn't work out that way. Waterbeds were viewed as part of the Hashbury hippie culture. "People saw these undulations and there were all these hippie and sex connotations," he said. "Actually, although I hate to say anything negative about waterbeds as far as sex goes, well, that's not the best part. Waterbeds are for sleeping."

Hall and members of what is now a $135-million-a-year industry are fighting "waterbed misconceptions" through a marketing and public relations campaign that the American Waterbed Council says "is designed to achieve the AWC's goal of obtaining consumer waterbed acceptance by skillful application of marketing techniques." The campaign was launched in late 1977.

Hall, who is now 34 and whose own waterbed company went bankrupt, never made much money from his patent. He has since returned to inventing and has marketed several other products. But he also leaves his Bay Area home for frequent waterbed promotions.

Waterbeds account for about 4 percent of national bed sales today, the American Waterbed Council says, with 15 percent of California's 20 million residents supposedly resting on them each night. Heavier vinyl and improved construction methods have eliminated leakage problems and today an "average" waterbed with accessories such as heaters costs between $500 and $1,000.

Questions

1. Do you believe that Charles Hall was following the basic dictate of marketing (find a need and then fill it) in connection with the development and marketing of his waterbed? Explain.

2. The American Waterbed Council, according to the case, is now embarked on a marketing and public relations program to "increase customers' acceptance and awareness of waterbeds." Within the framework established in Table 1-1, where would you say their effort best fits? What are listed as the primary tasks of marketing within this cell of the matrix in Figure 1-1?

3. How would you respond if you were asked by the president of the American Waterbed Council to provide some basic ideas and information for their impending campaign, especially to explain briefly the following terms?

   • Marketing

- Marketing strategy
- Marketing concept
- Marketing mix

4. What do you believe might be the most serious impediment to increased sales of waterbeds?

Case 1-2

The United States Post Office

The United States Post Office according to a mandate by the Congress is supposed at least to break even. That is, its revenues should equal, if not exceed, its costs. The Post Office now finds itself in conflict with a frustrated Congress, embattled postmasters, angered supervisors, militant workers, and an embittered consuming public. Some contend that the service is so large and in such a state of disarray that it may be impossible to manage. The system currently

U.S. Post Office activities are not highly automated.

employs nearly 1 percent of the entire American work force.

The Post Office is facing a complete new set of competitive realities. It must compete with private deliveries that are skimming off its most profitable business. It must contend with changes in individual consumers' habits and with new technologies like electronic banking that threaten the rest of its business. And the system must struggle to increase its own operating efficiency—most notably through twenty-one new bulk-mail centers that cost $1 billion.

To cope with these new realities and to operate more effectively, the Post Office is considering these possible alternatives:

1. Providing price concessions to big mailers. These concessions would reflect the fact that the cost of handling such items as utility bills is less than sending personal letters across the country.
2. Raising the price to small users by charging more postage on letters while also adding a surcharge for home delivery of mail. The average household mails only 135 letters, cards, and postcards annually. Meanwhile, per capita mail volume dropped last year only from 429 to 419 pieces. Some postal officials think a user fee similar to the one applied by telephone companies should be charged.
3. Home delivery will likely be cut from the present six days a week to five days a week or less. Business deliveries will be cut to one a day in fifteen Eastern cities.
4. Mail that is considered less important—including second-class periodicals, third-class circulars, and fourth-class parcels—may be delivered only three times a week. Periodicals might pay a premium to avoid the delays of alternate-day delivery.

To solve the problem, postal officials will need to be imaginative and innovative. It is not so easy as simply raising prices. As rates go up, the post office volume declines. So if rates are raised too high, the postal service could actually be destroyed. It may all sound unworkable, but Postal Service officials stress that these changes and more may have to come. If not, they say, the institution will either collapse or become an unendurable drain on taxpayers.

Questions

1. Are the problems of the United States Postal Service marketing problems? If so, why and how are they related to marketing?
2. What is the "product" of the United States Postal Service?
3. Who are the consumer-users of postal services?
4. Could the marketing concept be applied to the problems of the United States Postal Service?

Chapter 2

Marketing
in the Larger Setting

For nearly two decades, Madison Avenue has concentrated on selling products and services to a market of young people, aged 18 to 34, for the most part. But now it has awakened to the existence of a growing market referred to as the oldsters, "50 plus" or the "maturity" market.

Made up of people past the half-century mark chronologically, this group of men and women is getting consideration for the first time by such marketers as Procter & Gamble, Colgate-Palmolive, Bristol-Myers, and Coca-Cola. As a matter of fact, Coca-Cola has been considering making some significant adjustments in terms of how it views the market. Part of the change in thinking which is taking place in many companies is a result of analyses that show a slowdown in the rate of growth of younger segments of the population. For example, the heavy users of soft drinks in the United States are between the ages of 13 and 24. In early 1980 there were nearly 49 million such persons — you are one of them — and they are the lifeblood of the soft drink industry. On the average, each consumes 823 cans of soda pop each year, while the average for all groups is only 547 cans. But the market is changing, because it is shrinking. By 1985 there will be fewer persons in the 13 to 24 age group. And these 4.4 million fewer individuals would have consumed 3.3 billion cans of soft drinks annually.

America is becoming a nation with a greater mix of older citizens.

Soft drink companies will not be the only businesses concerned with the coming drop in the number of young people. Few industries in the years ahead will escape the impact of this shift in the demographics* of the United States' population. The baby food industry has already felt the effects and its marketing executives have hastened to diversify into other food lines; one of them has even bought an insurance company. Some industries—pharmaceuticals, for instance—stand to benefit from an aging population. Others—tobacco, record makers, and fast food outlets among them—will find themselves facing smaller markets in the future.

As we learned in the previous chapter, the real task of the marketing manager is to develop a comprehensive and dynamic plan of action, that is, a marketing strategy. The elements around which marketing strategies are formulated are the marketing mix. The marketing mix consists of the firm's policies concerning price, promotion, product and channels of distribution. The elements of the marketing mix are sometimes referred to as the controllable variables of marketing. There are constraints upon every firm's behavior and these constraints are sometimes referred to as uncontrollable marketing variables. Some firms may, under unique circumstances, be less affected by the uncontrollable variables than others. Coca-Cola can certainly not do much to change the fact that its core market segment is shrinking. However, it can, and is, aggressively responding to this change by a major push into foreign markets and by more product diversification at home.

The Coca-Cola Company, like all marketing oriented firms, exists in a larger setting or environment. And as this environment changes, the firm must adapt and accommodate to it.

The Market Opportunity

The marketing firm behaves in accordance with its market opportunity. The market opportunity has been called "a challenge to purposeful marketing action that is characterized by a generally favorable set of environmental circumstances and an acceptable probability of success."[1] What does this suggest? (1) The firm's success or failure depends to a great degree on how well management perceives its market opportunity. (2) The company does not operate in a vacuum. It takes its marching orders from the market, which is shaped and conditioned by a number of environmental forces. (3) A state of interdependency exists between the firm and its environment. (4) Environmental forces may be at times conducive to great success for a given enterprise and at other times not hold promise for even limited success. The essential point is that the business organization, in creating and building its strategy, must constantly monitor its environment.

Demography is the statistical study of human population, with special attention to matters like age, income, size, and density.

[1] Martin L. Bell, *Marketing: Concepts and Strategy* (Boston: Houghton Mifflin, 1966), p. 29.

Figure 2-1 Elements in the marketing strategy.

The Firm's Behavior Reflects Its Environment

All environments have behavior-shaping properties. The behavior of the business firm is affected by its environment. When the environment is favorable and supportive, the business firm may find it difficult to fail. Success may be virtually assured by a good business climate, or overall environment. On the other hand, consider the odds of a new marketing firm's succeeding when the climate is unfavorable. The firm that begins its operation where the social, economic, political, and technological environments are not well matched to its marketing program has only a limited chance for success. Hence, all well-conceived marketing strategies begin with an appraisal of the market opportunity, which is a direct outgrowth of the environmental forces and circumstances surrounding the marketing firm.[2]

Consider Figure 2-1, which is a modified and more complete version of Figure 1-4, which appeared in the first chapter. The marketing firm in Figure 2-1, is embedded in an environmental setting that will affect the company's performance. Its marketing strategy must reflect the impact of environmental constraints.

The Aggressive versus the Passive Firm

The firm's operating style and philosophy affect the way it perceives its marketing opportunity, and will also affect its reaction to its marketing environ-

---

[2] For an example of how strategic planning in relation to the environment affects company operations, see Stanley F. Stasch, "1980's Marketing to Require Wisely Chosen Strategies," *Marketing News,* May 30, 1980, p. 16.

ment. Passive marketing firms regard the environmental constraints confronting them as beyond their control and influence. If an organization programs its future to fit the prevailing and forecasted conditions, its behavior is characterized as passive. Such a company's success depends on the predicted environment.

On the other hand, many marketing firms plan to act vigorously in pursuing their goals and objectives. The behavior of such firms is best characterized as aggressive, or environment-shaping. The environmental forces that surround these enterprises are not viewed as fixed, but as flexible and, at least over the longer run, able to be molded to the enterprise's best interests. For such aggressive companies, "uncontrollable" variables are less formidable and may even be responsive to varying degrees of influence by the firm.

While perhaps in the minority of business enterprises, aggressive companies do exist. Examples are Renault in France, Fiat in Italy, Marks and Spencer in England, ASEA in Sweden, and Sony in Japan. In the United States we find 3M (Minnesota Mining and Manufacturing), the Bell Laboratories of the American Telephone and Telegraph Company, the Bank of America, and Sears Roebuck. There are without question others, but the firms mentioned apparently have little difficulty innovating and meet little resistance in getting change accepted throughout their organization.[3] Aggressive organizations, therefore, program change into their current operations, relentlessly sloughing off the old while emphasizing planned, systematic change.

The Environment of Marketing

The so-called climate of business consists, as is shown in Figure 2-1, of five major environmental influences. The firm, if passive, will simply respond to these forces in its own distinctive ways. The behavior of an aggressive firm, on the other hand, may affect, shape, and modify the elements of the business climate. In either case the firm must monitor its environment to understand it and evaluate it accurately.

Marketing takes place in an environment of interrelated factors, some of which are social and cultural; others, political and economic; and still others, technological. We shall examine these factors in some detail in the following pages and later, in Chapter 3, we shall build upon this discussion in exploring the implications of strategic market planning.

The Social-Cultural Environment of Marketing

All of us are part of a social-cultural fabric that affects our behavior. It is a basic part of our environment. We are surrounded by traditions, customs, and rules. All people and all institutions are part of a social-cultural network. They contribute to and influence it, and each in turn is affected by it. One authority

---

[3] See Peter F. Drucker, *Management: Tasks, Responsibilities, Practices* (New York: Harper & Row, 1974), p. 786.

has defined a social-cultural system in a much more elegant fashion, calling it a system of solutions to unlearned problems as well as learned problems and their solutions, all of which are acquired by members of a recognizable group and shared by them.[4]

Social-cultural systems affect marketing behavior primarily because such systems dictate what is proper and acceptable. No marketing firm can ignore the social-cultural context of its behavior and hope to succeed.

Dimensions of the Social-Cultural System

There are various ways of looking at the social-cultural system. Understanding its several distinctive dimensions will better enable us to grasp its significance as an environmental variable affecting marketing strategy. The social-cultural system is usually analyzed from the standpoint of its three dimensions: (1) The Demographic, (2) The Organizational, and (3) The Normative.[5]

The Demographic. The demographic dimension examines such things as age, income, educational levels, occupations, and geographic location.

The Organizational. The organizational dimension observes how the various institutions of the system participate and interact. It weighs the structure, power, and influence of the family, the church, the school, and the business organization. Social class structure and the power structure of cities and communities also lie within the organizational dimension.

The Normative. The normative dimension of the social-cultural system relates to values, customs, and norms; it is more concerned with political, religious, social, and economic values.

All the social-cultural dimensions important to marketers are seen in Figure 2-2.

As Figure 2-2 suggests, marketing strategy must reflect an understanding of the social-cultural system and its dimensions. The firm bases its strategy upon a host of considerations, chief among them its social-cultural environment. The firm's strategy, or its comprehensive plan of action, is based upon a thorough, on-going analysis of the various dimensions of the social-cultural system. Product policies, new-product development, pricing, promotion, and channel of distribution decisions are affected by such factors as age, income, geographic location, and the position in the life cycle of the firm's market targets. Strategy is also affected by customer occupations, life style, social class, and educational level, plus such important factors as the prevailing values, norms, and customs of the social-cultural system.

---

[4] Albert D. Ullman, *Sociocultural Foundations of Personality* (Boston: Houghton Mifflin, 1965), p. 181.

[5] This classification and approach was suggested in the work of Thomas S. Robertson, *Consumer Behavior* (Glenview, IL; Scott, Foresman, 1970), pp. 99–102.

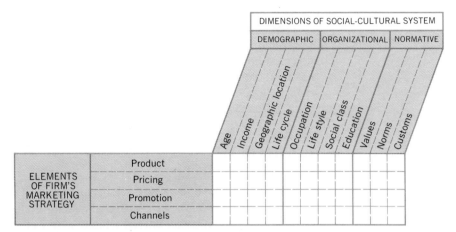

Figure 2-2 Social-cultural matrix of marketing behavior.

The Social-Cultural System and a Value Orientation

The chief function of the social-cultural network is to establish a value system as the foundation for behavior. Values, underlying all forms of human behavior, are individual or collective conceptions of what is desirable, that is, what I and/or others feel we justifiably want. Our social-cultural system is infused with values. Their basic purpose is to provide us with a means for choosing goals, or selecting one object over another.

Business basically has to serve consumer demands or it cannot sell its products. But the question is, What determines consumers' effective demands? The answer is two things: money and values. Money decrees the amount and quality they want. Values determine what type of goods and services they want. A few years ago, General Motors ran a very succcessful advertising campaign declaring that Americans liked "baseball, hot dogs, apple pie, and Chevrolets." The suggestion was that these things were uniquely American and therefore in keeping with the value orientation of our social-cultural system.

The Social-Cultural System and Conflicting Value

Not all Americans, however, share the same value orientation. Contrary to General Motors' notion, some—in fact many—Americans prefer "football, hamburgers, cherry pie, and Fords." Not all Americans march to the same drumbeat as far as core culture values are concerned. Despite a once-popular misconception, America is not a melting pot where all values are reduced to a few single common denominators. Actually, the United States' social-cultural system is characterized by cultural assimilation and structural pluralism. Cultural assimilation suggests that the major segments of our society share a common core culture value orientation. However, structural pluralism indicates that major groups or subcultures also retain a strong sense of group identity that makes them embrace some values that are counter to the mainstream culture.

A social-cultural system, a dynamic set of processes, changes as our values change. And American values are currently undergoing profound and radical changes, plunging our social-cultural system into a state of flux. Figure 2-3

Cultural assimilation.

Figure 2-3 Profile of significant value-system changes: 1969–1980 (as seen by General Electric's Business Environment section).

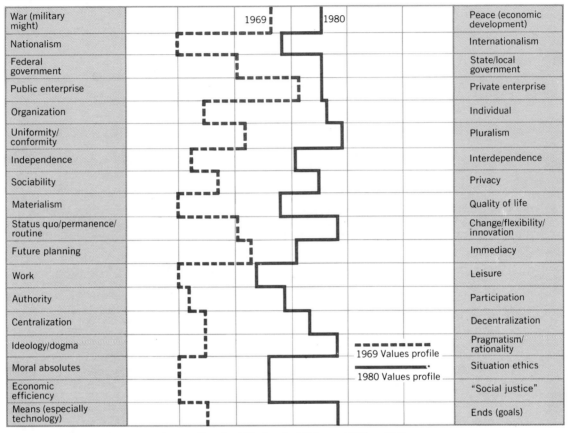

War (military might)			1969		1980				Peace (economic development)
Nationalism									Internationalism
Federal government									State/local government
Public enterprise									Private enterprise
Organization									Individual
Uniformity/conformity									Pluralism
Independence									Interdependence
Sociability									Privacy
Materialism									Quality of life
Status quo/permanence/routine									Change/flexibility/innovation
Future planning									Immediacy
Work									Leisure
Authority									Participation
Centralization									Decentralization
Ideology/dogma									Pragmatism/rationality
Moral absolutes									Situation ethics
Economic efficiency									"Social justice"
Means (especially technology)									Ends (goals)

1969 Values profile
1980 Values profile

Source: Ian H. Wilson. "How Our Values Are Changing," *The Futurist* **4** (February 1970), pp. 5–9.

shows how some of our most important values have been altered in recent years.

This transition in the value orientation of many Americans is having a profound influence on all dimensions of marketing, from the emergence of new products to promotional activities, choices of channels of distribution, and pricing decisions.

Mainstream Social-Cultural Values

Many have attempted to catalog and assess our core culture value characteristics. In such a complex and diverse society the task is difficult and, needless to say, such practices can even be dangerous, given the ready tendency to form stereotypes and overgeneralized images.

The basic value orientation of the American core social-cultural system centers on the following[6]:

1. *Individualism and achievement.* Americans place heavy emphasis on the dignity and welfare of the individual and the right of every person to achieve. Achievement and success are often equated with money, property, and life style. Life styles are basically a reflection of the goods and services one can command.

2. *Busyness.* Americans are a busy people who seem compelled to be doing things all the time. They extol the virtues of "active leisure" and consider idleness slothful. Leisure usually means doing things, which often means consuming things: drinking beer, taking pictures, riding bikes, going fishing.

3. *Efficiency.* Americans are schizophrenic about efficiency. We value it because it means that minimum resources are being used to produce maximum output. However, we are likely to ignore inefficiencies like environmental pollution, economic waste, and use of scarce resources. We revere efficiency in production, but indulge in great waste when we consume.

4. *Morality in conduct.* Americans see the world in simplistic moral terms—right-wrong, good-bad. The roots of puritanism still lie deep in our perception of the world and tend to make us feel guilty about our overconsumption, waste, and lack of concern for the environment.

5. *Material comfort.* Material comfort in America denotes one's standard of living. We are proud that we have reached the highest mass level of consumption of any place on the planet. We value consumption and literally compete with one another in consuming automobiles, vacations, pets, and countless other goods and services. Our desire for material comfort has led us to the threshold of a new consumption value, *hedonism*, the urgent desire for total sense gratification.

There are other core culture values of great importance: Americans believe in and value progress and change; we extol freedom and democracy; we have recently embraced the notion of equality more realistically, and, though slightly embarrassed about it, we still have strong values of patriotism.

Values of the Counterculture

Members of the so-called counterculture, the "other directed," spurn the core culture values and symbols of middle-class America. A large sector of young adults disdain and even resent the achievement drives and symbols of affluence so prevalent among the middle class. Hence, youth culture values tend to reject object accumulation.[7] However, once again there is nothing homo-

---

[6] For a greatly expanded assessment, see the following: Geoffrey Gorer, *The American People* (New York: Norton, 1964); David M. Potter, *People of Plenty* (Chicago: Phoenix Books, 1954); Daniel J. Boorstin, *The Americans* (New York: Vintage Books, a division of Random House, 1974).

[7] William Lazer, John E. Smallwood, et al., "Consumer Environments and Life Styles of the Seventies," *MSU Business Topics* **20**, no. 2 (Spring 1972), pp. 5–17.

geneous about subculture. Young people are not all alike. Many members of the youth culture, for example, are resisting the notion of rational restraint now, and demand instant gratification. Many, perhaps, are just as hedonistic, just as gadget-prone, as their middle-class parents. They buy massive numbers of stereophonic sound systems; cassette players for their autos and vans; imported ten-speed bicycles; expensive sporting goods; shoes, and clothing.

By the same token, blacks in America are making rapid social and economic progress. Many have abandoned the paths of protest and militancy to seek, along with their white counterparts, the "good life," "the sweet life" in America—suburban living, country clubs, credit cards, vacations, and outdoor summer barbecues. Others, in the ghettos and in rural slums of both the North and South, continue to live "lives of quiet desperation," projecting seething hostility toward a social-cultural system whose values they do not accept and that consequently excludes them.

In sum, the social-cultural fabric is an important environmental variable that impacts strongly upon the marketing strategy and behavior of all firms. It is essential that those who do the strategic thinking and planning for marketing firms understand this variable.

Before proceeding, can you answer these questions:
1. Why is the external environment important to marketers?
2. What is the difference between an adaptive and an innovative firm?
3. What role do values play in determining marketing strategy?

The Political-Economic Environment of Marketing

Political economy is a term that describes the philosopohy of government toward developing legislation to meet changing economic conditions.[8] Of course, such a term is subject to numerous interpretations. For some, it means little governmental interference with business. For others, it means increasing regulation and, in some instances, the actual suppression of business enterprise. American political economy is rooted in our cultural value of freedom.

Freedom means, literally, to be free from constraint. Marketers in the United States have a rich heritage of freedom, although it did not appear until nearly 300 years after the first settlers came here. The American Revolution was sponsored in part by the businessmen of the colonies who wished to trade free of English interference and taxation. American business was, from its earliest beginnings, a staunch advocate of laissez faire, a system of enterprise whose French name means "hands off." In other words, government must interfere as little as possible with business.

---

[8] For an extended discussion see H. H. Liebhafsky, *American Government and Business* (New York: Wiley, 1971), pp. 4–6.

The Role of Modern Government in Business

Today American enterprise is a form of "mixed capitalism." Basically, private firms using the price or market system of resource allocation respond to the economic questions raised in chapter 1: (1) What things will be produced? (2) How will they be produced? (3) For whom will they be produced? However, in our mixed capitalism, customs and laws dictate that government, rather than private firms in the market place, answer some of these basic questions. The role of government in the twentieth century is to create a political-economic environment that is favorable not just to business but to the entire society as well.

In short, government, for better or for worse, is playing an increasing role in the regulation and conduct of American enterprise. Through its power to write laws and so control behavior, government has become to a great extent the unloved partner of American business.

Government Attitudes toward Business

Government-business relationships have changed dramatically during the past several generations and even today vary with the political winds. On balance, the basic role of government is to support, strengthen, and encourage business, especially in its exports and its multinational efforts. In Japan it is fashionable to talk about "Japan, Inc.," that is, a system uniting corporations and government in supporting Japanese business and products throughout the world.[9] To some extent this attitude prevails in the United States today. Yet it is offset by a notion pervading government-business relations that business cannot be trusted. Therefore, the role of government is to act as watchdog—to see that business people, both at home and abroad, act according to society's best interests. Government is thus placed in somewhat of an adversary relationship to business, governed by laws rather than administered. The notion emerges that business is too important to be left to business people alone, and that society's welfare demands the regulation and increasing control of business enterprise.

The Regulation of Marketing Activity

The exchange relationships between buyers and sellers of goods and services are subject to a withering array of government regulations and legislative behavior. There are many groups working to increase the regulation of marketing and business activity. Individuals like Ralph Nader constantly advocate greater governmental control of business enterprise. Politicians, responding to the demands and complaints of their constituents, are calling for tighter federal and state regulation of product packaging; advertising and promotion; pricing practices; credit charges; food additives; automobile safety; emission stan-

---

[9] Peter F. Drucker, *Management*, p. 354.

Farmers march on Washington protesting over-regulation.

dards; stated gasoline mileage rates; meat processing; and laws requiring the disclosure of the composition of foods, soft drinks, and liquor. As a result of such agitation, numerous laws are passed each year that tend to regulate, constrain, and in many instances actually control, marketing activity. Sometimes the laws and regulations are genuinely in the best interests of the overall society. Unfortunately, some are petty and ambiguous and promote only the self-interest of a limited few.

History of Government Regulation

The history of governmental regulation in the United States has had two major phases. First, there was the antimonopoly era in the early 1900s, when the basic thrust of legislation was to preserve competition by slowing the alarming rate of concentration of business power in the hands of a few. Second, in the 1930s, a period of rapid chain store growth and development, government regulation emphasized preserving certain competitors rather than promoting competition. During this period the chain stores, with their massive buying power and well-developed buying skill, grew rapidly, sometimes at the expense of smaller, less efficient, independent merchants. Prices in chain stores were lower, and the quality of their merchandise and services often higher. Many independent merchants felt threatened by these newer firms and mobilized considerable political force to curb their development.[10]

[10] Godfrey Lebhor, *Chain Stores in America* (New York: Chain Store Publishing Company, 1959).

It is important that marketers understand both the philosophy and the context of government regulations. Nearly all aspects of marketing strategy are affected by government regulations and legal considerations.

Table 2-1 lists the major milestones in federal legislation affecting business in general, and marketing in particular. In the following pages some of these laws will be explained. The main provisions of the acts shown in Figure 2-1 are listed in the table itself. Our discussion will focus on those with an important bearing upon marketing practices.

Sherman Antitrust Act (1890).   After the Civil War, during a period of great business expansion and growth, the formation of trusts, cartels, pools, and joint ventures aroused suspicion among the general population that American enterprise was in the clutch of a small group of conspiring, elitist "robber barons." People feared that prices, output, and markets were being administered by these few in a way contrary to the general welfare. In 1890 the *Sherman Antitrust Act* was passed, the first law to establish a statutory public policy against restraint of trade and monopoly in interstate and foreign commerce. Prior to the passage of the Sherman Act, such situations were governed only by the provisions of the common law, which were, at best, ambiguous and unenthusiastically enforced. However, even the new act was less than clear, and the courts in early cases tended to favor the defendants. The cause of preventing monopolies and restraints of trade was taken up much more vigorously during the so-called "trust busting" era under President Theodore Roosevelt. Antitrust regulation, for the first time, became an express goal of federal regulation. In 1911, in a landmark decision involving the Standard Oil Company of New Jersey, the Supreme Court introduced the so-called "rule of reason."[11] This interpretation declared that the defendant's behavior must amount to an unreasonable restraint of trade to be unlawful. The decision was a substantial victory for bigness because it meant that each case had to be judged separately. If bigness in the form of monopoly that could interfere with trade and competition was to be curtailed, it was evident that stronger legislation would be needed.

Federal Food and Drug Act and Meat Inspection Act (1906).   For many years Americans had been warned that the food and meat products they consumed were prepared, packaged, shipped, and marketed under less than sanitary conditions. Upton Sinclair, in his novel, *The Jungle*, shocked the country into awareness of filthy conditions in the meat packing industry. Public indignation was aroused and in 1906, again led by Theodore Roosevelt, the Congress enacted two new pieces of legislation, the Meat Inspection Act and the Federal Food and Drug Act. The Meat Inspection Act empowered the federal government to inspect packing plants and meat being shipped in interstate commerce. The Federal Food and Drug Act made it unlawful to misbrand or to adulterate food and drugs. For the first time, government assumed responsibility for protecting consumers against deceptive and harmful business practices.

[11] *Standard Oil Company of New Jersey v. United States,* 221 U.S. (1911).

Table 2-1 Important Legislation Affecting Marketing

SHERMAN ANTITRUST ACT (1890)

Prohibited (a) "monopolies or attempts to monopolize" and (b) "contracts, combinations, or conspiracies in restraint of trade."

FEDERAL FOOD AND DRUG ACT (1906)

Forbade the manufacture, sale, or transport of adulterated or fraudulently labeled foods and drugs in interstate commerce. (Supplanted by the Food, Drug, and Cosmetic Act, 1938; amended by Food Additives Act, 1958.)

MEAT INSPECTION ACT (1906)

Provided for the enforcement of sanitary regulations in packing establishments, and for federal inspection of all companies selling meats in interstate commerce.

FEDERAL TRADE COMMISSION ACT (1914)

Established the commission, a body of specialists with broad powers to investigate and to issue cease and desist orders to enforce Section 5, which declared that "unfair methods of competition in commerce are unlawful." (Amended by Wheeler-Lea Act, 1938, which added the phrase "and unfair or deceptive acts or practices.")

CLAYTON ACT (1914)

Supplemented the Sherman Act by prohibiting certain specific practices (certain types of price discrimination, tying clauses and exclusive dealing, intercorporate stockholdings, and interlocking directorates) "where the effect...may be to substantially lessen competition or tend to create a monopoly in any line of commerce." Provided that violating corporate officials could be held individually responsible, exempted labor and agricultural organizations from its provisions.

ROBINSON-PATMAN ACT (1936)

Amended the Clayton Act. Added the phrase "to injure, destroy, or prevent competition." Defined price discrimination as unlawful (subject to certain defenses) and provided the FTC with the right to establish limits on quantity discounts, to forbid brokerage allowances except to independent brokers, and to prohibit promotional allowances or the furnishing of services or facilities except where made available to all "on proportionately equal terms."

MILLER-TYDINGS ACT (1937)

Amended the Sherman Act to exempt interstate fair-trade (price-fixing) agreements from anti-trust prosecution. (The McGuire Act, 1952, reinstated the legality of the nonsigner clause.)

ANTIMERGER ACT (1950)

Amended Section 7 of the Clayton Act by broadening the power to prevent intercorporate acquisitions where the acquisition may have a substantially adverse effect on competition.

AUTOMOBILE INFORMATION DISCLOSURE ACT (1958)
FEDERAL CIGARETTE LABELING AND ADVERTISING ACT (1967)
CONSUMER CREDIT PROTECTION ACT (1968)

Established new patterns of consumer protection in the areas of automobile retailing, cigarette packaging and advertising, and consumer credit lending.

Source: Philip Kotler, *Marketing Management* (Englewood Cliffs, NJ: Prentice-Hall, 1972), p. 74.

In 1938, the Federal Food, Drug and Cosmetic Act supplanted the Federal Food and Drug Act of 1906. The FDA (Food and Drug Administration) now had the power to issue injunctions and seize goods found to be in violation of the law. Such violations include failure to report the name and place of business of the manufacturer or distributor; inaccurately or falsely reporting weight, size, or ingredients; using a container whose size misleads customers; misstatements about artificial ingredients like sweeteners; and the use of extravagant descriptions like "giant half-pint." The agency is particularly watchful for problems of side effects of drugs and has the power to approve or reject all new drugs as well as the advertising used to introduce them.

Federal Trade Commission Act (1914). The Federal Trade Commission Act was a "get serious" commitment on the part of the federal government to regulate trade and promote competition. The passage of the Federal Trade Commission Act in 1914 launched a serious effort to promote genuine competition in the interest of individual and social welfare. Under this act a commission of economics and business specialists was established to oversee the more technical and complicated issues in antitrust endeavors. The commission's task was to aid the courts; it was also given the power to launch investigations and issue cease and desist orders. The Federal Trade Commission Act listed specific practices of unfair competition and this, of course, added objectivity and broadened the opportunity for prosecution. The act also specified that the commission delineate in further detail what it considered to be unfair methods of competition. After much frustrated effort, the commission eventually turned to the industries, many of which were already under attack, and asked them to develop their own trade practices to protect the interests of both individual firms and consumers. Needless to say, these efforts met with a marked lack of success.

From its earliest days the FTC directed its efforts toward eliminating and exposing false advertising and branding. But the courts soon ruled that the power of the FTC was limited to exposing injury to competition. Thus, protecting consumers from deceit was not considered to be the task of the FTC. In 1938, however, the passage of the Wheeler/Lea Act added the phrase, "unfair or deceptive acts or practices" to the provisions of the Federal Trade Commission Act aimed at unfair methods of competition in general. Today the FTC is an aggressive branch of the federal apparatus regulating a broad spectrum of business behavior that might hurt either consumers or other businesses. For example, recently the FTC issued a cease and desist order requiring Warner-Lambert, the company that markets Listerine, to spend a specified amount on advertising (called corrective advertising) that must state: "Contrary to prior advertising, Listerine will not prevent colds or sore throats or lessen their severity."[12]

As we enter the decade of the 1980s, the FTC has encountered stiff opposition from a Congress which believes that regulation has run amuck and therefore plans to weaken the FTC's overzealous efforts at curbing business enterprise. This may in part reflect the public's new anti regulatory sentiment.[13]

Clayton Act (1914). In some respects, 1914 was a vintage year for the passage of legislation regulating competition. In addition to the Federal Trade Commission Act enacted that year, Congress also passed the Clayton Act. This act broadened and hence strengthened the Sherman Act of 1890 by more specifically defining practices as unlawful, where such practices "...may be to substantially lessen competition or tend to create a monopoly." It was no longer the burden of government to produce proof of actual monopoly or conspiracy. The following practices now were all held to be illegal if they substantially lessened competition: (Section 2) price discrimination; (Section 3) tying and exclusive agreements; and interlocking directorates and intercorporate stockholding, (Sections 8 and 7, respectively). Still, there were a few loopholes in regulation and enforcement. The task remained of working out agreements and establishing precedents for what is meant by "competition" and what constitutes behavior that "tends to substantially weaken competition."

From the Regulation of Competition to Regulating Competitors

Not all regulation, as was mentioned earlier, was directed toward preserving competition. Some was more narrowly designed to curb the progress of new forms of competitors.

Robinson Patman Act (1936). The Robinson Patman Act was basically passed at the insistence of smaller independent merchants, who felt threatened by the growth and success of chain store merchandisers. This act stipulated that it was unlawful for a seller to discriminate in price between different purchasers of commodities of like grade and quality whereby the effect of such discriminatory practices may be to substantially lessen competition, to foster a monopoly, or "to injure, destroy or prevent competition." The last phrase seems to have caused great difficulty. Discriminatory pricing practices, which generally result in buying economies for large purchasers, were not just unlaw-

[12] Dorothy Cohen, "F.T.C. Orders $10 Million 'To Correct' 55 Years of Ads; Warner-Lambert to Appeal Case," in "Legal News and Views," *Marketing News*, April 23, 1976, p. 3. Also, see Dorothy Cohen, "The FTC's Advertising Substantiation Program," *Journal of Marketing* **44**, No. 1, (Winter 1980), pp. 26–35.
[13] "Open Season on the FTC," *Time*, December 3, 1979, pp. 85–86. Also see Ernest Gellhorn, "The FTC Under Siege," *Regulation,* January–February 1980, pp. 33–40.

ful if they tended to *lessen* competition, but were also unlawful if they *injured* competition, and the courts began to interpret this *to mean injury to competitors*. Here was an act that under the guise of promoting competition actually protected many inefficient firms from the rigors of a competitive market place. The Robinson Patman Act stated that sellers cannot give a lower price to a buyer

1. If the buyer takes commodities of like grade and quality
2. If the price difference
   - substantially lessens competition
   - tends to create a monopoly
   - injures, destroys, or prevents competition with vendor or buyer, or customer of either, and
3. If the price difference is not making due allowances for differences in the cost of manufacture, sales, or delivery resulting from the differing methods or quantities in which such goods are to such buyers sold or delivered.

There is one loophole, perhaps best termed an ambiguity, in the law that is called the "rule of reason." This phrase says you can sell to a buyer at a reduced price if the lower price is "to meet a competitor's equally low price." In addition to price differentials, the Robinson Patman Act regulates and prohibits discrimination through advertising allowances, brokerage fees, or any other special services or facilities.

The overall effect of the Robinson Patman Act has been to eliminate or seriously dampen much price competition.[14]

Miller Tydings Resale Price Maintenance Act (1937).   Resale price maintenance, known popularly as "fair trade," is an arrangement under which the seller of a product identified by a brand name or trademark sets a minimum price below which the buyer may not go in making a subsequent sale. The company that sets the price may be a producer or a distributor of the product in question. The firms whose prices are thus controlled are those who sell the product at retail. It is readily apparent that advocates of resale price maintenance are opposed to retail price competition. Prior to the 1930s resale price maintenance had repeatedly been condemned by the courts, which held that it violated both the Sherman Act of 1890 and the Federal Trade Commission Act of 1914. However, the first state Fair Trade Law was passed in California in 1931. In 1933, again in California, the so-called nonsigner's clause was added, which in effect provided that if one retailer in the state signed a contract with a manufacturer not to sell below a minimum price, all other California retailers were bound to that contract. Other states soon followed with similar legislation.

Resale price maintenance legislation aroused passions on all sides. It was a hotly contested issue throughout the court system, the state legislatures, and

---

[14] See Rom J. Markin, "The Robinson Patman Act: Regulatory Pariah" in *Contemporary Issues in Marketing Channels,* Robert F. Lusch and Paul Zinszer eds., Center for Economic and Management Research, University of Oklahoma, Norman, 1979, pp. 121–130.

the Congress. Small merchants favored it, arguing that their survival depended on its existence and enforcement. Competitive, price oriented merchants detested it as a haven for the sloppy, inefficient, nonagressive merchant.

In 1975, Senator Edward W. Brooke (R.) of Massachusetts introduced a bill (S. 408) to repeal provisions in antitrust laws exempting fair trade laws. The bill was passed in both houses and signed into law by President Ford in late 1975. Fair trade proponents could no longer muster much support, for consumers throughout the country were demanding more aggressive price competition. Hopefully, the uneconomic, wasteful, and inefficient concept of fair trade pricing is dead forever. May it lie undisturbed.

Proconsumer Legislation.   There is seemingly no end to the amount of legislation that regulates, governs, constrains, and affects marketing activity. We have made no effort to exhaust the subject, but as marketing students it is necessary that you have some familiarity with the laws. Many of these are designed to regulate certain practices; others regulate certain industries, and many, of late, add a fuller measure of protection for consumers.[15] A listing of several of these laws is shown in Table 2-2.

Some would argue that government is taking an overly protective position toward the consumer and that such an attitude is needlessly paternalistic. Others, including legislators, government agencies, and consumer representatives, claim that today's consumers are overwhelmed by marketers' blandishments; that too many products and too many promotional efforts are confusing customers. Today's consumers, they say, have less opportunity to evaluate merchandise before purchasing it and that manufacturers must therefore accept a greater responsibility for their products' reliability, safety, and performance.

So much new legislation has tended to alter marketing activities. Some firms are much less inclined than formerly to make claims about product performance. Marketers often complain, somewhat justifiably, that government agencies carrying out consumer protection laws have little real understanding of consumer needs. Consumers do not make choices solely according to economic criteria, but according to a host of criteria, many of which are subjective and psychosocial rather than strictly economic. Regulatory agencies often fail to take this into consideration, according to many marketers.

Is Marketing Overregulated?   The question is not so much whether there will be government regulation of the private enterprise system, for we have had a mixed, public-private system since the 1930s. We really must ask, How much government regulation is desirable? Some contend that in the 1970s, the pendulum of the mix swung further and faster toward central control, creating some undesirable side effects for Americans in general and business enterprise

---

[15] Dorothy Cohen, "Remedies for Consumer Protection: Prevention, Restitution, or Punishment," *Journal of Marketing* **39** (October 1975), pp. 24–31.

Table 2-2 Major Proconsumer Legislation

Year	
1960	Federal Hazardous Substances Act Color Additives Amendment
1962	Kefauver-Harris Drug Amendments
1965	Drug Abuse Control Amendments Fair Packaging and Labeling Act
1966	National Traffic and Motor Vehicle Safety Act Child Safety Act Cigarette Labeling Act
1967	National Commission on Product Safety Wholesome Meat Act
1968	Wholesome Poultry Product Act Consumer Credit Protective Act Hazardous Radiation Act
1969	Public Health Cigarette Smoking Act of 1969 Child Protection and Toy Safety Act of 1969
1970	Fair Credit Reporting Act Council on Environmental Quality
1971	Federal Boat Safety Act
1972	Consumer Product Safety Act
1974	Motor Vehicle Information and Cost Savings Act Transportation Safety Act of 1974
1975	Consumer Goods Pricing Act. Prohibited the use of price maintenance agreements among manufacturers and resellers in interstate commerce.
1975	Magnuson-Moss Warranty and Federal Trade Commission Act

in particular.[16] These effects were (1) a lessening of competition and competitive markets; (2) a growing consumer attitude that central control and government regulations are superior and necessary; and (3) public mistrust of the market system.

The opposing side, of course, would argue to the contrary. They would contend that business (1) has gotten out of hand, (2) has abused its power, (3) is too important to the national welfare to remain unregulated, and (4) that the interest of the consumer is best served through government regulation and control.

No doubt we will continue to have government regulation of marketing and business activity. Of late, though, American business may be suffering from

[16] See C. Jackson Grayson, Jr., "Let's Get Back to the Competitive Marketplace," *Harvard Business Review*, November-December 1973, pp. 103–113.

regulatory overkill. Some controls are confusing, illogical, contradictory, and unnecessarily costly. During the last fifteen years, 236 new federal regulatory agencies and departments have been created. During this same time only twenty-one have been eliminated.

Maintaining a Competitive Atmosphere

The role of government is to preserve and maintain a competitive atmosphere, not to stifle competition. A competitive market structure is important because it determines the behavior of firms in the industry, which in turn governs the quality of the industry's performance. Highly concentrated industries are likely to perform poorly because they allocate resources inefficiently, impeding our efforts to reach national economic goals. Too much concentration means flaws in the market system; prices are probably too high; assortments may be more limited; and other firms that would like to compete for the consumers' favor are discouraged by high barriers to entry in the markets.[17]

Maintaining a Favorable Business Climate

A favorable business climate is attained primarily through the government's monetary and fiscal policies, carried out through both the executive and legislative branches.

Through its agencies as well as through such quasigovernmental bodies as the Federal Reserve System, the government can affect money supplies and the cost of borrowed funds. Regulation of the nation's money affects business expansion, size of inventory buildups, remodeling, new-product introductions, and other business functions. Through its fiscal policies, the government can generate expenditures or withhold them, affecting the climate of business in such areas as employment, income, and inflation levels.

Employment.   People working constitute the basic ingredient of effective market opportunities. In 1980 the United States work force consisted of more than 103 million persons. More people today hold jobs than ever before in the history of United States employment. More than fifty percent of all households are characterized as two-income families, with both the husband and wife gainfully employed. Throughout the 1970s, with the exception of the recession year 1973–1974 when unemployment rose to nearly 10 percent, the average unemployment rate hovered at about 6 percent. Such programs as unemployment insurance, social security, and public assistance programs, while specifically oriented toward individual welfare, nonetheless act to buoy and maintain national consumption and expenditure levels.

Incomes.   The government also fosters a favorable business climate in order to assure consumers of both an adequate and a rising income level. Incomes

---

[17] See Richard Caves, *American Industry: Structure, Conduct, Performance,* 3d ed. (Englewood Cliffs, NJ: Prentice-Hall, 1972), pp. 16–35.

are, of course, basically an outgrowth of employment, but they also arise from past employment and income converted into savings and other asset holdings. In 1968, per capita personal income amounted to $2,672; by 1980, it stood at $6,421.[18] Personal income includes all wages, pensions, and other income received by Americans. The slow but steady climb in personal income throughout the decade of the 1970s meant substantial increases in the buying power of American consumers. For American marketers this meant more sales and profits.

Inflation. Inflation can be loosely characterized as a situation where too many dollars are chasing too few goods. This means that there is too much demand relative to supply, resulting in a rapid climb in the general price level. Inflation is a disease always harmful, and sometimes fatal, to both consumption and business activity. In one period of rampant inflation, the one that erupted in 1979 and 1980, the general price level shot up almost immediately by 17 to 18 percent. Such a steep rise can wipe out consumers' purchasing power, especially those on fixed incomes. It can lead to an "inflation psychosis," where everyone frantically buys now to avoid the price increases sure to occur tomorrow or next week.

The usual cure for inflation is to curb demand through restrictive governmental monetary and fiscal policies that tend to reduce government expenditures and maintain relatively high interest rates. As you will readily observe, these are the same policies adopted to restrict employment and so curtail incomes.

Hence, government, as we have seen, both gives and takes away. It works to create a climate conducive to business and marketing enterprise, and at the same time, through its laws, regulations, and agencies, it controls and constrains marketing activity.

Before proceeding, can you answer these questions:
1. How does the government affect the marketing environment?
2. Some government regulation affects competition; some affects competitors. Explain.
3. How does government policy on (a) employment, (b) incomes, and (c) inflation affect marketing?

The Technological Environment of Marketing

Technology is the way things are done; the methods and materials used to achieve commercial and industrial objectives. It is usually the product or outgrowth of scientific discovery, plus positive social attitudes and awareness. For example, consider the case of razor blades mentioned earlier. Scientific break-

[18] "Consumer Markets: Per Capita Income," *Across the Board*, Vol. XVII, No. 6., June, 1980.

throughs in developing special metal alloys and processes for coating blades with special plastic coverings have led to markedly improved blade quality and durability. If such improvement were not met by consumer groups willing to try new products, the effect would be negligible. The economy of the United States, oriented as it is, has been deeply and positively affected by technology.

Changes in ways of doing things, making products, the application of scientific progress and social innovation—all are constantly taking place, churning up new problems and new opportunities for marketing endeavors.

Hundreds of products now sold in great volume did not even exist ten to twenty years ago. Marketers today realize the importance of technology. As a consequence, many firms spend at least as much for research and development of new products as they do for sales and promotion of existing ones. The transistor, the integrated circuit, the computer, the jet plane, the automobile, the supermarket, and the sexual revolution all have had great impact upon marketing. Products, processes, promotion, and profits have all been affected.

An Object Lesson—The Automobile

In 1867, at the Paris Exposition, there was an interesting exhibit: a small engine in which gasoline and air were introduced into a combustion chamber and ignited by a spark.[19] The resulting explosion pushed a piston; the piston turned a wheel. It was the world's first internal combustion engine, invented by Dr. N. A. Otto of Germany. Soon thereafter every up-to-date farm, shop, and feedmill had its one-cylinder engine chugging away, pumping water, sawing wood, grinding meal, and doing many other tasks.

The gasoline engine led the way for an even more startling technological advance. In 1886, Charles E. Duryea of Massachusetts decided to install this new engine, instead of a steam generator, in a self-propelled road vehicle. Six years later he had produced the first gasoline-powered "automobile." By 1896, Duryea and his brother had sold thirteen cars. In that same year a 32-year-old tinker-mechanic named Henry Ford sold his first "quadricycle"—and the development of the automobile was underway. Its growth, as we all know, has been phenomenal.

Within the next decade, 125 firms, with 10,000 workers, were making automobiles. By 1923, the number of plants had risen to 2,471; the industry had become the largest in the country. In less than forty years, by 1960, the annual payroll was as large as the entire national income of the United States in 1890. And there is more. The automobile industry is the single greatest customer for sheet metal, zinc, lead, rubber, and leather. A major user of fabrics, carpeting, and plastics, it also buys one out of every three radios produced in the nation and absorbs 25 billion pounds of chemicals a year. It is the second largest user of American engineering talent, bowing only to national defense. The automobile industry is the originator of one-sixth of all

---

[19] Adapted from Robert L. Heilbroner, *The Making of Economic Society* (Englewood Cliffs, NJ: Prentice-Hall, 1962), pp. 102–104.

the patents issued in the United States and the object of one-tenth of all its consumer spending. No less than one out of every seven jobs and one business out of every six owe their existence directly or indirectly to the car.

Consider still further the impact of the automobile on Americans' life styles, the new businesses it has spawned, and its impact on various aspects of marketing. It has revolutionized the way people live, work, and play. The rise of the suburbs and the resulting decay of the inner city can be traced directly to the automobile. Our newfound mobility was largely responsible for the growth and development of the supermarket and, later, the controlled or planned suburban shopping center. Drive-in restaurants, laundries, and banking facilities as well as motels all have been developed to accommodate Americans on wheels.

The Automobile—Trouble Ahead?

Between 1940 and 1980, the number of automobiles increased in the United States from 22 million to 120 million, so that presently the ratio of autos to people is about 1 to 2. The automobile, without exception, has done more to transform American society in the twentieth century than has any other technological innovation. It has come to be thought of as a necessity, an essential ingredient for happiness, and an integral part of the American life style. But the auto, of late, has also come to be seen as a mixed blessing. It is the scapegoat for a host of modern problems such as air pollution, urban decay, congestion, and noise pollution. However, it is not the automobile that is guilty; the owners and manufacturers are at fault. The main problem is that automobile companies charge buyers only for the private costs of buying cars. Many of the social costs of owning and driving the car—the fouling of our environment—are not borne by the owner, but by society in general. When there is a divergence between social and private costs, economists say that an externality exists. Externalities occur because of the inability of all concerned to decide who will assume what costs.[20]

Today, Americans are looking at automobile transportation from a new, more realistic viewpoint. We are weighing its unmatched convenience against the heavy social costs it exacts. Social innovation or change, as we mentioned earlier, almost always impacts with technology. As citizens' awareness of the price society pays for automobiles grows, the automobile industry and many of its satellite industries are pressured into change. This new social awareness is spawning a whole generation of technological innovation: new fuels, cleaner burning engines, alternative forms of transportation (bicycles and mass transit systems) and perhaps new ways of living and shopping.

Changing Technology. Our technology is in a constant state of change, but the new developments do not come smoothly nor evenly. The technology

---

[20] For a fuller discussion of "The Economics of the Automobile," see Douglas C. North and Roger Leroy Miller, *The Economics of Public Issues* (New York: Harper & Row, 1973), pp. 74–78.

of the 1980s, especially in relation to fuel and energy, communication, transportation, and more widespread computerization, most likely will come on willy-nilly. Marketing managers who hesitate to stick their necks out stand a good chance of losing many marketing opportunities.

Perhaps twenty years from now, reflecting on the developments that moved marketing from the primitive days of the early 1980s to the streamlined systems of 1995, we will recount the many social and technological changes, and their consequences, that took place. These changes will have embraced not only new consumer and industrial products and services but equally dramatic developments in advertising, distribution, and selling.[21]

The Postindustrial Society

The economy of the United States is one of the wealthiest in the world. Its gross national product (the value of goods and services produced in a year) is more than $1.4 trillion. With slightly more than one-twentieth of the world's population, the United States possesses somewhere between a third and a half of all the world's wealth. Many factors account for this, but surely no less important than our natural resources, our climate, and geography are our technological orientation and our enterprising national character.

Our technology and industriousness have led us into what is called the postindustrial society, that is, one in which the production of services is more important than the production of goods.[22] However, the postindustrial society has many other important features that affect the marketing environment. Among these are:

1. *An increasing emphasis on technology.* The stream of scientific information from outer space exploration, comparable to the information given us by the microscope at the end of the nineteenth century, will revolutionize our thinking and patterns of living. A whole new generation of products will drastically alter our living and consumption patterns.

2. *There will be marked changes in demographic and economic trends.* Almost all advanced countries of the world will become overwhelmingly urban, preoccupied with the quality of life and leisure. The gap between rich and poor nations will widen and it will be harder for poor countries to provide their people with the necessities of living. In advanced nations, people will seek sensation and gratification through change—in careers, products and services, life styles, marriage partners, and geography. This means that new market opportunities will increasingly originate in the demand for novel experiences and fresh sensations.

3. *There will be marked changes in social-cultural traditions.* Consumers will be more knowledgeable. Exposure to an estimated 15,000 hours of televi-

[21] Theodore J. Gordon, "Changing Technology and the Future of Marketing," *The Conference Board Record,* December 1974, pp. 22–26.
[22] R. Joseph Monson, *Business and the Changing Environment* (New York: McGraw-Hill, 1973), pp. 259–284.

"I'm still reading it. When I'm finished, then you can recycle it."

Drawing by Modell; © 1974 The New Yorker Magazine, Inc.

sion by college age has made Americans more aware of the rest of society and the world than earlier generations ever were. Attitudes toward sexual behavior will move beyond the new morality that stemmed from the wide acceptance of birth control. Finally, a shrunken world, rapid communication, and higher levels of education will heighten consumers' social awareness. They will have new expectations and new standards for business behavior and will be more insistent that marketers act with meaningful *social responsibility*.

Social Responsibilities in the Postindustrial Society

Will the marketing firm's social responsibilities be greater in the postindustrial society? The answer is a clear yes. Social responsibilities of business are always related to the value orientation of the prevailing social-cultural system. For instance, during the emergence of the industrial era, businessmen, especially those at the forefront of expansion, were given the unsavory but apt name of "robber barons." Such a name says a great deal about the social responsibilities of the times.

The Rules Change.   Business ethics and social responsibilities do change, sometimes very quickly. Major political events like the "Watergate Incident" during the Nixon administration can quickly bring about a new set of expectations concerning social responsibilities and ethics in business and government.

The rules have changed. The rules of the game, which include social responsibilities and business ethics, are never absolute; they are relative to the value orientation of a given social-cultural system at a given time.

Emerging out of the value orientation of the postindustrial era in the United States is a new set of themes that are affecting marketers' social responsibilities and business ethics. These themes are the following:

- Social conscience, generally expressed as a concern for the preservation, restoration, and protection of the environment.
- More rational marketing, typified by such questions as "Should this product be sold?" and "Is it worth the cost to society?"
- An expanded role for marketing. Marketing service in the wider public interest; namely, marketing that takes account of consumers' notions about fuel conservation, protection of health, and other critical social ideas worthy of support.
- The responsibility of marketing to help regulate the shape and level of demand for a wide range of products and services.

Some marketing managers see the future as it is turning the corner, and others see it only after it arrives. However one sees it, it is important to recognize that marketing exists in a larger setting and this setting is an important determinant of the firm's performance and success.

Summary

Marketing strategy is a comprehensive plan of action in pursuit of company goals and objectives. What we have learned in this chapter is that planning and developing strategy does not take place in a vacuum, but rather, in a larger setting. It is important for marketers to understand the complex nature of the environment of marketing, because to a great extent the firm's behavior will be affected by these environmental variables and constraints. Some marketing firms, by virtue of their size and style, are more innovative and hence likely to be less constrained by environmental considerations. Other firms, being more adaptive than innovative, are more apt to be affected by environmental considerations. No firm, however, regardless of its size, influence, or style of operation, can afford to ignore the external environment that surrounds it. This environment has social-cultural, political-economic, and technological dimensions that must be studied, understood, and incorporated into a firm's thinking as the basis for interpreting its social responsibilities as well as its strategic marketing planning.

Review Questions

1. What is meant by marketing strategy?
2. What are the basic elements in the firm's marketing mix?
3. How would you describe the difference between an innovative marketing firm and an adaptive marketing firm?
4. What is a social-cultural system? How does it affect the behavior of marketing firms?

5. What is meant by "mixed capitalism?" Does this concept suggest something about the relationship of government and business in the United States?

6. Why does government attempt to regulate business through antitrust legislation affecting the size and structure of business organizations?

7. Some legislation attempts to regulate competition and some attempts to regulate competitors. Explain.

8. What are the main provisions of the Robinson Patman Act?

9. As a consumer, do you favor resale price maintenance legislation? Would you favor it if you were the product manager of Timex watches? The owner-manager of a drugstore selling Timex watches? Give your reasons.

10. Do you believe marketing is overregulated? From whose point of view are you considering the question?

11. In what ways does government attempt to create a favorable business climate?

12. What is meant by the "postindustrial society"? What are some of the trends emerging from the postindustrial society? How will they affect marketing strategy and the measurement of marketing performance?

Case 2-1

American Motor's Eagle

American Motors Corporation's new Eagle, which is America's first four-wheel drive auto, is just as much at home during regular driving as it is climbing a steep slippery hill. The Eagle is designed for comfortable driving on normal roads that are in average or rotten condition. It is classified as a light truck by the government but that is misleading. It offers all the comforts of AMC's compact size Concord from which it is derived. The major difference between the Eagle and Concord, besides the four-wheel drive system, is a stiffer suspension. Many motorists who buy high-priced imported sedans demand such a suspension.

The Eagle sits three inches higher than the Concord, which is the only significant visual tip that is different from the Concord. A car that is three inches higher, however, still looks considerably taller than other autos. To prevent a "jacked-up suspension" look, AMC put fender flares on the Eagle to bring the wheel openings down to where the top of the tires are. The flares are not noticeable.

The Eagle is not a fuel efficient automobile. The EPA (Environmental Protection Agency) estimates that it gets 19 miles per gallon on the highway and 16 miles per gallon in the city. The vehicle weighs more than a conventional compact and its four-wheel drive system results in fuel-robbing drag. Also hurting economy is the car's rugged but dated 258 cubic inch six-cylinder engine. The car also has an automatic transmission, which eats more gasoline than a manual. The car comes as a two- or four-door sedan and as a four-door station wagon.

The Eagle is not cheap, although a four-wheel drive truck can easily cost more than $10,000. The Wagon version of the Eagle has a $7,549 list price. The two door lists at $6,999, and the four door costs $7,249. When snow and ice are causing motorists to despair, the Eagle might seem like the bargain of the century.

An AMC spokesperson said demand for the Eagle has been so great since its introduction—especially in snow belt areas of the country—that the company is hiking production from 50,000 to 90,000 units during the car's first year on the market.

The Eagle is another attempt by AMC to find its market niche and to compete effectively with both domestic and overseas producers. For some years AMC has attempted to be America's small car specialist but with limited and measured success. The past five years have been a particularly critical period for AMC with repeated industry rumors that the company might not make it through the decade of the 1980s. The chairman of American Motors recently predicted that the domestic small car market will triple or quadruple by 1985. In early 1980, larger U.S. cars simply were not selling, while Japanese and European small car imports were in such demand that customers were paying premium prices and waiting as much as six to eight weeks for delivery. AMC officers believe it is better "…to fish in a pond of six to eight million small cars, instead of two million." Company spokespersons also assert that their company "…has new opportunities and that they hoped to be good enough and smart enough to take advantage of them," adding further that "…we've been facing tough competition and in a market much smaller than what is on the horizon."

Questions

1. To what extent is AMC's new venture with the Eagle related to "market opportunity"?

2. What share of the subcompact and compact car markets has AMC been getting? (You

Eagle Sedans

When your concern is how to get where you want to go, securely and comfortably, look to the driving alternative designed for the '80s . . . the 1981 Eagle 2-door and 4-door sedan models. Security . . . furnished by a built-in four-wheel drive system that handles on- and off-road driving situations with ease. Family-sized . . . with the roominess afforded by efficient design. And comfort . . . with all the conveniences and appointments of a luxury automobile.

There's no mistaking the styling refinements of the 1981 Eagle sedans either. On the outside the lower bodyside Kraton™ system blends neatly into the front and rear bumpers. The grille is re-styled with a textured rectangular insert. The 2-door sedan is also highlighted by a new distinctive opera window treatment in both the standard and Limited models. And a wide range of new options include 6-way power seats, aluminum wheels, floor shift console and gauge package, to name only a few.

The standard Eagle sedan powerteam is the 2.5 liter 4-cylinder engine with 4-speed manual transmission. Optional powerteam choices include both the 4.2 liter six and 3-speed automatic transmission.

An exciting Eagle Sport Package is also available as an option with the 2-door sedan. Features include a color-keyed leather sport steering wheel with woodgrain hub on the inside, low gloss black Kraton™ wheel flares, black bumpers and bumper guards, dual remote sport mirrors, black grille insert, silver 4x4 graphics and "Sport" nameplates.

Of course, at no extra cost you get the benefits of the 1981 Buyer Protection Plan. It includes Ziebart® Factory Rust Protection with galvanized steel on the inside of all exterior body panels. Full five-year No Rust-Thru™ Warranty. Full 12-month/12,000-mile New Vehicle Warranty. All yours as standard equipment on all new Eagles for 1981.

The American Eagles for 1981 . . . unbelievable motoring traction and control uniquely combined with automotive luxury. Experience driving in the 4th dimension.

will need to do some library research to discover this information.)

3. What major environmental factors will affect AMC's sale of automobiles during the 1980s?

4. If a given market increases, does that necessarily mean that a particular competitor's sales will increase also? Why or why not?

5. AMC executives contend that "we have new opportunities and we hope to be good enough to take advantage of them." Why would you think the company might be good enough and smart enough to take advantage of their new opportunities when they obviously were unable to do so in the past?

Case 2-2

Warner-Lambert
v. Federal Trade Commission

In the case of *Warner-Lambert v. Federal Trade Commission,* the FTC had issued an order requiring Warner-Lambert to cease and desist from advertising its product, Listerine mouthwash, as a preventive, cure, or palliative for the common cold. The FTC also directed that in all future advertising, both print and electronic, Warner-Lambert must include the following corrective statement: "Contrary to prior advertising, Listerine will not help prevent colds or sore throats or lessen their severity." The Circuit Court of Appeals for the District of Columbia upheld the use of the corrective advertising program by the Federal Trade Commission.

In addition, the FTC required that the statement be included in all Listerine advertising until the company has spent $10 million on advertising, a sum equivalent to that spent on publicizing Listerine from April 1962 to March 1972. The Court of Appeals upheld all the commission's orders except the required use of the phrase "contrary to prior advertising."

The concept of full disclosure in advertising and marketing has been well established, but corrective advertising is a new approach by the FTC. It warns that an advertiser may be required to make affirmative disclosure of unfavorable facts.

Listerine has been on the market since 1879 and Warner-Lambert has always claimed that the product has a beneficial effect. FTC found that Listerine did not alleviate colds or sore throats because it does not contain enough of its supposed therapeutic ingredients to do any real good. The commission stated that gargling does not permit the mouthwash to reach the affected areas of the body in a concentration sufficient to be considered medicine.

One of the critical issues that arises is the question, "If Listerine's advertising in the past was false, does the commission have the power to prescribe the remedy of corrective advertising?" The appellate court said yes. The court noted that a broad, modern interpretation must be given to Section 5 of the FTC Act. Therefore, the court said, it was not necessary to find express statutory authority for the power invoked. Warner-Lambert claimed that corrective advertising was improper because it (1) impinges on the First Amendment, and (2) has never been approved by any court. The Court of Appeals disagreed.

Thus, the court indicated, the remedy was proper. In printed ads, the statement must be displayed in type size at least as large as that in which the principal portion of the text of the ad appears, and it must be readily noticeable.

In television commercials the disclosure must be presented simultaneously in both the audio and visual portions. During the audio portion of the disclosure on television and in radio ads, no other sounds, including music, may occur.

Questions

1. Do you believe corrective advertising is a desirable form of government regulation and constraint?

2. Whose interests are best served by such FTC requirements as full disclosure and corrective advertising?

3. What logic or reasoning do you believe underlies the court's upholding of the FTC's corrective advertising approach? What does this imply about the power of advertising?

4. How might Warner-Lambert combat this ruling and still continue to market Listerine?

Chapter 3

The Elements of Strategic Marketing Planning

Marketing is the basic process by which any organization, be it profit oriented or nonprofit oriented, adapts and responds to its ever-changing market opportunity. To underscore this point, let's consider some of the new developments in three widely different areas.

- An operation that began as a public service has become a new and successful profit center for the Washington Natural Gas Company. Like many other utilities in the 1970s, Washington Gas found it desirable to shift the focus of its advertising efforts from consumption to conservation. As a promotional device to bring the idea of conservation to the attention of the public, the company decided to offer free home insulation throughout the Puget Sound Basin. The company estimated costs, provided financing, and hired firms to do the installation. However, the demand for these services turned out to be much greater than the company had anticipated, so it began to charge for them. In fact, it now has eight home insulation retail stores that supply both products and services.
- Many of the larger American commercial banks are beginning to broaden the range of their banking services considerably by moving into what is called merchant banking. They are no longer merely taking deposits and lending money; they are also—for a fee, of course—arranging financing from nonbank sources, offering customers financial advice, and helping companies with mergers and acquisitions. They are even becoming involved to a limited extent in the stock brokerage business. European banks have been carrying out such activities as these for years, as have some U.S. banks in their overseas operations. Now U.S. banks are moving into this wider market arena here at home.
- The management of the American Hospital Supply Company in Evanston, Illinois, realized that hospitals were being supplied by a large number of small firms, each selling only a few products. This made the purchasing activities of the hospitals difficult and cumbersome. The company felt that hospitals would be receptive to the idea of concentrating their business with a few firms that could supply most of their needs. It therefore decided to become such a company. Because its management saw a marketing opportunity and acted on it, the American Hospital Supply Company has now become one of the largest hospital suppliers in the United States.

As we saw in chapter 2, marketing is a dynamic process of change and response through which a firm is able to adjust to changes in environmental variables beyond its control. The link between the firm and the environment is its comprehensive plan of action—its **marketing strategy**. The examples just presented illustrate this concept in actual practice. They deal with real firms that have used imagination and creativity along with a planned, methodical approach to develop effective marketing strategies. These strategies have then allowed the firms to adjust their marketing programs to take advantage of new market opportunities created by changes in the business environment.

In the 1960s and 1970s, marketing success was relatively easy. It was most often the outgrowth of a firm's ability to detect the presence of a market or industry in which there was no strong competition and then to develop a product and a marketing program that made it the dominant competitor. Thus, a firm could be successful even when its efforts did not reflect a great deal of expertise. Still, a brief study of successful marketing firms suggests that they invariably do three things well:

1. They are the first, or one of the first, to recognize the existence of a marketing opportunity.
2. They are able to develop a strategy that is appropriate for the given situation.
3. They are able to execute that strategy with a high degree of proficiency.

Marketing firms will continue to rely on these proven management techniques in the 1980s. However, given the uncertain and rigorous competitive environment that appears likely to exist in the years ahead, market strategies that are astutely chosen and expertly implemented will become more and more crucial.[1] Marketers must therefore increase their proficiency in strategic marketing planning if they hope to survive and prosper. As a result, strategic planning will truly become the cutting edge of total corporate policy.

What is Strategic Marketing Planning?

Every enterprise ought to have at least two major objectives: (1) to do things right and (2) to do the right thing. The first of these objectives applies to the way the enterprise carries out its operations. It means that whatever is done should be done well. The second objective—to do the right thing—is of more fundamental importance, however. No matter how well something is done, if it is not the right thing to do, doing it well is of little or no value. Discovering what is the right thing is the purpose of strategic marketing planning.

All organizations, both profit and nonprofit, must plan effective strategies if they are to be successful. Not just business firms, but also charitable institutions, hospitals, and even Olympic committees all engage in strategic planning; political campaigns, in fact, are the essence of strategic planning. As one insightful commentary on the lack of success of many American enterprises puts it, "Without a strategy the organization is like a ship without a rudder, going around in circles. It's like a tramp; it has no place to go."[2]

But what, then, is strategic marketing planning? While the term *strategy* still has connotations of competitiveness, it is increasingly coming to denote an action-oriented program that has been designed to give an organization a unified plan for achieving specific goals. It indicates where emphasis is to be placed, what direction is to be taken, and what resources are to be used by the organization in carrying out its basic mission. The essence of strategy is deciding what needs to be done *in advance*. It is therefore a comprehensive,

---

[1] See Stanley F. Stasch, "1980's Marketing to Require Wisely Chosen Strategies", *Marketing News*, May 30, 1980, p. 16.

[2] Joll E. Ross and Michael J. Kami, *Corporations in Crisis: Why the Mighty Fall* (Englewood Cliffs, NJ: Prentice-Hall, 1973), p. 132.

"Then, too, of course, there's the damned human factor out there, and that, gentlemen, can be a wily little rascal."

Drawing by Zeigler; © 1978 The New Yorker Magazine, Inc.

long-range plan. The shorter-range, action plans used to implement a strategy are called tactics.

Strategic marketing planning, as the term implies, is an organization's application of the concept of strategic planning to marketing. It involves anticipating and evaluating coming developments in the marketing environment and deciding in advance how best to meet and profit from them. In short, it allows the organization to develop and maintain a viable mix of goods and services.

If the marketing environment were static, there would be little need for strategic marketing planning. But this environment changes rapidly. It is constantly affected by variations in customers' tastes and preferences, advances in technology, and, of course, the actions of intelligent competitors. It is therefore necessary for an organization to formulate a marketing strategy that allows it to respond to these changes quickly and effectively. This strategy will involve virtually every aspect of the organization's activities, from obtaining financing, through acquiring raw materials, designing new products, modifying existing products, updating production processes, altering promotional activities, developing new packaging, changing prices, establishing new channels of distribution and maintaining old ones, to broadening or streamlining services.

The Benefits of Strategic Marketing Planning

Marketing managers can ensure that strategic marketing planning has a specific bottom-line impact by developing careful strategies and taking conscientious steps for their implementation.[3] The general benefits of an effective marketing

---

[3] Robert T. Wetzler, "Management Theory Can Produce a Continuing Bottom Line Impact," *MSU Business Topics* **24**, no.1 (Winter 1976), pp. 5–10.

strategy include increased profitability, a better corporate image, and, sometimes, survival itself. In addition, there are a number of specific benefits. Among them are the following:[4]

1. *The coordination of the various activities within an enterprise strengthen it.* Strategic planning is a means of coordinating a firm's marketing, production, and financial activities. This leads to clearer corporate thinking, better utilization of the firm's resources, and a higher probability of attaining corporate objectives.

2. *Strategic planning allows an organization to specify expected developments.* Astute and disciplined executives are trained in the art of forecasting the future significance of what may be at the time barely discernible events. Through strategic planning, such events can be evaluated and placed in a better perspective for determining the organization's future course of action.

3. *Planning eliminates surprises.* Unexpected events can cause problems and even create havoc in a company. For example, the unforeseen rise in the price of gasoline, and the uncertain nature of supplies have forced thousands of independent service stations out of business. Corporate-affiliated service stations have fared much better, however, largely as a result of the strategic planning of the parent companies.

4. *Strategic planning creates an effective climate for managing change.* Strategic planning forces decision makers to think through what actions they would take if certain events occur. Such anticipation means that a firm's responses to actual events are more likely to be rational, deliberate, and in line with company objectives. In addition, strategic planning improves intracompany communication because it forces decision makers at all levels to exchange information. Such communication minimizes conflicts and facilitates the effective pursuit of those goals that best serve the company's overall interests.

Before proceeding, can you answer these questions:
1. Why is marketing the basic process by which an organization adapts and responds to an ever-changing market opportunity?
2. What is strategic marketing planning?
3. What are some of the benefits of strategic marketing planning?

The Elements of Strategic Marketing Planning

The basic elements of all strategic marketing planning efforts are shown schematically in Figure 3-1. A *schematic diagram* is an abstraction, or model, of a real-world system which shows the general relationships among a number of

---

[4] Another writer cites six benefits that a firm derives from strategic planning. See Alfred R. Oxenfeldt, *Executive Action in Marketing* (Belmont, CA: Wadsworth Publishing Company, 1966), pp. 36–39.

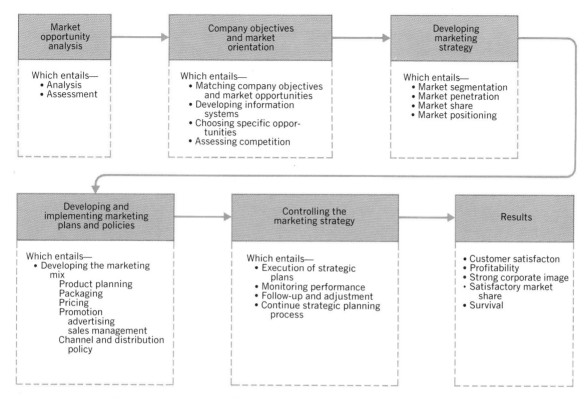

Figure 3-1 The Elements of Strategic Marketing Planning

complex variables. Though less than a perfect reflection of the actual system, it is easier to visualize and to work with than its real-world counterpart.

The process shown in Figure 3-1 is the most common approach to strategic marketing planning. It is a logical series of activities that can lead to an increase in an organization's success when they are completed with thoroughness and imagination. Of course, all firms do not approach strategic marketing planning in exactly the same way. Generally speaking, however, each of the major items shown will be considered by any firm that devotes serious attention to the development of an effective marketing strategy.

The remainder of this chapter will be devoted to an examination of the individual elements of strategic marketing planning. However, because subsequent chapters deal exclusively with some of these concepts, the treatment of them here will be relatively brief.

Market Opportunity Analysis

Markets and market opportunity will be discussed in depth in chapter 5. Nevertheless, a few general comments are warranted here.

The first step in strategic marketing planning is to identify and analyze market opportunities. Fortunately for businesses, the world is filled with countless potential opportunities. Many of them are presently disguised as insurmountable problems, however. For example, the world needs cheaper, pollution-free transportation and greatly increased amounts of energy of all types. We need synthetic products to replace scarce and expensive natural and organic products. Our supplies of high-calorie, protein-rich food must be significantly expanded. Faster and more effective means of personal and intergroup communication must be developed. We need more efficient and less expensive methods of mass education. And we must find ways of cleaning up our polluted rivers and lakes as well as our endangered oceans. In short, crucial problems exist in virtually every area of contemporary life—production, marketing, transportation, communication, government, and agriculture. Firms that are able to solve these problems through the development of new systems, products, services, or technology have great opportunities for growth and profit.

All of the problems just mentioned are definitely environmental opportunities. However, they are not necessarily company opportunities. A company opportunity is a set of marketing endeavors for which a specific company with distinctive characteristics is likely to have a competitive advantage because of its particular marketing approach.[5] For a good example of a company opportunity, let's look at powdered drink mixes.

By 1976, the market for powdered drink mixes had grown to $450 million a year, and no limits were in sight. Wyler's, Kool Aid, and Hawaiian Punch were the number one, two, and three companies, respectively, in this market. Their success intrigued Coca-Cola and Pepsi Cola, the leading marketers of carbonated soft drinks, and caused them to consider the advisability of entering the powdered drink market themselves. Before deciding, however, each firm did a little strategic marketing planning by analyzing the market opportunity such a move might afford.

The analyses Coca-Cola and Pepsi Cola completed were based on the following considerations. First, they determined that entering this market would satisfy certain *success requirements*. Powdered drink mixes offered both firms opportunities for growth and profit. Second, they found that the endeavor matched their particular areas of *distinctive competence*. In other words, both firms had already proven that they could market soft drinks successfully. Finally, the companies reasoned that their distinctive competence coupled with the success requirements for growth and profit gave them an advantage in this market equal to, if not better than, that enjoyed by the prevailing competition.

As a result of their respective analyses, Coca-Cola and Pepsi Cola decided that powdered drink mixes did indeed offer them viable market opportunities. Both firms therefore decided to move quickly into this market.

---

[5] Philip Kotler, *Marketing Management: Analysis, Planning and Control*, 3rd ed. (Englewood Cliffs, NJ: Prentice-Hall, 1976), p. 47.

Choosing the Right Market Opportunity

There is nothing of less value than the correct solution to the wrong problem. To a large extent, the crux of strategic marketing planning is choosing the right market opportunity. The wrong initial choice has often spelled near disaster. An example is the National Cash Register Company's early efforts in the computer field. The firm advertised its new line of computers with the slogan "NCR means computers." Initially, customers balked at this notion. To them, NCR meant cash registers and IBM meant computers. However, the consummate marketing skill of NCR's management coupled with very effective strategic planning eventually allowed the company to penetrate this market. Today, NCR has a broad line of computers and competes with IBM effectively.

Another well-documented example of how not to approach strategic marketing planning is provided by America's railroads.[6] Their insistence on viewing "railroading" rather than transportation in general as their major market opportunity led directly to many of the problems the railroads face today.

Classes of Market Opportunities

There are three major classes of market opportunities: intensive, integrative, and extensive. These three classes along with their various subclasses are shown in Table 3-1.[7]

Intensive market opportunities exist when all the possibilities of a particular market have not been exhausted. There are three main subclasses of intensive market opportunities: market penetration, market development, and product development.

In market penetration, a company seeks increased sales and profits from its existing line of products in its present markets through more aggressive marketing efforts. For example, Royal Crown Cola and Seven-Up are both attempting to increase their market penetration by developing larger and better-coordinated networks of distributor-dealers.

Market development occurs when a company seeks increased sales and profits by taking its present product line into new markets. Coca-Cola and Pepsi Cola are presently doing this by working to expand their overseas marketing operations.

Product development is what a company does when it tries to foster new growth by coming up with new or improved products for its present markets. Coca-Cola and Pepsi Cola are also doing this in developing their own lines of powdered drink mixes, which we discussed earlier.

Integrative market opportunities exist when a firm has the chance to grow by moving to a different level of distribution or productive services. **Backward**

[6] Theodore Levitt, "Marketing Myopia," eds. Edward C. Bursk and John F. Chapman, *Modern Marketing Strategy* (Cambridge, MA: Harvard University Press, 1964).
[7] This table and the accompanying discussion lean heavily on the treatment of the topic by Kotler in *Marketing Management*, p. 49.

Table 3-1 Major Classes of Market Opportunities

1. Intensive	2. Integrative	3. Extensive
a. Market penetration	a. Backward integration	a. Concentric diversification
b. Market development	b. Forward integration	b. Horizontal diversification
c. Product development	c. Horizontal integration	c. Undifferentiated diversification

integration occurs when the firm seeks greater control or outright ownership of its sources of supply, and **forward integration** occurs when it seeks greater control or outright ownership of its distribution network. In **horizontal integration,** a company seeks growth opportunities by acquiring its competitors. Can you think of some examples of these types of market opportunities?

Extensive market opportunities generally lie outside a company's traditional lines of endeavor. They are most often sought out when there are limits or unusual barriers to further growth through intensive or integrative opportunities. There are also three subclasses of extensive market opportunities: concentric diversification, horizontal diversification, and undifferentiated diversification.

Concentric diversification occurs when a company seeks new growth by adding new products that have technologies or marketing processes similar to those of present products. Normally, these new products will appeal to new types of customers. For example, when the Gillette Company acquired a home permanent firm, it could use the mass merchandising techniques, primarily television commercials, it had already developed for its other products even though it was reaching for a new group of consumers.

In **horizontal diversification,** a company seeks growth opportunities by adding new products which are basically unrelated to its present line but which will appeal to its present customers. Pepsi Cola, for instance, has developed an entire array of snack food products through its Frito Lay division. Although these products are quite different from soft drinks, the same people who buy soft drinks tend to buy snack foods.

Undifferentiated diversification, sometimes called *conglomerate diversification,* is what happens when a company seeks to grow by adding new products that are intended to appeal to new types of customers. These new products have little or no relation to the company's existing product line, technology, or marketing systems. Businesses that engage in this type of diversification might best be characterized as financial manipulators. Still, there are frequently sound financial or strategic reasons for exploring such market opportunities. For instance, a firm may need to offset seasonal or cyclical fluctuations in its current endeavors. Seeking market opportunities through undifferentiated diversification is, however, an extremely high-risk venture.

Company Objectives and Market Orientation

Strategic marketing planning is most successful when it is based upon clear, attainable, and verifiable objectives or goals. Objectives are verifiable when, at some specified future date, management can clearly determine whether or not they have been accomplished. Verification is easiest when the objectives can be quantified, as in dollars of sales or percentage of increase in profits. Unfortunately, such quantification is not always possible. Many worthwhile objectives can only be couched in qualitative terms. An example would be a marketing program with certain characteristics that is to be launched by a specific date.

Defining company objectives is not an easy task. However, consideration of the following questions can often help management to crystallize its thinking:

1. What is our business?
2. Who are our customers?
3. What do our customers want?
4. How much will our customers buy and at what prices?
5. Do we wish to be a product leader?
6. Do we wish to develop our own new products?
7. What are our specific competencies in serving our customer needs?
8. What are the strengths and weaknesses of our existing competition?
9. What are the legal restraints that might affect our future growth and development?
10. Is our organization structure and management strength adequate to meet the changing needs of our marketplace?

There are other pertinent questions, of course, but these are surely among the most important.

In choosing a company's objectives, strategic marketing planners must realize that all objectives have three properties: multiplicity, timeliness, and level. Multiplicity refers to the fact that organizations almost always have a number of objectives. The second property, timeliness, means that objectives are relevant only for a certain length of time. Therefore, the time frame for each objective should be clearly stated. The third property, level, recognizes the fact that a firm has many levels and each level has its own objectives. Inevitably, all the objectives of the entire organization are ranked in some kind of hierarchy.

Figure 3-2 shows the hierarchy of objectives that forms the strategic marketing plan of the Interstate Telephone Company. The chief objective, which appears at the top, is to "Increase Return on Investment." All of the other objectives in the hierarchy, such as the specific marketing objectives to "Increase Billings" and "Reduce Costs," are consistent with and supportive of the chief objective and are thus integral parts of the overall strategic plan. Quite likely there are also a number of implied objectives such as maintaining high levels of customer service, maintaining and updating customer equipment, and conforming to the standards of the state regulatory commission.

Figure 3-2 A hierarchy of objectives for the Interstate Telephone Company.

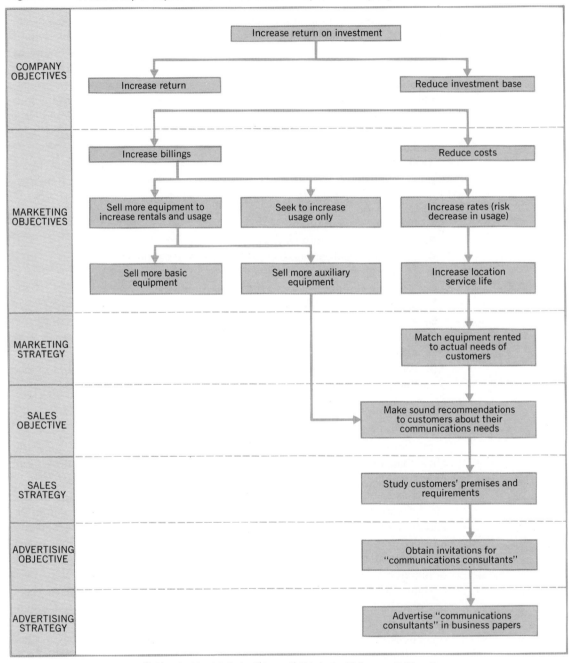

Matching Company Objectives and Market Opportunities

Effective strategic marketing planning requires a good marriage between the firm's objectives and those environmental opportunities that have been identified as company market opportunities. In other words, the strategic planners must ensure that the company's objectives and its opportunities are well matched. They should select opportunities for which objectives can be set, and the objectives decided upon should support the company's efforts to realize its opportunities. This process involves two very crucial steps. First, the planners must realistically analyze the company's situation. Second, they must accurately forecast the future business environment in which the objectives must be achieved.

Analyzing the Situation.   In setting a company's objectives, the strategic planners must analyze the company's situation to determine how and under what conditions those objectives can be achieved. Sometimes this analysis is accomplished through a situation audit. Basically, a situation audit is an assessment of where the company has been, where it is now, and where it is going. The future situation is evaluated in the light of two different assumptions. The first is that there will be no change in strategic planning; the second, that there will be a change in strategic planning at some level.

Forecasting the Environment.   If strategic marketing planners are to set realistic objectives and match them effectively with the company's marketing opportunities, they must have some sense of the conditions under which those objectives will probably be achieved. A forecast of the future environment is therefore of vital importance. Among the factors that the planners should consider are the following:

1. Population and demographic changes
2. New discoveries that may lead to competing types of products
3. New uses for the company's existing major products
4. Changes in business conditions
5. Changes in consumer tastes, attitudes, or purchasing habits
6. Developments relating to present and expected competition

There are, of course, many other factors that can affect a company's performance in the future. However, the more accurately strategic planners anticipate that future, the more likely it is that the company will be successful.

Developing Information Systems

Good strategic planning requires the development of an effective marketing information system. The intelligence such a system supplies comes from a wide range of information sources, including customers, potential customers, competitors, and the government. The relationship between information sources and the strategic planning process is shown in Table 3-2.

Table 3-2 Marketing Information Systems

Strategic Planning Process	Environmental Information Desired	Strategic Information Sources
Situation Analysis (What is our current situation?)	Firm Assessment image	Customers
Goal Development (What do we want our future situation to be?)	Potential customer attitudes	Potential customers
Constraint Identification (What constraints might inhibit us?)	*Competition Regulation*	Competitors Government
Selection of Strategies (What actions should we take to achieve our goals?)	Situation audit	Total environmental network

Source: Adapted from William R. King and David I. Cleland, "Environmental Information Systems for Strategic Planning," *Journal of Marketing* **38** (October 1974), p. 36.

Obtaining marketing information is normally the responsibility of a company's marketing research department. In some cases, however, a company may hire an outside organization, such as management consultants or firms that specialize in doing market research, to gather and assess marketing information for them.[8] The importance of information systems to strategic planning is discussed in far greater detail in chapter 7.

Assessing Competition

A firm's competition—whether heavy, light, or nonexistent—has an important influence on its market opportunities. In fact, no strategic planning effort that fails to assess the competition can possibly be effective.[9] Some firms even go so far as to construct a profile of each major competitor. Such a profile analyzes the competitor's business character, style, and methods of operation and assesses the competitor's past and present strategies. Obviously, the task of evaluating the competition is much easier if it proceeds along an orderly line of inquiry. Some of the pertinent questions that should be answered include:

1. How effective is each competitor's marketing strategy?
2. What are the strengths and weaknesses of each competitor's marketing

---

[8] For more on this topic, see William R. King and David I. Cleland, "Environmental Information Systems for Strategic Marketing Planning," *Journal of Marketing* **38** (October 1974), pp. 35–40.
[9] See, "Corporate Strategies," *Business Week*, July 7, 1980, pp. 40–41.

mix? Goods and services, channels of distribution, promotional activities, and prices should all be evaluated.

3. What are the backgrounds of the competitor's key personnel? Are they experienced? Are they industry trained? If not, from what nonrelated industries do they come?

4. In what areas does the competitor show the greatest and the least inclination to compete?

5. For what kinds of projects does the competition bid most fiercely?

6. How strong are the financial and organizational structures of the major competitors?

Developing Marketing Strategy

A strategic marketing plan is not a scheme concocted by a group of wily old men for the purpose of exploiting unsuspecting consumers. Instead, it is a comprehensive and well-reasoned program designed to respond to people's needs with the products and services that will satisfy them. Companies do more than merely provide bread, toothpaste, automobiles, cosmetics, apartments, motorcycles, clothing, and books. In the broader sense, they supply energy, health, security, status, transportation, shelter, means of self-expression, and escape. To this end, matching its objectives to its opportunities gives a company a strong sense of direction. However, the development of the plan itself requires consideration of several new factors. These include market segmentation, market penetration, market share, and market positioning.

Market Segmentation

Market segmentation, which is based on the fact that different people need different products and services, involves the splitting of larger markets with their diverse demands into smaller market segments in which the demands are more homogeneous. Or, put another way, segmentation involves selecting groups of consumers who would probably be most receptive to a given product and directing the marketing effort specifically to those groups.[10]

The firm electing a market segmentation strategy must consider the different degrees to which consumers in different segments will respond to changes in its marketing mix—its policies relating to product, price, promotion, and channels of distribution. This assumes, of course, that the incremental costs of serving specific segments are the same. The firm must then determine which segments it wishes to serve and offer those segments the marketing mixes they will accept.[11]

[10] Harold W. Berkman and Christopher C. Gilson, *Consumer Behavior* (Belmont, CA: Dickenson Publishing Co. 1978), p. 15.
[11] The comprehensive work on this topic is contained in Ronald E. Frank, William Massy, and Yoram Wind, *Market Segmentation* (Englewood Cliffs, NJ: Prentice-Hall, 1972), especially pp. 133–134.

Many firms practice market segmentation quite successfully. Almost all automobile manufacturers, for example, have a wide variety of models, styles, and price lines in order to appeal to different segments of their total market. Department stores recognize the different needs of various market segments by clustering their goods according to use, style, and price. The "budget basement" found in many department stores is designed to reach those customers who are at the lower range of the socioeconomic scale.[12] The Miller Brewing Company introduced Lite beer to cater to what it perceived as a distinct market segment of beer drinkers who want a lower-calorie, less-filling beverage. Witnessing their success, many other brewing companies quickly followed suit. And finally, Hugh Hefner, the publisher of *Playboy*, succeeded in creating a magazine with a strong appeal to a very distinct market segment—those men who have what he calls the *Playboy* philosophy.

Market Penetration

The firm that discovers a new opportunity and acts on it with dispatch has a chance for great success. General Motors, for instance, was quick to recognize the emergence of the luxury, small-car market segment and responded with its Cadillac Cimarron. Pepsi Cola reacted to the national craving for snack foods, which is particularly strong among active teenagers, by acquiring the Frito Lay Company, a marketer of potato chips, crackers, and other snack foods. And General Electric, sensing increased competition and saturated demand in the small appliance market, has deemphasized many of its traditional products. At the same time, the company has established a new Space Division and is developing products to meet the growing needs in the space, energy, and antipollution areas.

Once a firm identifies its market opportunities and establishes its objectives, then it must decide next how it will enter, or penetrate, the market it has selected. Normally, there are three options available. The company can go it alone and enter the market by developing its own marketing mix; it can acquire production and marketing facilities from another company; or it can collaborate with other companies in seeking to tap the market.

Going It Alone.   There are obvious advantages to the company that penetrates a market on its own. If the market develops successfully, the profits belong solely to that company. Another benefit, perhaps the most important from the executive point of view, is that the company has total control of policy decisions. The problems of meshing or coordinating the activities of a parent company with a number of subsidiaries having different management philosophies as well as different organizational and financial structures are often greater than some companies are willing to put up with. On the other hand, it can be risky and time consuming for an individual company to de-

[12] For more on planning in retailing see Bert Rosenbloom, "Strategic Planning in Retailing: Prospects and Problems," *Journal of Retailing* **56,** no. 1, Spring 1980 pp. 107–120.

velop a full marketing program geared to a rapidly growing new market all by itself.

Acquisition.   Market penetration through acquisition is a frequent occurrence. For instance, the Miller Brewing Company felt that there was a sizable market for a higher-priced, better quality beer. It therefore acquired the right to bottle and market the well-known German beer Lowenbrau for U.S. consumption. Miller's sales have borne out their expectations. In another instance, Playtex International, the nations's leading maker of women's undergarments, recently acquired Danskin Inc. through direct purchase. Danskin has well over half the market for women's dance costumes and has recently diversified into sleek swimsuits and clingy sportswear.

There are sometimes compelling reasons for a firm to seek market penetration through acquisition. The acquiring firm may have limited knowledge of the new market or industry. Also, time may be a critical factor—market opportunities, like vacuums, are filled quickly—and development lead time may be long. Or the company may face serious problems relating to patents, special skills, or complicated processes, and another company may already have the necessary technical or marketing skills. In such cases as these, merger or acquisition can be the best alternative available. However, legal constraints may sometimes block acquisition efforts as Procter & Gamble discovered when it was forced to divest itself of the Clorox Company, a manufacturer of household bleach, because of the antitrust laws.

An example of industrial collaboration.

Collaboration. Sometimes a company's best option is to achieve market penetration through collaboration. There are many reasons for such undertakings—high risks, large capital requirements, government pressures, complicated technology, or the size of the project. A recent example of a large scale collaborative effort was the development and production of the Concorde, the supersonic passenger jet. Many people believed that there was a considerable market segment of high-income passengers who would pay a premium fare to cross the Atlantic in only slightly more than three hours. However, building and producing this revolutionary new airplane was such a mammoth undertaking and the costs and risks were so great that no company was willing to tackle the project alone. Therefore, a number of French and English companies joined together in the venture to capture this market segment (and to establish Europe as the leader in air frame technology). This venture proved to be a dismal failure.

Market Share

Seldom will a company be the only one with a particular market opportunity, nor will a company often have a particular market all to itself. Most markets or market segments are divided up among a number of firms. That part of a market that a company controls is called its **market share.** The greater a firm's market share and the larger its total output of a product are, the lower its unit costs and the higher its profitability become.[13] Therefore, the essential purpose of a firm's marketing strategy is to create a differentiated, or specially designed, marketing mix that will allow it to capture a market share, or if it has already penetrated the market, to increase its market share.

As Table 3-3 indicates, market share is increased through a firm's marketing mix. Gaining significant market share increases requires carefully planned and well-executed market strategies along with specific tactical plans. The time for a company to emphasize planning for market share increases is when its profits are unsatisfactory, when its market share has dropped because of the competition's gains, or when the competition's marketing efforts have slackened. It is least expensive for a company to increase its market share during the growth and expansion phase of a product's life cycle. When the product has reached the mature phase or the decline phase of its life cycle, the costs of increasing its share of the market can be prohibitive.

Measurement of market share is a very convenient tool for marketers, especially in assessing a company's marketing objectives. Share figures eliminate most of the influence of forces over which marketers have little or no control, such as the amount of consumer disposable income—which influences sales—or the company's cost structure—which influences profits.

---

[13]. C. Davis Fogg, "Planning Gains in Market Share," *Journal of Marketing* **38** (July 1974), pp. 30–38.

Table 3-3 Strategies for Gaining Market Share

Strategy	When to Use	How to Apply in Market Place
1. Price	To gain a share in a product line (a) where there is room for growth or (b) by launching a new product, preferably in a growth market	A. Set general market price level below average B. Lower prices at specific market targets where reduced prices will capture high volume accounts and where competition is vulnerable on a price basis; lower price enough to keep the business C. Lower prices against specific competitors who will not or cannot react effectively
2. New Product	When a new product need (cost or performance) can be uncovered and a new product will (a) displace existing products on a cost or performance basis or (b) expand the market for a class of product by tapping previously unsatisfied demand	A. Develop and launch the new product, generally B. Target specific customers and market segments where the need for the product is strongest and competition most vulnerable, and immediate large gains in share can be obtained
3. Service	To gain share for specific product lines when competitive service levels do not meet customer requirements	A. Improve service generally beyond competitive levels by increasing capacity for specified product lines. B. Target specific accounts where improved service will gain share and the need for superior service is high C. Offer additional services required in general or by specific customers—information, engineering advice, etc. D. Expand distribution system by adding more distribution points

4. Quality/Strength of Marketing	When a market segment or specific customers are getting inadequate sales force coverage (too few calls/month) or inferior quality of coverage (poor salespeople or insufficient information conveyed by salespeople)	A. Add salespeople or sales representatives to improve call frequency above competition's in target territories or at target accounts B. Sales training programs to improve existing sales skills, product knowledge, and territorial and customer management abilities C. Sales incentive program with rewards based on share increases at target customers or in target markets or products
5. Advertising and Sales Promotion	(a) When a market segment or specific customers are getting inadequate exposure to product, service, or price benefits compared to competition (b) A change in the benefits offered is made and needs to be communicated	A. Select appropriate media to reach target customer groups B. Set level and frequency of exposure of target customers high enough to create adequate awareness of benefits and counter competitive efforts

Source: Adapted from C. Davis Fogg, "Planning Gains in Market Share," *Journal of Marketing* **38** (July 1974), p. 32.

Market Positioning

A new dimension in strategic marketing planning called **market positioning** has recently come to the fore. Today we are entering an era that recognizes both the importance of the product and the importance of the company image, but more than anything else, stresses the need to create a position in the prospect's mind.[14] Market positioning has it roots in the packaged goods field, where the concept was called product positioning. Basically, it refers to how a product's form, package size, and price stand out from the competition's. As applied to marketing strategy on the company level, product positioning involves creating a strong identity or image for a company and its products and vividly communicating this image to customers. The firm must therefore determine the market segment or segments toward which a product will chiefly be

[14] Jack Trout and Al Ries, "The Positioning Era Cometh," a three-part series in *Advertising Age* (Chicago: Crain Publications, 1972).

aimed and then decide on the appeals it will use to promote the product to those segments. Market positioning highlights the importance of selecting the specific pattern of market concentration that will give the company the best chance to attain its marketing objectives.[15]

Before proceeding, can you answer these questions:
1. What is meant by market segmentation?
2. What are the principal strategic ways of increasing a company's market share?
3. How does market positioning relate to marketing strategy?

Developing and Implementing Marketing Plans and Policies

The process of strategic marketing planning involves a series of decisions that lead ultimately to the development and implementation of a comprehensive marketing plan, the firm's marketing strategy. Earlier, in chapter 1, we discussed the marketing mix—a firm's unique combination of decisions concerning products, promotional efforts, pricing, and channels of distribution. We also discussed the fact that the firm's marketing strategy is built around this marketing mix. Now, in this chapter, we have seen that the marketing strategy is designed to enable the firm to determine its market segments, to penetrate these segments, to gain the desired market share, and to achieve strong market positioning. Therefore, the final marketing plan will consist of such major items as (1) sales targets for all of the company's divisions, product lines, and products; (2) a total budget of both money and resources for supporting marketing efforts; (3) a statement delineating how the firm will allocate its efforts among the four components of the marketing mix; and (4) the marketing budget allocation by products, which states in both dollars and effort—that is, work—how much emphasis each of the products will receive.

Controlling the Marketing Strategy

Control is the vital follow-up phase of the strategic marketing planning process. While the planning itself is concerned with deciding in advance what needs to be done, control is concerned with setting standards, measuring performance, and taking corrective action when performance falls too short of the stated objectives. Without a systematic and concerted effort to control the marketing strategy, the marketing plan is nothing more than an unproductive fantasy. Every firm therefore needs to examine systematically such measures of per-

[15] William D. Neal, "Strategic Products Positioning: A Step by Step Guide," *Business* **30**, no. 3 (May–June 1980), pp. 34–42.

formance as market share and expense ratios through comprehensive marketing audits, which are the firm's basic control tools.

Control has many purposes, but foremost among them is to make sure that the firm, if it is profit oriented, is making money. Management needs to know not only if the firm is making money but also where and how.[16] In turn, such analyses of profitability trigger further control efforts to assess whether planned results are actually being achieved and whether the company is pursuing the most desirable opportunities with respect to products, markets, and other aspects of its strategic plan.

Planning and control take place almost simultaneously. Strategic marketing planning is a repetitive process. Each plan ends with a control evaluation that then becomes the basis for the next round of strategic planning activities.

Nonprofit organizations that use marketing techniques to reach markets and to serve their clients better also need control procedures. Hospitals, churches, and health care foundations are all finding it necessary to monitor and control their marketing strategies more and more carefully. In addition, colleges and universities are increasingly being held accountable for delivering what they promise. Recently, a student sued an Eastern college because, the student alleged, a course that was taught did not deliver what was "advertised" in the college bulletin. If public service organizations promote their services, they must then use planning and control procedures to make sure that what is provided is what was promised. A marketing orientation demands no less.

Summary

The strategic marketing planning process consists of a series of sequential planning and control activities. The firm, whether a profit-seeking or a nonprofit organization, will benefit from strategic planning. The strategic plan is a major comprehensive assessment of a company's opportunities examined in light of company objectives and resources. It begins, therefore, with an examination of market opportunities and an effort by the firm's management to define the firm's objectives in relationship to its market opportunities.

Critical concepts that must be incorporated into the development of a marketing strategy include market segmentation, market penetration, market share, and market positioning.

The major strategic decisions become the basis for developing the firm's marketing mix. The application of its policies concerning price, product, promotion, and channels of distribution is the unique way each firm approaches its market situation. Most importantly, it must be underscored that marketing strategy—the firm's comprehensive plan of action—is the organization's way of responding to its shifting environment. Hence, as the environment changes, there is a constant need to monitor the firm's performance through control devices and processes. Control, while sometimes called the other half of plan-

[16] Frank H. Mossman, Paul M. Fischer, and W.J.E. Crissy, "New Approaches to Analyzing Marketing Profitability," *Journal of Marketing* **38** (April 1974), pp. 43–48.

ning, is really an extension of the planning process. Control consists of setting standards, evaluating performance and, if necessary, taking corrective action.

Review Questions

1. What is meant by market opportunity analysis? How is this related to strategic marketing planning?
2. What is the relationship between a firm's market opportunity and an assessment of that firm's competition?
3. Explain each of the following terms:
   a. Market segmentation
   b. Market penetration
   c. Market share
   d. Market positioning
4. What is the difference between information systems designed for control and those designed for planning?
5. Don't all companies have just one objective—to make money?
6. Is strategic marketing planning a relevant activity for the nonprofit organization? How and why?
7. What is the relationship, if any, between market share and market positioning?
8. Explain how the firm's marketing mix is related to its overall strategic plan.
9. Is control a separate and distinct activity from strategic planning? What are the essential elements or steps in the control process?
10. In your estimation, what is the bottom line, or critical results, that flow from the strategic marketing planning process?

Case 3-1

Cat Pause Kitty Litter

Phil Reinhardt and Larry Johnson are about ready to begin full-scale marketing operations to launch a product called Cat Pause, their entry into the $300-million-a-year cat litter business.

Reinhardt and Johnson lease 1,000 acres of federal land near Wickenburg, Arizona, a small desert community northwest of Phoenix. The land is rugged and covered with cactus and is virtually worthless for grazing or farming. However, just a few feet beneath the bone-dry surface lies a large vein of a brittle, white, rhyolite-like material that was formed by a volcanic eruption. This material is highly absorbent, which is a clear advantage in the cat litter market.

On the basis of a limited market research effort, Reinhardt and Johnson are convinced that

buyers look for three things in cat litter. It must absorb odor; it must absorb moisture: and, slightly less important, it must not produce a lot of dust when dumped into a litter box. In limited product tests, Cat Pause has proven itself superior to all the competition. It will absorb more ammonia, the major source of odor in cat urine, than will any of the leading brands. Although not sure why their rhyolite-like rock outperforms the clay used by their competitors, both Reinhardt and Johnson are convinced their product is best.

Having marketed Cat Pause on what amounts to an experimental basis in the Phoenix area, Reinhardt and Johnson feel that there is a superb market opportunity for their product. Therefore, they plan to set up an extensive regional distribution network in and around Los Angeles.

Reinhardt and Johnson believe that they stand on the brink of great marketing success. There are millions of people in the United States who have cats, so there is a sizable market for cat litter. The two men are now waiting for cat owners everywhere to beat a path to their door.

Questions

1. Do you believe cat owners will beat a path to Reinhardt and Johnson's door? Why or why not?
2. Do you believe Reinhardt and Johnson have discovered a market opportunity for their product?
3. Reinhardt and Johnson have limited marketing ability. Therefore they have sought your professional counsel and advice. Using the diagram in Figure 3-1, develop a marketing strategy for Cat Pause.

Case 3-2

McCall Publishing Company's *Your Place*

McCall Publishing Company is planning to introduce a new magazine called *Your Place*. Milton Lieberman, advertising director for McCall, thinks *Your Place* will be one of a new category of magazines known as dual service publications.

In launching this venture, the publisher can cite the record of one magazine that has blazed a trail to the dual audience. Since 1969, the Des Moines-based Meredith Corporation, (which markets 8 million copies of *Better Homes and Gardens* each month) has been steadily building up a magazine called *Metropolitan Home*. The magazine first appeared as *Apartment Ideas*, a one-shot, special interest publication. When the first issue sold out, the publisher turned *Apartment Ideas* into a quarterly. The following year it began to appear every other month, and in 1974, under a new title, *Apartment Life*, its

circulation hit 450,000. By 1978, circulation had exceeded 800,000, and the publication was made a monthly. In April 1981, the magazine's title was changed to *Metropolitan Home*.

The magazine is aimed at an audience that was largely ignored by traditional home or service magazines, which are specifically directed at either women or men. "We didn't think of our readers as either male or female," says Dorthy Kalins, executive editor of *Metropolitan Home*. "Although the present figures show us with about 60 percent female readership and about 40 percent male, we aim our editorial material at an audience that could be 50 percent female and 50 percent male."

The audience for *Metropolitan Home* is perceived as young (60 percent of the magazine's readers are 18 to 34), well educated, earning more than $15,000 per year, and living either alone or as unmarried couples. To the advertisers, the young woman sitting alone in her apartment is as much a prospect for a Sony stereo system as the young man sitting alone in his apartment is for Birdseye frozen peas.

The Census Bureau confirms that there are now more one- and two-person households in the United States than there are multiple-person households. With this in mind, the advertising directors of both *Metropolitan Home* and *Your Place* expect manufacturers to re-think traditional ways of reaching new prospects for their merchandise.

There is some anxiety on the part of McCall's management concerning their new venture. Despite the trend toward more similar clothing, jobs, and life styles for men and women, few magazine publishers have been successful in appealing to both female and male readers with a single periodical. Three years ago, *Family Health* publisher Hy Steirman saw $1 million go down the drain when he folded *Singles* after seven issues. Readers of both sexes have tended to shy away from new magazines whose advertisers might run the gamut from feminine hygiene products to saber saws. Still, McCall's

management is convinced that there is a whole new market out there that calls for new editorial and advertising approaches. "The success of our magazine, *Your Place*, will prove the viability of that market," says one executive. A dummy cover of a forthcoming issue features "Sex Fantasies" and "A Dating Guide for the Insecure" among the promised articles. But editor Kathleen Fury says the magazine will also tell readers how to shape up "the awful apartment kitchen" and how to give "a tiny office a powerful look."

Questions

1. Does McCall's venture in launching a new magazine call for strategic marketing planning? Explain.
2. In what way is McCall's marketing mix the organization's way of responding to the changing environmental situation?
3. What comparative advantage does McCall feel it must possess that equips it to launch such a new venture?
4. What elements of strategic marketing planning might be most prominently used by McCall in publishing a new magazine?

Chapter 4

Market Segmentation: The Basis for Market Targeting

The beginning of the 1980s saw the country, already awash in beverages, bracing itself for a flood of new products. The money being spent to promote and put these new products on retail shelves and, hopefully, into consumers' hands, was the largest sum ever spent by the beverage industry.

These new products represent something for all thirsts, from kinky new soft drinks to exotic waters. The carbonated soda pop industry is determined to regain its 6 percent growth rate which had declined to 4 percent during the final year of the decade of the 1970s.

Coke still reigns supreme in "Cola War."

The soft drink marketers are leading this new effort because they are growing increasingly nervous as they see their 36 gallon a year per capita consumption begin to flatten out. The major segment of the market, those between the ages of 13 and 24, is beginning to shrink as the U.S. population begins to age. Thus, Coca-Cola has boosted its advertising and marketing expenditures by two-thirds to nearly $70 million. Pepsico is boosting its marketing effort by 25 percent. Seven-up, with the vast resources of its new owner, Philip Morris Inc., is doubling its usual marketing-promotional figure to a $40 million annual rate.

Industry estimates that it costs $20 million to put a new soft drink on the market. The latest and anticipated products contain a touch of fruit. With the introduction and general success of Sunkist's new orange soft drink and Pepsi's Aspen (snap of Apple) others in the industry are taking up the hint of fruit theme.

Coca-Cola, which seems determined to enter every segment of the soft drink market, is adding Mello Yello which is described as a lightly carbonated drink. Mello Yello was found to be very popular with young males in test marketing and that is an important segment at which Coke is aimed as well. Mello Yello was designed to cut into the success and market share of Pepsi's Mountain Dew. Mountain Dew has been around well over 15 years but was revitalized when Pepsico changed the marketing theme and the product's image with the campaign that sung the phrase, "Hello sunshine, hello Mountain Dew."

Both Mello Yello and Mountain Dew will be competing against a product marketed by Cadbury-Schweppes to be called Rondo, another citrus-based soda. The word Rondo has no meaning. It was chosen by computer to sound familiar and macho. It, too, will be targeted for the young, sports-oriented male. All these lightly carbonated, cloudy lemon, green bottle concoctions are aimed at the 13 to 25 year old active male segment because they are the single biggest consumers of soft drinks. The marketing executives in this industry believe that these heavy users are seeking a thirst-quenching, less carbonated drink with less sugar.

The cola market segment is not being overlooked either. There are two new smaller companies promoting colas. Former executives of Pepsico and Coke are associated with King and CC Cola, both of which are geared to the idea that they taste as good as Pepsi and Coke but will appeal to the price-oriented segment of the market. The soft drink industry is a $13 billion a year business in the United States and the various firms and products that compete within this market all want an increasing share of the market.

Product Differentiation and Market Segmentation

The above narrative underscores what amounts to two, usually complementary, approaches to the development of a marketing strategy. These approaches are known as product differentiation and market segmentation.

Product differentiation is the attempt by marketers to differentiate or distinguish their product from those of competitors. The attributes of the product which are used as the basis for distinguishing are either real or imagined. For example, Mountain Dew may be projected as tarter, more lemony, more thirst-quenching, or generally more satisfying. It may be promoted along these lines using visual imagery. That is, Mountain Dew is shown in settings and surroundings where the drinkers are doing fun things such as hiking, biking, attending sporting events, swimming, skiing, boating, or roller skating.

Coca-Cola, early in its marketing history, pursued only a strategy of product differentiation. It marketed its product in the distinctive green seven-ounce bottle and for years used the basic unchanging advertising theme, "Coke, The Pause That Refreshes." Product differentiation largely assumes that there is little or no diversity on the demand side of the market. The marketer basically assumes that all buyers for the product are essentially the same and that the marketer's task is to make the firm's product different from all the others in the eyes of potential buyers.

Market segmentation is a somewhat different strategy based upon the growing sophistication and complexity of market development. It is the recognition that not all buyers for a product are the same. For example, soft drink marketers' reasoning along the lines of market segmentation would contend, quite correctly, that not all buyers of soft drinks are young, 13 to 25 years of age, active males. Their research and intuition would tell them, further, that many are young, 13 to 25 year old females; that many are older 25 to 50 year old males and females who buy Coke, Seven-Up, and other products as mixers to be used with alchoholic drinks. Other users might be preschoolers who prefer powdered mix soft drinks such as Kool-Aid or Country-Time. Still another segment might be comprised of young, aware mothers concerned about their children's health and who wish them to drink less carbonated sugary products and thus buy large amounts of such products as Hawaiian Punch or Cranapple Juice.

The marketer who pursues a strategy of market segmentation is concerned with the essential question, "What are the attributes or characteristics of the market and how should the market be divided into meaningful segments that can be pursued as profitable market segments?"

Product Differentiation is Product Oriented. From the strategy point of view, product differentiation is concerned with securing a measure of control over the demand for a product by promoting or advertising differences between a product and the products of competing sellers.[1] Attempts toward product differentiation generally tend to be characterized by the heavy use of advertising and promotional activities.

Market Segmentation is Market Oriented. Market segmentation largely rejects the notion of homogeneous overall markets. Instead, market segmentation views a heterogeneous market (one characterized as having considera-

---

[1] The classic and original article that dealt with these two concepts was written by Wendell R. Smith. See his "Product Differentiation and Market Segmentation as Alternative Marketing Strategies," *Journal of Marketing*, July 1956.

ble diversity or differences within it, as opposed to a homogenous market which means a market comprised of buyers whose demand characteristics are closely similar) as a number of smaller homogeneous markets in response to differing product preferences among important market segments. To return again to the opening narrative, the market for soft drinks is a heterogeneous market. There are clusters or segments within the overall market which are similar or homogeneous and these segments manifest similar demand characteristics and constitute important market targets. Much like differentiation, segmentation, too, often involves substantial use of advertising and promotion. This is necessary to inform market segments of the availability of goods or services produced for or presented as meeting their needs with precision. This then really is the crux of market segmentation. It is an attempt to adjust the firm's market offering to consumer or user requirements. Market segmentation is the adjustment and accommodation of the firm's marketing program to subgroups of the market.

Analyzing Market Preference Patterns

As we learned in Chapter 3 when discussing the elements of strategic marketing planning, the firm's basic task is to discover and understand its market opportunity and then to develop and implement an effective marketing program. Market segmentation lies at the heart of this task in many instances because it deals with the analysis of market opportunity.

The firm succeeds best not only when it perceives clearly what needs it might serve but, in addition, when it sees and understands clearly whose needs it should serve. For example, the petroleum industry of America perceives that its market task is to serve the energy needs of the nation. But more specifically whose needs are these and what are the characteristics of the energy markets? Some of the markets are relatively homogeneous. For example, high octane fuel needs make the jet passenger airline business virtually a homogeneous market and selling to such a market is basically straightforward. The market for diesel fuel was once relatively homogeneous, consisting principally of users in the long-haul trucking industry. However of late, this market is becoming increasingly heterogeneous and consists of the trucking industry, the American farm market, the railroad industry, and a growing share of the American passenger car market. In other words, this market is made up of customer groups who have different buying needs and interests and these groups are called market segments.

Market Targeting and Market Segments.   Market targeting is another aspect of the firm's strategic planning process. Targeting is concerned with the decision as to which segments to serve. Market targeting follows on the heels of market segmentation. While segmentation is the activity of identifying groups or clusters of buyers or users with different requirements or needs, market targeting is concerned with the choices or decisions as to which segments to approach with a marketing program.

Most firms usually discover that they can never successfully tap or reach all the available segments. When markets are heterogeneous or when overall markets are comprised of a number of distinct and identifiable segments, the marketer has three targeting options.[2]

1. The marketer can adopt a policy of *undifferentiated marketing*. With this policy the marketer can introduce only one product and strive to get as many people as possible to desire and buy it. This amounts generally to a firm having a single product supported by a single marketing program. A reasonably good example of such an approach is the Royal Crown Bottling Company and their me-too-tasting product, R.C. Cola. Although the marketer recognizes that not everyone will buy this product, the firm does expect to attract a sufficient number for profitable operations.

2. The marketer can adopt a policy of *concentrated marketing*. With this policy the marketer targets and attempts to develop the ideal product for one particular market segment. Examples of firms that pursue strategies of concentrated marketing would be the Dr. Pepper Bottling Company with their product which appeals to the soft drink segment that desires a different, snappy, peppery drink, or the A & W Company which markets a single soft drink to a specific segment of the market which prefers a root beer flavored soft drink.

3. The marketer can adopt a policy of *differentiated marketing*, or what we have called a policy of market segmentation. With this policy, the marketer introduces several product versions, each of which is designed and marketed to appeal to a different market segment. Examples, again in the soft drink market, would be the Coca-Cola Company's Coke, Tab, Mello Yello, and other product variations. Examples in other industries would include General Motors with its various car divisions. Chevrolet alone with its various models, body styles, and colors could operate at full production for more than a year and never make exactly the same car. In a not-so-extreme example, Procter and Gamble produces not only Ivory Snow, but Tide, Dash, Duz, Dreft, and other laundry detergents adjust to meet different consumer needs or perceptions.

Marketers are Increasingly Segmenting Markets. Numerous examples of segmentation can be cited; the cigarette and automobile industries are well-known examples, as are the soft drink, beer, and liquor markets. Most leisure product markets are segmented—for example, skis, boats, motorcycles, snowmobiles, and bicycles. Similar developments exist in greater or lesser degree in almost all product areas.

Strategies of segmentation and differentiation are often employed simultaneously, but increasingly they are applied in sequence in response to changing market conditions. Often segmentation is a momentary or short-term activity in that effective use of this strategy may lead to more formal recognition of the existence of market segments. This was classically illustrated by the Miller

[2] Philip Kotler, *Marketing Management*, 3rd ed., (Englewood Cliffs, NJ: Prentice Hall, 1976), p. 142.

Brewing Company's success with their product Miller Lite, a beer with about one-third fewer calories per can or bottle for the weight- and calorie-conscious beer drinker who enjoys drinking beer without getting filled up. Once the nature and extent of this market was realized by the other breweries, many began developing their own light beers to target at this market and now competition in large measure has swung back to differentiation. Each competitor is now, via heavy promotion and advertising, trying to convince the light beer users why their product is better than all the others.

Before proceeding, can you answer these questions:
1. What is meant by product differentiation?
2. How does market segmentation relate to marketing strategy?
3. Which comes first, market targeting or market segmentation?

Why Segment the Market?

There are many firms that do not follow a practice of market segmentation. Instead, they pursue a policy of undifferentiated marketing that offers certain advantages for them. Such firms reason, often correctly, that even though consumers differ, they are enough alike to treat as a homogeneous market target. Thus, such firms offer a more or less standard product that differs only slightly, if at all from competition. These firms usually make heavy use of advertising and sales promotion and the promotional effort is designed to convince buyers of the superior merits of their products.

Are there advantages to this strategy? For some firms, given the nature of some markets, the answer is clearly yes. By having demand conform to what these marketers are willing to supply, the major advantage gained is a reduced cost of doing business as a result of longer production runs with a single product. Other efficiencies or economies of scale may result from better media or advertising rates, or discounts that result from large-scale single-product promotional campaigns.

But on the Other Hand. However, undifferentiated marketing has it disadvantages. The biggest disadvantage is that such marketers are vulnerable to competitive efforts by other firms who are bent on serving unfulfilled consumer needs. Remember, the marketer has two primary objectives: to serve customer needs as expressed in the notion of "finding customer needs and then filling them" and secondly, to make a profit. The undifferentiated marketer, in the attempt to meet most consumer demands reasonably well, is often outdone competitively by the marketer who seeks to serve specific segments of the market very well.[3]

---

[3] See Ronald E. Frank, William F. Massy, and Yoram Wind, *Market Segmentation* (Englewood Cliffs, NJ: Prentice Hall, 1972).

The Benefits and Costs of Segmentation

To the extent that undifferentiated marketing works to bend demand to the will of supply, market segmentation is just the opposite. Supply, or the marketing program, is made to match the characteristics of demand. This, as can be seen, results in a more careful delineation of customers and would lead to more detailed knowledge and understanding concerning each segment's character-istics. Such an approach would therefore benefit the marketing manager in the development of the marketing program.

1. Segmentation improves management's understanding of the buyer and, quite importantly, why he or she buys.
2. Segmentation permits the marketer to quickly detect trends in what usually is a rapidly changing market.
3. Segmentation affords the marketer the opportunity to design and create products that truly meet the customer-buyer's expectations.
4. Segmentation permits management to better evaluate competitive strengths and weaknesses and to know where competition is most rigorous and where there is little hope of a true market penetration or market share increase.
5. Segmentation, and the analysis that precedes it, permits management to undertake more systematic planning for both present and future markets leading to better allocation of marketing resources for a more finely tuned marketing program. More specifically, product and advertising appeals can be better coordinated, media plans can be pursued which minimize waste through excess exposure, sharper brand images can be developed, and, of course, target customers can be ultimately better served.[4]

Benefits Usually Outweigh Costs.   Normally the benefits of segmentation outweigh the costs, otherwise segmentation would be considerably less desir-able as a marketing strategy. Still, the costs must be considered.

The added costs of segmentation stem from higher manufacturing costs as-sociated with shorter production runs; higher unit costs for promotion when quantity media discounts are lost, and, quite importantly, the higher cost of learning about the characteristics of the segments through marketing research efforts. The cost of acquiring such information is often exorbitant. Another cost that marketers must absorb which stems from segmentation and the conse-quent development of new or modified products to meet the demands of these buyers is the cost of "cannibalization" in the case where one product steals sales from another. When Miller first, and then other breweries such as An-heuser-Busch and Coors came up with light beers, their new products not only gained sales from buyers in the newly tapped segment, but they took some sales from their existing regular products. Market segmentation usually results in greater sales but also at somewhat higher unit costs. However, the profit-

---

[4] Suggested by James F. Engel, Harry F. Fiorilla, and Murray A. Cayley, *Market Segmentation: Concepts and Applications* (New York: Holt, Rinehart and Winston, 1972), p. 4.

seeking firm's goal is to increase sales more than costs, resulting in improved profits.

Service and Other Organizations Also Use Segmentation.   Service organizations and nonprofit organizations also use segmentation strategies to increase revenues, attract more clients, and better dispense user benefits. Doctors and lawyers sometimes practice segmentation strategies by specializing in only certain areas. Accounting firms may specialize in taxation, auditing, or estate preservation and trusts. They may also segment by user characteristics, that is private individuals, corporations, or government agencies. Morticians, hospitals, hair styling salons, even colleges and universities practice limited amounts of segmentation activities.

How the U.S. Army Uses Segmentation Strategies.   The United States has had an all-volunteer army since the early 1970s. However, from the beginning of this program, the Department of Defense has had some difficulty attracting recruits and keeping the ranks sufficiently manned. Each year thousands of new recruits are required and they must be attracted with a limited budget. Faced with this problem, the Department of Defense hired a marketing research organization to assist with the task. Preliminary investigation by the research firm revealed that the most likely candidates for army service possessed certain specific characteristics: (1) a desire to know what army life would be all about and "promise" of the reduction of uncertainty about where the recruit would be sent and what he or she might do by way of training or further education; (2) a desire to break away and to strike out on their own; (3) the desire or yearning for adventure, especially travel, and for new experience; and (4) the need for structure and limited discipline to assist those not quite ready to make it totally on their own.

Potential recruits for the volunteer army were then described on three dimensions: age, nature of current residence, and family economic status as shown in Figure 4-1.

The three-dimensional matrix of Figure 4-1 was helpful in devising a recruiting strategy for the all-volunteer army because it pointed out the significant segments from which recruits might be drawn, and it was therefore useful for market targeting activities, especially advertising and promotion. Such an approach underscores again the benefits and costs of marketing segmentation. The costs were those incurred by buying the services of the marketing research organization. The benefits to the Department of Defense were essentially those that accrue to others who use segmentation strategies. The army has only about $30 million each year to promote its recruitment program to more than 31 million males between the ages of 17 and 35. This figures out to be less than $1.00 to spend on each eligible male candidate, which is considerably less than the price of one direct mailing piece. Furthermore, it includes nothing for eligible females, prospective soon-to-be candidates under seventeen years of age, or parents who are important influencers/opinion leaders who would play an instrumental role in helping their children decide whether or not to enter the volunteer army.

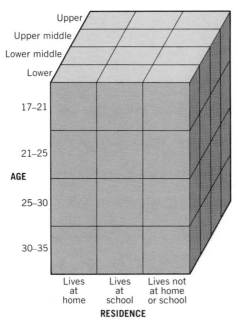

Figure 4-1 Potential groups of recruits for volunteer army.

The research suggested that the market segment with the greatest potential for recruiting was the male between 17 and 21, living at home and a member of a lower class family. With a total cost of recruitment averaging slightly over $1,000 per recruit, the army is eager to make every advertising dollar count.

Criteria for Meaningful Segmentation.   It is not enough simply for a marketer to know that market segments exist or that the firm may be able to increase its profitability or other measures of effectiveness by better serving a particular segment. The basic fact that a market segment is not being served or is being served badly is not sufficient. Four additional conditions must be considered.[5]

The Segment Must Be Measurable.   The market and other characteristics on which the segment is based should be both identifiable and measurable. In the volunteer army example, the segments were identified in terms of age, income, and residence, and these were also measurable criteria. Prospective buyers for surfboards and dune buggies could likewise be identified and measured. Criteria that are usually measurable include population, that is, young persons between the ages of 17 and 25; income, that is, those who earn between

[5] See T.P. Hustad, C.S. Mayer, and T.W. Whipple, "Segmentation Research Works If...," *1974 Combined Proceedings* (Chicago: American Marketing Association, 1975), p. 23 ff.

$10,000 and $20,000 per year; education level, that is, those who complete high school, and other factors. Then again, there are factors that are not easily measurable. It would not be too easy to measure, for example, how many persons volunteer to join the army because they don't get along with their parents, or dislike school or have had other difficulties.

The U.S. Army: It isn't just for men anymore.

YOU MIGHT BE PERFECT FOR A JOB YOU NEVER HEARD OF.

It's out there waiting for you. A chance to prove yourself in a way you might never have dreamt of. In Army Aviation. Right now, the Army has hundreds of openings for women in air traffic control, aircraft maintenance, radar and avionics. You might even get a chance to earn your wings. But it takes more than a high school diploma to make it in today's modern Army. It takes someone who's ambitious enough to realize her full potential in a really challenging skill. To be somebody special.

If you'd like to serve your country as you serve yourself, call toll free 800-421-4422. In California, call 800-252-0011. Alaska and Hawaii, 800-423-2244. Better yet, visit your nearest Army Recruiter, listed in the Yellow Pages.

ARMY. BE ALL YOU CAN BE.

"We thank thee, Lord, for this instant coffee, this Redi-Quick Cocoa, this one-minute oatmeal, and the pop-up waffles. In haste, amen."

Drawing by Whitney Darrow, Jr.; © 1973 The New Yorker Magazine, Inc.

The Segment Must Be Substantial.   Marketers often need to know if a potential market segment is large or small. Naturally the segment has to be substantial enough to justify the marketing effort that is to be made. The marketer must consider not only the number of customers available in a segment but also such additional factors as their purchasing power and frequency of use. Substantial market segments are those with enough potential buyers with sufficient dollars to cover the costs of producing and marketing the product and still generate a profit.

The Segment Must Be Accessible.   Buyers in market segments must be reachable with marketing efforts directed toward them with reasonably economical means. Some segments are reached via a process of controlled coverage. Stereo and audio buffs are sometimes reached by magazines such as *Stereo World.* Using such a selective media choice results in lower costs, eliminating waste coverage, and being able perhaps to use more detailed and informative copy with a consequently harder-hitting appeal. However, the firm might otherwise decide to use a marketing effort based upon customer self-selection. Stereo ads might be placed in such magazines as *Seventeen, Sports Illustrated, or Rolling Stone.* These more general market media would cover many consumers who are not interested in stereo components, but those who actually are or might be would be attracted to the ad. In short, buyers must be exposed to the products through the advertising and places where they do their purchasing.

The Segment Must Be Responsive. A well-delineated and defined market segment should respond favorably to changes in any elements of the firm's marketing mix. If, for example, a segment is determined by a reaction to price, a cents-off offer, couponing, or other price-oriented incentive, then these devices ought to create more purchases. Conversely, less price-oriented segments would respond more to nonprice-oriented inducements. Two buyers or two households may exhibit the same purchase behavior for a given marketing mix, yet they may respond differently to changes in the mix. Therefore, customer segments should be considered on the basis of response functions instead of a single variable. A response function is simply an expression relating a customer's buying behavior to levels of all marketing stimuli such as price, advertising, and product alternatives.[6]

Selecting a Segmentation Variable

Using a segmentation strategy involves the selection of relevant segmentation variables. A relevant segmentation variable is one that enables the firm to divide or segment the market. There are numerous bases upon which to segment a market. In most marketing situations there are large numbers of segmentation variables, and correspondingly a large number of segmentation schemes that could be utilized. The crux of the problem is, which scheme is best? The answer will vary according to product, market, customer, and competitive characteristics. Several segmentation variables can be used to select a segmentation strategy. Table 4-1 shows several alternative bases for segmentation.

The point to consider while looking at Table 4-1 is that the paramount criterion for selecting and evaluating segmentation variables is that the variable should pinpoint segments for which marketing programs can be implemented which will generate positive and sufficient market response in relation to program cost. The segmentation variables should be capable of stimulating ideas for promising marketing efforts. Truly effective procedures for selecting segmentation variables are based upon detailed performance analyses of each alternative segmentation option, given the marketing programs that are to accompany them.[7]

[6] The significant work in this area has been done by Parker Lessig and John Tollefsen, "Market Segmentation Through Numerical Taxonomy," *Journal of Marketing Research* **8** (November 1971), pp. 480–487.

[7] See Nariman K. Khalla and Winston H. Mahatoo, "Expanding The Scope of Segmentation Research," *Journal of Marketing* **40** (April 1976), pp. 34–41.

Table 4-1 Segmentation Variables

Variable	General Breakdown
Geographic region	New England, New York area, Mid Atlantic, Chicago area, West Central, Southeast, Southwest, Pacific
County size	A, B, C, D,
Demographic age	Under 6; 6–11; 12–17; 18–34; 35–49; 50–64; 65 and over
Sex	Male; Female
Family life cycle	Young, single; young, married, no children; young, married, children; older, married, children; older, married, no children; older, single; other
Family income	Under $10,000; $10,000–14,999; $15,000–24,999; over $25,000
Education	Some high school; graduated from high school; some college; graduated from college
Occupation	Professional and technical; managers, officials, and proprietors; clerical; sales; craftsmen, foremen; operative; farmers; armed services; retired; students; homemakers; unemployed
Social class	Lower; working; lower middle; upper middle; upper
Manufacturer's industry	Standard Industrial Classification Code SIC
Manufacturer's total assets	Under $25,000; $25,000–99,999; $100,000–249,999; $250,000–$1,000,000; Over $1,000,000
Psychographic	
Life style	Traditionalist, militant mother, suburbanite, etc.
Personality	Dogmatic, achievement oriented, persuasive, ambitious, hedonistic
Benefits sought	Economy, convenience, quality, prestige, social approval
User status	Never use, exuser, inclined user, first-time trier, regular user
Loyalty status	No loyalty, growing loyalty, strong absolute loyalty
Marketing response sensitivity	Price, quality, deal-prone, advertising, service, other sales promotion

Bases For Segmentation Strategies

As Table 4-1 suggests, there are indeed a large number of variables that can provide the bases for a segmentation strategy. It may be, for the moment, less confusing if we think of all segmentation variables as falling generally into two categories: consumer characteristics and product characteristics. Look now at Figure 4-2 which follows.

Figure 4-2 breaks down all the segmentation variables shown in Table 4-1 into two major classifications: general consumer characteristics and product-

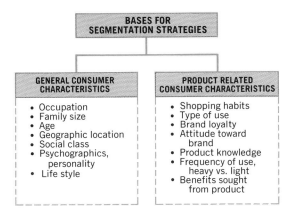

Figure 4-2 Bases for segmentation strategies.

related characteristics. We shall examine and discuss the importance of segmentation variables within the framework of these two broad classifications. Product-specific segmentations often offer deeper insights into the structure of a specific market, but segmentations based upon general consumer characteristics have other values such as versatility and overall economy, and such segmentation variables may suggest general shifts in value orientations.[8] Many companies base their segmentation strategies on a number of variables, some of which may be from the product-related customer characteristic category.

In order to add an element of greater realism to our analysis, however, let us consider again the soft drink industry of the United States. Assume that as a marketing or product manager for a major soft drink bottler and marketer, you were able to purchase a great deal of informative data about this industry. As a matter of fact, such data is available from various sources, but it is expensive. The data to be used in our illustration is hypothetical but nonetheless basically realistic. We shall call this data the Target Index Planning Survey, or TIPS for short. The data is the result of an annual survey of 20,000 persons (10,000 males and 10,000 females), all of whom are 18 years old or older. The data is the result of questions based upon demographic, sociological, social-psychological, and economic issues. Respondents are also asked to report the brands they buy when purchasing some 1,000 different goods and services. Such surveys also report respondents' media habits for television, radio, and magazines. Examples of the TIPS data for soft drinks are shown in Table 4-2.[9]

General Customer Characteristics.   The data in Table 4-2 show that 120 million adult Americans buy soft drinks. We can see also that 59 million adults

[8] Stuart Van Auken, "General Versus Product-Specific Life-Style Segmentation," *Journal of Advertising* (Fall 1978), pp. 31–35.

[9] This discussion follows that of G. David Hughes, *Marketing Management* (Reading, Mass.: Addison-Wesley, 1978), pp. 133–153.

Table 4-2 Profiles of Soft Drink Market Segments

	Needs Met					
	All Uses		Mixer Uses			
Profile Variable	Users (1)	Nonusers (2)	Users (3)	Nonusers (4)	7-Up (5)	Orange Juice (6)
Number of adults (millions)	120	18	59	78	26	23
Men	48%	45%	53%	44%	53%	51%
Women	52	55	47	56	47	49
Adults 18–25	20	6	21	15	23	28
26–34	22	8	24	17	26	23
35–49	27	19	28	25	26	24
50–64	21	31	19	25	18	16
65 or over	11	36	9	19	7	9
Northeast	24	25	28	22	21	27
North Central	26	26	26	26	32	25
South	32	38	26	36	24	26
West	17	20	20	16	23	22
SMSA central city	34	29	37	31	36	37
SMSA suburban	37	38	42	34	42	42
Non-SMSA	29	33	21	35	22	21
Graduated college	16	13	20	13	18	17
Attended college	21	16	24	17	25	25
Graduated high school	36	28	35	35	37	35
Did not graduate high school	27	43	21	36	20	23
Professional/managerial	17	12	20	13	20	17
Clerical/sales	15	11	17	13	17	17
Craftsmen/foremen	8	6	9	8	10	7
Other employed	19	14	17	19	18	20
Not employed	41	57	37	47	36	39
Household disposable income:						
$25,000 or more	8	6	10	7	9	8
$15,000–24,999	23	15	27	18	26	25
$10,000–14,999	30	22	30	28	32	29
$8000–9999	10	7	9	10	11	10
$5000–7999	16	19	14	19	14	16
Less than $5,000	14	30	10	20	9	12
White	88	87	87	89	90	84
Black	9	10	10	9	8	12
Other	3	3	3	2	3	3
Single	12	7	13	10	13	17
Married	78	72	79	77	80	74
Widowed/divorced/separated	9	21	8	13	7	8

Table 4-2 (Cont.)   Profiles of Soft Drink Market Segments

	Needs Met					
	All Uses		Mixer Uses			
Profile Variable	Users (1)	Nonusers (2)	Users (3)	Nonusers (4)	7-Up (5)	Orange Juice (6)
No children in household	45	69	43	52	41	43
Children under 2	10	3	11	8	13	11
2–5	20	10	22	17	23	21
6–11	26	13	27	23	27	26
12–17	28	19	28	26	28	29
Psychographic variables						
Affectionate	32%	24%	35%	28%	35%	37%
Amicable	22	18	24	19	23	22
Awkward	27	20	28	25	27	29
Brave	47	36	50	43	52	52
Broadminded	38	31	40	35	41	40
Creative	23	19	25	21	25	26
Dominating	34	23	38	29	38	39
Efficient	27	24	27	26	27	28
Egocentric	15	11	16	13	16	18
Frank	31	27	32	29	31	31
Funny	20	17	21	19	21	22
Intelligent	25	24	27	23	24	27
Kind	46	41	47	44	47	47
Refined	44	38	46	41	46	46
Reserved	21	21	20	21	20	19
Self-assured	24	21	24	23	23	24
Sociable	38	32	41	35	40	41
Stubborn	41	27	42	36	44	42
Tense	38	28	38	35	39	39
Trustworthy	60	53	62	57	63	59
Buying styles						
Brand-loyal	32%	31%	33%	31%	32%	32%
Cautious	38	35	37	37	38	36
Conformist	16	16	16	16	16	16
Ecologist	28	30	27	30	26	27
Economy-minded	36	34	33	38	33	34
Experimenters	26	22	27	25	26	28
Impulsive	22	15	23	20	23	23
Persuasible	31	26	31	30	31	32
Planners	45	36	45	43	46	42
Style-conscious	29	21	32	26	31	32

Source: Target Index Planning Survey (TIPS). Based on a hypothetical survey of 20,000 persons, 18 years or older (1982).

buy soft drinks as a mixer and the assumption would follow that the remaining 61 million persons use them as a beverage. You can also see that the South contains 32 percent of the users and this would be the largest segment in this category. The mixer market is largely located in the Northeast (28 percent) and mixer users tend primarily to live in suburbs (42 percent).

The data from Table 4-2 show that women buy more soft drinks than men and that the age group of 35 to 40 is the heaviest buying segment. Buyers tend to be unemployed, married, and have children between the ages of 2 and 17. There is little distinction among the occupations in terms of soft drink purchases. The data also show that the larger purchase segments for soft drinks are those whose incomes average between $10,000 and $15,000 per year and who have graduated from high school.

Thus our demographic profile suggests that housewives are the largest purchasers of soft drinks and that they purchase this item as part of their weekly shopping activities. These buyers are largely in the working, lower-middle, and upper-middle social classes, but people in all social classes buy soft drinks for whatever uses.

All of these factors would be important in terms of developing a marketing and promotional strategy. A point to be noted is that the data suggest that the buyers of soft drinks are not necessarily the users. Recall again the description of the major user profile in our opening segment. Housewives are the buyers, but the major users are the young active males. This could mean that we should have a promotional strategy directed toward both the housewife as the family purchasing agent, and the children and teenagers who are the principal users.

Other General Customer Characteristics. The data in Table 4-2 do not reveal much of significance in terms of such factors as *life cycle, life style, or personality characteristics*. Yet, again some insight about these factors is revealed or suggested.

Purchases of soft drinks seem to be spread fairly evenly among the various age segments with the exception of the over 65 category. While life styles of all users are not determined, some data that relate to this behavioral factor are shown in Table 4-2. By looking at the psychographic variables, we see that users regard themselves as brave, affectionate, dominating, stubborn, and tense. Further investigation of such factors, especially the tenseness factor, might lead to the development of promotional themes based upon the alleviation of tenseness or other forms of anxiety-reducing attributes of soft drinks. A comparison of users and nonusers of soft drinks suggests that users tend to be more impulsive, persuadable, style-conscious, and like to anticipate and plan ahead.

Product-Related Consumer Characteristics. The second major basis for segmentation strategy is very closely associated with the purchasing process itself. Such factors as brand loyalty, shopping habits, attitudes toward brands, user age rates, and benefits sought are, in many respects, situation-specific variables. That is, their influence and importance is a function more of the purchase situation than it is of the general consumer's characteristics. We shall discuss some of these factors here and others will be discussed more fully in chapter 6 which deals with buyer motivation and behavior.

From the data in Table 4-2 and the subsequent discussion, we can discern that shopping habits for soft drinks are a regular part of the housewife's weekly shopping experiences. Soft drinks are purchased mainly in supermarkets and the principal type of use is for consumption by teenagers and children, but adults also drink soft drinks and buy them for use as mixers with alcoholic beverages. From our earlier discussion, you could also conjecture that many consumers of soft drinks are highly brand-loyal; and thus the attitudes and images that buyers and users have of the product are extremely important to the brand's market acceptance and loyalty.

Usage Rate.   Many marketers discern that as much as 75 or 80 percent of their sales volume comes from as few as 20 to 25 percent of the buyers. To illustrate, 17 percent of the heavy half beer drinker consumes 88 percent of the total market; 37 percent of the heavy half market for cake mixes consumes 85 percent of the total market; 41 percent of the heavy half shampoo buyer consumes 81 percent of the total market; and 48 percent of the heavy half market for ready-to-eat cereals consumes 87 percent of the product.[10]

The heavy user segment is usually of extreme importance to the marketer, and therefore, it becomes important to examine the profiles of the heavy user. To continue our documentation of the bases for market segmentation, let us look now at Table 4-3 which again is an extension of the data related to the Target Index Planning Survey (TIPS) which we have purchased to aid us in understanding the market for soft drinks in the United States.

[10] These data, while dated, illustrate the nature of the heavy user segment. See Dik Warren Twedt, "How Important to Marketing Strategy is the Heavy User?," *Journal of Marketing* **28** (January 1964), p. 72.

Table 4-3   Profiles of Soft Drink Segments—Heavy and Light Users

	All Users		Soft drinks as a mixer	
Profile Variable	Heavy Users (1)	Light Users (2)	Heavy Users (3)	Light Users (4)
Number of adults (millions)	25	36	16	22
Men	53%	45%	59%	48%
Women	47	55	41	52
Adults 18–25	34	11	18	21
26–34	26	16	19	25
35–49	23	29	28	28
50–64	12	26	23	18
65 or over	6	18	12	8

Table 4-3 (Cont.) Profiles of Soft Drink Segments—Heavy and Light Users

Profile Variable	All Users		Soft drinks as a mixer	
	Heavy Users (1)	Light Users (2)	Heavy Users (3)	Light Users (4)
Northeast	23	25	30	27
North Central	24	27	25	27
South	38	26	27	26
West	15	22	19	19
SMSA central city	37	30	39	34
SMSA suburban	34	40	39	43
Non-SMSA	29	30	22	23
Graduated college	12	17	21	18
Attended college	24	20	21	24
Graduated high school	37	33	33	37
Did not graduate high school	27	30	25	22
Professional/managerial	15	18	20	17
Clerical/sales	17	13	14	18
Craftsmen/foremen	10	8	9	9
Other employed	22	17	17	17
Not employed	36	46	39	39
Household disposable income:				
$25,000 or more	7	8	12	9
$15,000–24,999	22	22	27	25
$10,000–14,999	29	30	25	33
$8000–9999	11	9	9	10
$5000–7999	19	15	15	14
Less than $5000	12	17	13	9
White	86	91	83	89
Black	11	7	14	8
Other	3	2	3	3
Single	20	8	15	10
Married	73	80	76	82
Widowed/divorced/separated	7	12	10	8
No children in household	38	51	47	39
Children under 2	13	8	8	12
2–5	25	16	18	24
6–11	29	25	25	28
12–17	28	28	29	28

Source: Target Index Planning Survey (TIPS). Based on a hypothetical survey of 20,000 persons, 18 years or older (1982).

Much can be learned by studying the heavy user segment of a given market. In our illustration, we can see emerge some rather sharp distinctions between the all-user segment and the mixer segment. Table 4-3 shows that 60 percent of the all-user segment is under 35 years of age, whereas only 37 percent of the mixer market is in this age bracket. The all-users market is concentrated in the South. The mixer market is concentrated in the Northeast. The mixer market contains more professionals, more college graduates, more black persons, fewer children in the household and, as would be expected, higher incomes. Heavy users of soft drinks are those who drink more than one soft drink per day, whereas the light user drinks a soft drink once per week or less. Naturally soft drink marketers will want to go after the "heavy half" of the market because every heavy user drinking his or her brand is worth several light drinkers. Too often, however, when all the companies go after the same heavy user, their campaigns seem to look alike and cancel each other. Isn't this largely the case with soft drinks and also for many of the fast food outlets such as McDonald's, Burger King, Burger Chef, Arby's, and Wendy's? Much the same holds true for beer. The marketer usually hopes that the heavy user of a product will have certain common characteristics and media habits and where this is true, these characteristics then become the basis for total marketing and segmentation strategies.

It should be emphatically pointed out, however, that the heavy user segment is not the only segment worth pursuing. The light user segment may be a market that would be receptive to a special product or a product that meets special needs. At one time, Seven-Up was just such a product. V-8 Juice is such a product, as Perrier Water. But each of these products has made some market penetration and has captured a significant share of a small but important market segment.

Another segment that should always be explored is the nonuser market. Referring again to Table 4-2, we see that there are 18 million nonusers of soft drinks in the United States. Can some of these 18 million nonusers be persuaded to buy a new or an existing product if it promises the right benefits or appeals to some special need of these persons? The data suggest that these nonusers are older, have less education, tend to be unemployed, have lower incomes, and have no children in the household. This does not answer the question, however, as to why they are nonusers of soft drinks.

Beware the Majority Fallacy.   Developing a marketing strategy that is always directed to the heavy user segment, while sometimes viable, is on other occasions not very successful. Remember that all the companies usually are striving for some share of the heavy user segment. So to avoid what is called "the majority fallacy," creative marketers do not overlook the light user and the nonuser segments. This majority fallacy can trap an unwary firm into simply duplicating existing characteristics and always following the majority. The fallacy is that competition is ignored. It should seem self-evident that the majority of consumers do not have to prefer a particular product in order for it to be successful.[11]

[11] See, Alfred A. Kuehn and Ralph L. Day, "Strategy of Product Quality,"*Harvard Business Review* **40** (November–December 1962), pp. 100–110.

Market Segmentation Is Planning

Market segmentation, as we have seen demonstrated throughout the soft drink example, is based upon analysis and planning. Inevitably there are limitations to each of the segmentation variables discussed. The lengthy example presented underscores the notion that a research study must be concerned with all the implications segmentation has for developing marketing strategies. The illustration has also suggested that a sequence of activities should be undertaken to make segmentation more useful to marketing executives.[12]

To summarize, how does the marketing decision-maker do a better job of selecting market segments and targeting the firm's strategy to these segments? By following three rather basic steps in the overall planning procedure:

1. Think small initially and begin with a small sample of potential consumers to investigate possible segment characteristics.
2. Move from the small and simple to larger, more complex samples. Be careful not to jump to conclusions. At this stage, findings are tentative and are not to be considered conclusive.
3. Use more than one measure for collecting data and submit your findings to a panel or group of judicious, even critical, fellow decision-makers. Seek agreement and satisfactorily answer all their objections.

By following such guidelines, a more objective picture of the market can be obtained and a more useful basis for segmentation strategies will emerge.[13]

Determining Buyer Benefits Sought

Market segments based upon general customer characteristics and even some of the product-related customer characteristics are far too broad to be useful in discriminating among users of different brands within a product category. Such segments may even turn out to be misleading. A personality or a lifestyle measure in its generalized form may simply not be related at all to a product under question. For example, a buyer may be price-conscious in making routine decisions, but will still purchase the most expensive brand of wine or perfume. An individual may perceive himself or herself to be aggressive, bold, and assertive and behave that way in terms of his or her professional behavior but may never choose to express this aggressiveness in the purchase of clothing[14] or in the type of automobile purchased.[15]

---

[12] Such a sequence is also suggested in the following work. See Henry Assael and Marvin Roscoe Jr., "Approaches to Market Segmentation Analysis," *Journal of Marketing* **40** no. 4 (October 1976), pp. 67–76.

[13] See Phil Levine, "Locating Your Customers in a Segmented Market," *Journal of Marketing* **39** (October 1975), pp. 72–73 and B. Stuart Tolley, "Identifying Users Through a Segmentation Study," *Journal of Marketing* **39** (April 1975), pp. 69–71.

[14] Elizabeth A. Richards and Stephen S. Sturman, "Life-Style Segmentation in Apparel Marketing," *Journal of Marketing* **41** no. 4 (October 1977), pp. 89–91.

[15] Joseph Pernica, "The Second Generation of Market Segmentation Studies: An Audit of Buying Motivations," in *Life Style and Psychographics*, William D. Wells ed. (Chicago: American Marketing Association, 1974), pp. 279–313.

In many purchase situations, the benefits the buyer seeks from products should serve as the major segmentation variable. For example, recreational skiers may be mostly interested in economy, comfort, and desirability in ski equipment. More advanced skiers may seek style and above all, performance. General Foods discovered that not all buyers of dog food sought the same benefits. One group of buyers, they found, was concerned with matching the characteristics of their dogs with specific attributes of the product. Consequently, General Foods developed its Cycle Dog Food. Cycle 1 was for puppies; Cycle 2 was for adult dogs 1 to 7 years old; Cycle 3 was for obese dogs—those that get too many calories; and Cycle 4 was for older dogs—those over 7 years of age.

The Boeing Company of Seattle, Washington, considers nearly every buyer for one of its 747 passenger jets as a separate and distinct market segment based primarily on the fact that each buyer is seeking unique and specific benefits when one of these products is purchased.

Benefits Sought Determine Strategy.   Therefore, each group of customers for a different product, or customers who buy similar or identical products may buy them because they seek certain benefits from the products. This may mean that each group will require a different type of product, a different advertising or promotion strategy, a different pricing strategy, and even a different method of distribution.

Benefit segmentation then is based upon the idea that it is meaningful for the marketer to look toward causal factors for segmentation variables.[16] Variables such as demographics, brand loyalty, and usage rates often tend to describe the kinds of people who make up a market, or how much of the product they consume, but they do not explain in a causal way why they buy the product.

The approach to benefit segmentation begins with a survey of users and potential users of a product in terms of what benefits they seek and what benefits are missing or deficient from the products they use. Table 4-4 is a listing of benefits consumers expressed a desire for in terms of a household cleaning product.

An analysis of benefits sought by consumers shows what types of product characteristics are perceived as being most closely associated with any single benefit or any group of related benefits and the importance of benefits as a basis for segmentation strategies as well as other aspects of the marketing program.[17]

Volkswagen, for example, has attempted to build a product line based essentially on the benefits sought by automotive users. For those who seek the basic benefits of economy, safety, and ecology, Volkswagen markets the Rabbit. For the segment that is more concerned with handling, maneuverability,

---

[16] Benefit segmentation was first described by Russell I. Haley. See "Benefit Segmentation: A Decision Oriented Research Tool," *Journal of Marketing* **32** (July 1968), pp. 30–35.

[17] James H. Myers, "Benefit Structure Analysis: A New Tool for Product Planning," *Journal of Marketing* **40** no. 4 (October 1976), pp. 23–32.

Table 4-4 Examples of Benefits in a Household Cleaning Product

Bleaches	Chrome sparkles
Removes stains	Doesn't dull
Removes grease	Doesn't hurt hands
Removes built-up dirt	Dissolves grease
Cleans tub ring	Doesn't remove gloss from paint
Less elbow grease	Boosts detergents
Can see it work	Strips wax
Cleans cracks (grout) better	Less buildup
Doesn't leave residue	Lets color come through
No rinsing necessary	Stands up to damp mopping
Doesn't damage surfaces	Seals porour floors
Kills mildew	Doesn't yellow
Disinfects	No streaking
Removes discoloration	Does two jobs at once
Removes soap scum	Leaves it "squeaky clean"

Source: James H. Myers, "Benefit Structure Analysis: A New Tool for Product Planning," *Journal of Marketing* **40,** no. 4 (October 1976), pp. 23–32.

performance, and speed, they have marketed the Scirocco. Bic Shaver's disposable twin blade razor was developed to meet the needs of the segment of users who wanted the specific benefits of convenience, comfort, and low price, while in shampoo, Body by the Numbers markets three different formulas it has developed for those whose hair requires such special benefits, that is, #1 is for normal hair, #2 is for oily hair, and #3 is for dry hair.

In the toothpaste market, four major segments have been discovered based upon benefit analysis. One segment is particularly concerned with flavor, another with brightness of teeth and freshness of breath, another with decay prevention, and another with price. As we shall learn shortly, sometimes a new product can be introduced which includes product attributes that will appeal to more than one benefit segment such as a toothpaste that is low priced, has a clean fresh taste, makes teeth whiter, and prevents tooth decay.

Benefit Segmentation Can Work for Most Markets. The belief underlying this segmentation strategy is that the benefits which people are seeking in purchasing a particular product or service are the basic reasons for true market segments. Hence, benefit segmentation is useful in a wide range of market-oriented situations. Benefit segmentation has been shown to be useful in nearly all profit-seeking marketing situations. Nonprofit organizations such as churches, hospitals, colleges, and universities can also use this approach to segment and better understand their markets. Benefit segmentation is a useful approach in industrial marketing. Industrial markets too can be segmented on the basis of general customer characteristics and product-related characteristics, but benefit segmentation, that is, such factors as assurance of continuity of supply, quality, speed of delivery, reduced operating and maintenance costs, and price protection are also important benefits sought by many market targets. Experience with this approach has shown that benefits sought by consumers determine their behavior much more accurately than do demographic characteristics or volume of consumption. With the use of benefit segmentation and modern statistical techniques, marketers can group respondents on the basis of the importance they attach to certain combinations of rational, sensory, and emotional benefits expected from the product.

Approaches to Benefit Segmentation.   The beginning point in benefit segmentation is to identify the benefits relevant to the particular product or product class. This is accomplished in a number of ways. Groups of potential users of the product are surveyed to discover what attribute or benefits of the product they deem to be most critical. Consumers are often asked simply to discuss a product; why did they buy it? what do they expect it to do? what are its basic deficiencies? where did they buy it? what do their friends think of the product? and other questions. From such discussions and surveys, the market researcher may produce a large number of phrases or word descriptions that consumers use in describing and evaluating products and brands. Then more sophisticated procedures of analysis are used to identify the significant attributes and eliminate the redundant ones.

For example, assume that we were interested in knowing how users perceived a particular brand of soft drink. Respondents may be asked to rate various brands on a number of scales or attributes. Such a procedure is shown in Figure 4-3.

Notice that consumers are asked to rate ten attributes of the soft drink and to note on a scale of 1 to 7 how important or unimportant each attribute is to the purchase situation. Observe also that in the illustrative example of Figure 4-3, the respondents' rankings and evaluations varied somewhat depending on

Figure 4-3   Customer ratings for a brand of soft drink.

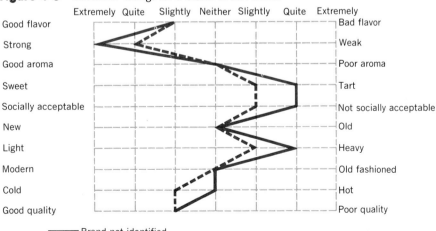

━━━ Brand not identified

▄ ▄ ▄ Brand identified

whether the product was identified by brand or was not identified. Many factors can readily affect the rater's judgment and evaluation.

The purpose of such schemes is to enable the researcher to group people on the basis of how they ranked various attributes in order that meaningful segment possibilities can be identified. Sometimes this is a relatively easy task and other times it is much more difficult. In soft drinks, for example, some persons like sweet flavors; others prefer their flavors to be more tart. Some, of course, fall in between and prefer flavors that are neither too sweet nor too tart. Such truly distinct preferences, however, often fail to occur. In some product classifications, distinct groups do not emerge. In such cases, computer-oriented statistical procedures are useful to help the researcher. It would be somewhat unusual for a single dimension such as "socially acceptable" to be so prevalent as in our soft drink example. Most of the time, the research suggests that for most groups several benefits or attributes are important to them.

Perceptual Space Mapping.   Sometimes it is useful to know, in addition to the relative importance of an attribute or benefit, where customers would like an "ideal" brand or product to be located. If the attribute were "sweet" versus "tart" as in the soft drink example, the answer is fairly clear from the data shown in Figure 4-3 since these respondents clearly prefer a brand that is basically tart. However, if soft drinks are being rated on a scale that extends from extremely sweet to extremely tart, an ideal brand could be anywhere along the scale. A procedure called perceptual mapping enables marketers to distinguish among competing brands and find unfilled market opportunities.[18] Thus by examining a brand on a perceptual map the marketer can determine the brand's strength or weakness. Figure 4-4 shows a set of ideal brand points for a midwestern soft drink market. The circles represent groups of ideal points. The size of the circle indicates the number of people who locate their ideal brand in that area.

Segments 1 and 2 are clearly the largest and segment 3 is the smallest. Our perceptual space map is shown for illustrative purposes and such a map, if done more realistically, would doubtless show a larger number of segments. Coke and Pepsi, as can be seen, are clearly the dominant products serving segment 1 and Seven-Up is the dominant product serving segment 2. While King and Shasta Colas seem to be meeting the requirements for sweetness, they clearly are perceived by many users, perhaps teenagers, as being much less socially acceptable. Segment 3, which consists of a cluster of users who want a soft drink that is tart but are not too concerned about its image of social acceptability, does not appear to be served by any of the existing products. Such a discovery makes it interesting to speculate on where a new brand might position itself or toward which area an existing brand might move. Perhaps

[18] Perceptual space mapping can be further explored by examining the following sources: Robert Krampf and John Daniel Williams, "Multidimensional Scaling as a Research Tool: An Explanation and Application," *Journal of Business Research* **2** (April 1974) pp. 157–176. Much of the pioneering work in this area was done by Paul Green; see, "A Multidimensional Model of Product-Feature Association," *Journal of Business Research* **2** (April 1974), pp. 107–118.

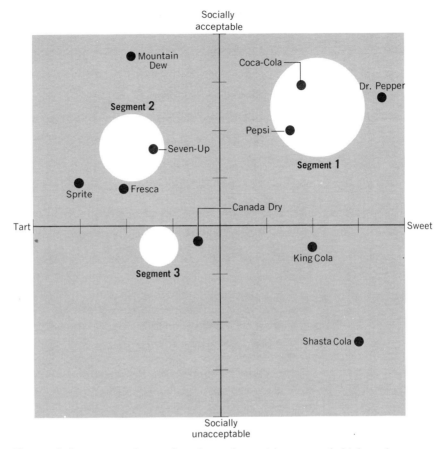

Figure 4-4   Perceptual space brand map for a midwestern soft drink market.

segment 3 is composed of many persons who buy soft drinks as mixers and if so, it would appear that Canada Dry would wish to move their product somewhat closer to the ideal point of segment 3. What strategy would you suggest that King and Shasta Colas pursue?

In Summary, Benefit Segmentation Is Useful.   Benefit segmentation, as we have seen, seldom fails to provide fresh insight into markets. When segmentation studies are undertaken, a number of smaller markets emerge instead of one large general market. When this occurs, each smaller market can be subjected to the same rigorous analysis to which large general markets have been subjected in the past. However, the segmentation analysis has now shown that the total market was a heterogeneous aggregation of subgroups. The so-called mythical average consumer exists only in the minds of some marketers. When benefit segmentation is employed, a number of distinct homogeneous segments are discovered. Therefore, because they are homogeneous, descriptions of them in terms of averages are much more significant as marketing guides.

Before proceeding, can you answer the following questions?
1. Why do marketers segment markets?
2. What are the two broad categories or bases for market segmentation?
3. How are the product attributes or benefits related to market segmentation?

Market Positioning

When the concepts of product and firm differentiation are merged with market segmentation, the resulting concept is called positioning. Remember from our brief discussion in Chapter 3 that positioning is an important part of the firm's overall strategic planning and it relates to how the firm and certain attributes of its products such as form, package size, and price stand out from the competition.[19]

Positioning means creating a strong identity or image for the company and its products and communicating this image vividly to customers. It is concerned with determining the market segment or segments toward which the product will be chiefly aimed and deciding on the appeals to be used in promoting the product to these segments. Thus, product position focuses upon buyers' perceptions and preferences about the place a product or brand occupies in a specific market. Product differentiation relates product positioning with market segmentation. Under such an arrangement, there is some change in marketing emphasis from "whom you reach" to "what characteristics do you build into the product."[20]

Head-on Positioning.   Head-on positioning is the strategy of comparing, or **positioning,** your product or company directly against the industry leader. It is sometimes a dangerous tactic, but the widespread use and practice of comparative advertising indicates that many firms consider it a viable positioning effort. For example, in a recent advertising campaign the major theme was "How do you improve a bottle of Chivas Regal?" The illustration showed how—by filling the bottle with Cutty Sark.

Other examples of head-on positioning include Coke's perennial battle with Pepsi; Gillette's Earth Born Shampoo confronting Clairol's Herbal Essence; Colgate's direct challenge to the well-entrenched Crest. Burger King's "Have it your way" campaign was a distinct success and it was directed at the McDonald's customers who were frustrated by having to wait too long for special orders.

---

[19] Jack Trout and Al Ries, "The Positioning Era Cometh," a three-part series in *Advertising Age* (Chicago; Crain Publications, 1972).

[20] John B. Maggard, "Positioning Revisited," *Journal of Marketing* **40,** no. 1 (January 1976), pp. 63–66.

Positioning with an Idea. Head-on positioning strategy is being applied in a number of different ways. The intent is, of course, to better satisfy customer demands, increase sales, and thus make better profits.[21]

In **positioning with an idea,** the notion is to bracket your product or company with a perceived leader, while at the same time pointing out why your product or company is better. The now classic example of positioning with an idea was that of Avis against Hertz, when Avis cast itself in the underdog position with "When you're No. 2 you have to try harder." Another recent example of this kind of positioning was the B.F. Goodrich Company's attempt to create an identity and position for itself separate from that of Goodyear by acknowledging the strong image of the Goodyear blimp.

Lever Brothers positioned their toothpaste Aim against both Procter and Gamble's Crest and Colgate-Palmolive's Colgate as a product that would be equally effective in preventing decay and at the same time would clean and whiten teeth. Thus, they combined two product attributes or benefits that were successful: stannous fluoride, the successful anticavity ingredient so long touted by Crest, and its patented clear gel process, which had proved to be successful in its earlier product Close-Up.

Repositioning Works Too. Miller's Beer was originally positioned or cast a woman's beer, but sales and market response were poor, so it was recast or repositioned as a good-tasting brew enjoyed by typical beer drinkers (blue collar workers, fun and zestful, adventuresome, and sports-minded). For another example, consider Johnson's Baby Shampoo, which was first positioned as a "no tears" shampoo for toddlers. It was later repositioned as a mild product for those who shampoo frequently. Many staple products are repositioned. Lysol was repositioned from a disinfectant to a product that promised "to kill household germs and odors as you clean." Vaseline was repositioned from a hair care product to a product designed to be a general "skin survival kit."[22]

Perhaps the greatest resuscitation of a dying product to one of renewed growth and vigor through repositioning is that of Arm & Hammer Baking Soda. Because of the decline of baking in the United States due to working wives and prepared cake and cookie mixes, there was a dramatic decline in the sales of baking soda. However, Arm & Hammer began promoting their baking soda as a refrigerator deodorant, a deodorant for cat litter boxes, and as a general powdered deodorant for rugs in family playrooms and living areas. Instead of using just a few teaspoons as required in baking, consumers were now using the product a few boxes at a time. One commercial persuaded more than 30 million buyers to put a box of baking soda in their refrigerators.[23]

[21] John H. Holmes, "Profitable Product Positioning," *MSU Business Topics* (Spring 1973), pp. 27–32.
[22] Bernard F. Whalen, "Marketer Designs Permanent Media to Position Firms," *Marketing News* **13**, no. 9 (November 2, 1979), p. 1.
[23] H.W. McMahan, "Alltime Ad Triumphs Reveal Key Success Factors Behind Choice of '100 Best'," *Advertising Age* (April 12, 1976), p. 78.

An example of repositioning.

Sometimes the original image of a product conflicts with a new image. Not too long ago, Geritol was repositioned. The name Geritol is based on the word geriatrics, which pertains to the care and health of the aged. Is Geritol promoted as an older person's product today? A product name that is appropriate when positioned for one market segment may be less appropriate when positioned for another segment.[24]

Managing Segmentation and Positioning Strategies

Market segmentation is based upon differences in customers' demand characteristics. Groups of customers with similar demand characteristics are market segments. Positioning is concerned with psychological characteristics such as how consumers perceive a product and what attitudes or feelings they have about it. Product differentiation is an effort to create distinctions between similar products. Segmentation, positioning, and differentiation are all integral aspects of marketing strategy and they are used by the firm in its effort to better target its product and service offerings to the marketplace.

When a company considers penetrating a market it must consider the following things:

1. It must ascertain those attributes with which to identify the possible existence of distinct market segments.
2. The firm must assess and evaluate the size and potential of the various market segments.
3. The firm must assess how the various brands are positioned in the market.
4. The firm must consider if there are market segments that are not being served by existing brands.
5. The firm must then decide what roles market segmentation, positioning, and product differentiation are to play in its own market targeting efforts.

Marketing managers must constantly assess which market-product strategy is most appropriate. An undifferentiated product or service permits only limited marketing creativity. With such products, the usual goal is to match competition, especially in terms of price and, perhaps, to offer better service such as faster delivery. By contrast, in connection with a differentiated product, a whole range of creative, innovative marketing efforts can be employed. When considering a differentiated product, the marketer must decide whether it should seek to penetrate the whole market or only some distinct market segment. In almost all cases, a product that is positioned with a knowledge of the consumer benefits sought has a tremendous advantage for segmentation and differentiation through marketing and promotional efforts.

Guidelines for Better Segmentation. Product differentiation and positioning efforts usually flow out of the firm's segmentation efforts. Therefore, it is imperative that segmentation be used properly. There are three ways by which

[24] See G.L. Urban, "Preceptor: A Model for Product Positioning," *Management Science* **21** (April 1975), pp. 858–871.

segmentation efforts can be generally improved. First, the firm should not pursue the wrong segment. The right segment is not necessarily the largest one. It is, instead, the segment that a specific company, given its skills and abilities, can best serve. Second, the firm should not engage in oversegmentation. Most firms can only effectively reach a few segments of each market. Few firms have the resources or marketing know-how to reach all segments.

As the costs of products and services soar and conservative lifestyles gain in popularity, the values and attitudes of many consumers seem to be changing. In return for lower prices, some consumers are increasingly willing to "accept a little less than I want"—to buy a product or service that is not as precisely tailored to their desires as it presumably would have been in an era of stable prices and plenty. For many marketers, this trend suggests the need for a new strategy: aggregating or clustering market segments. Such firms are offering simpler products with lower price tags and are identifying markets that are ready for combining.[25]

Third, and finally, some marketers must be admonished to avoid overconcentration. By concentrating so much on one segment, other important segments might be overlooked which could be profitable. Several of the carbonated soft drink marketers realized that they were overconcentrated in this market. Some have tended to correct this by developing noncarbonated drinks, some of which are dry mixes and some of which are fruit juice-based. Other soft drink marketers have begun to realize that they have overpromoted their products to the 12 to 20 year old youth segment and that as a consequence, the industry has lost many of its older consumers.

Summary

Product differentiation, market segmentation, and product positioning are three of the vital concepts upon which many marketing strategies are built. Product differentiation is the effort by marketers to differentiate or distinguish their products from those of competitors. The attributes of the products that are used as the basis for differentiation are either real or imagined. With product differentiation, the marketer largely assumes that all buyers for the product are essentially the same and that the marketer's task is to make the firm's products different from others in the eyes of potential buyers.

Market segmentation is the recognition that not all buyers of a product are the same. Market segmentation largely rejects the notion of homogeneous overall markets. Instead, the overall market is viewed as a heterogeneous market or one characterized as having considerable diversity or differences within it. A market segment is composed of a group of buyers or potential buyers whose demand characteristics are similar and who would be inclined to respond similarly to differences in the firm's marketing mix. Markets are

---

[25] Alan J. Resnik, Peter B.B. Turney, and J. Barry Mason, "Marketers Turn To Counter-Segmentation," *Harvard Business Review* (September–October 1979), pp. 100–106.

segmented on the basis of two major variables: general customer characteristics and product or situational-related consumer characteristics.

Market positioning means creating a strong identity or image for the company and its products and communicating this image vividly to customers. Positioning focuses upon buyer perceptions and preferences about the place a product or brand occupies in a specific market. Segmentation, positioning, and differentiation are used by the firm to better target its product and service offerings to the marketplace.

Review Questions

1. What is meant by product differentiation? How is it related to marketing strategy?
2. How does market segmentation differ from product differentiation? Does Bayer aspirin rely more on product differentiation than it does on market segmentation?
3. Why is product differentiation "product-oriented" and why is market segmentation more "market-oriented"? Explain.
4. How are product differentiation, market segmentation, and product positioning related to the concept of market targeting?
5. What are the advantages and disadvantages to the firm of pursuing a policy of undifferentiated marketing? Today, do most firms pursue a policy of undifferentiated or differentiated marketing?
6. List and discuss several of the benefits of following a segmentation strategy.
7. What are the major criteria that are used to determine if a market can be meaningfully segmented?
8. Recalling the information from Table 4-2, list first the two major bases for segmentation strategies and then list several of the variables that marketers use under each of these bases for segmenting markets.
9. In marketing segmentation efforts, marketers are sometimes warned to beware of the "majority fallacy." What are they being warned about?
10. What is the basic distinction between head-on positioning and positioning with an idea? Why would the Florida Orange Growers Association attempt to reposition orange juice with the theme "It isn't just for breakfast anymore"?

Case 4-1

Toyota Motor Sales—U.S.A.

In the fall of 1979, Toyota Motor Sales U.S.A., Inc. launched a $65 million, 51-week TV and print advertising campaign, one of the most expensive media blitzes in history. The Japanese automobile firm whose U.S. import base of operations is Torrance, California, has adopted a new theme for the current campaign. All Toyota ads will stress "Oh, what a feeling, Toyota." This theme replaces the well-worn theme "You asked for it, you got it—Toyota."

"Oh, what a feeling—Toyota" was developed to "best convey the strong feeling of satisfaction among Toyota owners." E.B. Brogan, national advertising manager for TMS commented, "We think the jingle is extremely up-tempo, and the entire mood of the commercials is uplifting. The theme will appeal to our market segment."

Toyota is the number one selling auto imported into the United States. Toyota has been met with enthusiastic customer acceptance in the United States and the TMS Company has achieved enviable market penetration and has a significant share of the overall U.S. car market. Toyota products are generally considered to be high quality. In the era of high energy costs, many U.S. car buyers are looking increasingly to high-mileage imports as one way of lowering their overall transportation costs. The new front-wheel drive Tercel is Toyota's latest entry in the low-cost compact field. Several of the major and popular Japanese import models such as Honda and Subaru are designed around the front-wheel drive technology which reduces the car's overall weight by eliminating the drive shaft which in turn usually means greater efficiency.

Nine new TV commercials were developed to lend support to the company's redesigned Corolla Series, including the new front-wheel drive Tercel, the Celica series, and Toyota trucks.

Independent surveys and market research showed that Toyota owners were near the top in terms of automobile owner satisfaction. Toyota owners indeed possessed a special feeling that came with driving and owning Toyota cars and trucks.

Thus, through both product differentiation and market segmentation, Toyota planned to develop its major marketing and promotional strategy for the early 1980s.

In addition to its TV campaign, Toyota bought space in numerous national magazines such as *Time, Newsweek, Sports Illustrated, People Weekly, Playboy, National Geographic, Car and Driver, Motor Trend,* and *Road and Track.* Each of these carried six-page color ad units promoting Toyota's 1980 models. Toyota also placed single-page ads in magazines such as *T.V. Guide, U.S. News and World Report, Life, Psychology Today, Scientific American, Sunset,* and *Reader's Digest.* It was estimated that 90 million people read these magazines for each issue.

Newspapers also were slated to carry Toyota's new model message with insertions planned for more than 800 papers across the country. The most Toyota ever spent on an advertising campaign previous to this one was about $50 million.

Questions

1. There are usually two complementary approaches to the development of marketing strategy. These are product differentiation and market segmentation. What evidence of these two approaches do you see in Toyota's strategy?

2. Describe to what extent you believe Toyota's market segmentation strategy is market-oriented.

3. What would you consider to be Toyota's major benefits and costs of segmentation?

4. What essential segmentation criteria do you believe might be best for Toyota?

Case 4-2

Landor Associates, Inc.

Landor Associates, Incorporated is a staff of 175 designers, researchers, and marketing specialists stationed in eleven offices throughout the world. The organization exists by performing corporate facelifts, by repositioning companies, and by designing new images.

John Diefenbach, 42, is president of Landor Associates, Inc., San Francisco, and he is a specialist when it comes to nonverbal communication. His vocabulary includes such terms as "permanent media," "visual pollution," "corporate identity resource management," and "integrated product concepts."

Diefenbach's client list is long, impressive, and diverse. It includes hundreds of companies from Coca-Cola to Colgate-Palmolive, from small Wisconsin banks to multibillion-dollar retail chains in Japan. However, they all had one thing in common—they were suffering from corporate identity crises—and they called on Landor for help. Such help costs $50,000 to $250,000 and according to clients is well worth it.

Diefenbach suggests that such help is needed because corporations must take a position to be visible and reflect their personalities to society. He asserts that the need for an acceptable image came about because of the age of overcommunication. Overcommunication is the result of more than 300,000 brand names in circulation, a montage of too many company logos which has resulted in visual pollution. His argument is that there is a dramatic need for corporate and product identity and that to assure survival in an age of overcommunication, positioning and corporate image development are imperative. Corporate image, to his way of thinking, is a marketing tool for positioning your products.

One of Landor's repositioning efforts is Allegheny Airlines, which had grown to become the sixth largest U.S. carrier in terms of passengers flown. Yet the company suffered from a "rinky-dink" image. Research showed that when it comes to airlines, the consumer feels that "big is better" so Landor set out to reposition Allegheny as a big carrier. The name of the carrier was changed to "U.S. Air," the jets and ground vehicles repainted in bright modern colors, terminal stations refurbished, and employee uniforms redesigned. The new ad campaign stressed the slogan "It takes a big airline to fly more flights than TWA…"

The results of Landor's facelift have been dramatic, according to Jack King, the airline's vice-president of public affairs. He said U.S. Air has benefited from increased passenger traffic and improved employee morale.

Another Landor success involved the introduction of "Lite" beer which the Miller Brewing Company inherited when it bought Meisterbrau Breweries. Lite was positioned and packaged as a low-calorie feminine product, a category tainted by failure.

In an effort to successfully market Lite, Landor decided to position it as an independent brand capable of standing on its own strengths. The new concept for Lite would project a premium brand image and a broad appeal. To overcome the low-calorie, feminine product stigma, Landor created a new logo type letter style and graphics for Lite. They had a traditional Germanic feeling which evoked the country's heritage of masterful brewing.

The inherent excellence of Lite was further reinforced by the package's strong bulls-eye design, emphasizing natural ingredients by focusing attention on the prominent hops illustration.

The introduction of Lite turned out to be one of the most successful market stories in history, and Miller credits the work of Landor.

Although the redesigning of logos is important, it is only the tip of the iceberg in terms of total repositioning. When Landor goes to work for a new client it spends months conducting marketing, demographic, and psychological research before recommending any creative changes.

Brand names, company names, divisional/subsidiary names, and system organizing names are all studied. Product packaging and styling are reviewed, as is the firm's advertising, sales promotion, publicity, and permanent media. A company's personnel are even researched. Environmental and social factors are also weighed, as are the positionings of the company's competitors. When all these factors are put together, Landor develops a variety of plans and executions. The entire identity resource management program is presented to the client and a final decision is made.

Diefenbach believes that the keystones to a successful design program are "personality, permanence, honesty, believability, and appeal."

"Positioning is the single most important element in successful marketing today," Diefenbach insists. "You don't redesign an airplane or anything else simply for the sake of aesthetics." The ultimate goal of positioning is to create an image that will place the company at its proper position within the market it serves.

Diefenbach believes that repositioning and designing of corporate identities is necessary not only to overcome visual pollution but also to combat negative social factors. Positioning and creating the proper image can overcome the general public's distrust of corporations.

Questions

1. Does Mr. Diefenbach's (of Landor Associates, Inc.) notion of positioning square well with the discussion of positioning presented in the text?
2. What does Diefenbach mean when he talks about "overcommunication" and "visual pollution"?
3. Do you agree with Diefenbach's statement that "Positioning is the single most important element in successful marketing today"? Why might one take issue with this statement?
4. Do you believe that positioning or repositioning can combat negative social factors? How might Mobil Oil or Exxon use positioning to combat negative social factors?

Chapter 5

Knowing Your Market

Without people—consumers—there would be no demand or market opportunities. For strategic marketing planning to succeed, marketers must know their markets. But the endless diversity of human beings greatly complicates this essential task. There are young people, old people, people who live in large cities, and those who live in small rural communities. Some have almost staggering incomes; others find their modest earnings more than adequate to supply them with all the necessities and even some of the luxuries of this affluent society. And there are those whose incomes can purchase little more than a dismal misery.

These trends will offer challenges for marketers in the 1980s:[1]

- A sharp decline in the number of children and young adults
- A population growing at a slower rate
- A 50 percent increase in the number of consumers age 75 and up
- Immigration will account for a greater proportion of population growth
- Hispanics will outnumber blacks by 1990
- A great increase in the number and diversity of households accompanied by a decline in the average size of household and gains in nonfamily households
- Population in Sunbelt states will increase dramatically while population in Snowbelt states will grow slowly or decline
- By 1990, more than 60 percent of all wives will be employed outside the home. This will affect a family's standard of living, expectations, and expenditure patterns. Products that ease the burden of housework and provide convenience will be even more in demand.

These changes and trends will create both problems and opportunities for marketers but most importantly, change often is the cause for the emergence of new markets.

Why New Markets

Marketing planners and developers, after assessing technological and environmental changes, deliberately try to exploit and enlarge new markets. Faced with a shrinking market, alert managers stimulate other sources of demand. This underscores again the earlier point that successful marketing is knowing your environment.

New markets, expanding markets and shifting markets are the vital life force of American industry. An understanding of markets is an understanding of market opportunities. It is also the basis of much of strategic market planning. How the firm approaches questions of product differentiation and market segmentation as alternative marketing strategies depends largely on how markets are perceived and defined. In this chapter we will explore in some detail the characteristics of markets in general. Following that, we will analyze three

[1] William Lazer, "Lucrative Marketing Opportunities Will Abound in the 'Upbeat' 1980s," Marketing News, XIV, 1, (July 11,1980), pp. 1 and 14.

kinds of marketing targets: consumer, business-industrial, and government. The balance of the chapter will then focus on two of the more crucial dimensions of markets, population and income. In the chapter to follow, we will explore the third critical dimension of markets, buyer behavior.

What Are Markets?

Markets Facilitate Exchange

A market consists of the forces of supply and demand facilitating an exchange process between people. When we go to the market, we exchange money, or a promise to pay, for goods or services. The job market implies suppliers and users of services and skills. A housing market is the sum total of supply and demand forces for given kinds of housing services: condominiums, leisure homes, apartment buildings, or single-family dwellings. Markets may be local, regional, national, or, increasingly today, international in scope. A market implies a set of conditions that affect the exchange process, thus determining prices and the other terms of trade. However, the essential characteristic of a market from a seller's perspective is that it is an opportunity to seek success through the development and implementation of a marketing program.

Markets are complex, many-sided concepts, including geography, demographic characteristics, social-psychological descriptions of consumers, and many other considerations.

Demand Characteristics of Markets

It is often easier to convey the meaning of a concept by description than it is by simple definition.[2] The concept of a market, for example, can be better understood if we think of its characteristics. The two operating forces of a market are the selling, or supply, side and the buying, or demand, side. Naturally, those with a marketing perspective will tend to see markets as a set of demand characteristics, and will view them within the framework of market demand. Such demand orientation means that markets can be described in terms of three major characteristics:

- People
- Income or purchasing power
- Inclination to spend

Andrew Carnegie, the nineteenth-century steel and railroad magnate, is supposed to have said that he would rather have a market than a mill. In light of our discussion about market opportunity, you can surely appreciate his sentiments. A mill means productive capacity and potential while a market means consumption capacity and marketing potential. Because consumption is a vital

Andrew Carnegie: "I'd rather have a market than a mill."

[2] See Jack Z. Sissors, "What is a Market?" *Journal of Marketing* **30** (July 1966), pp. 17–18.

prerequisite to production, a market would have greater value than a mill. To Carnegie, a market, quite rightfully, meant people, with income to buy and the inclination to spend. To study and understand markets, then, we must start by studying people and learning about the demographic aspects of markets. Demography is the analysis of human population in terms of its size, distribution, composition, density, and other relevant characteristics.

People alone, however, do not constitute markets; another critical demand factor must be present. People must have purchasing power—income, wealth, and credit. They must also have an inclination to buy. There may be vast numbers of individuals with adequate purchasing power; but unless they are inclined to spend their money for goods and services, we still don't have a market opportunity. Thus, as we shall increasingly come to appreciate, there are several aspects of a market—demographic, economic, and behavioral.

Kinds of Marketing Targets

As situations in which supply and demand operate, markets are targets at which marketing programs are directed. There are a number of ways of classifying markets and the opportunities they offer. For logic and convenience, they may be classified as consumer, business-industrial, or government markets. This is a ranking preferred by the federal government.

The use to which a product or service is put determines whether it is a consumer; business-industrial, or governmental expenditure. Government purchases are easy to identify because the buyer is either a local, state, or federal body. However, it is sometimes more difficult to differentiate between consumer and business expenditures. For instance, when you buy a new steel-belted radial for your Porsche, that tire is a consumer good and the purchase amounts to an increase in the consumer expenditure category. Yet the tires Ford, GM, or Volkswagen buy as original equipment for their new cars are industrial goods, and the expenditures for them would be included in the business-industrial category.

There are other ways of classifying the total market opportunity, but this is at least the starting point for basic marketing analysis. Later, we shall explore international market opportunities and discover that as the world shrinks, markets actually expand.

Table 5-1, which makes use of these classifications, contains much useful information. The total market for goods and services in the United States including all sectors—consumer, business-industrial, and government—continues to grow apace.

Notice that the consumer market segment grew in 1978 by $140.8 billion, or 12 percent, and in 1979 increased by $159 billion, or 12 percent again. Contrast the growth in the consumer segment in 1979 with the growth in the business industrial market segment. Business-industrial markets are exceedingly volatile during periods of economic fluctuation. Expenditures in this category tend to fall rapidly during the first stages of economic recession, while the start of an upswing is apt to stimulate a surge of business buying. Can you

Table 5-1 Total U.S. Expenditures by Major Market Categories, 1977, 1978, 1979 (Billions of Dollars)

	Gross National Product (Annual Rates)	Consumer Markets (Spending by People)	Business-Industrial Markets (Spending by Business and Industry)	Government Markets (Spending by Federal, State, Local Governments)
1977	1,899.5	1,210.0	303.3	396.2
1978	2,127.6	1,350.8	351.5	435.6
$ Increase	228.1	140.8	48.2	39.4
% Increase	12	12	16	10
1979	2,368.5	1,509.8	386.2	476.1
$ Increase	240.9	159.0	34.7	40.5
% Increase	11	12	10	9

Source: *Survey of Current Business,* United States Department of Commerce, Bureau of Economic Analysis, January 1980.

explain this situation and what it would mean to marketers catering to this segment?

Consumer Markets

Beginning students of marketing are likely to think primarily in terms of consumer markets. The distinctive characteristic of these markets is that the goods and services sold there are purchased by ultimate consumers, those who buy for their personal use. Thus, your purchases of Cokes, bicycles, books, movie tickets, and clothing are all included in the consumer market category.

The United States consumer market, in numbers of people *plus* purchasing power, is the largest mass market in the history of the world. It consists of 220 million people who buy and consume more than $1509.8 billion worth of goods each year. This amounts to more than $6,000 for each man, woman, and child in the country. Furthermore, the market continues to expand—by more than $100 billion and 1.7 million people each year.

What Consumers Buy.   Another way of looking at consumer markets is to look at the categories of consumer expenditures. First of all, consumer expenditures can be classified according to product characteristics, particularly the product's length of life. The United States Department of Commerce divides consumer expenditures into three classifications:[3]

Durable Goods. **Durable goods** are physical, tangible, products which have an extended period of use. Such things as automobiles, boats, and major household appliances are included in this category.

Nondurable Goods. **Nondurable goods** are physical, tangible products which have a short or abbreviated period of use. As a matter of fact, they are considered to be consumed at the very moment of purchase but, of course, that is merely a statistical or accounting convention and not really the actual case. Nondurable goods include such items as food, clothing, gasoline, shoes, fuel oil, and coal.

Services. **Services** are intangible products such as activities, benefits, satisfaction, and behaviors which are purchased. Ther service category includes housing, transportation, household repairs, hair styling, and tickets to rock concerts and other entertainment.

The magnitude of the total of consumer purchases was shown earlier in Table 5-1. Table 5-2 breaks down the 1979 consumer expenditure category into durable, nondurable, and service expenditures.

Marketers often look at consumer expenditures from a different perspective. Whereas the durable, nondurable, and services categories are based essentially on product characteristics, marketers classify consumer expenditures by purchasers' buying habits—how, where, when and how often consumers shop. Hence, consumer goods categories based upon buying habits consist of:

Convenience Goods. **Convenience goods** are bought frequently and have a high replacement rate, although consumers are willing to spend only a minimum of effort and shopping time for these purchases. In relation to the other categories, convenience goods are low in unit value. Grocery fill-in items (bread, milk, snacks, soft drinks), tobacco products, soap, newspapers, and magazines are common examples.

Shopping Goods. **Shopping goods** are bought only after a certain amount of comparison shopping, during which the consumer evaluates alternative products on the basis of style, suitability, quality, and price. Many items of clothing, as well as furniture, hardware, and major appliances are normally considered to be shopping goods.

Specialty Goods. **Specialty goods** are those which consumers perceive to be unique and for which they exhibit unusual shopping-buying behavior. A

[3] Based upon, but not identical to, *Marketing Definitions: A Glossary of Marketing Terms*, Committee on Definitions, American Marketing Association (Chicago: American Marketing Association, 1960).

Table 5-2 Breakdown of Personal Consumption Expenditures by Major Categories, 1979 (Billions of Dollars)

Consumer spending (personal consumption expenditures)	1,580.4
Durable goods	215.5
Motor vehicles and parts	88.6
Furniture, household equipment	89.4
Other	37.6
Nondurable goods	631.0
Food	315.1
Clothing and shoes	105.0
Gasoline and oil	73.4
Fuel oil and coal	20.0
Other	117.5
Services	733.9
Housing	255.7
Household operation	105.6
Electricity and gas	50.5
Other	55.1
Transportation	58.9
Other	313.7

Source: Survey of Current Business, United States Department of Commerce, January 1980, p. 16.

special purchasing effort is put forth to acquire those goods for which the consumer has particular brand or product loyalties. Specialty goods are in many ways important to the life style and images of their purchasers. Well-known brands such as Brut toiletries for men, sophisticated photographic equipment, high-priced luxury autos, high-fidelity sound equipment, and men's and women's fashion clothing are standard examples.

By any standard regardless of how segmented, the American market for consumer goods is a lucrative one that is fervently pursued by marketing managers.

The Business-Industrial Market.   Despite its vastness the consumer market is greatly dependent on the **business-industrial** market. Although, as shown in Table 5-1 this segment spends far less than the consumer market (16 percent of the total gross national product*) 55 million consumers employed by private and nonprofit enterprise derive their incomes from this segment. The business-industrial market consists of those individuals and organizations who buy goods and services for use in the production of other products or services. In

*Gross national product is the dollar value of all goods and services produced in the United States in a one-year period.

other words, industrial goods are not sold to ultimate consumers for their personal consumption satisfaction. Instead, they are bought by many kinds of business organizations: agriculture, transportation, public utilities, construction industries, extractive industries (those that mine ores or explore for oil),

Industrial marketing: Raw materials, major and minor capital equipment, fabricated parts...

nonprofit organizations (hospitals, schools, church groups, and recreation-oriented firms), and the whole host of service industries. Altogether there are nearly 10 million different producer units who buy industrial goods and business services.

The business-industrial market is clustered in the eastern Atlantic states; the midwestern states of Ohio, Pennsylvania, Michigan, and Illinois; and, on the West Coast, in California. However, the stranglehold that these states have historically had on manufacturing activity is rapidly weakening because of the heavy exodus of business to the Sunbelt states such as South Carolina, Georgia, Alabama, Mississippi, Florida, and Arizona. In the decade from 1970 to 1980 the number of American companies in *Fortune's* list of 500 that were based in the South and West rose from 82 to 125. The available land and materials in the South, along with an advantage many business executives are reluctant to admit—few labor union related difficulties—surely have been a lure to manufacturers in both the United States and from abroad.

About 50 percent of all manufactured goods are sold to the business-industrial sector, making it an extremely potent market segment. What is more, about 80 percent of all farm products and nearly 100 percent of all mineral, forest, and sea products are industrial goods.

Business-industrial products are classified into five major categories. These are:

Raw Materials. Raw materials have undergone no processing other than the minimum amount necessary to harvest, extract, or protect them in their physical handling. Forest products, minerals, and agricultural products are examples of raw materials. Raw material prices around the world are rising rapidly because of worldwide shortages stemming from increasing demand and diminishing supplies.

Fabricated Parts and Materials. Fabricated parts and materials become part of a manufacturer's finished product. They are materials which have already undergone some processing so that their form has been altered, and may undergo still further alteration in the manufacturing process. The carpet used in automobile production is an example of a fabricated material; a spark plug is an example of a fabricated part.

Installations. Installations are large items of industrial manufacturing equipment commonly called capital goods. They have a long life, are usually very expensive and often are technical in operation. Machine tools and dies, steam or diesel generators, computer complexes, point-of-sale cash registers, and trucks for a transport company are all examples of installations.

Accessory Equipment. Accessory equipment is much like installations, except that it consists of smaller items of lower unit value. The productive life of accessory equipment is shorter than that for installations. Desks, typewriters, filing cabinets, fractional horsepower motors, portable electric generators, and small power tools are examples of accessory equipment.

Operating Supplies. Operating supplies are used to conduct the business. These are items of small unit value which facilitate the firm's operation but do not become a part of the finished product. Cleaning products, office supplies, heating and cooling equipment, and bathroom supplies are typical examples.

The markets that emerge from business-industrial purchases are thus extensive and very diversified. Each of the above categories has distinct and unique marketing characteristics. For example, raw materials often move through lengthy channels of distribution that include many specialized intermediaries, especially agents and brokers. Installations are sold through shorter channels of distribution, in many instances direct from manufacturer to user. Marketing programs and strategic marketing planning directed to the business-industrial user must consider that the demand for products and services arising from the segment is basically inelastic—which means that the quantity purchased will not change materially with price fluctuations. Yet, business expenditures do fluctuate along with the general level of the overall economy. Finally, the buyers of business-industrial products and services are usually astute, knowledgeable professionals. They are well informed about what they are buying, have excellent knowledge about supplier reliability, and are hard-nosed, cost- and value-conscious customers.

The Government Market.   Not to be overlooked as a major and almost constantly growing market for goods and services is government at all levels. Again referring to Table 5-1 federal, state, and local jurisdictions bought $476.1 billion worth of goods in 1979. Government purchases account for approximately 20 percent of the total gross national product or, looked at another way, total yearly government purchases amount to more than $2,000 for each man, woman, and child in the United States. Expenditures by the national government by far overshadow those at the state and local levels, with the federal share amounting to 65 percent of the total expenditures of all government.

Government purchases of goods and services have increased six times since 1955. And the prospect appears certain, given the magnitude of the country's social, economic, technological, and defense needs, that these expenditures will increase even more in the future.

The Diversity of Government Markets.   The range of products and services bought by all levels of government is wide. Table 5-3 shows some selected expenditures by the various areas in 1979.

Table 5-3 suggests that government at all levels is a ready purchaser of a near-staggering variety of goods and services. Government is America's biggest single customer and its largest spender.

Marketing to Governments.   The mere size of the government market makes it a desirable sales target. The government market is somewhat centralized, given the importance of the federal bureaucracy in Washington, D.C.; however, government purchases are widely scattered throughout the United States.

Table 5-3 Selected Expenditure Categories by Various Levels of Government, 1979 (Millions of Dollars)

Expenditure Category by Function	All Government	Federal Government	State and Local
Total	763,327	459,751	303,576
National defense	109,742	108,798	944
Space research and technology	4,072	3,997	75
Education	128,694	12,574	116,120
Postal services	2,204	2,204	N.A.
Health and hospitals	36,839	9,085	27,754
Labor	29,166	22,163	7,003
Regulation of commerce	2,811	712	2,099
Transportation	39,311	16,476	22,835
Natural resources	17,193	9,448	7,745
General revenue sharing	7,723	7,723	N.A.

Source: Statistical Abstract of the United States, United States Department of Commerce, 1980. Aggregates exclude duplicative transactions between levels of government. N.A. = not applicable.

Every arm of government at every level, from rural counties to vast metropolitan jurisdictions such as New York City and Los Angeles, is a purchasing unit for goods and services.

Government purchasing agents are guided in their decisions by stringent considerations of cost and value. A great many of the purchases are made on the basis of bid contracts with rigid product or service specifications. The General Services Administration (GSA), which operates only at the federal level, is responsible for supervising the buying of large quantities of general purpose supplies. Nearly all states as well as many local bodies have similar agencies to plan and control the buying process for products and services needed by their governmental operations.

Because the government market has unique characteristics, needs, and processes, in many instances a marketing program must be specially designed to service this ever-growing marketing opportunity. Most government bodies are anxious to expand the competition for their business. An increased number of firms bidding for public contracts means, in many instances, lower bid prices and a greater range of products, services, and features from which to choose.

The federal government, along with many state and local units, has encouraged private firms in the United States and occasionally even a few foreign ones, to participate in these marketing opportunities. They have done this in a number of ways, especially by providing directories or pamphlets explaining the procedures involved in selling to government agencies.

Derived Demand and Need Satisfaction

Before leaving this section, another important and related concept needs to be underscored. Remember that earlier we stated that a market results from the existence of people (consumer-users) with purchasing power (money, wealth, and credit), plus the inclination to buy (predispositions that arise from personality needs, culture, and certain situational factors).

In other words, demand originates in the needs of people. Goods and services are produced because they have need- or want-satisfying utilities. Thus, in the case of consumer markets, the basic determinants of demand—the rock bottom forces that create a need or demand for goods and services—are people, income, and inclination to buy. The people and income determinants are demographic and economic in character. The inclination to buy and consume is behavioral or social-psychological in character.

To meet people's demands for goods and services, businesses and industries spring up. Government expands to serve as a balance among the business organizations, as well as between consumers and business. But running businesses, turning out merchandise, and balancing the various economic segments all call for additional products and further assistance. Thus, the demand for industrial-business goods and the demand for goods and services purchased by the government market segments are derived demands. They are outgrowths of the needs of the ultimate users, consumers. For example, you might say that the industrial-business market generates no demand for steel, plastic, or wood—there is only the basic consumer demand for cars, houses, washing machines, and refrigerators. Steel, plastic and wood are purchased by industrial-business firms only because these products can be converted into the cars, houses, and home appliances that consumers want. The case of government purchases is basically the same. Government units buy goods and services that they deem necessary to maintain a healthy society. But society ultimately means people. Hence, the satisfaction of the needs of the people determines the level of government purchases of goods and services.

Industrial goods markets tend to follow directly the level of spending in consumer markets. Government expenditures for goods and services are not so positively linked to consumer market expenditures; they may be even inversely related. That is, when there is great unemployment or a downturn in effective consumer demand, government purchases of goods and services are quite likely to increase. Can you explain why?

Before proceeding, can you answer these questions:
1. What is a market?
2. What, in your estimation, is the relationship between marketing and markets?
3. What are the three primary characteristics of markets?
4. What is the implication for marketing strategy of the concept of derived demand?

Population and Income—The Major Determinants of All Marketing Opportunities

Markets are people, plus purchasing power, plus an inclination to buy. In the pages that follow we shall examine in some detail the first two of these important market determinants. In the following chapter we shall learn more about the significance of the notion "inclination to buy" when we explore the topic of buyer behavior.

Demographic Factors Affecting Markets

There are many population-related factors that affect market opportunities. The total number of persons, the mix among age groups, mobility, location, and the number of households are all important indicators of market opportunities. Shifts in any or all of these measures impact heavily on marketing possibilites.

Sears Roebuck and Company, in the early 1970s, ran a very successful promotional campaign based upon this theme: "We know you've changed. So have we." Sears' message was clear. The American market had changed. Sears' customers, who were at one time lower middle-class wage earners or farmers, had become middle class and largely urban or suburban. Sears' customers had changed their life styles; they had more income and were looking for better quality, more fashion-oriented merchandise. Sears wanted its customers and potential customers to know that it was aware of these demographic and economic changes and that it was responding with adjustments in its marketing program and market offerings.

All marketers would be well advised to remember that the character of markets does change over time. Some startling changes have occurred in the overall character of the American market in the last 200 years. Family size has decreased; we have a much older mix within the population; we are today a nation of great wealth , the largest affluent market in the world. Our population has moved from farm to city. Most striking, almost ominous, has been the 85-fold increase in our population since our founding more than 200 years ago.

Table 5-4 Past and Projected Population Growth of the United States (1850–1990)

Year	Total Population[a] (Millions)	Increase Over Past Decade (%)
1850	23,261	35.9
1860	31,513	35.5
1870	39,905	26.6
1880	50,262	26.0
1890	63,056	25.0
1900	76,094	20.7
1910	92,407	21.4
1920	106,466	15.2
1930	123,188	15.7
1940	132,122	7.3
1950	151,683	14.8
1960	180,670	19.1
1970	204,879	13.39
1980	220,132	7.4
1990 (projected)	240,531	9.2

[a]Includes members of the armed forces.

Source: Compiled from U.S. Bureau of the Census figures.

The Growth in Population.   Table 5-4 shows the growth in the population of the United States from 1850 projected to 1990. You will observe that the largest percentage increase in population from one ten-year period to another in the more recent past occurred from 1950 to 1960.[4]

Population in the aggregate, and the rate of population increase, are two indices of market opportunity. As babies are born and grow up, they generate a continuing need for various kinds of goods and services. Marketers in all lines of enterprise must plan their longer-term strategies according to the changing nature and composition of the population.

The idea of an ever-expanding economy fueled by steady population growth is tightly embedded in the minds of many marketers. Every child born is viewed as a potential customer to stimulate sales. Marketers are aware that each new baby can be expected to consume in a seventy-year life span: 21,000 gallons of gasoline, 10,000 pounds of meat, 28,000 pounds of milk and cream, $10,000 in school building materials, $10,000 in clothing, and $10,000 worth of furniture, plus many other goods and services.

Projections Are Unreliable.   Population projections have been wrong, sometimes not just a little, but grossly wrong. Few anticipated the huge bulge

---

[4] The discussion that follows is based upon *Population Characteristics: Population Profile of the U.S.*, Current Population Reports. Special Studies, Series P-20, No. 292, U.S. Department of Commerce, Washington, D.C., 1976.

in fertility between 1947 and 1961, and not many foresaw the great decline in births we are currently experiencing. In demographics enormous, often puzzling, changes can occur almost overnight. For example, in 1971 Americans were having babies at a rate of 2.9 for each family. Since 1972, however, the rate has fallen below the replacement rate of 2.1 children per family to an all-time low of 1.8. Should this rate continue for about sixty years, the American population would actually decline.

Other Changing Population Characteristics. Figure 5-1 shows some additional population factors that are important to marketing planners. Between 1974 and 1984, the percentage of people over 65 will increase by 3.8 million or 17.5 percent. The number of children and teen-agers will decrease by 2.1 million, or 3 percent. Massive shifts in the mix of the population can be foreseen in the years ahead and these shifts will have major significance for marketers. Firms such as Gerber Foods and H.J. Heinz have already begun to include in their product mix foods for senior citizens and special-sized containers for younger adults living alone.

Households. Two hundred and twelve million people in the United States in 1980 lived in what are called ordinary households such as homes and apartments.

In 1980, there were 77 million such households in this country. About 4 million people lived in various institutions such as army barracks, rooming houses, and hospitals.

Two out of three households were maintained by a married couple. Of the others, approximately 12 percent were formed by a group of relatives, but not by a married couple. Those maintained by a person living entirely alone, or

Figure 5-1 The changing population age mix.

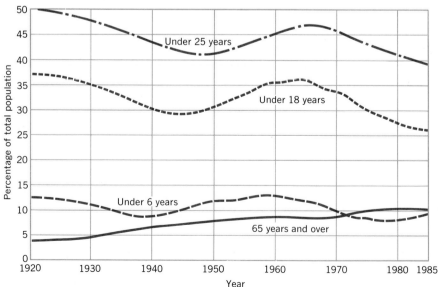

with nonrelatives, accounted for 22 percent of all households. There was a dramatic 57 percent increase in single-person households between 1970 and 1980—from 10.9 million to 17.2 million—a trend among Americans toward more separate living quarters with fewer occupants per unit. Official studies forecast an increase of at least 20 million households by 1990, suggesting that more men and women will be living alone or with nonrelatives instead of in family groups. Of the one-person households 49 percent were occupied by men or women under 35 years of age. Declining birth rates, increasing divorces (more than 1.5 million in 1980 compared with the 740,000 recorded in 1970) and marital separations, and a rise in the number of women who have children without husbands has helped to reduce the number of Americans who live together. The increasing number and changing character of American households means, in turn, changing market opportunities—a decline in the strength and size of some market segments, a rise in the strength and size of others.

Where People Live.   It is a well-known principle that marketers follow markets—and markets shift geographically over time.

American consumer markets are located primarily in urban places, but most consumers live not in the major central cities, but rather in the suburbs, the smaller central cities of urbanized areas, and the urban fringe surrounding the country's major cities. This is supported by Table 5-5. The Middle Majority American consumer may or may not like to shop in the central city, but clearly does not want to live there. The downtown urban area, while it possesses many attractive retail stores, is sometimes a difficult area in which to shop. The crime rate is high, walking can be hazardous, while traffic congestion and inner city neglect make a grim environment. Although suburban consumers do, on occasion, shop downtown, their general preference tilts toward the outlying planned shopping center.

Table 5-5   United States Population by Selected Residence Categories (1979)

Area	Population, 1979 (Thousands)	Percentage of U.S. Population
Total population	219,467	100.0
Metropolitan areas	146,046	66.5
In central cities	58,723	
Outside central cities	87,324	
Nonmetropolitan areas	73,421	33.5
Farm population	8,000	

Source: Current Population Reports, U.S. Department of Commerce, Bureau of the Census, Population Characteristics. P-20 Series, no. 336, April 1980.

However, the realities of the energy shortage could restore America's cities in the decades ahead. If the growing public demands for more mass transit are heeded, efficient systems may soon be developed. Spiraling fuel costs will make an automobile drive too extravagant a way to reach stores; downtown trading centers will come alive once more. When the central urban cores are humming with the exchange of goods, services, and ideas, once again, more people may be drawn back from the suburbs to "where the action is."

Consumer Mobility.   A shifting population results in many changes in the composition of consumption expenditures. There is evidence to suggest that a move from farm to urban places leads to a higher ratio of spending to disposable income, for example. A mobile population has a marked effect on consumer demand. Table 5-6 gives some indication of the percentage of the population who do move within given periods in the life cycle. Observe that "geographic mobiles," as they are sometimes called, are those basically in their early twenties to the early forties along with their children. This is the time when careers are established, earnings increase, households are formed, and consumer capital goods (housing, autos, home furnishings, major appli-

Table 5-6 Percentage of United States Population Moving Within and Between Counties in One Year, 1979, in Millions.

Age	Population	Percent Moving Within Counties	Percent Moving Between Counties
Total 2 years old and over	206,419	16.1	10.3
Under 5 years	9,113	26.5	15.9
5–9 years	17,192	18.8	11.8
10–14 years	19,246	13.0	7.4
15–19 years	20,767	14.0	7.5
20–24 years	19,230	30.7	21.4
25–29 years	17,460	30.5	20.6
30–34 years	14,824	20.9	14.6
35–44 years	23,108	13.3	8.6
45–54 years	23,302	9.1	5.5
55–64 years	20,076	6.9	4.8
65 and over	22,100	5.8	3.6
Median age 30.1		Median 24.7	Median 25.1

Source: U.S. Bureau of the Census, unpublished data average from successive March Current Population Surveys. Survey questions refer to mobility status during preceding 12 months.

ances) are bought. Moving one's residence creates a need for goods and services and this in turn leads to increasing and shifting market opportunities.

Where Americans Are Going. As we see in Figure 5-2, Americans are rapidly leaving the cast iron gray of the northern and eastern regions, the old industrial quadrant stretching from St. Louis and Chicago to Philadelphia and Boston, and heading south and west.

The fastest growing states (markets?) in the nation are Arizona, Florida, Nevada, Idaho, and Colorado. By far the nation's fastest developing new boom region is the area called the Sunbelt—the lower arc of warm lands stretching from Southern California to the Carolinas. Between 1970 and 1980, 2.53 million people migrated from the northeastern and north central states to those in the south and west. These modern-day migrants, in changing their geo-

Figure 5-2 Where they're going—percent population gains 1970—1979.

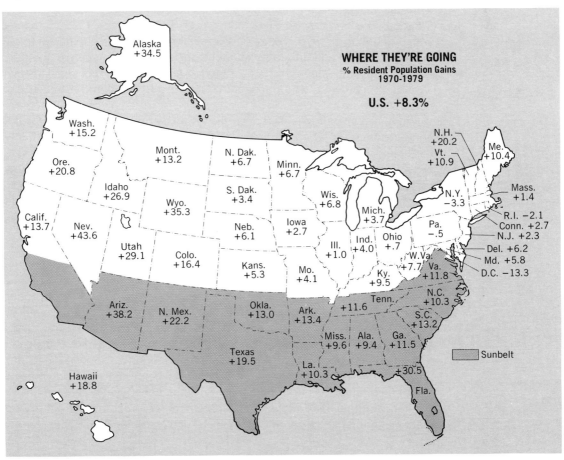

Source: Current Population Reports, Population Estimates and Projections. P-25, no. 875, January 1980, U.S. Department of Commerce, Bureau of the Census, p. 12.

Berry's World

Copyright © 1977 by NEA, Inc. Jim Berry

graphic locations, are also looking for new bundles of goods and services with which to express their altered life styles. This means not just a gross increase in the quantities of goods and services, but more and different qualities than what they already have.

Market Segments Based on Demographic Characteristics

Demographic and income variables are most often used by marketing managers as a basis for segmenting their markets. They are generally considered a sound basis for *market segmentation* because they have proven to be good indicators of different degrees of buyer response. Two important new consumer segments have emerged as a result of the changing demographic structure of the United States: the teen-age market and the senior citizen market.

The Teen-age Market.   The number of children and teenagers will increase by only 2 percent during the 1980–1990 decade. Yet the absolute number of teenagers makes this a formidable market opportunity. Teen-age expenditures for goods and services are expected to reach $35 billion by 1985, compared with $20 billion in 1975. Today's adolescents have a strong inclination to buy durable goods in addition to nondurables such as clothes, records, and other items of low unit value. One study reported that nearly all teen-age girls own a radio, 70 percent own a phonograph, and nearly one-third have their own personal television set.[5]

Much teen spending is, however, discretionary and principally confined to nondurable goods. The youthful spender has often been associated with low-cost items such as soft drinks, phonograph records, home permanents, magazines, and minor items of clothing and accessories. Many retail stores, however, are experimenting with "teen centers" in which the young customers are tempted with a wider range of merchandise and are sometimes granted credit. Marketers would be well advised to watch the buying behavior of this young, yet reasonably affluent, group.

The Senior Citizen Market.   Some marketing firms have found the senior citizen market a readily available and fertile field receptive to special product and service offerings tailored to their needs. A whole new class of product offerings, generally listed as geriatrics, has been created to be merchandised to this group. These product lines include general medicinal tonics, dietary supplements, digestive aids, cathartics, diuretics, oral and external analgesics and antirheumatics, and denture cleaners and adhesives. Special marketing programs for senior citizens are also being developed in the field of health care, continuing education, retirement housing, travel, and entertainment.

Although population projections suggest that the proportion of old persons will remain relatively constant (at about 10 percent of the total population) for

[5] From *Characteristics of American Youth,* Current Population Reports, Special Studies, Series P-23, no. 51, U.S. Department of Commerce, Washington, D.C., 1974.

the next quarter century, their absolute numbers will increase to about 27 million by 1990. And they will have more money to spend. In the future, a growing number of older people will probably receive larger incomes through a widening participation in pension plans, social security, and other benefits. Health plans such as Medicare will release savings and income for other consumption purposes. The upshot is that senior citizens will remain desirable customers for a longer period than was heretofore possible. Participating in consumption activities at more than a subsistence level, they will be a market segment of continuing and increasing importance.[6]

Income and Related Factors Affecting Market Opportunity

One of the key determinants of consumption and, hence, market opportunity, is income. If marketers could know but one fact about consumers they would be wise to choose consumer income. Its size would probably reveal more than any other single factor.

Income is an important stimulus to purchasing and so too is *wealth,* or *assets* and *credit.* Wealth includes such liquid (readily available) assets as money in savings and checking deposits as well as stocks and bonds. Physical assets that are less liquid (taking somewhat longer to convert into actual money), include all the consumer's personal goods such as clothing, jewelry, automobiles, houses, and furnishings. The American consumer's stock or inventory of assets has increased dramatically in recent years and this tends, to a degree, to bolster consumers' confidence, add to their financial security, and to motivate still more buying. Simply owning a larger stock of goods seems to generate a correspondingly higher level of purchases. For instance, owning a second home or a second car will generate the need for more insurance, additional equipment, and larger outlays for service and maintenance.

Credit is the ability to buy now with the promise to pay later. It is wealth in that, like assets, it can command goods and services. Credit is simply money that a person can borrow from someone else—a friend, a bank or a credit-lending institution. By 1980, outstanding consumer credit in the United States, not including home mortgages, was more than $275 billion, or well over $6,000 per household unit. The availability and use of credit make purchasing and consumption easier, thus stimulating *personal consumption expenditures.* However, the basic determinant of consumer expenditures is income.

Despite double-digit inflation throughout the 1970s and a dramatic dip in productivity, total income and consumption levels have continued to show a vital buoyancy which, of course, bodes well for marketers. Table 5-7 depicts this growth in the consumer's ability to purchase goods and services. This is also shown more graphically in Figure 5-3.

[6] From *Social and Economic Characteristics of the Older Population,* Current Population Reports, Special Studies, Series P-23, No. 57; and *Demographic Aspects of Aging and the Older Population in the United States,* Current Population Reports, Special Studies, Series P-23, No. 59, May 1976. Both published by the U.S. Department of Commerce, Washington, D.C. See also, "The Graying of America," *Newsweek,* February 28, 1977, pp. 50–65.

Table 5-7 Disposable Personal Income and Personal Consumption Expenditures 1969–1979

Year	Disposable Personal Income (Billions of Dollars)	Personal Consumption Expenditures (Billions of Dollars)	PCE/DPI[a] (%)
1969	634.2	577.5	91.05
1970	687.8	615.8	89.53
1971	744.4	664.9	89.32
1972	802.5	729.0	90.84
1973	903.7	805.2	89.10
1974	966.5	870.0	90.01
1975	1086.7	979.0	90.08
1976	1184.5	1089.8	92.00
1977	1305.1	1209.9	92.70
1978	1458.4	1350.7	92.61
1979	1623.2	1509.8	93.01

[a]Personal Consumption Expenditures divided by Disposable Personal Income.

Source: Compiled from U.S. Department of Commerce, Office of Business Economics, Survey of Current Business, Washington, D.C. U.S. Government Printing Office.

Figure 5-3 Personal consumption expenditures.

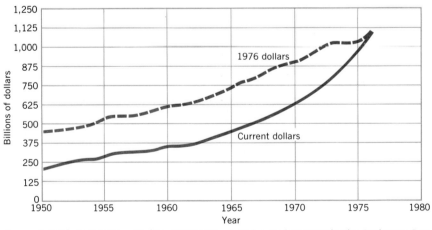

Source: A Guide to Consumer Markets, 1977/1978, ed. Helen Axel (New York: The Conference Board, 1977). Extrapolated by the author.

Note: The concept of disposable personal income as used in this table embraces three closely related ideas: personal income, disposable personal income, and personal savings. *Personal income* consists of people's income from all sources. *Disposable personal income* is what remains after they pay their income taxes. That portion of disposable income not used to buy goods and services forms *personal savings*.

From 1969 to 1979, disposable personal income increased from $634.2 billion to $1,623.2 billion. In just ten years disposable personal income nearly tripled. This was truly a remarkable growth period in the economy and, of course, in the market opportunity for many firms.

Personal consumption expenditures during this same period increased from $577.5 billion to $1,509.8 billion. Disposable personal income (DPI) is a major barometer of marketing activity. It is of utmost significance in analyzing variations in total consumption over periods of time and the demand for various categories of goods and services at any particular moment.

Disposable personal income is the wherewithal that supports consumer expenditures, or what is more recently called personal outlays. *Personal outlays* subtracted from *disposable personal income* equals *personal savings*. As can be seen from Table 5-7, personal consumption expenditures had been running about 90 percent of disposable personal income. In the 1976–79 period, however, there was some variation from the longer-run trend; and the savings rate had fallen to less than 7 percent. This may seem insignificant, but it is important to realize that each change in the savings rate of one percentage point is roughly equivalent to $5.5 billion in consumer spending. When consumers choose to spend a larger amount of total current income, we say that there has been an increase in their average propensity, or inclination, to consume.

For example, in early 1979 and early 1980, confronted by tapering incomes and other economic and political uncertainties, consumers cut back sharply in their spending. There was a deep cut in spending for automobiles, an industry basic to America's economy. Sales of new cars plunged to a rate of about 9.5 million units in early 1980, down from the 1977–1978 figure of about 11.5 million. The consumers' concern with unemployment and runaway inflation affected their confidence in the future and hence, their propensity to consume.

The general effect in the late 1970s was a considerable curtailment of expenditures for consumer durable goods. However, in an economy such as ours where a sizable portion of disposable personal income goes to buy consumer durable products, the savings rate will vary more than in economies where durable goods purchases are less important. By the same token, the more durables consumers have, the more their saving and spending behavior will fluctuate.

Changing Patterns of Income.　Despite economic ups and downs, ordinary families have become richer in recent decades. This is shown clearly in Table 5-8.

In 1965, about 66 percent of all families had incomes above $5,000 a year. In 1980, about 82 percent of all families had incomes in excess of $5,000

Table 5-8

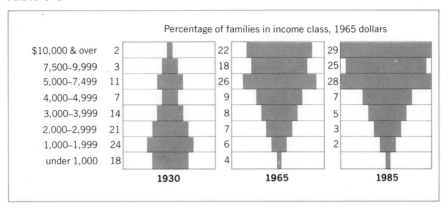

		Percentage of families in income class, 1965 dollars				
$10,000 & over	2		22		29	
7,500–9,999	3		18		25	
5,000–7,499	11		26		28	
4,000–4,999	7		9		7	
3,000–3,999	14		8		5	
2,000–2,999	21		7		3	
1,000–1,999	24		6		2	
under 1,000	18		4			
		1930		**1965**		**1985**

annually. Table 5-8 gives another insight concerning the changing patterns of income in this country: in 1965, roughly 22 percent of American families had incomes higher than $10,000 per year, eleven times the number in that bracket thirty-five years before. By 1985 the figure is expected to approach nearly 30 percent. Thus, the income revolution that began in the earlier postwar years will be essentially completed, with the income pyramid turned upside down. What we have typically called poverty will be virtually eliminated.

Despite the increases over the years, however, the present relatively high poverty-line standard still allows no dental care, no entertainment, very little meat, and very little clothing. It is hoped as we move through the decade of the 1980s the efforts of government in terms of employment, negative income tax and other social welfare programs will increase substantially the purchasing power of low-income Americans and make them a more viable market segment. So, while the level of American income is quite high, the distribution of that income is such that large numbers of people earn barely enough to subsist. The average is brought up by the extremely high incomes of a small number of individuals. Compared with other nations, American income distribution is more equal than in some countries, less than in others. Most importantly, however, those on the bottom have been getting an increasing share of the total national income, even though the very rich have also been getting more.

Helping to swell family income is the increasing incidence of working wives. In 1980, over 30 million wives were on the nation's payroll—representing about 50 percent of American families. About 40 percent of the spending power in these households is attributable to the women's income. Interestingly, half of all families in the $10,000 to $15,000 income bracket have attained this level through the wife's earnings.

These patterns of income change shown in Table 5-8 and their resulting consequences to marketers will likely continue for these reasons: (1) a projected 50 percent increase in the number of young families within ten years;

and (2) the configuration of the prevailing income distribution curve.

In the United States today, one out of every four, or more than 17 million, households, has earnings in excess of $15,000. Quietly and subtly we are experiencing a dramatic realignment of income distribution. This shift will affect merchandising strategies and will compel marketers to modify their over-all company images as well as their merchandising policies so that they may keep abreast of their market opportunities.

The remainder of this chapter will underscore the important implications that income and income changes of consumers hold for strategic marketing planning. These implications affect such strategic considerations as product planning, pricing, promotion, product positioning, and channels of distribu-tion. Most importantly, income and income variations among various con-sumer groups will affect the firm's market segmentation practices and policies.

Before proceeding, can you answer these questions:
1. Is population growth the primary reason the United States market is such a rich and important one?
2. What is the impact of the changing mix of population on market segmentation strategies?
3. What is one of the main reasons for the rapid rise in United States family income during the past ten years?

Family Expenditures For Major Categories of Consumption

Consumption, you will recall, is largely a function of income. Therefore, the "package" of goods and services a family buys and how they buy it ought to reflect the family's income bracket. It will also reflect such earnings indicators as life cycle, social class, and life style.

Examination of the data appears to confirm a previous generalization bearing on income and food consumption: namely, that as income increases, the percentage spent for food tends to decline. However, the absolute amount spent for food increases rather significantly as we move from lower-to higher-income families.

As family income rises, the amount spent for occupancy and operation of households (when viewed as a single expense category) consistently increases from the lowest to the highest income bracket. However, when related to total income, the percentage for this category declines markedly as each higher level is reached.

Clothing outlays also reveal some interesting characteristics. Although they absorb an increasing percentage of total expenditures, once household income reaches $15,000, the relative amount allotted for clothing declines. Not surprisingly, families in the higher income brackets buy a greater variety of clothing of better, longer-lasting quality.

The automobile, the major form of family transportation, tends to siphon off large amounts of family income. As a share of total spending, automobile expenses increase consistently until the $20,000 income bracket is reached. But the relative amount of income spent for automobile transportation declines once annual earnings of $20,000 are reached.

From expenditure patterns shown by United States families in different income categories, it seems safe to generalize that as income grows, there are marked shifts in the demand for different categories of goods and services. Spending patterns of families in different income categories have been observed for many decades. Possibly the earliest study was by Ernst Engel, a German statistician, who in 1857 compared the budgets of individual working-class families. He observed that rising family income meant generally rising spending in all categories, but with the following qualifications:

• The proportion of income spent on food tended to decline.
• The proportion of income spent on housing and household operation tended to remain constant.
• The proportion spent on other categories such as clothing, transportation, recreation, health, education, and savings tended to increase.

These generalizations are usually referred to as *Engel's Laws of Consumption* and have been fairly well validated in several subsequent budget studies.

Income not only has an effect on the amount and kinds of goods purchased, but also affects buyer attitudes and frustrations. Higher-income shoppers tend to put more emphasis on being able to get what they want when they want it. They are more experienced in shopping and therefore more discriminating in their desires. These buyers feel more secure in their knowledge and shopping experience and are therefore less likely to rely on the marketer for advice. In short, affluent shoppers are more independent, less loyal to a given merchant and particular brands of merchandise; and they expect more store services.

Other Related Concepts

With income such an important determinant of consumption, and consumption the real crux of the market opportunity, it behooves marketing managers to know as much as possible about income groups and their respective consumption patterns. However, income alone is not a complete indicator of consumption expenditure patterns. To pinpoint the market opportunity more sharply, one must consider other relevant factors. In the following paragraphs we will examine the concept of life style and the marketing opportunities originating in income class.

The Family Life Cycle Concept. To understand more fully an individual's consumption and buying behavior, it may be necessary to consider what stage in the family life cycle he or she has reached, rather than the person's specific

The young marrieds.

age. Family life cycle (FLC) is generally regarded as explaining buying behavior better than age or income alone. People change both their attitudes and their behavior as they grow older, but these changes reflect not only increased age, but also the influence of age upon the individual's family relationships.

Thus, the family life cycle concept has an important bearing on expenditure and shopping patterns. Households with young children are likely to exhibit a much different pattern of expenditure from childless households or those in which the children have grown up (sometimes called the empty nest stage). A family headed by a male wage earner between 35 and 40, with three children, ages 10, 7, and 5, will probably show one pattern of expenditure; a man and wife 60 and 55 years of age, respectively, will follow a different pattern of expenditure. Furthermore, a household composed of a man and wife 25 and 23, respectively, with an infant child will have still a third spending pattern—even though the incomes of all three families are identical or nearly so.

In the United States, it is generally acknowledged that most households pass through an orderly progression of stages:

1. The bachelor stage: young, single people
2. Newly married couples: young, no children
3. The full nest I and II: young married couples with dependent children
   a. youngest child under 6
   b. youngest child over 6
4. The full nest III: older married couples with dependent children
5. The empty nest: older married couples with no children living with them

      a. head in labor force
      b. head retired
  6. The solitary survivors: older single people
      a. in labor force
      b. retired

It is easy to visualize the family life cycle concept and its various stages as an important means of identifying special market opportunities and market segments. Table 5-9 highlights the various stages in terms of both income and expenditure patterns. One can conclude from Table 5-9 that newly married couples are highly involved in capital and asset formation. More than likely, they are buying household furnishings, small appliances, and accessories. Before children arrive, they are more apt to be entertainment and recreation oriented—inclined to be on the go and thus concerned with style and fashion

The empty nest.

Table 5-9 An Overview of the Family Life Cycle

Bachelor Stage; Young Single People Not Living at Home	Newly Married Couples; Young, No Children	Full Nest I; Youngest Child Under Six	Full Next II; Youngest Child Six or over Six	Full Next III; Older Married Couples with Dependent Children
Few financial burdens Fashion opinion leaders Recreation oriented Buy: Basic kitchen equipment, basic furniture, cars, equipment for the mating game, vacations.	Better off financially than they will be in near future Highest purchase rate and highest average purchase of durables Buy: Cars, refrigerators, stoves, sensible and durable furniture, vacations.	Home purchasing at peak Liquid assets low Dissatisfied with financial position and amount of money saved Interested in new products Like advertised products Buy: Washers, dryers, TV, baby food, chest rubs and cough medicine, vitamins, dolls, wagons, sleds, skates.	Financial position better Some wives work Less influenced by advertising Buy larger-sized packages, multiple-unit deals Buy; Many foods, cleaning materials, bicycles, music lessons, pianos.	Financial position still better More wives work Some children get jobs Hard to influence with advertising High average purchase of durables Buy: New, more tasteful furniture, auto travel, nonnecessary appliances, boats, dental services, magazines.

Empty Nest I; Older Married Couples, No Children Living with Them, Head in Labor Force	Empty Nest II; Older Married Couples, No Children Living at Home, Head Retired	Solitary Survivor, in Labor Force	Solitary Survivor; Retired
Home ownership at peak Most satisfied with financial position and money saved Interested in travel, recreation, self-education Make gifts and contributions Not interested in new products Buy: Vacations, luxuries, home improvements.	Drastic cut in income Keep home Buy: Medical appliances, medical care, products that aid health, sleep, and digestion.	Income still good but likely to sell home.	Same medical and product needs as other retired group; drastic cut in income Special need for attention, affection, and security.

Source: William D. Wells and George Gubar, "Life Cycle Concept in Marketing Research," *Journal of Marketing Research* **3** (November 1966), p. 362.

in clothes as well as decorating. Children alter this orientation somewhat. Now a major concern is with the nursery, more space—a house perhaps, rather than an apartment. The need for savings and insurance becomes clearer. The wife, who may have been working, may now decide to stay home and, hence, family income declines.

Thus family needs, which arise out of the various problems that emerge at the different stages of the life cycle, change over time. Income, expenditures on durable goods, assets and debts, and feelings about financial position differ from one stage of the life cycle to the next. In many ways the young to middle-aged couples with and without children are concerned with building up the proper inventory of goods, in assembling an appropriate and adequate bundle of social symbols. These symbols are expressed in cars, homes, furniture, clothing and recreation items such as boats, vacation cabins, and campers. The older family, especially after children are gone, may begin to look at travel, trading up in assets, moving out of the family home into an apartment, and shifting resources from physical goods to more near-liquid assets in anticipation of retirement. Younger couples, in buying furniture, are likely to look for functional pieces, modestly priced and contemporary in style. If they buy furniture at all, older couples are more concerned with quality and fine construction and are apt to choose Early American, or some other distinctive period style.

As we have seen, population and income are important determinants of consumption and hence, market opportunity. It becomes obvious, however, that income alone, while essential, is not the single most important element of consumption. Other factors, behavioral factors, which transcend the basic demographic characteristics of consumer markets, must also be explored.

Summary

All marketing planning is based upon the firm's assessment of market opportunities, which originate in markets. Markets are many things, but mainly they are mechanisms or forces which facilitate exchange processes. There are three basic characteristics of markets: people, purchasing power, and willingness or motivation to buy. In this chapter we focused upon two of these three determinants—population and income. Our basic task was to become familiar with the major kinds of markets in the United States: consumer markets, business-industrial markets, and government markets. A key concept of the chapter, derived demand, stipulates that the market for business-industrial goods and to a great extent, government purchases of goods and services, stems from the demand of ultimate consumers.

The United States economy undergoes constant change. The overall population has increased significantly during the past twenty-five years, and there have been remarkable changes in the mix of the population. In addition, there has been great consumer mobility from region to region, dramatic changes in the growth of consumer income and, more importantly perhaps, changes in the pattern of family income brought about largely by the increasing incidence of working wives. In sum, these population and income factors become important focal points in the development of the marketing strategies of many firms.

Review Questions

1. What are markets? List and discuss the three characteristics of a market.
2. One of the fastest growing consumer markets in the United States is that for services. Can you explain this growth?
3. During periods of economic recession, expenditures for consumer durable goods usually fall off more rapidly than those for nondurable goods. Why?
4. Marketers selling to business-industrial buyers need to understand the concept of derived demand. What is derived demand? Why is it important to marketing planners selling to business-industrial buyers?
5. What is the relationship between market segmentation and factors such as population and income?
6. What is the importance of disposable personal income as a barometer of marketing activity?
7. In what way does the change from a rural to an urban economy affect the marketing system?
8. If population is such an important part of market opportunity, wouldn't India and China be considered very important markets?
9. What are some important generalizations that can be made about family expenditures as related to income?
10. How do family consumption patterns reflect the concept of the family life cycle?

Case 5-1

Johnson Products Company

The Johnson Products Company was started in 1954 by George E. Johnson in a Chicago storefront. He borrowed $250 from a friend and began mixing with wooden poles, a hair straightener for blacks. Twenty-two years later his firm had an expanded line of health and beauty products, $39 million in annual sales volume, and became the first black-owned firm to be listed on the American Stock Exchange.

Competition has recently quickened for Johnson's products, however, as a result of a badgering from federal bureaucrats and stiff competition from cosmetic giants like Revlon. Johnson's sales in 1979 were down to $31 million. However, Johnson Products Company still maintains a 40% share of the market for black hair care products. His Ultra Sheen No-Base hair relaxer was the first product to contain a protective cream that shielded the scalp against powerful acids. Advised that patenting the new product could take two years, Johnson decided to put it directly on the market in 1965 without that legal protection. Competitors quickly copied his formula; nonetheless, Johnson Products continued to dominate the sales of all hair relaxers, substances that straighten curly hair.

In 1975, the Federal Trade Commission mandated that the company warn consumers that Ultra Sheen contained lye, which could harm the scalp and cause eye damage. Johnson was, he asserts, told by the FTC official that the other straighteners would also have to print a warning about lye on their packages. Yet for nearly two years, while Ultra Sheen's label carried the notice, competitors like Revlon continued to merchandise their "safe," "gentle," and "natural" products. During this period Johnson's share of the market fell from 60% to its current level of 40%.

Revlon meanwhile began going after black consumers with its Realistic hair straightener, in addition to marketing cosmetics for black women under the Polished Amber brand. By the early 1980s, sales of these beauty products were up 70 percent. Revlon has also launched Dermanesse, a line of skin care products aimed especially at blacks.

Johnson Products launched, in early 1980, Precise, a product that both straightens and conditions hair. The company has also launched an expanded line of products for blacks under the name Moisture Formula, to compete with Revlon.

The company's most promising new prospect, though, is the lucrative African market. In Nigeria, Ultra Sheen has become the generic name for all hair conditioning products. Johnson recently opened a $2 million manufacturing plant in Lagos. He is optimistic that his African venture will clear the way for the sale of a whole range of black health and beauty products in Africa and return the company on its high road to revenues and profits.

Questions

1. What role do such factors as income and population play in assessing the market opportunity for a firm such as Johnson Products Company?
2. Why were Revlon and other companies tempted to compete with Johnson Products Company and penetrate this market for black health and beauty care products?
3. In addition to Africa, what other ethnic groups or geographic regions might Johnson consider in looking for additional markets? What factors might the firm need to consider in approaching or avoiding particular target market groups?

ULTRA SHEEN® GIVES YOU A CHOICE

SMOOTH AND SLEEK.

Smooth, sleek, and classically chic. It's the kind of relaxing you've always wanted. And the kind of relaxing you always get with Ultra Sheen® Original Formula Relaxer. And the special Rinse N' Set® Lotion helps to condition as well as set your hair any way you like. Ultra Sheen Original Formula for that smooth, sleek look you love.

OR WITH LOTS OF NATURAL BODY.

Introducing soft natural body with new Ultra Sheen Natural Body Formula Relaxer. It takes the natural curl out, but leaves natural body in. And it has a separate penetrating conditioner to make your hair feel healthier and look bouncier. Plus a special setting lotion that adds even more body.
New Ultra Sheen Natural Body Formula, for that full-bodied look you love.

Warning: Follow directions carefully to avoid skin and scalp irritation, hair breakage, and eye injury.

STORE COUPON
SAVE $1.00
ON YOUR NEXT PURCHASE OF
ULTRA SHEEN®
PERMANENT CREME RELAXER
ORIGINAL FORMULA OR NATURAL BODY FORMULA

MR. RETAILER: This coupon may be redeemed by you at face value plus 5¢ for handling if terms hereof are followed. Retail customers must pay sales tax on your regular price. Coupon is void if proof of sufficient purchases to cover coupons redeemed is not produced upon request; if redeemed other than by retail customers; if presented by non-retail distributors; if prohibited, restricted, or taxed by law. Any other use may constitute fraud. Cash value 1/20 of 1¢. Ship redeemed coupons to Johnson Products Co., Inc., P.O. Box 1178, Clinton, Iowa 52734 for payment. Expiration date: March 31, 1982.

From the Johnson Products Research Center.
©1981 JOHNSON PRODUCTS CO., INC., CHICAGO, ILLINOIS 60620

Case 5-2

Declining Food Store Sales

Food store operators are faced with a serious problem. Instead of eating at home, an increasing number of Americans are eating in restaurants or fast food shops like McDonald's and Burger King, or eating Kentucky Fried Chicken at home. Currently, American consumers are spending one of every three food dollars in "eateries" whereas ten years ago they spent one in every five. This shift in consumer expenditure patterns has the American supermarket industry concerned because it is depressing their sales. A Harvard study sponsored by a supermarket trade association predicts that food store sales will increase annually at a maximum rate of 2 percent through 1985. In the 1960s and early 1970s, supermarket sales increased 3.5 percent. The Harvard study concluded that it was most likely that spending for food away from

home will increase at a faster rate than food store sales in the period 1975–1985. The Harvard study made no attempt to analyze or describe the reasons for this phenomenon.

Questions

1. What factors do you believe are contributing to the general decline in food store sales and the increase in the number of Americans who are eating out in restaurants or fast food shops?
2. If you were advising the supermarket industry, what would you suggest they do to alter this trend?
3. If you were advising the restaurant industry, what advice would you offer them in order to continue or even accelerate the trend?

Chapter 6

Buyer Motivation and Behavior

Consider two well-known consumer products—Coca-Cola and Pepsi Cola. Which one do you prefer? Do you know why? Can you really distinguish the difference in a blind test, where the products are presented in identical glasses distinguished only by number or letter? Would you believe that the results of such a test might be affected by the choice of letter used to represent one of the products? Well it might, and here is how. In 1975, Pepsi decided to challenge Coke's 3-to-1 sales lead in the Dallas, Texas, area. (Nationally, at that time Coke held about 26.2 percent of the market, compared with Pepsi's 17.4 percent.) Pepsi developed a promotion showing that more than half the Coke drinkers in the test preferred Pepsi's flavor when the two drinks were stripped of brand identification.[1] During the test, Coke was served in a glass marked Q and Pepsi in one marked M. Within a year, Pepsi had reduced Coke's lead in Dallas to 2-to-1. Naturally, Coke officials conducted their own consumer preference tests. However, instead of testing the colas, they tested the letters. Their tests showed that people like the letter M better than Q. Too many unpleasant words begin with Q (quack, queer, quitter). Pepsi Cola's tests, claimed the Coca-Cola researchers, were invalid. But this didn't end the matter. Coca-Cola's people then put their own cola in the glasses marked Q and M. Sure enough, most people tested preferred the drink in the M glass over the one labeled Q. Pepsi's staff responded by switching the letters on their glasses to S and L. Again, people preferred Pepsi, which was always in the L glasses. Coca-Cola's people called "foul" once again contending that just as people prefer M to Q so they like L better than S. And the battle goes on!

The impact that these tests and the corresponding advertising campaigns are having on sales of the two products is inconclusive, but executives on both sides were fearful that the confrontation might backfire—fuel the public's cynicism about all advertising, attract unwanted attention from government regulators, and turn consumers against both soft drinks.

The Meaning of Buyer Behavior

Studying *buyer behavior* is the attempt to understand and predict human actions in the buying role. It is a discipline that examines both *consumer-buyers*, those who purchase and consume goods as individuals or as members of individual household units, and *organizational buyers*, those who purchase goods and services for business firms, industrial groups, nonprofit organizations, and governmental units.

The theoretical basis for buyer behavior is primarily found in the behavioral sciences: psychology, sociology, and cultural anthropology.[2] More explicitly, buyer behavior describes the individual's activity in obtaining and utilizing

[1] "Coke-Pepsi Slugfest," *Time*, July 26, 1976, pp. 64-65.
[2] Harold Kassarjian and Thomas Robertson, *Perspectives in Consumer Behavior*, rev. ed. (Glenview, Il: Scott, Foresman, 1973), p. 12.

"Confound it, men! If they don't respond to hard sell and they don't respond to soft sell, what the hell sell <u>do</u> they respond to?"

Drawing by Ed Arnow; © 1975 The New Yorker Magazine, Inc.

goods and services, including the sequence of decision processes associated with these acts. [3]

There are many meaningful and useful theories of buyer behavior that improve our ability to predict behavior. A clearer understanding of buyer behavior can give marketers a better idea of how marketing works, enabling them to devise more potent marketing strategies. From a wider viewpoint, a greater ability to predict buyer behavior can provide information and insight for public decisions concerning consumer affairs. For instance, the Federal Trade Commission, as well as private organizations, is concerned with such issues as: (1) the use of fear appeals by television advertisers to scare consumers into buying various kinds of protection; (2) the use in commercials of sound, lighting, and staging techniques that deceive viewers; (3) the way in which people receive and process information, and the attitudes they consequently develop, about products, political candidates, and social concepts such as racism; and (4) the impact of television commercials addressed to children when their concepts about violence, materialism, work, and other aspects of life are developing. [4]

Audience-viewer reaction is largely within the domain of buyer behavior, as is voter reaction. Nonprofit organizations like schools, churches, and hospitals

[3] There are many definitions of buyer behavior, most of which center around the notion contained in the above definition. For example see Del I. Hawkins, Kenneth A. Coney, and Roger Best, *Consumer Behavior: Implications for Marketing Strategy* (Dallas, Tex.: Business Publications, 1980), pp. 11–18.

[4] Scott Ward and Thomas Robertson, *Consumer Behavior: Theoretical Sources* (Englewood Cliffs, N.J.: Prentice-Hall, 1973), p. 8.

also need to understand the behavioral characteristics of their users so they can provide better services. A politician needs to know the behavioral characteristics of his "market"—not to change his convictions to suit them, but to identify potential supporters and reach them better. A congresswoman might learn that voters have failed to perceive the implications of a policy issue on which she and her opponent differ. Or she might discover which issues are most important to the voters. Marketing oriented drives to inform and persuade people are almost invariably based upon behavioral considerations. Quite often these campaigns are not designed to "sell" products and make money. Many are meant to convince people to "join a union," "prevent forest fires," "support your local police," or "fight mental illness."

There are behavioral dimensions to nearly all purchase choices. Figure 6-1 depicts these dimensions. Not even highly trained professional organizational buyers are immune from behavioral considerations; they are not solely eco-

Figure 6-1 Behavioral factors in purchase decisions.

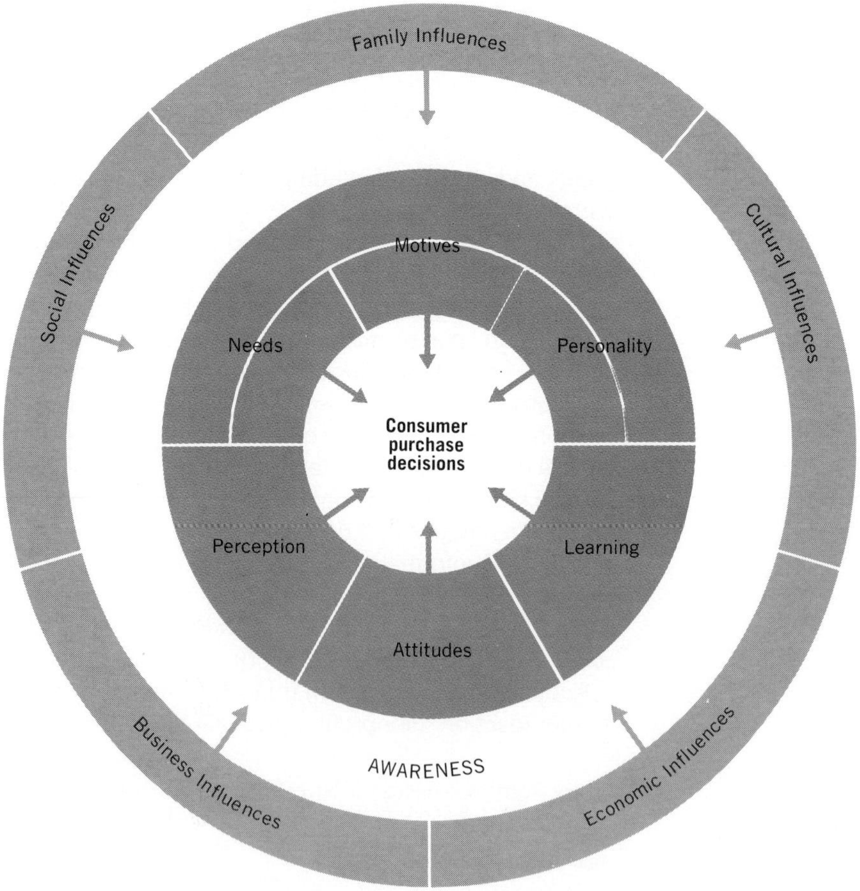

Source: Glenn Walters, *Consumer Behavior: Theory and Practice*, rev. ed. (Homewood, IL: Irwin, 1974), p.16.

nomic people motivated by purely rational appeals based upon the single logic of cost and efficiency. For example, those who buy for a supermarket chain are influenced by their perceptions of food wholesalers (which may not be accurate), by their interactions with wholesalers' representatives, and by their own personal tastes.

Marketing and Buyer Behavior

Today, marketing at all levels and in many kinds of organizations has changed markedly because executives have become aware of consumer behavior. Many innovations are not major items, but just little pluses that make for greater user satisfaction. Nevertheless, they are proof of business' new awareness of what makes a consumer buy. Some of these changes are:

- Drive-in windows at banks; more convenient banking hours.
- Appliance guarantees written in clear language rather than legal jargon.
- "Cool lines" for receiving customer complaints to which a genuine response is made.
- "Tell-tags" on appliances that give specific facts to help the customer make comparisons.
- Price labels that peel off, leaving the merchandise undamaged.
- Packages that protect their contents, while permitting the user to get at them easily.
- Hospitals that accord patients and visitors the dignity of cheerful, well-decorated rooms instead of the sterile atmosphere of a test tube.
- Advertising that both informs and entertains, without insulting the intelligence and sensitivity of the viewer.
- Products that meet basic standards of performance, safety, and health.

Marketing and the study of buyer behavior are both emerging disciplines. The flaws that exist in marketing programs may in part be attributable to our incomplete understanding of buyer behavior phenomena. Surely, no firm would knowingly build a marketing program based upon a false conception of buyer behavior. In this chapter, we will explore the various dimensions of behavior that are believed to be important variables in buyers' decision processes. We will look first at these factors as they affect the consumer buyer, and later we will examine their role in organizational buyer behavior.

What Causes Behavior?

Marketers and others are interested in understanding "causes," because if they are understood, behavior can to a great extent be predicted and influenced. Thus, the social and behavioral sciences are full of theories about what causes behavior. Many of these are only partial theories; some have been abandoned; others still linger and spread confusion; and some are still evolving. A brief review of some of these notions about what causes behavior would appear warranted.

The Superman Model

For many years, the principal model in analyzing buyer behavior centered around a kind of superman notion. Consumers were credited with having the logic of supermen, perfect knowledge of the market place; a perfect ability to judge the suitability of products and firms. Buyers' behavior was supposedly motivated solely by their desire to maximize utility. Consumers would buy products in such quantities that the marginal utility per dollar's worth of any product would equal the marginal utility* per dollar's worth of any other product for a given period of time. This model and its supporting assumptions were based upon the idea that consumers derive satisfaction from consumption and that they wish to maximize these satisfactions within the limits of their incomes. It assumes that the consumer is a fully rational, logic-bound human computer, ever alert to the sound of a falling price. This superman, or economic, model of consumer behavior ignored completely the social-cultural character of consumption. It also ignored the basic fact that utility cannot be measured and that consumers are emotional as well as rational in their attitudes about consumption.

The Inner Man Model

This model of behavior is based upon the belief that behavior is caused by an assortment of psychic forces within the individual including drives, instincts, needs, motives, and reflexes. Normal behavior represents a socially acceptable expression of these inner forces, or the development of socially acceptable traits. The inner man model of behavior constitutes a kind of "medical model" of human behavior, so called because it is similar to a doctor's view of disease. From a medical viewpoint, internal conditions of the individual (for example, bacteria, virus, or malfunction) show up in symptoms such as fever, infection, and discomfort. Yet, however distressing these symptoms may be, the real problem is the internal condition that interferes with normal functioning. Behavior, in the medical model sense, is thus considered to reflect basic underlying motives or drives; it is a function of internal mind states as seen in attitudes or motivations. Yet, it should be pointed out that, unlike a disease and its symptoms, these mind states are themselves the products of behavior and not necessarily the other way around.

The Whole Man Model

The model of behavior causation most widely accepted today and the one most relevant to buyer behavior is the whole man model. As its name suggests, this model sees behavior as caused by a number of factors, including (1) genetic endowment, (2) history of previous behavior, and (3) the current situation. The whole man (holistic) model of behavior acknowledges that genetic

---

*Marginal utility is the additional, or incremental, utility or satisfaction the user receives from consuming or buying the next additional unit.

factors such as intelligence affect behavior, but it also assumes that few, if any, drives, instincts, or motives are inherited traits. The holistic model stresses the individual's capacity to think, reason, process information, and so solve problems. Finally, this model of buyer behavior implies that the causes or reasons that initiate and direct behavior are related to the individual's capacity to process information and to solve problems in an ongoing interaction with his or her surroundings. In other words, this notion of behavior causation emphasizes social learning and social influence—that is, the capacity of culture and immediate environment, including the transactions among people, to shape behavior.

A Basic Model of Buyer Behavior

We can now conclude that behavior, including that important subset which is our concern, buyer behavior, is caused by two important and interrelated variables, person-centered factors and situation-centered factors. This can be shown a number of ways. First, $B = f(P,S)$.

The above equation states, simply, that buyer behavior (B) is a function (f) of person-centered factors (P) and situation-centered factors (S). This view of buyer behavior is based largely on the whole man model. Figure 6-2 is an expanded statement of the model.

The Basic Model of Consumer Buyer Behavior illustrates the two central, all-important variables that determine consumer buyer behavior. This model, while marginally applicable to the industrial or organizational buyer, is more valid for the ultimate consumer. The two central variables in the models are the person (the actor) and the situation (the social environment surrounding a given event). Notice that the relationship between the person and the situation, or the social environment, is referred to as the transactional nature of buyer behavior. This relationship has a special meaning.

Figure 6-2 Basic model of consumer buyer behavior.

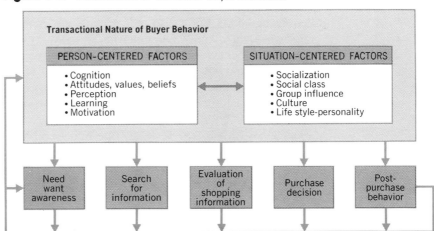

The Transactional Nature of Buyer Behavior

The transactional nature of buyer behavior takes its name from the notion that the proper unit of social-psychological analysis is the *transaction*. The transaction consists of a stimulus by one person and a response by another, which in turn stimulates another response from the first person. This interaction becomes a kind of psychological exchange process whereby we *give* reinforcing behavior in order to *receive* it in our turn. Isn't this the very essence of marketing as an exchange process? The basic, or transactional, model asserts that buyers initiate and originate behavior, but that their behavior is also a reaction and response to forces in their environment. Hence, the transactional model acknowledges the dynamic interplay, the mutual stimulation, and interaction of the person and the environmental situations.

Person-Centered Factors

The basic model of consumer buyer behavior as shown in Figure 6-2 underscores the importance of the person-centered variables. Consumers are people with needs, wants, and aspirations, who are subject to moods, sentiments, anxiety, and frustration. Consumers reason, that is, they process, store, and retrieve information to solve problems. Their behavior is affected by their past experience, which means that they learn from experience and modify their behavior accordingly.

Cognitive Factors of Behavior. The word *cognitive* has the same root as *recognize*, which means "to know." Cognitions are bits of knowledge, values, beliefs, attitudes, and images. Consumer behavior is a function of cognitions. Think about it this way. Your behavior, in all its roles and manifestations, is largely a function of what you know (your cognitions). Marketers, therefore, in their efforts to modify your behavior, spend nearly $40 billion per year persuading you to buy a host of products and services. Almost all marketing tries to communicate something (knowledge, images, values, attitudes, beliefs) to you so that you will respond favorably. Our behavior depends on what we know (cognition), but it also reflects what we think we know, and what we think we ought to know. Our behavior, in short, is cognitive in its orientation.[5]
  Cognitive behavior also assumes that persons reason (cogitate) by seeking, processing, and storing information (perception) and modify their responses on the basis of the insights thus gained and prior experience (learning). There is a dynamic interplay between the person and his or her situation.

Attitudes, Values, and Beliefs. Our values constitute the foundation of our cognitive structure. Our personal values carry expectations about our own behavior and the behavior of others. Values, like attitudes, define what is worthwhile and what is expected. Individuals usually hold many more atti-

[5] Uric Neisser, *Cognitive Psychology* (New York: Appleton-Century-Crofts, 1967), p. 10.

tudes than values. A given consumer has tens of thousands of beliefs and hundreds of attitudes, but perhaps only a few dozen values. To illustrate, a consumer may *value* thrift. As a consequence, the careful spending of his or her resources becomes an integral part of his or her belief system. Such a person would be reluctant to buy any but the largest items, like a home or car, on credit.

Attitudes, a very special kind of cognition or bit of knowledge, are predispositions to respond in specific ways to specific stimuli. Or looked at another way, attitudes are learned, long-lasting sets of beliefs about an object or situation, disposing a person toward some response.[6]

Marketers have long sought to create favorable attitudes for their poducts and services on the assumption that:

- The more favorable the attitude, the higher the incidence of product usage.
- The less favorable the attitude, the lower the incidence of usage.
- The more unfavorable the attitude toward a product, the more likely the consumer is to stop using it.

These are reasonably good assumptions by marketers, but it does not always follow that favorable attitudes will lead to the purchase of a particular product. Do you have a favorable attitude toward a Porsche, or a Mercedes? Are you in the market for one?

Attitudes are a complex kind of cognition with several components layered something like a cake. First, there is a cognitive or knowledge component. In terms of our previous example, the knowledge component of the Porsche would suggest that, yes, I know about this car, its turbo-charged engine, speed and acceleration, fuel economy, durability, quality construction, and craftsmanship. Second, there is an *affect* component to attitudes. Affect refers to liking or disliking something. Your attitude about the Porsche 924 may embrace a significant element of knowledge, but you may dislike its shape, or not care to own it for other reasons. Third, all attitudes have an action tendency component, consisting of your behavior toward the object. Thus, your attitude about the Porsche 924 may be based upon adequate knowledge and you may like it. But if you are not actually moved to purchase it or consider purchasing it, then your behavior, from the marketer's standpoint, becomes more important than your attitude.

Is Behavior a Function of Attitudes?   The answer is sometimes yes, and sometimes no. Occasionally the flow of influence is the other way around. Our attitudes are also a function of our behavior. Marketers often try to influence the attitudes of consumers by attempting to modify their behavior: urging them to "Visit the store," "Take the car out for a test drive," or "Try this free sample." Recognizing that behavior can and often does lead to attitude change, alert managers do not wait until their customers acquire attitudes requiring them to act. Instead, they work on the now firmly established psychological

---

[6] See Milton Rokeach, *Beliefs, Attitudes and Values* (San Francisco: Jossey-Bass, 1968), p. 112.

principle that attitudes change following a commitment to behavior.[7] This underscores again the important point that behavior is seldom caused by any single determinant, either person-centered or situation-centered, but is instead the outcome of many variables working interdependently.

Perception. Perception is the process by which we extract information from the environment and use it for problem solving—to make sense out of our experience. Perception involves reasoning, memory, and vast amounts of information processing. Figure 6-3 illustrates the concept schematically.

The transactional nature of buyer behavior emphasizes the importance of familiarity and value in the way consumers perceive a product. Our assumptions about objects, events, and relationships affect our judgments about their actual characteristics. If we think we are not going to like a product, the chances are good that when we actually try it we won't. If our next door neighbor tells us that a certain salesperson in a suburban store is a snob or a wise guy, we will most likely perceive the salesperson to be just that.

Perception pervades the entire range of marketing activities. Products are perceived differently. Brand loyalty largely depends on how different market segments perceive different products. For example, many consumers are loyal to Lysol because it is perceived as strong and therefore, effective in killing germs. Others may perceive the strong odor as offensive, and therefore may be more receptive to a disinfectant like Pine Sol, which has a more pleasant aroma. Pricing is often an exercise in the psychology of perception. Thus, we have "psychological prices" that are chosen for their known impact on the consumers' perceptions. For example, a shopper is apt to perceive a $2.00 item priced at $1.98 as lying within the $1 price range. Store location, design, and layout, as well as product development, and promotional activities are no less concerned with perception than are the other elements of the marketing mix.

Learning. Learning is the product of reasoning, thinking, information processing and, of course, perception. It is the process by which an activity originates or is changed through reacting to an encountered situation. People learn from all sorts of encountered situations. Shopping, reading advertisements, trying samples, listening to the experiences of one's friends and family are all learning and hence behavior modifying, experiences.

There are many approaches to learning and a considerable controversy simmers as to what extent consumers are coerced by outside forces of persuasion.[8] Consumers undoubtedly "learn" or acquire much of their behavior through simple association or trial and error. A product found to be rewarding or reinforcing is purchased again and again until such time as the consumer, seeking variety or simply curious, decides to try a different one.

---

[7] For more on this idea, see Philip Zimbardo and Ebbe B. Ebbesen, *Influencing Attitudes and Changing Behavior* (Reading, MA: Addison-Wesley, 1970), pp. 63–94.

[8] Sidney R. Bernstein, "Persuasive Methods Won't Change in 80's, But Ad Styles and Media Will," *Marketing News*, July 11, 1980, p. 11.

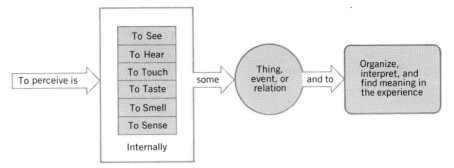

Figure 6-3 A schematic illustration of perception.

Consumers learn many things. For instance, they learn that the blimp is associated with Goodyear tires and that the "other guy," the company without the blimp, is Goodrich. Learning is concerned with *generalizing*. The information that Safeway supermarkets have lower prices than Seven-Eleven drive-ins will probable lead the shopper to conclude that A&P, and Grand Union supermarkets probably also have lower prices than Seven-Eleven. When consumers find that one store gives excellent service and value and another store does not, they learn to discriminate. Consumers practice brand loyalty as a result of what they've learned about a reliable brand. They also practice brand switching, which really means that consumers can unlearn as well as learn. Behavior that was once rewarding and satisfying is *extinguished* as a result of new experiences with new or different products which are more gratifying than the old ones. Consumers learn where to seek information, to use *Consumer Reports*, or to rely upon the judgment of friends and opinion leaders. Consumers adapt, accommodate, and cope, and in so doing learn to modify their behavior. Thus, learning is an important part of the person-centered factors that generate behavior.

Motivation.   It is becoming less fashionable, in the literature of both social psychology and consumer behavior, to talk about motivation as a special kind of arousal event. The term was often used in older theories of psychology to refer to inner causes of behavior. More recently, motivation is simply a label identifying a whole series of factors that help to explain behavior. In this sense it is concerned with the reasons that impel people to undertake certain actions. In every aspect of their lives, including consuming, people are always doing something. There is no such thing as motivated or unmotivated behavior. The explanation for behavior lies not so much in the motives for people's actions at a particular time as in explaining why they persist in them and why, after persisting so long, they begin doing something else. Behavior is thus seen as a stream, or continuity of acts, and changes in behavior reflect changes in cognitive and situational processes. Motivation, in buyer behavior, suggests that the reasons behind consumer actions are basically cognitive, but that they involve a dynamic interaction between the person and his or her surroundings.[9] The real issue is that variations in buyer behavior stem mainly from differences in the situations people encounter rather than from stable traits within the individual.

Situation-Centered Factors

Motivation refers only to reasons why buyers behave. Much buyer behavior is brought about by situational factors; therefore, marketers must understand what constitutes a motivating situation. Physical environments and situations induce and shape behavior. Retail stores must be made attractive, satisfying places to shop.[10] A suitable atmosphere in museums, libraries, restaurants, supper theaters, and department stores can create the appropriate mood for each activity. Altering a consumer's mood can in turn alter his or her behavior. Marketers arrange space, and space in turn, helps to shape a situation. Television commercials almost always project situations—Mrs. Olson showing a young bride how to make coffee, the friendly old druggist telling the boy to brush his teeth with Crest, Joe Namath talking with someone about the good smell of Brut. Cognitive approaches to buyer behavior are concerned with action sequences that are instigated by some source of information. We think about previous behavior, remember events, and transform them into attitudes, values, and beliefs that predispose us to act.

Consumer behavior varies so widely over time because situations change so frequently. The environment, consisting of everything that surrounds the consumer, is obviously also an important influence on behavior. Consumers are, in great part, products of their social environment; hence, the social environment is basically a motivator or producer of behavior. Consumer behavior is a function of the socialization process, of group influence, of social class and culture.

Socialization.   We learn the ways of society through socialization. We watch other people; we emulate role models and folk heroes as well as brothers, sisters, parents, and significant others. Socialization is the process by which people influence one another through exchanges of thought, feelings, and actions. So that we can fit into the society that sustains us, we are taught to value and esteem particular actions. Such reinforcement leads to repeating these actions; thus through watching, imitation, and reinforcement we learn what our society expects of us. Several of the more important means for achieving socialization deserve mention.

The Family.   Most of our attitudes, habits, and tastes are acquired within the family setting. Consumption patterns, likes and dislikes, attitudes regarding the

[9] Rom J. Markin, "Motivation in Buyer Behavior Theory: From Mechanism to Cognition," in *Consumer and Industrial Buying Behavior*, ed. Arch G. Woodside, Jagdish N. Sheth, and Peter D. Bennett (New York: Elsevier North Holland, 1977), pp. 37–48.
[10] Rom J. Markin, Charles Lillis, and Chem Narayana, "The Retail Store: The Social Psychological Significance of Space," *Journal of Retailing* **52**, no. 1 (Spring 1976), pp. 43–54 and p. 94.

Media socialization.

roles of goods, and habits of spending and saving are largely inculcated within this primary group.

The Mass Media.   Never have so many been exposed to so much information that is spread so rapidly. As an example of the impact of one mass medium, television, on socialization, consider the case of the American adolescent. Television consumes 64 percent of the average American preschooler's day. By the age of fourteen, this child will have seen 18,000 murders on television, by the age of seventeen, some 350,000 commercials. It has been estimated that television will consume ten years out of the lifetime of today's children. Television, to some extent, has replaced both parent and teacher as the primary socializer of children. The American child, during the critical preschool years, spends more time watching television than he or she will spend in the classroom during four years of college.

Other environmental-situational factors that influence behavior are group influence, social class, and culture.

Group Influence.   Groups are instrumental in casting the individual consumer in a series of roles. Group activity and association play an important role in social learning, and groups largely set accepted standards of purchase behavior. There are few persons whose purchase and consumption decisions are not to some degree affected by group activity. The influence that groups exert on our total individual actions and psychological state gives them a place of unparalleled importance in our study of consumer-buying behavior. For in great respect, once an individual identifies with a group and its collective action, his or her behavior is in a major way determined by the direction of the group's action.

Sociologists have divided groups into three categories: *primary*, or face-to-face, groups like the family; *secondary* groups, which are larger and more impersonal, such as college living groups, fraternities and sororities; and *reference* groups, those to which an individual looks for opinions, evaluations, and aspirations. All shape and affect the consumer's motivations (reasons for buying), aspirations, and expectations.

Reference groups are collections of people, real or imaginary, to which one looks for guidance in structuring individual behavior patterns. Marketing research studies have demonstrated, in varying degrees, the impact of reference-group influence on many aspects of consumer behavior and predispositions. It has been shown that:[11]

- Reference groups definitely influence their members to conform with respect to brands preferred.
- In more cohesive reference groups, the probability is much higher that the members will prefer the same brand as the group leader. Therefore the value of the cohesiveness is that it provides an agreeable environment in which informal leaders can effectively dominate.
- Leaders influence group members in two ways: First, the higher the degree of brand loyalty exhibited by a group leader, the more likely are the members to prefer the same brand. Second, the higher the degree of leader brand loyalty, the larger the percentage of the group also becoming brand loyal.

Such findings have important implications for marketers. When neither product nor brand appears to be affected by reference group influence (laundry soap, water heaters and lawn fertilizer), marketing programs should emphasize the product's attributes, price, and advantages over competing products. However, where reference group influence is strong (appliances, clothing, and automobiles), marketing programs should stress the kinds of people who buy the product, reinforcing and broadening whenever possible the existing image of heavy users. The strategy of the marketer should include learning what the stereotypes or images are and what specific reference groups enter into the picture so that appeals can be tailored to each main group reached by the different media.

Social Class. Social classes are distinct groups of persons who have similar socioeconomic positions and whose political-economic and purchase-consumption interests consequently tend also to coincide. Warner, whose work in social class is perhaps the classic in this field, determines class standing by using what he termed an index of status characteristics (ISC). This index consists of four determining factors: (1) occupation, (2) source of income, (3)

---

[11] See James E. Stafford, "Effects of Group Influence on Consumer Behavior," *Journal of Marketing Research* **3** (Chicago: American Marketing Association, February 1966) pp. 68–75. Also, M. Venkatesan, "Experimental Study of Consumer Behavior, Conformity and Independence," *Journal of Marketing Research* **3** (Chicago: American Marketing Association, November 1966), pp. 384–387.

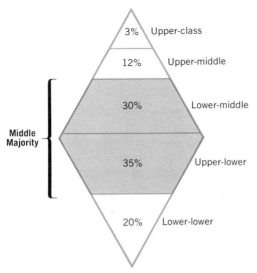

Figure 6-4 A breakdown of social class in America.

residential area, and (4) type of dwelling.[12] He concluded that there were six social classes in America. However, because of the very few people in Warner's top class, which he called Upper-Upper, marketing researchers have tended to use a five-fold classification. Figure 6-4 projects the proportion of the American class structure that fits into each of these widely used classifications.

Social class is a very special kind of reference group, suggesting adherence to a whole set of values, attitudes, perceptions, and life styles. For example, the consumption budget of a family is, in part, a symbol system that expresses the social values of membership in the life of a specific group. Being a member of a given class implies that money must be translated into socially approved behavior and possessions. Social class is an important element in a consumer's store choice. From a marketing standpoint it is an important factor in advertising and other forms of marketing communication. Class determines, in part, what is read, listened to, and watched. It also determines, in great measure, who saves and who spends; who uses credit cards and how; and who pays cash or buys on installment credit. Lower-class consumers seem to be especially sensitive to matters concerned with the body like upset stomachs and problems of constipation. They also buy great amounts of pleasure foods—beer, soft drinks, snack foods—and spend large sums on spectator sports such as baseball, football, and hockey. Middle-class consumers spend a large portion of their resources on furniture and the ornaments of life: a home and its decor, major appliances, television, cars, clothing and college education for children. The upper-class budget reflects a concern for aesthetics and life expanding products: books, magazine subscriptions, country club memberships, travel, leisure homes, and recreational equipment—goods interpreted as the necessary cost of a stressful life oriented toward peak competitive

[12] Lloyd Warner, M. Meeker, and K. Eels, *Social Class in America* (Chicago: Social Reseach, Inc., 1949).

achievement. In a section to follow, we will see how the idea of social class has been recently expanded into a rich new concept called **psychographics,** an important barometer for evaluating consumer behavior.

Culture.   Culture is the seedbed from which almost all behavior emerges. It is the vast, largely unseen, unfelt process by which we are "shaped up," by which we take on the characteristics and behavior of those who are like us. Culture, as we learned in chapter 2, is a system of solutions to problems both known and unknown, all of which are acquired and shared by members of a recognizable group. Culture is, in short, our nonbiological heritage—our systems of laws, customs, norms, and institutions. It is a mold that forms and transforms our personalities, our life styles, our attitudes, values, and belief systems. Since every human being is the product of a culture, aware managers of a business enterprise will study the cultures of its customers so as to pinpoint and fill their needs.

America is not a melting pot. It is rather a kind of tossed salad. American society is characterized by a great deal of cultural assimilation —most, but not all, Americans share a basic core culture. Yet our country also exhibits great diversity and pluralism. That is, there are many subcultures in the United States whose behavior is often at great variance with that of our dominant culture—middle majority, white, Anglo Saxon Protestant America. The Jews, Irish, Poles, Spaniards, Latinos or Chicanos, and blacks all have important and quite distinct subcultures. There is much cross-cultural borrowing in America, but marketers would make a gross mistake by assuming that all Americans, or all people throughout the world, are basically similar. Marketers are well advised to remember that culture is a guide to a person's behavior. People will solve their problems according to the unique set of value-laden responses and standards acquired from their respective cultures.

As more and more American firms turn their attention to foreign markets as well as to various domestic subcultures, the need to understand cross-cultural differences becomes clear.

Before proceeding, can you answer these questions:
1. What is the relationship between buyer behavior and marketing strategy?
2. Describe the transactional nature of buyer behavior.
3. Consumer behavior has two important determinants, one set of determinants is called person-centered factors. The other set is called
   _____ .

Buyer Behavior Is Problem-Solving Behavior

Consumer buyer behavior is a special form of problem solving. When consumers go into the market place, they are looking for solutions to problems. Some of these problems are basically functional—how to give the family an adequate diet, receive minimum health care, obtain basic shelter, protect oneself from the ravages of existence. Most consumer problem solving in the United States and other industrialized countries with a free market involves a great deal of symbolic significance. Consumers in these nations are searching for solutions to social-psychological problems as well as economic ones. This is what recently prompted the president of a large cosmetics firm in this country to state that in his factories they produce cosmetics, but in retail stores they sell hope.

Consumer behavior as problem solving activity is characterized by cognitive activity and information processing. Consumers buy goods because they are important as symbols to the individual's need for self-identity, self-enhancement, and self-extension.

Maslow contends that all persons have a hierarchy (order) of needs, ranging from lower or basic needs to higher, more complex ones. He asserts that the **needs-wants hierarchy** includes the following:

1. **Physiological needs**. These are the essentials that must be fulfilled if the body is to survive. They include the need for oxygen, water, food, waste elimination, relief from pain, and protection from the elements.
2. **Safety needs**. These are the needs for security, protection, order, stability, and routine.
3. **Social needs**. These needs include affection and affiliation—warm, satisfying, and fulfilling human interactions with family, friends, and other groups.
4. **Esteem needs**. These are the needs for self-respect, prestige, success, achievement, and self-validation (appreciating who one is).
5. **Self-actualization needs**. These are needs associated with the desire for self-fulfillment, for the satisfaction of one's curiosity, and the urge to deal effectively with one's environment.[13]

In a high consumption economy geared to the individual, marketing helps the consumer satisfy this total range of needs: marketing makes it easier to satisfy consumer needs and solve consumer problems. Once a given need is satisfied, it is no longer an important source of motivation, so the consumer moves constantly up and down his or her own needs-wants hierarchy. At each of the five levels, notice the significance of goods and marketing services. We buy food, clothing, and shelter to nourish and protect our bodies. But instead of filling basic or simple sustenance needs, we buy goods to satisfy acquired tastes consistent with our income and life style—sirloin steaks, redwood houses, and Pendleton jackets. We buy goods that stress safety—steel beams in automobile bodies and steel-belted radial tires that will get loved ones home safely. We buy insurance for the safety it gives, but we also buy it because we love certain people and want to protect them. We want to be more likable and more socially acceptable and advertisements consistently stress appeals to both the social and esteem reasons for buying products. Finally, given the increased awareness, education, and income of the average American consumer, a large

[13] Abraham H. Maslow, *Motivation and Personality* (New York: Harper & Row, 1954), especially Chapter 5, pp. 80–107.

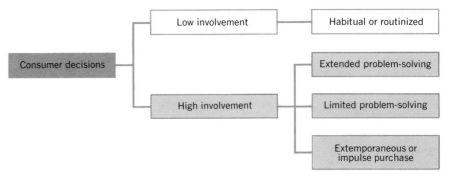

Figure 6-5 Kinds of consumer decisions.

amount of marketing effort is directed toward consumers' urges for self-actualizing, self-expression, and individuality. Products offering luxury, recreation and leisure, and aesthetic satisfaction, such as concert tickets and travel, are all marketing responses to this dimension of consumer needs. Each person's needs-wants hierarchy is the crystallization of that individual's person-centered and situation-centered factors. Hence, to the extent that consumer buyers have similar life styles, they will also have similar needs-wants hierarchies and will exhibit similar purchase consumption behavior.

Consumer Decision Processes

Consumer buying behavior must be purposeful and problem solving in order to satisfy the needs-wants hierarchy. Consumer behavior is thus goal oriented; and because consumers seek goal objects—products, services, satisfactions, and amenities—from among many alternatives, *consumer decision processes* have frequently been studied.[14]

Consumers make a number of different kinds of decisions, as shown in Figure 6-5.

Basically consumer decisions are either *low involvement* or *high involvement* decisions. High involvement decisions or ego-involved decisions are made in conjunction with important, significant problems. They involve significant purchases such as clothing, appliances, automobiles, expensive sporting equipment, and stereophonic sound equipment. High involvement decisions are nonroutinized decisions and they are often novel, unstructured, and consequential either monetarily or psychologically. The behavior-purchase process for high involvement decisions suggests the following sequence of activities: problem recognition, search, evaluation, trial, adoption, and conviction.

Low involvement decisions are so-called because there are relatively few ego considerations surrounding the purchase. Such purchase decisions are usually made with a routine process and the items are often of low unit value.

---

[14] Chester R. Wasson, "Consumer Choice Processes: Search or Automatic Response," *Journal of the Academy of Marketing Science* **7**, no. 4 (Fall, 1979), pp. 350–373.

An example of choice and consumer decision processes.

Much consumer behavior is low involvement behavior relating to trivial problems. For example:

1. whether to have a Coke or Pepsi
2. whether to buy Viva or Scott paper towels
3. whether to buy Rolaids or Tums
4. whether to buy Dial or Irish Spring soap

Behavior related to low involvement decisions is less cognitive and relies more extensively on simple affect (like or dislike). It does not involve processing large amounts of information. Instead it consists of a sequence of behavior whereby awareness and minimal comprehension occur first, followed by trial and then attitude change. Marketing's task for low involvement decisions is to provide the customer the opportunity to shop, to compare, and to learn about various products and product attributes. In the case of impulse purchasing, displays and other point-of-purchase stimuli become important decision factors; here the entire consumer decision process is a kind of explosive and telescoped procedure. Psychological suggestion and the provision of adequate cues are the marketer's basic tools.

Consumer Behavior—A Process Rather than a Single Act

Consumer behavior is more than simply buying or rejecting a product. Buying behavior is a series of related, somewhat sequential, stages or activities. This was shown diagrammatically in Figure 6-2. Consumer behavior begins with problem recognition which arises from a desire for need satisfaction. Consumers then begin a search for information, followed by a purchase decision. However, even then the process is not complete because there follows a period of postpurchase behavior, during which the consumer evaluates his or her purchase and the satisfaction it is or is not delivering.

Is Consumer Behavior Rational or Rationalizing?

Do women shoppers get that worked up over squeezing the Charmin, or over the paper towel that is one-third more absorbent? Are men all that excited by White Owl cigars or by Gillette's Atra razor blades? Do you buy Coke because you really believe "Coke is Life"? Do you go to McDonald's because "they do it all for you" or for the hamburger made from 1.6 ounces of meat? Or do you use the phone to communicate or to "reach out and touch someone"? Customers who buy these products or use these services are not morons—they are *you* and *me* and a great many other people.

It was once fashionable to talk about whether customers were rational or emotional, and buying and patronage motives were almost always characterized as one or the other. Modern consumer behavior studies contend that such a classification is not only needless, but foolish as well.

The cognitive buyer is rational in the sense that he or she has reasons for acting. These reasons, therefore, constitute a sufficient account of the whole matter as to why customers behave. We hold buyers personally responsible as the authors of their actions and we may ask them to describe their intentions, awareness, and purpose. We may also expect buyers to engage in a great deal of *rationalization*, which is nothing more than their unique verbal account of their own behavior which, incidentally, may not be very useful for our understanding.[15]

We All Try Not to Be Absurd.   Have you ever fallen down in a public place? Embarrassing, wasn't it? The first thing we do when something like this happens, is look around to see who's watching. You've probably seen a television commercial where a trained interviewer asks a customer, "Why do you shop in this store?" Even if this is the customer's first trip, and even if she doesn't like the store after going there, will she say so on camera? Probably not. Why? Because it would make her appear absurd. If she doesn't like that store, what is she doing there? In this behavior, is her response rational? Yes. In the broad-

---

[15] Rom J. Markin, "The Role of Rationalization in Consumer Decision Processes: A Revisionist Approach to Consumer Behavior," *Journal of the Academy of Marketing Sciences* 7, no. 4 (Fall 1979), pp. 316–335.

est sense it is, because it is reasonable for people not to wish to appear absurd. So we look for reasons to justify our behavior.

Motives Are Operational and Psychological

Motives are reasons for behaving and there are an infinite number of reasons why consumers act as they do. Some reasons for buyer behavior are operational in character. Formerly, operational reasons might have been called rational buying motives. Operational reasons are those describing the satisfactions hoped for from the physical performance of the product. These might include low cost, durability, dependability, and efficiency.

At the other end of the scale, reasons or motives for buying are often rooted in psychology. These reasons are related to satisfactions to be derived from the consumer's social and psychological interpretations of the product and its performance. Earlier these reasons would have been called emotional buying motives and would include such factors as sex, fear, status, achievement, pride, and anxiety. Motives for consumer buying behavior are never clear-cut, nor are consumers ever "motivated" by single reasons—motives are multiple and complex. But most importantly, reasons for behavior originate not only from within the individual, but from the situations in which individuals find themselves.

Marketers and advertisers almost never use single appeals to induce a single motive or reason for buying. Most advertisers use combinations of emotional and rational appeals to reach and persuade customers. We all are emotional, maybe more than we are rational. We all respond to appeals to the senses: joy, laughter, sex, love, sensations of speed, power, and excitement. Marketers address these desires and emotions, but at the same time subtly provide enough "rational," "logical," or "operational" appeals to enable us to justify our behavior so that we will not appear absurd.

Self-Concept

Every one of us possesses a set of feelings about ourself. That is, the organization of our ideas, beliefs, emotions, motivations, and behavior is centered on ourselves. Hence, consumers act in a way to maintain their pride and to enhance their *self-image*. Most of us need an acceptable self-image, which is a personalized, internalized, idealized conception of who and what we are. However, we also have multiple selves. There is a *perceived* self, which is how one sees oneself. There is an *ideal* self, which is the model person one strives to be; it is an image of self to which many persons aspire. There is a *social* self, which is how we think others perceive us and, finally, there is an *apparent* self, which is how other people actually see us. The *actual* self is a kind of composite of all the self-concepts. The actual self is defined as what one is seen to be objectively, but the true characterization of self-concept is that it is largely a subjective notion. Since all persons are always in a state of changing or becoming, there is no lasting or permanent actual self. Figure 6-6 is a diagram of these various notions of self.

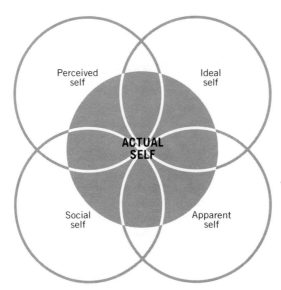

Figure 6-6 Conceptions of self.

These notions about consumers' self-images have important implications for consumer and buyer behavior. For example, consumers buy goods that are consistent with their various self-images. Conversely, they avoid products that are inconsistent with certain self-images. They use the occasion for purchasing and consuming goods as a means of changing, establishing, or reinforcing a given self-image. Consumer goods are really social tools or symbols that serve as a means of communication between the individual and his or her social environment. Goods enhance the *self* inasmuch as their purchase and use (1) sustain and boost the individual's self-concept—social, perceived, ideal, and apparent; and (2) prompt desired reactions from other individuals. In short, goods are one way we express our personalities.

All goods have a high symbolic character and making a purchase involves at least an implicit assessment of this symbolism, of deciding whether or not a given good dovetails with our perceived self-image. The good is purchased and enjoyed when it matches, adds to, or reinforces the positive way we think about ourselves.

Psychographics—Getting It All Together

Marketers have recently developed a technique for analyzing and predicting consumer buyer behavior based upon an approach known as **psychographics** or *life style* marketing. Used together with demographics, psychographics is a means of more fully understanding the psychological aspects of consumer behavior. Demographic analysis, which looks at age, sex, market size, and income, can tell marketers who is apt to use a product, and how heavily, and how the users of one brand vary from those of another in these quantifiable characteristics. This information is important but it tells us little about why products are purchased.

Psychographics seeks to describe the human behavioral characteristics of consumers that may have a bearing on their response to products, packaging,

Life-style dictates many consumption and purchase patterns.

Same lawn
35 days later.

Now you see them.

Now you don't.

Dandelions are a real problem. They can have roots up to two feet long. And if you don't get rid of every last bit, they just grow back.

Fortunately, there's a simple so-lution. And it won't take you much time. Thirty minutes or so with your spreader and our Turf Builder Plus 2* weed and feed will do the trick. Plus 2 is made to get rid of dandelions and 41 other broadleafed and vine-type weeds. Just apply it when the dandelions are in bloom. In a matter of days, the stems and leaves will curl and wither. In a few weeks, they'll dis-appear, root and all.

At the same time, you'll be giv-ing your lawn a good feeding of our Turf Builder* fertilizer. This will help your lawn thicken up, to help prevent new weeds from gaining a foothold.

We've tested Plus 2 on our own grass research farms as well as on lawns like yours, so we can make you this promise:

The results you see in the pic-ture will be the results you see on your lawn.

advertising, and public relations efforts.[16] Such variables span a wide spectrum of both person-centered and situation-centered factors, from self-concept and life style to attitudes, interests, opinions, and social interaction processes, and through perceptions of product attributes. Psychographic analysis focuses upon person-centered factors by analyzing the role of personality on use behavior—consumer traits and role related conduct. Psychographics also focuses upon the part played by the situation in buyer behavior by emphasizing the importance of *life style* in purchasing decisions. Life style is a pattern of living expressed as interaction with one's environment or situation. Thus, psychographics is a portrait of consumers as human beings; including the dimensions of personality, attitudes, and life style.

A Psychographic Portrait.   Demographics has been and will continue to be useful, but it is not as deep a source of information as psychographics. Psychographics provides a rich, hands-on dimensionality that puts flesh on the bare statistical bones of demographics.[17]

Psychographic analysis begins by asking questions about the consumer's activities, interests, and opinions. If the consumer is a housewife with a part-time job and three teen-age children, what does she think of her outside job versus her role as mother and homemaker? Is she interested in fashion? Does she have an exercise program? To what clubs or groups does she belong? Does she watch sporting events, participate in sports activities? How does she spend her leisure time, assuming she has any? Is she involved in her children's school activities? What are her opinions of community organizations? Is she a member of the PTA? Does she watch television? What are her attitudes about advertising? What does she read? Whom does she interact with? Does her life revolve around her husband and children? Or do her central interests lie elsewhere? How does she feel about the future? Is she optimistic? How does she save? Regularly? Not at all? Where does she bank? How and where does she shop? Is she outgoing, enjoying parties and other social functions?

Much can be learned about life styles and probable consumption behavior by building a profile of consumers based upon such an analysis of their activities, interests, and opinion statements.

Such AIO (activities, interests, and opinions) inventories, as they are called, reveal vast amounts of information concerning consumer attitudes toward product categories, brands within product categories, user and nonuser personality traits, and user and nonuser life styles.

Psychographic or life style studies focus upon how people spend their money; their patterns of work and leisure; their major interests; their opinions of social and political issues, institutions, and themselves. Finally, this psychographic information is combined with basic demographic information like age,

[16] Emanuel Demby, "Psychographics and from Whence It Came," in *Life Style and Psychographics*, ed. William Wells (American Marketing Association: Chicago, IL, 1974), p. 13.

[17] William D. Wells and Douglas J. Tigert, "Activities, Interests, and Opinions," *Journal of Advertising Research* **11** (August 1971), p. 35.

Blacks are increasingly adopting middle class values and consumption patterns.

Table 6-1 Life Style Dimensions

Activities	Interests	Opinions	Demographics
Work	Family	Themselves	Age
Hobbies	Home	Social issues	Education
Social events	Job	Politics	Income
Vacations	Community	Business	Occupation
Entertainment	Recreation	Economics	Family size
Club membership	Fashion	Education	Dwelling
Community	Food	Products	Geographic
Shopping	Media	Future	City size
Sports	Achievements	Culture	Stage of life cycle

Source: Joseph T. Plummer, "Applications of Life Style Research to the Creation of Advertising Campaigns," in *Life Style and Psychographics,* ed. William Wells (Chicago, IL: American Marketing Association, 1974), p. 160.

sex, income, and place of residence to give a rounded portrait of a person as a consumer. What is included in each major dimension of life style is shown in Table 6-1.

The purpose of psychographics is the better understanding and, of course, more accurate prediction of consumer buyer behavior. It is a major method for identifying the behavioral reasons—both person- and situation-centered—for purchasing and consuming goods.

Using psychographic or life style analysis, the Chicago advertising agency of Needham, Harper and Steers has identified ten major life style classifications and the percentage of the population in each life style segment.[18]

- Thelma, the old-fashioned traditionalist (25%)
- Mildred, the militant mother (20%)
- Eleanor, the elegant socialite (17%)
- Candice, the chic suburbanite (20%)
- Cathy, the contented housewife (18%)
- Herman, the retiring homebody (26%)
- Fred, the frustrated factory worker (19%)
- Dale, the devoted family man (17%)
- Scott, the successful professional (21%)
- Ben, the self-made businessman (17%)

Each of these segments or life style types is characterized as having unique activities, interests, and opinions and these, in turn, condition their individual product preferences and media habits.

Such profiles are extremely useful to market planners. For example, in developing a marketing strategy, the marketer would want to know what life style

[18] Peter W. Bernstein, "Psychographics Is Still an Issue on Madison Avenue," *Fortune,* January 16, 1978, pp. 78–84.

segments are most likely to find a new product appealing. For example, read Case 6-1 at the end of this chapter. Wouldn't the advertising copywriter appeal to Dale, the devoted family man, differently than he would to Fred, the frustrated factory worker, in developing appeals for a lightweight pickup truck?

Thus, we have seen how psychographics, or life style analysis, can be used, and most especially how this approach can produce multidimensional portraits of consumers which help the marketer to better understand and communicate with consumers in ways that are relevant to their lives. Psychographic studies are costly and the technique is not without limitations. However, psychographics can remove at least some of the mysteries that surround buyer behavior. It is an integrated attack on the specific problems of buyer behavior.

Before proceeding can you answer these questions:
1. Why is buyer behavior problem solving behavior?
2. List and discuss the five "needs" in Maslow's needs-wants hierarchy.
3. Contrast psychographic analysis with demographic analysis.

Organizational Buying Behavior

In addition to ultimate consumers, there are others who buy goods and services. Retail store buyers, industrial buyers, government buyers—all those who purchase goods and services for purposes other than ultimate consumption are referred to as **organizational buyers**. The question is, Are the factors that affect organizational buying behavior different from those that affect consumer buyers? And, therefore, is the buying process for organizations different from that for consumer buying? The answer is that there are differences, but they are more of degree than of kind.

Decisions by Professionals

Organizational buying, like consumer buying, is a decision making process. Unlike consumers, however, organizations buy through designated, often professional, individuals. And, to a much greater extent than individual consumers, professional purchasers must interact with other people. Business, industrial, and government buyers must operate within a formal and informal organizational framework built on shared responsibility, lines of command, and delegation of authority. Inevitably it also includes status and power conflicts. Hence, as in our consumer buyer model developed in the preceding pages, organizational buying behavior is affected by both person- and job- or situation-centered factors. In this kind of buying, however, these variables are somewhat different because of the nature of the job. Table 6-2 summarizes the important variables governing organizational buying.

Table 6-2 Examples of Variables Influencing Organizational Buying Behavior

	Job Centered Factors	Person-Centered Factors
Individual	desire to obtain lowest prices	personal values and needs
Social	meetings to set specifications	informal on-the-job interactions
Organizational	policy regarding local supplier preference	methods of personnel evaluation
Environmental	anticipated changes in prices	political climate in an election year

Source: Based upon Yoram Wind and Frederick E. Webster, Jr., "A General Model for Understanding Organizational Buying Behavior," *Journal of Marketing* **36** (April 1972), pp. 12–19.

The distinction between job-centered factors and person-centered factors is not an easy one to make.[19] Almost all conditions affecting organizational buying behavior—individual, social, organizational, and environmental—will have both job-centered and person-centered variables. Just as consumer buyers are affected by rational, operational reasons—the logic of cost and efficiency—as well as the logic of emotion, so too are organizational buyers.

Multiple Purchasing Influence.   Organizational buying, more frequently than consumer buying, involves a complex interaction of many individuals; purchasing agents, engineers, accountants, and users all have different goals and expectations that often lead to conflict in the buying process. More often than not the decision process is an extended one, taking a long time.

Problem Solving Behavior.   The buying process begins in organizations when members perceive a problem—when a need-want situation arises. Such occasions are generated by assortment deficiencies, the need to replace stocks, changes in production techniques, pressure to lower costs, competitive developments, and new programs. The buying process begins as members of the enterprise define and structure the buying situation. This includes defining the problem, seeking and then weighing information, and examining alternatives in brands, specifications, and suppliers. All who participate in the organizational purchasing process have varying roles in the buying tasks. Sometimes members are users, sometimes they are influencers, buyers, or "gatekeepers" who control the flow and amount of information to the buying situation.

---

[19] Yoram Wind and Frederick E. Webster, Jr., "A General Model for Understanding Organizational Buying Behavior," *Journal of Marketing* **36** (April 1972), pp. 12–19.

Summary

Buyer behavior is the cornerstone of marketing strategies. The objective of marketing is to create customer satisfactions. This means that firms must understand buyer behavior so that their marketing programs are an adequate and acceptable response to buyer needs. Marketers are, of course, interested in what causes behavior on the assumption that if causes can be understood and controlled, behavior, in turn, can be predicted. Modern concepts of buyer behavior, both for consumers and organizational buyers, embrace the notion that behavior largely results from certain person-centered factors and environmental, or situation-centered, factors. To take advantage of the person-centered factors, marketers attempt to understand buyer motivation, learning, perception, and cognitive states such as attitudes, values, and belief systems. Marketers must also be aware that behavior is shaped by socialization processes—people's interaction with each other and with their environment. Hence, marketers must look carefully at social class, group influence, and culture as important elements in their planning.

Psychographics is a technique for combining behavioral insights with demographic data to build a more complete and more human portrait of the consumer. This, in turn, opens up the possibility of serving distinct market segments of consumers.

Organizational buying behavior differs from consumer buying behavior more in degree than in kind. Organizational buying behavior is characterized by larger, more formal, informational sources, multiple purchasing influences, multiple buying goals, and a considerable need for resolving conflicts.

Review Questions

1. Why is an understanding of buyer behavior important to marketing planners and decision makers?
2. Define buyer behavior and explain what it means.
3. Is buyer behavior a single act or a process? Explain.
4. What is meant by the transactional nature of buyer behavior?
5. Briefly explain the main characteristics of
   a. the superman model   b. the inner man model
   c. the whole man model of buyer behavior.
6. What "causes" buyer behavior? List and discuss the major person-centered factors and the major situation-centered factors in consumer buying behavior.
7. Describe Maslow's needs-wants hierarchy. How is it related to consumer buyer behavior?
8. Is buyer behavior rational or rationalizing?
9. How does psychographic analysis differ from demographic analysis of buyer behavior?
10. In what ways does organizational buying behavior differ from consumer buying behavior?

Case 6-1

The Hot Rod Pickup

The phenomenal demand for light trucks and truck-like vehicles, which automobile manufacturers gleefully accommodated through the decade of the 1970s, all but dried up with the dwindling supply and soaring price of gasoline in the spring of 1979. But manufacturers, who again report a slow but steady increase in sales, are not about to give up on a lucrative market in these multipurpose vehicles which have become as familiar a sight on the streets of suburbia as on country roads. Actually these vehicles seem to be everywhere. They are rough, rugged, adventure vehicles of the period, with bucket seats, standard transmissions, and roll bars. They are often shag-carpeted on the inside and rakishly decorated on the outside. They come with the comforts of AM and FM sound and assert their individuality with names like "Thud Pucker," "Little Red," "Patty Sue," and "Easy Living" painted on their flanks.

To nudge sales back toward their 1978 record levels, Detroit is keeping what the public liked while modifying the things that kept customers away. Thus, the 1980 models are lighter, more fuel efficient, more stylish, and even more comfortable. "The light truck sales boom was fantastic in the first quarter of 1979," said a manager of truck sales for Chevrolet. But then came the gas lines in the spring and summer of 1979, he commented, and the bottom fell out. "People seemed not so much concerned about fuel efficiency as they were about availability. The summer of 1979 was not a time when people were buying cars—they were waiting in lines to fill tanks of the cars they already had."

In 1978, nearly 4 million lightweight trucks were sold in the United States, a considerable jump in sales from 1970 when 1.4 million trucks were sold.

In some parts of the country the demand in the late 1970s exceeded supply and in some markets in the South, Midwest, and West, light trucks outsold passenger cars.

According to a spokesperson for Ford, which like Chevrolet holds about 35 percent of the light truck market, total industry truck sales were down by more than 35 percent after the fuel crisis of 1979. The sale of Ford's light trucks increased by 71 percent between 1975 and 1978, but the company expects to see annual growth in the 1980s of about 3 percent a year.

"The future looks good," said another Chevrolet spokesperson. "We've given a lot of thought to fuel economy. Where mileage used to be about 8 or 9 miles per gallon, now we've brought it up to 18 or 19, and more improvements are to come. Vehicles will be lighter, perhaps smaller, and will have even more options. People want vehicles that serve several functions, and that is what they get and will continue to get in a truck."

Some of the hot rod magazines have hailed light trucks as the "super cars of the 1980s." And hence, truck marketers are promoting vans, pickups, and four-wheelers as the sporty new vehicles for everyone.

A Dodge advertisement refers to them as "adult toys." The ad is also sprinkled with such words as "macho," "sexy," and "bright and bold like the people it'll turn on most." This appeal comes on top of (and grows out of) the obvious popularity that vans and enclosed pickups have been demonstrating since the mid-1970s. Increasingly they have been identified with pleasure, such as going camping, boating, and attending road races and rallies.

Many buyers are switching to trucks or vans because of their utility. They have the space that a large family needs. They cost about the same as a passenger car and now many deliver comparable mileage. The truck makers have done their best to make them as luxurious as possible.

Virtually every known accessory, comfort, and option available in a car can be found on light trucks—and more. Few cars, for example, have the swiveling captain's chair and lush carpeting that give some vans an extra touch of luxury. Songs and even movies have been made which emphasize the hedonic, erotic pleasures the vans afford.

They have been made so fancy and have become such status items that you can go to the most elegant hotel or restaurant and find as many pickups and vans in the parking lot as you do luxury cars. Some owners confide that their light trucks lend themselves to individual expression better than cars. With vans especially, they state, there is so much more surface to decorate.

Questions

1. Do the buyers of pickups, vans, and other light trucks constitute a distinct market segment for these items? Why or why not?
2. What do you believe are the main demographic characteristics of such buyers?
3. List and discuss what you would consider to be the major buying motives of those who purchase such vehicles. Do you believe these motives are more "operational" or more "psychological"? Why?
4. What are the major "person-centered" factors that contribute to the purchase of such vehicles? What are the major "situation-centered" factors? Explain.
5. How could psychographics help you to explain buyer behavior for such commodities?

Case 6-2

S.C. Johnson & Son, Inc.

Samuel Curtis Johnson, named after his great-grandfather who founded the wax company that Johnson now runs, knows well the problem of attempting to transfer the power of a name long famous in consumer products to a new market. A few years ago, the 48-year-old chairman and major owner of S. C. Johnson & Son, Inc., tried to diversify his company beyond its broad assortment of household waxes, polishes, foams, and sprays. In a dramatic move into the highly competitive personal care field, the firm introduced four new toiletries—and quickly bombed on three of them.

S. C. Johnson has had a considerable success in marketing household products. Many of them have become leaders in the field, making the company the nation's top marketer of nonlaundry household products. These products include Glo-Coat, the first self-polishing floor wax (1932); the first house and garden bug killer, Raid (1956); the first aerosol insect repellent, Off (1957); Pledge, the first aerosol furniture polish (1958); the first aerosol air freshener, Glade (1961); and the first home carpet cleaner, Glory (1968).

In 1971 the company moved into the faster-growing personal care field and ran up against such successful consumer product firms as Bristol Myers, Gillette, and Revlon. S. C. Johnson's first grooming product, a gellike shave cream called Edge, appeared in 1970 and become an instant success. It was followed by three shelf-warmers, or duds: Crazy Legs, a more fragrant version of Edge for women; High Seas, is an aftershave lotion; and a unisex deodorant called Us. Consumer needs for these products had not been well researched. "It was quick, cheap and dirty marketing and it was a mistake," said W. Robert Peterson, executive vice president of S. C. Johnson. "We started ignoring some of the standards we have always had in introducing new products."

In February 1977 the company again launched a massive new offensive into personal care products with a major new toiletry, a huge marketing campaign, and a fresh desire to make it big in the personal care field. S. C. Johnson's new personal care product is Agree, a cream rinse and hair conditioner. The fastest growing segment of the $1 billion hair care business, rinse and conditioner sales have burgeoned at an annual rate of 20 percent, reaching $250 million in 1977. With Agree, S.C. Johnson hopes to capture 15 percent of the market the first year. To achieve this goal, the company began with a $7 million television and magazine campaign along with a $7 million sampling program that put small bottles of Agree into the hands of 31 million women. In fact, S. C. Johnson spent almost as much promoting Agree as the $18 million that went to promote all other hair conditioners in 1977. S. C. Johnson is determined to create a strong image for its new product. To accomplish this, the company launched an extensive consumer research study that sought a number of psychographic profiles from a panel of 2,000 housewives and working women. These women were asked 214 questions about their activities, interests, and opinions. They were also asked about the products they bought. One clear area of interest to the researchers was the women's concern about personal cleanliness and appearance. Many consumers, it was believed, are highly motivated to buy certain products that are perceived as reducing anxiety about cleanliness and appearance. One study

came up with six categories as most meaningfully classifying housewives and noncareer working women:

Outgoing optimists	Self-indulgents
Conscientious vigilants	Contented cows
Apathetic indifferents	Worriers

It was discovered, for example, that the Conscientious Vigilants and the Worriers were more likely to be receptive to products that promised personal cleanliness and better appearance. Contented Cows were described as relaxed, unworried, relatively unconcerned about germs and cleanliness, neither innovative nor outgoing, very economical, not self-indulgent. The study produced clues on the kinds of appeal to use in selling messages beamed at each category of women for various kinds of products.

Behind S. C. Johnson's new product is the classic problem of a company that suddenly woke up to find its established markets maturing. As women have become more involved in activities outside the house, S. C. Johnson executives note, they have become more concerned with personal grooming than with fastidious housekeeping. So the floor and furniture polish markets that S. C. Johnson dominates with a 60 percent market share are growing at less than 5 percent a year. That compares with a 15 percent steady annual growth in the 1950s and 1960s. "We looked around the house and found we were running out of markets to conquer," said Sam Johnson. "We were already polishing the floors and furniture, cleaning the rugs, killing the bugs, sweetening the air and waxing ole Dad's car."

Questions

1. Do there appear to be sound behavioral as well as economic reasons for S. C. Johnson to launch into personal care products?

2. S. C. Johnson's promotional campaign for Agree seems to rest on two assumptions:
- Advertising creates attitudes and attitudes create buying behavior, and

- Sampling leads to behavior and behavior leads to attitudes.

Are these two assumptions sound? Do they jibe with current understanding concerning the role of attitude and the causal nature of attitudes and behavior?

3. Would psychographic analysis seem a wise basis for launching and merchandising the new product, Agree? How are psychographics and demographics related?

Chapter 7

Marketing Research and Marketing Information Systems

It is not always easy to separate myth from reality. Several years ago a college instructor, introducing the topic of marketing research, told his class a mythical story about "Pushcart Tony." Tony Natalie, so the story went, was an Italian immigrant who arrived at Ellis Island like millions of others—penniless, barely able to speak a few words of English, but hopeful for the future. Tony and his family settled in Newark, New Jersey. He could find little available work, so he did what many others like him in those days did—he became a scavenger of other people's trash and junk. Tony fashioned himself a pushcart out of wheels and some spare boards, and he became a familiar junk man in the neighborhood.

However, like other immigrants of those days, Tony had higher ambitions. He yearned to be a grocer and to have his own retail store. From his meager earnings as a junk man, he fed and clothed his family but still managed to save a little money. But Tony did something else that was clever and unique—he carefully looked through the garbage he collected. He examined all the labels of the discarded empty cans, boxes, and packages. He noticed the brands and package sizes people bought most frequently, and he also noticed the prices of the commodities that were most popular. Subsequently, when Tony abandoned his pushcart and became "Tony the Grocer," he used this information as a basis for merchandising in his new operation; he knew the customers of his neighborhood; knew the merchandise they purchased most frequently, the price lines, brands, package sizes, and many other aspects of their purchase consumption behavior. Tony soon became a successful and prosperous merchant. The marketing professor made his point with this mythical story. But remember, it is not always easy to separate myth from reality!

The story of Pushcart Tony highlights the fact that to be successful, business decision makers must constantly be on the alert for leading indicators of business activity: signals and signs that will alert them to possible changes—new markets, changes in competitors' strategy, or general developments in the overall environment holding danger or opportunity for the firm.

Information: The Basis for Decision Making.   All business decisions are based upon information. Sometimes the information is based upon experience, sometimes on hunch or intuition, and sometimes on formal *marketing research studies*. The quality and quantity of information are often good indicators of the quality of the decisions that will be made and the resultant success or failure of the firm. Remember that marketing strategy is a comprehensive plan of action. Planning is deciding in advance what needs to be done. Making decisions is choosing from among alternatives in order to reach specified goals. This means that decision makers need information on which to base their decisions. In short, to manage is to assess the future and to assess the future is to weigh information that points to the firm's options. Because marketing is the firm's response to external opportunities, marketing decision making is disastrous without accurate information about those opportunities. The gathering, processing, and delivery of information is both complex and costly. But a company would be making a grave mistake if it should omit this essential activity.

The Increasing Importance of Research. Most firms and organizations today succeed or fail on the basis of their information. Service organizations must study trends and developments so that they too can meet market demand. For example, firms like H and R Block which specialize in completing private individuals' income tax returns, have found that the demand for their service is directly related to (1) rising consumer incomes, (2) the incidence of working wives in the household, and (3) the complexity of the income tax return forms.

Nonprofit organizations such as the large evangelist organizations of Billy Graham and Oral Roberts feel that they too must engage in market research studies. Before such evangelistic campaigns are taken to particular communities, research is often undertaken to estimate the probable number of persons likely to attend, their present church affiliations, the proportion of population in various age groups, people's attitudes and receptiveness to such programs, and any special characteristics of the people in the community or region.

The Role and Scope of Marketing Research

Marketing research, in the strict sense in which that term is used by the American Marketing Association means "the systematic gathering, recording and analyzing of data about problems relating to the marketing of goods and services."[1] This definition may be a bit too restrictive, but it nonetheless conveys a reasonably good notion about the range and scope of marketing research activities. The basic role of marketing research is to provide, in an orderly and systematic way, the information that will help to identify and solve marketing problems and so help in marketing decision making. This suggests that marketing research is a special kind of project and study effort. Because it is, marketing research efforts are often, though not always, undertaken by outside agencies. The objectives of marketing research are to improve decision makers' understanding of their environment, especially such factors as buyer behavior, reseller behavior, channel organization and function, and the behavior of competitors. Marketing research is used not to replace, but to complement, the judgment and experience of marketing managers, and to aid in the planning and implementation of marketing programs.

The Origins of Marketing Research

Marketing research, as the formal, objective, systematic gathering and analysis of data to facilitate decision making, is relatively new. The field as we know it today began in 1911, with the appointment of Charles Coolidge Parlin as manager of the Commercial Research Division of the Advertising Department of the Curtis Publishing Company. Parlin was the first to gather, analyze, and interpret systematically information that then became the basis for managerial decision making. Parlin's studies stressed such information as incomes, age,

---

[1] *Report of the Definitions Committee of the American Marketing Association* (Chicago: American Marketing Association, 1961).

Figure 7-1 The evolution of marketing research.

1930s	• Sales analysis • Sales forecasting

1940s	• Customer analysis • Store audits • Distribution analysis • Promotional research presentations

1950s	• Product testing • Advertising research • New product analysis • Customer behavior research

1960s	• Marketing info systems • Marketing planning • Marketing models • Marketing experiments

1970s	• Management science • Management info systems • Diversification/acquisition • Economic and tech. forecasting • Consumerism and ecology • Financial analysis

1980s	• Marketing information systems • Futurism

Source: *Marketing Strategies; A Symposium,* ed. Earl L. Bailey
(New York: The Conference Board, 1974), no. 629.

occupation, and educational levels of readership groups, but also included extensive studies of such factors as readership habits and other less demographic factors.

In rather quick succession, marketing research departments were established by the United States Rubber Company in 1915 and the Swift Packing Company in 1917. In 1919 the first book on the new field was published.[2] Figure 7-1 summarizes in chart form the evolution of marketing research.

Since the early 1960s, with the emergence of the marketing concept, marketing research has had near-phenomenal growth and development. Why is this so? Remember that the marketing concept stresses customer orientation and integrated marketing programs designed to produce customer satisfaction. The marketing concept also emphasizes the role of information as the key to both customer satisfaction and profitability. Thus, marketing research has grown apace with the expanded role of marketing as the focus for all business decision making.

With the expansion of the term marketing to include the design, implementation, and control of programs calculated to influence the acceptability of

[2] These facts are from Harper W. Boyd, Jr., and Ralph Westfall, *Marketing Research: Text and Cases,* 3d ed. (Homewood, IL: Irwin, 1973), pp. 15–17.

social ideas,[3] marketing research is increasingly being used as a tool in marketing social ideas, practices, and products. Examples of such marketing research efforts include studies relating to the makeup of consumer panels for an educational research and development center; using research techniques for developing advertising appeals to assist in international family planning; identifying and measuring various market segments for a political campaign; research for locating a new church; and market testing various package designs for oral contraceptives.[4] Marketing research is increasingly being used to aid in the solution of ecological and environmental problems as well as social ones.

The Expanding Role of Marketing Research

An extension of bank marketing services.

By far the most frequent marketing research activities are the determination of market characteristics, the measurement of market potential, the development of sales forecasts, competitive product studies, the study of business and environmental trends, and market share analysis.

In 1947, when the American Marketing Association began its surveys of marketing research by firms in this country, it was estimated that some $50 million a year was being spent on this activity. Present expenditures may now be approaching an annual total of $800 million. Despite this growth, however, marketing research budgets are still low in relation to company sales, advertising expenditures, and money spent on engineering research and development for new products. Expenditures by all firms for marketing research are far less than 1 percent of sales.

Yet today marketing-based business and social problems are getting bigger and more complex. Launching new products entails considerable business and social risk and may require the commitment of millions of dollars. Inadequate or outdated information and intuitive decisions are simply too risky for these ventures. More formal, systematic, and objective efforts are called for. Top management is well advised to recognize the role and importance of marketing research as the necessary backdrop for marketing decisions. The marketing research department is an important reservoir of managerial talent and the marketing researcher an increasingly important link in the decision making structure of the organization.[5]

Marketing Research and Science

Marketing research, which substitutes *science* for intuition, depends upon the scientific method for its validity and reliability. The real test of marketing

[3] Philip Kotler and Gerald Zaltman, "Social Marketing: An Approach to Planned Social Change," Journal of Marketing **35**, no. 3 (July 1971), pp. 3–12.
[4] Gerald Zaltman and Philip C. Berger; *Marketing Research: Fundamentals and Dynamics* (Hinsdale, IL: Dryden Press, 1975), p. 16.
[5] Robert J. Small and Larry J. Rosenberg, "The Marketing Researcher as a Decision Maker: Myth or Reality," *Journal of Marketing* **39** (January 1975).

research, as in all research endeavors, lies not so much in the results of the research as it does in the credibility of the research methods.

The scientific method is thus the hallmark of marketing research; it is characterized by two critical features. First of all, it is based upon careful and accurate classification of facts and observation of their relationships, and sequence. Second, and most important, it seeks to discover scientific laws through observation, the formulation of hypotheses, testing, and the drawing of inferences and conclusions through the use of creative imagination.

Thus, the scientific method is a set of procedures for establishing general laws about observed events and for forming an opinion about events that are yet to happen. The specific steps or procedures of the scientific method are:

1. Ask well-formulated and appropriate questions.
2. Devise testable hypotheses that will answer the questions.
3. State all assumptions.
4. Relate the logical consequences of the assumptions to the problem.
5. Design procedures and techniques to test the assumptions.
6. Test procedures and techniques for relevance and reliability.
7. Test the hypotheses; measure and interpret the results.
8. Evaluate the results.[6]

To illustrate how such a procedure or series of steps might be utilized, consider the following: Suppose a product manager in a cereal firm proposes a packaging change for a cereal. The proper question is, "Will it increase sales?" The hypothesis is that it would. The stated assumptions are that the cost estimates for production and marketing are accurate. The task is then to develop or design a procedure and set of techniques for testing the hypothesis. If the studies support the hypothesis, management can then use this information to decide whether or not to change the cereal package.

It is generally agreed that research means, basically, the systematic investigation of some problems. "Systematic" refers to the scientific method.

Creativity in Marketing Research

One should not necessarily conclude that creativity and imagination play no role in marketing research, nor that good results can be obtained through a kind of automatic, routine, and blind process. Creativity and imagination are essential ingredients in today's marketing research setting. For example, consider the following instances where creativity and imagination played a most important role in market research studies and subsequent marketing programs.

Mail order houses suffer burdensome expenses from their policies of liberal goods-return privileges. Returned merchandise not only means loss of the sale but also results in unusually high operating expenses from excessive handling of merchandise, reinventorying, repackaging, and returning the item to central warehouse facilities. To cut down on the large number of returns, one firm

[6] Mario Bunge, *Scientific Research* **1** (New York:Springer-Verlag 1967), p. 8.

requested its marketing research manager to study this problem and make appropriate recommendations. One critical hypothesis that he formulated and tested led to significant reductions in returned goods; the hypothesis was that the longer the customer waited for goods ordered, the greater the probability the merchandise would be returned. With more efficient order processing, the wait for merchandise was noticeably shortened.

The Ball Corporation provides another example of imaginative, effective marketing research. Several times in the past twenty years, this company had tried, without great success, to expand its line of consumer products beyond home canning jars. One of its items, a toilet bowl cleaner called Bonnie Johnny, was a dismal failure. The marketing research department was then asked to do some studies pointing up promising leads for new consumer products that could be sold through supermarket outlets. One researcher, considering the phenomenal success of Tupperware, sold only through home parties, wondered if Ball might produce and sell a similar high-quality line of food containers to women who disliked or didn't have time for Tupperware parties. After a six-month trial in supermarkets that capitalized on one of the best consumer product names in the United States, Ball was more than confident that it could deeply penetrate Tupperware's 66 percent of the $400 million market in plastic food containers. Ball's new line of food containers, called Freshware, has succeeded because of the correct assumption that many buyers want the convenience of buying food containers when they need them, in supermarkets.

Who Does Marketing Research?

Marketing research is not always done by the firm's own marketing research department. Firms (and there are many) that have no marketing research department can purchase this specialized service from outside organizations. Advertising agencies sell large amounts of marketing research to their clients. These studies are not related simply to advertising, but are also often designed to aid the firm in a wide range of strategic decisions as well as operational problems.[7] In addition, there are many firms that specialize in market research and assist in the design and development of marketing research projects. Major magazine publishing companies and some newspapers, along with radio and television broadcasters, are increasingly supplying marketing research services to their clients on a fee basis. Some banks as well as other lending institutions are also doing this. Finally, academic researchers are frequently called on by private and public institutions to conduct marketing research investigations.

There are both disadvantages and advantages to using outside organizations to carry out the research effort rather than the firm's own talent. The company's personnel are probably more familiar with the company's operations and the complexities of its problems. It may also be cheaper to use the firm's staff, especially if they are already underutilized. On the other hand, a highly spe-

[7] "'Strategic' Research Role Makes Grey Unique," *Advertising Age,* June 14, 1976, p. 20.

cialized outside organization may actually be able to do the research project more efficiently (because of their concentrated abilities and resources) and thus at a lower cost. The real value of using an outside firm or agency, however, is that it places the problem in the hands of independent, objective, unbiased thinkers.

The Marketing Research Process

The marketing research process closely parallels the series of steps outlined earlier in connection with the scientific method. It should be pointed out, however, that the marketing research process will vary with the nature of the

"WE'RE JUST NOT REACHING THE GROUP BETWEEN YOUNG MARRIEDS AND SENIOR CITIZENS."

problem, the amount of money to be spent, and the accuracy of the results desired. Although each project must be firmly rooted in the scientific method, there is no one single marketing research process.[8] Instead, there is a general loose format of procedures that are normally included in marketing research efforts. Figure 7-2 is a detailed illustration of the steps and procedures that may be involved. While following this general outline, a more detailed discussion of some of the elements in the marketing research procedure will be presented.

Statement of Problem

There is no more useless information than the right answer to the wrong problem. Problems that are ill defined and vaguely worded result in an incorrectly focused research effort and produce results that lead neither to increased customer satisfaction nor increased profits. Problem definitions too often focus upon symptoms rather than the issue itself. Sometimes marketing research is not designed to solve a specific problem but, through systematic and objective analysis, to discover *if* and *where* a problem exists. Sometimes information is actually misleading. For example, suppose a marketing manager is well pleased with sales and profits. The firm has shown a steady growth during the past ten years. Yet, a systematic study of the competition shows that almost every other firm in the industry is expanding more rapidly and that their profits are considerably higher. Does our marketing manager have a problem?

Jockey International, Inc., the maker of Jockey underwear, has been using television for the past several years, trying to convince American shoppers that men's underwear does not have to be white. They have had only moderate success. But they have discovered that the real problem was "to put over the basic idea that underwear is as much a fashion item for men as shirts, ties, and suits; to show the variety of colors, styles, and patterns in which Jockey briefs and shirts are available." Having defined the problem, Jockey International then decided to shift their advertising budget of more than $1 million from television to magazines.[9] Why? They simply couldn't show male models wearing these items on television. Here, then defining the problem altered the firm's complete promotional strategy.

The Situational Analysis.   The problem definition emerges out of what is often called "a situational analysis." The final and actual statement of the problem evolves from discussions with those who want the research conducted, the client or user; a review of research on related products; and a study and review of competitive products and markets. This is all part of situational analysis—it requires studying the firm's history, what it has done and with what success. It also demands a careful scrutiny of what the firm is doing now and with what results.

---

[8] See, David A. Aaker and George Day, *Marketing Research,* (New York: Wiley,) 1980, especially Chapter 3, pp. 44–57.
[9] "Why Jockey Switched its Ads from TV to Print," *Business Week,* July 26, 1976, p. 140.

The Development of Ideas or Hunches.   The development of ideas or hunches rests on both the problem definition and the situational analysis. The researcher observes other people for the purpose of generating additional ideas and for getting a "feel" for how consumers behave in purchase situations; their

Figure 7-2   Steps and activities in the marketing research process.

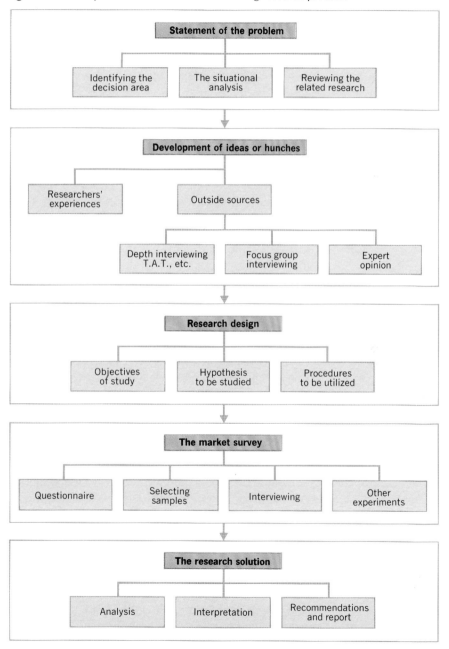

attitudes and learning processes; the frequency and place of purchases; and their reactions to advertising appeals and media.

It is possible to obtain ideas and hunches through a number of methods. It has been fashionable to use depth interviewing and other clinical psychological devices such as projective techniques which utilize word association devices and thematic apperception tests (T.A.T.) as possible sources of insight. These devices, while still in use, have rather questionable results. Depth interviewing, which involves a long drawn-out nondirective process (not directed by the interviewer), is supposed to bring out subconscious motivations or behavioral insights. In thematic apperception tests the subject is shown a picture that is somewhat ambiguous, and asked to project meaning to what he or she sees. To the extent that such devices provide us with additional knowledge about people, they are useful. Nonetheless, in the hands of an untrained researcher, these methods are not only useless, but dangerous as well, because too often they draw erroneous conclusions from too small a sample of people.

More recently an approach called *Focus Group Interviewing* has been used to gain insight into consumer thinking and gather useful information for product development, promotional activities, and other marketing related problems. In this procedure a small group of persons (usually no more than ten) meet to discuss products—categories, attributes, or concepts; consumer needs and uses related to products, or a company; or some other stipulated, or "focused," topic. It is hoped that out of this discussion will emerge useful information based upon first-hand consumer experience, its satisfactions and frustrations.

As is the case with many qualitative marketing research procedures such as depth interviewing, word association tests, and thematic apperception tests, focus group interviewing has its enthusiastic advocates as well as its critics. The detractors claim that the method has serious limitations. They argue that the group situation itself and the personalities of the participating consumers and researchers are variables that influence the opinions expressed and directly affect the outcome. Critics also point out that there are often discrepancies between what the members say in the group and what they do in the market place.

Expert Opinion.   Some persons simply know more than others and some, by virtue of training and experience, know so much more as to be called experts. Almost all managers who need to make decisions on the basis of limited information seek the advice of experts. Experts may be trade magazine editors, industry suppliers, retailers, wholesalers, staff members in advertising agencies, bankers, or economic and marketing consultants. Such people may not be able to solve the marketing manager's particular problem but they can provide valuable insight and help to formulate the specific nature of the problem more precisely. They can also direct the researcher to related studies done in the past or put him or her in touch with others who may have faced similar problems in other trade areas or industries.

Research Design

The research design, the most critical dimension of a marketing research study, is a kind of blueprint that specifies in written form the objectives of the study and the way the information will be gathered; it also gives a clear statement of the hypothesis to be tested.

An integral part of the design of every marketing research study is the determination of what facts are needed and the sources from which these facts will be obtained. Most marketing research studies use a combination of both primary and secondary data.

Primary data is original data gathered for the specific project underway. It either has not previously been published or is not readily available, and is gathered for the explicit purpose of solving a current problem. Such data is obtained from customers, salespeople, competitors, intermediaries, and a host of other sources. Needless to say, primary data is both costly and difficult to obtain. When a researcher observes a number of customers in a supermarket and records the number of items purchased, the average amount spent, whether a shopping list is used, and the amount of shopping time spent, he or she is gathering primary data. On the other hand, this type of information is readily available from a number of published trade sources such as *Progressive Grocer* or *Supermarket Merchandising,* or from studies by the Supermarket Institute. Other industries have similar publications to save marketers time and expense. Information already published is called **secondary data.**

Too frequently, marketing researchers overlook excellent secondary sources and launch studies to generate primary data. Before seeking primary data, all secondary sources should be exhausted. Secondary data does, however, pose difficulties. If a researcher were interested in the in-store shopping behavior of supermarket customers who were single working women earning $15,000 a year or more, the sources listed above would not be very useful. Futhermore, secondary data is frequently outdated. For example, if you need facts about the number of retailers and their sales volume, you might use *The Census of Business—Summary Statistics Retail Trade* which is published every five years by the federal government. Yet, this information is invariably two years old before it is ever published simply because of the staggering complexity of gathering and publishing such enormous amounts of data. Besides, other secondary data may well be biased, or it may have been collected for a purpose alien to the research being conducted, and so irrelevant on two counts.

Collecting Primary Data

There are three ways of collecting primary data: *observation, experimentation,* and *survey.* It is important to recognize that we are talking simply about data-gathering methods and not research design.

Observation.　A trained observer can learn a great deal by noting customer behavior, sales force behavior, product movement, or the buyers' responses to changes in a firm's marketing mix. Observation may be personal or impersonal. For example, a hidden camera may record a customer's in-store movement or his or her eye movements as the customer approaches a given display. An electric recording device stretched across a highway, or at the entrance to a parking lot will tell a trained researcher a great deal about customer traffic movements. Recorders or microphones hidden in the closing rooms of automobile showrooms have been used to monitor customer reactions to proffered deals. This is a questionable practice, however, and has been prohibited by a number of states.

The observation method has many merits, it is relatively inexpensive, it can be done without disturbing or annoying those observed, it is reasonably accurate if done by skilled personnel. It also reduces somewhat the possibility of interviewer bias, although field observer bias can arise. These two kinds of biases can weaken a market research study. The observers must be accurate, diligent, and inconspicuous. Tape recorders and cameras, both of which can be concealed, are often used to improve observational accuracy without changing the behavior of those being observed. This method, however, is limited in its application. The observer can readily report *what* happened, but cannot report *why* it occurred.

Experimentation.   For some, the very notion of marketing research conjures up a vision of elaborate experimentation. The experimentation method of gathering primary data relies upon introducing a selected new variable into a controlled environment, evaluating the results, and drawing relevant conclusions. Experiments are used to discover the best ways for salespeople to allocate their time or to cover their territories; to assess reader reaction to advertising messages, or space devoted to advertising; or to evaluate how "deal prone " customers are and how they react to special prices, promotion events, displays, packages, and many other marketing devices.

An example of experimentation in marketing research is provided by Thomas Coffin in reporting an experiment conducted by the National Broadcasting Company. NBC interviewed a sample of more than 2,400 household heads (both male and female) in a medium-sized market in the Middle West to determine their purchases of twenty-two brands in eleven different household product categories during the preceding four weeks. The results constituted the "before" measurement. At the time of the second interview, a new variable, advertising, was introduced. The sample was divided into two parts—those respondents who had been exposed to television and magazine advertising of the products, and those who had not.

The results generated are shown on the following page.[10]

Another design might assume that the two groups are so closely matched that the "before" measurement of the control group can be inferred from that

[10] Thomas E. Coffin, "A Pioneering Experiment in Assessing Advertising Effectiveness," *Journal of Marketing* **27** (July 1963), pp. 1–10.

	Experimental group (exposed to advertising)	Control group (not exposed to advertising)
"Before" measurement (first interview: percentage who purchased the brands during past four weeks)	19.4 percent (r_1)	19.4 percent (r_1)
Introduction of experimental variable (advertising)	Yes	No
"After" measurement (second interview: percentage who purchased the brands during past four weeks)	20.5 percent (y_1)	16.9 percent (y_1)
Effect of experimental variable	$= (20.5 \text{ percent} - 19.4 \text{ percent})$	$- (16.9 \text{ percent} - 19.4 \text{ percent})$
	$= (1.1 \text{ percent}) - (-2.5 \text{ percent}) = +3.6 \text{ percent}$	

Source: Thomas E. Coffin, "A Pioneering Experiment in Assessing Advertising Effectiveness," *Journal of Marketing* **27** (July 1963).

of the experimental group. The major disadvantage of this alternate design is that it does not permit the researcher to study the effect of the variable on individual members of the sample, because the same group does not receive both "before" and "after" measurements.

Market tests are frequently undertaken as a part of the experimentation approach to marketing research.[11] In such a test, the product is marketed in one or a few areas under conditions that are as similar as possible to the actual market conditions that the product will face. Market tests are usually done for new products, but other elements of the marketing program such as price, packaging, retailer acceptance, displays, and advertising are also sometimes scrutinized. The test market is an opportunity to weigh the marketing plan as a whole. After the test, certain changes in the marketing strategy for the product will likely be considered. Bic Pen Corporation, for example, tested its new Bic Shaver, a low-priced throwaway razor, in Canada. The Bic razor was supported by a $1 million advertising campaign that included television spots, ads in business publications, cross-product sampling, and coupon mailings.[12] The result of this test marketing was used as a basis for launching the product in the United States.

Experiments are always somewhat risky. Researchers may focus upon the wrong variables or draw the wrong conclusions, or a test market may not be representative of actual market situations. Yet again, some problems may lend themselves only to experimentation and, without it, the marketing decision maker may have no meaningful information on which to base strategic decisions.

[11] See Harper W. Boyd and William F. Massy, *Marketing Management* (New York: Harcourt Brace Jovanovich, 1972), pp. 260–261.
[12] "Bic Mum on U.S. Plan, But Razor Expected Soon," *Advertising Age*, June 14, 1976, p. 4.

The Survey.   Much primary marketing research information is collected by survey. A survey consists of gathering data by interviewing (either in person, by telephone, or through the mails) a select number of people (called a sample) from a larger group (called a universe). The sample respondents may be firms, retailers, heads of households, housewives, residents of certain census tracts, or others who might supply information useful to the research inquiry. Most scientific research is probabilistic; that is, although it is impossible to be certain about the future, the probability that a given result will occur is a sufficient guide to action. The degree of probability of the survey results, or the likelihood that they can be said to be typical of the entire universe, is a function of the sample size selected. Quite accurate results can be generated from a reasonably small sample if the sample is selected properly. To be useful, research results must be both *valid,* that is, they must measure what they are supposed to measure; and *reliable,* they must possess a sufficient degree of confirmation.

To use survey methods of marketing research one must make a number of decisions concerning the sampling plan. Several important questions arise at this stage: (1) Who is to be surveyed? (2) How many are to be surveyed? (3) How will those who will be surveyed be selected? (4) How will those to be surveyed be contacted?

Deciding Whom to Survey.   This can often be the critical part of the sampling plan. At this juncture, the researcher must decide what information is needed and who possesses it. Manufacturers of ski equipment, for instance, have discovered that "key influentials" are most important in determining the market success of new models and new additions to the product line. These "influentials" are the ski instructors, members of the ski patrol, and young "hot doggers" and "free-stylers." Hence, any effort to foretell the success of a given line should include surveying persons in these categories.

Some persons are influencers, some are actual buyers, while some are only users of certain products. For example, in industrial products, a purchasing agent may be the actual buyer, the engineering staff may influence what products are bought, but a technician or operator may be the actual user. Consequently, the market success of a given industrial product may ultimately rest with the technician or operator and a market survey that ignored this fact would clearly be flawed.

Choosing Sample Size.   Large samples are usually more reliable, but smaller ones can also yield statistically significant results. Seldom, if ever, are entire universes sampled. With sound experimental design and good sampling procedure, samples of 1 to 2 percent of a total universe or population can be most reliable. The time and money costs of market research studies often lessen the advantage of large samples over small. For this reason small samples are usually preferred. Some studies of an introductory or exploratory nature rely on extremely small samples yet still produce good results.

Choose every fifth student at random.

Deciding How to Select the Sample.   The sampling procedure selected is determined by questions of cost, convenience, and the degree of accuracy desired. Many surveys are based upon random samples, in which every unit in the universe has an equal probability of being selected. A random sample permits the use of statistics to judge the extent to which the data collected is representative of the total universe. Random sampling techniques are used to select a subset (or part) of a total population in such a way that all members of the population, however it is defined, have about an equal chance of being selected for the experiment. Clearly, collecting data this way is less expensive than if every unit were surveyed. The selection of a subset in this manner generally permits more to be known about the reliability of the information obtained from the subset of the total population.

A stratified random sample permits the researcher to use his or her knowledge about the distribution of characteristics in the universe to ensure a more representative sample than could be had with a simple random sample.

Not all samples are randomly selected, however. A nonprobability sample is one in which not everyone has an equal chance of being selected. Some nonprobability samples, called convenience samples, do not lend themselves to the use of statistical inference, nor is an estimate of sampling error possible with this type of sample.

Choosing Ways of Contacting Those to Be Surveyed.   This is a question of sampling method. Those chosen to be surveyed may be contacted by personal interview, by telephone, or by mail questionnaire. Each procedure has its hazards. Many respondents contacted by mail simply refuse to answer, postal costs are rapidly increasing, and mail questionnaires (that are not ambiguous, or even offensive, to some respondents), are exceedingly difficult to construct. Telephoning is costly, but WATS lines (Wide Area Telephone Services) can reduce this factor. Not all those selected for interviewing will have telephones, and those who do may not be at home, or may not wish to be bothered either at home or at work. Personal interviews are threatening to some people, they are extremely costly, and they generally require the use of trained interviewers. Nonetheless, in spite of its shortcomings, each of these methods has its own unique merits when used with particular research projects.

Not all surveys are directed to individual respondents. Surveys are also based upon **consumer panels** and **trade audits**. *Consumer panels* are made up of a preselected group of individuals who regularly report on their buying-consumption behavior. On many panels members keep a running record or diary of their purchases, shopping behavior, media habits, group contacts, or other items of interest to the researcher. These diaries, or purchase inventories, are returned periodically, either weekly or monthly, to the company sponsoring the panel.

Trade Audits   Some surveys simply measure stocks and flows in distribution channels. Many of these trade audits are used to measure the volume of store traffic in particular items. Two of the most prominent firms engaged in store audits of movement of grocery and drug products are Audits and Surveys, Inc., and the A.C. Nielsen Company. Changes in product stocks and flow can also be done at the wholesale level. For example, SAMI (Selling Areas Marketing, Inc.), a division of Time, Inc., regularly reports warehouse withdrawals of all major food chains in a number of metropolitan areas. Their data reflects the movement of as much as 90 percent of total food sales in some markets. In addition, the F. W. Dodge Company collects data concerning the construction of houses, apartment buildings, and office structures throughout the United States, while the Dun and Bradstreet Corporation collects financial data from almost all American firms who wish to use credit.

Some Final Considerations

The marketing research process is concluded with the analysis, interpretation, and recommendations, which are presented to management as a final written report. Like any factual writing, it should be readable, clear, and straightforward. The report should begin with a restatement of the problem and a summary statement of the major research findings. More lengthy and reasoned portions of the report are presented next and the statement concerning the experimental design along with other statistical materials are usually reserved for the appendix.[13]

---

[13] For a detailed update on several facets of marketing research, see "Special Marketing Research Issue," *Marketing News* XIII, **23** (May 1980).

The Limitations of Marketing Research. Marketing research has a number of distinct limitations. It is not magic.[14] Neither is it a cure-all. It will not solve all problems, it alone will not stymie an aggressive competitor nor save a poorly conceived marketing program.

The first of its limits is **time**. It takes time to launch a marketing research effort, and the company may not have time. It may need to respond to a given marketing development now. Second, market research is not an exact science. There are too many variables, too much uncertainty and complexity in the market place to expect marketing research to provide all the right answers. Even if it were an exact science, many organizations lack personnel who are capable of undertaking marketing research. Furthermore, many persons, even high executives, are incapable of judging the quality of marketing research efforts bought from outside research organizations. Third, and finally, marketing research is an aid to management decision making, not a substitute for good management. If used judiciously, it can improve the effectiveness of management decision making and thus lead to improved customer satisfaction and greater profitability. However, marketing research alone does not make such results inevitable.

Figure 7-3 shows the role of marketing research in the company's strategic plan.

Before proceeding, can you answer these questions:
1. Why do marketers feel the need for more and better information?
2. What is the relationship between the scientific method and marketing research?
3. What are the three ways of collecting primary data?

Sales Forecasting: The Key to Integrated Marketing Planning

The key to all integrated planning and decision making within the firm is forecasting. To plan is to decide in advance how to meet or initiate change. Forecasting is anticipating and predicting that change. To be meaningful, forecasting must come before planning. Forecasting is not guessing; rather, much like marketing research, it is the orderly, systematic analysis of trends projected from immediate and past conditions. Forecasts of market conditions and company sales volume are used for the following purposes:

1. Regulating employment, inventories, and purchasing
2. Setting sales quotas, managing the sales effort, and determining the size and character of the advertising appropriation

[14] John A. Martella and Davis W. Carvey, "Four Subtle Sins in Marketing Research," *Journal of Marketing* **39** (January 1975), pp. 8–15.

Figure 7-3 Contribution of marketing research to strategic positioning.

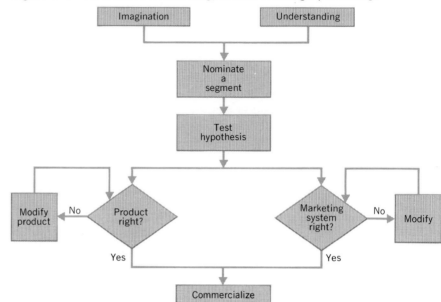

Source: Marketing Strategies; A Symposium, ed. Earl L. Bailey (New York: The Conference Board, 1974), no. 629.

3. Estimating standard costs
4. Budgeting and controlling expenses
5. Planning cash requirements

What Is a Forecast? Marketers try to forecast all those uncontrollable variables that affect the firm's market opportunity. Only by studying the conditions that affect the market opportunity, can the decision maker plan a strategy that will best enable the firm to cultivate that opportunity. Forecasting is a special kind of marketing research. Broadly viewed, forecasting is a progressive activity, moving from an aggregate assessment of massive economic forces to a more refined and specific assessment in the form of a **sales forecast**. Forecasting begins with a wide range of environmental research activities including such macroscopic forces as sociocultural changes, changing consumer tastes, consumer motivation and behavior, broad-gauge economic and demographic changes, and even changes in the political climate. From this broad level of forecasting activity, attention is usually then narrowed to forecasting changes in the industry. From here the focus shifts to the individual company and then, perhaps in the case of multiunit organizations, to the individual unit, and even to single product lines.

Figure 7-4 depicts the kinds of forecasting activity that might be undertaken by a marketing firm. It also shows how, as the forecasting progresses, it becomes much narrower and more explicit in its orientation.

Figure 7-4 Types of forecasting activities.

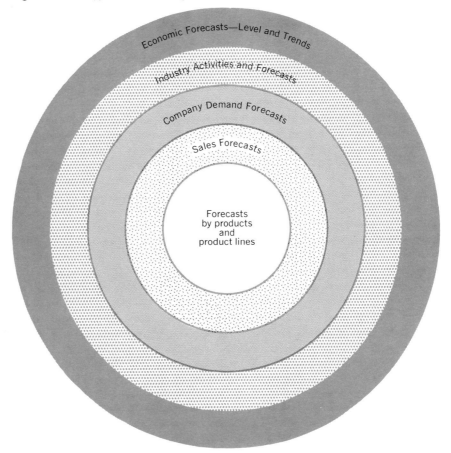

Economic Forecasting and Demand Analysis

Forecasts of the general economy are undertaken by only a few of the larger marketing firms. Others simply use forecasts prepared by government or quasi-government agencies, such as the President's Council of Economic Advisors or the Federal Reserve System. They can also consult the Fortune Poll, and the McGraw-Hill Survey or study the many industry and trade association forecasts and build their own forecasts around these. In addition to providing general economic data, these types of projections focus on such key economic indicators as gross national product, personal income, personal disposable income, and, of course, consumption expenditures.

Market Demand, Company Demand, Sales Forecast.   Market demand is some theoretical upper limit of sales for an entire industry. For example, automobile manufacturers in the United States and abroad are interested in the total market demand in this country for new automobiles in a forthcoming new model year.

Company demand is the total volume of sales expected under given environmental conditions for a specific firm. Thus, the Chrysler Motor Corporation can expect to receive some share of total expected or forecasted industry sales for the given year. Its share of industry sales may be running at about 5 percent of the total. So, if total market demand is forecast at 10 million units for the year, Chrysler Company's demand would be 0.5 million units. The sales forecast, then, is the expected or planned level of sales based upon a given marketing strategy. For example, look closely at Figure 7-5.

Figure 7-5 Company demand and the sales forecast.

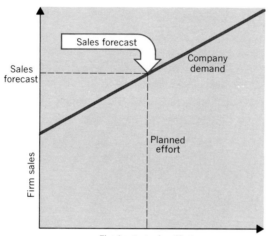

Figure 7-5 shows that company demand is a function of the firm's strategic marketing effort. In other words, demand for the firm's output, as measured by sales volume, increases as the firm intensifies its marketing effort. The sales forecast is the specific level of sales that is expected to result from a given level of planned marketing effort. So, to return to the example, Chrysler's actual sales forecast will depend in large measure on the kind of marketing effort Chrysler executives decide to mount. Should they choose to expand this effort, they will increase their planned effort as shown on the horizontal axis of the diagram, and because company demand is expected to increase positively with increases in its effort, the sales forecast would consequently be higher. Marketing effort determines the sales forecast, not the other way around.

Approaches to Forecasting Company Demand

Forecasting company demand can be accomplished by basing the forecast on (1) what people say, (2) what they do, and (3) what they have done. You will quickly recognize now that gathering information and building a specific forecast of company demand based upon these three approaches require many of the tools of marketing research.

Forecasts Based on What People Say.   Forecasting company demand based upon what people say must obviously focus on finding out what that is. Analysts taking this approach therefore sound out attitudes and opinions of customers, potential customers, sales personnel, intermediaries, industry and trade executives, or any others whose opinions are apt to be valuable. Thus, obtaining such information is basically a marketing research job calling for surveying techniques.

Knowing customer intentions can be an excellent foundation for building a company forecast. However, several important questions do arise in connection with this approach: (1) Are consumers aware enough of their purchasing intentions to be reasonably able to predict their purchases in advance? (2) If they are, can they communicate this information to an interviewer meaningfully and accurately? It is clear that estimates of company demand based upon consumer attitudes and intentions should be used with a great deal of caution.

Forecasts Based on What People Do.   If consumer intentions lack the stability necessary for a company forecast, then a better approach is actual observation of what consumers are doing—buying or not buying—under real or even simulated buying conditions. From these observations, the researcher then extrapolates the findings to a larger body of consumers. As we saw earlier in the chapter, there are several techniques for observing or gathering information on buyer behavior: test marketing, market audits, consumer panels, and fashion boards.

Forecasts Based on What People Have Done.   The more sophisticated and perhaps more objective methods for forecasting company demand consist of the systematic analysis of past behavior in relationship to some variable. This relationship is then projected into the future to produce an estimate of company demand. There are two basic techniques for undertaking such an analysis. The first is referred to as **time-series analysis,** and the second as **statistical-demand analysis.**

Time series is a set of observations on the same variable, such that the observations are ordered in time. The data of the series is regarded as being composed of four elements: a secular trend (T), a seasonal variation (S), a cyclical movement (C), and an irregular variation (I). The most common practice is to multiply these elements together so that the relationship is expressed by the formula $O = TSCI$. This is best explained as follows:

O = original data
T = trend component (the activity underway)
S = seasonal component (the effect or impact of the season or time of year)
C = cyclical component (the effect or impact of cyclical changes such as the business cycle)
I = irregular component (the effect or impact of changes not related to cyclical activities or seasonal variation)

Sometimes the elements are just added together, in which case the formula would be $O = T + S + C + I$. Figure 7-6 is a simple example of trend projection

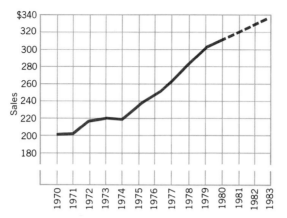

Figure 7-6 Four State Distributors.

on the basis of time series data. Sales figures for the Four State Distributors are shown for the years 1970 to 1980. A freehand line has been drawn from 1980 to 1983 to show what is hoped will be the future values of sales.

The projection of trends from time series data assumes that conditions in the past will continue largely unchanged in the future. This is often the case. However, the greatest danger in such a technique is that it is highly unreliable at the turning point. The turning point is that point where there is a marked or pronounced shift in the trend, say from an increase to a decrease, or vice versa, or a marked acceleration in a direction already underway. Time series analysis must be used with caution and skill. Trend, cycle, and seasonality factors all play important roles in forecasting a company's demand.

Statistical Demand Analysis.   Statistical demand analysis is based primarily on correlation or linear regression analysis. Linear regression analysis rests on the assumption that a dependent variable like sales is related to an independent variable like income. The relationship is thus expressed by a simple linear equation,[15]

$$y = a + bx$$

in which y represents the dependent variable, sales; x the independent variable, income; a represents a constant; and b, the slope of the line. Values of a and b are estimated and by substituting values for x, the equation may be solved for y. Figure 7-7 shows a graphic representation of the relationship between sales and income.

Point A represents the sales, $40,000, that would be realized when average family income is $20,000. As can be observed, the remaining dots represent other relationships between sales and income. Oftentimes a relationship is sought between a dependent variable such as sales and several independent

[15] Not all the relationships are necessarily linear.

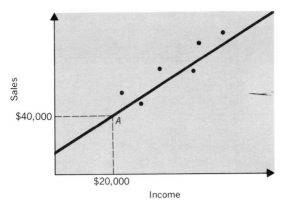

Figure 7-7 Regression relationship—sales and average family income.

variables like income, population, geographic location, employment, and so forth. In this case, the technique is known as *multiple regression analysis.*

The greatest danger of correlation analysis lies in the fact that the system we are attempting to forecast is highly unstable and dynamic. There is real danger that an equation that has worked well in the past may not work well in the future. The forecaster must be careful not to be mesmerized by the formula approach. No equation can ever be a complete substitute for imaginative thinking.

Forecasting, while vital to business success, can wreak havoc with management planning if it is improperly done. Errors can often be reduced by bringing more resources to the forecasting task. When marketing firms involve more people in this aspect of their operation, hire consultants, and use computer analysis, forecasting errors decline.[16]

Before proceeding, can you answer these questions:
1. Why is sales forecasting the key to integrated marketing planning?
2. What is the relationship between company demand and the sales forecast?
3. "Forecasting is a special kind of marketing research." Explain.

Toward Comprehensive Marketing Information Systems

Today, most firms are faced with a unique problem concerning information. While vitally needed in all firms, it is costly to obtain, process, and utilize. The paradox of information is that there is both too much and too little of it. Or,

---

[16] Douglas J. Dalrymple, "Sales Forecasting Methods and Accuracy," *Business Horizons,* **18,** no. 6 (December 1975), pp. 69–73.

rather, there is often too much data and too little information. Data becomes information only when it is available to management in a form useful for both operating and strategic decision making. The quality of information greatly affects the firm's dollar payoff in several ways.[17]

1. It can and does spell the difference in product acceptability to buyers and, ultimately, the product's total market success.
2. It is needed to guide the firm toward suitable and profitable projects, product development, and market opportunities.
3. It suggests to managers and decision makers where promotional dollars and efforts will bring the greatest results.
4. It leads to the setting of optimal prices and the development of creative price lines.
5. By providing insight into competitors' activities, information can prevent unwanted surprises and disruptions in the firm's marketing efforts.
6. Finally, information can create new customers and so maintain the firm's viability.

Given the importance of information, it is no wonder that many firms go to great lengths and suffer great expense to get reliable marketing research studies and market and sales forecasts. Inevitably, the ultimate in gathering and processing information is now being undertaken by some firms.

Marketing Information Systems

In a limited sense, every firm has a crude kind of **marketing information system.** Internal records from the accounting, sales, finance, and production areas constitute a kind of data base from which decision makers can, if they wish, draw information. Many firms, however, using complex management science models, have developed sophisticated computer-based information systems. These systems consist of large data banks; numerous statistical tools or programs for analyzing data; and computer oriented devices for information retrieval, display, storage, and computation. Such systems are truly **marketing information systems,** usually abbreviated MIS.

The MIS is an interacting, on-going, future oriented complex of people, equipment, and procedures designed to generate and process information flows in order to facilitate decision making in the overall marketing program of a company. Instead of seeking information only to solve specific problems, a company will use an MIS continously to solve problems as they arise and to plan future courses of action. Marketing information systems are thus specially designed methods of providing management with a steady flow of needed information on a regular basis—the right information, for the right people, at the right time. A marketing information system underscores the importance of the need to perform research systematically rather than plunging into projects in a panic. A simpler way to look at this array of definitions is to consider MIS

[17] See Zaltman and Berger, *Marketing Research,* pp. 529–530.

as a *system for providing information to management.* Looking at these concepts individually, we observe that[18]

A *system* means order, arrangement, and purpose. It is not an *ad hoc,* "one-shot" procedure.

Information is not just data. As explained earlier, data is raw facts in isolation and does not become information until someone has a need to know and utilizes the data to become informed.

Management requires information and encompasses routine operations, allocating and controlling resources, and the development of creative marketing strategy.

The General Marketing Information System

A general marketing information system is a combination of stored data, computer procedures, and computer hardware systems designed to facilitate the decision-making process for marketing managers. When these components are properly designed, the result is a computer-based system for processing and evaluating information which achieves the following results:

1. The search for and gathering of market and marketing data
2. The editing, sorting, and summarizing of data
3. The processing of data in terms of percentages, ratios, comparative analysis, and tests of statistical significance
4. The storage and retrieval of information
5. The assessment of the data value, reliability, and significance
6. The dissemination of processed data to the relevant decision makers

How It Works.   Let us consider a simple example of how such a marketing information system might actually be used in retail merchandising. A department manager has a great deal of data on the department's past performance. The department manager may very well have a great deal of external information obtained from a survey of people living within the store's market area. This information describes such facts as life styles, newspapers read, television viewing habits, and the other stores they patronize. The manager has most of this information, which constitutes the firm's data base, stored in the company's computer. Now suppose the department manager for young women's wear wishes to know how many units of the new jeans moved last week. She asks the marketing information system and it supplies the answer. Finding that the actual sales of the item were below planned sales, she wonders why the item failed to move fast enough. She may now ask the MIS how much was spent for advertising and where the money was spent. She also asks the computer to specify the number of potential buyers in her trading area and their media habits. The computer then "accesses" (retrieves) the survey data it con-

---

[18] See John T. Small and William B. Lee, "In Search of an MIS," *MSU Business Topics,* Autumn 1975, pp. 45–47.

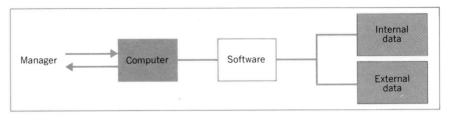

Figure 7-8 A simplified MIS.

tains and "outputs" the information requested. The department manager then redesigns her promotional strategy based upon this information. The procedure and the relationship that exists between the manager-decision maker and the internal and external data are shown in Figure 7-8.

It Is Not Yet 2001. The use of marketing information systems as originally envisioned is not yet widespread, even though the technology and systems design are now available. Yet after many years of attempted development and application, many managers feel that MIS systems benefits do not yet justify the costs. In spite of its apparent lack of overall success to date, many companies feel that the total MIS concept will ultimately be achieved.[19] There are many possible benefits to be gained from the proper use of sophisticated marketing information systems. Great successes have already been achieved using these advanced approaches for evaluating sales territory performance, managing personal selling efforts, and other sales management tasks.

Possibilities never before imagined now exist for banks and retailing firms to develop and utilize exceedingly sophisticated MIS concepts based upon current electronic computer-based innovations. Electronic funds transfer (EFTS) is a system for exchanging value via electronic entry, with no paper processing, and is primarily used for exchanging information among consumers, retailers, and financial institutions. Consumers are being linked to the information systems of retailers and financial institutions within the general framework of EFTS with the growing number of installations by retailers of point-of-sales cash registers (POS), and by banks of automatic teller machines (ATM).

POS devices range from an ordinary telephone for verbal checking of account status to high-speed electronic cash registers that are really the computer basis for a retailer's total marketing information system. Instead of paying cash for goods and services, the customer presents a debit card. When the card is fed into the POS device for processing, the specified amount of money is electronically transferred from the customer's bank account to that of the retailer. When POS devices are combined with orbital scanning devices and the newly adopted universal product code technique, a company has the basis for an elaborate marketing information system to aid its managers in all their decisions: merchandising, inventory, pricing, customer analysis, sales scheduling, and advertising and promotion.

---

[19] See David B. Montgomery and Charles B. Weinburg, "Toward Strategic Intelligence Systems," *Journal of Marketing* **43** (Fall 1979), pp. 41–52.

The automatic teller machines now handle 80 percent of the functions normally performed by regular bank tellers. However, the real potential of such devices is twofold: They permit the electronic storage and retrieval of massive amounts of information useful in every aspect of the economy. And they can become part of an interrelated information system linking consumers, marketers, and financial institutions. No, it is not yet 2001—but we are on our way.

Summary

Organizations thrive and succeed on information. Too much uncertainty, the lack of adequate knowledge or information, hampers marketing decision making. Increasingly, marketing firms are utilizing research as a means of generating information on which to base both their strategic and operating decisions.

Marketing research is the systematic gathering, recording, and analyzing of data about problems relating to the marketing of goods and services. Much current marketing research is being undertaken in order to provide intelligent information on which to base social programs. Marketing research, for whatever purpose, is an orderly and systematic approach to the gathering and use of information. Marketing research, therefore, makes use of the scientific method. A special kind of marketing research activity carried out by many business organizations is called market and sales forecasting. A sales forecast is the expected or planned-for level of sales based upon a given marketing strategy. It is an integral part of all of the firm's strategic planning.

Some firms are moving toward the development of total marketing information systems. An MIS is an on-going, future-oriented complex of people, equipment, and procedures interacting to generate and process information flows in order to enable a firm to make more effective decisions in its overall marketing program. Management information systems have not yet been widely adopted, but they are expected to be more widespread in the future.

Review Questions

1. What is meant by the term marketing research?
2. Explain and discuss the steps in the scientific method.
3. How does marketing research make use of the scientific method?
4. Outline the basic marketing research procedures.
5. What is the difference between primary and secondary data?
6. List and discuss the three chief ways of gathering primary data.
7. Marketing research strives for reliability and validity. Explain.
8. What is meant by market demand, company demand, and the sales forecast?
9. What is the importance of the sales forecast to the firm's overall strategic planning?
10. What is a marketing information system? List and discuss its main components.

Case 7-1

Weber Grills

George Stephen had a hearty appetite for just about anything cooked over a charcoal fire. However, he could not find a smokeless barbecue grill that delivered the slow even heat he wanted. So in 1951, he selected a steel spinning from the Chicago sheetmetal factory, Weber Bros. Metal, of which he was part owner. He instructed the foreman to shape it into a bowl, fashioned a spherical cover, and began using the new utensil in the backyard of his home in Prospect, Illinois.

At the time Stephen had no intention of starting a new business, but today, twenty-six years later, after steady but unspectacular sales, his grill has caught on with consumers and demand for it is accelerating. It is now one of the fastest-selling outdoor cookers in the country, and Ste-

phen's factory in Arlington Heights, Illinois, is struggling to keep up with demand. The suggested retail price for the Weber Barbecue Kettle is about $80 for the popular 22 1/2-inch model, more than for many competing grills. Sales, increasing at about 35 percent a year, approached $25 million in 1977. The market for Weber grills is now worldwide and they are hot sellers in Europe, Australia, New Zealand, and Japan. With all the furor over energy saving, many consumers have an added incentive to shun the gas, electric, or microwave oven in favor of open air cooking.

Weber Barbecue Kettles' distinguishing characteristic is their versatility. Their dome distributes heat uniformly, making it possible to cook anything from a suckling pig to the traditional

hamburger. It will even bake bread or cook an entire dinner. Another desirable attribute is that the grill is a penny-pinching charcoal miser. When the dampers are closed, the fire is quickly extinguished for lack of oxygen and the partially burned charcoal can then be reused. Seeing these features, Stephen's neighbors requested copies of his first grill. After he made a few of them, demand became so strong that in 1958 he left the sheetmetal company to found Weber-Stephen Products Company and make the grills full-time. In 1964, the company took over an old factory in Arlington Heights so as to increase their capacity and output.

The grill has been promoted in television spot commercials and in live cooking demonstrations in shopping centers and department stores around the country. During the commercials "Sammy Scorch" messes up a meal on an old-style barbecue while a jaunty, nattily dressed "Freddie Flavor" prepares smokeless but tasty dinners on his Weber.

Stephen's grill has made him a millionaire and his firm now employs more than 200 persons, including five of his twelve children. His present plans are to start a promotion campaign to make Weber grills a product to be purchased and used year-round. Before beginning this effort, however, Stephen, who really has little background in marketing, is considering hiring

a marketing research consultant or contracting with his advertising agency for a research study to gather information on the relative wisdom of this undertaking.

Assignment

You are to advise Stephen, by written report, on the following:

1. The advantages and disadvantages of the three principal ways of collecting primary data: observation, experimentation, and by survey.
2. After this initial report and a discussion with Stephen, he tells you that he plans to go ahead with a market research study based upon a consumer survey. He then instructs you to prepare for him, prior to a meeting with his advertising agency, a position paper briefing him on the fundamentals of consumer surveys, what they are, what they attempt to do and how.
3. Finally, Stephen has requested that you outline in detail the procedure and steps to be followed in launching a marketing research study to determine the feasibility of promoting the Weber Barbecue Kettle as a year-round product.

Case 7-2

Sears DieHard Battery

In 1966 Sears was in the battery business—in a big way. Sears, as a matter of fact, sold quite a few batteries in the fifties and sixties but these were basically low-priced. The early Sears battery, like most competitive models, was the basic black box with two poles, and it did a good job of starting a car. Sears then perceived an op-

portunity to introduce a product at the top of the line, make it the best replacement battery on the market, advertise it aggressively, and perhaps increase their market share—not only in batteries but in other automotive lines as well. One Sears executive, Judd Sackheim, national merchandise manager of automotive

products, commented, "We knew this was risky, because low-end batteries were a very good percentage of our automotive business." Sears therefore began to work with its supplier, Globe-Union, to develop this superior battery. What emerged was the Sears DieHard Battery. It soon was beating anything on the market at the time.

At that time, of course, all batteries were black. Sears felt that a distinctive exterior would be an asset to an aggressive marketing program. So after consumer testing, it was decided to make the battery white to set it apart from all others. And because Sears wanted to make their premium battery a household word—and today it largely is—they searched for a name they felt would stand for the best battery on the market. Consider the following portion of a position paper put together some ten years ago by Sears' advertising agency. It sums up Sears' feeling about the name they eventually gave to their battery.

No one has really tried to capture the spirit of a battery. The first thing we'd like to do is throw away the battery book and talk about batteries as people think about them. A bat-

tery has life. A battery is created and goes to work and dies. A battery needs water. Thus let's talk about it the way people think about a battery: the heart of the car. Let's give the Sears' battery a name that talks to the point. The DieHard. Do you know what a diehard is? Well, according to the dictionary it's "one who resists vigorously and stubbornly till last." According to the popular vernacular, a die-hard is a tough old coot who just doesn't know the meaning of defeat. The perfect battery is something like the perfect husband. He's a tower of strength when you need him. He lives a productive life. And he doesn't get sick when the weather gets cold. He's Mr. Strong. Mr. Silent. Mr. Tough. Clint Eastwood would make a hell of a battery. A DieHard.

So Sears created their tough battery and named it the DieHard. They then decided that to get on the map as a premier battery retailer, they had to tell as many people as possible, as quickly as they could, how great the Diehard actually was.

Their marketing effort was pegged to a massive research program. As Sackheim put it, "We used all kinds of research, primary and secondary: exploratory groups, concept tests, selling proposition screens, commercial testing—pre and post, campaign trading, brand trend analysis, and attitudinal studies. We may not be the most sophisticated (market researcher) but we try."

From this research, Sears learned what they believed was the principal reason people buy batteries—or more importantly, what people consider the most important benefit of a battery purchase. This finding was simple but profound. It was the ability to start the car in all kinds of circumstances or, as Sears now puts it "The DieHard starts your car when most batteries won't."

Sears' market share began to skyrocket and today the company remains number one in the battery replacement market. The company's management believe that the measurable benefits of the DieHard's success are probably only a fraction of the intangible boosts for corporate image, store traffic, and consumer perceptions of overall Sears' product quality.

Sears has developed a reputation for aggressive marketing tactics that they believe serve to keep them awake to product improvements, competitive activity, advertising and promotion, and all other facets of the marketing mix. Sears calls this "constant attention to the total marketing concept" (TMC), and they believe it has kept the DieHard number one in the battery business for a long time. The DieHard has become a part of the American language, an institution.

Questions

1. Does Sears, based upon the facts presented in this case, appear to be a firm committed to (a) the marketing concept, (b) consumer orientation, and (c) marketing research? Explain.

2. What does this case illustrate about the linkage between marketing research and decision making?

3. Because of Sears' success with building and marketing batteries, some have suggested that the company build and market an electric car. How could marketing research help Sears decide this issue?

Chapter 8

Product Planning
and Development

Each year, the American Marketing Association (AMA) presents an achievement award to a company outstanding for marketing leadership, successful and sustained marketing performance, good corporate citizenship, and innovativeness. Recently, the AMA's achievement award was won by Walt Disney Productions.[1] This company has a corporate philosophy that emphasizes quality and customer satisfaction. The Walt Disney Productions Company, whose films and recreational playgrounds are known throughout the world, is typical of firms whose success rests on customer satisfaction through effective *product planning and development.*

A synergistic approach, "total marketing," is the concept employed by Walt Disney Productions since the early days of Mickey Mouse cartoons. This total marketing system embraces a unique brand of product development combined with effective merchandising and promotional activities. From its early beginnings, Walt Disney Productions has catered to family recreation and entertainment that is clean, wholesome, fun, and educational. The company stresses the importance of such basic marketing activities as market research, careful tailoring of products and services to customer needs, well-targeted advertising, and quality implementation of total corporate effort.

As you will observe, these are the basic hallmarks of many successful companies; their key element is "finding and meeting the needs of customers."

Finding and meeting customer needs is in large measure the essence of *product planning and development.* Walt Disney Productions, like so many successful companies, constantly renews its commitment to develop, make, and market innovative, easy to use, high-quality *products.*

Product planning is the originating, evaluating, and development of new ideas that can be profitably sold in the market place. Clearly this is one of management's central tasks. Without "products" there is nothing to market, and without marketing there is no business enterprise. The firm largely succeeds or fails on the basis of this activity. Promotional effort, pricing tactics, and management of channels of distribution are all activities that are basically designed to facilitate product and service movement for the purpose of satisfying perceived customer needs. Products, those "bundles of goods and services," are the reasons for the transactions and exchanges which transpire between the firm and its customers. The way it plans and develops its products is, in many ways, a measure of the firm's consumer orientation. Firms that are truly consumer oriented make a concerted effort through management initiatives, marketing research, consumer studies, and internal organization to put out the products and services that customers demand.

Product Policies and Company Success. Product policies, that series of preliminary decisions regarding what to make and sell, always underlie effective market performance. A look at leading marketing organizations, both American and international, reveals that market success inevitably rests on

---

[1] "Walker Accepts AMA Achievement Award for Disney," *Marketing News* XIV, 1, July 11, 1980, pp. 1 and 9.

their ability to bring forth a stream of desired **new products.** To do this, they must have a well-organized system for developing new products, well-balanced and coordinated **product lines,** and an effective and balanced **product mix.** In most companies, new products do not occur by accident. They are the result of strategic planning, beginning with a careful assessment of customer wants.

Today product planning and development is a high-risk management effort in an increasingly hostile environment. Yet, this vital activity, if successful, wins for the firm increased market share, greater profitability, and survival itself. During the past twenty years, a rising proportion of both sales and profits have come, essentially, from expansions of product lines.

Fundamental changes in Americans' life styles have dramatically upset the historic stability of consumer product offerings. Change is inevitable. Perhaps 70 percent of successful new products will be obsolete in ten years; 60 percent of a company's sales may come from products not in existence five years ago; the oldest model in a firm's catalog may be only three years old. And one out of every five people working for a company owes his or her job to a product unheard of ten years ago. To adjust adequately to dynamic markets, a firm's product and service lines must reflect the new consumer demands. Its product is important in creating the firm's overall corporate image. Whether customers see a corporation as progressive and geared to serving their needs depends in large measure on how they perceive the firm's products. As far as most customers are concerned, the company is the product.

In this as well as the chapter to follow, we will analyze product planning and development as part of the overall marketing strategy.

Product Planning and Development: Basic to Strategic Marketing

Risks and Gains

Creating, testing, and developing new-product ideas are enormously risky and absorb a great deal of management time and company resources. Yet a successful new product can bring the firm tremendous profits as well as other benefits. It is the possibility of such large gains that entices business people into high-risk ventures. An examination of the successful firm shows that their achievement can be largely attributed to the size and intensity of their research and development efforts. For example, Dr. Edwin Land, founder of the Polaroid Corporation, spent $500 million developing the SX-70 camera.[2] His huge success led to Kodak's response—spending six years and millions of dollars to produce a similar instant picture camera.[3]

Firms can lose millions of dollars with new product introductions. Polaroid's venture into Polavision was a monumental financial disaster. Ford's failure

[2] Dan Cordtz, "How Polaroid Bet Its Future on the SX-70," *Fortune*, January 1974, pp. 82–87.
[3] Kodak's Instant Picture Camera," *Popular Science*, July 1976, p. 55.

with the Edsel is still a classic, often quoted, example of new product failure, as is Dupont's experience with synthetic leather which it called Corfam.

Spending large sums by no means guarantees that a new product will find a market. A new home incinerator that cost the Dravo Corporation $200,000 to develop was completely ignored by customers when it reached the market place.[4] Another study of 125 companies showed that 20 percent of new industrial products, 18 percent of new services, and 40 percent of new consumer products failed to meet company profit and sales expectations.[5] These statistics are for products and services actually launched. And for each one of these entries, fifty or more alternatives may have been abandoned somewhere earlier in the product planning and development process. For example, a leading management consulting firm studied new-product success in fifty-one companies. Of every fifty-eight ideas presented for possible development, only one eventually wound up as a product meeting new-product acceptability criteria.[6] The results of this study are shown in Figure 8-1.

Of the fifty-eight ideas, an average of twelve pass the initial screening test. Of these twelve, an average of seven remain after an evaluation of their profit potential. About three survive the actual product development process, two of these three survive test marketing, and finally, one is successful. The price of new products, of course, must carry the burden of the entire management effort and expense devoted to all the products—even the ones that failed.

Thus, we see that product planning and development bear considerable risk, stemming from several factors.[7] First, the investment required for product development is continually climbing. In some industries, it has doubled or tripled during the last ten years. Most new-product ventures have high breakeven points, meaning that the sales revenue required to cover the fixed and variable costs is high. It also means that the period needed for recouping the money devoted to product development (the payback period) is long. Finally, competitors react swiftly to successful new products, shortening the **product life cycle**. For the initiating company this means a short period in which to reap the rewards of their market success.

Management Is Reducing Risks.   The real test of management ability is how well its decisions reduce risk. The new environment of marketing—energy shortages, high interest rates, increased competitiveness, shorter **product life cycles,** higher breakeven points and extended payback periods—has made new-product development more risky. This function is in large measure the business of asset management—utilizing the limited resources of the firm in the most economical way possible. It must be done with great care. To keep risk at a minimum, many companies are carefully reviewing the entire new-

[4] New Products: The Push Is on Marketing," *Business Week*, March 4, 1972, pp. 72–77.
[5] David Hopkins and Earl Bailey, "New Product Pressures," *The Conference Board Record*, June 1971, pp. 16–24.
[6] *Management of New Products* (Chicago: Booz, Allen and Hamilton, Management Consultants, 1968), p. 9.
[7] Thomas A. Staudt, "Higher Management Risks in Product Strategy," *Journal of Marketing*, **37** (January 1973).

Figure 8-1 New-product success and the stages in the product development process.

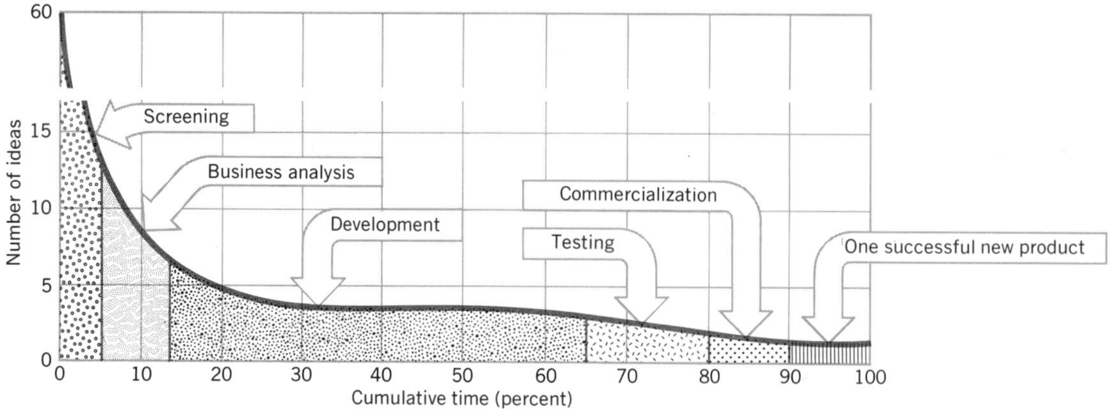

Source: *Management of New Products* (Chicago: Booz, Allen and Hamilton, Management Consultants, 1968), p. 9.

product process. Consequently, more checkpoints are being established during projects so that those with low odds for success can be aborted early enough to prevent wasted funds.[8]

The Role of Product Planning and Development

The purpose of product planning and development activities is to assure the firm that it will have a balanced assortment of goods to meet the anticipated needs of the market place. The firm produces and sells what it perceives is needed and desired. Product planning and development activities are thus a vital bridge between the economic and technological capabilities of the firm and the aesthetic, social, and economic perceptions of consumers.[9]

All Members of the Distribution Channel Are Affected.   Product planning and development affects all members of the distribution channel, not just manufacturer-marketers. What is called product planning and development by manufacturer-marketers is called *merchandising* by resellers such as whole-salers and retailers. Whatever the process is called, the goal is to have a balanced assortment of goods to meet expected customer demands. When retailers and wholesalers speak about their merchandising efforts, they are alluding to all the activities aimed at having the right goods, at the right time, in the right quantities, at the right prices and in the right places. Retailers and wholesalers who fail in their merchandising tasks are failing in their total marketing responsibilities.

[8] "Conference Tells Marketers, Researchers How to Cut New Product Development Risks," *Marketing News*, **9**, no. 20 (April 23, 1976), p. 6.
[9] Edgar A. Pessemier and H. Paul Root, "The Dimensions of New Product Planning," *Journal of Marketing* **37** (January 1973), pp. 10–18.

Industrial marketers must be equally alert to their product planning and development duties. Their market success is also dependent upon having a well-defined and -implemented product planning and development procedure.

Terms and Concepts

It is time now to discuss more precisely some of the terms and concepts marketers use in product planning and development.

What is a Product?

We all have an intuitive notion about what a product is—or do we? A product is *Playboy Magazine*, or Pillsbury's layer cake mix, Pillsbury Plus, or Ford's Escort or Mobil Oil's Mobil 1, or Water Pic's series of antismoking filters called "One Step At A Time." Yes, these are products, but only in the narrow sense of the word. A hair trim and styling is also a product. The removal of a dent in your automobile fender is a product, as are banking services, home maintenance, security systems, travel, and a host of other services. As mentioned in another chapter, services, of infinite variety, will become more important, actually larger in dollar volume, than tangible products in the postindustrial society. Innovations in services are already beginning to compete in the market place with new products. Many firms are now searching for areas of social improvement that match their capabilities—and marketing, in its broadened responsibility, will be expected to sell these services at a profit.

Expanded Definition of Product.   We need an expanded view and an expanded definition of a product. *A product is really a bundle of expectations.* From the standpoint of a user, a product is the right to own or use a bundle of need satisfactions. A product is all those things offered to a market, including physical objects, services, amenities, and satisfaction not only from the physical product or services offered, but from personalities, ideas, and organizations as well.

Marketers sometimes talk about the "core" or the "generic" product. Someone buying cosmetics is not buying just the product's chemical ingredients; that person is buying beauty, acceptance, and approval. The householder who buys an electric drill is buying holes and the camera buff who buys photographic supplies is buying nostalgia, a chance to be creative, and happy memories. The actual "product" is simply the packaging and marketing of a core product whose attributes are converted into customer benefits. The marketer's task is to merchandise benefits, not necessarily features. Thus, a porcelain interior (a feature) on GE's "pot scrubber dishwasher" is converted into "longer product life," "greater cleaning ability," and "lower maintenance," all of which are benefits. Successful marketing usually means "benefitizing" the product. Have you seen a Midas muffler ad on television? Do they benefitize their products? Now for another question: What is their product? You should find the answer in the next paragraph.

Products, more broadly conceived, are benefits offered to consumers by both profit-seeking and nonprofit organizations. Education, entertainment, even religion, are products. A funeral consists of physical products (burial plot, vaults, caskets, clothing), services (embalming, cremation, cosmetic treatment, hair styling), and other amenities or satisfactions (softening grief, assuaging guilt). Products are goods like tape recorders and jeans. Products are also services such as preparing a tax return, servicing a car, or counseling students at a sex education clinic. In addition, products are ideas such as the need to drive defensively, prevent child battering, pass the Equal Rights Amendment, or to "think metric."

The broadened concept of a product is often referred to as the **total product concept.** It means that when marketers talk about products, they are not referring just to a physical good or service, but have in mind the physical product (if there is one); the services; and the total complex of want-satisfying attributes or desired benefits, including branding, labeling, and packaging.

New products are simply those that are basically different from the goods, services, and bundles of benefits already in the market place.

Product line is a group of products closely related either because they satisfy a class of need, are used together, are sold to the same customer groups, marketed through the same outlets, or fall within given price ranges.

Product mix is the aggregate of products offered for sale by a firm or business unit.[10]

For example, the Kodak EK6 and EK4 instant picture cameras are new products; all of Kodak's cameras, on the other hand, constitute a product line. Eastman's product mix consists of literally thousands of products marketed through six major market divisions—business systems, consumer graphics, motion picture and audiovisual, professional, finishing, and radiography.

Product Planning and Development Objectives

There are many other reasons why firms deliberately originate, evaluate, and bring to commercial success a constant stream of new products. New products are the bridge between the firm and its future. Combined with existing successful offerings, they are the building blocks of the firm's marketing mix and strategy. Product planning and development policies must also take account of the firm's technological capabilities, engineering competence, financial structure and needs, and most importantly, its distribution capabilities (field sales force, advertising, channels of distribution, and physical distribution facilities). Thus, product planning and development policies depend on many factors. However, in most instances the decisions concerning planning and development of new products will be analyzed according to the following considerations.

[10] The terms *product line* and *product mix* are from American Marketing Association, Committee on Definitions, *Marketing Definitions: A Glossary of Marketing Terms* (Chicago, 1960).

1. The possibility for utilizing existing marketing know-how and facilities, such as:
   a. the same distribution channels for both new and old products
   b. existing field sales organization or other distribution methods
   c. existing physical distribution facilities such as warehouses and shipping and transportation facilities
   d. securing market advantage by having a more complete line, thus acquiring greater dealer or distributor support and/or gaining multiple sales because the sale of one product makes it easier to sell related items

2. The chance of stabilizing the firm's sales curve. Additional sales can supplement seasonal merchandise, as Jantzen Swim Wear proved when they introduced a line of year-round sportswear for women. If a product is subject to cyclical downturns, a broadened product line would offset such fluctuations.

3. Production, engineering, and financial savings.
   a. using the same production facilities for new products as for old
   b. eliminating or reducing excess or idle capacity
   c. utilizing by-products or raw materials common to both new and old products
   d. utilizing a greatly accelerated cash flow or idle capital
   e. replacing products whose profit possibilities have shrunk

Always, of course, the overriding consideration in determining new-product planning and development policies is their impact on customer satisfaction and company profit.

Product Planning and Development Strategy

There are a number of ways companies can answer the strategic questions surrounding product planning and development. In many instances a firm will expand its product offering by buying out other companies. In others firms seek merger opportunities enabling them to offer an expanded line or mix of products. At other times, firms enter into venture agreement with other companies, as was done on a grand scale in the building of the English-French Concorde, the supersonic passenger airplane. Finally, of course, there is the "do it yourself" route. The company undertakes on its own initiative, and with its own resources, the expansion and development of its product line or mix. Figure 8-2 shows, in a very basic sense, how the firm may respond to market opportunities.

As shown in Figure 8-2, the firm has a number of product policy alternatives in relationship to its perceived market opportunity. First, the firm can market its present products to existing markets (Cell A). This may be a steady-state market opportunity, or it may be a mature, if not a declining, one. The firm may offer its existing products or product mix to new markets (Cell B). This is a way of expanding market opportunity and prolonging product life cycles,

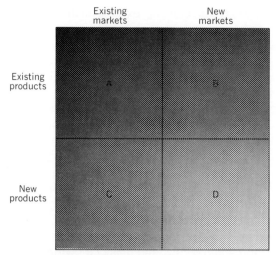

Figure 8-2 Product strategy and market opportunity.

Existing product/new market.

profitability, and even survival. The promotion of Arm and Hammer baking soda as a deodorant for refrigerators and as a safe cleaner for fiberglass products is an example of this strategy. Or, the firm may decide to create new products for existing markets (Cell C). Vicks' Day Care, the counterpart of its highly successful Nyquil; Purina's dog food, Fit and Trim; Procter and Gamble's Puritan cooking oil; and Bristol-Meyers, Datril 500 are all examples of a

Existing market/new product.

"Tommy and I used to get our raisins in raisin bran. But then we discovered Wheat & Raisin Chex® cereal. It has plenty of plump, juicy raisins. But it's made with toasted squares of wheat. They taste better than bran flakes and stay crispier in milk. It tastes absolutely delicious. To us, Wheat & Raisin Chex® is definitely a better way to get our raisins."

product strategy whereby well-known firms with high customer acceptance built new product additions upon existing market successes. Finally, a daring strategy with a small probability of gaining a very large market and satisfactory profits is the creation of new products for new markets. Successes with this strategy can be spectacular. Television was once in this category, as video cassette recorders are now. Some firms shun this approach completely, while others consider their hallmark to be that they are always in the forefront, creating new products for new markets.

New products/existing markets.

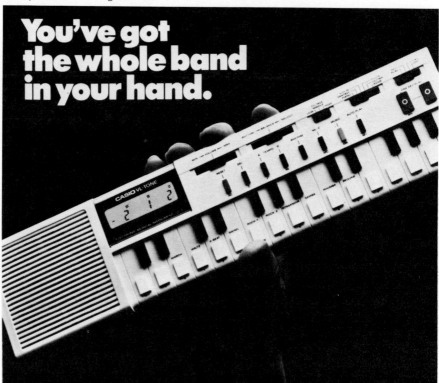

You've got the whole band in your hand.

Now Casio introduces five instruments and a rhythm section–in the new VL-Tone.

The Casio VL-Tone is an amazing new instrument that's so advanced, even a person who's never tried playing Chopsticks can compose a recognizable song, the first time out.

The secret is Casio's development of a very small computer chip that has a very large capability. With it, the VL-Tone lets you pick any one of 5 different instruments to play; record up to 100 musical notes and play them back; select pitch and tempo; go up and down 2½ octaves; and if you want to hear the beat of a different drum, choose from 10 pre-programmed rhythms that swing from rock to rhumba.

The VL-Tone is battery operated and has its own speaker or can be plugged into a hi-fi or professional amplifier. And, so portable you can take your act anywhere.

Even more amazing, in addition to being an incredible musical instrument it's also a full-function calculator.

So, if you're known as a one-fingered player or an accomplished musician, the Casio VL-Tone can put a whole world of music in the palm of your hand. As well as a song in your heart.

AT CASIO, MIRACLES NEVER CEASE.

Casio, Inc. Consumer Products Division: 15 Gardner Road, Fairfield, N.J. 07006 New Jersey (201) 575-7400, Los Angeles (213) 923-4564.

Maintaining Viability

There are few products that remain constant over time. The highly touted and successful Volkswagen (Beetle), while changing little in exterior for fifteen years, underwent extensive engineering changes. This is the case with many products and it is an important element of the strategy of many firms: to begin with a basic product, establish its market acceptance, and continue to improve it over time. Some firms extend this strategy by broadening their line of products or service assortments, thus reaching a larger segment of the market. Automobile and appliance manufacturers follow this route extensively. Another strategy frequently employed is to broaden the assortment or product mix. General Motors not only produces a whole series of passenger automobiles, but they also make trucks, diesel locomotives, tanks, armored personnel carriers and, through their Frigidaire division, a whole line of major household appliances.

Some companies attempt to minimize the risks of product development by practicing only imitative differentiation, or "me too-ism." They simply wait until a new product has won a solid market and then copy, to the extent possible, the better features of the successful product. Then, through promotion and other marketing efforts such as labeling, branding, packaging, or pricing, they attempt to differentiate their product in the minds of prospective customers. In any event, firms maintain their viability and survive in large measure through their product planning and development strategies.

The Product Planning and Development Process

Product planning and development is a systematic process for originating, evaluating, and developing new-product ideas, and adopting those showing promise so that they can be profitably sold in the market place. Thus, management procedures must be employed that generate, collect, and screen ideas for new products, and then develop, test, and commercialize the new items. Figure 8-3 shows a flowchart that depicts, step-by-step, the sequence of product planning and development procedures.

Figure 8-3 is a rich source of information, showing in detail not only the steps in the product planning and development process, but also the relationship of product planning and development to a whole host of other marketing strategy activities such as pricing, promotion, channel selection, market opportunity analysis, and sales forecasting.

In the pages to follow, we will examine some of the key points in each of the major steps in the product planning and development process.

The Search for New-Product Ideas

New product ideas come from many sources. Some originate within the firm itself: suggestions from salespeople, engineers and designers, and other company personnel. Some even come from customers who write in to say, "Why

Figure 8-3 Flowchart of the product development process.

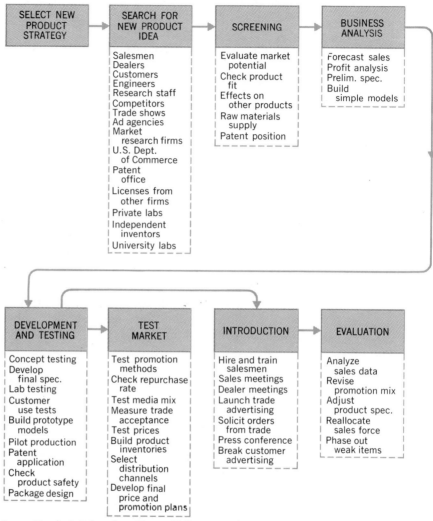

Source: Douglas J. Dalrymple and Leonard J. Parsons, Marketing Management Text and Cases, New York: Wiley 1980, p. 256.

don't you make a product that does thus and so?" For many companies there are literally thousands of new product suggestions which must be screened, evaluated, and reviewed. Trade shows, competitor activity, patent developments, and inventor efforts are all possible sources of new product ideas.

New technology is always an important source of new-product ideas. The telephone, the light bulb, the radio, the automobile, the transistor, the electronic chip, nuclear power—all have given rise not only to new products, but to vast new industries as well. Perhaps the most spectacular example of this is the United States space program. It has spawned among others, Teflon, weather and communication satellites, hand-held computers, and electronic wrist-

"Looks like R. & D. is onto something big."

Drawing by Chas. Addams; © 1973 The New Yorker Magazine, Inc.

watches. Other lesser-known by-products of the space effort include freeze-dried food, battery powered tools, lubricants and quality control techniques that extend product life, monitoring systems in hospitals, traffic control devices, and grooves in pavements to drain off excess water. Football teams wear helmets lined with a foam padding developed for NASA to reduce shock from impact. Electronic ignition was first developed for use in space vehicles. These are only the benefits consumers see. More than 99 percent of the benefits of new products, services, or processes generated by the space program are hidden from the layperson's view. Many of them are not related to consumer markets, some are dull, and most are complex. Nonetheless, in industrial markets and in manufacturing processes, these by-products have added billions of dollars to the American economy, providing jobs, saving lives, and making things more comfortable for all of us.

The starting point in the search process for new ideas, however, is not technology, company salespeople, or competitors' activities, but the *consumer*. Two points should guide firms in their search: (1) Marketing begins with the customer, and (2) products must fill needs.[11] The exceedingly high failure rate of many new products is testimony enough that these two factors are often overlooked.

The key to generating new-product ideas is the ability to visualize consumers' needs through their eyes rather than through the eyes of the company's engineer. It is important that each idea be investigated with a clear understand-

---

[11] John G. Hughes, "Marketers Must Focus Upon Future Consumer Behavior," *Marketing News* XIII, no. 16, Feb. 8, 1980, p. 6.

ing of what need that new product must satisfy, how important the need is, who has it, and under what conditions.

Many new-product ideas result from pinpointing consumer problems or dissatisfactions with available products. One large New York-based advertising agency, Batten, Barton, Durstine, and Osborn, uses what they call "problem research" to pinpoint deficiencies that consumers perceive with existing products and services. The use of such a "problem research" approach led BBD&O to devise the "Dry Look" of Gillette and Burger King's "Have it your way."

Screening New-Product Ideas

Ideas for new products must be carefully screened at an early stage. They are generally converted into what is called a simple **concept statement**—a two- or three-paragraph description of the product idea and the benefits it will supposedly provide.

The concept statement is then subject to a preliminary screening analysis that determines the practicality of the ideas—amount of investment required, market possibilities, customer reactions, and channels of distribution to be employed. The screening process is usually a two-step procedure. First, all new-product concepts are examined and those that are obviously unsuitable are rejected. The next step screens for those product concepts that might be feasible.

Product screening is the time to ask a series of "what if" questions.

* What if the product should not live up to its volume forecasts?
* What if competitors should introduce a similar product immediately?
* What if prices must be dropped 25 percent below planned levels?
* What if the product cannibalizes sales from other products of the company?
* What if existing company technology or plant capacity is insufficient to handle the added volume from the new product?

Many companies develop exhaustive checklists for use during the screening process to evaluate the candidate product's suitability to the company's marketing environment, to determine if the proposed item can survive under conditions different from those forecast, and to estimate the range of conditions under which the suggested product might succeed.

The proposed products are ranked by the new-product planning and development committee (or whatever group has been structured for managing this process). Table 8-1 shows a representative form used by some companies for this ranking process. What is desired is to separate the very best prospects from the worst. The use of such a rating device has many obvious flaws but remember, at this stage only crude approximations are required. Certainly not all factors are of equal importance, nor will all raters be equally adept.

Business Analysis

The next step in the product planning and development process is the systematic, formal analysis of the economic and financial implications of the new-product idea. Such an analysis is tied directly to the potential profitability of

Table 8-1 New Product Marketing Index

	5 Very Good	4 Good	3 Average	2 Poor	1 Very Poor
I. Marketability— Required chan- nels of distribution	Present channels can be used	Mainly through present channels	Half through present channels otherwise new channels	Mainly through new channels	All new channels needed
II. Durability— Stability	Long product life	Better than presently used machines	Normal product life	Relatively short product life	Early obsolescence
III. Productive ability— Equipment necessary	Produced with idle equipment	Produced with presently used machines	Some additional equipment needed	Some present equipment can be used	All new equipment needed
IV. Growth potential— Place in market	New need filled by new product	Substantial improvement of existing products	Some improvements	Minor improve- ments over existing products	Equal to existing product

Source: Adapted from John T. O'Meara, "Selecting Profitable Products," *Harvard Business Review* (January–February 1961), pp. 84–85.

the proposed undertaking. The analysis is basically one of costs and benefits: What will be the out-of-pocket and total costs for developing and launching the product, and how will these compare with the additional sales it is expected to generate?

The business analysis stage in product planning and development seeks to provide the answers to these most essential questions:

- If development, test marketing, and market introduction are successful, can the proposed product bear the costs of these procedures?
- Are the products currently scheduled for development and introduction, the prospective dates at which existing products will be replaced, and the nature of the desired product line such that the proposed product fills a realistic profit objective?

In many instances traditional and unsophisticated product planning and development processes provide little guidance for making these decisions. Too often in the past planning and development processes have ignored the competitive setting of the product, the relevant profit considerations, and the fact that sales depend on the firm's marketing efforts as well as on forces beyond its control. Today's competitive environment demands that these variables be taken into account and that management have the necessary product evaluation information for making these critical decisions.[12]

[12] See Yoram Wind and Henry J. Claycamp, "Planning Product Line Strategy: A Matrix Approach," *Journal of Marketing* **40** (January 1976), pp. 2–9.

Focus group interviewing, which was discussed briefly in chapter 7 is increasingly used at this stage of the product planning and development process. The technique is useful at this juncture because it makes it possible to get ideas on product refinement, it may help in recognizing difficulties with the product itself and in locating problems in making channel decisions, or other problem related areas.

Development and Testing

Remember that to this juncture no product has been developed—only a product concept has been created, a written description of the product and its benefits. Most product concepts that successfully pass the business analysis stage are tested with potential consumers before actual development begins.

For example, when Sunfield Foods, a division of Sunmark Company, a St. Louis candy and confections firm, was considering developing a new granola bar, it concept-tested the idea with a number of consumer groups in the test market. The participants were shown the following concept statement:

> *Here is a candy bar composed of rich natural ingredients, essentially peanut butter and granola. These new barlike snacks can be eaten at breakfast, brunch, or anytime you need quick energy and nutrients. They are conveniently packaged, can be carried readily on hikes or any kind of outdoor outing. They are filled with essential proteins, vitamins, and minerals.*[13]

When consumers are shown the concept statement, they are asked to evaluate the product idea from the standpoint of their need and use of it. They are asked, further, to evaluate the idea, suggest improvements in the product, and to indicate general features or attributes they would like to have either added or deleted.

Concept testing by market research studies can greatly facilitate the shaping of a product for development as well as provide the information needed to facilitate positioning. Concept testing has taught more and more companies that it is the "swing" attributes, the benefits beyond the standard ones that people expect from a given product, that are the keys to the product's success.[14]

Swing attributes are those largely responsible for shifting a significant number of buyers to a given product or brand. A solid-state (no moving parts) tuner may be the attribute that draws many buyers to a particular brand of television. Anacin, with twice the pain reliever of asprin and which doesn't upset your stomach, is promoted on the basis of two swing attributes.

The Consumer Products Safety Act of 1972 demands that products brought to market be safe. The Consumer Product Safety Commission can require that the responsible firm pay for necessary repairs, or even order the company to

---

[13] "Granola Again 'Hot'—Now as Solid Snacks, Breakfast Bars," *Advertising Age,* June 14, 1976, p. 1.
[14] "Determine Appeal of Concept, Positioning, Use Several Measures," *Marketing News,* April 23, 1976, p. 8.

take back unsafe products. If its orders are disregarded, the commission has the power to levy fines and start court action that can mean jail sentences. This new responsibility for safety must be considered when the marketer is planning the product.[15]

Once prototype models of the products are built, they are frequently tested in the home or in other in-use testing environments. Large companies test many prototype products extensively in their own laboratories and often conduct customer use tests of their products.

Test Marketing

Until now we have screened, evaluated, and tested only a concept—a product idea. In this way we determine the product's probable profitability and its physical characteristics or actual physical specifications. In market testing, the firm observes consumer responses to the product and to the marketing strategy that will guide it through actual market conditions.

As we learned in the previous chapter, **test marketing** is a special kind of market research—a scientific attempt to market a product on a limited scale under rigidly controlled conditions that tells the firm what will likely happen when full-scale distribution is undertaken. Test marketing is the last opportunity for the company to modify the product or the marketing strategy. If test marketing is unsuccessful, the product may even be withdrawn from further consideration or shelved for changes and later introduction.

Products should be tested in areas whose population resembles the one likely to be the market for the new product. Such tests allow a firmer definition of the target group and prevent defining a market too narrowly. There are many cities throughout the United States that are frequently used as test markets—Seattle-Tacoma, Columbus, Syracuse, Spokane, Boise, and many others.

Usually, only those products which are distinctly new or have unique features never before offered to consumers are likely to be test marketed. It is important to understand that test marketing is undertaken more to assess the efforts of the marketing program for the new product than to evaluate the product itself. Test marketing can be extremely expensive. Most such programs cost more than $1 million. In addition to the money cost, test marketing also can be time consuming, time that can mean a long delay in getting a product to market. Furthermore, test marketing exposes the new product to competition and sometimes a competitor may rush a similar product to market before the original idea gets there.

Introduction and Evaluation

With the final decision to introduce the product for national distribution, the product planning and development process has virtually ended and the new item is ready to take its place as part of the firm's existing line and total mix.

---

[15] William L. Trombetta and Timothy L. Wilson, "Foreseeability of Misuse and Abnormal Use of Products by the Consumer," *Journal of Marketing* **39** (July 1975), pp. 48–55.

The marketing program designed to support the new product will be, in large part, determined by the information generated in the early phases of planning and development. The sales forecast and the newcomer's estimated market share, in conjunction with the company's expectations for it based upon industry trends, will also affect the marketing strategy and the level of support provided for the new product. Remember, however, that the process works in two ways; the new product's market success in great measure depends on the strength of the marketing program. Coinciding with the introduction, or the new-product "roll out" as it is called in the trade, is the need to have salespeople already trained and apprised of the new offering and its benefits, to have the advertising campaign designed and launched, and to have inventories adequate to meet expected demand throughout all levels of the channel of distribution.

During the early stages of the introduction, management will wish to analyze carefully all the relevant sales and market data generated. Adjustments may be needed in the promotion mix or in distribution activities. Minor changes may be made during this phase in the product itself, or in packaging or labeling. A given market response may require a reallocation of sales force effort or, of course, the ultimate disappointment—withdrawal of the product itself.

> Before proceeding, can you answer these questions:
> **1.** Why is product planning and development such an important marketing activity?
> **2.** What is the objective and role of product planning and development in the overall marketing strategy?
> **3.** Can you list and briefly discuss the steps in the product planning and development process?

Why New Products Fail

Despite elaborate and diligent efforts throughout the product planning process, many new products fail. Perhaps as many as 50 percent of those actually launched have only a brief period of market success—if any.[16] But why, given all the care and attention, do new products fail? The answer is that many are not given that much care and attention. Many firms have no formal product planning and development procedure. Some companies ignore scientific, rational procedures in favor of management hunches and intuition. In others, management fails to recognize the importance of a rapidly changing market environment. Time passes and conditions in the market place change. Failure to recognize these changes can mean product failure.

Products that consumers perceive as not really new or not having sufficient benefits to justify trial usage are destined at the outset for market failure.

---

[16] This figure has recently been disputed by one study, see David Hopkins, "Survey Finds 67% of New Products Succeed," *Marketing News* XII, no. 16, Feb. 8, 1980, p. 1.

Who Manages the New Product Planning and Development Process?

Firms have many different ways of managing the new product planning and development process.

New-Product Managers.   Some corporations (Johnson and Johnson, General Foods, Procter and Gamble) have initiated new-product manager positions or product planners. These new-product managers work with **product managers** of existing products in an attempt to extend product lines, generate new ideas, and make top management aware of new-product possibilities.

New-Product Committees.   Many firms have a new-product committee of top management people from marketing, engineering, finance, and other areas to administer the product planning and development process. Such committees bring a broadened perspective to the task but they are often handicapped by all the shortcomings typical of leadership by committee: divided authority, lack of clear-cut responsibility, conservatism and, oftentimes, a lack of any real interest.

Product Managers.   Some firms, especially industrial marketers, use product managers to supervise the product planning and development process. In the consumer goods field, particularly where advertising is a major factor, product managers are called "brand managers"; they have marketing backgrounds and are completely responsible for the success of products in their jurisdiction. The product manager in industrial marketing organizations has the primary responsibility for coordinating all elements that affect the profitability of his or her product line. This individual's central responsibility is to straddle the gaps between marketing, manufacturing, and engineering, interpreting the needs of the marketplace to research, engineering, and manufacturing organizations.

New-Product Departments.   New-product departments have emerged in some companies. These departments have sufficient status to command the attention of top executives and to secure the cooperation of people throughout the organization. New-product departments are frequently given complete control of the product planning and development process, from the generation of ideas through concept and market testing. New-product departments can easily secure the cooperation of marketing research departments and, when the product reaches the roll-out stage, it is turned over to the regular marketing department.

The Venture Team.   The **venture team** is another space age by-product. Many companies like Ford, Westinghouse, and Monsanto have delegated responsibility for product planning and development to these venture, or special project, teams. Venture teams are organizational arrangements employing a "synectics" approach to creative problem solving that utilizes highly trained people from different disciplines.* The value of the venture team in many organizations is difficult to estimate. They have the magic in many instances of uniting people in a common, one-time effort, turning the job into a mission, and possibly even into a crusade. Yet, the venture team has its drawbacks.[17] Its life span is limited, it usually does not concern itself with routine on-going processes, and it is not always given due recognition by the traditional management and in-place (permanent) organization.

Increasingly, top level corporate executives are seeing to it that the new-product planning and development process is managed carefully. The heavy costs, high failure rate, and the shortened life cycle of many new products all seem to demand greater attention when the groundwork is being laid. No one organizational arrangement seems predominant at present and much experimentation is underway.

The Product Life Cycle

An important concept in the product planning and development process is that of the **product life cycle.** Few products last forever. Products are originated, developed, and launched. Some, like Gillette's Nine Flags cologne, have minimum market success; others, like the same company's Trac II razor are so successful that they spawn a flurry of competitive activity. Occasionally a product, such as peanut butter, grows to great maturity and enjoys prolonged market success. Others have their "moment in the sun" only to be replaced by new ones offering new potential and different customer benefits. The stages in the market success of products are referred to as the product life cycle. Figure 8-4 shows a typical product life cycle.

As suggested in Figure 8-4, products move through a series of stages and growth, and conditions in each of these stages markedly affect both sales and profits. An understanding of the three basic assumptions upon which the product life cycle concept rests will establish more clearly the relationship between product planning and development processes and the product life cycle.

1. The speed with which products move through the four stages in their life cycle (introduction, growth, maturity, and decline) varies from one product to another. Some move through very rapidly; others never even make it through the introductory stage to the growth period. Still others move steadily and predictably through each stage, while a few linger in what appears to be a period of everlasting growth.
2. Profits (per unit) rise steadily in the growth phase and start to decline during the maturity stage because of consumer satiation and strong competitive pressure. During the later stages of the maturity phase, increases in volume are most likely to outstrip profit increases.

---

*Synectics is based upon the concept of synergistics. Synergistics means "working together." People who work together effectively produce a result which collectively is greater than the sum of their individual efforts.

[17] Thomas A. Staudt, "Higher Management Risks," p. 8.

Figure 8-4 A product life cycle.

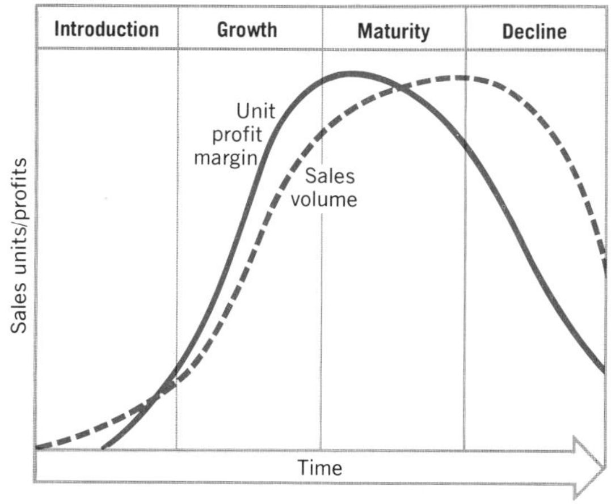

3. The marketing emphasis required for successful exploitation of the product life cycle will vary, depending upon the nature of the product, competitive behavior, and many other market related variables.

Stages in the Product Life Cycle

A firm must make many strategic decisions as a product moves through each stage of its life cycle.

Introduction. In its introductory phase, a product often faces stiff market resistance, or even indifference, especially items that are not particularly new or distinctive, or in which consumers perceive few meaningful attributes or benefits. The product at this juncture is burdened with large development costs and the costs of special marketing programs. Profits are usually nonexistent at this stage; sales come slowly as the firm attempts various penetration strategies. Occasionally there is the "wonder product" that takes off quickly, gains immediate customer favor, and begins generating profits late in its introductory period. Such products give their developer the chance to skim the market opportunity by setting higher than normal prices and lowering them later to attract less enthusiastic buyers or to reach other market segments.

Growth. Products enter the growth phase of their life cycle as the market expands through increasing awareness of the new items and repeat purchasing by initial buyers. Careful monitoring of a product's performance late in the introductory period and early in the growth period can signal marketing managers as to its ultimate success and profitability. As it moves up on the curve during this period, its sales and profits are rapidly increasing. This fact does not escape competitors, who are often quick to enter the market with similar or identical products. As shown in Figure 8-4 unit profit margins rise most rapidly during this phase.

Maturity.   During this period sales volume continues to grow as the market, too, reaches full maturity. Sales may continue to increase, but at a decreasing rate. Competitors are now sharing the market; if their marketing strategy is really effective, their market share may even be greater than that of the originating company. It is the marketing manager's responsibility to see that the company's products take full advantage of differences in profitability at different stages of market development. Several options are often available. First, the marketing manager may decide to try to increase the product's market share by actually investing more company resources in promoting and distributing it. Second, the company may decide to hold its market share (the proportion of total industry sales it obtains) at a consistent level. Third, the company may decide, if the product's prospects appear dim, to reduce its market position (the way customers perceive a product) slowly by reducing its market share.[18] This practice, called disinvestment or "milking the product," means gradually reducing expenses while increasing or maintaining present price levels. Timing is quite important. Disinvestment over a period of several years may bring a very high contribution to profit from the product.

Decline.   In the decline stage the product is making a smaller and smaller contribution to profit and overhead. In some cases, profits have totally disappeared and the item is carried only for the convenience of the firm's customers or to have a full assortment and a well-developed product mix. In the interest of efficiency and profitability, there comes a time when a product must be carefully scrutinized for possible deletion from the line. Usually consumer interest has shifted to other products because of innovations or improvements. Without sufficient customer interest, the costs of carrying the product or rejuvenating it are unwarranted. The product is through commercially and should be abandoned.

The product life cycle suggests that all firms must consider generating a continuous stream of new products in order to maintain market position, solidify their corporate image, and hold profitability at desired levels. As shown in Table 8-2, the product life cycle governs strategic marketing planning at all levels. This means not only product planning and development, but price, promotion, and distribution policies as well.

Before proceeding, can you answer these questions:
1. Give several reasons why so many new products fail.
2. Describe several organizational arrangements for managing new-product developments.
3. What is meant by the product life cycle concept? How does it relate to new-product planning and development?

---

[18] Bernard Catry and Michel Chevalies, "Market Share Strategy and the Product Life Cycle," *Journal of Marketing* **38** (October 1974), pp. 29–34.

Table 8-2   How Product Life Cycle Advocates View the Implications of the Cycle for Marketing Activities

Effects and responses	Stages of the PLC			
	Introduction	Growth	Maturity	Decline
Competition	None of importance	Some emulators	Many rivals competing for a small piece of the pie	Few in number with a rapid shakeout of weak members
Overall strategy	Market establishment; persuade early adopters to try the product	Market penetration; persuade mass market to prefer the brand	Defense of brand position; check the inroads of competition	Preparations for removal; milk the brand dry of all possible benefits
Profits	Negligible because of high production and marketing costs	Reach peak levels as a result of high prices and growing demand	Increasing competition cuts into profit margins and ultimately into total profits	Declining volume pushes costs up to levels that eliminate profits entirely
Retail prices	High, to recover some of the excessive costs of launching	High, to take advantage of heavy consumer demand	What the traffic will bear; need to avoid price wars	Low enough to permit quick liquidation of inventory
Distribution	Selective, as distribution is slowly built up	Intensive; employ small trade discounts since dealers are eager to store	Intensive; heavy trade allowances to retain shelf space	Selective; unprofitable outlets slowly phased out
Advertising strategy	Aim at the needs of early adopters	Make the mass market aware of brand benefits	Use advertising as a vehicle for differentiation among otherwise similar brands	Emphasize low price to reduce stock
Advertising emphasis	High, to generate awareness and interest among early adopters and persuade dealers to stock the brand	Moderate, to let sales rise on the sheer momentum of word-of-mouth recommendations	Moderate, since most buyers are aware of brand characteristics	Minimum expenditures required to phase out the product
Consumer sales and promotion expenditures	Heavy, to entice target groups, with samples, coupons, and other inducements to try the brand	Moderate, to create brand preference (advertising is better suited to do this job)	Heavy, to encourage brand switching, hoping to convert some buyers into loyal users	Minimal, to let the brand coast by itself

Source: Nariman K. Khalla and Sonia Yuspeh, "Forget the Product Life Cycle Concept," *Harvard Business Review* (January–February 1976), p. 104.

The Adoption of New Products

New products are adopted and diffused through the general population in a rather predictable pattern. Once this diffusion process[19] is understood, the marketing decision maker can better manage his or her own product planning and development activities as well as the product life cycle. Marketing managers study the adoption and diffusion of new products in order to answer such questions as:

1. Does diffusion occur in a predictable manner?
2. Who are the consumer **innovators** and how can they be identified?
3. How are people persuaded to adopt new products or services?
4. How can the many activities of marketing be better coordinated with the adoption and diffusion process?

The Diffusion Process

Starting with minor acceptance by the early adopters—a very small percentage of the total population—an innovation gathers adherents at an increasing rate through the early majority and late majority categories. Finally it tapers off as it moves through the last category, referred to as laggards. Thus, diffusion begins slowly, snowballs, and then subsides. What is most important is that the same behavior that causes the adoption and diffusion of new products is, in great measure, responsible for the product life cycle.

Thus, if marketers understand diffusion and adoption of new products and if they are in any way able to control the process, they can better manage the revenues and profits flowing from their marketing strategies. Especially important are their product planning and development activities as they affect the life cycles of the firm's product line.[20]

Innovators.   Innovators are extremely important to the success of new products even though they constitute only about 2½ percent of the adopting market. They are "risk takers" in many respects, experimenters, seeking the reinforcement and reward of being first. There is some evidence to suggest that innovators are markedly different in personality and life styles. They are *forerunners* often upscale (slightly above average in income for their age group), young, well-educated consumers. They tend to hold new values and are frequently opinion leaders, key figures in a network of personal and social influence.

Early Adopters.   Early adopters, the next 13½ percent to start using a new product, are also opinion leaders in their communities, often having positions

---

[19] An early discussion of this process can be found in Everett Rogers, *Diffusions of Innovation* (New York: Free Press, 1962). An updating of the work can be found in E.M. Rogers and F.F. Shoemaker, *Communication of Innovations: A Cross Cultural Approach* (New York: Free Press, 1971).

[20] See Vijay Mahajan and Eitan Muller, "Innovation Diffusion and New Product Growth Models in Marketing," *Journal of Marketing* **43** (Fall 1979), pp. 55–68.

of some social prominence. They are the better-educated managerial and professional people, with high incomes and considerable mobility. Early adopters are the *new conformists*. These people hold values that they espouse and drop regularly, depending upon what is "in" or fashionable at the time. While not the first to adopt new products, this category's cool reception usually means a new product will have only limited market success.

Innovators—early adapters.

Quick, name five people who drink Kirin Beer.

Don't give up.

Maybe you'll think of one or possibly even two. But most importantly, did you think of yourself? If you haven't discovered the distinctively delicious flavor of this exclusive imported beer, it's probably because you haven't discovered Kirin in the first place. Unless you're in an Oriental restaurant, it's usually hard to find. So, look for it, experience it, and tell your friends about it. And remember that once you find Kirin, the largest selling beer outside America, it'll be the last imported beer you'll ever want to look for.

Kirin Beer. It's worth the effort to find it.

IMPORTED BY THE CHERRY CO., LTD., NEW YORK, NY, LOS ANGELES, CA, HONOLULU, HI

Early Majority.   People in the early majority category, 34 percent of a product's adopters, make up the first half of America's mass market. They are solid citizens, people who may be slight overachievers. They have good educations, well-paying jobs, and spend their money for the good things of life. These are the people who validate the new products—make them an accepted part of the middle-class system of symbols. The early majority are autonomous consumers, people who form their own judgments. They are people who have made it. They are astute shoppers, articulate and demanding because they are more thoughtful about themselves and their behavior.

Late Majority.   The late majority category (34 percent) constitutes the other half of America's mass market. These people are somewhat older, not quite as well off financially, less well educated; often they are blue collar tradespeople or white collar clerical supervisors. They are sometimes "overprivileged" in that they have high incomes but have not learned how to spend their money to gain the most status. They strive, however, for social acceptance and in this sense they are *traditionalists* still trying to win a place in the system. Clinging to the old values and traditional ways, these people are among the last to try new products.

Laggards.   The last category, the final adopters (16 percent), are called laggards. They are society's *retreaters*. They have less education and are not really well integrated into the social structure of the community. They are often the misfits, the social dropouts, and the nonconformists. They are also made up in part of older people who essentially have given up their ambitions and struggle along on low, often fixed incomes. Few firms would deliberately develop products for this category, though it does represent a market segment for some goods and services.

Implications for Marketers

The meaning for marketers is that consumer behavior, as reflected in the adoption and diffusion of new products, can and does affect the firm's product planning and development process and the market programs that support it. Products are frequently designed and launched to take advantage of the diffusion process. Innovators are often asked to sample new products; concepts are tested by the early adopters; and the opinions of early adopters and sometimes late majority adopters are sought by survey and market tests. Alert companies direct their marketing programs, especially promotional activities, to the opinion leaders and key influentials in the diffusion process. Management also chooses its channels of distribution and retail outlets for their compatibility with the appropriate adopter and life style categories.

In industrial marketing, especially in such categories as installations and capital equipment of high technology, it may be particularly important to the successful launching of new products, processes, or services to identify the innovator adopters. Without a positive response from a few farsighted companies, the diffusion of the new product may be forestalled for many years.

Summary

New product marketing is the ultimate test of marketing skill and daring. Product planning and development is in many respects the essence of marketing, for products and services are the bridge linking the firm to its market opportunity.

Product planning and development is a high-risk venture. Much uncertainty surrounds the process and the landscape is littered with product failures. Yet product planning and development is a pivotal part of the total marketing effort. Careful management of the process is essential to preserve and strengthen the assets of the organization.

Product planning and development is the orginating, evaluation and development of new-product ideas, including the adoption of those showing the greatest promise of being sold profitably in the market place. It is a strategically necessary activity because it enables the firm to have a balanced assortment of goods to meet anticipated customer demand. Product planning is essential throughout every level of the distribution channel.

Products are bundles of expectations—they may be physical, but services and processes are also products. The total product concept is a broad term which encompasses the notion that "products" are composites of benefits derived from the product itself, as well as from packaging, product labeling, branding, and other marketing activities. The management of the product planning and development process must be coordinated with both the product life cycle of existing products and the adoption and diffusion process for new products.

Review Questions

1. How does product planning and development contribute to the well-being of the firm?
2. Are the costs of product planning and development high or low? Why?
3. Why do so many firms appear to have an increased interest in product planning and development activities?
4. Define product planning and development. Does it mean the same to manufacturers as it does to resellers such as wholesalers and retailers?
5. What is the objective of product planning and development? Why is this important?
6. What is a product? What is the total product concept?
7. What does product planning and development accomplish for the firm?
8. What are some of the organizational arrangements used by firms to manage the product planning and development process?
9. Discuss the stages in the product life cycle. What is the significance of the product life cycle in product planning and development?
10. What is the parallel between the product life cycle and the adoption and diffusion process for new products?

Case 8-1

The Weed Eater

Years ago George Ballas got so frustrated trying to keep his lawn neatly trimmed around the gnarled roots of two giant oak trees that he stormed the garbage can with an idea in mind. He was about to begin the George Ballas success story.

From the trash bin he retrieved a discarded popcorn can, punched holes in it, and threaded them with nylon fishing line. Then he removed the blade from his lawn edger, bolted the popcorn can device to the long handle and plugged it in. It made considerable noise but it also did the job—it ripped up the turf and tore the grass away from the tree roots. Ballas worked to improve his machine, which he called the "Weed Eater," and shortly thereafter took it to market, where it met with great success. He claims his was the first practical device that eliminated the back-breaking work of hand-cutting weeds and overgrown grass around all those hard-to-get-at places like fences, stone walls, walkways, and tree roots.

All this started in 1971. A year later net sales of Weed Eaters, Inc. were $568,000. By 1974, they were $7.79 million. In 1975 they reached 16.3 million and in 1976, according to audited statements, the company had sales of $54 million. Sales were projected at approximately $85 million for 1980.

There are now twenty or so similar devices on the market. However, in the early 1980s Ballas's Weed Eaters, Inc. was riding the crest of string trimmer sales with seven models, excellent distribution outlets, and a $10 million advertising program. The units range in price from $29.95 to $289.95.

One of the biggest advantages of the string trimmer invented by Ballas is its safety factor. It uses no blades and will not cut flesh. Unlike bladed devices, the string is not damaged by striking an obstruction like a rock or sidewalk edge. A major disadvantage of the string trimmers, however, is that the weeds and grass are whipped rather than cut and they tend to turn brown on the ends like grass cut with a dull rotary mower.

Questions

1. Does Ballas appear to have followed the procedures outlined in the product planning and development process as discussed in the text?
2. To what do you attribute the success of Ballas' Weed Eater device?
3. Why don't most large companies follow Ballas' example and just rush their good ideas to market?
4. Why do you suppose Ballas decided to forego market testing his product and instead launch the Weed Eater directly?

Case 8-2

"George," The Voice-Activated Toy Volkswagen Van

Thousands of toy Volkswagen vans may soon be rolling off a production line in Waterville, Connecticut. That is, they will roll off if the actual product meets with the same enthusiasm and excitement as the prototype model. "It's a magnificent toy, a super toy!" raves Gilbert M. Oelbaum, a principal of Northeastern Marketing Group, the New York sales organization that is orchestrating the toy's debut. Oelbaum's enthusiasm is shared by others who have seen the van. To them the reason is plain. The toy "hears" and responds to voice commands.

What makes "George" run is an apparent breakthrough in the economics of voice control that will allow "George" to be produced and retailed for about $30 per unit. "George" is the brainchild of an inveterate California tinkerer, Robert McCaslin, still in his twenties. "Our high school electronics teacher told us to come up with something unique," he recalls. So McCaslin created "George's" forebear, a vehicle simply called "It," as a project for his Pacifica, California, High School electronics class. It was little more than a brown blob of urethane foam with two eyes and a red tongue mounted on a toy truck chassis. In response to whistle blasts, it would move right, left, straight, and then stop. Later, as a student at Diablo Valley College, McCaslin refined It for another class. The new, more reliable model was voice-activated and named "George" after McCaslin's landlord.

What really makes "George" work is that the voice commands are picked up by a small crystal microphone in the roof of the van. If the sound is loud enough, it triggers an analog-to-digital converter—a simple integrated circuit that activates a relay switch, sending battery power to the motor that drives a fifth wheel, or "rud-

der," behind and between the front wheels. The rudder controls "George's" direction. The sounds cause the rudder wheel to rotate for a prescribed number of degrees, which creates a certain movement to the left, straight, or right in that programmed sequence.

"George" has been shown extensively to outsiders since the technology which is its heart is securely patented. Those to whom it has been shown are primarily investors and marketers, not consumers or buyers. Recently, "George" was exhibited at the Consumer Electronics Show in Chicago and the enthusiastic reaction to the toy prompted one of the product's developers to claim: "The potential annual market is 10 million units by 1985." Even before the American product rolls out, some foreign firms are negotiating for a license to manufacture "George" for European markets. One executive, anxious to introduce the product without further product planning and development efforts, said, "If we can deliver a quality product in quantity, this product is really novel enough to take hold." Yet there are others in the marketing group who urge a more cautious approach. They believe that the product should be put to further market tests and a careful economic analysis undertaken before launching the toy.

Questions

1. Who is right? Should the product be launched now or should it undergo further tests?
2. Briefly outline the major steps in submitting "George" to an economic analysis or assessment.
3. Would the normal consumer adoption process apply to an item such as "George"?

Chapter 9

Total Product Strategy

Americans have a "hang-up" about halitosis. American consumers spend nearly $255 million annually for mouthwashes, more than the rest of the world combined. This converts to 28.6 million gallons—a lake-sized amount—the equivalent of 366 billion one-ounce doses. Canadians, the world's number two mouthwash users, consume only 256 million one-ounce doses yearly. For a more easily understood comparison, each American swishes 1,500 times per year as compared to each Canadian's 11 times. Nearly 72 percent of adult Americans use a mouthwash. People who do are usually considered to be more independent, more compulsive, more concerned with leadership, and somewhat more anxious than nonusers.

Mouthwash users fall into two rather distinct market segments: those who prefer a product like Listerine, and those who prefer a pleasant flavor that promises only to sweeten the breath, such as Lavoris and Scope. Medicinal *brands* currently have about 58 percent of the market and the pleasant-tasting brands about 42 percent. The two major companies—Warner-Lambert, the manufacturer of Listerine, and Procter and Gamble, who make Scope—have been positioning their products head-on in a battle to win customers and increase market share.

Recently each company altered its product and marketing strategy. Procter and Gamble test marketed and introduced a mouthwash called Extend that was designed to compete with the "mediciney" Listerine, while Warner-Lambert countered with one that falls into the "soda pop" category. At the time, Listerine had about 50 percent of the entire mouthwash market and Scope about 20 percent. Yet, Warner-Lambert, in spite of their market success with Listerine, developed Listermint, a green sweet mouthwash after their research showed that those who chose mouthwashes for their good flavor tended to be younger and more urban than those buying therapeutic brands. They also discovered that new users are more likely to begin with the more pleasant, sweet products.

It's the Total Product that Counts

What this incident shows is that from a marketing as well as a consumer's point of view, it's the total product that counts. Consumers do not buy products just for their usefulness; they buy total bundles of expectations. For example, consider the two categories or market segments for mouthwash. The medicinal users probably are looking for health attributes—antiseptic qualities and better breath. The "soda pop" user is most likely seeking pleasure, the sense-gratifying attributes of pleasant taste, sweet-smelling breath, and social acceptance. It appears that each company wished to attain market dominance by creating a product that, in the minds of most consumers, combined the best qualities of each of these products. What is more important, however, in this incident is the **total product concept.** What are these consumers buying? A mouthwash? No. Each consumer segment was seeking a bundle of product benefits. And each company was attempting, through its own problem research, to discover the benefits people desired, the benefits the various products lacked, and the

UGH! MORNING BREATH, THE WORST BREATH OF THE DAY.

Overnight, a pasty film covers your mouth, teeth, gums. You wake with the worst breath of the day. But Scope® will help fix it.

Scope fights bad breath and leaves it minty-fresh. Not even the mediciney mouthwash cleans your mouth better.

And Scope doesn't stop there. Lab tests' prove that Scope, with anti-bacterial T₅, kills germs, too. Tomorrow, give yourself the pleasure of waking up to Scope.

Minty-fresh Scope. Fights bad breath, doesn't give medicine breath.

© 1981, The Procter & Gamble Company

benefits buyers actually received.[1] Consumers buy expectations; not just "products." When buying a product, the shopper makes assumptions (generates expectations) about the future performance of the product; mouthwash promotes greater sociability, social acceptance, sweet-smelling breath, and

[1] See James H. Meyers, "Benefit Structure Analysis: A New Tool for Product Planning," *Journal of Marketing* **40**, no. 4 (October 1976), pp. 23–32.

has a pleasant taste. As a given product is used, the consumer compares the quality of its performance to his or her expectations for it. If the product performs as well as, or better than, expected, the customer will be satisfied. If, on the other hand, the performance is below expectations, the buyer will be dissatisfied. [2]

Expectations are created in large part through "the total product strategy." The product or service is the nucleus around which expectations are created, but expectations are also created by such marketing devices as branding and trademarks, **packaging, warranties,** and informative labeling. All these things, because they are closely related to the entire product planning and development activity, need to be considered as a whole in devising the total product strategy. Combined, they create and promote the consumer's sense of expectations.

Hence, in considering the role of product planning and development in overall marketing strategy, branding and trademark policy and related activities of packaging, product labeling, warranties, and repair service also need to be explored. These facets of a product in themselves yield certain benefits—brands and trademarks create customer expectations of value, service, durability, and quality. Packaging enhances the product. Some goods, for instance toiletries, are purchased as much for the package as for the product itself. Sometimes it is difficult to distinguish between the product and the package. (Drano's instant pressure plunger comes to mind.) Product labeling, warranties, and the provision of service are all product related marketing efforts that tend to expand the customers' expectations concerning a purchase.

In the pages to follow, after a discussion of the importance of managing the product life cycle, we will explore these other issues and their overall importance to product planning and development.

Managing the Product Life Cycle

In discussing the role and importance of product planning and development in marketing strategy in the previous chapter, we also introduced the concept of the product life cycle (PLC), referring to the stages in the market success of products. This concept suggests that products move through several stages of growth, and that conditions in each of these stages markedly affect sales and profits.

Although we discussed the concept of the product life cycle rather extensively, there are some important analyses and implications that remain to be made.

The Optimal Product Mix

All firms attempt to create what for them is an **optimal product mix,** that combination of the firm's products that best meets the needs of its customers

---

[2] John E. Swan and Linda Jones Combs, "Product Performance and Consumer Satisfaction: A New Concept," *Journal of Marketing* **40** (April 1976), pp. 25–33.

and maximizes its profits. **Product mix strategy,** like product planning and development, is obviously related to the nature of the firm's resources, its perceived market opportunity, management philosophy, and competitive constraints. There is a wide array of product mix strategies. Some of the more prevalent ones are as follows:

1. Extensive full-line strategies. Some firms attempt to reach many market segments by producing and distributing a wide, even unrelated number of products.
2. Intensive limited-line strategies. Some firms delineate and define a limited number of market segments, or even a single one, and then develop a full range of products for them.
3. Selective product lines. Companies using this strategy specialize in the production and distribution of a few products of a single type. These products may be aimed at one particular market segment or scattered throughout a number of different ones.
4. Single product firms. Some companies produce and distribute a single product. They often disregard market segmentation and because of a special success or competence, either in the production-engineering or marketing-distribution sphere of their operation, quite literally put "all of their eggs in one basket."

Is any one of these strategies likely to lead to the greatest market success and profitability? The answer is no. Success and profitability depend on many factors. Good market performance most often results not so much from choosing a particular strategic option, as from the skill used in developing and carrying out marketing programs. The great diversity of needs in the market place gives businesses a wide choice of alternatives with which to pursue market success and profitability. Whatever strategy they choose, however, marketers must have a product or a product line that meets customer demand.[3] Because customer demand changes over time, the marketing manager must constantly monitor the company's product line and/or its product mix to ensure that it will not be left behind as market conditions change.

Product Phasing Strategy

Each company's potential for sales growth and profitability depends on the way its product mix is distributed among the six following phases:

1. Tomorrow's breadwinners. These are either new products with strong appeal and great market potential, or today's breadwinners, modified and improved.
2. Today's breadwinners. These are currently in the advanced growth phase of the product life cycle and account for the bulk of the firm's present sales and profits.

[3] See, "When a New Product Strategy Wasn't Enough," *Business Week*, February 18, 1980, p. 142.

3. Today's near winners. These products have good sales success and market acceptance generally, but can be made more profitable for a particular firm through better management. "Near winners" suggest modifications in strategy, that is, branding, packaging, advertising, or changes in distribution channels.

4. Yesterday's winners. Products in this group still have good volume but have slipped over into the latter stages of the product life cycle. Sales are now uneven, sporadic, and order size is diminishing.

5. Yesterday's also rans. These products once were thought to have great potential but never completely fulfilled management's hopes. They were not total failures, yet both profits and sales were greatly below planned levels.[4]

6. Yesterday's and today's "bombs." Perhaps "duds" would be a more appropriate term than bombs for these products, which never made it past the introductory phase of the PLC. Their development, production, and launching costs greatly exceed the revenues they generated. They are products which were met by market apathy and rejection.

Of course, the optimal phasing is one with most of its products in the first three categories. However, the dynamic nature of the market place suggests again, does it not, that product planning and development itself must be a dynamic process and that the effectiveness of product mix phasing can be evaluated in terms of several dimensions—sales growth, market share, and profitability. Figure 9-1 graphically portrays these dimensions expanded into high and low categories.

By analyzing product mix according to Figure 9-1, several important implications for managers become clear. Cell 1 shows products with high sales growth, high market share, and high profitability—an enviable position for any product. Cell 2 shows products with low sales growth, high market share, and high profitability. These may soon become "yesterday's breadwinners" as sales continue to decline, or they may be revitalized with changes in market strategy such as an improved model, better packaging, and a new brand name. Cell 3 products are those with high sales growth, low market share, and high profitability. Such products can have a promising future if stronger marketing efforts are exerted to push them up into the higher market share category. A product in this cell might be competing with a number of other successful products, but in spite of its crowded category, it enjoys good market acceptance. Cell 4 products have low sales growth and low market share. These are likely candidates for deletion from the product line. Managers would be wise to scale down their commitment to products in this category.

The analysis of a firm's product line that examines the three criteria of sales growth, market share, and profitability tends to focus attention on these vital product planning and development issues: (1) How well is the firm managing

---

[4] These categories and some of the labels were suggested by Peter Drucker, "Managing for Business Effectiveness," *Harvard Business Review*, May–June 1963, p. 59. Several of the labels, however, as well as all of the descriptions are the author's.

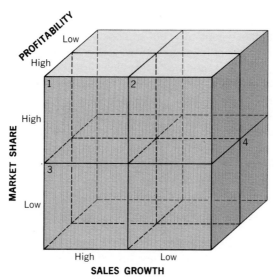

Figure 9-1 Products by sales level, market share, and profitability.

the life cycles of its products? (2) Is the company's rate of new-product development sufficient? (3) Is the product mix overloaded with exhausted products that should be deleted? (4) What objectives should be established for each product? (5) What resources and adjustments in total strategy does each of the company's products require?[5]

The PLC Under Control

The product life cycle is not an independent variable. Sales in units and profits are plotted against time. Instead of placing time on the horizontal axis, however, suppose you plotted sales against marketing effort. Would the product life cycle look the same? Perhaps it would, but perhaps it would not. The point is that the product life cycle is a dependent variable—it depends on the firm's marketing effort, the marketing and managerial system that supports the product. Marketing management can alter the shape and duration of any product's life cycle.

Many successful products have never entered the terminal stages of the product life cycle. For example, consider the following:

- The Franklin stove, invented by Benjamin Franklin in the mid-eighteenth century, is a cast iron fireplace made with a special flue arrangement that increases its capacity for heating a room. The stove has been slightly modified, but the design remains much the same as it was in its inventor's day. The Franklin fireplace, which can burn either coal or wood, is used exten-

[5] See Philip Kotler, *Marketing Management*, 3rd ed. (Englewood Cliffs, NJ: Prentice-Hall), p. 188.

sively today in vacation homes and as an auxiliary source of heat in many recreation rooms.

- Chain saws used by professional as well as weekend foresters, vacation home owners, and do-it-yourselfers, were first produced in the early 1930s. These early models weighed upwards of 100 pounds and required two men to handle them. Even after much modification, the early models still weighed nearly forty pounds. However, chain saws have been constantly improved, made lighter, quieter, and safer, with less vibration and at a lower cost. There is little likelihood that their market will diminish in the future.

- Ipana toothpaste, marketed by Bristol-Myers, was once a leading seller. In 1968, the company abandoned it in favor of new brands. Yet, in early 1969, two Minnesota businessmen bought the Ipana name and created a new formula for the toothpaste, but left the package unchanged. With a minimum of promotion, the "written off" dead product generated $250,000 in sales volume in the first seven months of its new life. A recent survey showed that Ipana was still being used by 1.52 million adults.[6]

Products and brands do go sour. Some products are short-lived, generating only a limited market response. Others receive a strong consumer franchise and thrive for a long time. However, management can extend the product life cycle through its marketing effort. Many product classes will continue to enjoy an already long and prosperous maturity. Good examples are Scotch Whiskey, Italian Vermouth, French perfumes, automobiles, radios, mouthwashes, soft drinks, cough remedies, and face creams. Some of these, which satisfy basic or strongly felt needs, appear to be almost immune to normal life cycle pressures. When the product no longer solves a customer's problem or satisfies a need is when it becomes a candidate for termination. Products, unlike human beings, are not necessarily destined to be born, flourish, and die. The product life cycle is manageable.

Deleting the Exhausted Product

Not all products are destined for perpetual life, however. Some become exhausted—worn-out for a number of reasons. Overexposure, failure to continue satisfying a need, inability to match competitors' offerings, new technology, a competitor's more aggressive marketing strategy, changing consumer tastes, and new or altered channels of distribution all drain product strength. Telltale signs of product exhaustion are lower profitability, decreased market share, and slow or stagnant rates of growth.[7]

Many firms discover upon analyzing their product mix for profitability, market share, sales growth, and other factors (as suggested in Figure 9-1) that 20

[6] The Ipana illustration, as well as other discussions in this section, is based upon the article by Nariman K. Dhalla and Sonia Yuspeh, "Forget the Product Life Cycle Concept!" *Harvard Business Review*, January–February, 1976, pp. 102–110.

[7] See Stanley T. Burkoff, "Don't Amputate New Product Programs During Recession," *Marketing News* XIII, no. 16, February 8, 1980, p. 1.

percent of their product lines are often contributing 80 percent of the profits or sales. This 20–80 problem, as it is called in sales management, suggests that the multiple product firm usually has a number of drones in its total assortment mix.

Obviously firms could increase their profitability by monitoring their product lines and developing systematic procedures for eliminating the depleted products.

There are many benefits to be gained from eliminating exhausted, nonprofitable products: the managerial time released can be spent in more fruitful efforts; scarce resources can be devoted to more promising products and ventures; and a periodic review of the total product line forces management to consider systematically, thoroughly, and critically why its products fail. Such a procedure strengthens the overall product planning and development process and leads as well to greater sales and profitability.[8]

A Procedure for Eliminating the Exhausted Product. Procedures for recognizing and eliminating the weak or exhausted product vary widely from company to company depending on their internal situation, competitive environment, and objectives.

Invariably, executives focus on at least three sets of decision variables: (1) financial indicators, (2) marketing indicators, and (3) managerial indicators.[9] *Financial indicators* include the trend of contribution to overall profitability, profitability trend, sales volume trend, price level trend, and present versus potential use of funds.

Marketing indicators are projected market growth, market share trend, how well the product fits into the total product line, the product's distinctiveness from its competitors, and the customer loyalty it commands.

Managerial indicators are the response of marketing and sales personnel, distributor and dealer reactions, machinery and facilities utilization, production personnel response, and present as opposed to potential user of the work force.

In many respects, the decision process for eliminating weak or exhausted products parallels that of planning and developing new products. The product line is screened for candidates for elimination; the criteria for possible discard are based upon financial, marketing, and managerial factors that are often weighted, and even computer analyzed; and the products with the poorest prospects are then dropped.

Weak performers are often subjected to supplemental evaluations weighing their prospects for revitalization through design changes or product improvements; or by marketing related changes such as new brands, new packaging, and further promotional or other support efforts.

---

[8] See Richard T. Hise and Michael A. McGennis, "Product Elimination: Practices, Policies and Ethics," *Business Horizons* (June 1976), pp. 25–32.
[9] See Parker M. Worthing, "Improving Product Deletion Decision Making," *MSU Business Topics* (Summer 1975), pp. 29–38.

Product Elimination Team.   The product abandonment process in many companies is handled by a high-level and broadly representative management team that meets periodically to set and evaluate objectives and procedures for eliminating weak products, and develop a phasing-out program for pruning the product line. This systematic and careful procedure often uses computer processed information.[10] Each member of the team generates a brief data sheet for each product under scrutiny, using a weight and rating for each relative factor. These ratings ultimately yield a retention index which indicates how weak the product is and, in turn, suggests the choices management has. Such an approach permits management representatives to take part fully in a formal procedure based upon solid accounting-financial inputs.

Recalling the Defective Product

The current atmosphere surrounding product planning and development is charged with increasing attention to product safety, environmental concern, and greater consumer awareness. This means that many new products are being challenged by consumer advocates and governmental agencies. Those found wanting are candidates for recall. In 1975, the Matsushita Electric Corporation of America recalled 300,000 color television sets because of radiation emission difficulties and General Motors recalled 234,000 Cadillacs in that model year after a faulty hood latch was discovered.

Under this increasing government and consumer pressure for product safety, business is beginning to develop more sophisticated methods for product recall. In trying various systems, companies are considering (1) the type of internal organization best suited for performing a product recall, (2) the kinds of information necessary to implement an effective recall program, and (3) how to finance product recall activities.

Needless to say, the costs of recall programs can be staggering. General Motors recently spent $3.5 million in postal expense alone when a problem with motor mounts was detected in 6.5 million cars.[11] These facts underscore an important axiom of new-product planning and development: namely, careful attention must be devoted to doing it right! Mistakes, especially those requiring a product recall, may be fatal to a company.

The movement for safer products is gaining momentum and the more alert companies are paying greater heed to the effect of their products on safety and health. Procter and Gamble now devotes more than 10 percent of its technical organization's efforts to safety testing; and the Gillette Company has appointed a "vice president of product integrity," who wields full power in enforcing high standards of safety and quality on all of Gillette's 850 products.

---

[10] Paul W. Hamelman and Edward M. Mazze, "Improving Product Abandonment Decisions," Journal of Marketing 36 (April 1972), pp. 20–26.

[11] Roger A. Kerin and Michael Harvey, "Contingency Planning For Product Recall, *MSU Business Topics*, (Summer 1975), pp. 5–12.

The increasing concern with product safety and the constant threat of an expensive, image-shattering product recall mean that each market offering must be tested during the progressive stages of development, production, distribution, and beyond. Safety and environmental considerations are increasingly important criteria in managing the product planning and development process.

Planned Product Obsolescence

Our discussion of product planning and development would not be complete without at least a brief treatment of **planned product obsolescence.** Basically, this concept asserts that products are designed, engineered, produced, and marketed with a deliberate attempt to make them obsolete or less useful before their "real" usefulness has been exhausted.

The issue of product obsolescence has far-reaching social, economic, and cultural implications. Planned product obsolescence is the deliberate attempt through product planning and development to make customers dissatisfied with existing products so that they will seek and buy the new. Do companies practice planned product obsolescence? The answer is obviously yes. Much of marketing is an effort to arouse and stimulate demand for new products and services.[12] Does this mean, however, that firms build shoddy products that will wear out quickly, forcing consumers to buy new ones? Not necessarily. Most products are built in a range of qualities to meet demand throughout all levels of the purchasing spectrum. Do customers want batteries or tires that will last the life of the automobile? Some do, and for these the products are available at a price. Do customers want razor blades that will last three to six months through dozens of shaves? Some do. And they can find such blades, at a price. But some prefer disposable razors and these are also available, at twenty-five cents each.

Do homemakers want refrigerators, washing machines, and food freezers that will last indefinitely? Apparently not too many do, because many of these appliances that are traded in after an average use of about ten years have at least five to six more years of useful life remaining. Customers want new models. Product obsolescence is often discussed as if it were some kind of conspiracy that marketers are perpetrating on the consuming public. That is a doubtful notion. Obsolescence is more a reflection of consumers' psychology than of a product's usefulness. Ours is a materialistic, goods-oriented culture. Our standard of living and our style of life are largely measured by our consumption expenditures. The American consumer, and increasingly the world consumer, demands "newness."

Of course, providing consumers with new products that are stimulating and different costs money and uses up resources. Perhaps we have been too self-indulgent in the past and new constraints will force us to act more prudently.

---

[12] See George S. Day, Allan D. Shocker, and Rajendra K. Srivastava, "Customer Oriented Aproaches to Identifying Product Markets," *Journal of Marketing* **43**, (Fall 1979), pp. 8–19.

Thus far, consumers have not shown much inclination to alter their buying habits to any great degree or to worry about planned product obsolescence. It is the consumer who is responsible for our system of product obsolescence, not the marketer. Marketers, it is true, can shape behavior, but they certainly cannot control it completely. When consumers no longer accept psychological obsolescence, marketers will find ways to accommodate this change.

In the mid-seventies appliance manufacturers were requested by government agencies to cut the total energy consumption of their products 17 percent by 1980. To comply, nearly every major manufacturer of household appliances added energy efficient models to its line, including washers, dryers, dishwashers, refrigerators, and ranges. However, householders are not buying energy-saving appliances, because they cost more initially. Apparently, the typical consumer just isn't interested in something that doesn't pay back its additional cost in two or three years.

Product obsolescence is a fact of life. However, planned product obsolescence, which implies that products have a built-in self-destruct mechanism so that new ones will have to be purchased, is basically a myth created by people who fail to understand the character of the American consumer and the American culture. Product obsolescence, which mirrors the consumer's desire to discard what is no longer reinforcing, is not solely a marketing problem—it is a part of the American character and culture.

Before proceeding, can you answer these questions:
1. Can the product life cycle be managed? Does this mean that the PLC is a dependent variable? Explain.
2. List and discuss three criteria for evaluating products in the firm's product assortment.
3. What is meant by planned product obsolescence?

Brand Strategy and Policy

An important part of many firms' product planning or management activities is the pursuit of a brand strategy and policy. In a company's strategic marketing planning, brand strategy is part of the development and carrying out of marketing plans and policies. Brand strategy relates to how the firm chooses to use branding, if at all, as part of its overall marketing strategy. Brand policy relates to the preliminary decisions made in regard to whether or not to use brands; whether to produce only its own **manufacturers' brand** or whether to produce **distributor or private brand** merchandise as well; whether to generate a single brand name for the firm's products or to create **family brands** in conjunction with distinctive brand names for each product produced.

What Is a Brand?   The word brand is used in several contexts. Basically a brand is a name, word, mark, term, symbol or device, or a combination of these things, used to identify the goods or services of one seller or group of sellers and to differentiate them from those of competitors.[13]

A brand name is a word that can be spoken such as "Coke" or "Coca-Cola." A brand mark is a symbol, design, or distinctive color or lettering closely identified with the product. McDonald's golden arches, the austere looking gentleman on the Quaker Oats box, and Chrysler Corporation's five-pointed star are examples of brand marks.

Trademark is a special legal term. It refers to a brand or brand mark which has been given legal protection, either by the common law provision of prior usage or by registration with the United States Patent Office. A trademark, that distinguishing sign that separates a product from every other product on the market, does not have to be a name to warrant protection. Among the trademarks that cannot be imitated for commercial purposes are the shapes of the Haig & Haig pinch bottle and the Coke bottle, the Playboy Bunny, the CBS Eye, and the NBC chimes. Trademarks and brand marks are sometimes referred to as the company's "logo." The logo is the trademark or other figure frequently associated with an enterprise.

The Coca-Cola Company places the value of its trademark at over $1 billion and, like Xerox and many other corporations, spends large sums of money each year defending its trademarks and brands from competitor infringement.

The Importance of Identification

The use of brands and trademarks therefore has advantages for both the buyer and seller of commodities. From the buyer's point of view, branding aids in identifying and recognizing the product, thus speeding up the shopping chore. Brands also afford buyers fairly good protection against risks. By purchasing branded goods that have a high degree of market acceptance and with which they are familiar, buyers are reasonably sure of getting at least minimum standards of quality and, to some extent, reasonable prices.

Brands Assist the Marketing Program

There are a number of reasons why sellers consider branding so important.

Advertising and Promotion.   Advertising and promotion are much easier if products are branded. Undifferentiated, unbranded commodities are difficult to promote because they are not easily identifiable. The brand becomes an important attribute in and of itself—it is a focal point around which other product attributes can be grouped to form a clear product image. Consumers are ordinarily faced with a host of products. The branded ones are often those with which the shopper is most familiar. Many items are purchased quickly; the customer wishes to spend a minimum of time shopping and, hence, the

---

[13] American Marketing Association, Committee on Definitions, Marketing Definitions: A Glossary of Terms (Chicago, 1960), p. 8.

"I can't remember the brand name, but it has a commercial with a lot of people running in all directions."

branded product that has been well advertised is, to a great extent, presold. Self-service stores rely heavily on customer acceptance of their products by promoting branded commodities.

Preferential Demand.   Branding makes it possible for a company to create a preferential demand for their product in a class of products. If a firm convinces buyers, through their combined branding and promotional efforts, that their product is significantly better, then they may also be able to convince the buyer that it warrants a higher price, or that the customer should be loyal to that brand and actually prefer it over other similar products. Branding therefore reduces direct price comparisons. How else could Bayer aspirin command a price 50 to 100 percent higher than an unknown or unbranded product when, chemically speaking, all aspirin is really the same? Branding also helps to stabilize prices. Prices of branded commodities tend generally to fluctuate less than those of their anonymous counterparts.

Expanding the Product Mix.   The successful branding and marketing of one product can make it easier to expand the product mix. Many successful multiple-product firms today began with a single item whose success created an umbrella under which additional products could be launched with less risk. Customers remember the familiar and the successful. Firms like General Foods, General Electric, Nabisco, General Mills, and General Motors have a considerable edge when it comes to launching a new branded product. They have already, to a great extent, won the battle of customer recognition—with new offerings they simply have to win market acceptance.

Some Firms Shun Branding

Not all firms brand their products. There are some strong reasons why branding is not always a desirable practice. First of all, it creates an assumed responsibility and something of a liability to manufacture and market a product of consistently high quality. If the firm wants to avoid such a responsibility, it is probably better that it not brand its product. Such firms often supply goods to resellers (retailers or wholesalers), who may choose to put their own label on the merchandise. In these cases, the reseller rather than the manufacturer vouches for the item's quality.

Some commodities do not lend themselves to branding. Agricultural products like wheat, peas, beans; extracted products such as coal, crude oil, natural gas; iron ingots, beams, sheet metal, fabricated parts, and other industrial products; and other items which are difficult to differentiate such as nails, nuts and bolts, and some building materials are not generally candidates for branding by either producers or sellers.

Types of Brands

In light of the confusion surrounding the different kinds of brands, the language of branding greatly needs simplification. Two of the more popular terms relating to branding are *national brands* and *private brands*. These terms suggest that the former are distributed nationally and that the latter are local or regional. Such is not the case and, in the interest of clarity, these terms might well be abandoned.

The most realistic and useful way of classifying brands is by ownership.[14] National brands have generally been associated with manufacturers and private ones with resellers (retailers and wholesalers). Hence, a brand is best classified as either a manufacturer's brand, one that is owned and controlled by a firm whose primary function is production; or a distributor or reseller's brand, one owned and controlled by an organization that is primarily in distribution or marketing. The brands of General Electric, General Mills, and Procter and Gamble Company are thus manufacturers' brands. Sears' DieHard battery, the Easy Rider shock absorber, and the Coldspot refrigerator are distributor or reseller brands.

Family Brands Versus Individual Brands.   When a manufacturer has more than one item in its product line, management must decide whether to identify the product with either a family or blanket brand, or to use individual brand names for each commodity. To some extent, the same problem confronts

---

[14] See Thomas F. Schutte, "The Semantics of Branding" *Journal of Marketing* **33** (April 1969), pp. 5–11.

National or manufacturers brand.

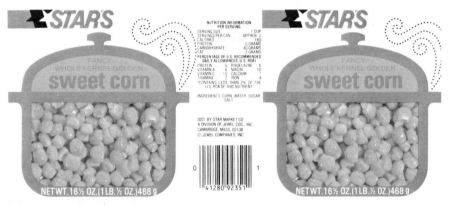

Private or reseller's brand.

A generic label.

resellers as well. For example, Sears' products are not identified with just the Sears name alone—many of their products also bear individual and distinct brand names such as King's Road men's wear, Craftsman tools, Step Lively panty hose, Junior Bazaar women's wear, and Sears-o-pedic bedding.

Some manufacturers use just one blanket, or family, brand to identify all products in their assortment mix. Such well-known firms as Libby, Del Monte, Heinz, Tupperware, Avon, and Johnson and Johnson are largely advocates of blanket, or family, brand practices. However, firms such as Procter and Gamble, General Motors, and International Shoe Company are more inclined to designate each of their separate products with individual brands.

Many manufacturers promote their family brand name along with the individual brand for each of their commodities, as well as model names; for example, the Camaro by the Chevrolet division of General Motors, or the same company's Delco Freedom Battery, which is advertised with the theme "Go with the names you know—AC, GM, and Delco."

The Increase in Distributor Brand Use

Reseller or distributor brands have played an important role in retail merchandising policies for many years. Resellers have developed their own labels in part to curb the strength and market dominance of manufacturers' brands. For example, about 80 percent of J.C. Penney's sales come from their own reseller brands. About 90 percent of Sears' sales and about 25 percent of A & P's are of their own branded commodities. More and more department stores, food chains, general merchandise houses, catalog stores, service stations, drug stores, and other retailers and wholesalers are developing and promoting their own distributor brands. The resellers who do this hope for better control of the total merchandising effort surrounding the product and for the higher gross margins and profits that can result. While manufacturers' brands are sold through a number of competing outlets, the reseller's label is available only through its own stores. These brands are not subject to direct price comparisons with those of the manufacturers.

The Battle of the Brands. Historically, manufacturers' brands have tended to win the greatest consumer acceptance and market success. This is also true today, but reseller and distributor brands are gaining in popularity. Nor are all manufacturers fighting this development very hard. Sometimes, product identification through branding is an important way to achieve market success; sometimes it is not. Manufacturers' brands compete not only with reseller brands, but also with those of other manufacturers. Similarly, resellers' brands also compete with each other. Branding is simply another dimension of marketing strategy.

Many manufacturers, even those with their own well-known products, willingly supply resellers with merchandise which will ultimately carry the resellers' own private brands. Thus, R.C.A. Whirlpool manufactures Sears' major appliances, and Westinghouse makes J.C. Penney Company's. Michelin supplies Sears' radial tires, while General Tire manufactures Atlas tires, which are merchandised through Chevron and other Standard Oil service stations. Why do manufacturers do this? To make money—to reap economies of scale by utilizing excess capacity, to avoid seasonal layoffs of workers, and to smooth out production schedules.

Remember, ours is a diverse, heterogeneous economy with many market segments, each with its own demand characteristics. In some instances the manufacturer's brand is not competing head-on with the reseller's brand—they are appealing to different market segments. Sometimes they are in a head-on positioning battle, but this, in a competitive society, provides the consumer with a wider range of choices and stimulates both resellers and manufacturers to strengthen their product offerings.

The Generic Product.   Some firms are experimenting with what are called "generic products." Generics are unbranded, plainly packaged, less expensive versions of common products. Generics can be found among many supermarket items such as canned foods, paper towels, soft drinks, and frozen foods. They offer standard quality at a price that may be as much as 30 percent lower than that of nationally advertised brands and 15 percent lower than private or distributor labels. Customer reaction to generic products has thus far been mixed.

There is no doubt that the price savings of generics have strong appeal to many consumers during this continuing era of double-digit inflation. Most shoppers believe the lower prices of generics are the result of reduced advertising expenditures. Only a few believe that the lower prices are the result of lower quality products. Yet lower quality is often the principal reason for the price differential. In spite of this, many consumers are impressed by the possibility of savings and many generic products such as beer, razor blades, shaving lotion, laundry detergent, and peanut butter have won widespread customer acceptance.[15]

What Makes a Good Brand Name?   A critical part of brand usage and strategy is choosing the brand name. A good brand name is *distinctive*, easily *vocalized*, highly *descriptive* of the product's attributes, and has significant *cue value*, which means it suggests the product's desirable features. Brand names must be descriptive without unduly appropriating ordinary English words. Many brand names have some of these characteristics, while some, even though successful, do not. Frigidaire, Beautyrest mattresses, Spic and Span cleaner, Taster's Choice coffee, Rain Barrel fabric softener, Sheer Energy panty hose, and Glade air freshener come close to meeting all the requirements for a brand name. However, Kodak, Xerox, and Exxon are brand names which really fit few of the criteria except that they are not descriptive English words and therefore have not appropriated any words unfairly from the language.

---

[15] "Generic Groceries Keep Adding Market Share," *Marketing News*, February 23, 1979, p. 16.

A brand name can be too successful. When it is, it becomes a synonym for the product itself. Aspirin, cellophane, cola, nylon, kerosene, linoleum, and even shredded wheat were once brand names. Currently, Frigidaire, Xerox, and Coke are all being challenged. The argument is that these terms have become so descriptive and generic that they ought to be in the public domain.

Implementing Brand Strategy

Branding is undertaken to enhance the firm's overall marketing program. Like any part of the marketing program, branding is costly and entails risks. However, it is pursued because the firm believes that its benefits—brand loyalty and better recognition by customers, increased sales, and higher profits—will outweigh the added cost of developing the brand through promotion and the risk and responsibility assumed in maintaining its quality image.

Consumers respond to a firm's brand offerings in a number of ways. They may be unaware of the brand's existence. They may be aware of the brand's existence, but it may not be included in those brands which the buyer will actually consider when making a specific brand choice. Or for various reasons, the buyer may completely reject the brand. The brands that become alternatives to the buyer's choice decision are generally small in number. Marketers categorize these consumer responses to brand offerings as "sets."

At any given time all brands constitute a total set, which is broken down into an awareness set and an unawareness set. With changes in marketing effort, a brand can move from the unawareness to the awareness set. The awareness set has three subsets: an *evoked set* $(+)$, an *inert set* (0), and an *inept set* $(-)$.[16] The evoked set includes the few brands the consumer considers in his or her purchase choice.[17] Naturally, all sellers of branded products want their merchandise to be part of the buyer's evoked set. The inert set consists of those brands in the product category for which the consumer has neither a positive nor a negative evaluation. And the inept set comprises those brands the consumer has rejected from purchase consideration, either because of a previous unsatisfactory experience with the brand, or because of negative feedback received from other sources. Each of these subsets has different marketing implications and the brands within each of them require different marketing emphasis. Figure 9-2 illustrates the concept of the relative positioning of brands within the consumer's perception.

The essence of brand strategy is, of course, to produce and market a brand so that it winds up in the consumer's awareness set, it is hoped in the evoked set category.

Marketing managers of branded products strive to create one of three situations for their products that have earned a place in the consumer's evoked set. First, the primary, most desired objective is that the product qualify for *brand insistence*. That is, consumers so prefer a given brand that they will insist upon

---

[16] Based upon Chem L. Narayana and Rom J. Markin, "Consumer Behavior and Product Performance: An Alternative Conceptualization," *Journal of Marketing* **39** (October 1975), pp. 1–6.
[17] John Howard and Jagdish N. Sheth, *The Theory of Buyer Behavior* (New York: Wiley, 1969).

Figure 9-2 A conceptualization of consumer behavior regarding perceptual preference for brands

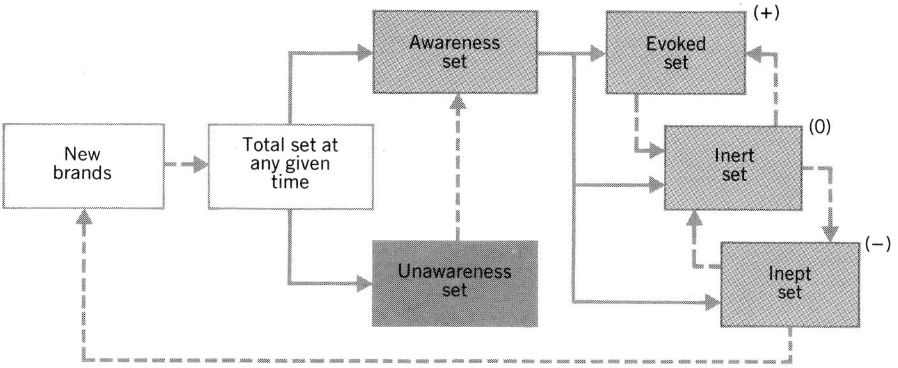

Source: Chem L. Narayana and Rom J. Markin, "Consumer Behavior and Product Performance: An Alternative Conceptualization," *Journal of Marketing* **39** (October 1975), p.2.

purchasing it and be reluctant to accept a substitute. Second, if brand insistence cannot be achieved, the next best situation is *brand preference*. Brand preference suggests that consumers favor that brand over most others, although if it is out of stock, they will accept a substitute. Finally, the next level to be attained through branding is *brand recognition*, which implies not just awareness, but favorable disposition toward the brand. This means that consumers will at the minimum consider the brand for possible purchase and that it is not perceived as being in either the inert or inept categories.

Strategy Implications.   The concept of consumer response sets can be an effective tool in the management of brands. Through marketing research a marketing manager could learn what percentage of the market was aware of the company's brand, as well as the relative breakdown into each of the three subsets—evoked, inert, and inept. If a high proportion of shoppers were unaware of the brand, this of course would signal the need for more advertising and promotion. Even if the brand were in the evoked set for a large part of the market, this would not necessarily be cause to relax. Advertising and promotional support for the brand would still be needed to reinforce the consumer's present acceptance and to ward off competition. Should the brand be in the inert set for a large group of consumers, a promotional campaign such as comparative advertising or free samples, widely distributed, might be warranted. Products in the inept set of too many consumers need careful evaluation and review and may be likely candidates for abandonment.

Packaging: It Is Both Product and Promotion

Packaging is an important part of product planning and development; it is, therefore, important in the total marketing strategy. Packaging is that part of product planning and development which relates to the design of a product's container or wrapper, whose purpose is both to protect the item and enhance its value to the consumer. Modern packaging designs are a sophisticated blending of viewpoints—marketing, design theory, and even research—into an aesthetically pleasing package. The package is an integral part of the product, in many instances, as well as a means of projecting the product in the

In the factory we make cosmetics—in the store we sell hope.

most favorable way. Packaging is often as vital to the effectiveness of the marketing program and the product's profitability as are branding, labeling, the product warranty, and service. In a vast number of consumer goods, the package is critically important to the buyer's recognition of the product. This is especially true with snack foods, soft drinks, chewing gum, cosmetics, toiletries, and some items of clothing and accessories like panty hose and men's jewelry.

Both seller and buyer benefit by packaging. For the seller, it permits protection of the product, more efficient physical distribution, lower total costs, and ultimately higher sales and profits. The buyer gains similar advantages. Packaging enhances the product and sometimes provides storage for it when not in use. It also helps the customer recognize the product, provides information concerning its use, and helps keep it fresh and undamaged until it is needed.

Packaging as Part of the Marketing Strategy

The Systems Approach to Packaging.   Packaging as a part of marketing strategy is today largely approached from a systems point of view, namely, packaging must be treated as a part of marketing management rather than as a strictly technical problem in physical handling. Seen this way, packaging must be judged from the following criteria: (1) the state of goods on receipt by the customer, (2) the package's informative and promotional value, (3) the role of package design in physical distribution, including the handling problems at all stages in the marketing channel, and (4) the ecological and environmental aspects of packaging.[18]

Within the context of marketing management, the company packaging objective is stated simply: an attractive, simple container that can be produced, stored, physically handled, and marketed for the least cost. Customers are not always willing to pay the price of what an engineer considers the best packaging method. Because sales revenue with the right profit margin is the goal, the customer's reaction always carries more weight than that of the packaging engineer.

Physical Distribution Requirements.   One of the package's essential requirements is that it protect the product while simplifying its physical handling and distribution from the time it leaves the production line to when it reaches the ultimate consumer. The cost of physical handling and distribution, which includes storage and shipping throughout the distribution channel, is an enormous part of the total cost of marketing a product. Goods that are damaged in shipment and arrive in poor condition at the retailer's store are a burdensome expense to manufacturers. If the retailer or other intermediary receives merchandise in a satisfactory condition, but it is damaged or its value in any way diminished because of improper packaging after its receipt, the reseller must

---

[18] See Gordon Wills, "Packaging as a Source of Profit," *International Journal of Physical Distribution* **5**, no. 6 (1975), pp. 306–333.

"The new package looks so good on the shelves the customers are leaving it on the shelves."

bear the loss. In any event, packaging as a part of the physical distribution function should result in:

1. Lower costs for handling, shipping, and other labor requirements
2. Lower packing costs through proper packaging design
3. Lower inventory holding costs
4. Lower space costs
5. Less damage in transit and storage

Customer Purchase Appeal. Marketing information systems will frequently yield all kinds of important data on customer responses to pricing and point-of-sale merchandising, yet the effect of the package on sales is only recently being assessed. The package is an important informational cue to many buyers. Products that enjoy unusual sales success also score high in recognition by shoppers. The marketer who packages creatively will have a considerable advantage in securing a meaningful market share.

Many firms attribute the market success of their products to management's close attention to packaging. For example, Ore-Ida Foods, the Boise, Idaho, subsidiary of the H.J. Heinz Company, ascribes much of its success in its product mix to competitive packaging.[19] Each season the company reevaluates consumers' needs, their changing tastes, and its product positioning and then evaluates the effectiveness of each of its packages in communicating the product message. Ore-Ida's packaging is based upon the following guidelines:

- Create a strong brand name and symbol association
- Establish an overall family association for each package
- Develop a clear differentiation for each product variety within an overall package design which contributes to the total impact of the package system
- Adopt a package system with a shelf or in-cabinet look unmistakably high-quality and dramatic

Such attention to the role of packaging is based upon the understanding born of intense competition that packaging must do a powerful selling job at the point of purchase. All products clamor for the buyer's attention. Because shelf space in retail stores is particularly scarce, retailers are inclined to take on products with high packaging impact, the result of manufacturers' careful planning.

Package designers are studying consumer behavior to assess the impact of packaging on buyers' search and find efforts, to discover how packaging fits into today's more complex shopping environment, how packaging reduces shopping time, and the impact of package design on customer eye movement.

Ecological and Environmental Consequences of Packages

Many social critics view packaging as a waste of national resources and a scourge to the environment—a fetish of convenience and luxury whose costs outweigh its benefits.

The opposition to packaging stems from its contribution to the solid waste problem and the difficulty of disposing of the container after its functions of product protection and consumer convenience are finished. A few years ago, the packager's response to critics of the "throwaway culture" was that it was simply easier and more economical to do it that way. Today, however, greater social awareness and sensitivity have led many marketers to realize that they have a responsibility not to squander resources needed by future generations and that all packaging programs must weigh environmental and ecological issues carefully.

Some companies, for example, Coors Brewery in Colorado, have taken the initiative in promoting returnable containers and in developing a beverage can that opens without a throwaway ring tab. Some legislatures are accelerating this trend by passing laws against throwaway containers, while lawmakers and private companies are promoting more responsible public attitudes toward recycling waste and encouraging more responsible packaging by industry.

---

[19] "Capitalizing on Presold Image," *Modern Packaging*, July 1976, p. 40.

Before proceeding, can you answer these questions:
1. What is a brand? What is a trademark?
2. What are the two principal types of brands?
3. What are the strategic reasons why a firm brands its products?
4. What are the main purposes of packaging?

The Total Product Concept and Full Utility

Consumers, we have learned, buy bundles of expectations. If their expectations are fulfilled, they are satisfied and their purchase behavior is rewarded. If their expectations are not fulfilled, consumers are dissatisfied and thus, not fully rewarded. The product or service is not just the benefits consumers seek, but the total product. The total product includes the basic product and all those other attributes which enhance or create *utility* for the consumer. Remember that *utility* is the ability of something to satisfy a want or a need. Utility is value. Marketing creates product value for consumers by providing goods when and where they are wanted, and by aiding in the exchange process that puts the goods or services in the possession of those who want them.

Marketing activities also create another very important value—the utility of information. Marketers inform consumers about a product's attributes; what it will do; what its limitations are; how it should be used; what it contains; and what hazards, if any, surround its use.

We purchase cars, furniture polish, boats, and most consumer and industrial goods because of their ability to do something. Possession alone is not sufficient; the product is purchased to be used. Therefore, to minimize the buyer's risk, especially in certain kinds of products, the performance of the product should be *warranted* by the seller. And, to ensure that the product lives up to the buyer's expectations, the seller can provide adequate maintenance or *service* facilities to repair products that develop defects or break down. These things too, then—information, warranties, and services—are part of the total product concept.

Packaging Information

The consumer's rights to safety and product choice have been broadened to include the right to know. This right to know developed through the combined efforts of more militant consumers, responsive state and federal legislatures, and enlightened business communities. Consequently, information about efficiency and comparative performance is given much more frequently and for a much broader array of products.

The most far-reaching piece of legislation to date has been the federal government's Fair Packaging and Labeling Act of 1967. This bill "requires labels and packages to disclose sufficient information regarding product ingredients and composition as will establish or preserve fair competition between competitive products by enabling consumers to make rational comparisons with respect to price and other factors or to prevent consumer deception.[20] In something of a departure from its usual practice, Congress thus legislated to protect the economic interests, rather than the safety or health, of the consumer.

Clearly, this bill established Congress as a champion of the consumer's right to know. Packages and their labels should give buyers accurate information as to the quality of the contents and such information should make it easy to compare value.

Many consumerists believe that such legislation has been badly needed. Informed customers are essential for the efficient functioning of the free market economy. Too frequently, label information has been both inadequate and confusing.

There is reason to believe that buyer behavior is greatly altered or improved with the provision of more information, because such information enhances the consumer's confidence in his or her choice. This confidence creates additional satisfaction (utility) with the purchase, assuring the buyer that the product is right for the purpose intended, and that the price is justified.[21]

The Product Warranty

A warranty is an obligation assumed by the seller. Basically it is an expressed or implied statement of responsibility that promises the buyer certain services or satisfactions. The product warranty has become, increasingly, an important dimension of competitive strategy. It is seen by many buyers as an added assurance of product quality and value, even though this is not always the case.

Most tangible goods are covered by implied warranties. An implied warranty of merchantability, under the **Uniform Commercial Code** in effect in all states except Louisiana, warrants that a product is fit for the ordinary purpose for which it is sold, is properly packaged and labeled, and conforms to any promises or claims made on the label.

Warranties have become, in many instances, mere promotional devices for promising customers more than ever is delivered.[22] As a result of numerous complaints by consumers and agitation by consumerist groups, the Congress passed in 1975 the Magnuson-Moss Warranty-Federal Trade Commission Improvement Act. Under its provisions, the FTC is directed to require the warrantor to make the terms of the warranty available to the consumer before the product is sold. The FTC is also empowered to specify the manner and form in which warranties may be used in advertising and other promotional material.

[20] U.S. Congress, Senate Committee on Commerce, *Fair Packaging and Labeling,* 89th Cong. 1st session on S. 985 (Washington, D.C.: Government Printing Office, 1965), p. 471.

[21] George S. Day, "Assessing the Effects of Information Disclosure Requirements," *Journal of Marketing* **40** (April 1976), pp. 42–52.

[22] Lawrence P. Feldman, "New Legislation and the Prospects for Real Warranty Reform" *Journal of Marketing* **40** (July 1976), pp. 41–47.

Table 9-1 Extent of Difficulties Experienced or Anticipated with Repair Service

Product	Adler-Hlavacek Study February 1975		
	Had a Great Deal or Some Trouble	Had Little or No Trouble	Don't Own
Automobile	22%	73%	5%
Television	19	75	5
Stereo	19	56	25
Refrigerator	18	74	8
Vacuum cleaner	17	75	8
Stove	19	71	11
Toaster	15	78	8
Electric can opener	20	53	27
Typewriter	18	52	30
Pocket calculator	12	26	61

Source: Lee Adler and James D. Hlavacek, "The Relationship Between Prices and Repair Services for Consumer Durables," *Journal of Marketing*, 40, no. 2 (April 1976), p. 81.

Other provisions stipulate that warranties provide consumers with necessary and meaningful information. A seller giving a full warranty is required, under the act, to remedy the defective product within a reasonable period of time. Another important provision is an outright prohibition on disclaiming implied warranties. The intent of this provision is to prevent a warrantor from escaping obligations under the Uniform Commercial Code upholding the implied warranties of salability and fitness. In capsule form, the intent of the act is to increase the consumer's awareness and understanding of warranty terms and to strengthen consumer recourse when products don't work.

Product Service

To enhance the customers' satisfaction and reduce their sense of risk, many companies provide extensive service facilities in support of their marketing programs. One study reported that servicing costs amounted to 35 percent of the total dollars spent on color television sets.[23] Furthermore, many marketers have learned that no matter to whom customer complaints are directed, they often boil down to dissatisfaction with service.[24] Table 9-1 shows the results of two studies of consumer experiences with repair services.

It is important to note the improvement in these statistics from 1972 to 1975. This may be the result of greater consumer and government pressure for better

[23] *The M.I.T. Report—Consumer Appliances: The Real Cost*, Washington, D.C.: National Science Foundation, 1973.
[24] *An Examination of Consumer Problems and Business Responses*, Sub-Council on Performance and Service, National Business Council for Consumer Affairs, September 1973, p. 4.

service and the positive response from business. One of the great unfulfilled market opportunities appears to exist in after-the-sale product service. The typical customer is tremendously disadvantaged in this area and is at the mercy of the person servicing the product. Repair costs are invariably regarded as "too high" for most products.[25] Many marketers, recognizing the need for greater responsibility on their part as well as the opportunity to generate increasd customer satisfaction and company revenues, are now providing better repair services at reasonable cost to their customers. Some manufacturers and resellers, for a set price, will make all repairs and adjustments not already coverd by the warranty. Even after the expiration of the warranty, they will continue to service the product for an annual fee. Offering such repair services benefits both buyer and seller. The seller may use service as a genuine promotional strategy, similar to a warranty or other product attribute. If the repairs are provided through a service contract, revenues and profits may actually be increased. At the same time, the seller's obligation to keep the product in good working condition increases buyer satisfaction as well as product and store loyalty because it reduces the customer's actual and perceived purchase risks. Repair services are therefore an important part of product strategy because they extend a product's life and add to its value.

Summary

Consumers buy total bundles of expectations. This total bundle of expectations is what marketers refer to as the total product concept—the basic foundation of product strategy. It is important for marketers to manage their total product assortment. Managing implies the planning needed in designing and creating new products, as well as in balancing the product line (having an assortment of goods available to meet expected customer demand) and assessing each product by such important criteria as sales revenue, market share, position, and profitability. Management of the product planning and development process requires an understanding of each product life cycle. The shape and duration of the product life cycle is affected by the firm's marketing strategy.

Furthermore, product planning and development includes methods for deleting products that no longer contribute significantly to the firm's marketing program. There must also be a procedure for recalling and modifying products whose defects detract from their safe use. The concept of planned product obsolescence is basically a cultural-social problem rather than exclusively a marketing problem.

Branding, packaging, product labeling and information, the warranty program, and the provision of after-the-sale repair services are all part of the total product strategy, because each of these activities adds to the customer's total bundle of product expectations.

[25] Lee Adler and James D. Hlavacek, "The Relationship between Price and Repair Service for Consumer Durables," *Journal of Marketing* **40**, no. 2 (April 1976) pp. 80–82.

Review Questions

1. What is the meaning of the term "total product concept"?
2. What is meant by the statement that consumers buy total bundles of expectations?
3. Why is it important for marketers to manage the product life cycle?
4. In your own words, what is meant by "product mix strategy"?
5. What is meant by "planned product obsolescence"? Is this a marketing or a cultural problem? What are the social costs of planned product obsolescence?
6. Why do many firms not have a systematic procedure for deleting sick or unproductive products?
7. What is a brand? How do brands differ from trademarks?
8. What are the marketing advantages of branding? Are there disadvantages? What are they?
9. What are the basic provisions of the Fair Packaging and Labeling Act of 1967 and the Magnuson-Moss Warranty-Federal Trade Commission Improvement Act of 1975?
10. After a product is sold, repair services extend its life and add to its value. Who should pay for the addition of these attributes?

Case 9-1

Blue Ribbon Sports

Like the ski parka and the ten-speed bicycle, fancy-colored running shoes have become part of the "leisure" hysteria of modern America and much of the world. Many buyers of specially constructed running or jogging shoes do little more with theirs than walk from the parking lot to the inside of the supermarket to shop or move from their easy chair to change the channel on the TV set to watch *Wide World of Sports*. Many of these new breed of running shoes cost as much as $70 per pair, but they have virtually replaced the old sneaker or tennis shoe as America's leisure time footwear.

The most successful U.S. manufacturer of this fancy new footwear is Blue Ribbon Sports of Beaverton, Oregon, a privately held company founded by running enthusiast Phil Knight, 42, and Bill Bowerman, 69. In slightly more than 8 years, Blue Ribbon Sports and their Nike (Nī-́kē) shoes have gone from a standing start to sales of nearly $400 million. Nike is now in the

starting blocks hoping to overtake Adidas, the West German sport giant. Nike already has 136 models for every sport from running and tennis to volleyball and wrestling. The company plans to add another 50 varieties to cover everything from hiking to leisure wear—running shoes, in effect, for the nonrunner.

Knight and Bowerman, the former University of Oregon track coach, met in 1958, when Knight was a business student at Oregon and a mile runner of considerable ability. For years coach Bowerman had been working to design a better running shoe in his kitchen. Existing shoes, he believed, were too heavy and lacked adequate cushioning.

In 1964, Knight and Bowerman each put up $500 and went into business importing Japanese running shoes. They produced their own prototype model in 1972, naming it after the Greek goddess of victory. They persuaded several marathon runners, just before the Olympic

trials in 1972, to try their new shoes. Runners wearing Adidas finished one, two, and three, but the next four finishers were wearing Nikes.

The big design and construction break-through came as a result of some Sunday morning fiddling by Bowerman in 1975. He began tinkering with the waffle iron that had just been used to make breakfast. Using some urethane rubber, he fashioned a new type of sole whose tiny rubber studs made it springy. The waffle iron was ruined but a new running shoe was created that was soon in high demand by the army of weekend runners and leisure enthusiasts suffering from bruised feet.

Along with its successes, Blue Ribbon has had a few problems. A much touted "air-sole" shoe, which had a tiny gas-filled bag in the sole, at first fizzled because of too little gas pressure. One of the biggest problems facing the company now is how to raise larger and larger amounts of capital so that it can continue to introduce new products and keep ahead of the pack. Perhaps the most critical activity within the company is related to product planning and development.

Questions

1. How does the notion of the total product concept relate to Blue Ribbon Sports?
2. What kind of product mix strategy does it appear is being pursued by Blue Ribbon Sports?
3. Does brand strategy appear to be an important element in Blue Ribbon Sports' marketing effort?
4. Would the development of a walking shoe be considered a viable possibility for Blue Ribbon Sports? To whom might it appeal?

Case 9-2

Sherwin-Williams Company

Sherwin-Williams Company has long been known as a paintmaker whose slogan has traditionally been "We cover the earth." However, that image is being changed by a new marketing program which SW hopes will enable it to recoup some of the earnings it has been losing. Throughout the late 1970s and the beginning of the 1980s, company sales have been flagging and profits as a percentage of sales have been down as much as 55 percent. Chairman Walter O. Spencer, 49, is hoping that the new marketing program for the 110-year-old company will rejuvenate the operation.

The new approach is a change in marketing strategy related to expanded product offerings and mix of assortments. All of this centers around transforming the Cleveland company's nationwide chain of paint stores into "home decorating centers." Boosting sales in these stores is important, for last year they provided about 77 percent of the coating group's total revenues of $598 million. The remainder of the group's volume comes from direct sales to industrial users, "house brand" retail chains, and independent dealers.

Sherwin-Williams has thus revamped some 600 of their stores and has plans for 1,000 others in the chain. Making over units that once sold paint almost entirely to local painting contractors, the company has lured homemakers and do-it-yourselfers with expanded lines of consumer oriented merchandise such as carpeting and drapes. Many stores have been enlarged and are now located in higher-traffic areas. The company has steered clear of opening units in large shopping malls and has put most of its stores on major traffic streets in "strip" shopping areas.

Spencer readily acknowledges that, in the past, the company was short on marketing know-how. "We weren't going out and asking our customers what they wanted to buy, how they wanted to buy it, and where," he says. "We were not aggressive enough in the marketplace and we had not upgraded our stores." Now Sherwin-Williams has gone from basically a paint contractor approach to a do-it-yourself approach that a majority of people seem to want today.

To accomplish these changes, Spencer first installed a marketing research department then, moved to alter the entire marketing operation through a changing merchandising concept. In the last five years, SW closed 100 of its stores in poor locations. It next added new ones or extensively modernized older stores in suburban areas, increasing their size from an average of 5,000 square feet per store initially to 6,000 square feet and most recently to 10,000 square feet. Over the next five years, eighty to one hundred Sherwin-Williams stores will be brought up to date each year. New lights, new shelving, new floors, and new display fixtures will brighten up units not closed or relocated.

The stores now carry carpeting and resilient floor covering plus made-to-measure draperies that shoppers order from in-store samples. The basic store formula for floor space now is 25 percent paint, 25 percent floor covering, 15 percent draperies, 15 percent wall coverings, and 20 percent accessories. The larger outlets—typical of the ones currently being opened now with 10,000 square feet of space—also carry decorator mirrors, lamps, unfinished furniture, and such seasonal items as lawn furniture and outdoor cooking utensils.

The new plan has yet to prove itself totally because more time is needed to assess it thoroughly. In 1977, sales were up 18 percent but earnings in the consumer sales division were down 46 percent.

Questions

1. How would you assess the marketing plan at Sherwin-Williams?
2. What is the relationship between product planning and development and the term "merchandising"?
3. What are the major risks in Sherwin-Williams' new approach?

Chapter 10

Understanding and Managing Channels of Distribution

Pantyhose began to appear on supermarket shelves about 1969. Up until that time, the Hanes Corporation had been selling its pantyhose through department stores.

However, based upon a market study costing $400,000, Hanes' marketers decided that supermarket buyers of hosiery were not interested just in price, and that many of them were frustrated by uneven quality and poor fit.

Hence, L'eggs were introduced as well-made, properly fitting hose to be sold basically through supermarkets at $1.39 per pair—a premium price compared with the other brands being merchandised in food chains. Pantyhose give supermarkets and drugstores about a 40 percent **gross margin** on a retail price of 99 cents. There is widespread private branding of pantyhose in supermarkets and this tends to accelerate the price competition. At the time L'eggs were introduced, most private brands were selling for 79 cents. A&P was selling its private label pantyhose for as little as 39 cents a pair, while some supermarkets offered price specials of three pair for a dollar. Hanes was firm with its $1.39 price and worked feverishly to establish a clear-cut identity for its L'eggs brand. The *product* was launched with an initial hefty $10 million introductory *promotional* campaign—more than double the amount spent by the entire hosiery industry. The advertising theme was tied to the distinctive egg-shaped, point-of-purchase *packaging* display and used with the catchy slogan "Our L'eggs fit your legs." The company spent an additional $5 million on national consumer promotion, using introductory coupons worth 25 cents or 35 cents off on each pair of L'eggs purchased. The concern of those in charge of the advertising campaign was that consumer brand awareness of hosiery was basically nonexistent in supermarkets and drugstores. Brand permanency for L'eggs had to be reinforced to the consumer and to the trade as well.

At the time, supermarkets were a new outlet for pantyhose, and Hanes designed a completely revised marketing program to sell the product through the new **channel of distribution.** Only 2½ square feet of selling space are required in the supermarket. The pantyhose are placed in the store on consignment, so the retailer is not required to make any investment in inventory at all. Each store is able to generate about $1,300 a year in profits from a single L'eggs display.

Hanes, with its L'eggs pantyhose, thus has turned a highly fragmented chaotic market situation into a unique market opportunity. Careful planning and strategic market action have created a very profitable situation which Hanes completely dominates.

There is much about this example that bears analysis. First of all, central to L'eggs' success was Hanes' tailoring of its marketing program to the particular channel it chose.[1] The supermarket, because of its customer acceptance, its ability to generate traffic, and to merchandise convenience items at relatively low prices, has become an important outlet for many commodities.

---

[1] See Robert E. Weigand, "Fit Products and Channels to Your Market," *Harvard Business Review,* January–February 1977, pp. 95–105.

Understanding Channels of Distribution

The story of L'eggs pantyhose tends to emphasize once again that marketing strategy is a comprehensive plan of action that consists of at least two major steps. The first is the identification of a market target to which the given company wishes to direct its appeal. The second is the development of a marketing mix—deciding on the relative emphasis to be placed on the different aspects of the marketing effort. Decisions must be made about product planning and development, branding, and packaging; the role of promotion and the kinds to be used; how to price the product; and the kinds and numbers of outlets through which the products will be merchandised. This last set of decisions relates to what marketers call "channels of distribution."

Most of us have a fairly good idea of what channels of distribution are. The phrase itself is descriptive. "Channels" are routes, avenues, or pathways, suggesting movement or flow. "Distribution" means to distribute, disseminate, or spread about. Hence, when related to marketing, channels of distribution refer to the routes, avenues, or pathways through which goods and services flow, or move from producers to consumers. Though formal definitions may differ, this is what channels of distribution essentially are. It is critically important that marketers understand channels of distribution and that they are able to create distribution facilities that will enable them to reach their market targets effectively.

Defining Channels of Distribution

There are many definitions of channels of distribution. A few will be cited because each definition in its own way conveys a bit of meaning about the concept.

Channels of distribution are often likened to pipelines through which a product flows on its way to the consumer. Channels are also seen as the agencies through which the seller, who may or may not be the manufacturer, markets a product to the ultimate user. In another view channels are a group of firms that together make up a loose coalition exploiting a joint opportunity in the market. Channels of distribution are also sometimes defined as the group of intermediaries who move goods from producers to consumers. Channels are perceived by a final group as made up of those merchants who own the goods and those intervening agents who facilitate sales. This last definition conforms most closely to that established by the American Marketing Association. In this text we shall define channels of distribution as the path taken, as evidenced by title or ownership, by goods in moving from producer to consumer.[2]

The channel of distribution, therefore, in its most meaningful and simple form, is the course taken in the transfer of title by a commodity. This route includes both the manufacturer and the ultimate consumer, as well as anyone in between. Intermediaries in the channel include both merchants who take

[2] American Marketing Association Committee on Definitions, *Marketing Definitions: A Glossary of Marketing Terms* (Chicago, 1960), p. 10.

title and market on their own account, and various kinds of agents such as brokers, manufacturers' agents, or commission sellers who do not take title but who still aid marketing flows and exchanges.

The difference between merchants and agents can be illustrated by an example such as coffee. South American growers own the beans and they sell them to buyers throughout the world. United States buyers include the coffee companies who merchandise their own manufacturers' brands and the large food chains who package and merchandise their own reseller brands. Most sales are arranged by brokers. Brokers do not take title to the coffee, hence, do not own the product; they are agents whose principal task is to smooth the way for (or, as marketing professionals say, facilitate) the transactions between the seller (the South American grower) and the buyer (say Hills Brothers, Folger's, or a food chain such as Safeway, A & P, or Kroger). Therefore, channels of distribution are made up of agents and merchant middlemen. In this example the agent is the coffee broker and the merchant middlemen are the United States coffee companies and the retailers who market both the manufacturers' and distributor brands.

Functions and Institutions versus Rivers and Pipelines.   Channels of distribution are best understood not so much as rivers or pipelines but as coalitions of **marketing institutions** cooperating in a series of complementary **marketing functions.** Marketing functions are the activities of buying, selling, transportation, storage, standardization and grading, financing, risk bearing, and circulating market information.[3] Such a listing of marketing functions is more relevant to physical products than it is to our expanded version of "product" under the generic concept of marketing. In this expanded concept of product, which includes intangibles such as services, marketing functions might be viewed more appropriately as follows:

1. *Contactual*. The searching out of buyers and sellers.
2. *Merchandising*. Matching the goods to the market requirement.
3. *Pricing*. Determining the optimum price: high enough to make production and distribution possible and low enough to induce users to accept the *goods*.
4. *Promotion*. Influencing the buyers to favor the product or its sponsor.
5. *Physical distribution*. The transportation and storage of goods.[4]

With the exception of services, which are usually characterized as being produced at the point of consumption and therefore having telescoped channels of distribution, the above list of marketing functions seems much more compatible with our notion of modern marketing as an organized system of

---

[3] See Theodore N. Beckman and William R. Davidson, *Marketing,* 8th ed. (New York: Ronald Press, 1967), p. 424.
[4] This list was suggested by the works of Edmund D. McGarry in "Some Functions of Marketing Reconsidered," in *Theory of Marketing,* eds. Reavis Cox and Wroe Alderson (Homewood, IL: Irwin, 1950), pp. 269–273.

transaction and exchanges. Each of the five functions is a major activity intended to facilitate exchange processes.

Marketing institutions are those firms or agencies that perform marketing functions. Most frequently, marketing institutions emerge through the need for specialization and division of labor in carrying out a set of marketing functions. For example, retailers are specialists in contactual, merchandising, and promotional functions. Wholesalers are also experts in finding buyers and merchandising and, in addition, are skilled in physical distribution. A given channel may utilize both retailers and wholesalers whose efforts complement one another in a particular market situation. Often, the total set of functions is best performed by a group of intermediaries working together.

Contrary to what the following cartoon depicts, intermediaries are not pompous "fat cats" who siphon off large profits and rob the marketing system of its efficiency. They are important marketing institutions, performing essential marketing functions.

Kinds of Channels

Goods and services simply cannot be marketed without the performance of marketing functions. An easy way to understand this is to remember that marketing is the performance of functions (activities) to facilitate exchange processes. Thus, when thinking about channels of distribution, it is important to keep two things in mind: (1) channels are coalitions of marketing institutions (firms or agencies) that (2) collectively or independently perform marketing functions (contacting, merchandising, pricing, promotion, and physical distribution) in order to move goods from producers to consumers. Channels of distribution may be long, short, or intermediate. These terms do not refer to distance but rather to the numbers of intermediaries within each channel. For example, in Figure 10-1, channels 1 and 2 are basically short channels. Chan-

Drawing by Stevenson; © 1976 The New Yorker Magazine, Inc.

nels 3 and 4 are of an intermediate length, that is, they contain a moderate number of channel members, and channel 5 is a relatively long one because of its rather large number of intermediaries. Channels of distribution are sometimes also described as either direct or indirect. A direct channel of distribution is best equated with the term "short." Hence direct channels, like shorter channels, are those with few if any intermediaries. Channels 1 and 2 in Figure 10-1 are clearly direct channels. Channels 3 through 5 would be best classified as indirect channels. You may eliminate certain intervening merchants, such as wholesalers, or agent middlemen, such as brokers, but you absolutely cannot eliminate the marketing functions.

Examples of Channel Types.   Figures 10-1 and 10-2 illustrate rather typical channels for the distribution of consumer and industrial goods. These two examples, however, do not exhaust all the possible ways of setting up channels.

The first channel in Figure 10-1 is a direct channel of distribution between the manufacturer and the ultimate consumer. Such channels are established when manufacturers sell through mail order, by catalog, or with their own field sales organizations. Avon cosmetics and Tupperware are examples of products sold by manufacturers directly to ultimate consumers. The second channel has one intermediary. A merchant intermediary who sells to ultimate consumers is called a retailer. Retailers who sell products at wholesale prices are not wholesalers. Instead, they are retailers selling at discount, because they are selling to ultimate users. Channel 3 has two intermediaries, a merchant middleman—the retailer—and an agent or broker. Agents or brokers do not take title to the goods they handle, but assist in the performance of certain marketing functions. The fourth channel also has two intermediaries, but both

Figure 10-1   Channels of distribution for consumer goods.

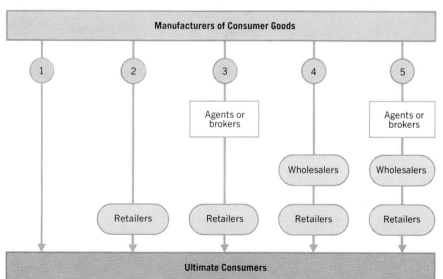

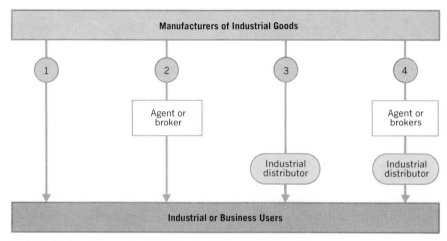

Figure 10-2   Channels of distribution for industrial goods.

are merchants. A wholesaler is a merchant middleman who sells to others, who in turn plan to resell to someone else. Retailers and wholesalers can therefore be distinguished by the purpose for which they buy and accumulate inventories. Retailers plan to sell to final consumers or users, whereas wholesalers' customers buy not for final consumption, but for resale. Channel 5 is the longest of the channels shown, consisting of both agent middlemen and two kinds of merchant middlemen—wholesalers and retailers.

Here is an interesting point for you to consider. Long channels of distribution generally indicate a high degree of specialization within the channel, and specialization usually means lower cost through efficiency and economies of scale. Long channels therefore are often a cheaper way of distributing goods than shorter channels. This can be easily illustrated with the case of bread, one of our most staple and taken-for-granted items, which goes through a seven-segment channel. The wheat is grown by the farmer (1) and when harvested sold to a local elevator (2). The elevator operator's main function is one of storage but this individual then sells the wheat to a wholesale dealer, (3) who in turn sells to a mill (4) that grinds the wheat into flour. The milling company then sells the flour to flour jobbers (another wholesaler) and wholesale bakers (5) who in turn convert the flour into bread products, which are then sold to retail stores (6) who sell them to consumers (7). Thus, this rather long distribution channel contains many specialists throughout its various stages, but these specialists are quite efficient and the result is relatively low prices for the consumer.

In Figure 10-2 the channels shown are similar to those of Figure 10-1, except that we are concerned here with channels for industrial goods. Notice that in Figure 10-2, channels 3 and 4 contain industrial distributors. These are merchant wholesalers who specialize in marketing industrial products (parts needed in fabricating, minor equipment, accessories, and operating supplies) to industrial or business buyers.

Which Kind Is Most Prevalent?   Unfortunately, it cannot be stated with any accuracy which kind of channel is most prevalent, or popular. As we shall learn, the type of channel employed and the number of intermediaries in it depend on a whole host of considerations—the nature of the product and its market; the size and financial strength of the manufacturer; consumer preferences, attitudes, and buying habits; the retailer's size and financial strength; and other environmental and situational considerations. Certainly, many manufacturers today seek to market directly, at least directly to the retailer. Many retailers likewise wish to buy direct from manufacturers and eliminate wholesale intermediaries. Yet, the wholesaler in many lines of trade is still a viable part of the channel of distribution.

Many firms have discovered that they can achieve greater market success by utilizing two or even more channels of distribution. For example, RCA Whirlpool markets a great part of its output through independent appliance wholesale distributors who in turn sell to retail appliance stores and small department stores. Large department stores and general merchandise discount stores buy RCA Whirlpool products direct from the manufacturer. Finally, a large portion of RCA Whirlpool's output, sold directly to Sears Roebuck and Company, is marketed under the Sears brand names of Kenmore and Coldspot.

Intermediaries Perform Valuable Functions

The presence of intermediaries in the marketing channel is an attempt to reduce the cost of performing marketing functions through specialization. Specialization arises from what economists call "division of labor." Simply stated, division of labor is an attempt to break down a complex task into a series of simpler ones that can be more routinely performed. In many respects this is what happens within the trading channel. The various intermediaries, and the producer as well, become more efficient when the total marketing effort is broken down into a series of functions, some of which are performed more competently by one member of the channel, while others are carried out better by different members. The total cost of marketing may therefore be lowered as a result of the combined efforts of all channel members.

Intermediaries Facilitate Exchange.   The use of marketing intermediaries facilitates the exchange process.[5] If every consumer had to seek out the manufacturer of each item consumed and had to examine and evaluate each offering at its place of manufacture, it would be an impossible task for consumers. Even if the retailer from whom consumers purchased was forced to seek out the individual products that might be suitable for his or her assortment, search, travel time, evaluation, and processing would be a crushing burden, Yet, without intermediaries, such would be the case.

[5] See Bert Rosenblum, *Marketing Channels: A Management View* (Hinsdale, IL: Dryden Press, 1978).

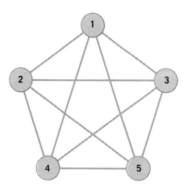

Figure 10-3 Decentralized exchange process with five manufacturers.

Consider this example. Suppose we have just five producers of five different commodities and each worker can make more of each item than he or his family can use. Therefore, to acquire commodities other than those the individual produces, each one must trade with another. Ten exchanges are required for each producer to acquire one of every product. Figure 10-3 diagrams the exchanges among the producers.

Now suppose we replace this form of exchange by putting a "trading specialist" in the exchange system. Our trading specialist is not a producer but a marketer who specializes in the buying and selling of producers' commodities. All the producers bring their surplus to the trading specialist, who accumulates an inventory of merchandise from which to sell the others commodities they need. As shown in Figure 10-4, only five trips, or exchanges, are now necessary. Buyers and sellers can come to the trading specialist at a convenient time and place an order for the exchange to take place.

In Figure 10-5 you can clearly see how the wholesaler simplifies the tangle of relationships through which manufacturers and retailers would otherwise have to pick their way.

Figure 10-4 Centralized exchange process with a trading specialist.

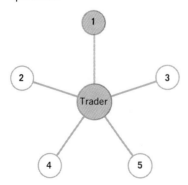

Figure 10-5 The role of the wholesaler in the channel of distribution. (a) Direct marketing. (b) Distribution through wholesalers.

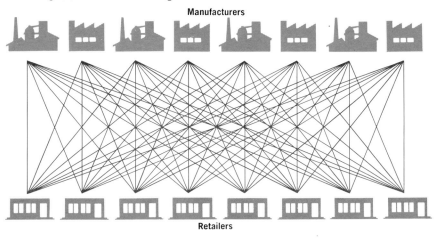

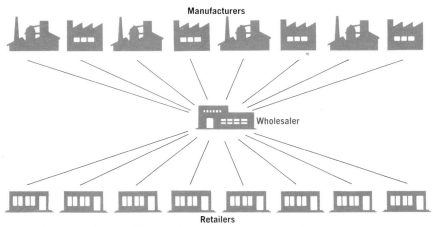

Source: Theodore Beckman, William Davidson, W. Wayne Talarzyk, *Marketing,* 9th ed. (New York: Ronald Press, 1973), p. 307.

Intermediaries create these utilities basically through a matching and sorting process. Each intermediary seeks a balanced stock of goods from the total of all goods available (sorting) in order to meet (match) the needs of the customers. Intermediaries perform several kinds of sorting activities. One is the sorting out or breaking down of a large varied supply into separate stocks which are basically similar. Another form of sorting is *accumulation,* or bringing similar smaller stocks together into a larger similar supply. *Allocation* is another form of sorting that consists of breaking down a uniform supply into smaller and smaller lots. Finally, *assorting* is building up assortments of items for use with each other. Now, to test your understanding, ask yourself: Which of these sorting activities is practiced most by (1) manufacturers, (2) wholesalers and retailers, and (3) consumers?

Before proceeding, can you answer these questions:
1. What are channels of distribution?
2. What is the relation of marketing functions and marketing institutions to marketing channels?
3. How do channels of distribution contribute to the exchange process?

What Determines the Choice of Channels?

Avon and Tupperware obviously believe that short, direct channels are best suited to their marketing programs. Sears also has found that they can best serve their customers through integrated and more direct marketing. The widespread popularity of new forms of retailing, such as catalog showroom stores and franchised fast food services, has altered the channels of distribution for many products. For example, so-called traffic appliances (small energy and time saving devices like toasters, mixers, and coffee makers) were once sold primarily through wholesalers to retail appliance dealers, drugstores, and department stores. Such items are still distributed this way, but vast numbers are also sold direct by manufacturers to large chain discount houses, department stores, supermarkets, and catalog showroom stores.

What determines a firm's choice of channels of distribution is in many ways related to several other fundamental marketing questions. "What determines the firm's decision regarding product planning and development?" or "What determines the firm's price or promotion strategy?" The answer, unique to each firm, is based upon company objectives, the strengths and weaknesses of the firm, customer and product characteristics, and many other situational factors.

Company Goals and Objectives.   Every marketing firm has a number of explicit, almost self-evident objectives: to reach the market, minimize cost, maximize revenues, generate profits, and satisfy customers. Yet, each company must specify its objectives according to its particular situation. J.C. Penney, for example, decided to move ahead into catalog merchandising to compete more successfully with Sears Roebuck. Sears has integrated and acquired many manufacturing facilities primarily to assure its customers of consistently high-quality merchandise. Hallmark's response to the impact of changing social needs on customer buying behavior was the principal reason for their decision to franchise Hallmark shops.

Company Characteristics.   The characteristics of both manufacturers and retailers affect the choice of channels of distribution. Large size and financial resources to match have led many retailers to seek more direct channels of distribution, including the development of extensive buying organizations, central warehousing and distribution centers, even their own manufacturing capacity. Contrariwise, manufacturers with a strong financial base may forego the wholesale distributor and establish their own field sales organization, warehousing and storage facilities, and elaborate physical distribution systems.[6] Smaller firms, both manufacturers and retailers, who lack adequate financing, are frequently unable to develop specialized efforts that could enable them to bypass intermediaries.

The firm evaluates each channel alternative from the standpoint of its cost and how much control over the marketing effort it either gains or relinquishes through using it. Frequently, the channel decision consists of a series of trade-offs. Maximum control is usually assured with a direct channel because with these there are few intermediaries with whom to negotiate. However, direct channels are often the most costly. Most channel decisions are therefore a compromise or balance. In the interest of lowering costs, some control is relinquished. But where size, financial strength, and other factors permit, direct channels are sought to ensure maximum control over the marketing effort.

Consumer Consideration.   The central role of the consumer in dictating marketing decisions has already been established. When consumer buying habits change, channels as well as other marketing decisions change also.

We have already documented the many changes underway in consumer behavior that are likely to affect marketing planning. Many of these impact directly on the firm's decisions regarding channels of distribution. Changing economics, altered life styles, population sprawl, shifting economic fortunes, and changing buying habits all affect a firm's choice of channels of distribution. The number of working women, the desire for more leisure time, and the overlapping roles of men and women have created the need for new products, new marketing services, and new channels of distribution. The increasing use of credit cards and checkless money systems (EFTS)—electronic funds transfer systems—has added to the popularity of discount stores, catalog showrooms, direct mail, and other forms of direct contact marketing.

Whether products are destined for the ultimate consumer, the industrial buyer, or the government will in turn affect the channels of distribution ultimately chosen. Industrial and government buyers have a strong tendency to buy what they require direct from manufacturer-suppliers. Ultimate consumers, however, buy only a small percentage (less than 3 percent) of the things they need from manufacturers.

The geographic concentration of many industrial and government buyers tends to promote the use of direct channels of distribution, while the widespread dispersion of ultimate consumers fosters more indirect channels for such markets. Finally, it must be pointed out again that in our complex, sophisticated economic system there is much diversity—large numbers of different kinds of buyers, whose needs and requirements are as varied and changing as their characteristics. Such diversity on the demand side of the market gen-

---

[6] "Switchover for Bigger Profits," *Sales and Marketing Management,* November 8, 1976, pp. 47–48.

Every home is an inventory of goods.

erates the need for comparable diversity in marketing institutions, product offerings, promotional appeals, price lines, and channels of distribution.

Characteristics of the Product. The characteristics of the products, too, play a strong role in determining the channels of distribution to be employed.

Consumer goods, as was discussed in chapter 4, are sometimes classified on the basis of customer shopping habits as either convenience, shopping, or specialty goods. This classification is clearly intended as a guide in determining marketing strategy, including channel selection. On the other hand, consumer goods may be classified on the basis of the product's marketing characteristics in conjunction with consumer buying habits.

Consumer goods classified according to buyer behavior, you will recall, fall into three categories:

Convenience goods: Those goods for which the consumer regards the probable gain from making price and quality comparisons as small compared with the effort of making those comparisons. Items such as bread, milk, cigarettes, toothpaste, and aspirin are good examples.

Shopping goods: Those goods for which the consumer regards the probable gain from making price and quality comparisons as large relative to the effort of making such comparisons. Most clothing items, appliances, and building supplies are examples of such products.[7]

Specialty goods: Those consumer goods which have such a unique or special character in the perceptions of some buyers that they will make a special or extended effort to purchase them.[*] Cameras, ski equipment, outboard motors, and recreation vehicles may qualify for this classification.

On the basis of patronage motives—the reasons customers shop at particular stores—retail establishments can be classified as convenience, shopping, and specialty stores; and some automobile agencies, boutiques, and camera shops are clearly specialty stores. A three-by-three matrix, representing nine possible types of buying behavior, results from a cross-classification of each product shopping motive with each patronage motive.[8]

1. Convenience store–convenience good: The consumer in this category prefers to buy the most readily available brand of the product at the most accessible store.
2. Convenience store–shopping good: The consumer selects his or her purchase from the assortment carried by the most accessible store.
3. Convenience store–specialty good: The consumer purchases his or her favored brand from the most accessible store which has the item in stock.
4. Shopping store–convenience good: The consumer is indifferent to the brand of product, but shops among different stores to secure better retail service and/or lower retail prices.
5. Shopping store–shopping good: The consumer makes comparisons among both retail controlled factors and factors associated with the product (brand).
6. Shopping store–specialty good: The consumer has a strong preference as to product brand, but shops among a number of stores to secure the best retail service and/or price for this brand.
7. Specialty store–convenience good: The consumer prefers to trade at a specialty store but is indifferent to the brand of product purchased.
8. Specialty store–shopping good: The consumer prefers to trade at a certain store, but is uncertain which product to buy and examines the store's assortment for the best purchase.

[7] Richard H. Holton, "The Distinction between Convenience Goods, Shopping Goods, and Specialty Goods," *Journal of Marketing* **23** (July 1958), pp. 53–56.

[*] The definitions of convenience goods and shopping goods are Holton's (footnote 7). The definition of specialty goods is the author's.

[8] Based upon Louis P. Bucklin, "Retail Strategy and the Classification of Consumer Goods," *Journal of Marketing* **27**, no. 1 (January 1963), pp. 50–58.

9. Specialty store–specialty good: The consumer has both a preference for a particular store and a specific brand name.

Such an extended classification scheme clearly provides additional information and important guidelines to manufacturers in the overall strategy of channel management. Channels may be chosen according to the character of the goods, the consumer's seeming preference for store types, and the extent of market coverage to be achieved. The channel decision must consider the total combined support system or marketing effort to attain the desired penetration and coverage.

Marketing Characteristics of Products.   Recall that we mentioned that consumer goods are classified basically around two sets of criteria: customer buying behavior and the characteristics of the product themselves. When classifying consumer goods on the basis of the nature of the goods themselves, you will notice that consumer buying behavior is still considered an important variable.

A characteristic of a good or product is a distinguishing quality or attribute relative to its performance in the market and its relationship to consumers for whom it has the ability to satisfy wants. Based upon this definition, five characteristics of consumer goods have been selected as important distinguishing criteria for classification purposes.

Replacement Rate.   The rate at which a good is purchased and consumed by users. Replacement rate is related to the idea of turnover, or sales velocity. Bread has a high replacement rate; that for grand pianos is very low; and men's and women's shoes have a medium one.

Gross Margin.   Selling price minus the cost of goods sold. From the standpoint of channel management, the total cost of all the intermediaries is the relevant figure. It is the total sum of money cost necessary to move a good from its point of origin to the final consumer. There is usually an inverse relationship between replacement rate and gross margin. Whenever replacement rate is high, gross margin is apt to be low and when replacement rate is low, then gross margin will most likely be high. Can you explain this relationship?

Adjustment.   Services applied to goods so they will meet the exact needs of customers. Adjustments include measuring and fitting, alterations, installation, dissemination of information such as operating and use of instructions, and minor and major repairs. Large requirements for adjustments are usually associated with goods with low replacement rates—autos, appliances, televisions—and with high gross margin. Any notions now about why the need for the higher gross margin? Goods with high replacement rates usually have little need for adjustment.

Time of Consumption.   The length of time over which the good yields its desired utility. Aspirin gives up its utility in a brief period of time; a record or

Table 10-1   Characteristics of Goods—Convenience, Shopping, and Specialty

Characteristics	Convenience	Shopping	Specialty
Replacement rate	High	Medium	Low
Gross margin	Low	Medium	High
Adjustment	Low	Medium	High
Time of consumption	Low	Medium	High
Searching time	Low	Medium	High

a new tape for the sound system may give up its utility over an intermediate period.

Searching Time.   The average time and distance from the retail store, including the inconvenience spent in getting a certain product or brand, or in evaluating alternative products or brands. Hence, search time is related to the convenience afforded the consumer by the total marketing system.[9]

These characteristics of goods can now be used to provide an additional set of dimensions to our classification of consumer goods. For example, in Table 10-1 these characteristics are shown as they apply to convenience, shopping, and specialty goods.

How does all this affect channel management? Because transactions that occur very frequently lend themselves to standardization and specialization, convenience goods (which are sometimes bought daily) call for long channels and mass promotion efforts. Because they require the most personal and direct promotional efforts to match their high characteristics, specialty goods call for short channels with only limited standardization and specialization. Shopping goods, with their moderate characteristics of replacement, margin, adjustment, and time, will support less standardization and specialization of function than convenience goods, but more than specialty goods. So they need a channel of intermediate length.

Our analysis here has focused mainly on consumer goods characteristics and their impact on marketing channels. Try now to apply this knowledge to how the characteristics of industrial goods and the behavior of their buyers would in turn, affect their distribution. Think first of the parallel between consumer convenience goods and industrial goods such as operating supplies and raw materials. What is the relationship between consumer shopping goods and industrial accessory equipment items such as buildings and other capital equipment? In your analysis of these problems, would it help to think in such terms as replacement rate, gross margin, adjustment, time of consumption, and search time? And finally, ask yourself "To what extent will marketing

[9] These ideas are based upon the classic work of Leo Aspinwall. See "Characteristics of Goods and Parallel Systems Theories," in Eugene Kelly and William Lazer, *Managerial Marketing* (Homewood, IL: Irwin, 1958), pp. 434–450.

transactions for each of these classes support standardization and specialization of functions."

Managing Channels of Distribution

Managing channels of distribution is concerned principally with aiming for effective market penetration and market coverage by choosing the appropriate kind and number of channel intermediaries and by properly controlling and evaluating each member's contribution to the total marketing effort.

Another relevant decision is whether a single channel or a number of marketing channels may be required. Specialization and standardization of function appear to favor single channels of distribution. Yet, the many varied market opportunities and the possibilities for multiple positioning of products in a number of different market segments, suggest that management consider setting up multiple channels.

Do We Have a Choice?

Our discussion has tended to suggest that a manufacturer always has the option of using a general line wholesaler, a manufacturer's agent, or selling through mass merchandisers such as Sears or J.C. Penney. Is such the case? No! Quite frequently, manufacturers or resellers are not chosen to be in a channel. Although sometimes they are, they can also be rejected in favor of other alternatives. Channels are not always put together like a major league football team. The best participants are not inevitably drafted, nor are all those who are simply eager to "play the game" permitted to take part. Some manufacturers and some retailers, because of their unique product, large financial resources, or overall marketing skill, are able to program their own marketing channels. The more usual situation, however, in choosing channels of distribution, is that firms take (1) what is available and (2) what they get by careful bargaining and negotiation.

All firms must bargain their way into a channel arrangement. They may offer efficiency and cost reducing capabilities, better markups, or rapid turnover. Additional incentives are promises for direct mail, newspaper, magazine or television advertising, or missionary sales work performed (by manufacturers) for wholesalers.

The Extent of Market Coverage

The manufacturer-seller firm must decide upon the number of outlets through which to merchandise its output. In great measure this question is answered according to (1) consumer-buyer behavior and (2) the characteristics of the goods to be marketed. Manufacturers can choose from these possibilities: (1) **extensive distribution*** (2) **selective distribution**, (3) **exclusive distribution**.

---

* Some writers insist upon calling the first option *intensive distribution*. Any dictionary definition of the two words would more logically support the term *extensive distribution*.

Extensive Distribution.   Extensive distribution is called for in the case of consumer convenience goods and those industrial goods whose marketing characteristics closely resemble those of consumer convenience items. What is sought is maximum exposure of the product to sales possibilities, or saturation of the market opportunity. Convenience items such as food, soft drinks, snack items, cigarettes, candy, chewing gum, and similar products call for the use of a wide network of marketing intermediaries, including wholesalers and different kinds of retail outlets. Especially suitable are supermarkets and places of high traffic density like concession stands at recreation facilities and sporting events, airline terminals, restaurants, and all places where people congregate in large numbers. The need to attain mass market coverage at a relatively low unit price calls for long channels and an extensive network of alternative retail outlets. The effort required to market convenience goods, as well as shopping and specialty goods, is clearly intensive (that is, concerted, coordinated, and managed, to the extent possible) but the network of channels for convenience goods is extensive in nature.

Selective Distribution.   When the number of outlets for distributing a product is scaled down and only the more preferred outlets are chosen, manufacturers are practicing a form of selective distribution. By selecting a few, better retail outlets and working more cooperatively with them, manufacturers may feel that they can lower the total cost of distribution and create a more receptive climate for their merchandise. Manufacturers engage in selective distribution channel strategies for a number of reasons: retail salespeople and service personnel are more easily trained, drastic price cutting of a nationally promoted branded item as a loss leader may be more easily discouraged, cooperative advertising and other promotional considerations are more easily attained and managed, and a smoother and mutually advantageous channel arrangement is more easily secured.

Exclusive Distribution.   The ultimate in selective distribution is exclusive distribution. A manufacturing firm chooses one or two distributors or outlets for its products and excludes all others. You may be most familar with exclusive distribution as seen in the marketing of automobiles, boats, boat motors, some major appliance lines, and high fashion or highly advertised branded items of men's or women's clothing. Some brands of sporting goods such as AMF tennis racquets, Head and Olin skis, or motorcycles like Honda and Kawasaki are sold through exclusive distributorships that bar other firms from selling these products within the assigned territory. Exclusive distributorships are desired by manufacturers for a very special reason: so they can exert as much control as possible over the marketing effort surrounding the product. Some marketing costs may be reduced by a policy of exclusive distribution inasmuch as the manufacturer has fewer outlets with which to deal, but the real issue is basically one of the manufacturer's maintaining control.

There are many legal headaches associated with exclusive distribution. These problems are of great concern: exclusive dealing contracts, closed sales territories, and tying contracts.

An *exclusive dealing contract* is covered by Section 3 of the Clayton Act. This section prohibits leasing or selling a product with an agreement, either explicit or understood, that the purchaser shall refrain from handling competing products in those cases where such an understanding or agreement might have the effect of substantially lessening competition or would tend to create a monopoly.

The *closed sales territory* exists when a manufacturing firm restricts the geographic territories for each of its distributors. The legal issue is whether such restriction decreases competition and therefore violates provisions of the Sherman, Clayton, and Federal Trade Commission Acts. Territorial restrictions are usually either vertical or horizontal. Vertical restrictions (a manufacturer allows only one authorized dealer for a product in a specified area) have usually been accepted as promoting competing brands. Horizontal restrictions (agreement among retailers or wholesalers not to compete in marketing products from the same manufacturer) have been aggressively policed and judged consistently to be unlawful.

Tying contracts require a dealer or distributor who wishes to market a given product also to carry other lines of the manufacturer's that may not be as desirable. Such contracts are generally viewed as violations of the Sherman and Clayton Acts because they tend to bar competitors from major markets.

Figure 10-6 is a graphic summary of the three types of market coverage which a manufacturer might consider in establishing and planning channel strategy. Each circle represents a market opportunity in a given geographic location. As can be seen, the first market is saturated with outlets in order to attain maximum exposure to sales. The second circle shows a pattern of selective distribution, where a more select group of outlets carries out the marketing effort. In the third circle, an exclusive distributor or retail outlet is the only supplier for each segment of the total territory in which the product is marketed.

Evaluating and Controlling Channels of Distribution

When a company plans and develops its channels of distribution it must make a series of coordinated decisions concerning four general questions: (1) What types of intermediaries will be involved in marketing and assisting in the phys-

Figure 10-6 The three types of market coverage.

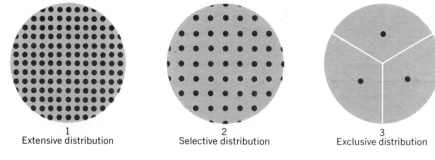

1	2	3
Extensive distribution	Selective distribution	Exclusive distribution

ical movement of the goods to markets? (2) How many intermediaries will there be and how will they cooperate at each stage of the total distribution system? (3) What will be the specific tasks of the participating intermediaries? Finally, (4) What will be the terms of our transactions with the intermediaries and what responsibilities will we require each of them to shoulder so that the total channel effort is successful and profitable?

Sound management practice does demand that firms—both manufacturers and resellers—should attempt to control their channel operation in the interest of attaining company goals and objectives. Control, of course, means setting standards for each member's performance, as well as standards or goals for the entire network; monitoring each channel member's performance and judging whether it meets the established standards; and, when necessary, correcting any weaknesses.[10]

All evaluations or judgments of channel effectiveness must take into account the objectives of each channel intermediary as well as the overall marketing function. The manufacturer has several principal criteria in planning and controlling channels. Among them are the following:

1. How will the various reseller possibilities benefit our marketing program, and what will each cost?
2. How much market penetration will each one achieve for us?
3. How will the potential contribution of each alternative reseller help the company gain customer recognition, market share, and acceptance of its promotional campaign?
4. Which of the various possible resellers will weaken the company's market position? Which will strengthen it?
5. How much aggressiveness can each channel alternative add to the firm's marketing program?

Retailers and wholesalers have a somewhat different point of view regarding the planning and control of channels. Recall that planning pertains to structure; it means shaping events and processes. Control pertains to authority and power; it means convincing others to do what you may wish them to do. Thus, as seen from the retailers' and wholesalers' vantage point the main objectives in channel management involve the following:

1. How much freedom will the various channel alternatives allow the intermediary in managing products handled, territory covered, and functions?
2. How much expansion will the channel arrangement and commitment permit each intermediary?
3. To what extent will the channel setup allow each intermediary who wishes to do so to take part in the managerial struggle for control of the channel?
4. How much of an operational identity will the channel intermediaries be able to maintain? Or will they be played off against each other?

[10] Mary A. Higby and Edward W. Smykay, "Marketing Channels: An Efficiency Approach," *Contemporary Issues in Marketing Channels*, eds. Robert F. Lusch and Paul H. Zinszer, Distribution Research Program, Center for Economic and Management Research, University of Oklahoma, Norman, OK, 1979, pp. 27–39.

5. Will the intermediaries' profit margins or commissions satisfy their cost profit requirements?

The primary marketing management tools for evaluating and controlling channels of distribution include such concepts as comparative sales analysis, special techniques of distribution cost accounting, and marketing research studies.

Before proceeding, can you answer these questions:
1. Discuss several factors which affect a firm's decisions regarding channels of distribution.
2. How does the nature of the goods affect marketing channels?
3. Do all firms have a real choice in determining the channels of distribution for their products?

Managing Power and Conflict in Channels of Distribution

The desire to plan and control channels of distribution leads in many instances to considerable conflict of interest among the manufacturer, the wholesaler, and the retailer and a struggle for power in the channel. Member firms of a marketing channel operate in a dynamic field of conflicting and harmonious objectives. If the conflicting objectives outweigh the harmonious ones, the effectiveness of the channel will be reduced and efficient distribution impeded. Therefore, the implementation of certain methods of cooperation will lead to increased channel efficiency.[11]

In marketing there is always inherently a great deal of conflict. This conflict takes basically three forms:[12]

- *Horizontal competition.* This is competition between intermediaries of the same type; for example, discount store versus discount store.
- *Intertype competition.* This is rivalry between intermediaries of different types in the same channel sector; for example, discount store competing with department store.
- *Vertical conflict.* This occurs between channel members at different levels, for example, discount store versus manufacturer.

Vertical conflict usually arises because of the various channel members' myopic view of their self-interests. Oftentimes one channel member's gain is at the expense of another. Conflict will invariably arise in the vertical marketing channel when it is composed of members of unequal strength and the stronger members attempt to dominate the channel distribution policies. Con-

---

[11] Bruce Mallen, "Conflict and Cooperation in Marketing Channels," in *Reflections on Progress in Marketing,* ed. L. George Smith (Chicago: American Marketing Association, 1964), p. 65.

[12] Joseph C. Palamountain, *The Politics of Distribution* (Cambridge, MA: Harvard University Press, 1955).

flict is also likely to emerge in the channel network simply because of basic differences in the operating and management philosophies of the various channel members. There is a great tendency today for the manufacturer and the large-scale retailer to cooperate in order to eliminate the wholesaler from the vertical marketing network, while the wholesaler fights to remain a continuing part of the distribution flow through voluntary chain efforts (discussed later in this chapter).

Managing Vertical Channel Conflict.   There are primarily three ways of managing conflict in organizations such as vertical channels of distribution. One way is by a system of *autocracy*, where a powerful group leader determines policy and dictates or assigns tasks. Another way is through *democracy*, where members jointly decide policies and assign tasks, and leaders are chosen by consensus. The final way is *anarchy*, in which each member of the group has complete freedom and the group lacks leadership and a common sense of direction.

If anarchy prevails in a channel, the results are often haphazard or even chaotic. Such channels are usually short-lived because of their built-in self-destructive tendencies.

Autocracy provides a better climate for managing conflict. Management in such an arrangement is based upon power and authority. While democratic management of vertical marketing networks may be on the increase, it is probably safe to assume that the basis for managing most channels, historically and today, is autocracy.

Channel Management Through Captaincy.   An idea long advanced about the conflict and cooperation within vertical channels of distribution is that whether a network is run autocratically or democratically, there is a *channel captain* or leader who either guides, directs, or demands that member behavior conform to certain accepted standards.

It has been pointed out that channel members have a hierarchy of individual goals and, as a result, pursue the channel goals that they perceive as furthering their own ends.[13] Channel leadership emerges primarily from channel power— the ability to make things happen in a desired way, or to bring them more in line with a specific goal or set of goals. Conflict must be managed and when it arises in the channel, members try to reduce or eliminate it.[14]

There are convincing arguments for assigning the leadership (captaincy) role to retailers and equally convincing ones championing manufacturers.[15]

The Retailer as Captain.   The argument for the retailer as channel captain assumes that the retailer dominates consumer goods marketing and brings

[13] Robert W. Little, "The Marketing Channel: Who Should Lead This Extracorporate Organization?" *Journal of Marketing* **34**, no.1 (January 1970), pp. 31–39.
[14] Larry J. Rosenberg and Louis W. Stern, "Toward the Analysis of Conflict in Distribution Channels: A Descriptive Model,"*Journal of Marketing* **34**, no. 4 (October 1970), pp. 40–47.
[15] Louis P. Bucklin, "A Theory of Channel Control,"*Journal of Marketing*, **37**, no. 1 (January 1973), pp. 39–48.

greater net benefits to consumers than do manufacturers. Retailers are closest to the consumer markets, so the argument goes, so if retailers are channel captains, consumers should benefit, with goods better matched to customer demand, and at lower prices.

The Manufacturer as Captain. The argument for manufacturer captaincy is based upon the fact that the final decision in channel selection most often rests with the manufacturer-seller and will continue to do so as long as the manufacturer has the legal right to sell to some and refuse to sell to others. It is also contended that channel decisions are primarily problems for the manufacturer and that of all the historical trends in marketing, none is so self-evident as the tendency for the manufacturing company to assume greater control over the distribution of its product.

No given channel member is likely to dominate the channel in all marketing situations. Instead, more likely there exists a tendency toward equilibrium in vertical marketing networks, resulting from a continually shifting balance of power among components in the system.[16] Perhaps the consumer's best interest is served by a balance of power, rather than any one member's domineering in the marketing channel.

The Development of Programmed Vertical Marketing Systems

Channels of distribution as loose coalitions of independent units that bargain with each other, maneuver for power and dominance, terminate their commitment at will, and generally behave independently are, in many instances, being replaced by **vertical marketing systems**. These are programmed distribution networks designed as integrated, consciously cooperating systems.[17]. Such vertical marketing systems are professionally managed, predesigned, and engineered to achieve operating economies and maximum impact by completely integrating the market effort throughout the distribution network. These systems take three primary forms: corporate, contractual, and administered.

Corporate Systems. **Corporate systems** in retailing are well represented by the multilevel merchandisers like Sears, Ward's, and Penney's. In their effort to control the total marketing network better, these firms have integrated backward toward their sources of supply. Sears, for example, has an ownership equity in production facilities that supply nearly 40 percent of its inventory requirements. Furthermore, these companies and others like them have developed extensive warehouse, storage, and other physical distribution facilities for the distribution and processing of merchandise throughout the network. The enthusiasm of many firms to merge with or acquire other firms is simply

---

[16] See Robert F. Lusch, "Channel Conflict: Its Impact on Retailer Operating Performance," *Journal of Retailing*, **52**, no. 2 (Summer 1976), pp. 3–12,89.

[17] See Bert C. McCammon Jr., "The Emergence and Growth of Contractually Integrated Channels in the American Economy," in *Marketing and Economic Development*, ed. Peter Bennett (American Marketing Association, 1965), pp. 214–232.

the desire for better control of the distribution of products through corporate vertical marketing systems.

Administered Marketing Networks.   In **administered marketing networks** the components remain semiautonomous (somewhat independent), but the channel efforts are directed, or administered, by a channel leader or captain. Such networks are structured alliances where individual firms, through initiative and leadership, influence the behavior of other channel members. As a result, vertically aligned companies work closely with each other to achieve control over transportation, warehousing, accounting, finances, and inventory, as well as realizing advertising economies. Administrative arrangements like this are designed to reduce friction within the channel and to produce a coordinated marketing effort.

Perhaps the greatest success in administered vertical marketing systems is in automotive marketing. This is the system in the United States, which has influenced its adoption throughout the world.

Contractual Vertical Marketing Systems.   In **contractual marketing systems** independent firms on different levels of the distribution ladder can coordinate and balance their efforts through formal agreements. This cooperation enables them to enjoy systematic economies, market penetration, and market share that could not be achieved as easily through individual action. Contractual systems, involving either forward or backward integration, have grown rapidly in recent years. Such systems are often sponsored either by wholesalers or retailers.

Wholesaler-sponsored voluntary chains are contractual attempts by wholesalers to assure themselves a place in the distribution network by entering into a formal agreement with a number of retail merchandisers. Such arrangements are interesting examples of survival strategies by threatened channel members.

Some wholesalers, to protect their own markets (the smaller retailers whom they service) have attempted to standardize their operations, their names, their marketing practices, and facilities. The wholesaler then coordinates the marketing programs of these retailers, providing distributor brand merchandise and an array of marketing services. Such wholesaler sponsored merchandising groups as IGA (Independent Grocers Alliance) with its 5,000 stores, is a well-known example of a contractually integrated marketing system.

Retail Cooperatives.   Retail stores, in integrating backwards toward sources of supply, often band together with a set of contractual arrangements and operate their own wholesaling facilities. This form of vertical marketing network is called a *retail cooperative*. In this scheme, the retail firms who participate buy shares of stock in the wholesaling operation and commit themselves to purchase some minimum percentage of their merchandise requirements from the firm. Often, though not always, the member stores will adopt a common name and even develop their own distributor brands which they advertise cooperatively.

Vertical marketing systems are unique responses to market conditions, the struggle for power and dominance within channels, and the drive not only for profits, but for survival. In an increasingly competitive marketing world with its relentless movement toward large-scale enterprise, such systems are proof of the creativity of marketing enterprisers.

A Conceptual Approach to Channel Management

Channel management, in the basic sense, involves making decisions concerning structural and functional changes within the channel.[18] In functional changes channel tasks are reallocated among the various members. Recall that the functions that must be performed throughout the channel are (1) contactual, (2) merchandising, (3) pricing, (4) promotion, and (5) physical distribution. A functional change within a channel might therefore consist of having the retailer take a more active part in pricing the product, promoting it, or carrying a larger inventory (storage-physical distribution). A structural change is one that results in the addition or deletion of some channel intermediary. For example, if a manufacturer discontinues marketing through wholesalers and goes to a system of direct marketing to large-scale retail stores, this is a structural change.

If channels of distribution are in balance or equilibrium, the marketing manager can make no structural or functional change that would add to the total channel profit. This can be illustrated with the example in Figure 10-7.

Figure 10-7 shows a rather conventional channel of the producer, wholesaler-retailer type. Each channel member makes a combined set of decisions on price, advertising, and distribution, shown as P, A, D. It is assumed that each channel member's decisions relating to P, A, D affects the succeeding stage. The producer makes decisions $(P, A, D)_1$ which influence the quantity (Q_1) ordered by the wholesaler. The producer computes profits (Z_1) by subtracting his costs from his revenue from the wholesaler. Each channel member makes similar decisions and in the same way computes his individual profit subtracting costs from revenues received from the next channel member. From the standpoint of the channel as a whole, a set of independent decisions is made $(P, A, D)_1, (P, A, D)_2, (P, A, D)_3$ that collectively result in some total channel profit $(Z_1 + Z_2 + Z_3)$. The channel is out-of-balance and needs either a structural or functional change if an alternative set of decisions $(P, A, D)_1, (P, A, D)_2, (P, A, D)_3$ would generate a channel profit greater than the current set of decisions is producing. Furthermore, the more that profits currently generated by the decisions being made within the given structural and functional arrangement are below profits that would result from a different set of arrangements and decisions, the greater the incentive for change. Such a change might consist of cooperative planning, or some channel member might acquire one or more of the other members in order to achieve additional profits from coordinated or integrated decision making.

[18] Based upon Philip Kotler, *Marketing Management: Analysis, Planning and Control,* 4th ed. (Englewood Cliffs, NJ: Prentice-Hall, 1980), p. 444.

Figure 10-7   A conceptual model of channel management.

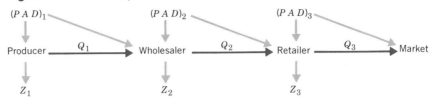

Source: Philip Kotler, *Marketing Management Analysis, Planning and Control* 4th ed., (Englewood Cliffs, N.J.: Prentice-Hall, 1980), p. 444.

Summary

Channels of distribution are the routes or pathways that goods follow in getting from producer to consumers. More importantly, they are marketing firms, agencies, and institutions which facilitate the transfer of goods by the performance of marketing functions.

Decisions about channels of distribution rank with product planning and development activities as a critical marketing variable. Channels, without question, are an important part of the firm's strategic marketing program.

Channels of distribution are affected by a host of factors, foremost of which are (1) consumer buyer behavior, and (2) the nature and marketing characteristics of the goods. Other factors, however, also affect the decisions made by manufacturers and resellers about their channels of distribution. Most channel decisions are based upon the marketing firm's need to reach its markets at low cost, to generate sales revenue, penetrate and cover markets, earn profit, and satisfy customers.

Channels of distribution, involving the use of marketing intermediaries, demonstrate the need for specialization and standardization of tasks in the marketing of goods. Marketing intermediaries facilitate the creation of time, place, and possession utilities. Although there are numerous issues that arise concerning the management of channels of distribution, the three principal areas of management concern are what channels to use, the extent of the market coverage, and how to evaluate channel performance.

Power centers and conflict are found in many channels. To manage this conflict and attain more harmony, vertical marketing systems are increasingly replacing the independent, loosely structured, more conventional channels of distribution.

Review Questions

1. Use the illustration at the beginning of the chapter ("Our L'eggs Fit Your Legs") to demonstrate the comprehensive and interrelated nature of channels of distribution.
2. What are channels of distribution? Why are they often likened to rivers and pipelines?

3. Channels are best explained in terms of marketing functions and marketing institutions. Discuss.
4. Why are some channels long, some short, and some of intermediate length?
5. What is the purpose of marketing channels? How do marketing intermediaries facilitate the creation of time, place, and possession utility?
6. List and discuss three factors which affect a manufacturer's choice of channels of distribution. Are these factors relevant to wholesalers? To retailers?
7. What does channel management consist of?
8. Do firms always have a choice concerning channels of distribution, or must they sometimes take whatever is available?
9. Describe your approach to evaluating channels of distribution if you were a marketing manager for a midsize manufacturing firm.
10. What are multilevel merchandisers? Often such merchandisers have established vertical marketing systems. What are vertical marketing systems? What do they achieve? How?

Case 10-1

Jaicam, Inc.

"Jaicam" stands for Japanese Appliance Importing Company of America. The firm is a major importer of appliances made in Japan and distributed widely throughout the United States. Jaicam is, for all practical purposes, the United States marketer for the parent company's appliance distribution in this country. The products are shipped in large quantities to Jaicam in Paramus, New Jersey, and from Paramus, Jaicam distributes the products through franchised dealers all over the United States. The hottest item in Jaicam's total assortment now is microwave ovens. Jaicam's oven is high quality and has met with reasonable market success. Recently, however, microwave ovens have become much more price competitive and, increasingly, more are being sold through large mass-merchandising operations such as Sears and J.C. Penney. Major department stores are also an outlet from which these appliances are now being sold.

Except for very large cities, it has been the policy of Jaicam to limit representation in any community to one dealer by an exclusive agency arrangement. The typical dealer for Jaicam appliances is the conventional appliance store. Almost no dealers are department stores and Jaicam has never sold direct to large national chain stores or mass merchandisers. However, in a recent sales meeting, the general sales manager proposed to several other executives of the firm that the company change its policy by permitting a number of dealers to be franchised in all but the smallest cities. He contends that one agency or outlet cannot cover or penetrate heavily populated areas extensively. Furthermore, he claims that items such as appliances and, increasingly, microwave ovens are today more of a shopping good than formerly because of the many competitors now in the field and the increased emphasis on price competition.

One of the vice presidents takes a point of view contrary to the proposal. He argues that the appliance business is still a question of "making the sales presentation and closing the sale" and that this can be better accomplished by one large exclusive agency in an area. The vice president contends that the sales manager's proposal would lead to price cutting among local representatives and could lead to large amounts of intertype competition and that this was undesirable, especially as the company tries to maintain uniformity of prices within divisional areas. He added, that if department stores, discounters, and other nonspecialized retailers are allowed to carry the line, they will not carry the entire product line and they will likely not give each item its proper emphasis or aggressively promote the products. The final thrust to his argument was that such a change in channel strategy would antagonize the existing dealer-agencies, which had spent much time, money, and marketing effort in building goodwill and creating demand for the Jaicam line.

Questions

1. Evaluate the sales manager's proposal in light of the arguments advanced.
2. As an assistant to the sales manager, develop a set of guidelines for structuring an effective channel strategy for Jaicam.
3. The principal criterion for establishing channel policy and strategy is consumer buying behavior. From this point of view, whose arguments do you most favor? Why?

Case 10-2

The Rack Jobber

The rack jobber is the firm, or merchandiser as they prefer to be called, that supplies food stores with such items as small housewares, toys, soft goods—impulse items retailing for under $5. Currently, the rack jobber is deep in a swirling controversy. The controversy has two aspects. One is the food chains' question: Is this intermediary the best channel for distributing nonfoods or should the supermarkets handle them directly? This is a persistent question and one which is growing more insistent. Tied in with this dispute is the argument between the rack jobbers and store operators over the rack jobber's contribution to store profits.

To some extent the resolution of this controversy will affect the future growth of this offbeat and unique breed of distributor. The controversy, furthermore, has undoubtedly helped put pressure on the rack jobber from two directions. First even heavier demands are being placed on the rack jobbers' own merchandising skills to stay in the running, and, second, there is pressure which is forcing concentration of rack jobbing into fewer, but bigger, concerns. In spite of some threats to their existence, rack jobbers have earned themselves a substantial place in food retailing. Many rack jobbers belong to the American Research Merchandisers Institute (ARMI), formerly the American Rack Merchandisers Institute. This association claims that its members are responsible for the major increase in nonfood sales in supermarkets across the country. According to the institute's figures, rack jobbers are responsible for about two-thirds of the total supermarket volume in nonfood item sales.

Grocers, especially supermarkets and convenience stores, first opened their doors to rack jobbers when, in their search for higher profits, they began to scramble their merchandise lines and to spread deep into merchandise other than

food. They needed help because they were getting into a world that they didn't know. Rack jobbers "guarantee" sales. That means they take the inventory risks. If the items don't sell, back they go to the jobber's warehouse. The jobber preprices the merchandise, sets it up on the shelves, keeps the display clean and filled, and takes over the labor and administrative costs involved in maintaining an inventory often in excess of 5,000 items.

The only responsibility the supermarket manager has in nonfoods when a rack jobber handles them is to allocate space and ring up sales at the checkout counter.

Food merchants, especially the larger supermarkets, agree that nonfoods will continue to be important. Where they disagree with the rack jobber and the ARMI is over profits. The Supermarket Insitute reckons that supermarkets' gross margin on a typical assortment of nonfood items is 35 percent, about twice the margin on groceries. A representative of ARMI contends that nonfoods supplied by rack jobbers bring stores a 33 percent profit—and that this is practically net profit since the jobber assumes so much of the cost.

According to a Supermarket Institute official, "A large majority of chains are dropping jobbers and changing over to direct buying." Yet the ARMI people say, "They'll be back. We've had chains try direct buying in the past and they've come back to the jobber when they realize he can do a more efficient and profitable job."

Now rack jobbers face a new hazard. Big food chains are moving into discount merchandising and even large omnibus stores called "hypermarkets" or "super supers." Speculation is that when a food chain has an interest or control in a discount house, it will use the same suppliers for the nonfood lines in the supermarkets.

Questions

1. What do you believe are the major reasons for the emergence and success of rack job-bers to date?

2. Do you believe that the dissatisfaction of the large chain supermarket with the work and profit contribution of the rack jobbers is a serious threat to their continued use by the markets? Explain.

3. How do you assess the controversy as to whether (1) the rack jobber is the best inter-mediary for distributing nonfoods, and (2) the rack jobber's merchandising effort con-tributes sufficiently to store profits?

Chapter 11

Principal Channel Intermediaries: Wholesalers and Retailers

For twenty-three years Alberto Romaine and his wife, Rosinita, have owned and operated a small corner grocery a few miles west of downtown Providence, Rhode Island.[1] After so long a time, the Romaines regard their regular customers almost as part of the family.

But now, Alberto and Rosinita have decided to call it quits. There is no longer a future in the business. All over the country similar small grocery operators are saying the same thing. Competition from the large, more efficient supermarkets has made their lives difficult. Many of the tiny grocery outlets, often called "mom and pop" stores because they are usually family owned, have bowed to the same pressures.

Such small stores are also competing with superette stores, the increasingly popular convenience stores such as 7-Eleven that are scaled-down versions of the larger supermarket.

Some "mom and pop" stores continue to flourish. Often they are run by members of minority groups, eager to get started in American business by catering to specific ethnic neighborhoods.

For the most part, though, such stores belong to a vanishing breed. According to the Bureau of the Census, "mom and pops" in operation dropped sharply, from 89,455 in 1967 to approximately 64,500 in 1977. This is not surprising because the number of their customers had also dropped sharply. In 1967, small groceries accounted for more than 30 percent of all food purchases. However, by 1977, this figure had slipped to slightly less than 15 percent.

"Mom and pop" stores are victims of the growing efficiency and changing structure of retail and wholesale distribution. These stores are too small and nonspecialized to compete with a giant supermarket that carries 10,000 items. And the convenience superettes, which are frequently franchises, are filling the distribution niche once occupied by the family run grocery. The superettes are well designed, well stocked, better managed, and carry a streamlined but still fairly broad assortment of items like cold beer and snack foods as well as the usual fill-ins like bread, milk, and frozen foods.

The "mom and pop" stores are not even well served by the wholesalers, who often refuse to sell to them because they buy so much less than larger customers. Some wholesalers even attempt to discourage these small operators by charging them greatly inflated prices, refusing delivery on orders less than $500, and demanding cash rather than extending trade credit. Such conditions, combined with the normal inefficiency of small-scale enterprises, means that they have high operating expenses, due in part to the fact that they often offer credit. In order to make a small profit, they must charge much higher prices than supermarkets or the superette convenience stores.[2] For example, a gallon of milk at one "mom and pop" market in Pittsburgh sold for $2.25 while

[1] This incident and the related facts are true. The names and the places are fictionalized.

[2] For more on this topic, see, "Those Mom and Pop Stores are Still Going Strong," *U.S. News and World Report*, July 24, 1978, pp. 59–62.

the A & P price down the street was $1.98. Pampers diapers cost $2.75 in another such store, but only $1.89 in the competing supermarket.

Could the "mom and pop" stores stage a comeback? It is doubtful. The environmental conditions that once fostered the growth and development of the small, family owned corner grocery store have changed. And this has brought modifications in the overall structure and functioning of retailing and wholesaling institutions.

Marketing Structure and Functions

Marketing structure changes over time as marketing functions shift from institution to institution. A generation or two ago, the small corner grocery was a dynamic marketing institution, while today it is rapidly vanishing from the American scene. However, depending on the level of economic development, marketing struture can vary from one country to another. In many developing countries, the small family owned grocery store is still the mainstay in the distribution structure for food commodities.

Retailers and wholesalers earn their place in the marketing structure by performing vital marketing functions. These are the functions necessary to move goods through the marketing channels from manufacturer to ultimate or industrial users. In the ever-present urge to lower costs and reach more buyers, activities which are not essential will inevitably be abandoned. If and when marketing intermediaries such as wholesalers and retailers no longer earn their place in the distribution network, they are eliminated from the marketing structure or become much less important.

Marketing Intermediaries Create Value

The very presence of marketing intermediaries in the distribution network is conclusive evidence that they are creating needed services through the performance of marketing functions. In other words, they create time, place, possession, and information utility.

Efficiency Leads to Lower Costs.   Retailers and wholesalers, by practicing specialization and division of labor, reduce their operating expense ratios; they then can lower their gross margins and so operate on relatively small profit margins. Too often we look upon marketing institutions as firms which raise our cost of purchasing. A retailer with a gross margin of 40 percent is mistakenly accused of being a parasite who raises our cost of consumption. We think the same way, perhaps, about a wholesaler with a gross margin of 20 percent. Our naive temptation is to eliminate wholesalers so we can eliminate their margin and thus buy our goods more cheaply. Mostly such desires are based upon ignorance about the importance of wholesalers' and retailers' functions.

Remember that Sales − Cost of Goods = Gross Margin; and Gross Margin − Total Expense = Net Profit. Actually, while retailers and wholesalers do exact a gross margin, their actual profit ratios are exceedingly small in relation to their gross margin and their operating expense ratios. Their gross margins reflect in many respects the value of the marketing services they perform. To a great extent, firms with high gross margins are those undertaking higher risks through the performance of marketing functions.

Tables 11-1 and 11-2 show net profit as a percentage of net sales for selected lines of wholesaling and retailing operations for 1978. In only two categories of wholesale trade does the net profit percentage exceed 3 percent of sales.

And, in retailing, there is only one category where the *net profit* percentage exceeds 5 percent of sales. Observe that the net profit ratios for both wholesaling and retailing establishments are mostly around 3 to 4 percent. In the case of standardized goods such as groceries, observe that the wholesaler's profit margin is less than 1 percent of sales, and that the net profit for grocery retailers is under 2 percent of sales.

It should be pointed out, however, that retailers and wholesalers in general have rather rapid merchandise turnover, which, when combined with the low profit margins as a percentage of sales, tends to generate an overall return on investment usually around 10 to 15 percent. Even this would not necessarily be called bountiful or generous profits.

These small profit margins are the reward for the successful and efficient performance of marketing functions: having goods and services at locations convenient to customers when customers wish to purchase them; helping manufacturers search out and find buyers for their products; for helping consumers find the merchandise and commodities they want at prices they are willing to pay. Wholesalers and retailers are important merchandisers—they both work to match the supply of goods to the market requirements. Wholesalers and retailers are a major force in keeping prices within reach of the mass

Table 11-1 Net Profit as a Percentage of Net Sales for Selected Lines of Wholesaling—1978

Line of Business	Net Profits on Net Sales
Automotive parts and supplies	3.31
Beer, wine, and alcoholic beverages	2.23
Clothing and accessories:	
women's, children's, infant's	3.07
Dairy products	1.85
Drugs, drug proprietaries and	
sundries	2.00
Footwear	3.00
Fresh fruits and vegetables	1.45
Furniture and home furnishings	3.03
Groceries, general line	0.99
Meats and meat products	1.43

Source: "The Ratios of the Wholesalers," *Dun's Review,* October 1979, pp. 144–146.

Table 11-2 Net Profit as a Percentage of Net Sales for Selected Lines of Retailing—1978

Line of business	Net Profits on Net Sales
Auto and home supply stores	4.26
Clothing, furnishings:	
men's and boys' wear	4.05
Department stores	2.00
Furniture stores	4.42
Gasoline service stations	2.95
Grocery stores	1.79
Household appliance stores	3.62
Jewelry stores	7.71
Variety stores	3.74

Source: "The Ratios of Retailing," Dun's Review, October 1979, p. 143.

of consumers. These merchant intermediaries buy in large quantities from manufacturers and often receive quantity, as well as functional discounts.* Buying in large quantities cuts transportation costs and other transaction costs, and the savings are then passed on to consumer buyers in the form of lower prices.

You Can Eliminate Intermediaries but You Can't Eliminate Their Functions

What all this means, simply, is that you can eliminate any particular marketing institution, but not the marketing functions that institution performs. The functions performed by the "mom and pop" stores have been taken over by the supermarkets or the superettes, or pushed even further forward in the channel to the consumer. Supermarkets emerged as a lower cost form of distribution based upon what were, at the time, two radical marketing innovations: self-service and cash and carry merchandising. Clerk service was largely abandoned in favor of customer self-service; and credit and delivery were almost universally replaced by cash and carry merchandising. Marketing functions were not eliminated by supermarkets; they were simply transferred to the consumer buyer through the inducement of lower prices. Intermediaries earn their place in the channel by carrying out certain marketing functions. A retailer may decide to assume those functions and bypass a wholesaler intermediary. A manufacturing firm may decide to bypass both wholesaler and retailer by marketing its products directly to ultimate consumers. The cost of distribution may be reduced by eliminating a channel member if the marketing functions are discharged more efficiently as a result of reallocating the total channel effort.

* Quantity discounts are based on the quantities purchased, functional discounts on the duties or functions performed.

Wholesalers and Retailers in the Distribution Channel

Wholesalers market products to retailers, to manufacturers, and to other wholesalers. In 1977, the latest Census of Business figures reported that there were 382,837 wholesalers operating in the United States, compared with 311,000 in 1967. In the same period wholesale sales rose from roughly $500 billion to $1,258 billion. That is, in those 10 years sales volume increased by over 2.5 times while the number of establishments increased by about 20 percent. Evidently, the average size of wholesaling institutions is increasing.

Retailers Versus Wholesalers. The word "retailer" comes from the French *retaille*, which means "to cut down," Wholesaling literally means selling in "whole" or large quantities. These distinctions, however, are only marginally helpful today in distinguishing between wholesalers and retailers. Clearly, at an earlier point in marketing history, wholesalers usually bought and sold in larger quantities than retailers. It is no longer quite so easy to make that generalization. The most useful and convenient way to differentiate between retailers and wholesalers is by the *motive of purchase*. All sales made to ultimate consumers who buy the goods for their own use, are *retail sales*. All goods, regardless of quantity that are purchased by a customer for resale to his or her customer are *wholesale sales*. In the simplest sense, then, wholesalers are engaged in marketing transactions leading to retail sales.

Wholesalers in the Distribution Channel

Wholesalers perform a broad spectrum of marketing activities. However, their most important function is *breaking bulk*, that is, buying in large quantities from manufacturers and selling in smaller quantities to other resellers who have more limited needs. Breaking bulk requires wholesalers to develop specialized abilities and expertise which tend to generate operating economies in the transportation and storage of goods. Therefore, in many respects, the wholesaler becomes a specialist in particular distribution functions. Wholesalers provide many different valuable services for their customers as well as for their producer-suppliers. However, all wholesalers do not offer all services.

Wholesalers must anticipate their customers' demand and buy accordingly. They must also regroup goods in order to provide adequate assortments. Furthermore, wholesalers often deliver the merchandise, provide credit for its purchase, offer information and management advisory services, and assume a large portion of the buying function for retailers and industrial users by anticipating their needs.

The wholesaler is an important part of the marketing support system for manufacturers, producers, and growers taking on much of the selling effort of these organizations.

Table 11-3, "Links in the Chain of Distribution," is a convenient summary of the major methods of wholesaling, as well as a brief description of the major types of wholesaling establishments.

A link in the channel of distribution.

Wholesaling by Manufacturers.   Manufacturers do a great deal of wholesaling. As shown in Table 11-3, manufacturers often devote much of their marketing efforts to the sale and distribution of their products to independent wholesalers, retailers, other manufacturers, and government buyers.

Wholesaling by manufacturers is becoming an increasingly important form of distribution. Many manufacturers are finding it necessary and desirable to establish their own wholesaling facilities in order to develop better control over their marketing programs. Wholesaling activity by manufacturers takes two forms: manufacturer's sales office and manufacturer's branch office.

Manufacturer's Sales Office.   A **manufacturer's sales office** is located either right at the firm's manufacturing facilities, or in an area strategically located for marketing contacts between the firm's sales staff and its buyers. The sales office is literally that—an office for salespeople from which they solicit orders by telephone and by personal selling contacts. The manufacturer's sales office carries no inventory and thus needs no warehousing or storage facilities. By having a sales office close to the firm's major markets and customers, both costs and travel time for selling are reduced, and better "on the spot" service is offered. Many manufacturers of technical products train their sales personnel to provide customers with high levels of technical support. IBM uses both the sales office and the branch office arrangement with great success. In smaller communities, IBM customers are serviced primarily through sales office arrangements. In larger areas, the sales office is augmented by branch offices. Like IBM, many other firms find that in order to service their customers adequately and to provide full distribution to a large number of accounts, they need a variety of marketing-selling arrangements.

Table 11-3   Links in the Chain of Distribution

Type of Operation	Specialization	Function
Producers, fabricators, growers	Manufacturers: Sales office	Solicits orders; transmits orders to central facility; maintains no inventory
	Branch office	Solicits orders; fills orders from onsite inventory
Wholesalers: (jobbers, merchant wholesalers) Own goods		
Full service wholesalers: extend credit, deliver, carry stocks, sell	General line Specialty Line Distributors Rack jobber	Carry broad lines: dry goods, groceries, etc. Carry narrow lines: rubber goods, electrical goods, fancy foods, etc. Carry lines of one or a few noncompeting manufacturers Full service wholesaler, specializing in helping food chains sell nonfood items
Limited function wholesalers: cut expenses by eliminating some functions, e.g., credit, storage, delivery, personal selling	Cash and carry wholesaler Drop shipper Wagon distributor	No delivery or credit Arranges direct shipment from manufacturer to broker; takes title, assumes market risks; deals in carload lots. Carry much of their inventory on a truck; deliver purchases immediately
Agent intermediaries Do not own goods; often deal in limited lines	Broker Commission merchants (agricultural commission) merchants, selling and manufacturers' agents, distributors	Brings buyer and seller together but does not have possession of goods. *Selling broker* represents seller; *buying broker* represents buyer. Have possession of goods but do not own them; have authority to make deal.
Assemblers		Deal mainly in agricultural products and seafoods. Buy in small quantities from many producers; sell in large quantities.
Petroleum bulk stations and terminals		Transfer, store, and distribute gasoline and other petroleum products

Manufacturer's Branch Office.   **Manufacturers' branch offices** are sales offices plus physical facilities for warehousing, storing, and shipping merchandise. The major distinction between a manufacturer's sales office and a manufacturer's branch office is that the sales office has no inventory, while the branch office does. For example, a salesperson working out of a manufacturer's sales office solicits orders and transmits them to the manufacturing headquarters or to some central distribution facility. Here, the order is processed and shipped from stock directly to the wholesale buyer. A salesperson working out of a manufacturer's sales branch follows essentially the same procedure, but the order is processed right at the branch and merchandise shipped from the local inventory. Delivery is therefore much quicker and a higher level of overall support can generally be provided.

Independent Wholesalers

Independent wholesalers are autonomous, that is, they are owned by neither manufacturers nor retailers. They account for nearly two-thirds of the total volume of wholesaler sales.[3]

Independent wholesalers are essentially of two types—**merchant wholesalers** and **agent wholesalers**. The distinction is based upon whether the wholesaler owns, or takes title to, the goods being sold. Merchant wholesalers do; agent intermediaries do not. Merchant wholesalers account for slightly more than 50 percent of total wholesale trade, while agents and brokers account for little more than 12 percent.

Merchant wholesalers in turn fall into two major classes—full service, or limited service. As Table 11-3 shows, there are several types of wholesalers within each class.

Full Service Wholesalers

Full service wholesalers are also called full function wholesalers. Such intermediaries buy merchandise for resale, operate warehouses and many other physical distribution facilities, maintain large assortments of merchandise, and sell through their own sales force, who call on customers frequently. They also extend credit and other financial services, make deliveries, and provide management services such as accounting and inventory control assistance. In addition they provide vast amounts of marketing information to buyers as well as important feedback to manufacturers and suppliers of the merchandise carried. Thus, the full service wholesale firm offers a broad range of services to two of its principal partners in the channel of distribution—the retailer and the manufacturer. For the retailer, the full service wholesaler assists in planning for customer requirements, assembling merchandise items on a broad scale from many suppliers, purchasing in large quantities, and maintaining inventories where they are needed most. The wholesaler also extends much support to the retailer through management service and trade credit.

Full service wholesalers perform these important services in both the consumer and industrial goods market. In the industrial goods field, they are most frequently called **industrial distributors.** These distributors stock the products

---

[3] For the reader who may wish a more comprehensive treatment of wholesaling, the truly definitive work is that of Theodore N. Beckman, Nathanael H. Engle, and Robert D. Buzzell, *Wholesaling,* 3rd ed. (New York: Ronald Press, 1959). This work is partly updated in the following sources: Theodore N. Beckman; "Changes in Wholesaling Structure and Performance," in *Marketing and Economic Development,* ed. Peter D. Bennett (Chicago: American Marketing Association, 1965), pp. 603–618; and Theodore N. Beckman, *The True Facts About Wholesaler-Distributors* (Washington, DC: The National Association of Wholesaler Distributors, 1971).

they sell, and carry out a broad variety of marketing channel functions including customer contact, extending credit, stocking, delivery, and providing a full assortment inventory.[4]

The Rack Jobber. The rack jobber or service merchandiser, as this intermediary is sometimes called, is a special kind of full service merchant wholesaler who emerged primarily to offer supermarkets special merchandising assistance in selling nonfood items such as books, records, drugs, toilet articles, housewares, hardware items, and small hand tools. Rack jobbers also supply many discount stores with similar lines of merchandise. The term "rack" jobber relates to this wholesaler's practice of supplying a near-total merchandising service—preticketed (priced) products in an attractive point-of-purchase display that also serves for storing. This merchandising service is a form of simplified selling for the retail outlet. No investment in inventory is required. The display is set up by the rack jobber and periodically restocked. The merchandise is sold on a consignment basis and the salesperson inventories the assortment on each visit and collects for the items that have been sold. Merchandise that is damaged, shopworn, or doesn't move is simply removed and replaced with other items.

Limited Function Wholesalers

The marketplace is a great force for bringing about change and accommodation. To scale down operating expenses and compete more succesfully when the motive for patronage includes lower prices, **limited function wholesalers** have eliminated, reduced, or modified the more conventional functions or services performed by full service wholesalers.

Cash and Carry Wholesalers. Cash and carry wholesalers were historically especially strong in the grocery trade, where competition from chain supermarkets was the most severe. Cash and carry wholesalers employed few, if any, outside salespersons, carried narrower lines of merchandise with fewer offerings in each category, and sold strictly on a cash and carry basis, thus eliminating credit and delivery service. Many cash and carry operations were set up as special departments of the full function wholesaling company. This arrangement afforded buyers another option. If they wanted to take care of more of the marketing functions themselves, thus lowering the cost of goods sold, they could do so.

Drop Shippers. Drop shippers usually have an office but no warehouse and most often do not have possession of the goods they sell, even though they take title and have legal ownership. Drop shippers, also called desk jobbers, primarily buy carload lots of merchandise from producers and have the shipment "dropped" to a buyer or buyers along a designated transportation route.

[4] See Frederick E. Webster, Jr., "The Role of the Industrial Distributor in Marketing Strategy," *Journal of Marketing* **40** (July 1976), pp. 10–16.

In earlier days buyers were located along railway lines; today, many drop shippers use truck transportation. Drop shippers deal in various kinds of merchandise, but much of their sales volume is concentrated in coal, coke, lumber, and construction materials. Volume or carload lot purchasing is rather standard with these commodities.

Wagon Distributors.   Truck jobbers, or wagon distributors, are another form of limited function wholesaler. Wagon distributors are wholesalers who carry much of their representative inventory on the delivery truck. The driver-salesperson solicits business from customers, many of whom are in the grocery trade, and purchases are delivered immediately from the wagon distributor's mobile inventory. Wagon distributors deal primarily in fast moving but highly perishable specialty goods. Such items carry rather large merchandising risks and therefore often have sizable gross margins. Because of the specialized nature of the inventory, the risk, and the special services offered by wagon distributors, their operating expenses are relatively high.

Agent Intermediaries

Agent, or functional intermediaries do not take title to the goods in which they deal. Numerically, and in sales volume, they are not as important as merchant wholesalers. Yet, they constitute a series of very important links in the chain of distribution, representing, in many respects, the ultimate step in marketing specialization.

Selling Agents.   Selling agents specialize in the performance of marketing services for manufacturers. They generally work under a continuing contractual arrangement with a manufacturer, selling the entire output and handling the total marketing program for their principals. Selling agents are used by manufacturers who have production capabilities but lack marketing skills. An expert marketer, the selling agent receives a commission on each item sold. These agents carry on the most varied and complete marketing services of any of the functional intermediaries. In essence, the selling agent's activities are a substitute for a manufacturer's own complete marketing program.

Manufacturers' Agent.   The **manufacturers' agent** is a functional intermediary who acts as a salesperson in a defined territory. While the selling agent usually represents only one client or manufacturer, the manufacturers' agent may represent a number of noncompeting clients or manufacturers in the assigned territory. Manufacturers' agents have limited control over the marketing or sales program for the products they sell; selling agents have virtually unlimited control. The latter sell the entire output of the manufacturer they represent; the former sell only a portion of the manufacturer's output. Manufacturers' agents are often used as the sole distributor of a particular line of merchandise.

Brokers.   Brokers are specialists in the contactual function of marketing. They act principally as "go between" to bring buyer and seller together and are seldom permanent representatives of either. Brokers neither take title to, nor possession of, the goods in which they deal; they do not store, handle, or process the merchandise and they offer no financial services to buyers or sellers. Brokers are simply, but importantly, persons who are well informed about market conditions, terms of sale, and sources of credit. The broker expedites the negotiation between buyer and seller, although he or she has only marginal authority to complete a transaction without formal confirmation by the principal.

Assemblers and Commission Merchants.   Assemblers are agent intermediaries who deal mainly in agricultural products and seafoods. They assemble small quantities of a product from numerous small producers and sell the accumulated amount to buyers in central markets and other collection centers. The main problem for assemblers is to know prices in the central market so that they may buy from local sources at a price low enough to enable them to cover their acquisition costs and operating expenses and make a small profit.

Commission merchants are somewhat akin to brokers. They are functional, or agent, intermediaries who operate principally in agricultural markets for livestock and grain. Commission merchants usually have physical possession of the goods they trade. They contact buyers, performing a limited kind of overall marketing or sales service for sellers, and work especially hard to receive the most favorable price possible for the commodity. Commission merchants have more freedom than brokers: as long as they exert a "best effort" approach, they can negotiate the selling price with a buyer, providing that the price does not fall below the seller's stated minimum.

Current Developments and the Future of Wholesaling

The wholesaler's position as a principal marketing intermediary is sound and secure. Of course, success is not guaranteed; neither is it certain that particular kinds of wholesaling institutions will not pass out of the distribution structure. As conditions in the marketplace change, manufacturers and retailers will alter their marketing strategies and wholesalers will have to adapt accordingly.

Wholesalers have worked hard to reduce their costs of operation and to expand and broaden their appeal to both retailer and manufacturer. While becoming more adept at both buying and selling functions, wholesalers have made really significant strides in physical distribution. They have made concerted efforts to lower costs through better storage, warehousing, packaging, and shipping with the result that wholesalers move literally tons of merchandise at relatively low unit costs. New efficiently streamlined warehouses, containerized storage and shipping and computer assisted warehousing and inventory control systems have all tended to lower operating costs and to enable wholesalers to offer faster, better service.

The Continuing Tendency for Direct Marketing.   Not everyone is delighted, or even basically satisfied, with the wholesaler's services. There is a growing tendency on the part of many manufacturers and retailers to avoid wholesale intermediaries when establishing their marketing programs.

Large manufacturers have become increasingly disgruntled with wholesalers' weak or indifferent efforts to promote their individual products. Large retailers, many of whom have integrated, see the wholesaler as an unnecessary intermediary whose services can best be performed and controlled by the retail organization. Several things thus tend to support direct marketing: (1) the manufacturer's desire for greater sales volume and more aggressive promotion of individual company products, (2) the perceived inadequacy of wholesalers' services, and (3) the desire of some retail organizations to buy directly from manufacturers.

Are Wholesalers Doomed? No, wholesalers are not doomed. As we have said, their existence is virtually assured. Not all manufacturers can sell direct; neither do all retailers wish, nor can they afford, to buy direct from manufacturers. The diversity of our economy and our marketing system assures us of continuing diversity in our overall channels of distribution.

Before proceeding, can you answer these questions:
1. What is meant by the functional value of wholesalers?
2. Are wholesalers important links in our distribution system? Why?
3. Doesn't the increasing tendency for direct marketing threaten the continued existence of wholesalers? Explain.

Retailers in the Distribution Channel

Every day each of us feels the effect of retailing activities. The food we eat, the clothes we wear, the automobiles we drive, the services we use—our total life styles—are dramatically and positively affected by retailing and retail merchandising endeavors. Because retailers must be located close to the customers they serve, it is difficult to remove oneself from the presence of some sort of retailing activity.

Retailing is the act of selling goods or services to ultimate consumers. Thus, the motive of the buyer, as we said earlier, becomes the fundamental criterion for distinguishing sales at retail from other forms. Retail selling can be performed by many individuals, firms, or companies. Manufacturers can make sales at retail; so, too, can wholesalers or private individuals whose primary vocation is *not* retailing. Our concern, at this point, will be with sales and other activities of institutions that, as classified by the Bureau of the Census, are primarily *retail stores or retailing institutions*. In 1967 there were approximately 1,934,666 retailers in the United States with sales volume of $471 billion. By 1977, the actual number of retailing institutions had declined to 1,855,068 but sales volume had increased to $723 billion, or by nearly 54 percent. Much of this was real growth, yet some of it was, of course, related to the unprecedented increase in the inflation rate during the period.

The Growth and Development of Retailing Institutions

The United States meets the needs of its consumers today with the most stream-lined and efficient retail distribution system in history. Such, however, has not always been the case.

In matters of economic development, it is generally true that specialization is limited by the extent of the market. For example, early rural, sparsely settled America could support only the most rudimentary of retailing institutions. With population in cities and towns expanding, and with highways and other forms of transportation developing and so increasing mobility, retail stores became more and more complex. The changing nature of the economy brought about such institutions as the department store, which served the needs of the urban and close-in rural consumer; and the mail-order house, which focused its services on rural residents and brought them large selections of merchandise unavailable in their local area.

The surge in manufacturing and its consequent ability to pour forth an un-ending stream of low-priced goods in turn spurred the growth and develop-ment of such specialized retail operations as the variety store, specialty shops, supermarkets, and other modern forms of retailing institutions.

Improved methods of communication and better managerial techniques are largely responsible for the appearance of the corporate chain organization, a development that once threatened the conventional pattern of both retailing and wholesaling activities, but that has been somewhat stymied largely by the independent's flexibility and capacity for change.

Supermarkets and Discount Houses. The supermarket emerged in the early 1930s, largely as the result of consumers' increased mobility brought about by the automobile and their urgent desire to reap price advantages by performing some of the marketing functions themselves.

At least to date, it was one of the last great retailing institutions to emerge. With its emphasis on simplified selling and cash-and-carry merchandising, the supermarket has had a cataclysmic effect on the entire structure of retail distri-bution, leading to self-service merchandising strategies in many other kinds of retailing institutions and to the widespread adoption of discount selling.

The discount house is largely a post-World War II merchandising phenom-enon. The many types of this institution are discussed in several places throughout this book. Basically, the *discount house* is a merchandising firm that attempts to expand sales by featuring low prices. As a matter of fact, the hallmark of discount store operations is that their prices are usually considerably lower than those of conventional retailers. Some would question if discount houses really represent a new way of retailing or if they are simply retail stores that adopt special merchandising tactics such as low prices and fast turnover. Most authorities, however, treat discount houses as if they were a new and unique merchandising institution.

Retailing: The Current Scene. Retailing remains today an unsettled indus-try—buffeted by distressed economic conditions, especially unprecedented levels of inflation. Yet the industry is dynamic and undergoing near-constant change; each year brings some new development, expansion, and diversity. It is an industry of contrasts, one that features continued scrambled merchandising in some outlets while others strive to hold down inventories and operating costs by narrowing their merchandise lines. However, today, merchandise lines have become "scrambled." Food stores carry clothing items, clothing stores stock food items, hardware stores have become "building supply centers" where one can buy sporting goods items, small appliances, housewares, lawn and garden supplies and an array of often nonrelated items. In New Orleans or Baltimore, a drugstore may be a major outlet for liquor. In San Francisco, Dallas, or Peoria, the drugstore may be a place to buy lunch, pick up picnic supplies, shop for lawn furniture, or examine a variety of merchandise ranging from digital watches to books, records, and stereo tapes.

The trend to scrambled merchandising has had a dramatic impact in the food field and has affected both the retail supermarket and the wholesale operations which supply them. It has led to a closer examination of consumer shopping patterns and a reevaluation of the kinds of products a firm can offer to potential customers, the "proper" outlet through which goods can best be merchandised, and the channels and intermediaries best suited to move particular kinds of goods and services to market.

Energy shortages, the probable curtailment of the automobile, the push to develop more urban transit systems, the attempt to rebuild our central cities, and costs and profit squeezes are all manifestations and causes of the continuing turmoil in retail trade.

Classification of Retail Stores

The field of retail distribution is in many respects a hodgepodge of different kinds of establishments of different sizes, each possessing its own distinguishing characteristics. Table 11-4 helps to clarify the different classification schemes that may be employed. Compare this table with Table 11-3, shown earlier.

For most purposes the important criteria for classification center around (1) ownership, (2) extent and nature of lines handled, and (3) location.

Another revealing classification of retail institutions is that of location. Retail establishments and sales volume conform rather closely to the distribution of population and disposable income. Retail trade, although somewhat dispersed, has tended to focus around the major standard metropolitan statistical areas of the United States.

The Shopping Center. One of the truly important trends today in retail merchandising has been the increasing decentralization of retailing. Retail stores and trade centers follow the development of the better residential areas; decentralization of retail shopping areas has therefore been a natural evolution of urban expansion.[5]

[5] This trend is referred to as "the decentralization of retailing." See Gruney Breckenfield, "'Downtown' Has Fled to the Suburbs," *Fortune*, October 1972, pp. 81–85, 158, 162.

Table 11-4 Classification of Retail Stores

I. On the basis of merchandise carried:
1. General stores.
2. One-line stores and specialty stores. One-line and specialty stores may derive the majority of their business from a single line of merchandise, such as groceries, shoes, filling station supplies, and so on, or from a number of lines of merchandise that are closely related.
3. Multiple-line or convenience stores. This type is a limited edition of the old general store. It carries related merchandise but on a much wider base than the one-line or specialty store. Examples of such stores are those that carry all home furnishing items, present day auto accessory stores, drugstores, supermarkets, and so on.
4. Department stores.
5. Variety stores.
II. On the basis of functions performed or services rendered:
1. Self-service stores.
2. Cash-and-carry stores.
3. Service stores.
4. Supermarkets.
5. Mail order houses.
6. Direct selling.
7. Automatic vending.
III. On the basis of ownership:
A. Extent of ownership.
1. Independent retailers.
2. Voluntary chains.
3. Ownership groups.
4. Chain stores.
5. Branch stores.
B. Character of ownership.
1. Manufacturers' retail outlets.
2. Leased departments.
3. Company stores.
4. Utility operated stores.
5. State stores.
6. Consumers cooperative associations.
7. Franchising.
IV. On the basis of location:
1. Neighborhood stores.
2. Secondary shopping district stores.
3. Shopping district stores.
a. In shopping centers.
b. In central downtown districts.
4. Market stalls and stands.
5. Roadside stands and markets.
6. Mobile stores.
7. Country stores.
8. Pushcarts.

A revitalized urban center.

The principal magnet drawing retail trade away from the central business district has been the suburban shopping center. Although a few of these complexes date from more than forty years ago, the majority have been built since World War II. From approximately 1,000 centers at the end of 1955, the number jumped dramatically to 4,500 by 1960, topping 21,500 by 1980. Planned or controlled shopping centers at the end of the 1970s accounted for 37 percent of all retail sales and by 1985 their share may approach 50 percent.

The planned, or controlled, shopping center is a commercial development that is designed, developed, controlled, and operated by a single ownership, with off-street parking at the site to serve all establishments in the development.

A midwestern shopping center.

Shopping centers, or malls, are planned for a specific trading area through their site location and the proper mix of store types.

The planned retail center is designed and located to make shopping as convenient as possible. It is built close to large residential complexes so that shoppers have easy access to it. The planned shopping center is also designed to meet another dimension of convenience, namely clustering. These malls offer the consumer large assortments of goods in a concentrated variety. Such clustering makes shopping very convenient and permits what appears to be, from the standpoint of many consumers, the ultimate convenience—one-stop shopping.

The Changing Nature of Retail Merchandising

Retail merchandising is one of the most dynamic and responsive of industries. It is constantly changing, adapting, and accommodating. In many respects it is a reactive industry—it reacts and adjusts to all kinds of wide social and economic changes. Shifts in the population age mix, increased mobility, suburban living, changes in personal income, consumer credit uses, and many other changes all bring corresponding changes in retailing. Furthermore, retailing must accommodate to technological and cultural developments in our society: energy shortages, urban renewal, equal opportunity, women's liberation, new modes of travel and of living.

The retailer's general responses to such pressures and changes in the environment can be readily traced throughout the recent history of retail merchandising. For example, consider the following:

1. Stores are being relocated in various regions, some in suburban and outlying areas, but many are also being reestablished in the downtown central business district. Whenever there are shifts in people's location, their places of residence or work, and wherever people gather, there will be retail facilities to serve them.

2. Recently there has been a double-barreled trend toward the establishment of both larger and smaller stores. The larger ones are usually department stores or branches, general merchandise stores, or large super-supermarkets, sometimes called family centers. The smaller ones are often specialty and limited-line outlets, sometimes called **boutiques**, which emphasize **thematic merchandising** or merchandising to a theme.

3. There has been a constant effort toward store improvement, modernization, revitalization, and the updating of older buildings to meet the high aesthetic demands of today's critical shopper.

4. All kinds of organizational changes and restructuring have been undertaken in retailing to make the administration and operation of stores more responsive to the rising level of both retail customers' and retail employees' expectations.

5. Compulsive changes in styles of operation for retail stores have taken place. Many merchandisers have adopted night and Sunday openings, with employees working on flexible schedules.

6. The frenetic effort to find novel, exciting merchandise lines to meet the greater expectations of today's affluent consumer goes on, with an increasing emphasis on leisure time merchandise, antiques, art objects, and high-quality imported items. All this tends to swell the already well-established tendency toward broadened product lines and scrambled merchandising.

7. Rising operating expenses and decreasing gross margins and profit levels have caused retailers to apply new technology to control inventory shortages and manage and control overall inventory levels better through closed circuit monitoring devices and information retrieval and processing equipment.

8. Finally, many new forms of organization, such as franchising, have emerged to meet the capital needs of those businesses wishing to expand rapidly and the needs of the smaller manager-entrepreneur. The increasing development of nonstore retailing, telephone and catalog selling, mail order merchandising, and vending machine selling are all responses, answers, if you will, to the increasing and changing demands of today's aware and affluent consumer.

Retailing: An Industry of Contrasts

It is not easy to generalize about retail merchandising. Retailing is an industry of contrasts born of size, location, management style, and organization arrangement. The student of retailing must never overlook the importance of diversity. Diversity on the demand side of the marketing equation requires diversity on the supply side. Different market segments, each with its own set of demand characteristics, will require different kinds of retail distribution facilities.

Now that we have dramatized the importance of change and underscored the contrast and diversity it leads to, let us examine some of the major changes in retail merchandising that are likely to shape retailing well into the late 1980s. We shall explore, therefore, three major and significant trends. These are (1) franchising; (2) nonstore retailing, which includes a whole range of both older and newer approaches to retail distribution; and (3) thematic merchandising, which is the way some retailers generate significant consumer responses by merchandising to special categories of buyers through the use of themes. These themes almost always have certain style and fashion implications and entail generally high price and quality to match.

Franchising Operations

Throughout the late 1960s and early 1970s there was a virtual groundswell of retailing activity. One form this took was the expansion of franchised operations. Franchising is a rather simple, yet in some ways complicated, organizational and operating arrangement. It requires a legal contract between two parties, one known as a *franchisor* and the other as a *franchisee*. The franchisor in return for payment licenses the franchisee to carry on certain activities.

Let us look at a simple, though not unrealistic, example. Suppose Joe McIver, a mythical student at Pacific Northwestern University, decides to go into business for himself with a hamburger, fries, and shake shop. He opens his establishment; streamlines the production of hamburgers; develops a special, secret-recipe sauce; learns a new way of creating crisp, nonsoggy French fries; and packages his commodities uniquely for carryout sales. He then widely and successfully promotes the name of his firm and his principal product, the "Fantastic McI. Hamburger," along the theme, "You deserve to try the Fantastic McI." Flushed with success, McIver wishes to expand. However, in spite of his success, he lacks both capital and a highly motivated, trustworthy, experienced person to run his next unit. What can he do? He can sell a franchise to an interested person with sufficient capital, whom McIver and his existing staff can then train. The next unit, situated in a strategic location, is a carbon copy of the first. It is completely standardized in appearance, style and method of operation, and uniformity of product. The new franchise is sold to and operated by Sharon Davis. McIver is the *franchisor* and Davis is the *franchisee*. What McIver sold Davis is a franchise and all that is entailed in a franchised operation.

Franchising is the creation of a continuing business relationship in which a franchisor, in return for payment, licenses a franchisee to do business using the franchisor's business name and methods. Included in the on-going exchange is assistance in management, organization, training, and control.

The History and Development of Franchising. Although it has recently mushroomed, franchising as an organizational and operating form has been around for a long time, supposedly since the Middle Ages.[6] It emerged in the United States just after the Civil War, when the Singer Sewing Machine Company used franchising as a way of expanding sales facilities and controlling the operators of the outlets. Franchising has been extremely popular in the United States, where both automobiles and gasoline are sold extensively through franchised dealers or agencies.

Vertical Versus Horizontal Franchising. The kind of franchising used by the automobile manufacturers and the large petroleum refiners is a form of *vertical franchising*. It is called vertical because it involves operations on two or more different levels of distribution. For example, the manufacturer of the automobile seeks retail outlets and what is franchised is the right to sell the manufacturer's products, not to produce them. However, more recently franchising has expanded through *horizontal franchising* in which retail sellers of products and services license or franchise others on the same level of distribution to duplicate these products and services in some other place. This kind of franchising is also known as a *service-sponsor-retailer franchise* in which

---

[6] Ernest Henderson, Sr., "Franchising Yesterday," in *Franchising Today*, ed. Matthew Bender (Albany, NY: 1966-1967), p. 239.

the *franchisor*, who is the service-sponsor, sells and licenses the franchisee an established method for operating a retail business. It is in this area of service-sponsor-retailer franchise, or horizontal franchising, that recent growth has been so phenomenal. Much of this expansion has occurred in nontraditional areas like the following:

1. Coin-operated laundries and self-service dry cleaning establishments
2. Temporary employee and assistance agencies
3. Specialty food and beverage retailing
4. Ready-to-eat carry-out food facilities
5. Tool and equipment rental
6. Automobile, truck, and trailer rental units
7. Carpet, upholstery, and general cleaning services

In the future consumer products and retail outlets may increasingly be franchised operations. To a great extent, the growing success of franchising may well be linked to the increased mobility, restlessness and changing life styles of American consumers—highly dependent on the automobile for travel and daily use, on the move and on the go—who want their needs for cleaning, eating, travel, leisure, and sleeping to be met quickly and efficiently. Franchising may owe its success in part to the greater emphasis on customer services rather than on goods, and to a diminishing interest in owning goods as opposed to simply utilizing them.

The Range of Service-Sponsor Retailer Franchises.   A wide range of business opportunities beckons the aspiring franchisee. Depending upon one's ambitions, capital, and other factors, a person can find any number of franchising opportunities. Table 11-5 depicts several of these, showing the probable capital requirements and some of the main elements of the franchisor's package of service.

Whatever franchising's specific future, it has already had a strong impact on retail merchandising. It has greatly improved the quality of many smaller scale retail operations, while the generally excellent service and operating efficiency of the franchise affiliates have produced many imitators among smaller independents. Even the larger chain organizations have, given the competitive nature of some franchised operations, been forced to modernize their facilities and upgrade their operations in order to keep their place in the market.

Nonstore Retailing

Nonstore retailing—merchandising directly to ultimate consumers without benefit of the intervening physical store facility—is an increasingly important way of doing business for many retailers. Americans' changing life styles, increased mobility, and active nature are bringing about important changes in shopping and purchasing habits and patterns. Retailers' response to these changes, in part at least, is to provide a number of alternative shopping-purchase options, many of which lie in the realm of nonstore retailing.

It is important to understand that a person can go shopping without necessarily visiting a retail store. Merchandise can be ordered by telephone, examined in a catalog, or displayed on closed-circuit television. A salesperson can visit the customer's home or office, or merchandise can be purchased directly from a machine by paying cash, or, maybe very soon now, by inserting one's bank credit card.

Table 11-5 Franchising Opportunities—Franchisee Requirements and Franchisor's Package of Service

Franchise Offering to Customers	Items in the Franchise Package	Financial Requirements
Holiday Inn: Food and hospitality services	Training for management and key employees, workshops and retraining conferences, promotional and operational services.	Total investment, approximately $1,500,000. Royalty payments of 3% of gross room service.
Shakey's Pizza Parlor: Pizza, beer, entertainment	Complete training and instruction by Shakey's Corporate Training Personnel at Shakey's University. All skills needed to create and operate Shakey's Pizza Parlor. Promotional and total operating services.	Total investment, $220,000. For full-scale operation, approximately $35,000 cash requirements. Franchise royalty payment of 5½% of monthly food sales.
McDonald's Hamburgers: Fast food, french fries	Training at Hamburger University. Follow-up retraining and update seminars—complete, comprehensive operations manual, broad training materials by field service staff.	Total investment, $140,000 including $75,000 cash requirement. Service fee of 3% monthly of net gross sales, and rental of 8.5% of monthly gross sales.
Rent-All stores and United Rent-All	Management training, inventory and control planning, merchandising, and accounting consulting service. Comprehensive manual of operations.	$25,000 to $50,000 total investment, with $10,000 to $15,000 cash requirement. Royalty payment of 4% to 5% on monthly sales.
Kelly Girl: Management or help assistance agencies	Personnel selection assistance service, training and procedural assistance. Advertising and promotional assistance. Accounting methods and tax assistance.	$10,000 to $25,000 investment. Usually no more than $10,000 cash requirement. Sign rental and royalty fee of 5% of monthly billings.

The distinction between in-store and nonstore retailing is not as tidy as one might desire. Much merchandise is sold, for example, by telephone and mail order from the retail store premises. Thus, we must be careful not to push the distinction between store and nonstore merchandising too far.

Nonstore retailing takes two major forms; personal nonstore selling and nonpersonal nonstore selling. As you would surmise, the basic difference between the two is the minimal personal, face-to-face, or oral contact between seller and buyer in the nonpersonal, nonstore retailing category.

Personal, Nonstore Retailing

Personal, nonstore retailing is chiefly of two types, telephone sales and direct selling in the customer's home or office. Once again, it should be emphasized that *personal* connotes either a face-to-face or oral transactional process.

Telephone Selling.   Telephone selling may take place either from a retail store, or from a firm which has no store itself but acts in behalf of a store; or a person or persons may simply try to sell merchandise via telephone. In either case the items sold are delivered from a central warehouse facility.

Telephone selling is becoming a major marketing tool for a number of reasons: (1) Compared with other forms of promotion and advertising, it is inexpensive. (2) It can effectively support and complement in-store merchandising efforts. (3) It makes excellent use of employees otherwise slack time.

Retailers increasingly are moving toward more telephone solicitation, finding it raises the efficiency of their in-store sales personnel. Every day there are usually slack periods, when customer in-store traffic is slow and housekeeping and inventory chores are caught up. These periods can be made productive by shifting efforts to telephone solicitation. Furthermore, each telephone sale or store visit that is added as a result of such effort is an incremental merchandising gain. Each sale thus obtained is added, or plus, revenue and of course plus profit. It may be a significant profit too, especially if such a sale does not add appreciably to the direct costs of attaining it. Telephone solicitation is also an important way of complementing the firm's advertising and its overall promotional effort.

In-Home Selling.   The home has characteristically been an important point of purchase throughout the history of retail merchandising. Today, door-to-door selling continues as an important means of distributing some goods (such as cosmetics, personal care products, appliances, and magazines), but the frequency, range of goods, and general success of this form of selling as a percentage of total sales has diminished somewhat in importance, especially in comparison with earlier periods.

However, the home is a desirable atmosphere for the buying and selling of services and commodities. In its reinforcing and familiar environment customer-buyers often feel less intimidated by an aggressive seller. For several reasons many customers are quite willing to have sellers call on them in their home.[7] First, when other family members are present they can be consulted

[7] Marvin A. Jolson. "Direct Selling: Consumer vs. Salesman." *Business Horizons,* October 1972, pp.87–96.

about the merits of the proposed product. Second, some customers contend that because of their personal reluctance they might not have bought a given product had it not been persuasively and effectively demonstrated in their home by the salesperson. Third, many customers prefer to try out the product and actually use it at home before making the purchase commitment. Direct-in-the-home buying permits this kind of product use and evaluation. Finally, the retail store, for some shoppers, seems a hostile place to be shunned, a place where one encounters discourteous and poorly trained sales personnel. Many customer-buyers, by contrast, see their home as an unhurried, casual shopping environment where they control what is happening.

Nonpersonal Nonstore Retailing

We shall discuss briefly three forms of nonpersonal nonstore retailing: mail order retailing, catalog selling, and vending machines.

Mail Order Selling.   Many retailing organizations use direct mail advertising, but this form of promotion should not be mistaken for mail order selling. Direct mail advertising is often used by retail stores to attract customers to the store; it also serves to encourage customers to order items by mail *from the store*. However, for our purposes we are discussing a form of selling and retail distribution that sells merchandise directly to consumers by *mail* and in which there is no store facility as such.

There are several reasons why mail order selling has much general customer appeal. More important among them are the following:

1. Lower prices. Mail order selling as a form of direct distribution can sometimes be an efficient and inexpensive method of selling. Customers are often stimulated by the low selling prices, which are in many instances the result of low overhead and low operating expense ratios.
2. Uniqueness. Many mail order items that are merchandised successfully can attribute their success, in part at least, to their novelty and the shopper's curiosity. Items that are successfully merchandised by mail are often unusual articles with strong reinforcing qualities or, in the case of some personal items, those which customers might desire but which might cause some embarrassment to buy in a conventional store.
3. Convenience. The foregoing statement underscores the importance of convenience. Many buyers, for obvious reasons that have already been explained, wish to shop, buy, pay for, and use items in the privacy of their homes. This eliminates all the problems associated with shopping in a store.

Problems of Mail Order Selling.   This kind of selling continues to gain popularity and success in spite of some serious problems.

A major difficulty is with the postal service itself. People are finding the mails increasingly slow and unreliable. Postal fees have soared during the past five years and are likely to climb even higher in the future. This will raise operating costs and, of course, the prices of the commodities sold.

Also, it is difficult for a buyer to return items purchased by mail, and other adjustments are equally complicated. There have been, not surprisingly, some problems with fraud and misrepresentation, such as an ad which read, "Complete sewing machine kit $3.98" but which turned out to be a needle, thread, and thimble. Finally, mail order selling is a more sophisticated kind of merchandising effort. The products themselves must be promotable by mail, and must be mailable, dependable, reliable, and somewhat exclusive.

Catalog Sales.   There are various forms of catalog selling. Some combine direct selling with in-store merchandising. Some retailers are successful merchandisers without benefit of stores at all. And finally, a recent development that is gaining popularity is the catalog store, which we shall examine in some detail.

Catalog selling offers business an excellent opportunity to create sales and profits without benefit of sales personnel, store facilities, physical assortments, or displays of merchandise. Catalog selling is a means of getting plus, or incremental, business. For example, United Airlines has arranged a tie-in agreement with a catalog merchandiser. United dispenses to passengers a twenty-four page, slick paper, high-quality catalog illustrated in full color, which United calls its *Friendship Store-Shopping Service*. Items are chosen by how well they fit passengers' socio-economic life style. Another firm, the House of Webster, which specializes in what they call "old-fashioned gifts" and replicas of early American household appliances and tools, distributes its catalog, called a "scrapbook," at major air terminals throughout the United States.

Catalog selling will undoubtedly continue to grow as techniques for creating highly attractive and successful catalog merchandising opportunities become more sophisticated. Its growth in turn is related to the increasing selectivity and preference of many emerging market targets.

Catalog Stores.   Catalog stores are a novel blend of catalog selling techniques and in-store merchandising. Such stores are sometimes called *catalog showrooms*. They combine the atmosphere and service of a general merchandise operation with the convenience of a catalog and the savings of a discount store.

Conservative estimates placed annual catalog showroom sales at approximately $5 billion in 1980 and forecasts are that they may reach $25 billion by 1990. Historically, such stores were the bastion of the mail order houses, discount houses, department stores, and the premium stamp companies.

Most of these outlets are free standing units and are dressed in eye-pleasing color schemes, plushly decorated with full carpeting and expensive fixtures. Well-managed catalog showrooms are recording profits of 5 to 10 percent of sales based upon 25 to 30 percent margins. Sales per square foot range from $85 to $200. Operating costs are lower than the average supermarket, averaging 15 to 20 percent.

Catalog stores are basically order houses where customers shop from 400-page catalogs that include some 8,000 different items. Only one or two of each item are displayed in the store. When a customer makes a selection the order is filled from the store's warehouse stock. These operations have several advantages:

1. Using the catalog as a shopping guide eliminates the need for a large sales staff.
2. Display of one-of-a-kind merchandise described on its price ticket reduces showroom pilferage to about 1 percent of sales, as compared to as much as 5 percent of sales in stores which have more merchandise in open displays.
3. Direct take-home of purchased items by customers nearly eliminates delivery costs.
4. The pulling power of the attractively displayed, discounted merchandise allows showrooms to be located on less expensive land and in low-rental areas.
5. Payment in cash or customer's bank credit card lowers the cost of credit.
6. With the catalog as the primary advertising medium, promotional costs are kept to a bare minimum.

By the end of the 1980s there may be as many as 3,500 of these outlets. Just how significant this special new breed of retailer will become is uncertain. However, catalog selling in especially attractive surroundings in stores, as well as in customers' homes, appears destined to be a significant part of retailing for the future.

Vending Machine Selling. The ultimate, in many respects, of nonstore, nonpersonal retailing is the automatic vending machine. Given our highly automatic, almost robotized, society, selling by machines seems to hold exciting possibilities for both buyer and seller. Machines do not go on strike; they do not require coffee breaks and rest periods, or ask for salary increases, or pilfer merchandise. From the customer's perspective, they neither ignore nor insult. They are perennially available and do not talk back. Not being overly persistent or aggressive, they do not sell unwanted merchandise to reluctant customers. Given all these desirable features, it is small wonder that so many forecasted such a rosy future for machine selling during the 1970s. Yet, sales from automatic vending machines will reach slightly more than $300 million by the mid-1980s and the prospects for future growth seems somewhat dim.

Automatic machine vending is ideally suited for many convenience items of low unit value. Machines for off-hour selling of bread, milk, and other fill-in items were installed in supermarket parking lots during the 1960s, but with very marginal success. Machine selling is common at bus terminals, air terminals, college and university locations outside classrooms and in dormitories, factories, offices, and almost all places where people congregate and need snacks, beverages, or personal care items. Problems of pilferage and machine malfunction have been the greatest barriers to success in this kind of retailing.

The 1970s brought no really new technological breakthroughs, and machine selling has just about kept pace with food and beverage production and the increases in the total population.

Furthermore, the market for machine vending appears to have reached a point of near-saturation. There is an equipment surplus and the rapidly rising price levels of the 1980s have generated real merchandising difficulties, especially in the areas of pricing.

In the future there may be new developments in machine design or in packaging that would tend to accelerate sales. Vending machines depend greatly for their success on eye-catching appeal, which leads to impulse and reminder buying. Without striking packaging and machine design, plus good locations, machine vending is at best a speculative merchandising venture.

Thematic Merchandising

American merchandising has always had its themes—the central scripts and settings which cast a given store into some kind of alliance with its target customers. The overwhelming theme of twentieth century retailing in the United States has been mass merchandising, with the emphasis usually on price, good quality, and undifferentiated facilities and services. This tends to generate a kind of sameness, a blandness, with a capacity for quick satiation and dullness. Given the increasing diversity of the American market, this merchandising theme no longer satisfies all market segments. Some customer groups, because of vastly different socioeconomic characteristics which support varied life styles with different interests and activities prefer different themes—hence, the concept of *thematic merchandising*. These themes are as varied as the customer segments they cater to: leisure, youth, travel, recreation, hobbies, sports, education, gourmet foods, ecology and environment, affluence. Almost every special interest of any magnitude can in turn both generate and support merchandising institutions to cater to it.

Boutique Merchandising.   A boutique is a shop-within-a-shop. The essence of the boutique is individuality. Boutique merchandising is the essence also of theme oriented retailing. Atmosphere is exceedingly important, and most boutiques, although not necessarily in the luxury category, are certainly not price oriented. They are for discriminating people with highly individual views of fashion or special product needs. Identifying a discerning customer group is the first step to success in boutique merchandising. The second most important step is creating a unique store image through merchandise assortment and atmosphere. Boutique assortments usually include relatively unusual, hand-crafted clothes, gifts, jewelry, crafts, and furnishings, with a few choice items in each category. As a matter of fact, a boutique means the opposite of plenty of everything; it means a few of different things.

Boutique merchandising is another example of retailing response to meet particular needs, in this case the preferences of a selective clientele. As giant retailers are expanding, fashion has become more uniform. However, there are always those who resist uniformity and who will pay for more individual merchandise. The major advantage of the boutique is that it helps to personalize; this is important to those who feel lost in a large store.

Boutiques located in air terminals and major hotels have become highly successful. Many department stores are now attempting to emulate the successful independent boutiques by establishing their own shops-within-a-shop. The next decade may see many more follow suit.

It is hoped we have projected something of the atmosphere and the psychology of "The Changing Nature of Retail Merchandising." Retailing, in our culture at least, is almost never static. Marketing institutions come and go. In the next, and last, section of this chapter, we will look briefly at a few alternative explanations of why marketing institutions emerge, grow, and then often decline.

Before proceeding, can you answer these questions:
1. Retailing is often characterized as more dynamic and fast paced than wholesaling. Can you explain why?
2. List and discuss several of the more important trends in recent retailing operations.
3. Why are nonstore retailing activities successful?

Theories of Institutional Change

Why do marketing institutions emerge, develop, change, and sometimes lapse into extinction? Several theories or general notions have been advanced that partly explain this process.

Marketing Institutions as Social Systems

One theory holds that marketing institutions are parts of social-economic systems. Each new institution comes into existence to meet a social-economic need. Hence, marketing institutions exist in a state of regular interaction with other institutions. The importance and well-being of a particular organization will depend on its internal management, plus how well its efforts are coordinated with the larger network of which it is a part.

The general conclusion is that marketing institutions emerge and develop in response to the needs of the social-economic system and, when they no longer fulfill those needs, become obsolete and eventually extinct.

The Wheel of Retailing

Professor Malcolm P. McNair introduced the **"wheel of retailing"** concept to explain the dynamics of institutional change within the overall retailing sys-

art forms
Wear them. Live with them. They're a part of your life.

The Greengrass Gallery in the Cellar: Whether you're inclined to trend-setting moderns or enduring classics, we've a finely edited collection of reproductions and posters.

The Perry Ellis Shop on 3. Perry turns dressing into an art form. To find his inspirations, head to his new shop on 3 and get a look at the innovative looks you'll be seeing (and wearing) on the sidewalks of New York.

The Great American Supermarket on 4. Is it pop art? Probably. Most assuredly, it's the most super market you'll ever cruise through, with a veritable crazy salad of fun, easy things to wear and give. (You may even find Brand X).

New Country Gear on 5. American design is finally at home with itself. It'll fill every room in your home with beauty. Come see this new line of home furnishings and see how to go back to the country without ever having to leave the city.

The shop-within-a shop concept.

tem.[8] In this theory, the wheel is always revolving and moving forward. The cycle begins with an innovation. These "innovators" enter the market as low-status, low-margin, low-price operators "in bad odor, ridiculed, scorned, condemned as 'illegitimate'."[9] Gradually, they acquire more elaborate establishments and facilities, and so become top-heavy and vulnerable with both increased investments and higher operating costs. This process of change, often referred to as "trading-up" in marketing terminology, leads to what some have termed an invariable tendency for rising margins. Do you know why?

The process of trading up is a form of nonprice competition and nonprice competition tends to raise operating expenses. If operating expenses go up and profits are not to fall, gross margins must be increased. Finally the cycle or revolution of the wheel is completed when the new institutions mature as vulnerable, high-cost, high-price merchants. Then comes the next innovation or revolution of the wheel, beginning with the next merchant with a bright idea, starting business on a low-cost basis, slipping in under the umbrella the old-line institutions have hoisted.

The wheel concept of institutional change is intriguing and to some extent descriptive of the changes which take place in the structure of retail institutions. Nevertheless, it does not explain why new institutions emerge; it is only an explanation of why institutions change or adapt, and has not been very useful in predicting their changes. As a matter of fact, the theory, even in its more descriptive aspects, does not appear to hold for all types of retailing institutions. The department store is one worrisome exception. The "wheel of retailing" concept, however, has been an influential one in retailing and will continue to undergo refinement and further development.[10]

The Life Cycle Concept

Not too subtly hidden in the "wheel of retailing" concept is the old notion of life cycle. Remember, we first encountered this idea in our discussion of product planning and development. We learned that products may go through a cycle from "birth" to widespread adoption and popularity, to decline, and eventually total or near-total demise. Some see the life cycle concept at work among marketing institutions. New institutions come about as a result of innovation, move through a period of accelerated development, from there to maturity, and then on to their ultimate decline. The life cycle concept, contrary to some opinions, is not an inevitable, inflexible evolutionary process.[11]

[8] Malcolm P. McNair, "Significant Trends and Developments in the Postwar Period," in *Competitive Distribution in a Free High Level Economy and Its Implications for the University*, ed. A.B. Smith (Pittsburgh: University of Pittsburgh Press, 1957), p. 17.
[9] McNair, "Significant Trends," p. 17.
[10] The theory has recently been updated. See Malcolm McNair and Eleanor May, "The Evolution of Retail Institutions in the United States," Marketing Science Institute, *Research Briefs*, August 1976, p. 1.
[11] William R. Davidson, Albert D. Bates, and Stephen J. Bass, "The Retail Life Cycle," *Harvard Business Review*, November–December 1976, pp. 89–96.

It is doubtful that the life cycle concept is a really significant explanation of the growth and development of marketing institutions. People do move through an unalterable life cycle; in a very loose sense, so do some marketing institutions. But many do not. The life cycle seems highly relevant as an explanation when looking back on failed products or extinct institutions, but for looking ahead, its usefulness is dubious. The life cycle, remember, is not an independent variable, but a dependent one.

The department store as an institution is relatively ancient—the first one in the United States, the A.T. Stewart Store in New York City, was opened in 1863. Stewart's long ago closed its doors, but department stores generally continue to prosper and are a viable part of the structure of retail distribution. The first supermarket opened in the early 1930s and in a short time its breed dominated food retailing. Today, they remain the principal outlet for food and related products and capture the largest share of the consumer's dollar. Department stores and supermarkets have shown a remarkable capacity for adaptation. Some individual stores or chains fail to adapt and therefore decline in importance and eventually pass out of existence. But there is no unalterable pattern of innovation, maturity, decline, and extinction. Patterns of growth and development are simply reflections of how well marketing managers adapt to environmental changes. Any marketing institution can survive and grow for a long time if management is diligent in its efforts to remain flexible. Such efforts require a constant search for new market opportunities coupled with an awareness of emerging technological and social changes.

Summary

The success of our United States system of marketing can, in large measure, be attributed to the sophistication and efficiency of our marketing institutions. Marketing institutions are firms or agencies which perform marketing functions, activities essential to facilitating and consummating (completing) marketing transactions. Thus, without marketing institutions, there would be no performance of marketing functions and without marketing functions there is simply no marketing.

Marketing intermediaries are evidence of specialization and division of labor within the distribution network. Marketing institutions lower the costs of distribution by standardizing and routinizing the performance of certain essential marketing tasks. Wholesalers and retailers work to create utility—the added value of having the right products and services at the right time and place in order to facilitate their consumption or use.

Both wholesaling and retailing institutions are part of a larger social-economic system, whose needs they exist to serve. When they no longer do so, they tend to be replaced by more innovative and responsive institutions. There are several theories of institutional growth and change. Two concepts, the "wheel of retailing" and the "life cycle," are broad descriptive theories useful for discussion and some analysis, yet limited for explanatory purposes.

Numerous trends and developments are underway in both wholesaling and retailing. Mainly, these developments are responses to the fast-paced, competitive, rapidly changing environment within which these institutions operate. Survival of any given institution most likely depends on managerial effort and attention to social-economic, technological, and demographic forces. Survival dictates the necessity to remain flexible, to monitor emerging marketing opportunities constantly, and to adapt and accommodate to these changes.

Review Questions

1. What is the importance of wholesalers and retailers?
2. What is the relationship between marketing structure and marketing functions?
3. In marketing institutions, how does efficiency lead to lower costs?
4. What is meant by "gross margin"? By "profit"? Can you illustrate these terms?
5. "You can eliminate intermediaries, but you can't eliminate their functions." Explain.
6. Distinguish between merchant wholesalers and agent wholesalers.
7. What is a full service wholesaler? How does this intermediary differ from a limited function wholesaler?
8. What is the basic difference between a wholesaler and a retailer?
9. List and discuss three major trends which appear to be underway in retail merchandising.
10. What is meant by franchising?
11. What are the causes of the increasing popularity of nonstore retailing?

Case 11-1

Hard Time Tools

Bill Stack lives with his wife, Velma, and their two children in the Green Monarch mountains of northern Idaho. Bill and his family are members of the counterculture. They live an austere but comfortable life far from the city and, to the extent possible, they are largely self-sufficient, living on the produce from their garden and on a modest income generated by Bill's trapping and his work as an outfitter and hunting guide.

The Stacks live in a hand-hewn log cabin which Bill and Velma built themselves. In the process of building the log cabin, Bill used his chain saw and ax but found that there were many jobs which required more specialized tools. Bill made many of the specialized tools himself, improvising some and copying some from pictures found in old catalogs and from illustrations shown in stories and histories of pioneering families.

Bill's craftsmanship has been widely admired and many have asked him to duplicate for them some of the tools necessary to do good quality woodwork, especially those used for building log cabins. As a matter of fact, Bill was not surprised to learn that there is something of a "back to nature" trend underway and that thousands of people are building log cabins either as permanent, basic, year-round structures, or as leisure time homes such as lake cabins or ski houses. The request for Bill's specialized tools was beginning to grow and he was getting as many as two to three letters a week inquiring about them, their availability, price, and so on.

Bill was anxious to respond to these inquiries for several reasons. First, he was genuinely interested in promoting his own life style among other people. Second, he was flattered by the growing recognition and his reputation as a designer and craftsman of high-quality tools. Third, he was pleased that he was able to sell these tools at a very generous profit. He began calling his tools Hard Time Tools and was seriously considering expanding the scope of his operations. He arranged for a large machine tool and welding shop in Spokane, Washington, to make up his tool designs and he also had a small printer, "Good Earth News" in Spokane design and print up a small illustrated brochure which not only showed his tools but gave detailed directions about how to build your own log cabin. More recently, as output has expanded, Hard Time Tools have been distributed through a limited number of wholesale supply houses in the Pacific Northwest, Rocky Mountain region, Alaska, Northern California, and in the East, especially in Maine, Vermont, and New Hampshire. All the products bear the "Hard Times," brand which is only moderately well known because little or no money has been spent on promotion. Stack is not too satisfied with the way his product is moving. Wholesalers carry the tools reluctantly, and they make no attempt to "push" or aggressively promote them. Retailers likewise, except in rare instances, take a passive interest in these products. Stack is intrigued and enthusiastic about doing the best he can with his products. He is even considering hiring sales people who would sell directly to retailers.

Questions

Suppose you have been hired as a consultant to advise John Stack as to the wisdom of such a change.
1. What factors would you consider in determining whether or not the proposed method of distribution would be feasible?
2. Would such a change lower or raise the cost of distributing the product?
3. Finally, develop for Stack an "ideal" channel of distribution for his product and explain why your channel is ideal.

Case 11-2

K-Mart Corporation

Since 1962, the S.S. Kresge Company, which now calls itself K-Mart, has been expanding and transforming itself from a slow-paced variety store chain into one of the new breed of super merchandisers offering low prices, value, and service based upon fast turnover of its multi-merchandise lines.

The formula has worked well for K-Mart because the company today has more than 1,900 units blanketing the country and has catapulted past the J.C. Penney Company to become the nation's second largest retailer. K-Mart's annual earnings of $358 million last year even exceeded the $349 million in merchandising net income by Sears Roebuck and Company, and some industry sources are predicting that by 1985 K-Mart will surpass the Chicago-based giant in dollar sales volume. K-Mart's 1979 sales amounted to $127 billion while Sears' merchandising revenues were $175 billion.

Yet K-Mart faces, like many retailers, an uncertain and perhaps even hazardous future. Economic recession, high rates of inflation, increasingly fierce competition, saturation of major markets, and soaring operating costs are making it nearly impossible for K-Mart to maintain its 20 percent annual growth rate. As a result, the company is now projecting a more modest 12 percent annual growth rate for the early years of the 1980s. K-Mart executives are now worried about this loss of momentum. Preoccupied over the past five years with building more than 175 new stores annually, the company, some industry analysts contend, lost sight of the need to maximize profit from every square inch of store space. One immediate goal of present management personnel is to boost inventory turnover in the stores by 50 percent within five years. Inventory turnover is a key measure of a retailer's success and at K-Mart turnover has dropped from 8 times a year in the 1960s to 3.8 in 1979. By comparison, general merchandise retailers on the average turned over their stocks 4.7 times in 1979. K-Mart's earnings growth is lagging behind sales, and profit margins dipped from 2.9 percent in 1978 to 2.8 percent last year. Target profit figures are set at a 3 percent minimum. Selling, general, and administrative expenses rose from 21.5 percent of sales to 22.5 percent, a trend the company fears will continue.

Much of K-Mart's growth came at the expense of Sears during the 1970s as the Chicago giant first upgraded its merchandise lines and then slashed its prices when its customers be-

PUT ON THE K MART PERFORMER
Put off repainting for up to nine years

Brush on The Performer and coat your house with nine-year, all-season protection that won't chalk, yellow, blister or peel. The tough acrylic latex finish is washable, resists fade and mildew, too. Apply The Performer to wood, metal or masonry surfaces; it goes on smoothly, cleans up easily. The K mart Performer comes in more than 40 colors. But choose carefully! The Performer will be with you for a long time. The Performer, our best exterior paint, available only at K mart, is on sale at over 1,800 K mart stores across the U.S.A.

$9.96 PER GALLON SAVE 33%

ON SALE MAY 18 THROUGH MAY 30

Quality at a K mart price. Nice.

Kmart

The Saving Place℠

came confused and turned to other alternative retailers. From 1974 to 1978, K-Mart revenues grew 21 percent and the company accounted for 6.1 percent of total general merchandise, apparel, and furniture sales. During that period, Penneys' sales grew only 12.6 percent and Sears' 11 percent. When Sears engaged in heavy promotional activity in 1977 to win back lost market share, it triggered a price war among the nation's 28 leading retailers. These leaders now account for 41 percent of general merchandise, apparel, and furniture sales, up from 36 percent in 1974. Major retail markets have to some extent become saturated. At the beginning of 1980, some 276 of the country's major metropolitan areas have outlets of at least five of the leading 28 retailers. The development is prompting many retailers to explore prospects in smaller towns and the suburban fringes. K-Mart believes it is well positioned to plumb both the urban and small town markets. It claims that only 60 percent of its urban market potential has been reached. Moreover, with 400 units in operation, K-Mart is one of the few major retailers that already has a strong presence in smaller market areas. These scaled-down units—40,000–73,000 square feet, compared with the typical K-Mart of 84,000 square feet—will account for nearly half of the company's new stores in the future.

K-Mart's primary consumer is between 25 and 44 years old, with a household income ranging from $15,000 to $35,000, a demographic group that is growing rapidly. The company is also optimistic because shoppers are becoming polarized between low-margin and high-margin or high-priced stores, a trend that is expected to accelerate as the economy worsens and middle-class families are forced to trade down for goods.

One K-Mart executive, however, expressed concern about the company's image: "We still suffer from the image that our shoppers are blue-collar, low-income people. So we are in a series of constraints in adding better quality and yet not improving our gross margins."

Questions

1. Contrast the recent operating experience of K-Mart with the "Changing Nature of Retail Merchandising" as discussed in the text.
2. Why is turnover of such concern to retailers?
3. What is meant by the notion that retail markets are becoming saturated? How does K-Mart propose to react to this strategy?
4. What economic factor bearing upon consumer behavior is likely to bode well for the success of K-Mart, at least in the near future?

Chapter 12

Physical Distribution: Marketing's Other Half

Japan invades America.

In 1970, Japanese automobile manufacturers' total sales in the United Kingdom (Great Britain and Northern Ireland) amounted to barely 5,000 units. Ten years later, in 1980, British imports of Japanese cars and trucks had swelled to nearly 150,000, or approximately 15 percent of the total United Kingdom market. Elsewhere in Europe Japanese car imports have equaled this performance only in countries lacking important automotive industries. To explain the increased market share won by the Japanese, the British have cited numerous problems in their own economy: lower productivity, not enough productive capacity, and shortages and disruptions caused by labor disputes, among other problems. However, Japanese officials and the British car buyer reject these explanations, contending that English and Irish motorists buy the Japanese cars because of superior quality and reliability.[1]

Japanese Automotive Revolution.   The issue has a clear focus: how do the Japanese manage to produce a better car and deliver it to a customer halfway around the world at competitive prices? The answers are not in the "inscrutable Asian" methods of production and organization. The simple but profound truth is that the Japanese automotive industry has achieved a revolution in the economics of motor vehicle production, marketing, and *physical distribution* as fundamental as the inventions of Henry Ford or the scientific management innovations of Frederick W. Taylor, father of scientific management.

Nowhere is their innovativeness so clear as in their approach to the *physical distribution* and *transportation* of their automobiles. The Japanese have responded uniquely to these aspects of overseas selling. Fitting out special automobile-carrying ships with test and repair facilities, they can deliver some 5,000 cars per vessel to overseas markets, fully serviced and checked enroute, thus ensuring high levels of customer service and satisfaction. Backing up their

[1] Based upon an original article by Gene Gregory, "From Nissan with Love," *Business Topics* (Winter 1976), pp. 47–59. Data for 1980 updated by the author.

streamlined method of distributing their cars are outstanding strategic marketing planning, highly efficient production techniques, and a superlative quality control regime.

Japanese automakers pay minute attention to (1) doing the right thing, and (2) doing things right. Even their competitors acknowledge that their *marketing* and *strategic planning* are superb. Strong market planning divisions using proven analytical techniques have succeeded every year in *forecasting* accurately the cyclical growth and contraction of demand throughout the world. Japanese marketers have also developed a finely tuned responsiveness to changes in *consumer behavior* and preference in key markets. This, in turn, has assured the development of the right products and the right models to match changes in each *market opportunity*.

The concentration of highly automated, zero-defects production in a manufacturing facility serving markets 12,000 miles away has been made possible primarily because of the Japanese auto industry's conquest of *space* through a revolution in *shipping*. Using shipping time and facilities as stages in quality control enables Datsun to compete effectively in markets halfway around the world. Japanese auto manufacturers can ship a car from Tochigi, sixty miles north of Tokyo where Datsun produces 180,000 cars a month, to Middlesbrough, in England, for less than it costs Mercedes to send a car from Stuttgart, Germany, to London, England.

The Importance of Physical Distribution

Marketing as an integrated whole must be concerned with the delivery of a complete range of desired customer benefits. Especially important are maintaining product quality, competitive prices, adequate inventory assortments, alternative transportation modes, and facilities for product storage within the channel. Furthermore, to compete effectively, every firm must monitor and control its costs carefully so as to offer the lowest possible prices consistent with accepted levels of industry service. This means a well-designed and managed system of physical distribution.

Physical Distribution Creates Time and Place Utility

Marketing, as we learned earlier, creates time, place, information, and possession utility and thus justifies its existence, both economically and socially. Marketing makes exchanges possible and thus adds value. Sales promotion and advertising create information, or the utility of knowing about products, services, and firms. Time utility is created through storage, and place utility is the result largely of transportation. Therefore, distribution, or more specifically, physical distribution, is not something apart from marketing, but is a vital part of the total effort.[2]

[2] Robert Bartels,"Marketing and Distribution Are Not Separate," *International Journal of Physical Distribution* 7, no. 1 (1976), pp. 22–29.

What is Physical Distribution?

Physical distribution consists of those activities related to the physical handling of goods, order processing, inventory management, transportation, and storage. Physical distribution is essential not only for the *effective* performance of total marketing activities—attaining the marketing goals and objectives established—but also for the *efficient* performance of total marketing activities— getting the most output per unit of input, given an established level of customer service.

Physical distribution, therefore, is concerned with transporting finished inventory and/or raw material assortments so they arrive at the designated place when needed and in usable condition.

Physical distribution has been formally defined by the National Council of Physical Distribution Management as:

> *A term employed in manufacturing and commerce to describe the broad range of activities concerned with the efficient movement of finished products* from the end of the production line to the consumer, *and in some cases includes the movement of raw materials from the source of supply to the beginning of the production line. These activities include freight transportation, warehousing, material handling, protective packaging, inventory control, plant and warehouse selection, order processing, market forecasting, and customer service.*[3]

Physical distribution within this framework is literally the distribution of goods after they are produced, as the logical follow-up to the search for and stimulation of buyers. In short, physical distribution is a company's activities and arrangements for efficiently locating, storing, transporting, and moving goods to meet the service requirements and standards of the market place.[4]

What Better Physical Distribution Can Accomplish

A company's marketing effort can be notably improved by distribution policies that lead to consistent and dependable customer service. Customers are concerned with the length of the order cycle (how long it takes from the time an order is placed until it is received); the consistency of the order cycle (if it is supposed to be ten days, is it usually within that time, or often twenty days?); and the time and effort needed to get order progress reports. The knowledgeable marketing manager realizes that increased sales are not the only way to improve company profitability. James L. Heskett, an authority on physical distribution, and his associates have summarized case studies of five firms

---

[3] From a published statement of the National Council of Physical Distribution Management, Chicago, IL (author's italics).

[4] The literature of the field is developing widely. There are several good textbooks, among them, Edward W. Smykay, *Physical Distribution Management* (New York: Macmillan, 1973), and Donald J. Bowersox, *Logistical Management* (New York: Macmillan, 1974). There are also several good professional journals, including *Transportation and Distribution Management*, *Transportation Journal*, and the *International Journal of Physical Distribution*.

Movement and storage are important elements of physical distribution.

whose profits and sales were increased as a result of changes in physical distribution methods.

1. A large retailer noted an immediate 15 percent increase in sales of white goods when a newly established distribution center reduced delivery time.
2. A large general merchandise chain put in a new ordering system for catalog sales which increased on-time delivery from 30 to 100 percent; this change

led to savings above and beyond the breakeven point because of fewer canceled orders.

3. A producer of chemicals used in fertilizers instituted an extensive customer service program which led, a year later, to a 20 percent increase in sales, a 21 percent increase in earnings, and a 300 percent increase in the number of customers purchasing the company's full line of products.

4. A manufacturer spent $200,000 on warehousing changes that led to a profit increase of $500,000 due to a rise in annual sales from $45 million to $50 million.

5. A large retail chain with sales in excess of $1 billion increased sales by $100 million, and net profit by $10 million, by consolidating its distribution centers.[5]

Other examples could be quoted to demonstrate the importance of physical distribution in increasing sales and profits through improved levels of customer service.

The implication is clear. If physical distribution is truly a part of marketing, then the marketing concept must apply to the management of physical distribution.[6] Thus, the utility added by physical distribution, derived from customers' needs, is availability (the right products at the right time and place).

The Cost of Physical Distribution

In an earlier chapter, total marketing costs were said to amount to about 50 percent of the price of all goods. Physical distribution costs amount to about one-half the total marketing costs, or about 25 percent of the finished, or total, price of most goods.[7] The importance of these costs can be more forcefully demonstrated by the data in Table 12-1.

The Emergence of Physical Distribution Management

The idea of physical distribution as a planned, integrated, and managed approach to lowered distribution costs and more desirable customer service levels emerged during the late 1960s and throughout the 1970s, as a result of several strong pressures.

Skyrocketing Costs. The costs of transporting, by all carrier modes, increased rapidly during this period. Many factors were responsible: the rising level of prices in general; higher costs for repair, maintenance, and expansion of transportation facilities; and the impact of spreading unionization and the higher wage rates accompanying it. Other physical distribution costs were

[5] James L. Heskett, Nicholas A. Glaskowsky, and Robert M. Ivie, *Business Logistics* (New York: Ronald Press, 1973), pp. 249–250.
[6] William D. Perrault, Jr., and Frederick A. Russ, "Physical Distribution Service: A Neglected Aspect of Marketing Management," *MSU Business Topics* **22**, no. 3 (Summer 1974), pp. 37–45.
[7] For a broader discussion of this point see Richard J. Lewis, *A Logistical Information System for Marketing Analysis* (Cincinnati, OH: South Western Publishing Company, 1970).

Table 12-1 The Relative Significance of Distribution Costs for Each Dollar Spent for Consumer Convenience Products

Cost Activity	Value Added by Stage of Activity			Total Value Added	
	Manufacturer	Wholesaler	Retailer	Actual	Percent
Material cost	$0.08	—	—	$0.08	18.5
Manufacturing cost	0.105	—	—	0.105	43.5
Selling cost	0.265	$0.025	$0.145	0.435	38.0
Distribution cost	0.150	0.075	0.155	0.380	
	$0.60	$0.10	$0.30	$1.00	

Source: Compiled by the author. The data in this table is a composite of data for many products. The table illustrates relative, not absolute, levels of cost. As Table 12-1 shows, the costs of physical distribution are high, nearly as high as selling, advertising, and the other normal demand stimulation activities of marketing that are often criticized. Such high costs obviously have important economic and social consequences. Almost two-thirds of the GNP consists of physical goods. So, in a trillion-dollar-plus economy, such as in the United States, the marketing costs (50 percent) of physical goods would amount to $333 billion. Of this amount, nearly $170 billion would pay for physical distribution. A reduction of only 1 percent in these costs would permit either a price reduction or a profit gain of $1.7 billion.

Physical distribution is thus a major marketing activity. The effectiveness with which its functions are carried out has an important impact on customer satisfaction, while its efficiency is reflected in the level of operating costs. Competing effectively requires not only the search for and stimulation of buyers but the provision of adequate distribution services as well. As business becomes increasingly international in scope, success in foreign markets often boils down to the effectiveness and efficiency of a company's physical distribution activities and methods.

climbing accordingly: the costs of warehousing, materials handling, and storage as well as the "hidden" costs of carrying inventory and processing orders. Customers were demanding higher, and thus costlier, levels of physical distribution service.

Scientific management and large-scale production, with its routinized assembly lines, had led to lower average unit costs. Many companies were convinced that similar "scientific" approaches to physical distribution would lead to lower overall physical distribution costs. Physical distribution was thus tagged as the last frontier for cost economies.

Broadened Scope of Marketing. Another stimulant to an increased interest in physical distribution at that time was the broadened scope of marketing. No longer considered as just "buying and selling," the marketing functions of storage, transporting, warehousing, and handling were coming to be seen as a series of activities that could be managed as an integrated whole. Furthermore, this aspect of marketing was subject to even greater pressure by the explosion in product lines and general inventory assortments.

Increased Competitive Demands. Some firms quickly saw the benefits of managed physical distribution systems (lower costs and higher levels of customer service) and led the way in adopting them. Other firms, as is so often the case in a competitive enterprise system, were compelled to "get on the bandwagon" to remain competitive. Hence, when industry leaders set up integrated physical distribution systems, many other firms began to pay more attention to the quality of their physical distribution operations.

The Sales Generating Potential of Physical Distribution.   Many managers realized that there was a positive connection between product merchandising programs on the one hand and adequate delivery service and order processing on the other. In short, a well-run physical distribution program was actually a tool for generating more sales, higher profits, and better satisfied customers. One study has recently shown that physical distribution service is more important to customers than price and the quality of supplier management. It is second only to product quality as a reason for buying from a particular firm.[8]

Integrated Physical Distribution: Product of Management Science

The concept of a managed (planned and controlled) physical distribution system was dependent on new technology. Physical distribution management is in many respects an outgrowth of what is sometimes referred to as "management science," or "operations research." Both terms mean, loosely, a **systems approach** to the solutions of problems by using reasonably complex mathematical models, computer technology, and a team of specialists. It was the development of these "management science" techniques and concepts which made possible the integration of physical distribution functions.

The Computer.   Revolutionary new computer technology permitted the accurate, high-speed processing of vast amounts of information—the location of a railroad car in transit between Chicago and Seattle; how many items of a given product had been shipped since a given date, how many remained in inventory, how many were on order and their expected delivery date; how many additional warehouses would be required to enable a firm to reach 80 percent of its customers with one-day service; how much more inventory would be needed in a given business to fill 95 percent of the customers' orders out of stock than to fill only 80 percent. Computers could be used to maintain local inventory balances, forecast demand, calculate item orders, propose tentative purchase orders, and to aid routine decision making. Computers not only do what intelligent clerks were formerly trained to do, but they do it faster and more accurately.

The Total Cost Approach

Total cost was developed a a measure of all expenditures required to accomplish a firm's physical distribution mission. The logic of the total cost concept is that it is less important to minimize the cost of any one component than to minimize the costs of all components in the physical distribution system. Man-

---

[8.] William D. Perreault, Jr., and Frederick A. Russ, "Physical Distribution Service in Industrial Purchase Decisions," *Journal of Marketing* **40** (April 1976), pp. 3–10.

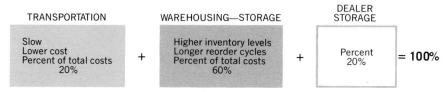

Figure 12-1 Physical distribution components.

agement chooses a level of desired customer service and then creates a physical distribution package that achieves this level while minimizing total cost. A study of air freight economics was one of the first to emphasize the **total cost approach.** Its authors suggested that the high freight rates of air transport could be more than justified by **cost trade-offs** from lowered inventory and reduced warehouse operations. Consider the illustration in Figure 12-1.

As shown in Figure 12-1, a lower cost form of transportation often leads to high warehousing and storage expenses for both the supplier and the dealer-purchaser. A faster means of transportation speeds up order processing and reduces reorder cycles, thus requiring less inventory in the channel. The possible results are diagrammed in Figure 12-2.

As shown in Figure 12-2, a faster means of transportation can lead to lower storage and warehousing costs. The total cost approach can reduce costs in actual dollars and at the same time provide better customer service. The total cost principle is frequently employed by firms today in establishing their physical distribution arrangements.

The Concept of Cost Trade-offs.   The total cost concept contains the notion of cost trade-offs: while some costs in a given physical distribution arrangement may be higher, others may actually be lower. Figure 12-3 illustrates the trade-offs that are necessary when establishing customer service levels, purchasing policies, transportation policies, and warehousing systems if maximum company profits are to be realized.

It is important in evaluating cost trade-offs to realize that at no time should costs be cut if the result will be substandard levels of customer service.

Suboptimization.   Things that are optimal are at their most favorable point. Therefore, things that are below their best, or most favorable, point are *suboptimal.* Very often, decisions made in one sector of an organization are not the

Figure 12-2 Physical distribution components.

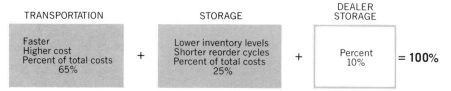

Figure 12-3 Cost trade-offs required in physical distribution systems.

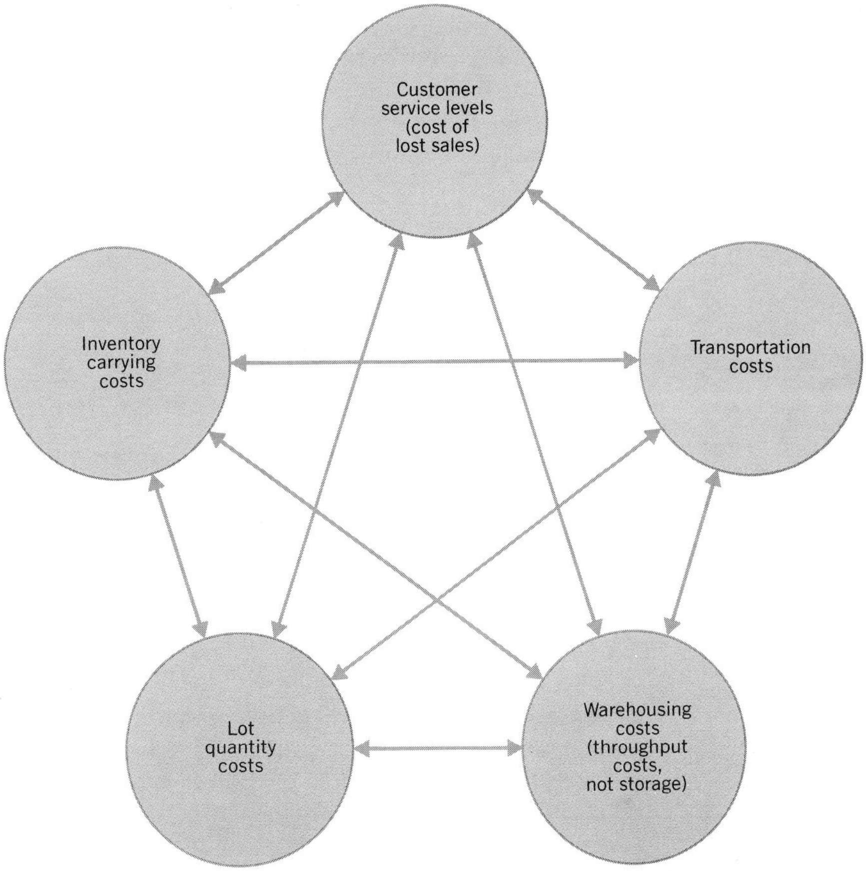

Source: Bernard J. LaLonde and Douglas M. Lambert, "Inventory Carrying Costs," *International Journal of Physical Distribution* **6**, no. 1 (1975), p. 30.

best from the standpoint of the overall firm. Suboptimization is to be avoided in managing physical distribution systems. In a given unit of the firm, the traffic manager may attempt to do the best job possible for that department by minimizing the cost of shipping the firm's products. This may be a suboptimal practice, however, leading to increased customer stock-outs, longer reorder cycles, and lost customers. Or, a shipping department may use cheap containers to hold down shipping costs, but then suffer a high damage rate. An inventory manager who holds down stocks on hand to reduce total inventory costs may cause frequent stock-outs, back orders,* additional order processing, special production runs, and special shipments. As you can see, suboptimization, the total cost concept, and the idea of cost trade-offs are closely intertwined. Physical distribution management, as an integrated set of activities, is designed, in part at least, to avoid suboptimal decision making.

*Unfilled orders held for future delivery.

Planning and Managing Physical Distribution Systems

The planning and subsequent management of physical distribution systems is generally undertaken in two phases: (1) study and analysis and (2) development.

In phase one, the existing system is studied to gain insight into its operation, to determine the relationships within it, and to assess its limitations, problems, and capabilities. Information about the firm's output, in terms of products and markets served, must be gathered and analyzed. Other information that must be studied is of an operational nature, such as records of accounts payable and receivable, analysis of past sales, inventory control costs, wages, and customer service commitments.

In the second phase, the designer of the physical distribution system ponders the various system requirements, both at present and in the longer run. Often a checklist like the following is used:

What must the system do?

How much of each product will or can the firm sell?

Where will or should goods be warehoused and, if warehoused, for how long?

Is there a significant relationship between certain of the firm's products and its market areas?

When must the firm have its inventories at high levels? That is, is demand at all seasonal, and where is it seasonal?[9]

By answering these and similar questions, the firm will begin to grasp the dimensions of the physical distribution system it needs.

Each physical distribution designer also needs to know how well the proposed system must perform. Oftentimes one of the major criteria of performance is time. However, there is a trade-off between speedy performance and cost. Some examples will illustrate this point.

—Very fast or overnight delivery depends upon a number of distribution alternatives, some of which are
  - centralized warehousing with high-speed, high-cost transportation
  - slower, lower-cost transportation with many dispersed warehouses
  - many sales outlets close to points of demand

—Reducing the frequency of stock-outs calls for
  - high inventory levels within the system and the associated high costs of:
    inventory carrying
    storage and handling
    increased risk of obsolescence and merchandise deterioration
    high losses from pilferage and inventory shrinkage

[9] From C. G. Chentnik, "Movement Considerations for Physical Distribution," *International Journal of Physical Distribution* **6**, no. 1 (1975), pp. 39–51.

—Full line product availability at points of demand minimizes stock outs, but also carries high operating costs.

Additional factors to be considered are dependability (many customer firms would rather have consistent service than very fast, but sporadic, delivery); capacity (should the physical distribution system be geared to handle peak loads or only the upper average loads?); and management acceptance (if managers do not believe in the system, they may find it difficult to accept the need for certain tasks to be performed in specific ways).

Customer Service Levels

Because physical distribution is an extension of the marketing concept, it must be customer oriented. Thus the starting point for the design and management of every physical distribution system is the customer for whom it is intended.[10] The service of physical distribution includes many factors. Some have even attempted to rank these factors in order of popularity.

1. Time from order receipt to order shipment
2. Order size and assortment constraints
3. Percentage of items out of stock
4. Percentage of customer orders filled accurately
5. Percentage of customer orders filled within X days from receipt of order
6. Percentage of customer orders filled
7. Percentage of customer orders which arrive in good condition
8. Time from order placement to order delivery (order cycle time)
9. Ease and flexibility of order placement [11]

A given physical distribution system is effective if it accomplishes the firm's objectives and gives its customers the service they expect. That same system is efficient if no reorganization of its components or inputs could reduce the costs while maintaining the existing service level.

To summarize and at the same time provide an overview of the steps in planning and managing a physical distribution system, a visual diagram of the process is shown in Figure 12–4. The process involves seven major steps:[12] (1) delineate relevant elements of PDS package; (2) determine current levels of service provided by the firm and its competitors for each PDS element; (3) propose specific changes in PDS elements; (4) pick new PDS package; (5) establish PDS performance controls; (6) promote and test new PDS package; and (7) measure and evaluate results.

[10] See Philip B. Schary, "Customer Service as a System Process," in *Contemporary Issues in Marketing Channels,* eds. Robert F. Lusch and Paul Zinszer, Center for Economic and Management Research, University of Oklahoma, Norman, 1979, pp. 165–176.
[11] James I. Heskett, Nicholas A. Glaskowski and Robert M. Ivie, *Business Logistics* (New York, Ronald Press, 1973), pp. 250–251.
[12] Perreault and Russ, "Physical Distribution Service Neglected," p. 41.

Figure 12–4 Overview of the process for designing and managing a physical distribution system.

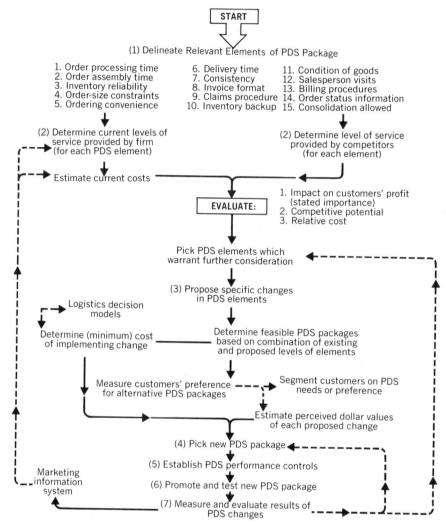

START

(1) Delineate Relevant Elements of PDS Package

1. Order processing time
2. Order assembly time
3. Inventory reliability
4. Order-size constraints
5. Ordering convenience
6. Delivery time
7. Consistency
8. Invoice format
9. Claims procedure
10. Inventory backup
11. Condition of goods
12. Salesperson visits
13. Billing procedures
14. Order status information
15. Consolidation allowed

(2) Determine current levels of service provided by firm (for each PDS element)

(2) Determine level of service provided by competitors (for each element)

Estimate current costs

EVALUATE:

1. Impact on customers' profit (stated importance)
2. Competitive potential
3. Relative cost

Pick PDS elements which warrant further consideration

(3) Propose specific changes in PDS elements

Logistics decision models

Determine (minimum) cost of implementing change

Determine feasible PDS packages based on combination of existing and proposed levels of elements

Measure customers' preference for alternative PDS packages

Segment customers on PDS needs or preference

Estimate perceived dollar values of each proposed change

(4) Pick new PDS package

(5) Establish PDS performance controls

(6) Promote and test new PDS package

Marketing information system

(7) Measure and evaluate results of PDS changes

Source: William D. Perrault, Jr. and Frederick A. Russ, "Physical Distribution Service: A Neglected Aspect of Marketing Management," *MSU Business Topics* 22, no. 3 (Summer 1974), p. 22.

Before proceeding, can you answer these questions:

1. What utilities are created by marketing? What role does physical distribution play in creating utilities?

2. List and discuss three factors that contributed to the emergence of physical distribution management.

3. What is the focal point in designing and planning a physical distribution system?

Components of the Physical Distribution System

A physical distribution system, as we have learned, consists of a set of individual components such as inventory, storage, transportation, and other activities related to the physical movement of goods. Together, the components create utility of time and place for the buyers, and ensure form utility. To this point, we have looked broadly at physical distribution as an integrated system. To better understand that system, we will turn now to a more detailed examination of several of its individual components. We must be ever mindful that each of these components is to be managed within the context of a system's framework which requires (1) total cost analysis, (2) the consideration of cost trade-offs, and (3) the avoidance of suboptimization.

The day-to-day management of the stocking and flow of merchandise deals with controlling inventories, creating storage facilities, or depots, in locations strategic to customers' needs, and directing the transportation of the merchandise. The aim of these components is to replenish inventories and make the desired customer reorder cycles easier to attain. In the subsections that follow we will look at each of these activities in some detail.

Inventory Management

All marketers of tangible goods are concerned with problems of managing inventories. Inventories themselves are of great value; they constitute a generous portion of the total assets of many firms. Through the merchandising cycle sellers work to convert cash into inventories, inventories into accounts receivable, and accounts receivable into cash. The process of conversion leads to profits. Through a similar process manufacturers convert cash into raw materials, components, and fabricated parts, which are then made into finished goods. Finished goods in turn are converted into accounts receivable and then cash, all for the purpose of gain.

Principal concerns of *inventory management* are to determine how much stock on hand is necessary to meet customer needs, the most economical or efficient size of order to place, the frequency with which orders should be placed and the appropriate safety stock for preventing stock-outs.[13]

Inventory management aims at having a balanced assortment of merchandise for sale to meet expected customer demand. The key word is "balanced." Too small an inventory, or one lacking in breadth of assortment, will mean stock-outs and lost sales.[14] However, maintaining too large a one is equally undesirable because this entails too great an investment, lower turnover, and an increase in inventory operating expenses.

An optimum level of inventory is consistent with customer demand as shown in rates of sale and other factors such as safety stocks and length of the reorder cycle. Figure 12–5 depicts an ideal inventory situation.

---

[13] For a treatment in greater depth, see James Don Edwards and Roger A. Roemmick, "Scientific Inventory Management," *MSU Business Topics* (Autumn 1975), pp. 41–45.
[14] For the effects of a stock-out, see, C.K. Walter and John R. Grabner. "Stockout Cost Models: Empirical Tests in a Retail Situation," *Journal of Marketing* **39** (July 1975), pp. 56–68.

At the beginning of each month period, 100 units of an item are ordered into stock. It is assumed that delivery is instantaneous, that is, there is no waiting time. The rate of sale is constant. At the end of thirty days the inventory is exhausted and is instantly replenished. There are never any stock-outs and average inventory is found by dividing 100 by 2.

In Figure 12–6, an equally unrealistic situation, observe that changing the order period from thirty days to fifteen reduces the size of the average inventory. By reordering more frequently, reorder costs go up, while the cost of carrying inventories declines. Take a minute to think about this. Why is it so?

However, inventory cycles are usually more erratic and sales rates are uneven stair-step curves. Figure 12-7 is a more realistic picture of inventory. The sales rate varies and new merchandise seldom ever arrives at just that instant when old stocks are sold out.

Figure 12–5   A theoretical inventory cycle.

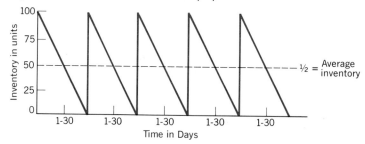

Figure 12–6   A theoretical inventory cycle.

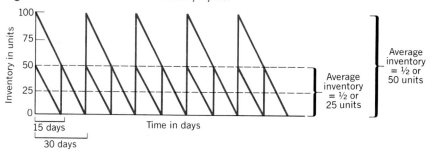

Figure 12–7   A more realistic inventory cycle.

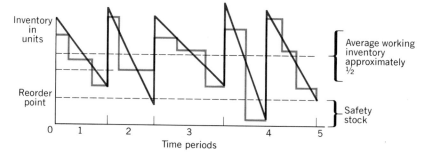

Figure 12-7 shows that safety stocks are needed because of variations in the rate of sale and in the time required to receive new shipments of stock. In period (1) slow sales permit a stock buildup. In (2) a late shipment depletes stocks; in (3) there is a slowing in the rate of sale; in (4) peak seasonal demands require a rapid reorder; and in (5) early receipt of an order brings inventory levels back to normal.

The Classification of Inventories.   Inventory management systems are best geared to the specifics of the stock to be managed. In establishing procedures for controlling inventories, planners seek a balance between the methods employed and the benefits to be received. This is a kind of "cost-benefit" approach. Such balanced systems usually:

1. *Are selective*. Energy, time, and money are allocated to control items with the highest dollar sales and value.
2. *Include ordering rules*. A rule or policy is set to determine when and how much of an item to order.
3. *Are economical to manage*. The chosen procedure minimizes inventory carrying and ordering costs within the established constraint of customer service levels.
4. *Minimize stock-outs*. Merchandise is aged and inventory assortments are balanced in accordance with demand forecasts.
5. *Seek flexibility*. The system should be easily adaptable to changing conditions.
6. *Are easy to operate*. The system may be readily routinized and computerized.

These characteristics are often attained in part through the systematic classification of inventories. For example, the manager knows that there are some items of inventory which are extremely important because of their high value. These may be the 10 percent of the assortment that account for 70 percent of its total value. Another 40 percent may account for only 20 percent of the inventory's total value. Finally, there may be 50 percent of the entire stock that represents only 10 percent of its total worth. This type of inventory classification by value is often called *A B C analysis*. A items are low in value and call for only loose and inexpensive inventory planning and control procedures. At the other extreme, C items are high in value, requiring careful, more costly, observation and control. The B, or medium-value, merchandise requires a system of management that is neither as low-cost, impersonal, and automatic as A items, nor as expensive, personal, and frequent as that for C items.

The cost of carrying a merchandise inventory consisting of many low-value items is minimal. For high-value items, the opposite is true, and the goal of inventory management for medium-value items is to strike a balance between ordering costs[15] and inventory carrying costs.[16]

[15] Order costs are the variable costs of placing an order: writing the order, mailing or phoning it to a supplier, and so forth.
[16] Inventory carrying costs are much higher than many of us assume. Inventory carrying costs include capital costs, inventory service costs, storage space costs, and inventory risk costs. Such costs often amount to as much as 20 to 35 percent of the value of the inventory. See Bernard J. LaLonde and Douglas M. Lambert, "Inventory Carrying Costs: Significance, Components, Means, Functions," *International Journal of Physical Distribution* **6**, no. 1 (1975) pp. 51–64.

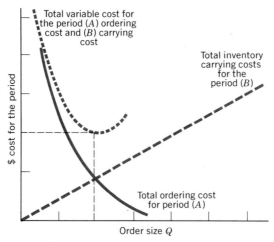

Figure 12-8 A graphic EOQ model.

The inventory manager tries to minimize total variable cost by controlling its two components: total inventory carrying costs and total ordering costs. Figure 12-8 shows that total variable cost $(A + B)$ is minimized when the cost curves of A and B intersect.

Figure 12-8 demonstrates graphically an important concept in inventory management; namely, the concept of trade-offs. The logic of the figure is that there is a trade-off between ordering costs and inventory carrying costs. By using such EOQ models the inventory manager can determine not only the correct order size but also the optimum number of orders to place, and the optimum turnover for an item during a period.

Storage

Acquiring inventories invariably leads to a need for storage facilities such as warehouses and distribution centers. Factories are usually located near supplies of raw materials or a well-trained or otherwise suitable labor force, both of which are often far from manufacturers' markets. Resellers, especially retailers, locate close to their major markets. Storage and transportation are two vital links in the chain of physical distribution activities required to meet market opportunities. Both manufacturers and resellers require fixed facilities for storage and related activities. Such facilities are needed for:

1. Inventory availability to eliminate the discrepancies that occur between supply and demand
2. Raw material and fabricated parts storage to facilitate the scheduling and production of finished products
3. Finished goods storage to permit a smooth production schedule and marketing activities
4. **Distribution center** storage, which cuts down on the shipment of small

orders by using volume transportation to move large shipments from factory to storage centers close to large markets

5. Stock blending to provide customers with an assortment of all products desired by assembling a full line of merchandise at one point

Storage activities—receiving, transferring, assembling, and shipping merchandise—are usually connected with a special storage facility called a warehouse. This is a fixed facility designed to provide storage and physical distribution at the lowest total cost. Many warehouses today emphasize product flow rather than "dead" storage. In other words warehouses speed the movement of goods to points of assembly and, ultimately, consumption.

Types of Warehouses According to Function. **Distribution warehouses** are places where orders are assembled and then distributed. Sometimes referred to as distribution centers, they are designed to promote rapid movement of high demand items.

Storage warehouses are fixed facilities where products are stored for relatively long periods. Storage warehouses contain stocks of goods beyond the inventory needed for normal replacement. There are a number of reasons why stocks are stored for relatively long periods: seasonal production; erratic demand; product conditioning such as the ripening of fruit or the aging of whiskey; and speculation, the expectation that demand will rise in the future and bring higher prices than at present.

How Many Warehouses Are Needed?

Here again is the issue of trade-offs. Every firm needs the number of warehouses required to maintain a desired level of customer service and at the same time to minimize its total physical distribution cost. Notice that it was not recommended that we minimize the costs of warehousing and storage. Why?

Too many warehouses would raise costs, and too few would mean lowered levels of customer service, longer reorder cycles, and increased costs of transportation to speed products to points of demand. Usually, as shown in Table 12-2, customer service does not rise appreciably when the number of warehouses increases beyond a certain number.

In this example, 90 percent of the firm's market can receive first-day service with 12 warehouses, and all of its market (100 percent) can be given second-day service. With 50 warehouses—more than the original 12—only a small percentage of the total market served (9 percent) receives any appreciable benefits in better service.

There are a number of management decisions concerning warehouses which are as crucial to physical distribution activities as the number of such facilities. The actual location of the structures, storage requirements of the product mix, the need for expansion and contraction of warehouse facilities, the selection of the materials handling system, and the extent of warehouse automation—

Table 12-2 Number of Warehouses and Resulting Impact on Customer Service Level

Number of Warehouses	Percentage of Market Served	
	First Day	Second Day
50	99	1
25	95	5
12	90	10
8	80	20
2	30	70

all are factors with strong impact on the effectiveness and efficiency of storage and warehousing services.

The Distribution Center. The distribution center is a special kind of warehouse facility, strongly market related, and so, emphasizing the rapid movement of merchandise rather than its storage. As in many mass marketing operations, sales velocity and high turnover, combined with minimal handling and storage of merchandise, are a clear way to minimize the expenses of warehousing and storage. Reducing these costs can boost profits and have a significant effect on the overall distribution task. The physical distribution center is located close to a firm's principal target areas. Many firms have such installations in strategic cities like New York, Chicago, Minneapolis-St. Paul, Atlanta, Houston, Salt Lake City, San Francisco, Los Angeles, Portland, and Seattle.

There are many varieties of physical distribution centers. While some are used in industrial goods markets, most are related to consumer products, especially high-volume, price oriented merchandise, where fast turnover is essential in generating profits. Firms such as Sears, J.C. Penney, Zayre's, and K-Mart, have generated great successes with their distribution center concepts.

The Pillsbury Company was an early adopter of the distribution center concept. This company, which manufactures flour and a wide assortment of baking mixes, formerly moved its products primarily by carload lots directly to wholesalers or retailers from its production facilities. Plants, each producing the company's entire line, were located close to customers. However, the growth in number of product lines made this a cumbersome policy. It also became difficult for the company to ship mixed carloads to its customers. Despite nearly 100 branch warehouse facilities and a third as many sales offices, materials handling and order processing were excessive and the Pillsbury customer's order cycle was more than one week.

With distribution centers, Pillsbury now offers 90 percent of its customers third-morning delivery anywhere within the United States. Each plant specializes in a limited line of the company's products and thus ships in full carload lots to its distribution centers. Warehousing and storage are practically unnecessary at the various points of production. Now the field sales organization can concentrate more on sales and less on physical distribution. The distribution centers are controlled primarily by four regional data processing centers, which manage the important communication aspects of physical distribution. High-speed automatic data processing accounting systems speed invoices to customers, resulting in quicker payments and a faster "merchandising cycle." Each distribution center has adequate flows of all merchandise lines, thus avoiding stock-outs while providing economical shipments and better customer service. The whole system is under the control of a director of distribution who is equal in rank to the heads of marketing and manufacturing. Pillsbury's distribution centers have reduced distribution costs and increased profits, as well as enhanced the firm's ability to search for and stimulate demand for its products.

Transportation

It should be apparent by now that a physical distribution system is a network of activities consisting primarily of one or more storage points interconnected by a series of transportation linkages. The costs of transportation have soared throughout the last decade. Shipping some items—sand, cement, and building stone, for instance—often costs more than manufacturing or extracting them. Transportation costs for many industrial capital goods, and for big-ticket consumer items such as appliances, automobiles, and boats may amount to as much as 10–20 percent of the sales price of the commodity. Magazines cost five times more to deliver today than they did ten years ago.

Managers and buyers of physical distribution services must possess an encyclopedic knowledge of the various transportation modes, the legal classifications of carriers and their significance, various freight classifications, and be familiar with the specialized transportation intermediaries.

The Transportation Modes.   Merchandise is transported by five means: railroads, water, highway motor carriers, airplanes, and pipelines. The proportion of traffic carried by each mode of transportation has changed in the recent past. Table 12-3 shows the distribution of total revenue ton-miles of domestic intercity freight traffic for a number of years.

As shown in Table 12-3, railroads continue to be the principal carriers of intercity freight in the United States, followed by motor carriers and oil and gas pipelines. Although not shown in the table, prior to the 1950s railroads were an even more significant carrier than they are today. For instance, in the 1930s, nearly three-fourths of the total intercity freight moved by train. However, the 1950s, 1960s, and 1970s witnessed a continuing round of competitive activities, with each carrier striving to increase its share of the transportation market. In essence, each carrier competes on the basis of the average cost per ton-mile of merchandise moved. This cost will vary widely within specific modes depending on the characteristics of the product being transported. Transportation carriers are evaluated on the basis of specific criteria, including,

Table 12-3 Distribution of Total Revenue Ton-Miles of Domestic Freight Movements in the United States for Selected Years

Year	Total Ton-Miles (millions)	Railroads	Motor Truck	Inland Water Ways	Oil Pipelines	Air Carriers
1960	1,314.3	44.3	21.7	16.8	17.4	0.1
1965	1,620.8	43.5	23.1	16.0	17.3	0.1
1970	1,901.4	40.8	21.0	16.2	21.8	0.2
1973	2,231.0	38.4	22.6	16.0	22.7	0.2
1976	2,565.6	37.2	23.6	16.0	23.0	0.2

(1) speed, or the time required to transport the goods from point of origin to destination; (2) frequency of service, or the number of scheduled vehicles moving from origin to destination per time period; (3) dependability, or the ability to perform consistently according to schedule; (4) availability, or the number of geographical points between which a given carrier provides service; and finally, (5) operational capability or flexibility, which is a carrier's capacity to handle all kinds of merchandise from large, bulky, durables to more fragile and perishable commodities.

Each transportation mode ranks both high and low, depending on the operating criteria chosen, and the physical distribution manager is once again forced to consider the trade-offs for the company's products, the relative costs of shipping, and customers' expected levels of services.

The total cost of transportation in the United States now nearly equals 10 percent of our total GNP and is rapidly climbing. The deepening energy crisis is impacting dramatically with the rising transportation costs and each carrier is being affected.

Railroads are working to reassert themselves as the cheapest and most efficient way of moving massive quantities of goods relatively quickly. Our network of inland and coastal waterways is still important in both domestic and international trade. Vast shipments of grain, lumber, and raw materials are received from abroad, and equal amounts are shipped from inland ports, on the St. Lawrence Seaway in the east. Vessels laden with oil, chemical products, and food ply the Ohio and Mississippi. Today, thanks to a series of locks and dams, barges and other shallow draft carriers can travel up the Columbia and Snake rivers in the West as far as Lewiston, Idaho, to take on shipments of grain and lumber destined for eastern ports of entry.

Our railroads and waterways opened the western part of our nation for settlement. Our early merchant marine made the United States a worldwide shipping competitor. Transportation is still our country's lifeblood. But today, our efforts are geared increasingly to holding down the cost of moving goods, thus permitting us to cope with staggering increases in the cost of energy.

Transportation Carriers Are Marketers Too. Transportation carriers are basically marketers who sell service, compete through pricing, and deliver a satisfactory level of customer service. Many transportation companies have established specialized services and facilities. Often, carriers help their customers lower transportation costs. They train customers' transportation managers in how to audit their bills, or in using freight bill auditors to eliminate the mistakes that arise so frequently from the complicated rate system. Carriers also train managers in the intricate processes for categorizing cargo and assigning routes.

The carriers' desire to help customers has even led to a relatively rapid adoption of new methods and new technology. Railroads have worked to develop "soft cars," which absorb the shocks of switching and jostling, thus protecting commodities not built to withstand such stress. The railroads have also worked to achieve faster delivery of some commodities. Shippers who need such services can ship on "through trains," which average 60 miles an hour and are routed by computer around major switching centers. Railroads have both pioneered and promoted the use of containerization to facilitate the materials handling aspect of transportation. By using containers, the various modes of carrier are able to cooperate, making the entire transport process more flexible and efficient. Shipping in intermodal containers that fit onto both trucks and railroads is called "piggyback," using trucks, railroads, and ships in this way is called "fishyback." Goods transported in containers adapted to both trucks and airplanes are going "birdyback."

Understanding the Complex World of Transportation

Every transportation mode has its advantages and disadvantages and each has its baffling complexities. There are literally millions of different freight classifications which determine the rates charged. A modern transportation manager must be thoroughly versed in the features of the alternative modes of transportation, the characteristics of the different classes of carriers, and the various cumbersome rate structures. In addition, as one of America's most overregulated industries, transportation suffers from needless confusion and unjustified higher prices.[17]

Marketing, transportation, and physical distribution managers can, like Alexander the Great, cut this Gordian knot if they work diligently at all times to match their transportation needs with the various alternatives available. Most carriers are not attempting to compete for all the nations' transport business, but instead usually cater to the special jobs that each can do best. The physical distribution manager must therefore capitalize on this carrier specialization to move merchandise as efficiently and economically as possible.

[17] Robert C. Lieb, "Promoting Change in Transportation Regulation," *Business Horizons* **18**, no. 3 (June 1975), pp. 91–94.

Before proceeding, can you answer the following questions:
1. What is the goal of inventory management? What is meant by inventory carrying costs?
2. What is the distinction between a warehouse for storage only and a distribution center?
3. A commonly held view of physical distribution is that it is a system of one or more storage points connected by a series of transportation linkages. Explain.

Trends and Developments in Physical Distribution

Physical distribution is moving to the forefront in every major firm's overall strategic planning. While cost reduction may have been the original motive behind the concern with getting products to their users, today and in the future the emphasis will most likely stem from the necessity to meet the customer-buyer's rising level of expectations of service. Reliability, dependability, shorter order cycles, smaller inventories, and faster delivery have all become important aspects of physical distribution services. For firms hoping to compete in foreign markets, a well-planned and -managed physical distribution system is an absolute must. The paper work alone in marketing overseas from an American base of operation is staggering. Faster communication and automated order processing are helpful in attacking this problem.

Physical distribution is no longer something that can be tacked on after the marketing program is established. In many instances, physical distribution *is* the marketing program, or so vital and integral a part of it that it must be planned and incorporated step-by-step with the firm's other efforts to search for and stimulate buyers.

As we move ahead in the decade of the 1980s, we can see several likely developments unfolding. First, the distribution function will almost certainly become more important in marketing oriented firms. Second, firms will increasingly change their organization to strengthen their physical distribution services. Shipping departments, warehouses, packaging, and other distribution activities are now being combined in a total systems approach to the management of distribution processes. Many companies are appointing distribution managers whose rank is equivalent to that of corporate officers in production, finance, and marketing.

Physical distribution will rely even more in the future on automation, computers, and scientific problem solving techniques because its processes tend to be repetitive and therefore readily routinized. Because distribution activities are often easily quantified, objective measures can be used to evaluate their effectiveness.

Quite likely, the future will bring many changes in physical distribution. Intermodal transportation systems will become more common. The railroads, for example, instead of competing with the trucking industry may join it in promoting total movement systems. Efficient terminals, better materials handling systems, and more widespread containerization will lead to more efficient total systems of distribution.

Specialized physical distribution companies are already on the scene. These firms provide a whole package of integrated distribution services including physical handling and storage of goods; inventory management; all paper work such as purchase orders, invoices, and freight bills; all transportation including consolidation of shipments and local delivery to the client's customers; and computer and management systems capability that can develop the most efficient distribution program for any given client.[18] Some companies who compete aggressively in the market place may even find it advantageous to cooperate more by sharing services with rivals: consolidating shipments, using common warehouse space, and sharing materials handling equipment.

Many studies show that the physical distribution concept is being widely applied throughout American business. As the concepts on which physical distribution is based become better understood, this meaningful scientific management approach should 'ᵣ come even more widespread.

Summary

Physical distribution has been called "the other half of marketing." This is because its activities are not quite so visible to the average consumer as are those related to the search for and stimulation of buyers. Yet the importance of physical distribution increases each day as marketing strives to deliver high levels of customer satisfaction at low costs. The products people consume have value because they satisfy customer needs for goods at a particular time and place. Physical distribution adds value to products by bestowing on them time, place, and possession utilities.

Physical distribution management emerged as a result of efforts to lower the costs of transporting, storing, materials handling, and order processing. As part of the marketing concept, physical distribution services are designed to generate a competitive level of customer services while working to hold down costs. Physical distribution management requires an undestanding of a number of supporting concepts: the total cost approach, the idea of cost trade-offs, suboptimization, and the systems approach to managerial decision making. The physical distribution system is an integrated network of components for moving goods, linked by intervening storage points. Such activities as inventory management, storage and warehousing, transportation, and materials handling, therefore, are the basic building blocks of a well-designed physical distribution system.

[18] Walter F. Friedman, "Physical Distribution: The Concept of Shared Services," *Harvard Business Review*, March–April 1975, p. 195.

Review Questions

1. Describe in your own words what physical distribution is. How is it related to marketing?
2. What role did physical distribution play in permitting Japanese auto makers to penetrate the automobile market of the United Kingdom?
3. How does physical distribution contribute to the firm's marketing program?
4. Should society be concerned with physical distribution and its costs? Why?
5. What are the reasons for the emergence and dramatic growth of physical distribution?
6. Explain the following concepts:
   a. total cost approach
   b. the idea of cost trade-offs
   c. suboptimization
   d. the systems approach
7. What are the implications of the concepts in question 6 for physical distribution?
8. Why must a firm work to manage its inventory? What are the two critical elements in inventory management?
9. What is a distribution center?
10. What trends and developments are likely to characterize physical distribution efforts in the future?

Case 12-1

Sound House

Sound House is a fast growing Texas-based chain of consumer electronic stores. The firm has more than 5,000 United States and Canadian outlets and claims 15 percent of the market in citizens' band radio equipment. CB enthusiasts accounted for almost 25 percent of the chain's $750 million in revenue in 1980. Experts forecast sales in 1981 of at least 10 million of the CB models and Sound House is expecting to take home to its parent, Dandy Corporation of Fort Worth, an increasing share of the firm's profits. Sales of hi-fi and stereo equipment are also booming and the chain is expanding at a pace that puts it further and further ahead of its

rivals. Columbus Radio Electronics, for instance, was once bigger than Sound House but now is only about one-eighth as large.

The driving force behind Sound House's success is Dandy Corporation Chairman and President, Robert D. Dandy, a Texan who attended Harvard Business School. After World War II, Dandy went into the family plastics business and later bought the small Boston-based Sound House chain thirteen years ago, when it was $1.5 million in debt.

When Dandy acquired Sound House, the stores sold 25,000 different products including sporting goods and pots and pans. Inventory

management problems were horrendous and Dandy insisted on streamlining inventory assortments and increasing turnover. Dandy cut the store's lines by 90 percent.

He then set out to blanket the country with small but attractive stores in new shopping centers. The stores were extensively stocked with radio merchandise and the merchandising program placed a heavy emphasis on intensive advertising, especially television. Dandy has worked hard to create a strong incentive system for store managers. His system now permits store managers, whose average age is 25, to earn low salaries but to make up to $30,000 a year through profit sharing and bonuses tied to sales.

After a decade of solid but fairly slow growth the chain suddenly began to experience rapid growth in both sales and profits. Between 1972 and 1980 the number of stores more than tripled. During the company's fiscal year 1977, which ends in June, profits rose 120 percent to over $64 million. Sound House has almost cannibalized its parent firm. Dandy Corporation has spun off most of its other businesses into separate companies chaired by Robert Dandy and now has only minor operations other than Sound House.

Dandy is confident of his company's future but does worry a bit about the possibility of a slowdown in sales and profits as many of the firm's products move into the more mature phases of the product life cycle. Dandy also feels that his company executives have mastered reasonably well that part of marketing concerned with the search for and stimulation of buyers but feels that the company could greatly strengthen its operations concerned with physical distribution. Nearly 75 percent of the firm's sales come from products which are manufactured overseas. This means high costs for transportation, storage, and other activities necessary to have balanced stocks. Dandy places great store on being the first to merchandise a new product line. For example, one manager, T. M. Whitehead of the Guam Sound House, personally journeyed to Japan to pick up new forty-channel CB radios so he could be the first to sell them on United States soil January 1, 1977—which was still December 31 on the American mainland.

Dandy and the other corporate level executives of Sound House, in order to give greater recognition and attention to physical distribution, have considered adding a vice president of physical distribution. The new vice president would be equal with the vice president of marketing and would report directly to Dandy himself.

Questions

1. Would you recommend a vice president of physical distribution for this firm?

2. What problems are likely to arise if such an organizational change were implemented?

3. The vice president of marketing has resisted the proposal to add a vice president of physical distribution. What do you suppose his reasons are?

4. Dandy has requested that the vice president of marketing, the company sales manager, and the manager of new-product development work as a committee to recommend a policy for emphasizing physical distribution within the company more strongly. What suggestions (in detail) do you believe the committee should make?

Case 12-2

Moped Mobility, Inc.

Calvin Duncan is the owner and manager of Moped Mobility, Inc., a recently formed organization whose purpose is to import and distrib-ute—eventually nationally within the United States—a line of mopeds which are manufac-tured in Japan by Nipponese Industries, a sub-

sidiary of Musuki Motors.

Mopeds are the near-beer of the motorcycle world. They are more than bicycles but considerably less than the roaring machines straddled by Marlon Brando in *The Wild One* or Peter Fonda in *Easy Rider*. No self-respecting Hell's Angel would be caught dead on one. Yet mopeds (the word comes from "motorized bicycle-plus-pedals") are coming on like gangbusters and are one of the hottest selling new wheeled vehicles in America.

Lenient laws are being passed favoring mopeds, instead of treating them like the bigger motorcycles or cars. One Department of Transportation study estimates that 3 million mopeds a year may be sold between 1980 and 1985. Sears Roebuck, which sold an Austrian-made moped briefly in the early 1960s and then dropped it because of poor sales, is planning a return to the moped business.

The moped's chief appeal is economy in an energy and inflation conscious age. With small engines (no more than 2 h.p., usually 1), most models get about 150 miles per gallon. Prices range from $300 on up to $550 for models with cast alloy wheels, special suspension, and cushy seats. Pedals are used to start the machines and to assist them on hills.

No fewer than thirty moped manufacturers have jumped into the United States market. Only one, Columbia of Westfield, MA, is American-headquartered; all the rest are based in Europe, where mopeds have been popular for decades. France's Motobecane has 5 million of its Moleylettes on foreign roads (including Bermuda, as legions of American tourists have discovered); Austria's Steyr Daimler Puch and Holland's Batavus are doing nearly as well. All have set up United States subsidiaries and are racing to open moped dealerships. Duncan, however, with his firm, Moped Mobility, Inc., has become the exlusive importer for Nipponese Industries' entire line of mopeds. Nipponese is, in turn, a marketing affiliate of Musuki, the big Japanese maker of motorcycles and cars.

Other Japanese motorcycle makers are reportedly gearing up for American sales.

Duncan is convinced that mopeds will have strong market appeal in the United States. His headquarters in Los Angeles will be the central receiving point and staging area from which he will distribute. He proposes to franchise authorized dealers in the West Coast and Rocky Mountain regions but plans eventual national distribution for the product. The mopeds will be shipped, partially assembled, by containerized ocean carriers from Japan to the United States. Duncan's plan is to transship the mopeds via motor freight in selected lots to regional distribution and warehouse points in Denver, Colorado, and Portland, Oregon. In such an operation, Duncan is aware that much of the success of his venture will depend in part upon the success of his physical distribution effort. He is prompted to this belief by his conviction that customer service (rapid deliveries to dealers, adequate assortments, and complete inventories of spare parts) will be a prerequisite for success. Also, his business acumen has taught him that efficient management of inventories in a business such as this is the secret to profitability.

Questions

1. How would you assess Duncan's plans? Do you believe his priorities concerning the preeminent importance of physical distribution are correct?

2. How does the customer service provided by physical distribution fit into the marketing mix? How can changes in elements of the marketing mix affect physical distribution?

3. In terms of physical distribution, what trade-offs result from the following marketing decision which Duncan might consider?
   a. Adding more products to the product line.
   b. Building and establishing more distribution warehouses so stocks will be closer to markets.

Chapter 13

Promotion: Advertising in the Marketing Strategy

During the late 1960s, STP was one of the "go-go" stocks and its engine oil additive, one of the hottest products in America. Relying heavily on the hard sell, STP advertising blitzed the country and sales skyrocketed. In 1971, *Consumer Reports,* the consumer advocate magazine, charged that STP's oil additive was a useless concoction, and shortly thereafter the Federal Trade Commission charged the company with deceptive advertising.[1] STP was suddenly about out of gas. Revenues fell, and stock prices plummeted. However, the company came back. It agreed to document its *advertising* claims (the FTC had charged that STP's advertising was not substantiated by research), and the company is once again watching its profits climb.

The real heart of STP's marketing strategy is still consumer advertising. On the comeback trail, STP directed its advertising agency, J. Walter Thompson Company, to come up with campaigns that use test results to document the claims made for the additive. One such effort appeared in a $200,000, four-page spread in *Reader's Digest,* detailing what STP does for an auto engine. The effect in many of the new ads is to tell people more than they may care to know about the product and the testing it has undergone. Finally, in a further attempt to regain its market position, the company switched its principal channel of distribution away from service stations and garages to supermarkets. Today, 65 percent of its products are sold in supermarkets—A&P, Colonial, Kroger, and Safeway—compared with 30 percent in service stations and garages. Five years ago the reverse was true. Television and magazine advertising to direct users has the capacity to "pull" the product through the channel; so given sufficient shelf space in the supermarket, and the power of advertising virtually to presell a product, STP once again appears to be on the road to market and sales success.

There is a powerful moral in the STP story, however, which we should not miss. First of all, advertising is an important part of the marketing program. It creates awareness; informs us about new products, or new uses for existing products; creates likes and dislikes; and actually alters our attitudes, our product preferences, and our behavior. Most of us still remember Alka Seltzer's theme, "Try it, you'll like it"; Lay's potato chips, "Bet you can't eat just one"; Noxzema shaving cream's, "Take it off, take it all off"; or the Coca-Cola Company's "It's The Real Thing," and "Coke adds life."

Neverthless, it takes more than just advertising to sell a product. When the product is perceived by consumers as weak, or lacking the attributes claimed, sales fall off and advertising loses its punch. Advertising is only a small, though important, part of marketing. To be really effective, it must be carefully integrated into the firm's overall marketing strategy. It must relate to the firm's target market and address their specific needs. Advertising must also make it easier for the company to sell through its chosen channels. Although advertising is the most conspicuous activity in calling buyers' attention to products, it is only one of several important elements in the promotion process. A com-

---

[1] Based upon "What Craig Nolan Did to Turn STP Around," *Business Week,* January 10, 1977, p. 38.

pany's promotion policy, like its branding, packaging, and distribution policies, must be coordinated within the marketing effort.

The Significance and Forms of Promotion

Broadly, promotion means "to push forward," to advance an idea in such a way as to gain acceptance and approval for it. If Americans decide to attack national problems, whether they be mental illness, crime in the streets, or energy conservation, the thrust of the attack is often a promotional campaign. If a local school levy is being proposed or the downtown needs renovating, public awareness and support are sought through promotional activities. Nearly everyone promotes. Doctors combat the rising costs of malpractice insurance through promotional activities to garner public support. Churches advertise and promote to gain favor and increase their congregations. Colleges and universities promote to create favorable images, attract more students, and increase their endowments.

A review of the television commercials of the past twenty years or so would, in many ways, reveal the large part promotion has played in our lives. The University of Arizona has created an archive for old television commercials. Advertising agencies and sponsors have already donated 1,000 commercials which document the recent twenty-five year rise of "the affluent society." These commercials are considered cultural artifacts and research material, reflecting the mood and times of our contemporary culture. Future generations of Americans will see how we conquered the scourges of underarm odor and stomach distress. They will also be able to share the joy of the pre-lib housewife over her sparkling kitchen floor and her triumph over balky sink drains and stubborn dirt.

Kinds of Promotion

Promotion in the broad sense consists of coordinated seller-initiated efforts to establish channels of information and persuasion to foster the sale of a good or service, or the acceptance of ideas or points of view.[2] There are a number of different kinds of promotion, including the following: advertising, personal selling, sales promotion, and publicity or public relations.[3]

Advertising is defined as any paid form of nonpersonal presentation and promotion of ideas, goods, and services by an identified sponsor.

Personal selling is an oral presentation in a conversation with one or more prospective puchasers for the purpose of making a sale.

Sales promotion consists of marketing activities other than personal selling, advertising, and publicity that stimulate consumer purchasing and dealer effectiveness. (It includes such intermittent activities as contests, premiums, dis-

[2] See Edward L. Brink and William T. Kelley, *The Management of Promotion* (Englewood Cliffs, NJ: Prentice-Hall, 1963), p. 6.
[3] The definitions are those of the American Marketing Association, Committee on Definitions: Marketing Definitions: A Glossary of Marketing Terms (Chicago, 1960).

plays, shows, exhibitions, demonstrations, and various other nonroutine selling efforts.)

Public relations is nonpersonal stimulation of demand for a product, service, or business unit by placing commercially significant news about it in a publication or obtaining favorable presentation of it upon radio, television, or stage that is not paid for by the sponsor.

Many promotional campaigns are built around all four of these principal activities. Each year, for example, in the early fall, when new car models are introduced, the campaigns will be launched with the release of news stories and public relations events relating to the new models. The advertising will extol the virtues of the new entries, often showing them in elegant settings. Prior to the introductions, dealer sales staffs may be called to regional meetings to be given special training in selling the new features. Special sales promotional devices are often used, such as displaying the new models at fairs, exhibition halls, in banks and in airports, or using contests and rebates as sales incentives.

Every product will likely warrant its own unique package of promotional activities. The ones chosen will depend on the nature of the product, its intended market, the characteristics of the consumers in various market segments, and the particular goals and objectives of the promoting firm, all balanced against the campaign's financial resources.

Promotion as Communication and Persuasion

While most people realize that promotional efforts are almost always persuasive, it is easy to overlook the fact that promotion is a very important form of **communication**. Communication is a process by which people attempt to create a *commonness* of understanding between them. Slightly more formally, communication has been defined as "the study of who says what to whom in what settings, by which channels, and with what purposes and what effects. It deals with messages designed to influence human behavior, the media that carry such messages, and the market that responds to such messages."[4]

Everything the marketing firm does, in a sense, communicates, or sends a message to someone. Its products, as symbols of the company, become important messages. The firm's employees, especially its salespeople, communicate; the firm's prices contain messages which say in effect, "We're reasonably priced, or high priced." Or the price may convey a message which says, "At $2.95, the price for this product is too low and you ought to worry about the quality."

Promotion as a planned marketing activity is persuasive communication. Marketers develop their messages and their total promotional effort to have a positive impact on the attitudes and behavior of the target audience.

Consumers Are Receptive to Persuasion.   Much of the time we are really receptive to being sold—that is if it is done subtly, intelligently, and without

4 Joel P. Bowman and Bernadine P. Branchaw, *Successful Communication in Business* (New York: Harper & Row, 1980), p. 6.

making us feel we are being coerced. Buying, for most consumers, is a pleasurable experience. When we buy, someone's promotional and selling effort has succeeded. Contrary to what many critics of promotion say, most of us do not have a deep aversion to or resentment of promotional efforts which are projected to us as persuasive communications.

The Persuasive Process

Most people are avowed behavior shapers. We all fancy ourselves as having certain "selling abilities"—dominant personalities, persuasiveness and charm, or an ability to converse and convince. We all try from time to time to influence someone else's decisions. What happens when someone attempts to influence the decision process and, hence, the behavior of another person? The answer, within a psychological context, has been at least partially provided by Cartwright. He suggests that:

> To influence behavior, a chain of processes must be initiated within the person. These processes are complex and interrelated, but in broad terms, they may be characterized as (1) creating a particular cognitive structure, (2) creating a particular motivational structure, and (3) creating a particular behavioral or action structure. In other words, behavior and decision processes are determined by the needs, goals and values a person has; and by features of his cognitive and motivational structure. To influence behavior...requires the ability to influence these determinants in a particular way.[5]

Remember our discussion of buyer behavior and our notion of the cognitive consumer in Chapter 5. We laid down then the basic groundwork for a "theory" of behavior. Behavior, you will recall, is a function of cognitions (knowledge, attitudes, values, belief systems), one's affect (what one likes and dislikes), and the person's particular state of arousal or motivation in a given situation. Cartwright goes on to specify four particular steps that must be taken to influence behavior.

1. *The communication of information must reach the sense organs or cognitive mechanisms of the persons who are to be persuaded or influenced.*
2. *Having reached the sense organs or cognitive mechanisms, the information must be perceived as compatible with the person's existing cognitive structure and belief system.*
3. *To induce action by communicating information, the suggested action must be seen by the person as a path or alternative to some goal that he has.*
4. *To induce a given action or to alter a given decision process, an appropriate...motivational system must gain control or dominance over the person's behavior at a given point of time.[6]*

[5] Dorwin Cartwright, "Some Principles of Mass Persuasion," *Human Relations*, **2** (1949), p. 255.
[6] Cartwright, "Mass Persuasion," p. 255.

The concept of a **hierarchy of effects,** or the fact that consumer decision processes occur in a series of stages or activities, is generally well accepted. Look carefully at Table 13-1. The sequence, or hierarchy, of mental or behavioral processes that consumers are likely to move through is carefully illustrated. Notice how the consumer is moved from a state of unawareness to one of awareness; from awareness to more knowledge; from knowledge of the product, service, or firm, to liking; from liking to preference; from preference to conviction; and ultimately to purchase.

There is more to observe in Table 13-1. Look at the left side of the table. What you see there is basically Cartwright's four stages of behavior change. To create awareness and knowledge, promotional efforts must emphasize the *cognitive aspects* of behavior. The promotion must provide information and facts. As the consumer moves from knowledge to liking and preference, the promotional activity must emphasize the *affective*—the realm of emotions must be entered because the promotion must change attitudes and feelings. Finally, to activate the consumer to purchase the product, the promotional effort must emphasize the conative, or *motivational*. The consumer must be given sufficient incentive actually to make the purchase commitment. The two columns on the right side of Table 13-1 show some types of promotion that are relevant to the various steps in the hierarchy of events and some research approaches that can measure and evaluate the effectiveness of the promotion at each relevant stage.

Persuasion, Not Coercion.   What we have been discussing is persuasion, not coercion. Persuasion relies upon inducements, rewards, or reinforcements by advising, urging, or providing reasons. Coercion relies upon force, compelling people to do our bidding. Some critics of promotion—often those who do not understand the promotional and persuasive process—confuse the two. No firm has the power to coerce in its promotional program.

Ironically, many promotional campaigns even create a dislike for their product and a preference for brand X. We all know that we don't run out and buy everything that we see advertised. At each stage of the hierarchy shown in Table 13-1, there is a relatively low probability that the promotional effort will move the consumer from any one stage to another. The notations $P_{(A)}$ by awareness, $P_{(K)}$ by knowledge, and so on, mean "the probability of creating awareness and the probability of creating knowledge," and so on. If there is a low probability at each stage, then the combined probability $(P_{(A)} \cdot P_{(K)} \cdot P_{(L)} \cdot P_{(P)} \cdot P_{(C)} \cdot P_{(P1)})$ of the promotion's success is indeed very low.[7]

---

[7] Here is an example that might help clarify the concept. Suppose the probability at each stage is .25, or one chance in four, that the person will be moved from one step to the next, then the probability of a person making an actual purchase is .25x.25x.25x.25x.25x.25 = .0002441—a very low probability. This low probability and the example are appropriate only if the customer is moved completely through the hierarchy in *one* exposure. If, however, the customer is in the conviction stage, that person's probability of purchase after exposure to promotion is .25 (using the figures from the example).

Promotion Is Not a Hypodermic.   Some have viewed mass advertisng as having a hypodermic effect, that is, creating a compulsion to buy. However,

Table 13-1 Advertising and The Hierarchy of Behavior Effects

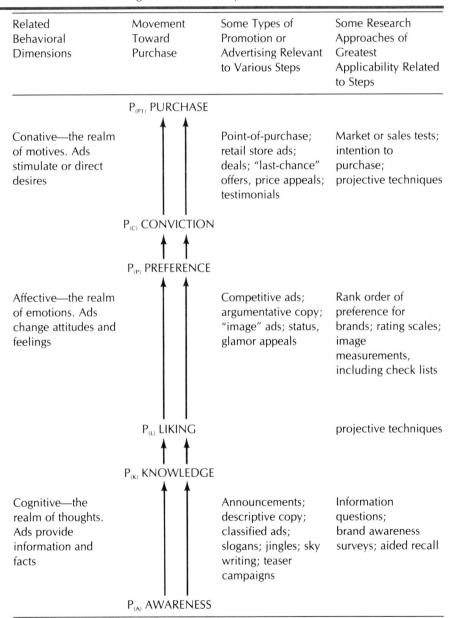

Related Behavioral Dimensions	Movement Toward Purchase	Some Types of Promotion or Advertising Relevant to Various Steps	Some Research Approaches of Greatest Applicability Related to Steps
	$P_{(P1)}$ PURCHASE		
Conative—the realm of motives. Ads stimulate or direct desires		Point-of-purchase; retail store ads; deals; "last-chance" offers, price appeals; testimonials	Market or sales tests; intention to purchase; projective techniques
	$P_{(C)}$ CONVICTION		
	$P_{(P)}$ PREFERENCE		
Affective—the realm of emotions. Ads change attitudes and feelings		Competitive ads; argumentative copy; "image" ads; status, glamor appeals	Rank order of preference for brands; rating scales; image measurements, including check lists
	$P_{(L)}$ LIKING		projective techniques
	$P_{(K)}$ KNOWLEDGE		
Cognitive—the realm of thoughts. Ads provide information and facts		Announcements; descriptive copy; classified ads; slogans; jingles; sky writing; teaser campaigns	Information questions; brand awareness surveys; aided recall
	$P_{(A)}$ AWARENESS		

Source: Adapted from Robert J. Lavidge and Gary A. Steiner, "A Model for Predictive Measurement of Advertising Effectiveness, *Journal of Marketing,* October 1961, p. 61.

this notion is being abandoned in favor of the situational or functional approach which views promotion as one persuasive influence working amid other influences in a total situation.[8] This means that communication does not directly affect consumer behavior, but may positively or negatively affect it, given the presence or absence of certain mediating factors. In our examination of consumer behavior, we discussed these factors as the individual's cognitive structure, particular motivational or arousal state, and the need system, or problems (situations), confronting that individual at a particular time.

The Two-Way Nature of Communication

Whenever communication occurs, we say that the parts involved in the transfer of information constitute a communication system. Every communication must have a *source* and a *destination*. Between the source and the destination there is a connecting link called the *communication channel*. For the information to pass over the channel, it is necessary to operate on it in such a way that it is suitable for transmission; the component that performs this operation is the *transmitter,* or sender. At the destination, there must be a *receiver* that converts the transmitted information into its original form. These five components—source, channel, transmitter, receiver, and destination—make up the model communication system illustrated in Figure 13-1.

The source may be an individual, a spokesperson for a small group, or a multiunit organization. The message may be visual and/or audible, face-to-face, or impersonal. The receiver, like the source, may be an individual, a group, a crowd, or a mob. The channel or media may be visual or auditory, or a combination of both.

A capability that ought to be incorporated into every communication system is *feedback*. Feedback is an effort to monitor a part of the output of a system in order to correct, modify, or control the total system. Marketing firms may often be more interested in establishing a communication system to feed information back than to feed it forward. It is feedback that creates two-way communication systems and allows us to zero in on our marketing targets. Marketers get various forms of feedback from those who receive their messages. Customers write letters of complaint about the firm's products or about its advertising. Or they may write that they would like to try the product but it is unavailable from their local store. Sales of a product are feedback; so, too are declining sales or promotional activity that generates no customer response.

A message is much more likely to succeed if it fits the patterns of understanding, the attitudes, values, and goals of the receiver, or at least tries to reshape them only slightly.[9] This process is known in advertising circles as *canalizing,* or "starting where the audience is." It means that the sender provides a message that is compatible with the existing feelings and motives of the receiver.

[8] Joseph T. Klapper, *The Effects of Mass Communications* (Glencoe, IL: Free Press, 1960), p. 5.
[9] Raymond A. Bauer, "The Obstinate Audience: The Influence Process from the Point of View of Social Communication," *American Psychologist* **19** (1964), p. 327.

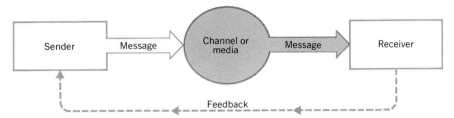

Figure 13-1 Communication components.

Determining the Promotional Strategy

Almost all firms doing extensive promotion find it advantageous to develop a promotional strategy. This is a comprehensive plan of action, geared to and coordinated with the firm's master plan, or overall marketing strategy. The promotion strategy ranks with the strategies adopted for product planning and development, pricing, and channels and distribution as a key determinant of market success.

The Promotion Quadrangle

Marketers like to speak of the **promotion quadrangle**.[10] When persuasive communication is used in marketing, the four sides of the promotional quadrangle are as follows:

1. The product. The thing featured in the advertisement
2. The potential buyer. The person to be persuaded or influenced by the promotion
3. The seller. The company or sponsor who undertakes the promotion
4. The distribution channel. The route along which the product will move from seller to buyer

A brief example of how these factors affect various aspects of the promotional strategy may be helpful.

The Product. Some products lend themselves readily to certain kinds of promotion. Children's toys can be shown in highly effective settings on television, whereas advertisements in newspapers and magazines mean little to small children who cannot yet read. Consumer products, especially convenience goods, can be readily sold through mass promotion such as television advertising. Complicated industrial equipment, on the other hand, can best be promoted through technical journals, news stories, or other publicity, and the use of well-qualified sales engineers.

---

[10] For more on the quadrangle notion, see John S. Wright and Daniel J. Warner, *Advertising* (New York: McGraw-Hill, 1966), pp. 92-94. The idea has been extended in the 1977 edition on pages 610 through 651.

The Potential Buyer.   Every seller needs to understand the needs, wants, values, aspirations, and expectations of potential customers. The makers of Grecian Formula 16 hair dye for men, for instance, understand their market very well. Few middle-aged men want to call attention to their lost youth by going from gray hair to brown overnight. By promising a gradual or partial disappearance of the gray, the company offers its customers an inconspicuous and believable youthfulness. This is the essence of communication. If marketers are to provide solutions, they need to understand buyers' problems.

The Seller.   Companies are often unique and this quality must be incorporated into the promotional strategy. Suppose you are E.F. Hutton in 1970 and the stock market is down and sour. Many other brokerage houses are failing. Investors confuse you with a small firm called W.E. Hutton and, relatively speaking, you are a self-described "murky fifth" in size on Wall Street. What should you do? Maybe you run a series of clever commercials that don't hawk a single stock, bond, or commodity directly, but simply establish your image among investors as the ultimate authority on securities with the message, "When E.F. Hutton talks…people listen." Institutional advertising almost never stresses products, but focuses instead on the character, reputation, reliability, and responsibility of the company.

The Distribution Channel.   The promotional strategy also hinges on the channel or channels through which the company's products will flow. Some products are almost literally "pulled" through the channel by mass promotional efforts aimed at ultimate consumers. The heavy promotion causes customers to look for these products, and retailers respond to the demand by including the items in their merchandise inventories. Other products, given the nature of the distribution channel, depend more heavily on "push type" promotional strategies such as personal selling. This sort of effort is directed to "gatekeepers" or "key influentials," persons who are pivotal in the adoption and diffusion process for new products. Many times, the best promotional strategy will demand a blend of both push and pull type promotional efforts.

In addition to the four elements of the promotion quadrangle, the promotional strategy will be determined by the assessments of the promotion budget available, nature of the market situation, the promotion targets (hoped for markets and sales), the stage of the product life cycle, the promotional activities of the firm's competitors, economic conditions, and, of course, the nature of the product itself.

Before proceeding, can you answer these questions:
1. What is meant by "promotion"?
2. Can you define and differentiate each of the major kinds of marketing promotion—advertising, personal selling, publicity, and sales promotion?
3. What is the relationship between promotion and persuasive communication?

The Role of Advertising in the Promotional Strategy

The Purpose of Advertising

Advertising is an impersonal presentation of goods, ideas, or services requiring a mass medium. These mass media—radio, television, newspapers, magazines—have the power to reach large numbers of potential users or buyers of a product with a persuasive message. Advertising, in the broadest sense, informs and sells.[11] Much more specifically, however, advertising has additional objectives. Among the more important are the following:

1. To create awareness of, and build consumer interest in, new products, new technology, and new companies.
2. To remind customers and potential customers constantly of the availability of existing products and companies and how they compare with other products and firms.
3. To alert and sensitize all members of a marketing channel to products, product improvements, special promotions, contests, and other features in a company's operation. This creates a more favorable company and product image and helps to obtain better dealer outlets and a more cooperative attitude throughout the channel.
4. To presell products and ideas. Advertising induces a state of mental readiness for the salesperson's call and inclines direct consumers to buy, either from impulse in self-service situations or from salespeople in service establishments.
5. To reach selected target audiences. Through the creation of unique messages and appeals, advertising communicates purchase solutions to those who need them most.
6. To reduce customers' dissonance* and eliminate some dissatisfaction. After purchasing a product, many people become highly selective of the ads to which they expose themselves. These ads tend to reassure them and they often find information in the ads that heightens their use and enjoyment of the product.

The more specific the firm's advertising objectives, the easier it becomes to measure advertising's effectiveness. Many companies have multiple goals for their advertising programs that embrace all of the objectives listed previously. The objectives, of course, will again depend on the company's assessment of its target markets, the product, the channels of distribution to be employed, and the other promotional activities to be used. Advertising that presells products destined for mass consumer markets might obviously be inappropriate for selling industrial products.

---

[11] See Saeed Samiee, "Elements of Marketing Strategy: How Important Are They from the Executive Viewpoint?," *Journal of the Academy of Marketing Science* **8**, no. 1 (Winter 1980), pp. 40–50.

*Dissonance is a state of anxiety that arises when a person has one or more ideas that are in conflict with other ideas or beliefs held by the person.

Here's three ways not to get mugged.

I hate to repeat myself—
but you're not listening!
So I'll say it again:
1. Walk on well-lit streets.
2. Don't walk alone late
at night.
3. Have your keys ready,
so you don't fumble
around at your door.
Find out what else you can
do to protect yourself. Write
to: Crime Prevention Coalition, Box 6600, Rockville,
Maryland 20850.
And help me...

TAKE A BITE OUT OF CRIME

Advertising and social marketing.

The Magnitude of Advertising Expenditures

Advertising costs an enormous sum of money each year. In 1980 advertising expenditures amounted to about $47 billion. At the turn of the century, we were spending only about $0.5 billion a year and, as late as 1960, advertising

Figure 13-2 Growth in advertising volume 1865–1985.

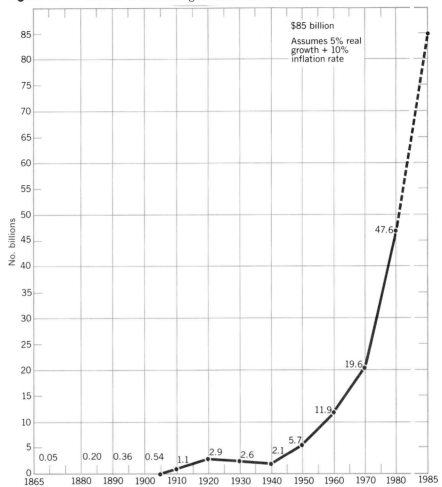

$85 billion

Assumes 5% real growth + 10% inflation rate

47.6

19.6

11.9

5.7

0.05   0.20   0.36   0.54   1.1   2.9   2.6   2.1

1865   1880   1890   1900   1910   1920   1930   1940   1950   1960   1970   1980   1985

Source: Based upon selected data from *Advertising Age*. The projection to 1985 is based upon author's estimates. Advertising expenditures increased 10 percent in 1979 and will continue to grow at about this rate for the next 5 years. *Advertising Age*, January 8, 1979, p. 4.

expenditures were slightly less than $12 billion. As the data in Figure 13-2 shows, advertising expenditures are expected to be about $85 billion by 1985.

When listing $47 billion spent for advertising in 1980, we need to remember that only about 20 percent of that figure was for actual advertising. The rest financed television and radio programming, and the editorial content of magazines and newspapers. The 20 percent applied directly to advertising messages went into direct mail advertising, contests, agency compensation, and all the things which must be considered the true costs of advertising.

Overall expenditures for advertising have been running at around 2 percent of Gross National Product for the past several years. American corporations spend about 1½ to 2 percent of their sales dollars for advertising. Table 13-2

Table 13-2 Advertising Expenditures of Selected Companies, 1979

Company	Amount Spent (millions)	Percentage of Sales
Procter and Gamble	$614.9	5.60
General Foods	393.0	6.55
Sears Roebuck & Co.	379.3	2.17
General Motors	323.4	0.49
Wm. Wrigley Jr. Co.	48.5	9.60
Anheuser Busch	160.5	4.90
Revlon, Inc.	101.0	5.90
Coca-Cola Co.	169.3	3.40

Source: *Advertising Age*, September 11, 1980, p. 30. Although the percentage spent on advertising by some companies is small, individual companies spend millions each year to promote their products.

shows advertising expenditures as a percentage of sales for some familiar American companies. When one considers that the overall cost of marketing to the consumer is about 50 percent of the consumer sales dollar, the proportion spent for advertising pales significantly. No more than about 3.5 percent of the consumer's personal consumption expenditures goes to pay for the cost of advertising.

Some firms are big spenders—others more restrained. Drug, cosmetics, and soap companies may spend as much as 20 to 25 percent of their sales revenue for advertising. The major automobile companies, by contrast, all average less than 1.5 percent of sales. Retail chains are modest spenders. Sears has the largest advertising budget in the industry, but this amounts to only about 2.2 percent of sales.

Of course, advertising expenditures mount rapidly when it costs as much as $50,000 for a single-page ad in *Reader's Digest* or $40,000 for a one-page spread in *Time*. A one-page weekday ad in the *New York Times* costs $12,000 and the advertiser will spend approximately $45,000 for thirty seconds of prime television time on ABC. Even radio and billboards are not cheap. It will cost upwards of $150 for one minute of prime radio time in Atlanta and as much as $1,200 for the monthly rental of a set of prime billboards in Los Angeles. But the real cost is the cost of reaching each person. Given television's mass audience during a program such as the Super Bowl game, each potential customer can be reached for only a few pennies. A direct mailing piece to similar customers, with the high costs of production and mailing, may run as high as $2 per person. In many cases, advertising is an even better buy when compared with personal selling. The average cost per call of a salesperson selling industrial goods is around $60; a sales call for consumer goods averages around $35. Personal selling expenses can run from 5 percent to as high as 20 percent of sales. By most any comparison, advertising is a relatively inexpensive promotional tool.

When E.F. Hutton talks, people listen.

Basic Advertising Strategy

Advertising strategy is the comprehensive planning for using advertising in implementing the firm's marketing strategy. All aspects of marketing strategy are integrated and coordinated, but advertising is a principal means for communication with perceived target markets. There are many different media through which the firm can attempt its communication—television, radio, newspapers, magazines, direct mail, and others. Choosing from among all the media will depend on many considerations, such as:

1. The markets or customers the firm is trying to reach
2. The distribution channels for the product
3. The size of the advertising budget
4. The behavior and current practices of the competition
5. The nature of the marketing strategy
6. The combination of media judged best for the program
7. Reach, or market coverage, versus frequency of the communication, and other desired measures of effectiveness

Obviously, having so many variables to consider suggests that we need a clearly structured plan of action, one that is carefully detailed and then executed. More than most other business functions, advertising is difficult to plan and implement because of a lack of commonly accepted standards for measuring its effectiveness. Advertising planning must therefore take continuous and close account of advertising feedback. In this respect it is difficult to isolate the point at which advertising planning stops and advertising control begins. Advertising planning most assuredly, however, must begin with advertising objectives.

Specify Objectives.   Advertising planning is most successful when based upon clear-cut objectives. However, advertising and marketing objectives are not always identical. While marketing efforts may be directed at increasing sales or market share, the advertising may be simply trying to change consumer attitudes, or encourage consumers to visit a store or return a coupon.

Relate Advertising to Target Market.   To whom is our advertising directed? The often quoted response is "Everyone!" But that is usually incorrect. The planning and development of most products evolve with a particular user in mind. The same consideration should prevail during the planning and implementation of the advertising program. When General Motors brought out the Cadillac Cimarron, they had in mind a certain kind of consumer: high income, prestige conscious, and having a privileged life style enjoyed by relatively few. Shouldn't the advertising and media chosen for this product reflect these considerations?

Most successful advertising possesses what is called the unique selling proposition (USP), a term describing such factors as "electric grind coffee" for automatic coffee makers. Another is Lipton's tea blend and filter for automatic coffee makers like Mr. Coffee, designed to appeal to those who own such appliances but resent exploding coffee prices. Unique selling propositions, as conveyed by advertising, can only be effective if they offer solutions to unique problems and unique problems are what make for unique market targets.

Selecting Media

The media selected will depend on the advertising objectives, the media habits of the target consumers, and the funds available to carry out the advertising program. Any sound advertising campaign must be based upon a thorough understanding of the various advertising media. Media have personalities, much like some products, retail stores, or corporations. For example, to many people magazines are an information medium, while television is often seen as a source of entertainment. Television advertising, therefore, is usually perceived as highly entertaining but not very informative. Magazine advertisements must do much the same thing that television commercials do: arrest attention and create awareness. Magazine advertising, however, because the reader is exposed to it longer, can also be more informative and move the reader through a wider span of steps in the consumer decision process.

The major advertising media include newspapers, magazines, radio, television, direct mail, outdoor advertising, and a few other specialty advertising outlets (such as calendars or pencils). Advertisers must choose from among the available media those that best suit their marketing and promotional objectives, in light of their particular needs. The combination chosen will constitute the advertising mix. A description of each of the available alternatives follows.[12]

Newspapers. Newspapers receive the largest share, about 30 percent, of all advertising revenues. There are 1,760 daily newspapers in this country, with a combined circulation of roughly 62.5 million. Their daily audience is actively seeking editorial and advertising information. Newspapers reach an accumulated 94 percent of all adults (eighteen and older) over five weekdays, and have been shown to be relatively free from false, misleading, and deceptive claims.[13] Newspapers reach specific target markets, especially local ones, and have strong penetration power at relatively low cost. The short lead time for newspaper advertising makes them ideal for rapid insertion of special promotional events. Newspapers, however, suffer certain mechanical or production limitations which sometimes affect the quality of their advertisements. Moreover, they have a brief life span and there is considerable waste circulation for many products.

Magazines. The most striking thing about magazines is their diversity. Magazine publishers are keenly aware of market segmentation and, as a consequence, there is a wide variety of magazines for both general readership and special audiences. Magazines, like newspapers, have generally high credibility but are neither as local nor time bound as newspapers. Magazines have very specific identities which permit an advertiser to reach a large number of identifiable prospects at relatively low cost. Most magazines today address themselves to special audiences. Their readers are highly selective in the information they seek, the attention they give it, and how long they will remember it.

Television. Television is the fastest growing advertising medium in the world. So quickly is it expanding in the United States that in spite of spiraling rate

12 These descriptions were compiled from numerous sources. For a much longer and more detailed characterization, see Maurice I. Mandell, *Advertising*, 2nd ed. (Englewood Cliffs, NJ: Prentice-Hall, 1974), pp. 314–397.
13 James R. Krum and Stephen K. Keiser, "Regulation of Retail Newspaper Advertising," *Journal of Marketing* **40** (July 1976), pp. 29–34.

Magazines are an important media for much U.S. advertising.

structures, advertising demands in this medium are about to outstrip the amount of available time.

The uniqueness and strength of television lie in its ability to combine many of the functions performed singly by other media. Television advertising can create drama, suspense, and emotion. Because it combines visual and auditory stimuli with movement and staging, it has the power to arrest attention, generate interest, inform, and teach by illustration and example. Advertising on television, however, is costly. Unless you are a national, or at least a large regional marketer, you may discover that its high cost and wasted circulation are prohibitive for your marketing program. Nevertheless, television advertising has a dynamic vitality and an enormous capacity to attract and hold large audiences.

Radio.   Radio has changed drastically since the advent of television. For a while, its future as a viable advertising medium was uncertain. That uncertainty of late, however, appears to have been dispelled. The value of radio lies in its ability to saturate a market. Its music and frequent news summaries are widely heard by young single persons, housewives and retirees, and all those who travel by automobile. The growing popularity of country western music stations makes radio an ideal vehicle for reaching members of this audience. Radio has a special capacity for presenting messages which promote ordinary everyday products. Small merchants find the radio particularly suitable for their promotional needs. It is a relatively inexpensive medium but even so, there is often a lot of wasted broadcasting.

Direct Mail.   Direct mail is a desirable medium for many advertisers. In spite of postage rate hikes and the rising costs of producing attractive direct mail pieces, it is still a relatively low-cost means of advertising. With the purchase of highly selected mailing lists, a company acquires a very effective tool for reaching a specific target audience with a minimum of wasted circulation. The big drawback to direct mail, and one which deters many from using it more frequently, is that its recipients are likely to throw it away unread. Direct mail pieces must have an unusual capacity to catch a person's attention and hold it. A great advantage of direct mail is that it can be made more personal than most other media, almost to the point of being absolutely confidential. Direct mail offers great flexibility with the possibility for novelty and realism. It presents an advertiser's message without having it contaminated by competing ads as in newspapers, radio, and television.

Outdoor and Transit Advertising.   Among the oldest forms of advertising is the outdoor sign. There are various types of outdoor advertising including posters, billboards, and transit advertising.* Messages can be delivered nationally, or on a market-by-market basis. They can be tailored to obtain specific frequencies and coverage, and can reach people on their way to work, to play, and to shop. The relatively low cost of outdoor advertising brings it within reach of users with small budgets. The copy, however, must be tailored to specific viewers and there is usually neither time nor space to develop lengthy messages. Such advertising is particularly appropriate in large urban areas with high concentrations of pedestrians, automobiles, or public transit users. There is a growing clamor to reduce "visual pollution" in these areas, however, and this form of advertising is its special target.

Balancing Costs with Coverage

A large part of advertising strategy consists of seeking a balance between the costs of advertising and the coverage we get in return. It does not necessarily follow that the advertising message is best told in only one medium. So, we need some way of comparing advertising costs and coverage for the various media so that we can judge the relative value of our expenditures in each of the media selected.

*Transit advertising consists of posters and other visual displays on buses, subways, and railroads as well as signs on panel trucks, vans, and other vehicles.

In speaking of coverage, advertisers speak of reach, frequency, and continuity. *Reach* refers to the total number of people to whom a message is delivered, and *frequency* describes the number of times the message is delivered within a given period. *Continuity* refers to the length of time a scheduled message runs. In other words, is the advertisement a single insertion, or will it run for some period, and if so, for how long?

For magazines, the attempt is to balance cost with circulation. This rate is designated as the *cost per thousand*, computed by multiplying the page rate in the magazine by 1,000 and dividing this figure by the magazine's circulation. For example:

$$\text{cost per thousand} = \frac{1 \text{ page rate} \times 1,000}{\text{circulation}}$$

For a magazine with a page rate of $50,000 per issue and a circulation of 8 million, cost per thousand would be $6.25.

In newspapers, the standard unit for measuring cost is the agate line. This is a line one column wide and one-fourteenth of an inch deep. To compare one large newspaper's cost with another for advertising purposes, a *milline* rate (cost per million) is used. This rate is the advertiser's cost for sending one agate line of advertising in a given newspaper to 1 million people. For example:

$$\text{milline rate} = \frac{\text{cost of 1 agate line} \times 1,000,000}{\text{circulation}}$$

A newspaper with a circulation of 500,000 and a line rate of $2 would have a milline rate of $4.

The cost per thousand concept is also used for radio and television. The base rate to be multiplied by 1,000 is the cost per commercial minute of a particular time slot. However, the circulation or coverage of radio and television is not nearly so easily measured as that for magazines or newspapers. To gauge the size of television and radio audiences, advertisers and broadcasters use rating services such as A. C. Nielsen and others.

How Much Should We Spend?

"How much should we spend?" is not a particularly good question, nor is it an easy one to answer. It depends on the answer to many other questions, like: What are the options to spending? What is the competition doing? What are our advertising objectives? And, most importantly, what kind of return will the firm get on its advertising investment?

Competitive Parity. Many advertisers answer the question by trying to spend about the same as their competitors. This method, called competitive parity, is really no rule for decision at all. Your advertising expenditure is simply determined by your competitor's decision on how much to spend. Nonetheless, it is the approach used by many advertisers. "Match the competition and spend a little more if we can." The real shortcoming of this approach is that it largely ignores the strengths, weaknesses, and market(s) of the advertiser.

The Percent of Sales Method.   One frequently employed rule of thumb for answering the question "How much should we spend?" is the percent of sales method. As the name suggests, for reasons of habit, custom, or good judgment, some percentage of either past or forecasted sales is decided upon as the figure to be appropriated for current advertising expenditures. For example, if 3 percent of sales is the figure selected, and sales last year were $500,000, then the amount for this year's advertising would be $15,000. Or if forecasted sales were the base, and sales were forecasted for the coming year at $550,000, then advertising expenditures would be $16,500. Is this a good method? No, not at all. And the reason is that it reverses the normal cause-effect relationships. Advertising presumably causes sales but with this method, sales determine the amount spent for advertising.

The Task and Investment Method.   This method suggests that the amount spent for advertising should be a function of the tasks to be attained (sales to be achieved) or that advertising expenditures, like any other expenditures, should be undertaken in order to generate a return on investment. It sounds good. But there is a problem. We don't know with much precision what the **advertising sales response curve** looks like. Many presume it looks like Figure 13-3.

In this figure the first advertising dollars are not very efficient, maybe because there are not yet enough of them to break through buyer resistance or induce sufficient awareness and purchase of our product. As the firm spends more, we reach a more efficient point on the curve that economists would call "increasing returns to scale." As we increase our outlay by a small increment, we get a rather large incremental increase in sales. Finally, at the upper reaches of the curve, after spending a considerable amount, our advertising efficiency begins to drop off and we come to a point of diminishing returns—advertising

Figure 13-3   A supposed advertising sales response curve.

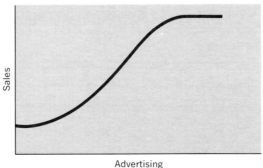

Advertising

dollars are not returned to us in the form of increased sales. Now, this is all rather hypothetical because we really do not know what the advertising sales response curve looks like. Marketers work on the assumption that it looks like the figure, but in actuality we are guessing. Why? Because there are too many other variables that contaminate the picture. There is no way to hold all the other market factors constant—price changes, competitors' behavior, new-product development, changes in consumer conditions, consumer attitudes and expectations—so that we can derive a single measure of advertising-sales relationships for any one firm, or for a whole industry.

This means that the task method of determining how much to spend on advertising is limited in application.[14] It is certainly true that a firm should attempt to link its advertising expenditures to the tasks and objectives at hand. From another standpoint, however, advertising expenditures should also be considered a long-term investment that will pay back dividends over a long period.

The Computer Can Help.   In recent years, advertising effectiveness has been enhanced somewhat by the development and use of media models. Such models establish optimum schedule recommendations according to reach, frequency, and continuity. The aim is to provide the most effective schedule of advertising activities based on the various media characteristics. Such a schedule is conditioned by characteristics of the prospects to be reached, the desired frequency of exposure among all the prospect audiences, and the chosen time intervals between exposures. The truly ideal model is one that attaches a dollar value to the optimum schedule, subject to the restraints of the prospective buyers. Most of these models are mathematical programming models and must be used in connection with an electronic computer. These models, to be sure, do not answer the question, "How much to spend?" But they do answer the question that arises after how much to spend has been decided. That question is, "What mix of media will give us maximum effectiveness for our expenditures?"

The Three Essentials in Effective Advertising.   We don't want to get the impression that it is only dollars that count. It isn't. Advertising, to be effective, must have three ingredients: information, stimulus value, and emphasis.[15] *Information* is news. *Stimulus value* provokes a consumer to evaluate, judge, and reach a decision. *Emphasis* prompts consumers to single out your product from all the other advertising messages surrounding them. This means that advertising must have:

1. *Stopping power*, revealed by the initial delivery of the message
2. *Holding power*, apparent in a receiver's continuing attention to the message
3. *Commitment power*, shown when the receiver takes the hoped-for action.

[14] See Gary L. Lilien et al., "Industrial Advertising Effects and Budgeting Practices," *Journal of Marketing* **40** (January 1976), pp. 16–24.
[15] Herbert E. Krugman. "What Makes Advertising Effective?" *Harvard Business Review* **53** (March–April 1975), pp. 96–103.

These things are not achieved with just money. They are largely the fruit of creativity, and sometimes a little money will buy lots of creativity and ingenuity. The numbers—neither the dollars spent, nor even how many people are watching or reading—will not tell you how an ad communicates, or how it really sells something.[16] Large differences in audience numbers are overshadowed by variations in the creative performance of specific ads. What really matters most is whether the right idea is expressed in the right way and in the right setting. So, the first priority in determining the effectiveness of an advertisement belongs to the creative communication process and its impact, rather than to the generalities about media.

Before proceeding, can you answer these questions:

1. What is the purpose of advertising?
2. What is the distinction between direct action advertising and institutional advertising?
3. Can you discuss the shortcomings of the competitive parity and the percent of sales methods for determining the size or amount of the advertising budget?

Managing the Advertising Program

The management of a company's advertising program is usually the responsibility of a high-level staff officer, generally designated as the advertising manager or the vice president for advertising. The organization of the advertising program, and the way the work of the advertising unit is carried out, will vary greatly among firms, according to size, product, customer orientation, and other factors.

Some firms have in-house advertising departments. This is especially true of smaller manufacturers, cooperative and voluntary retail chain organizations, and local and regional retail stores. In larger organizations, which are more likely to use an advertising agency, the promotional manager's main task is to help the firm select an agency that can best project a favorable image of the firm and attain its advertising and promotional objectives. When such specialized services are employed, the advertising director or manager works in-house as a coordinator among the firm's various departments. This executive's task is to help these people develop their own advertising and promotional objectives, which are then coordinated with the entire company's advertising goals and policies. Again, the advertising director, where an agency is involved, works directly with the agency's principal representative, called the account executive. Together, these two share the responsibility for carrying out the company's advertising goals and objectives.

[16] Leo Bogart, "Mass Advertising: The Message, Not the Measure," *Harvard Business Review* (September – October 1976), pp. 107–117.

The Advertising Agency

Quite often when we think of advertising we think automatically of advertising agencies. Advertising agencies are very important marketing intermediaries who specialize in selling advertising skills. These include such diverse activities as market research studies, product testing, the creation of individual ads and whole campaigns, the selection of media, and the follow-up evaluation of advertising effectiveness. In the United States there are approximately 4,000 advertising agencies. J. Walter Thompson, the industry's largest agency, had billings (value of advertising placed) in 1979 of $1.69 billion. Young and Rubicam and McCann Erikson, the numbers two and three firms, had billings that same year of $1.92 billion and $1.67 billion, respectively.[17]

The advertising agency is a team of highly skilled technical and creative people who develop and prepare advertising and place it in the various media for marketers. Because of intensive specialization, the agency can often perform these tasks for a firm much more cheaply than the firm can.

Advertising agencies began as space sellers or brokers who represented the medium (newspapers, primarily, in the early days). The commissions, though varied, have recently averaged about 15 percent. This commission, it must be made clear, comes from the medium selected, not from the client or marketer. The fee is retained by the advertising agency and the agency, in turn, bills the client. For example, if the rate for a page in a magazine is $25,000, the agency is billed by that magazine for $25,000 less $3,750 (15 percent), for a net amount of $21,250. The agency then bills the client for $25,000 and pays out to the magazine $21,250, retaining $3,750 as its gross margin.

Advertising agencies are today much more than space buyers and sellers. As mentioned earlier, they are in many instances complete advertising departments, performing a wide array of marketing services for their clients. Some years ago a growing clamor arose for a change in the way agencies were paid. Many firms complained because the agency received the 15 percent regardless of the amount of work performed. Marketers sometimes argued that this payment structure made it hard for agencies to be completely objective about low-cost media or economical advertising campaigns. Many agencies, on the other hand, especially those who performed a broad range of services for their clients, often felt that the standard commission was not enough to cover their full costs and provide them with a sufficient margin to justify the extra effort. In 1956, the American Association of Advertising Agencies agreed to a consent decree with the Justice Department that agencies would no longer depend entirely on the 15 percent commission fee. This opened the way to rate discounts as well as fee increases.

In some cases, where the costs of services provided by the agency are unusual, or where the agency agrees to provide services much beyond the normal level, the client is charged a fee for services rendered and the commissions received are then applied to these fees.

---

[17] Data is from *Advertising Age*. The Young and Rubicam total includes figures from the acquisition of another firm, Marsteller, Inc.

The Social and Economic Criticisms of Advertising

By most standards, advertising is effective. It sells merchandise. And most business executives use a kind of hard-headed logic—they don't spend money needlessly. Advertising works. Knowing just how it works or how to measure its effectiveness, however, is not an absolute science. There is probably a great deal of waste in advertising. Advertising is often condemned by social critics, some economists, and government officials, but overall, when examined closely, advertising is not counter to the public interest. We should, however, examine some of the criticisms in order to gain perspective on the issue.

Advertising Doesn't Create New Demand: It Simply Alters The Market Place.   This is a charge frequently leveled at advertising, yet the data in large part refutes it. Sales of such products as automobiles, appliances, televisions, and stereophonic equipment show that advertising raises total consumption levels. Even products like soft drinks, soaps and detergents, and coffee (until the 1977 price rise) have shown marked increases in their per capita consumption levels.

Advertising Promotes Planned Product Obsolescence.   Until recently the automobile industry changed styling about every year. Many people would argue that this made many of us want a new car each year, and if this practice were avoided we could save perhaps as much as $600 to $1,000. The facts show, however, that the automobile industry has never been successful in getting people to buy a new car each year. There are good statistics on new-car purchases indicating that the typical new car is traded in after about five years.

Advertising Promotes Trivial Differences.   Many claim that the features extolled in many advertisements are trivial and do not serve the customer's real needs. But is this really so? In automobiles, to continue the previous example, manufacturers have developed and promoted improvements like four-wheel brakes, the automatic shift, air conditioning, and electronic ignition. Automobiles are better products today than they were thirty years ago.

This is not to deny completely that advertising promotes trivial differences among products. Certainly in some cases it does. Much advertising does little more than point out slight product differences and continues to extol their virtues far beyond their value. However, despite some admitted triviality, much advertising is highly informative about significant product differences.

Advertising "Costs" the Consumer.   Some declare that advertising "costs" the consumer. Upon examination, that doesn't sound like too intelligent an indictment. Of course, advertising "costs" the consumer. Consumers pay the full cost of all products—production, design, engineering, marketing, and physical distribution costs. We don't hear anyone say: Why not eliminate engineering or design and reduce the cost of the product? But we do hear people say: Why not eliminate advertising and reduce the costs of the product? The real questions are: What is the impact of advertising on production costs? On selling costs? On the company's overall image and acceptance?[18]

The Beat Goes On. Advertising and its relative merits, if any, are debated frequently and hotly. Social critics point to what they see as massive waste and the growing power of advertising. They tell us that advertising makes people want things they can't afford; makes us a nation of conformists; is confusing because its claims are false and misleading; and that advertising creates monopolies that destroy free enterprise. Space simply will not permit examining all these charges in detail, but we can answer some of them. It is true that advertising has a stimulating effect on expectations, but is that bad? Given the varied character of the American people, it is really doubtful if we are, or ever will be, a nation of conformists. No one person, not even our best marketing scholars, can judge what is false, misleading or even deceptive.[19]

The Increasing Public Sensitivity to Advertising

The task of managing the advertising program, both from the agency and the marketer's standpoints, has become increasingly burdensome because of the public's increasing criticism of advertising. Many advertisers are weary from the battering they have been getting over such issues as truth in advertising, advertising to children, and the overall argument that advertisers have enormous power to shape tastes and modify behavior.[20] Other concerns are that advertising simply does not inform, but rather, attempts to entertain by intruding in a strident, loud, and offensive fashion.[21]

Thus it would seem that conforming to public policy and avoiding legal issues may occupy as much advertisers' time as do planning and implementing campaigns. Consumers, individually through feedback to advertisers, and collectively through organized consumer movements and government, are working to assert their rights for less offensive, more informational advertising and to insist that advertisers generally shoulder their social responsibilities.[22] Much has come of these developments, by way of both increasing government regulations and self-policing by the industry.

[18] See Paul W. Faris and Mark S. Albion, "The Impact of Advertising on the Price of Consumer Products," *Journal of Marketing* **44**, no. 3 (Summer 1980), pp. 17–35.

[19] See David M. Gardner, "Deception in Advertising: A Conceptual Approach," *Journal of Marketing* **39** (January 1975), pp. 40–46.

[20] Stephen A. Greyser, "Irritation in Advertising," *Journal of Advertising Research* **13,** no. 1 (February 1973), pp. 3–10.

[21] Alan Resnik and Bruce L. Stern, "An Analysis of Information Content in Television Advertising," *Journal of Marketing*, January 1977, pp. 50–53.

[22] For more on this subject, see Richard A. Posner, *Regulation of Advertising by the FTC,* American Enterprise Institute for Public Policy Research, Washington, DC, 1973, pp. 17–31; and Francesco M. Nicosia, *Advertising, Management and Society: A Business Point of View* (New York: McGraw-Hill, 1974), pp. 327–342. Also, see Priscilla A. LaBarbera, "Advertising Self-Regulation: An Evaluation," *MSU Business Topics* **28,** no. 3, (Summer 1980), pp. 55–63.

Affirmative Disclosure.   If information in an advertisement is considered insufficient by the FTC, the commission may require a company to disclose in its advertising some of the deficiencies or limitations of its product or service so the consumer can judge the product's negative, as well as positive, attributes. This is a sore spot with many advertisers because little is really known about how much information consumers seek, or how much they really consider in purchase consumption decisions. Some products, cosmetics and toiletries among others, do not lend themselves readily to **affirmative disclosure.** Then, too, what about the dilemma of the little girl in the cartoon? Does she really want all that additional information?

Substantiation.   In 1971, the Federal Trade Commission adopted a resolution that requires advertisers to submit on demand by the commission data to back up advertising claims for a product's safety, performance, quality, or price comparability. The intent of this **substantiation** is to help consumers make more reasoned choices by having information available to them. Members of many industry groups including automobiles, appliances, soaps and detergents, television sets, dentifrices, hearing aids, and all over-the-counter drugs have been ordered to provide the commission with documentation in support of their designated advertising claims.

Corrective Advertising.   **Corrective advertising** requirements have increasingly been a part of many FTC consent orders. Corrective advertising doctrines are based upon the notion that inaccurate information has already been communicated by advertisers, and that corrective advertising is needed to eliminate the lingering effects of such information. The provisions generally state that, for a limited period of time, a percentage of the firm's advertising budget for the misrepresented product must be devoted to messages designed to correct prior questionable claims.

Needed: Better Methods for Measuring Advertising Effectiveness

What is really needed most may not be more laws to regulate advertising but better methods for measuring its effectiveness. There are many consumers, as well as business people, who extol the virtue of advertising. As stated earlier, it has been shown that advertising actually lowers consumer prices.[23] Legislators throughout the country are considering removing the restrictions on advertising for retail prescription drugs,[24] as well as on the professional services of lawyers, doctors, and accountants, on the presumption that advertising spreads information and leads to more vigorous competition and lower prices.[25] Effective advertising can act as a significant stimulus to market competition through giving useful information to consumers. To ignore this effect would be damaging to consumer welfare.

Improving the Effectiveness of Advertising through Research

Much is being done through marketing research to improve the results advertising yields. Research may ultimately tell marketers more about:

1. The relationship between liking an ad and its effectiveness
2. The impact of repetition on customer irritability and thus, on sales
3. The impact of a product's setting in a television commercial on its adoption
4. The impact of advertising intensity, or customer reaction in terms of expenditure of advertisers' dollars and exposure
5. The value of segmentation (directing special messages to segmented and identified audiences)
6. The impact of the product life cycle on advertising effectiveness (is the advertisement of older products more likely to irritate than that of newer products?)

Research has invariably helped to increase advertising effectiveness.[26] For example, research showed that many people completely misunderstood Dr. Pepper. They thought it was medicated, contained pepper, and so on. So a

---

[23] Robert L. Steiner, "Does Advertising Lower Consumer Prices?" *Journal of Marketing* **37** (October 1973), pp. 19–26.

[24] John F. Cady, "Restrictions on Advertising and the Retail Price of Drugs," *Arizona Review*, College of Business and Public Administration, University of Tucson, Tucson, Arizona, November 1973, pp. 1–4.

[25] Jules Backman, *Advertising and Competition* (New York: New York University Press, 1967), pp. 40–79.

[26] Virginia Miles, "Research is Key in Changing Your Brand Strategy," *Advertising Age*, July 12, 1976, pp. 31–33.

new theme was introduced:"You've got to Try It to Love It." Research also has shown that customers liked Hamm's beer's old theme, so the company changed back and revived their sales with a live bear and the motto, "Land of Sky Blue Waters." Like all of marketing strategy, advertising begins with the consumer. Too often, advertising is ineffective, irritating, or simply ignored because it is not based upon an understanding of consumer needs. Marketing research is the vital bridge linking the firm's advertising strategy to its markets.

Summary

Promotion is a very important part of the firm's marketing strategy. Promotion means to "move forward" and, marketing promotion is a form of persuasive communication. Promotion consists of advertising, personal selling, sales promotion, and publicity combined into an effective promotion strategy. Effective promotion is based upon a sound understanding of the communication process and the persuasive process. Communication is concerned with sending messages. These initiate processes within a person which create motivation, in turn leading to a particular desired course of action. The sequence through which persons move in response to communication, from awareness to commitment, is known as "the hierarchy of effects." The promotional quadrangle suggests that effective promotion is carefully related to such factors as the product, the potential buyers, the seller, and the distribution strategy.

Advertising is the promotional method that often comes to mind when we think of marketing. Advertising expenditures are a significant cost to the marketing firm, and to the ultimate consumer, whose purchase price for the product must cover all costs. Advertising consists of two major types: (1) direct action advertising, and (2) institutional advertising. Effective advertising, whatever the kind, must be based upon carefully defined objectives and related to specific target markets. A knowledge of the characteristics of advertising media is also essential in the planning and implementation of the advertising program. Advertising agencies specialize in performing a wide range of services for their clients on a commission or fee basis.

There is, of late, an increasing public sensitivity to advertising that has led to such developments as affirmative disclosure, corrective advertising, and substantiation. The real problem with advertising, however, is the difficulty with which its effectiveness is measured and evaluated. Marketing research is increasingly being used to study customer reactions to advertising and to relate advertising more closely to customer needs.

Review Questions

1. What is meant by promotion? Define the term literally.
2. Define the following: advertising, selling, publicity, and sales promotion.
3. What are the principal components of a communication system?
4. How does promotion relate to persuasive communication?
5. What is the purpose of advertising? Does it fulfill its purpose?
6. What is meant by the term "promotion strategy"? What are some of the elements in the firm's promotion strategy?
7. Discuss the two major kinds of advertising. Is it always easy to distinguish between them? Why?
8. Why does the advertising manager need to know a great deal about the characteristics of the various advertising media?
9. Criticism of advertising by both economic and social critics has led to these developments: corrective advertising, affirmative disclosure, and substantiation. Discuss each of these developments and assess its impact on current advertising practice.
10. How might increased use of marketing research improve advertising effectiveness?

Case 13-1

Knudsen's Frozen Yogurt

Knudsen's Frozen Yogurt is a new, relatively low-calorie snack food and dessert. It combines to a degree the high-protein and low-calorie attributes of yogurt with the pleasing, sensuous, and appetizing qualities of ice cream or sherbet. Knudsen's Frozen Yogurt is sold two ways: in "push ups," which are advertised as fun to eat and which appeal to younger persons and are convenient for picnics and other outings; and in sundae cups, which lend themselves to slightly more formal consumption at the dinner table or for TV snacks.

The push ups sell for 99 cents for a box of six and the sundae cups sell for 39 cents and 69 cents, respectively, in packages of either two or four.

The ingredients for frozen yogurt are milk and nonfat milk solids, sucrose, corn syrup, fruit, citric acid, natural flavor, artificial flavor, modified starch, gelatin, cellulose gum, peptin, vegetable mono and diglycerides, polysorbate 80, artificial color, sodium benzoate and potassium sorbate to preserve fruit. Frozen yogurt is sold in strawberry, raspberry, orange, and pineapple flavors.

Since its introduction, the product has had considerable market success, but studies have shown that only a very small percentage of the total population or potential market has tried the product. The company advertises in several magazines, has had a limited amount of exposure on national television, but has concentrated its basic media strategy around newspapers. To accelerate the trial and adoption process, many of the advertisements have featured an introductory cents-off coupon.

In order to get "a better fix" on the company's product and customer reaction to it, a limited marketing research study was launched in a medium-size Midwestern city. Consumers were generally favorable to the product but there were

some negative reactions. A sample of consumer responses follows:

"It's a really good tasting product. But I thought the packaging was terrible. The cylinder was very hard to push down for the yogurt when it's firmly frozen. The plastic base has nothing to keep the yogurt on it. So it's really sort of tricky balancing it. But if they improve the packaging, they should have a really good seller there. It is a very good tasting product."

A homemaker commented: "Strawberry push ups are like a popsicle treat for children. I tried them on all the children that came to our home the last few days and the percentage of like and dislike was about 50 percent each way. I think I'll stick to popsicles as all our children like them."

Virginia Combs, an administrative assistant at a small college, commented: "I really haven't any idea how these taste because they didn't get past our grandchildren, who loved them. Our 9-year-old granddaughter gave us her verdict, "They taste just like real orange, only maybe a little more tart." Since they took the rest of the package home with them, I think we can safely assume they are a real hit with children."

Finally, Roger O'Neil, a music store manager, stated: "Believe me, I'm not one for yogurt! When I was asked to try this new dessert I thought I'd probably have to force it down, but after the first taste, I thought it was just great. I had the raspberry flavored push ups and I thoroughly enjoyed every bite. I'm anxious to try some of the other flavors. The nice thing about the dessert is that it can be eaten anywhere—at home, on the street, in the car, and so on, and

there aren't any dirty dishes to clean. Then, too, it's reasonably priced and, of course, it's a low-fat dessert! I like it and recommend it."

As part of the company's evaluation of its total marketing program, the managers are somewhat concerned as to what changes, if any, to make in their advertising program and media strategy.

Questions

1. What changes would you recommend in the advertising and media strategy for promoting Knudsen's Frozen Yogurt?
2. What appeals do you believe would be most effective for promoting the product?
3. In order to spread its limited advertising budget, Knudsen has considered using more cooperative advertising. Do you believe this would be advisable? Why? What are the features and advantages of cooperative advertising?
4. How might Knudsen utilize the results of market tests and consumer studies to improve not only its product but its advertising and promotion?

Case 13-2

Borden, Inc.— Measuring Advertising Effectiveness

A day of reckoning arrives each year for the six advertising agencies who work for Borden, Inc. One by one, the executives who run the agencies will parade through the main conference room in Borden's New York offices and field questions from Borden Chairman Augustine R. Marusi, President Eugene J. Sullivan, and other key company executives.

The questions by these top managers are tough and critical. If this or that ad campaign failed to

boost a product's market share by three or four percentage points, why? Was the ad theme wrong? Was the media selection wrong? Maybe it was the product. Was the price too high? Was the distribution too limited? The exchange between Borden executives and agency heads and account executives often gets peppery and both sides are intensely vocal. Yet, the idea is to nail down the answer to the question that haunts every advertiser, big and small: How do you measure the effectiveness of advertising?

Many companies, Procter and Gamble, General Foods, and other large packaged consumer goods companies have long monitored market share and correlated their advertising expenditures with market position. Yet Borden is perhaps the only major company to have set up a formal working relationship which makes the agency answerable for every dollar of ad spending and the achievement of specific market share objectives. On the final scorecard, any of Borden's six agencies that finishes in sixth place two years in a row stands a good chance of losing its Borden business. "We want growth," says Marusi, "and the agencies that surpass their objectives will be rewarded."

Borden's growth, even before the new advertising accountability program was initiated, has been impressive. Since 1967, the year Marusi became chief executive, sales have jumped from $1.6 billion to $4.3 billion in 1979 while earnings went from $55.3 million to $134.9 million. During this period, nondairy foods became the dominant volume producer for Borden, growing from 27 percent of sales in 1967 to 34 percent today. Now Borden's dairy products—long its main business—account for 20 percent of sales as opposed to 40 percent in 1967, while chemical operations are now 22 percent versus 19 percent in 1967.

Borden has produced, from all three of its businesses, a stable of strong brands that it plans to push with increased advertising expenditures. Their biggest selling brand names include: Elmer's Glue-All, Krylon paints, Cracker Jack carmelized popcorn, Wise Potato Chips, Wyler's powdered drink mixes, Bama jams and jellies, plus, of course, Borden's milk, ice cream, cheese, and other dairy products. From $66 million, or 2.6 percent of sales, in 1974, Borden raised its ad spending to an estimated $130 million, or 3.8 percent of sales, in 1978. This compares with 2.5 percent to 3 percent per year by such firms as General Mills, General Foods, and Kraftco.

Before Marusi stepped into Borden's top job in 1967, according to industry observers and

Goodbye, super-strong glues that are a pain to open, messy to use, and clog up.

Hello, Elmer's Wonder Bond Plus.

Sure, super-strong glues are great for bonding glass, metal, plastic and china. But most super-strong glue *packages* are as likely to put their glues on you as they are on the object you're gluing. That is, if you can get them open. And keep them unclogged.

New Elmer's' Wonder Bond Plus™ cyanoacrylate adhesive has the perfect solution to this sticky problem. It's a super-strong, fast-setting glue that's easy to open, easy to use and easy to keep clog-free. Here's how easy:

1. Twist and lift and the cap is off. 2. Twist the special plug on the applicator tip and the seal is broken (no pins!) so you're ready to glue. 3. Squeeze gently and the tip puts one drop of super-strong glue (bonds up to 5,000 lbs. per square inch tensile strength) right where you want it – even on the head of a pin! No mixing. No clamping. No problem. 4. Invert the special plug and snap it back on the tip to help keep your Wonder Bond Plus clog-free for the next use.

Look for Elmer's Wonder Bond Plus. And say hello to super-strong glue in a super-sensible package.

ELMER'S Wonder Bond Plus. Stick with a name you can trust.

company insiders, the company was dangerously short of measurements in general. Because of Borden's highly decentralized structure, there were almost no basic management and financial controls, very little coordination among divisions, and almost no earnings growth. As a part of Marusi's new management accountability approach, in 1976 the company cut its number of ad agencies from twenty-seven to the current six. "We had to get the number small enough so that our individual billings to each agency would make us a major client," said Treasurer Joseph E. Madigan. "That's the only way we could command the time of their top executives."

At Grey Advertising which handles Cracker Jack, this year's advertising goal is to increase Cracker Jack's market share from roughly 59 percent to 63 percent. Last year Borden spent $1.7 million on Cracker Jack advertising. To get another four percentage points of market share,

Borden and Grey figured the cost at $200,000 more in advertising.

"If a product has less than a 15 percent market share," says Borden executives, "it can rarely be profitable—at least for a company like ours. If it has more than 30 percent to 35 percent of the market, it is usually profitable."

Chairman Marusi sums up their new approach to advertising effectiveness with these comments, "The whole new thrust of our program," he says, "is to put a price on market share and then spend what it takes to get there."

Questions

1. What advantages and disadvantages do you see in Borden's approach to measuring its advertising effectiveness?
2. What other reasons for advertising might Borden have which would not be explicitly reflected in a concept such as market share?
3. What do you believe Chairman Marusi meant by his comment, "The whole new thrust of our program is to put a price on market share and then spend what it takes to get there?"

Chapter 14

Promotion: Personal Selling, Sales Promotion and Public Relations

When CR Industries (Chicago Rawhide Manufacturing Company) of Elgin, Illinois, a company that manufactures seals* for oil and hydraulic installations, developed a revolutionary design for the sealing element of oil and grease seals, top management began a full-scale production program. At the same time, the company's marketing group was asked to start a marketing and promotional campaign that would introduce the new line to distributors and their industrial customers.

The new product was called Waveseal. Outwardly it looked like most other seals. Even experienced technicians had to look very closely to see the difference. The primary user benefit of the new design was longer service life. Tests had confirmed a minimum life for Waveseal 30 percent longer than any other mechanical seal available. This feature became the keystone of the product's promotion—the unique selling proposition chosen to ensure market penetration and to attract customers for CR's new product. The company decided that it would guarantee a 30 percent longer life for Waveseal, and if the device fell short of the guarantee, CR Industries would replace it with any other seal the user chose. The introduction of this new product was considered to be the company's most significant development opportunity in ninety-seven years.

As strategic planning began, it became obvious that there were three major interrelated promotion tasks:

First, a communications program to introduce and support the new line had to be created. This effort would be targeted primarily to industrial users.

Second, distributor enthusiasm had to be generated.

Third, the company wanted to capitalize fully on this opportunity and establish a new company identity more consistent with its position, technology, and future plans.

To accomplish these results, CR Industries hired an advertising agency, Brand Advertising of Chicago. The agency people suggested that the central theme of the advertising program should be the longer life of its new seal.

The agency developed a comprehensive selling package, including a sales kit, mailers, and a slide and tape presentation, for the distributors. It was vital that the distributors be "sold" because they formed the critical links between CR Industries and the new product's ultimate users. The seventeen-piece distributor sales kit that was developed contained technical literature on Waveseal, detailed information on the guarantee, decals, ad reprints, catalog data, and merchandising aids. Distributors also received a series of direct mail pieces to use in promoting the new seal to their users and prospects. The mailers were designed around the theme, "Sometimes it pays to take a closer look." Each mailer contained a visual puzzle that required reader participation to solve—readers had to take a closer look.

A slide and tape presentation detailing the Waveseal properties and features completed the selling package. This was to be used at sales meetings with distributors, as well as at in-plant distributor presentations.

*Seals are gaskets made from various materials—leather, cork, rubber, and synthetic fibers—which hold in the oil and other lubricants used in hydraulic equipment.

The advertising campaign was kicked off through highly selective media geared especially to users of Waveseal-type products. Circulation of all the magazines used was carefully analyzed as to key industrial buying groups such as purchasing, production, design, and maintenance. The group of magazines that met the advertising objectives and audience requirements at the lowest cost per thousand (cpm) received the advertising account.

The product was designed, produced, and marketed to fill a specific industrial need. The promotion program that supported the whole project was as carefully designed and executed as the product itself.

The Moral.   The Waveseal example underscores a marketing axiom: namely, that all the firm's business functions must be coordinated efficiently to ensure proper performance and success. From that foundation, with a good product, and a good marketing strategy that includes an adequate promotion budget and a diverse promotional approach, merchandising excitement can be infused throughout every level of a marketing channel.

Remember the Promotional Blend

Waveseal's approach to communication and promotion as part of its marketing strategy demonstrates that integrated marketing strategy requires a blend or mix in which all the promotional elements are used effectively, with each one assigned adequate weight in the total effort.[1] The **promotion blend** combines advertising, **personal selling, sales promotion**, and **public relations**, all working harmoniously to reach the target audiences essential to the success of the firm's products. Promotion, as we said in the previous chapter, is the coordination of all seller-initiated efforts to establish channels or flows of information and persuasion to facilitate the sale of a good or service, or the acceptance of ideas, companies, or products.

As shown in Figure 14-1, advertising is usually considered a more important promotional activity for consumer goods, especially convenience and shop-

Figure 14-1   The relative importance of advertising and personal selling for consumer and industrial products.

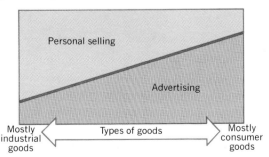

[1] See Stanley F. Stasch and Patricia Lanktree, "Can Your Marketing Planning Procedures Be Improved?" *Journal of Marketing* **44**, no. 3 (Summer 1980), pp. 79–90.

ping items, than it is for industrial products, where personal selling predominates. Sales promotion and public relations are of about equal weight in both consumer oriented and industrial oriented markets.

Advertising and personal selling each has its unique merits in every marketing program. The compelling argument for using personal selling is its effectiveness. Good personal selling delivers an individual sales message specially tailored to each prospective buyer, making the communication effort complete and persuasive. Advertising, however, given its indirect and impersonal approach, is less effective but more efficient. That is, it is efficient in that it reaches more potential buyers at a lower cost per prospect than does personal selling. Figure 14-2 shows the relative advantages of direct promotional efforts (personal selling) and indirect promotional efforts (advertising, sales promotion, and public relations) as measured in terms of effectiveness and efficiency.[2]

"Push" and "Pull" Strategies.   The exact blend of the promotional mix will depend on a number of factors: the stage of the product's life cycle, the nature of the product itself, the size of the promotion budget, and management's preferences among the various kinds of promotional activities. Some markets appear to lend themselves more readily to "push" strategies whereby personal selling is the dominant force. Others are more easily tapped by promotional efforts keyed to "pull" strategies, which emphasize mass communication in order to create strong consumer demand. This, in turn, will be expressed to resellers so that they, in turn, will stock the goods. Merchandise of low unit value with mass market appeal usually lends itself best to pull type strategies. Most companies, of course, use both push and pull strategies, but the nature of their markets and customers often suggests emphasizing one over the other.

Figure 14-2 The relative merits of alternative promotional mix activities.

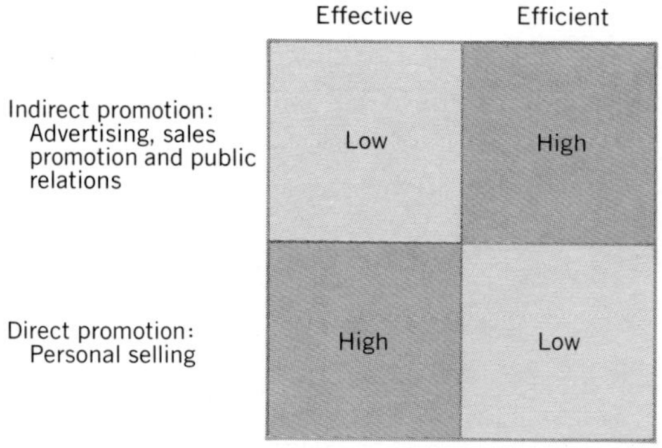

	Effective	Efficient
Indirect promotion: Advertising, sales promotion and public relations	Low	High
Direct promotion: Personal selling	High	Low

[2] For an extended view see Robert M. Prentice, "How to Split Your Marketing Funds Between Advertising and Promotion," *Advertising Age*, January 10, 1977, pp. 41–43.

Planning the Promotional Campaign

**VISIT
CON EDISON'S
CONSERVATION
CENTER**

an exciting exhibit
of energy-saving,
money-saving ideas.

Located at the corner of 42nd Street
and Lexington Avenue in the
Chrysler Building in mid-Manhattan.
Open Mondays through Saturdays.
No admission charge.

 conserve energy

Most promotional programs are organized and coordinated on a campaign basis. The campaign concept consists of a series of multiple activities carried out aggressively over a period of time. Campaigns sometimes last for only a few weeks but others may stretch over several years. For example, in the early 1970s, the utility companies' campaigns promoted using more gas and electricity and encouraged consumers to buy more energy-using appliances. For the past few years, however, the utility companies' campaigns have been stressing energy conservation, the value of home insulation, and more energy-efficient appliances. Most successful promotional campaigns are centered around some unifying theme and, of course, the promotional campaign is always considered an integral part of the overall marketing strategy.

Planning the promotional campaign should begin early and a realistic budget should be developed.[3] The first order of business is to do some market research to get an idea of customer attitudes, use behavior, brand loyalty, and consumption (or purchase) patterns. These factors will all have a bearing on marketing strategy, pricing, competitive position, distribution methods, outstanding product features and the promotional themes they suggest, media to employ, and, of course, promotional blend.

At this point, a blueprint or checklist of the promotional activities, their coordination, and timing should be developed. In a well-organized promotional campaign, material is available when it is required and all bases are covered. Good planning also is important in keeping promotional costs in line with budgeted figures.

Some Basic Questions in Promotion. Planning a successful promotional campaign usually involves a reliance on certain readily identifiable qualities. To assess whether the promotional campaign is based upon these qualities, promotion managers can ask themselves these critical questions:

1. *Is there a big idea, or unique selling proposition?* A genuine selling idea is basic and it must emerge clearly, emphatically, and single-mindedly. It should be an important idea such as Scope's "medicine breath," the positioning of Pledge furniture polish as a dusting aid, McDonald's "You deserve a break today," or AMF's "We make weekends."
2. *Can the big idea be converted into a promotional theme?* Provocative themes like "Thank you, Paine Webber," "Please don't squeeze the Charmin," "Try it, you'll like it," and "I can't believe I ate the whole thing" make it easy for the customer to remember your selling message.
3. *Is the promotion relevant?* If your promotion is remembered, but your

---

[3] For a comprehensive treatment of planning promotion, see L.C. Hooper, "How Advertising and Sales Promotion Can Make or Break Your New Product," *Industrial Marketing*, September 1976, pp. 133–139.

product isn't, you have missed the objective of promotion. Look for and project relevance in every promotional execution.

4. *Is it worn out?* Some promotional ideas get "tired blood." Effective promotion is fresh, innovative, original—not a carbon copy of somebody else's advertising. Such efforts are often costly failures that do little, if anything, to build strong consumer demand.

5. *Can the unique selling proposition (USP) be demonstrated?* Nothing works harder or sells better than a lively demonstration of a product's superiority. Promotion, if it doesn't demonstrate, should at least show the product in use, and sometimes provide customers with a free sample to allow them to test the product for themselves.

6. *Is the promotion believable?* There is much "promise" in promotion; but good promotion does not overpromise. In promotion, it is probably better to underpromise and be believable than to overpromise and lose credibility.

Truly good promotion is not made by rules nor created by a series of steps or guidelines. It is the product of creative imagination plus the skillful blend of advertising, personal selling, sales promotion, and public relations, all of which are market oriented and projected with a unique selling theme.

In the following pages, we shall explore more fully the roles of personal selling, sales promotion, and public relations in the overall promotional strategy, and we shall learn how each of these methods contributes to the attainment of the firm's promotional objectives.

Personal Selling

Personal selling is the most important of all promotional activities in magnitude of expenditures. According to industry figures, approximately $125 billion was spent in 1980 for personal selling, which absorbs about 13 cents of each dollar spent for goods in the United States. As many as 10 percent of the nation's entire labor force are engaged in this pursuit. Hard-headed logic suggests that so much would not be spent, nor would so many people be devoting themselves to personal selling if it didn't work. It does. Personal selling is an effective, results producing, promotional activity.

Personal Selling Isn't Dead, But It's Different

Personal selling as a tool for marketing goods, services and ideas, is not obsolete. However, it is often a different method of selling than it was twenty years ago. The use of personal selling as a promotional tool has changed. So, too, have personal selling appeals and approaches. Many of these changes stem from our clearer understanding of the personal selling function and buyer behavior.

In general, personal selling is considered vital when the product's size or cost make it important, when the buyer is likely to be very uncertain about what he or she needs or wants, and in all cases in which specialized requirements need to be filled. Advertising may be exceedingly effective in encouraging the buyer's initial interest in new products and services, but it often takes personal selling to convince the customer of the product's merit as against other alternatives.

The Status of Selling.   Would you like to be a salesperson? Surprisingly, in spite of the fact that so many people are already employed directly in some form of selling activity, many people—especially those of college age—quite frequently say NO! when asked if they would like to be in sales work. Why is that? Largely, it's because most of us have a distorted image of what selling is. Too often we confuse low-level with **high-level selling**. **Low-level selling** is hardly selling at all. It consists of performing sales related duties for customers who have already made up their minds to buy and who know, at least approximately, what they want. Low-level selling characterizes much of retail selling and the work of route salespeople who are basically delivery people. By contrast, high-level or creative selling involves arousing demand for new products, new brands, or new models of products, or influencing buyers to change patronage from one source of supply to another. Creative selling takes more persuasive initiative on the part of the salesperson.

There is a wide range of selling jobs in marketing, from the lowest level order taker to the highest level creative salesperson. Table 14-1 shows the range, from creative to maintenance, of various selling positions and describes the responsibilities of each.

In the everyday course of affairs, most of us encounter many low-level salespeople, but few high-level creative ones. We tend to generalize about selling and sales career possibilities from our limited experience. This view, an unwarranted holdover from the past, is a major reason for the low prestige of personal selling as an occupation.[4]

In many parts of the world, at nearly all levels, selling still implies pushing unwanted goods on unwilling buyers. For many years, this philosophy prevailed in the United States, too. By and large, however, such high-pressure, salesperson oriented selling has gradually been giving way to a newer kind of selling situation, one that is oriented toward the customer. This type of selling is based upon insights gleaned from social-psychological-economic lines of research into buyer motivation and behavior.

From Salesperson Oriented to Buyer Oriented Selling.   Successful selling today has come to be essentially "customer oriented." Sales authorities refer to this change as developing the "you" (as opposed to the "I") attitude. Personal selling is simply an extension of the marketing concept, the firm's total effort to help the consumer to solve problems. Salespeople today are *problem solvers*. Selling, as problem solving, assumes that purchases are made to satisfy needs and wants. Consequently, to make a sale the salesperson must discover the customer's need and demonstrate how the firm's products or services will best fill the need.

[4] John L. Mason, "The Low Prestige of Personal Selling," *Journal of Marketing* **29** (October 1965), pp. 7–10.

Table 14-1 The Creative-Maintenance Range of Personal Selling Situations

Emphasis	Work Environment	Responsibilities
Delivery	Field (outside)	Predominantly delivering products (e.g., milk, bread, and fuel oil); obviously, good service and a pleasant manner will enhance customer acceptance and lead to more sales, but origination of new business is rare.
Order taking:		
1. Inside	Behind the counter (inside)	Services customers, most of whom have already decided to buy; the salesperson may use suggestion selling to upgrade customer's purchase, but opportunities to go beyond that are limited.
2. Outside	Field	Takes orders from customers in the field (e.g., buyers of soaps and spices for a supermarket); this salesperson may actually be discouraged from applying the "hard sell," and has little opportunity for creative selling.
Emissary of goodwill and/or educator	Field	Order taking is not expected or permitted; rather, the salesperson is required to build goodwill and/or educate the actual or potential user (e.g., the distiller's "missionary" and the medical "detailer" representing an ethical pharmaceutical house).
Educator	Field	Emphasis is placed on technical knowledge that the salesperson communicates to counterparts at client companies as a consultant.
Creative sales:		
1. Tangibles	Field or behind the counter	A two-part function that involves (1) creating dissatisfaction for the customer with the present appliance or situation and (2) beginning to sell the product (e.g., refrigerators, siding, vacuum cleaners, and encyclopedias).
2. Intangibles	Field or behind the counter	Similar to selling techniques with tangibles, but more difficult as product or service is less readily demonstrated and dramatized (e.g., insurance, advertising services, and education).

Source: Adapted from Robert N. McMurry, "The Mystique of Super-Salesmanship," *Harvard Business Review* **39** (March–April 1961), p. 114.

Consider, for example, the case of Joanne Wilson, a saleswoman for the American Tobacco Company. On a typical call Joanne first checks American Tobacco Company products for appearance and location, rearranging the stock, putting it in order, and checking the quantities of the various items on hand. She also checks the store's order book to make sure that adequate stocks have been ordered from a distributor or the store's warehouse. She then attempts to increase the order if she thinks inventory levels will be inadequate to meet expected demand. She does this by means of a brief presentation to the store manager in which she details some of the current promotions underway in her company. Sometimes, when calling on smaller accounts, she may sell small quantities of products from stocks she maintains in her company car, receiving cash payment for them. Joanne makes a point of knowing on a first-name basis the managers of the nearly 250 stores on which she makes regular calls. She is seen by most of the store managers as a friendly, helpful person who aids them in their merchandising task and who often places their needs above her personal goals of simply selling more goods.

The Many Roles of the Personal Salesperson.   Personal salespeople have many roles to play in fulfilling their widening responsibilities. Traditionally, salespeople were thought of as having three tasks: (1) getting orders from existing customers, (2) getting new business, and (3) undertaking supporting activities. Today's salespeople are looked upon as account managers who have taken on a lot of duties other than just simply writing orders. Such salespeople become the company's broader marketing representatives.[5] Procter and Gamble salespeople, for example, keep abreast of industry developments and report these to their clients. They also monitor their customers' competition and attempt to learn what promotions are working so that similar efforts can be attempted in their clients' stores. The P&G salesperson advises customers on how to merchandise P&G products and shows them how a change in merchandising will increase store profits.

The increasing importance of personal selling, combined with the need to lower costs and raise selling efficiency, are causing more and more companies to reexamine the ways that they recruit, train, pay, and equip their salespeople. Some are experimenting with new compensation and incentive programs. Almost all companies today are carefully analyzing the selling process and working to integrate it better into their overall marketing effort.[6]

Understanding the Selling Process

Selling at all levels is a tough and demanding job, but the rewards for those who are successful and well suited to the occupation are substantial. It should be no surprise that many individuals show a distinct lack of interest in selling occupations. As a matter of fact, one study showed that lack of *initiative* is the chief cause of sales failures.[7]

The same study reported that *poor planning* and *lack of knowledge* are the second and third major reasons why people fail at selling occupations. Lack of native ability is not listed as a major cause of failure in selling, suggesting that proper planning and a thorough understanding of the selling process could lead to greater selling success.

---

[5] "The New Super Salesman: Wired for Success," *Business Week*, January 6, 1973, pp. 45–49.
[6] See Dan H. Robertson, "Sales Force Feedback on Competitor's Activities," *Journal of Marketing* **38**, no. 2 (April 1974), pp. 69–71.
[7] Charles Atkinson Kirkpatrick, *Salesmanship*, 5th ed. (Cincinnati: South-Western Publishing Company, 1971), p. 131.

The Steps in the Selling Process

A series of five activities normally make up most selling situations. These are (1) preparing and anticipating the sales situation; (2) the approach; (3) the presentation; (4) closing the sale; and (5) the follow-up.

Step One: Getting Ready—Anticipating the Sales Situation. Anticipating the sale means getting ready, finding out who your customers are, what their needs are, and how you plan to solve the customer's problem. When the customer spends money on your products, you want that customer to feel that it is a better investment than if the money were spent somewhere else. Salespeople often must go *prospecting*, that is, they must ferret out customers, and then when they are found, determine whether they should be pursued and approached further with a selling proposition.

Step Two: The Approach. Consider for a moment the dilemma of the buyer in Figure 14-3. He is a busy person. There are many demands on his time. Every salesperson the buyer agrees to see will have something to sell, some message to leave, or some commitment to secure. How will the salesperson penetrate the natural defense mechanisms of the buyer—the desire to use his time efficiently, to avoid harassment by an overzealous salesperson, to meet

Figure 14-3   The salesperson meets the buyer.

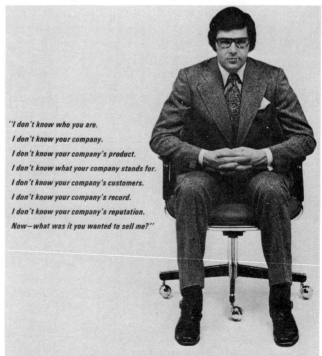

"*I don't know who you are.*
I don't know your company.
I don't know your company's product.
I don't know what your company stands for.
I don't know your company's customers.
I don't know your company's record.
I don't know your company's reputation.
Now—what was it you wanted to sell me?"

MORAL: Sales start **before** your salesman calls—with business publication advertising.

with other salespeople with whom he has already developed a long-range partnership? Part of the answer will come from the work done in Step 1. A good salesperson will know whether the buyer's company is having difficulty meeting quality performance standards or delivery schedules, and may use this knowledge as an opener. He might show the buyer how his company's new packaging machinery boosts the quality of the product and actually speeds up production and delivery schedules. Or the salesperson might approach the encounter by telling the buyer of his company's recent success. Something like, "Last year our sales increased 25 percent and our return on investment was up 15 percent. We think this reflects a growing recognition of our firm's ability to help solve problems for companies like your own."

A positive, businesslike, no-nonsense approach which is problem oriented will usually get the salesperson an audience with a buyer. The salesperson's physical attractiveness, grooming, and credibility are the primary influences during the approach to the prospect.

Step Three: The Presentation.   The presentation is the salesperson's opportunity to tell the company's story, to project its image, and to relate its products or services to the buyer's needs.

Effective presentations usually point out product characteristics, including the advantages and disadvantages of the product, and should provide examples of other customers' reactions and satisfactions with the product. Good presentations convince the prospect of a product's performance or of the dependability of the company's word to deliver. At opportunities to "show and tell," presentations should be clear, concise, to the point, and positive. A good salesperson learns from every encounter. Whether the sale is made or lost, the experience is an important form of feedback to be evaluated and the mode of presentation perhaps changed for subsequent selling situations. The presentation, of course, is always an outgrowth of the planning that preceded it. Proper planning means greater selling flexibility, better and more effective presentations, and better situation management overall.

Step Four: Closing the Sale.   Convincing the prospect and closing the sale is often just a matter of meeting the customer's objections.[8] An objection is a statement of uncertainty, but by meeting it squarely and answering it, a salesperson can reduce the buyer's uncertainty and make an order more likely. The salesperson's task in closing the sale is to meet the prospect's objections, reduce the uncertainty surrounding the purchase, and convince the buyer that a commitment will lower rather than increase the purchase risk. One last point: good sales presentations never last forever. There is a critical point during each presentation when the salesperson should ask for the order.

---

[8] See Charles W. Gross and Robin T. Petersen, "A Study of the Appropriateness of Various Means of Meeting Objections by Sales Representatives," *Journal of the Academy of Marketing Science* **8**, no. 1,2 (Winter–Spring 1980), pp. 92–99.

Step Five: The Follow-Up. The follow-up should be a part of every sales situation where there is an expectation of continuing or repeat business. In this step, the salesperson discovers whether everything that was promised was actually delivered, and has a chance to resell the customer in case any dissonance has arisen. The follow-up is a powerful reinforcement to the buyer and can lead to a satisfying long-term relationship. It also gives the salesperson an opportunity to learn of the customer's reaction to the purchase, information that may be useful in selling the product or service to another prospect. Finally, the follow-up can lead to increased sales by suggesting complementary products or accessories to accompany the original purchase.

Before proceeding, can you answer these questions:
1. What is meant by the promotion blend?
2. From a selling point of view describe situation management.
3. Of the steps in the selling process, why is preparing and anticipating the sale likely to be the most important?

Managing the Personal Selling Effort

Managing the personal selling effort consists essentially of recruiting, selecting, training, and maintaining an effective selling force, and coordinating their efforts with the overall marketing program of the firm. The discussion that follows focuses upon the principal tasks of **sales management** relating to the personal selling effort, namely, (1) recruiting, selecting, and training; (2) staffing the personal selling effort; and (3) controlling the selling function.

Recruiting and Selecting Sales Personnel. The nature of the selling situation will affect the firm's efforts in recruiting, selecting, and training its sales staff. Recruiting and hiring sales personnel is hampered somewhat by the low status of some selling jobs. Another problem also exists—how to recognize who has the aptitude to become a successful salesperson, given the nature and level of the sales position. Up to this point companies have not had much success with this effort. It may be well to consider in rather general terms the major conclusions that some social scientists have reached about the social and psychological characteristics of sales personnel.

1. There is no significant relationship between intelligence test scores and sales success.
2. No significant relationship has been found between independent measures of personality traits and sales success.
3. No correlation exists between age and sales success.
4. There is no apparent connection between measurable character traits and sales success.
5. There is no significant correlation between level of education and sales success.

6. Salespersons are more likely to succeed when chosen with regard to the kinds of customers with whom they will deal.[9]

Salespeople are made—they are trained and shaped to become successful at selling. They are not born to the calling. However, they do differ from nonsalespeople in that they:

1. Are persuasive rather than critical
2. Are intuitive rather than analytical
3. Have a higher average energy level
4. Have more drive or desire for status achievement, power, and prestige[10]

Most companies are discovering that it is vital to get more out of the sales dollar. For example, a company may spend $10,000 to $30,000 to train a salesperson and $35,000 to $45,000 to keep that person selling in the field. That averages out to $68.00 per sales call, which is about triple the figure of a decade ago. Obviously, recruiting and selecting the right person for the sales position are critical. The demand for salespeople will likely grow by 250,000 jobs a year over the next ten years and this increasing demand will magnify the difficulty of recruiting and training effective salespeople.

Training Salespeople. Because selling effectiveness often translates into marketing effectiveness, more and more firms are stressing sales training at nearly all levels. A growing number of companies, for good reason, offer continuing instruction for their sales staffs. Armour-Dial, Inc., a consumer goods division of the Greyhound Corporation, ran a study on salespeople who had attended a recent sales meeting at its Aurora, Illinois, sales training center. The results were staggering: a big 12 percent boost in the number of calls per day, 25 percent more new-product retail displays, a 100 percent increase in case sales, 62 percent more displays sold, and a 25 percent rise in sales to direct-buying, or chain, accounts.[11]

Training programs are becoming much more common, even in retail selling, which characteristically has lagged behind other fields. The principal methods used in sales training are shown in Table 14-2.

Several issues arise in setting up training programs and deciding upon the proper mix of sales training approaches.[12] Successful training programs generally have well-formulated, specific training goals, and objectives. Appropriate training devices are then geared to each of the goals and objectives sought. In addition, most effective sales training programs are conducted by special training personnel, rather than just sales managers or other salespeople. Finally, to maximize the program's effectiveness the results are monitored. Stu-

[9] Samuel N. Stevens, "The Application of Social Science Findings to Selling and the Salesman," *Aspects of Modern Marketing*, AMA Reports, No. 15 (New York: American Management Association, 1968), pp. 85–94.
[10] Stevens, "Social Science Findings and the Salesman," p. 88.
[11] "New Super Salesman," p. 49.
[12] Charles S. Goodman, *Management of the Personal Selling Function* (New York: Holt Rinehart and Winston, 1971), pp. 201–203.

Table 14-2 Training Methods for Salespeople

Learning Area	Structured Presentation*	Role Playing	Cases	Games	Conferences	Structured Experience†	Coaching on-Job	Demonstrator-Observer
Knowledge								
Products	✓							
Economic bases	✓		✓		✓			
Customer problems	✓	✓	✓		✓			
Customer rationale	✓	✓	✓		✓			
Markets	✓		✓					
Augmentation of market knowledge	✓	✓	✓		✓			
Sales policies	✓		✓					
History	✓							
Support activities	✓							
Selling methods	✓	✓	✓		✓			
Procedures	✓							
Skills								
Intercommunicative		✓		✓	✓			
Selling methods		✓	✓	✓			✓	✓
Intelligence		✓	✓	✓		✓	✓	✓
Work habits							✓	✓

*Includes lectures, audio and/or visual presentations, manuals, workbooks, and programmed instruction.
†Includes job rotation and other specific training assignments under direction of, but not necessarily in the presence of, a trainer.

Source: From *Management of the Personal Selling Function* by Charles S. Goodman, Copyright © 1971 by Holt, Rinehart and Winston, Inc. Reprinted by permission of Holt, Rinehart and Winston, Inc.

dents' performance is evaluated and measured against their skill before the training or against skills gained from alternative training measures.

Determining Sales Force Size.   Determining the size of the sales force is one of the most important aspects of managing the personal selling effort. Sales force size, or staffing, is concerned with the problem of balancing the number of salespeople needed to service explicit customer demand at a desired level of service against the firm's expense and profit constraints. Having too many salespeople means inefficient performance and too high a wage rate as a percentage of sales. When salespeople are employed and paid by commission, having more than are needed may mean low average earnings resulting in employee dissatisfaction and excessive turnover. However, with too few salespeople customer service will be limited, and sales and buyer patronage lost.

For field selling, a number of staffing methods are employed. One is called the "Equalized Work Load Method."[13] To determine sales force size with this

[13] The analyses for such decisions are increasingly being made by computer. For a more extended treatment, see Porter Henry, "Manage Your Sales Force as a System." *Harvard Business Review* **53** (March-April 1975), p. 75.

method, the sales manager must (1) multiply the number of customers in each class of buyers by the number of calls required annually to service customers in these classes effectively; (2) add the results for each class; and (3) divide this sum by the number of calls made annually by each salesperson. Here is how the method works. Assume that the company has two classes of buyers: 600 Class A customers, who require 20 sales calls annually, and 1,800 Class B customers, who require 10 sales calls annually. Also assume that the firm's average salesperson makes 500 calls annually. Then, given this data, the sales force size should be:

$$\frac{600(20) + 1800(10)}{500} = 60$$

Several problems are normally encountered when using such an approach. First of all, because it is only a formula approach, it should be used with flexibility and caution. It is difficult to estimate how many calls are required to service an account because each prospect's needs are different. A salesperson's load is not just a function of the number of sales calls, but it is also related to such factors as the size of the territory, travel time between customers, the amount of time spent with each customer, and the blend of selling and nonselling responsibilities shouldered by the salesperson. This means that sales managers must also guide salespersons in efficiently allocating their time. To this end, time allocation decisions are being increasingly assisted by the use of mathematical models and computer analysis.

In a sales territory or a retail store, it is usual for sales to increase with the number of salespeople. Of course, total selling costs go up as well. This suggests another approach to staffing. That is, management should always continue to increase the sales force as long as the incremental, or additional, sales increases are greater than the incremental selling cost. To use such a method, however, you must be able to estimate accurately how much sales will increase with additional sales personnel. Frequently, historical records may suggest some guidelines; but in the case of new stores or newly developed territories, a great deal of subjective judgment must be employed.

Designing Sales Territories.   The performance of field sales personnel is greatly affected by the design of the selling territory. Management must make several major decisions here relating to such factors as size of the territory, its shape, and the routing and scheduling of sales calls. Figure 14-4 diagrams the sequence of the sales manager's decisions under both short- and long-term conditions.

Whether selling insurance, computers, Boeing 747s, or wholesale cosmetics, today's salesperson has two important advantages: improved transportation and rapid communications. Together these allow the salesperson to cover more territory faster and to be ever present in the market. Both are drastically altering the way territory design and routing and scheduling problems are being managed.

Compensating Sales Personnel.   Historically, sales personnel were compensated in direct proportion to sales results. Consequently, most compensa-

Figure 14-4 A sales manager's territory decisions under short- and long-range conditions.

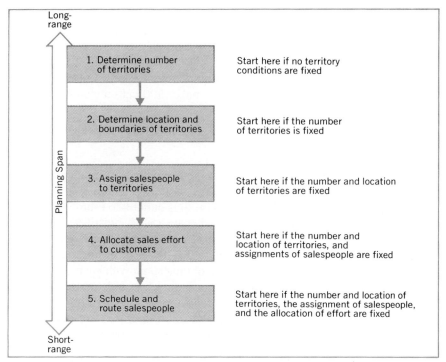

Source: Adapted from Thomas R. Wotruba, *Sales Management: Planning, Accomplishment, and Evaluation*. Copyright 1971 by Holt, Rinehart and Winston, Inc. Reprinted by permission of Holt, Rinehart and Winston, Inc.

tion plans were basically commission plans. Under *commission plans* salespeople are paid a percentage of the price of what they sell. A salesperson working on a 10 percent commission plan and selling $200,000 worth of merchandise a year, would earn $20,000. Some firms have what is called a *commission plus a drawing account plan*. Such plans are designed to eliminate some of the uncertainty from earnings based strictly on commission by allowing the salesperson to draw out some basic figure each week or month against expected commissions. To continue the example, suppose the commission rate of the salesperson mentioned above is 10 percent of sales. That person may also be permitted to "draw" a payment of $1,500 a month. At the end of the year, total commissions on sales are calculated and if $200,000 worth of merchandise was sold, commissions of $20,000 were earned. The monthly draw of $1,500 equals $18,000. Subtracting $18,000 from $20,000, the salesperson has earnings due of $2,000. If, however, sales amounted only to $175,000 what would be the situation then? Most companies would not require the salesperson to return the difference. In other words, the salesperson's draw amounts to $18,000 and commissions were $17,500 (10 percent of $175,000). Since the draw exceeded earnings, the company was the loser. Normally, a salesperson is permitted to draw more than his or her commissions warrant only for a few

Table 14-3 Characteristics of Compensation Methods for Sales Personnel

Compensation Method	Frequency of Use (Percent)*	Especially Useful	Advantages	Disadvantages
Straight salary	20.4	When compensating new salespersons; when firm moves into new sales territories that require developmental work; when salespersons need to perform many nonselling activities	Provides salesperson with maximum amount of security; gives sales manager large amount of control over salespersons; easy to administer; yields more predictable selling expenses	Provides no incentive; necessitates closer supervision of salespersons' activities; during sales declines selling expenses remain at same level
Straight commission	15.5	When highly aggressive selling is required; when nonselling tasks are minimized; when company cannot closely control sales-force activities	Provides maximum amount of incentive; by increasing commission rate, sales managers can encourage salespersons to sell certain items; selling expenses relate directly to sales resources	Salespersons have little financial security; sales manager has minimum control over sales force; may cause salespeople to provide inadequate service to smaller accounts; selling costs less predictable
Combination	64.1	When sales territories have relatively similar sales potentials; when firm wishes to provide incentive but still control sales-force activities	Provides certain level of financial security; provides some incentive; selling expenses fluctuate with sales revenue	Selling expenses less predictable; may be difficult to administer

*The figures in this column are from Jack R. Dauner, "Salesmen's Compensation: Have We Kept Pace?" *Akron Business and Economic Review*, Summer, 1972, pp. 33–34. These data are based on a cross-sectional survey of 375 companies.

Source: William M. Pride and O. C. Ferrell, *Marketing: Basic Concepts and Decisions* (Boston: Houghton Mifflin, 1977), p. 396.

times. If such a practice becomes persistent, the salesperson usually is discharged or decides to look for another job.

Many companies today pay their sales staffs a straight salary, or a salary plus commission, or a bonus over a predetermined sales quota. This plan is preferred by many salespeople and it often works to the advantage of the company. Compensation plans that rely too much on commissions tend to overemphasize the importance of selling, to the neglect of many important nonselling duties of the salesperson. A salary plus a bonus or commission can be matched more appropriately to the nature of the selling job and can be geared to stimulate a range of desired sales activities. Table 14-3 shows the basic kinds of compensation plans used to reward sales personnel, the frequency of their use, and the advantages and disadvantages of each.

Motivating and Controlling the Sales Effort

Compensation is an important means of motivating sales personnel at all levels and in different selling situations. However, too much emphasis on incentive payment plans often strike salespeople as both demeaning and risky. Thus, the extensive rewards of salary, bonuses, and other fringe benefits constitute the main "carrot" approaches in motivating a sales staff to high performance.

Really effective methods of motivating and controlling salespeople must take careful account of the nature of the selling job. Field selling, especially, is not an occupation of constant psychological reinforcement. Some sales are closed, others are not; some prospects are warm and receptive even if they do not buy; others may be cool, haughty, caustic, or even surly. Furthermore, salespeople often travel great distances and work alone, far from family, friends and colleagues. Thus, motivation from without is not enough and it is becoming increasingly necessary for sales managers to focus upon developing special motivating and control procedures for imparting inner rewards and satisfaction.[14] Increasingly, motivation and control efforts, which demand skilled qualities of leadership from sales managers, must be based upon solid feedback information from the salesperson's performance. Better control of the salesperson's performance is being achieved through increased understanding of the true nature of the selling job along with clear-cut standards and measures as to what constitutes good sales performance. In addition, reward systems in keeping with the level of difficulty of the task and each salesperson's general quality of performance are being adopted.

Sales Promotion: When 2 + 2 = 5

In our discussion of promotion, we have thus far talked about advertising and personal selling. Without question, these are the two primary means of presenting ideas, goods, or services to those who can use them. Yet, there are two additional promotional methods that, combined with effective advertising and personal selling programs, really add up to more than the sum of the parts. These methods are *sales promotion* and *public relations*.

Sales promotion is a broad label that is applied to special kinds of sales accelerating activities not necessarily classed as advertising, personal selling, or publicity. Sales promotion is often thought of as a special selling effort.

A Closer Look at Sales Promotion

Sales promotion consists of short-run inducements to buying action. The term is normally used to describe all promotional activities that supplement advertising and personal selling, are conducted for a limited period of time, and

---

[14] For a rundown on these new approaches, see Rom J. Markin and Charles M. Lillis, "Sales Managers Get What They Expect," *Business Horizons,* June 1975, pp. 51–58; and Robert Krietner, "PM—A New Method of Behavior Change," *Business Horizons,* ; December 1975, pp. 79–86. Also see Paul Busch, "The Sales Manager's Bases of Social Power and Influence Upon the Sales Force," *Journal of Marketing* **44**, no. 3 (Summer 1980), pp. 91–101.

seek to stimulate buying action. Such efforts are directed to three promotional targets:

Consumers who are offered samples, coupons, money refunds, price-off deals, contests, trading stamps, and demonstrations;

The *trade*, who receive free goods, merchandise allowances, cooperative advertising, buying allowances, dealer sales contests, and prize money for salespeople to accelerate sales of particular merchandise;

The *sales force*, who are motivated through sales meetings, bonuses, contests, and merchandise gifts.

Why use sales promotion? The answer is simple. Sales promotion is that "something extra" that can arouse enthusiasm, create a buying mood, or spark an immediate reaction from consumers, the trade, or the company's sales personnel. Sales promotion can establish and reinforce the feeling among intermediaries and consumers that they are getting a better deal.

Sales Promotion Objectives. Broadly considered, sales promotion has a double-barrelled objective: (1) to increase buying response by ultimate consumers and (2) to increase selling efforts and intensity by resellers and sales personnel. Sales success, the result of an effective total marketing program, depends on positive customer reaction and an intense, well-organized selling effort.

Another way of thinking about sales promotion is to consider it a method of accelerating product movement and increasing the stock of the firm's merchandise in the hands of its resellers—retailers and wholesalers—at all levels of the distribution channel from producer to consumer.

Overall, the most frequent use of sales promotion is to attract new buyers, penetrate new markets, and generate new customers. Yet it is not uncommon to use various sales promotion efforts to disrupt existing buying patterns, break the bonds of brand loyalty, or to provide better values and increased buying incentives for the firm's present customers. One study suggested the following reasons for undertaking sales promotional efforts.

1. Calling attention to product improvements
2. Informing buyers of a new brand
3. Improving market share
4. Accelerating usage rate by present users
5. Maintaining customer patronage and brand loyalty
6. Obtaining dealer outlets
7. Securing additional shelf space and added display
8. Creating talking points for sales force
9. Aiding in the product's positioning
10. Increasing dealer inventories of your products in lieu of competitors' (this is called "trade loading")[15]

[15] Donald R. McCurry, "15 Tips for More Effective Sales Promotion," *Business Management* **40**, no. 5 (August 1971), p. 33. See also John F. Luick and William L. Ziegler, *Sales Promotion and Modern Merchandising* (New York: McGraw-Hill, 1968), p. 15.

The Limitations of Sales Promotion.   Sales promotion efforts must, of course, be used judiciously, even sparingly. Some special promotion activities can be a signal to buyers that the seller is eager, maybe too eager, to move the product. A too-frequent scheduling of such events may convey the notion that the products being pushed are inferior, ill-designed, or even overpriced. Then, too, the repeated use of sales promotion activities may actually tend to extinguish the desired customer response by causing customers to tire of such appeals. Recognizing these facts, it is well to remember that sales promotion does have limitations. Among them are the following:

1. Sales promotions are short-lived, limited in durability, and not suitable for long-range or sustained marketing effort.
2. Sales promotion is a facilitating measure used to assist the main promotional activities of advertising and personal selling.
3. Some sales promotions may actually hurt the product's brand image. AMC automobiles may have been damaged by the excessive use of sales promotional efforts which tended to alert potential buyers to the cars' distinct lack of customer acceptance, poor styling, and small number of dealers.
4. Sales promotion is not always creative or innovative. Unimaginative, tasteless programs may project messages that unintentionally create negative customer attitudes, actually boost a competitor's product, or otherwise alienate the firm's dealer outlets.

Designing the Sales Promotion Program.   Designing and implementing the sales promotion program is basically the responsibility of the promotion manager or the vice president of promotion. Most importantly, the design and implementation of sales promotion efforts must be coordinated with the firm's advertising, personal selling, and public relations efforts and directed at the appropriate targets: namely, the sales force, the distribution network, and final buyers. A typical sales promotion program might include any or all of the following:

For the Sales Organization

1. Sales meetings
2. Sales manuals
3. Prototype models of the product
4. Sales literature
5. Contests and incentive campaigns
6. Exhibits and trade shows
7. Direct mailing pieces to customers

Before deciding on incentive programs for the sales force, most authorities agree it is wise to check with them first. Green Giant's sales vice president says, "The person who is going to do the selling job should have some say in setting the objective."[16] It is generally agreed that a company's salespeople

---

[16] "Sales Incentives: Tactics for a Tougher Market," *Sales and Marketing Management,* September 13, 1976, pp. 47–50.

should be asked about their own valuable ideas about incentives for selling activities. The firm's own salespeople are often the best judge of how distributors will react to a sales promotion program.

For the Intermediaries

1. Sales meetings
2. Point-of-purchase display material
3. Trade shows and exhibits
4. Contests
5. Trade deals
6. Push money
7. Advertising and display allowances
8. Buy-back allowances

The reseller will obviously be concerned with the economic and financial results of participation in a special effort. Sales promotions to dealers must present dealer benefits convincingly. Most resellers deal with many suppliers and if a sales promotion does not demonstrate clear advantages, it is likely to be ignored.

For the Consumer

1. Point-of-sale material, tell-tags, and shelf talkers*
2. Premium offers
3. Sampling programs
4. Cents-off and coupon offers
5. Sweepstakes, contests, games
6. Price-off deals
7. Trading stamps

Sales promotional activities for consumers are designed to build and strengthen consumer favor toward the firm. This means that the sales promotional effort should induce interest in new brands and products, create awareness of product improvement, and accentuate and reinforce a firm's advertising and personal selling programs. Sales promotion is designed to create sales revenue beyond the added total cost of the promotion. The actual promotion, while short-lived itself, may also create sales benefits that persist for a longer period of time.

Popular Forms of Sales Promotion

There are many forms of sales promotion.[17] For example, a selection of twelve of the various techniques listed above could result in 845,059,745 different

---

*Tell-tags are labels affixed to the merchandise that describe in detail the product's characteristics and unique selling points. Shelf talkers are similar labels that are attached to the shelves close to product displays.

[17] William A. Robinson, "12 Basic Promotion Techniques: Their Advantages—and Pitfalls," *Advertising Age,* January 10, 1977, pp. 50 and 55.

combinations. The job of selecting, combining, and timing sales promotional efforts reflects the decision maker's knowledge about the strengths and weaknesses of the available techniques. A brief examination of several of these techniques would appear warranted.

Sampling.   Sampling is useful for reaching new users—either when a product is introduced or improved, or at the opening of new markets. Sampling is generally more effective than other techniques when the product's features or benefits (such as flavor and aroma) cannot be fully conveyed in advertising. Sometimes the easiest way to get people to try your product is simply to put a package of it into their hands. Sampling, however, is expensive and imprecise. The firm may give away thousands of dollars worth of merchandise to people who are not even potential users.

Couponing.   Coupons are used to produce trial, to convert triers to regular users, and to reach large numbers of prospects. Sometimes coupons are used to convert regular users to larger sizes, to increase usage by present users, and to retain users in the face of competitive activity. There are some limitations to couponing. The method of distribution limits the nature of the response received. For example, in-pack coupons get the firm few new triers even when heavily advertised. Couponing works best with older, better-educated, urban, and married consumers; it is much less effective with young, single, and less educated consumers.

Free In-Mail Premiums.   Such premiums are used to boost sales, but their main purpose is to increase product awareness and to create a favorable product image. Such premiums themselves often have advertising and public relations value. Other premiums are a part of the product, like towels in boxes of laundry detergent. Others are called self-liquidating premiums and are offered to customers at the firm's volume wholesale price.

Refund Offers.   Refunds create interest and accelerate sales volume by suggesting good value at especially low prices. Refunds are a source of good talking points for salespeople, and are often used to "flag," or call special attention to, the product's package. Refunds are an excellent device for creating new users, and especially for reinforcing brand loyalty. They are also used frequently to stimulate multiple purchasing. For example, promotions like 1-cent sales (buy one at regular price and get another unit for 1 cent) tend to load the customers and, through extended product usage, create strong brand loyalty.

Sweepstakes and Contests.   Sweepstakes and contests attract unusually high customer interest. Using such sales promotion devices will tend to heighten the customer's interest in your advertising, expose the product to more people, provide a reason for getting your product off the shelf and on the floor display, and generate new triers for your product. However, there are some serious limitations. Sweepstakes and contests can be extremely expensive and often fail to produce mass trials.

Other Sales Promotion Devices.   There are other forms of sales promotion that can give sales a short-term lift while strengthening long-run market acceptance. However, each needs to be carefully tailored to the firm's special selling and marketing needs. *Demonstration* may be required to create awareness and interest in the product. Forcing samples was the technique used by one seller; he simply grabbed people off the streets and insisted that they sample his rice pudding.[18] And his sales increased from a few pounds to 900 pounds per day.

Stamp plans and continuity programs (longer-run premium redemption plans) can be used to create steady users. Such efforts are usually a small part of a larger program or a low-cost substitute for more expensive brand-image building. However, these devices usually appeal to only small segments of buyers and often create little, if any, retailer interest. The wise firm will promote its products, services, and brands rather than premiums or trading stamps.

Before proceeding, can you answer these questions:
1. What is meant by sales management? What are the sales manager's basic responsibilities?
2. How do you distinguish between promotion and sales promotion?
3. Who are the three main targets of sales promotion efforts?

---

[18] "'Forcing' Samples Proves Best Way for Factory Owner to Sell Rice Pudding," *Spokesman Review*, February 1977, p. 26.

Public Relations and Publicity

Public relations and publicity, taken together, constitute the fourth major component of promotion. These activities differ somewhat from advertising, personal selling, and sales promotion in that they are not totally controllable by the firm.[19] Every firm attempts to create good public relations so as to receive good publicity. Yet the firm has only a limited influence over whatever poor public relations and bad publicity it receives. It is important to realize that reducing the impact of bad news is as important as creating good publicity.

Public Relations: The Marketing Concept Extended

Public relations is a management activity, a planned effort to shape and affect the attitudes and behavior of the public. These activities (including publicity and institutional advertising) are an attempt to earn the understanding and the goodwill of the firm's customers, employees, and resellers, as well as government officials, and others. Public relations as a marketing function is a natural extension of the marketing concept, which says essentially that every decision in the organization should be made on the basis of its positive impact on customers. To create good public relations, that philosophy is extended to include the firm's larger public, not just its customers. Good public relations, like all marketing activity, puts the interest of the public first in matters relating to the conduct of the company and its business.

Why Public Relations?   Today's public is more aware of social responsibility and demands that business be held accountable for its behavior. Consumerism, environmentalism, women's liberation, the youth movement, and the new assertiveness of minority citizens are all part of this growing awareness.[20] The impact of business behavior on consumer well-being is being watched with increased concern. Along with their specific goals, these movements are seeking corporate openness as opposed to secrecy, cooperation in industry rather than harsh competition, and increased well-being rather than individual exploitation. Businesses are being judged not just on their products and prices, but on their conduct as members of society as well.

In summary, without public relations support, the money spent on all other activities never works as hard as it could, and the promotional team in general has to work harder than it should.

Market Oriented Public Relations

Market oriented public relations demands that the company concentrate heavily on activities that increase its chances of making sales. Such public relations projects then have the same objectives as the company's overall promotional

---

[19] See M. Wayne Delozier, *The Marketing Communications Process* (New York: McGraw-Hill, 1976), pp. 266–267.

[20] Leonard L. Berry and James S. Hensel, "Public Relations: Opportunity in the New Society," *Arizona Business* **20** (August-September 1973), pp. 14–21.

program. And, the public relations effort is therefore directed at much the same audience: people who recommend, buy, specify, represent, influence, or distribute the firm's products, or whoever is in a position to influence decisions on the sale or purchase of the firm's products or services.

Functions of Marketing Public Relations. Market oriented public relations serves many functions, both direct and indirect. Such public relations:

1. Obtains new sales leads. Trade publications, which are primary sources of product information in many industries, can be especially helpful in this.
2. Paves the way for sales calls to dealers. By creating awareness, public relations reduces the buyer's resistance to the visit with a salesperson.
3. Creates literature and articles as "ice breakers" and "talk pieces" with which to interest buyers, company executives, and others in the buying organization.
4. Facilitates point-of-purchase activities. When store executives are aware that an item has received favorable publicity, they are more likely to allow display material and allocate or increase shelf space.
5. Creates ready customer acceptance and presells many items. Public relations and publicity educate consumers to new products and their uses.
6. Finally, public relations and publicity provide wide exposure for sensitive new products (such as birth control devices) where advertising might be inappropriate or indelicate.

The universal business doctrine is simply this: "People can't do business with you if they don't know you're there, and people won't do business with you if your firm lacks credibility in the market place." Public relations is a highly effective method of dealing with both of these basic business requirements. If its public relations projects are intelligently planned for newsworthiness, a company can realize healthy promotion benefits at relatively little cost. Promotion and public relations are drawing inexorably closer as parts of marketing. Including public relations thinking and strategy in the initial stages of a company's marketing program often generates greater selling power.

Summary

Promotion is concerned with all the efforts used by a firm to communicate to its markets. Personal selling, sales promotion, and public relations are all important parts of the firm's overall promotion strategy.

Personal selling is a face-to-face presentation of the firm's products and services by a salesperson. It is a costly but important means of communication. Its chief advantage is its flexibility in reaching the firm's customers and potential customers. It is useful when buyers are reluctant to buy, when products are technical and sophisticated, or when customers generally are not well informed about the product's use. There are many approaches to selling, depending on whether it is low-level or high-level. Many sales situations call for a more creative and original kind of selling, such as situation management, in which the response of the buyer affects the response and tactics of the salesperson, and vice versa. Sales management is that part of marketing concerned with recruiting, training, and maintaining a sales organization as well as with the planning and control of the work of the sales force.

Sales promotion is a broad label that is applied to special kinds of sales-accelerating activities that are not necessarily considered as advertising, personal selling, or public relations. Sales promotion consists of a set of efforts designed as short-term inducements to buying; these may be directed toward consumers, the trade, and/or the firm's own sales force. Popular forms of consumer sales promotion are sampling, couponing, in-the-mail premiums, refund offers, sweepstakes and contests, and such activities as stamp plans and continuity programs.

Public relations and publicity together are the vital fourth arm of marketing promotions and communications. Public relations (including publicity and institutional advertising) is a management activity—a planned effort to affect the attitudes and behavior of the organization's public. Public relations as a marketing function is a natural extension of the marketing concept, which states that every decision in the organization should be made on the basis of its potential impact on customers. Hence, in this context, public relations is related to market-oriented behavior.

Review Questions

1. What is meant by the concept of "the promotion blend"?
2. What are some major factors that affect the firm's promotion blend?
3. Briefly characterize personal selling. What, basically, is the status of personal selling in today's marketing?
4. What is meant by "the transactional nature of selling"? By "situation management"?
5. List and discuss the steps in the selling process.
6. Briefly outline the responsibilities and major duties of sales management. How is the sales manager's role changing in more modern selling situations?
7. What are the objectives of sales promotion? Why is sales promotion often directed to consumers, resellers, and the firm's own sales organization all at the same time?
8. What are some of the popular forms of sales promotion directed toward consumers?
9. Public relations is often seen as something shallow, superficial, contrived, and not in keeping with the marketing concept. Is this a valid view of public relations from the point of view of the marketing oriented firm?
10. What is meant by market oriented public relations? Give some examples of the groups of "publics" to which market oriented public relations is directed.

Case 14-1

Port-A-Dolly

Bernard Saltz had an idea for a new kind of luggage cart. Saltz is a part-time inventor and also the vice president of American Maid, a family-owned business that markets lingerie. In 1958, Mr. Saltz invented the hand-held Dexter sewing machine, a venture that netted him about $100,000 in royalties before companies in other countries copied it and saturated the market. in 1979, Saltz was intrigued by luggage carts being sold through department stores at prices ranging around $25 to $30. He believed they were overdesigned and that he could make one with more appeal at less cost.

Saltz took his idea, along with $10,000 in start-up venture capital, to A. Eiecoff and Company, the Chicago agency that had helped him launch his Dexter sewing machine. The Eiecoff Company has several speculative accounts and has had considerable success in assisting small entrepreneurs in developing and promoting ideas and helping to convert them into marketable commodities.

The first step for new-product ideas is an evaluation by the agency's creative review board. The review board must decide whether the product's potential is sufficient to justify an investment by the agency as well as the investment by the inventor. The review board suggested a go-ahead decision and a prototype cart was produced by Hapco, a Chicago wire-forming company. The prototype was critically evaluated. Several of the company executives took the cart home to try it out. The evidence came back. The cart was too wobbly, its wheels were too small, the cart wouldn't stand by itself. The decision was made to redesign it. The original cart would hold only 100 pounds; the redesigned cart was strengthened to hold 200 pounds. Shortly thereafter another review session was held, a production model was ready, and the product was in need of a name. "Dolly" was

decided to be used as a descriptive term. Names that were suggested included "Grab-a-Dolly," "Fold-a-Dolly," even "Hello Dolly." Finally, the name "Port-A-Dolly" was selected.

The price of the product was then considered. The target entry price that was considered ideal was $19.95, but the executives worried that their costs would forbid pricing the product this low. After all costs—shipping, production, promotion, and so on—were calculated in light of several alternative sales projections, it was finally determined that the $19.95 price was a realistic pricing goal.

Packaging was also considered at an early meeting. Competing products were sold and packaged in clear polyethylene bags, which did not permit point-of-sale merchandising. Hence, it was decided to package the unit in a corrugated box which permitted showing the product's usage for greatest point-of-sale impact. The box showed various Port-A-Dolly uses: luggage, grocery cart, lawn cart, and hand truck.

Promotion was then considered. The promotion task was constrained by what Saltz could afford to spend. The agency's approach with such clients is to figure out what the client can spend and not to spend a lot of money on production, nor delve too heavily into creativity. Instead, the agency suggested that the ads just show what the product does and that ninety-second television spots be used whenever possible to allow maximum time for product usage explanation.

Thus, the agency shot a ninety-second commercial that included space for dealer names. The total cost of the commercial production was $4,000. The commercial shows a Port-A-Dolly being taken out of a suitcase. The script reads as follows: "How many times have you seen a new product and said to yourself, 'Why didn't I think of that?' Well, here's one of those products. It's called Port-A-Dolly. And it has 1,001 uses around your home, office and store. If you're tired of lugging suitcases out of the house...out of the car...out of the plane...Port-A-Dolly is the answer." The commercial then turns to a person who remarks, "Why didn't I think of that?" The remainder of the spot goes on with demonstrations of the cart's usefulness, with the "Why didn't I think of that?" question interjected several times. The advertisement also stresses a money-back guarantee. The agency believes that the money-back guarantee is a notable and worthwhile attribute to be promoted.

After the spot was finally edited and approved, the product was ready for launching. The agency used one of its standard marketing concepts—key outlet marketing. Instead of going to national or even regional distribution, with its high introductory marketing costs, the product was launched sequentially in a number of key markets. El Paso, Texas, was chosen as the first launch site and $1,300 worth of television time was bought. This buy included day time, early and late fringe and prime time Mondays through Fridays, and prime time on weekends. The schedule was skewed to reach females 18 to 49 years of age. During the first three weeks, 495 units were sold, and additional units were sent into the market. The agency is insistent that each market become self-supporting, maintaining a predetermined advertising-to-sales ratio that will sustain advertising expenses and provide the company a profit. The profits from the initial market are then used to expand production, widen markets, and buy more advertising. This then leads to the product being able to support more television time, and that's where the agency begins to make money.

After El Paso, the product was introduced into Sacramento, where it enjoyed a reasonably good market success. At each new market penetration, there is a continual monitoring and adjusting of product, advertising, merchandising, and distribution designed to correct situations where sales volume does not meet expectations. Port-A-Dolly has had no major reversals thus far; neither is it what might be called a "rousing market success." Production problems have somewhat held up expansion and there have been some minor problems with television spot availability. The next markets to be considered will likely be New Orleans, Los Angeles, and possibly Portland, Oregon. One of the great advantages of the key market concept and the leapfrog approach to distribution is that the client does not have too much money tied up in inventory.

Questions

1. Assess the promotional and distribution approaches of Port-A-Dolly. Is this approach a "push strategy" or a "pull strategy"? Explain.

2. Suppose after a period of using this approach, Saltz decided to emphasize more of a "push strategy" in his campaign. What would you recommend he do to change the emphasis of his campaign?

3. What other sales promotion techniques might lend themselves to the successful promotional effort of Port-A-Dolly? Give examples and specific recommendations for carrying them out.

4. a. Where might Port-A-Dollies be conveniently displayed in order to facilitate sales of the product? b. Are there possibilities for utilizing public relations efforts to promote the sale of Port-A-Dollies? How? Give some examples.

Case 14-2

The American Motors Eagle SX4

Low fuel economy no longer is a problem with American Motors Corporation's four-wheel drive autos. A new, subcompact, four-wheel drive car, the American Motors "Eagle" highlights the 1981 lineup from AMC.

AMC's subcompact 4WD is based upon its

EXPERIENCE WHAT LIES BEYOND THE SPORTS CAR. EAGLE SX4.

(The first sport machine that doesn't always need a road.)

Come, enter the 4th Dimension of driving with the spectacular new Eagle SX/4. Experience **22/29** * the near-ultimate in traction and control as all four wheels, not just two, power you over good or bad roads, wet or dry roads, even where there are no roads. 4-wheel drive Eagle SX/4 takes you places such sports cars as Trans Am, Mustang Turbo and Corvette can't. Plus, Eagle SX/4 beats the EPA estimated MPG of all three. Come, drive the new sport machine that takes you beyond the ordinary. Eagle SX/4...it's somewhere else.

Experience driving in the 4th Dimension.

*Use these figures for comparison. Your mileage may vary due to speed, weather and trip length. Actual highway mileage will probably be less. Calif. figures lower.

American Motors

Spirit model and is marketed as the Eagle SX4 two-door hatchback and the Kammback two-door sedan.

AMC officials said the cars are positioned for people who want "sporty styling, practicality and performance characteristics of four-wheel drive."

AMC became the first U.S. car producer to introduce a four-wheel drive with its 1980 Eagle, based upon its compact Concord model. The four-wheel drive system in the SX4 is the same found in the compact Eagle. Four-wheel drive often is associated with poor fuel economy. This certainly was the case with the 1980 Eagle with its standard six-cylinder engine and automatic transmission. It got only an estimated 21 mpg on the highway and 16 mpg in the city. However, the 1981 Eagle SX4 will get an estimated 29 mpg on the highway and 22 mpg in the city with a standard four-cylinder, 151 cubic inch engine and four-speed manual transmission. "These high 4WD mileage figures really constitute big news for us," said Gerald C. Meyer, President of AMC. When the SX4 was rolled out, it became, in AMC advertising, a car for buyers who want good handling, smooth ride, and roominess in a more compact package plus the convenience and desirability of four-wheel drive. Meyer commented in an interview, "We decided to position the Eagle SX4 clearly as a sporty, good handling vehicle with all the economy of a small car, but with the added convenience of 4WD."

AMC is the only domestic producer of 4WD compact automobiles. Subaru has done well with its 4WD compact sedans and station wagons as well as with its sporty runabout called the Brat.

The American Motors Corporation decided early in the 1980s to concentrate through its advertising and promotional campaign on the company's products and their attributes—a marked change from the previous heavy concentration on selling the "buyer protection plan" warranty.

AMC is determined to bring itself out of the prolonged slump which has seen it drop below the top five imported cars in sales since the late 1970s.

Questions

1. What is the role of positioning in advertising and promotional strategy?

2. What did Meyers mean by his statement, "We decided to clearly position the SX4 as a sporty, good handling vehicle with all the economy of a small car but with the added convenience of 4WD"?

3. Why do you believe AMC is switching its advertising and promotional theme from the buyer protection plan warranty to more emphasis on its products themselves?

4. Do you believe AMC's sales slump can be attributed to its advertising and promotional efforts or to other aspects of its marketing program? Explain.

Chapter 15

Pricing: Basic Considerations

Early in 1973, the Associated Press drew up a random list of fifteen commonly purchased food and nonfood items, checked their prices on March 1, 1973 at one supermarket in each of thirteen cities, and has rechecked them on or about the start of each succeeding month.[1] Among the findings in the August 1980 survey: the market basket bill increased in the checklist stores in all thirteen cities, up an average of 7.3 percent over the preceding month. Overall, the cost of the market basket at the checklist stores went up 5.6 percent in July over June 1980.

The steep rise in prices throughout the late 1970s and the early 1980s is attributable to several factors. Most importantly, prices are going up because costs are soaring. Prices are always somebody else's costs. Costs are going up because of inflation. Inflation is generally described as "too many dollars chasing too few goods." This means that *demand* is outstripping *supply* and unless supply increases to bid down prices, prices continue to go up.

Our capitalistic view of how markets operate leads us to assume that prices are determined by supply and demand. And they are. Normally we think of supply and demand as impersonal market forces, but supply can be controlled if there are too few supplies or if they collude, like the Organization of Petroleum Exporting Countries (OPEC). They have a unique product in strong demand, and these producers can effectively control the available quantity of their product for which there are no really close or acceptable substitutes. Of course, demand is not necessarily impersonally determined either. Why do Americans have such a love affair with their automobiles as personal modes of transportation and driving? Didn't Texaco, Arco, Shell, Union Oil, and many others spend billions through advertising, conditioning the American consumers to drive more, and fostering the heavy demand? Over a significant range of prices, from about 29 cents to 79 cents a gallon, gasoline consumption was relatively inelastic. Now, however, that gasoline has reached $1.50 per gallon in some areas, its demand has become more price-elastic. So, in discussing pricing, you must become accustomed to hearing such terms as *supply, demand, costs, prices, elasticity of demand,** and other alien-sounding terms. It's almost necessary to have a marketing education to understand the events one reads about in the daily newspaper.

The Significance of Price in Marketing Strategy

Pricing decisions are perhaps the most complex decisions confronting the marketing manager. Used wisely, price manipulation becomes a powerful tool for ensuring the success of a marketing program.

Today, overcapacity, increased competition from foreign-made goods, higher labor costs, rampant inflation, and many other factors have sharply increased price competition in many industries and given a new relevance to pricing

---

[1] Data for this illustration has been compiled from numerous sources.
Elasticity refers to the relationship between price changes and the change in quantity purchased which will occur if there are changes in price. This concept is discussed at some length later in the chapter.

An example of price specials.

strategies throughout all levels of the marketing channel. Pricing is an area of marketing decision making that increasingly concerns all Americans, from housewives and business executives to legislators and officials in government regulatory agencies. So, in today's setting determining price is a major decision area for business management. When done correctly, the rewards are increased sales, better product and company images, favorable market position, better public relations, and less government intervention and regulation. Poorly conceived and implemented price decisions are apt to result in a weakened market position generally and, in the extreme, outright business failure.

Price Wears Many Hats

Price plays a number of roles in most marketing strategies. It can be a key component in the company or product image; a powerful sales promotion device; or a versatile weapon in competition. It also serves as a balance wheel for the overall economy.

A marketer uses prices to accomplish multiple objectives. For example, price may be used as a clue to product quality. It can convey the notion to customers that a seller has high-quality merchandise, that the marketer is a medium-priced seller, or that prices for merchandise and service are simply "fair," or reasonable.

Price may be used, and often is, in sales promotion activities such as cents-off, couponing, discounted prices, two-for-one sales, trade-in allowances or other special discounts. Price is also sometimes used to project a strong snob appeal or an aura of exclusiveness—the $45,000 Mercedes and the $15,000 BMW 320i are just such examples.

The role of price is not only multifaceted, but, equally important, it is also a function of the overall marketing strategy. It is intricately related to the goals and objectives of the particular marketing institution. From the standpoint of the individual marketing firm, price is the mechanism that guides optimal input and output decisions.

One writer has dramatized the role of price in the overall marketing strategy of the firm, in the following way:

Pricing and price alone, more than any other single decision making activity, is responsible for most of the profit differences among similar firms....How the product is priced will in itself determine the product mix [that will be offered]. The pricing action will make the product more or less attractive to the buyer, the major factor which determines the buyer response. To the extent that costs of the mix produce both profit contributions and favorable responses from buyers, the volume sold will be profitable. The sales revenue, then, is a mixture of the various prices of the different products or orders, and the resultant profit is a mixture of their profit contributions.[2]

Much of this chapter will focus upon developing a background that will facilitate our understanding of these challenging propositions.

Price Has Many Names

Price goes by a lot of names. As students you pay **tuition** for your education, **rent** for your apartment or dormitory, or a **house bill** for your fraternity or sorority. When you travel between school and your home town, the airline, train, or bus charges you a **fare**. Local utility companies charge a **rate** for gas, water, and electricity; and if you borrow money from the local bank, or obtain a student loan, you pay an **interest** charge for the borrowed funds. You pay a **premium** for insurance on your car, and a **toll** in order to travel on certain highways or cross certain bridges. A special guest lecturer at your university may receive an **honorarium** and may discuss a legislator who took the **bribe** from a foreign official. If you belong to the Young Democrats Club you will pay **dues**, or if your parents belong to a country club, in addition to their dues, they may be required to pay a special **assessment** to cover the costs of repair to the clubhouse or the outdoor pool. Should you encounter legal problems and hire a lawyer, you may have to pay a **retainer** to cover his or her services. Or if you own property and sell it through a broker, you pay a **commission**. The price paid to executives for their services is called a **salary** but construction workers and lifeguards working at the beach for the summer are paid **wages**. Finally, almost everyone pays **taxes**, the price we pay for owning property and making money.[3]

[2] Spencer Tucker, *Pricing For Higher Profit* (New York: McGraw-Hill, 1966), p. 4.
[3] Suggested by David J. Schwartz, *Marketing Today* (New York: Harcourt, Brace Jovanovich, 1973), p. 468.

Price Defined

Price does then have many names but in spite of its many names and multiple personalities, basically the price of a good or service is derived from its exchange value. Exchange value is considered as the command one good or service has over others. The price of a good or service is an expression in monetary units of the command that the good or service exercises in exchange on the market. Price is an agreement between seller and buyer concerning what each is to receive, the mechanism or device for translating into quantitative terms (dollars and cents) the value of the product to the customer at a point in time. Pricing involves setting terms, like the time of payment; the currency used, which can be critical when exchange rates are changing; and the discounts, if any, which are offered.[4]

Price is based upon some assortment of goods and services and is probably easiest to visualize as a simple equation: Money or price (list, or quoted, price less deductions—discounts and allowances) equals a product or service with an attendant bundle of expectations (extra services, quality, delivery, credit, and other benefits). Therefore, price is a figure that equates a given amount of money to some total bundle of satisfaction or expectations. If the price in dollars and cents is altered, it is likely that the satisfactions side of the equation will be altered also.

The Notion of Demand

Demand for goods and services can be set down in the form of a schedule with one column listing various prices at which something may be sold and another column, the amount that would be purchased at each price. Consider a simple situation. Jimmy Barter's demand schedule for pants might look like the following:

Price per Pair	Pairs Purchased Each Year
$35	
30	1
25	3
20	5
15	7
	9

What can be put down in a schedule or table can also be shown in a graph. The price of the item is shown on the vertical axis and the quantity that would be purchased at each price is shown on the horizontal axis. By plotting the amounts Jimmy would purchase at the various prices, we come up with a **demand curve** as illustrated in Figure 15-1. The curve that results as the points are joined is useful for estimating the amounts that will be purchased at any

---

[4] This statement is a slightly altered version of a long-standing and well-received delineation and definition of "What is Price?" based upon Reavis Cox, "Non-Price Competition and The Measurement of Prices," *Journal of Marketing* **11**, no. 2 (April 1946), p. 376.

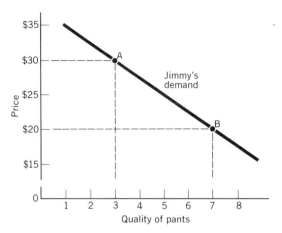

Figure 15-1

price along the curve even if it is not one of the specific prices listed in the demand schedule. Total demand curves can be estimated and drawn which are the summations of individuals' demand. Since the demand of each buyer is only a small part of the total demand for any item, each individual has little significance. Together, however, the millions of people whose families, firms and governments buy products like pants, autos, and rock concert tickets do have a great effect. Their combined actions make up the total demand for such things. Once the concept of demand and the demand curve are understood, it should be easier to grasp the difference between price and **nonprice competition**.

Price Versus Nonprice Competition: Do Marketers Have a Choice?

Before answering the question, "Do marketers have a choice?", perhaps we had better make a clear distinction between price and nonprice competition. Several of our chapters have dealt with nonprice competitive activities as elements in marketing strategy. Advertising and sales promotion are clearly examples of nonprice competition. To a great extent, so are product development, packaging, and physical distribution activities.

The folklore of competition suggests that a high degree of **price competition** marks our overall economic system. From such a general belief one is likely to conclude that marketing is also highly price competitive. It it? Well, yes and no. In some instances there is a great deal of price competition and in others it is decidedly absent. Price competition is a situation wherein a firm attempts to maximize total revenue, and thus profit opportunity, by manipulating the price variable. The counterpart of price competition would of course be nonprice competition, defined as an attempt to manipulate total revenue by manipulating nonprice variables such as product assortments, quality and design, promotion or personal selling, and channels of distribution. The two kinds of competition can be differentiated as shown in Figure 15-2.

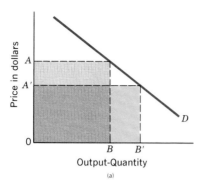 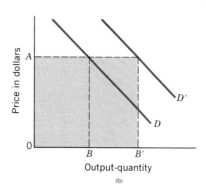

Figure 15-2 *(a)* Price competition. *(b)* Nonprice competition.

In Figure 15-2*a* total revenue (which is price times quantity sold) has been changed by a change in prices. Observe that: (1) at price *OA*, quantity *OB* is sold; (2) at the lower price *OA'*, quantity *OB'* is sold; and (3) the cross-hatched area of the rectangle *OA', OB'* is larger than the shaded rectangle *OA, OB*. Therefore total revenue is larger after the price reduction than before.[5] In Figure 15-2*b* although price remains unchanged, the demand curve has shifted upward and to the right as a result of the firm's nonprice competitive activities. Presumably customers now prefer this firm's goods, so that the total revenue— the area of the rectangle *OA, OB'*—is much greater than that of the rectangle *OA, OB*. Remember that profit is the difference between total revenue and total cost; because costs have not been included in this analysis, it has been assumed in each instance that the behavior that tended to raise total revenue was profitable. Close examination of the real world of marketing indicates that price is not always the critical factor in strategy that it is often thought to be. Surprisingly, nonprice competition probably plays a far more important role in total strategy considerations than does price competition.

Demand Oriented Pricing Models

Economic analysis has wrestled with the problems of pricing goods, seeking to shed some light on pricing in light of the problems just discussed. For example, economists have attempted to model the various market structures, or what the business community could call different kinds of competitive environments. Four competitive environments have been modeled: **pure competition, monopoly, oligopoly**, and **monopolistic competition**. From the models, we can deduce different pricing situations from which emerge various kinds of pricing behavior. The nature of the various market structures hinges primarily around two considerations: (1) the number and the size of firms in competition with one another, and (2) the nature of the products sold. It should be borne in mind that one of the principal things the price decision maker wishes to know is, "How much freedom do I have in determining price?" This freedom will depend on the nature of the market or competitive structure. Figure 15-3

---

[5] This would not be true in all instances but only if the product in question had an elastic demand.

"There are no prices listed, sir, because prices tend to put people off."
Drawing by Ross; © 1980 The New Yorker Magazine, Inc.

shows the demand curves for the four market structures discussed. A demand curve is the average revenue curve, or the price per unit received times the number of units sold at each alternative price.

Pure Competition. Pure competition is a market structure characterized by these features: (1) There are many buyers and sellers, none of whom is large enough to appreciably affect price, either by heavy selling or by heavy buying. (2) Pure competition is also characterized by a high degree of knowledge, mobility of resources, and instantaneous adjustment to changes in supply and demand conditions. (3) The products sold in the purely competitive market are homogeneous, that is, the product of each seller is perceived by each buyer as identical with those of other sellers. Therefore, there is no opportunity to differentiate the product. The market for many agricultural products often closely approximates pure competition. Because of these conditions the demand curve for a single seller is a horizontal straight line, or perfectly elastic, at the level of the going market price.

Figure 15-3 Demand curves for alternative market situations. *(a)* Pure competition. *(b)* Monopoly. *(c)* Oligopoly. *(d)* Monopolistic competition.

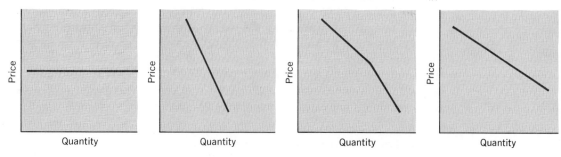

Why now does the demand curve for a firm in pure competition have no slope and why again is it a straight line at the going market price? The implication is that if firms operated in purely competitive markets, they would have no pricing freedom, no discretion to choose from among a range of alternatives. However, direct observation of pricing behavior of marketing firms in the real world indicates that most do.

Monopoly. Monopoly is like pure competition in that it is not a very realistic model. Both these models show what **might be** if the described conditions actually prevailed. Thus, they are used for theoretical analysis rather than as an operational analysis of real world conditions.[6]

Monopoly is a market or competitive situation in which there is a single seller of a product for which there are no reasonably close or acceptable substitutes. Therefore, the seller is a monopolist and constitutes the entire industry for that commodity. A monopolist would have a downward sloping, inelastic demand curve, meaning that the monopolist has a great deal of liberty to exercise in pricing decisions.

In the cases of pure competition and monopoly, we are talking about the extreme ranges of pricing freedom. There is none in pure competition, whereas the monopolist has virtually unrestricted freedom over a wide range of choices. Neither pure competition nor monopoly exists in reality, and there are no marketing firms (except regulated utilities such as the telephone, electric and gas companies, and public transportation) whose competitive condition could be realistically described by either of these models. Yet, because of active existing competitive situations, some marketing firms are likely to discover that their pricing freedom is considerably limited by large numbers of sellers and an inability to differentiate their products or product mix significantly. Thus, their market behavior will approach that of the purely competitive market. Contrariwise, where a firm has but few competitors, or has brought out a new product protected from competitive substitutes by special patent rights or secret technology, it will have a great deal of freedom in its pricing behavior. (For instance, the Polaroid camera was virtually a monopoly until Kodak came out with a similar device. Yet Polaroid, strictly speaking, was not a total monopoly. Why not?) Therefore, the competitive situation of some firms is not identical to monopoly, but it is at least closer to monopoly than to the purely competitive model.

In fact, there are two other models of competitive environments that characterize marketing price making behavior much more realistically. These are the models of oligopoly and monopolistic competition.

Oligopoly. In an oligopolistic market there exist only a few sellers producing a differentiated product.[7] Because there are so few sellers, the action of one is

[6] For a full discussion of each of these models see Mark I. Alpert, *Pricing Decisions* (Glenview, IL: Scott, Foresman, 1971), especially chapter 1, pp. 1–24.

[7] The type of oligopoly discussed here is what is called a heterogeneous, or differentiated oligopoly. A pure oligopoly is characterized by the inability to differentiate the seller's product. Hence, such an oligopoly (called a homogeneous oligopoly) is found only in a few industries producing raw materials.

likely to affect the behavior of others noticeably. In effect, behavior in such a market becomes quite interdependent. If a marketing oligopolist lowers a price, his rivals are quite likely to retaliate with matching price cuts. However, if an oligopolist raises prices above the level of the competition, the latter in all likelihood will not raise their prices and, therefore, the demand curve has a "kink" at the level of the going market price. The important consideration in oligopoly is that when sellers are few, each must take account of the actions of the others; one's behavior (pricing and otherwise) and that of one's competitors will be interdependent. The large automobile companies such as General Motors, Ford, and Chrysler are good examples of oligopolistic marketing firms, as are firms in the steel, tobacco, and gasoline refining industries.

Monopolistic Competition.   Monopolistic competition, as the name suggests, combines features from both the purely competitive model and the monopolistic model. Monopolistic competition is a market structure characterized by a relatively large number of sellers, but unlike conditions in pure competition, the monopolistic competitor sells a differentiated product and has some ability to differentiate the marketing mix offered. The monopolistic competitor has some degree of freedom in making price decisions. Such a firm's demand curve is downward sloping, but the range of prices from which it can choose is affected by its ability to differentiate its products in the minds of buyers when many alternative firms are offering their products and services. This means that each seller's product is confronted with a large number of reasonably close and acceptable substitute products from which all buyers can choose.

What Relevant Economic Model for Marketing?

Marketing is a very diverse activity with a wide range of different institutions (manufacturers, wholesalers, and retailers) of varying size, some of whom sell or market many products; some, single products; and many of whom sell to different markets. Given such diversity, can one single economic model possibly characterize market structure and its impact on pricing? Possibly not. Some firms are obviously differentiated oligopolists, but most operate under conditions more nearly like monopolistic competition.

Monopolistic Competition and Price Determination

The general theory of price determination under conditions of monopolistic competition can be briefly sketched as follows. Figure 15-4 represents the demand and cost structure of a marketing firm in a monopolistically competitive market. Such a firm has a degree of monopoly power because of its ability to differentiate its product in the eyes of some buyers. Bayer Aspirin is a classic example. All aspirin is alike but Bayer has convinced many buyers that its product is somewhat different, and thus better. Therefore, the demand curve or the average revenue curve of the monopolistic competitor slopes downward and to the right (a negative slope), which indicates that at higher prices the

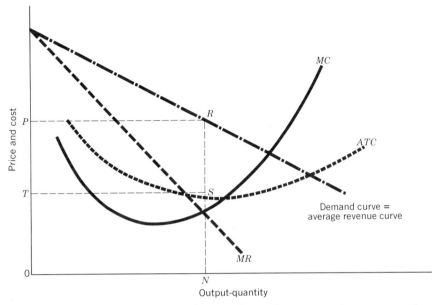

Figure 15-4 Price determination for a marketing firm in a market structure of monopolistic competition.

firm loses some sales, but not all. Recall that the seller in pure competition has a perfectly elastic demand curve, one that is a horizontal straight line at the level of the going market price. From the demand curve, the marginal revenue curve *(MR)* that represents the change in total revenue resulting from a unit change in output is derived. The average total cost *(ATC)* curve and the marginal cost curve *(MC)* are then drawn, and following the conventional decision rule of economic analysis, price is set at the point on the average revenue curve where *(MC)*, marginal costs = *(MR)*, marginal revenue.

Notice that this is the point where the rate of change in total costs equals the rate of change in total revenues. From Figure 15-4 it can be shown that the optimum output is *ON* units that will be sold at a price, *OP*. Total revenue is the price times the quantity sold, or the geometric area of the rectangle *OPRN*, and the total cost is the geometric area of the rectangle *OTSN*. Net profit (total revenue minus total cost) would be the area of the rectangle *PRST*. Net profits are only maximized when price and output are established where *MC = MR*.

Economic Analysis or Demand Oriented Pricing Has Its Limitations.   The rule for pricing and output determination, as shown in Figure 15-4 and for all the economic models discussed, is the same: namely, set price and determine output at that level where *MC = MR*. It is a normative decision rule inasmuch as it tells the decision maker what *ought* to be done. However, in actuality, economic price decision making has several serious limitations that restrict its usefulness for the marketing manager and the price decision maker.[8]

[8] For some further criticisms of the theory see Edwin Mansfield, *Micro-Economics*, 2nd ed. (New York: W.W. Norton, 1975), pp. 316–317.

Pricing: Normative Versus Realistic Considerations

We are often told what we ought to do. Such instructions are "normative." That is, they state that if you do what you ought to do, such and such will be the result. Pricing is plagued with such normative thinking, which states that marketers ought to price their products so as to generate certain results. However, when examined more realistically, these normative approaches are often found to have many deficiencies. For example, the question confronting the marketing price decision maker is, "What is the ideal price to charge?" From a normative point of view, the question can be answered easily. The price decision maker ought to establish a price that will promise the maximum total contribution to overhead and profits. For a multiple-product firm, as almost all firms are, the normative decision rule would state that the prices charged should generate maximum expected total contribution to overhead and profits of all products combined. It's a decision rule that is easy to state but rather difficult to apply and implement in the real world.

To set such an ideal price, both cost and demand schedules or estimates are needed. But cost and demand schedules are difficult to estimate and, as a consequence, many price decision makers attempt to set prices that will not so much maximize profit as maximize total revenue. Total revenue is Price times Quantity. The sticky point is that often the price that can be obtained depends on the quantity offered and, conversely, the quantity that can be sold depends on the offered price. Furthermore, the price and resulting output sold will affect unit costs given various sales levels. Thus, uncertainties surrounding price decision making begin to mount, preventing or hindering the price decision maker from setting the "ideal" price. Before proceeding further, however, it is necessary to outline more specifically the uncertainties facing the price decision maker and to explain why they are a part of the real world of marketing and how they impede pricing objectives and behavior.

The Real World Is Uncertain

Broadly considered, these uncertainties amount to the following:

1. The price decision maker is unsure about the nature of the competitive environment within which the company operates. Quite simply, the price decision maker no doubt recognizes that the firm has some discretion in setting the price for its products but, lacking perfect knowledge, does not know clearly either the upper or lower bounds of this pricing freedom.
2. Given the nature of most market structures, price decisions will not go unobserved by competitors, so the price behavior of one marketing firm is likely to be constrained to some degree by its rivals. The degree of constraint will depend upon the nature of the competitive market, that is, the number and size of sellers and the nature of the product.
3. The decision maker does not know what the effect of a price decision on sales is likely to be, whether the demand for a given commodity is elastic or inelastic. Therefore his or her ability to determine the optimum price for the product or product mix is severely limited.

Limitations of Demand Oriented Pricing

Upon close examination, demand oriented pricing (pricing decisions based upon the economic decision rule to set price where marginal cost equals marginal revenue) is not so easy as it appears. To use demand oriented pricing, the decision maker would have to know with certainty the marginal cost or incremental costs for each product in the total product mix. This would be difficult for many marketing firms because of the relatively unsophisticated state of their cost accounting systems; at best the decision maker is armed with a knowledge of only standard or average costs. Marginal costs are not normally available to many marketers, not to mention all the problems a multidivisional, multidepartmental or multiproduct firm would have with joint costs and cost allocation. Thus, determining marginal costs and marginal revenues for each product within the marketing system becomes a formidable task, one that may not negate, but at least seriously impede, the use of marginal analysis for marketing price decision making.

Price Determination: Upper and Lower Bounds

No firm can charge more for its commodities or services than is justified by the demand for them. On the other hand, no firm should charge less for a commodity or service than its incremental costs of producing and/or selling that product or service. (Incremental cost is the increase in the firm's total costs

Supply and demand are the determinants of price.

as a result of producing one more unit.) Somewhere between these upper and lower bounds (that is, the level of demand and the level of the firm's relevant costs) lies the "right" price for each of the firm's individual products or services.

Therefore, demand is the upper bound or constraint on the price decision maker, and a price that exceeds the upper bound can be ruled as "too high." Conversely, costs are the lower constraint on the pricing decision, and in the short run no price should be lower than the product's variable costs. If the price were set lower than these costs, it would mean a direct, out-of-pocket loss on all units sold of this particular product. In the long run all costs become variable costs and therefore price must exceed or at least equal total costs.

The realistic goal of the price decision maker is to know when a price is either too high or too low. The decision maker who can make this determination should thus have some insight as to when one price is better or worse than another.

Before proceeding, can you answer these questions?
1. What role does price play in marketing strategy?
2. What is the economic decision rule for demand oriented price setting? What are some of the shortcomings of this approach?
3. Describe the conditions that make for a market structure of monopolistic competition.

Cost Oriented Pricing Approaches

Most marketers confronted with price decisions will argue convincingly that they know considerably more about the nature of their costs of operation than they do about such abstract and difficult concepts as demand. Naturally, marketers' pricing behavior tends to reflect this attitude, and the result is a great emphasis in marketing on cost oriented decisions. There are two widely used and standard cost oriented pricing approaches: average cost pricing and target rate of return pricing.

Average Cost Pricing

In average cost pricing a reasonable or standard markup is added to the cost per unit to determine the selling price. Both average cost pricing and target rate of return pricing must sometimes rely on cost figures that are hardly more than crude approximations. Because of the large number and wide variety of products they market, many firms find it difficult to allocate costs accurately to specific products. Some companies, however, do have excellent cost accounting procedures that permit them to measure and allocate costs with great precision. Yet often the allocation of costs to particular products is largely arbitrary. Some marketers, retailers for example, are apt to be more interested in the overall gross margin of a department or a product line than in the gross margin or contribution margin earned by a single product. For this reason, exact costs associated with a particular product are not always considered crucial to a given price decision and average cost concepts are relied on frequently as guides to decision making.[9]

An Example of Average Cost Pricing.   The essence of average cost pricing is to determine the cost base for a recent or forecasted period by dividing total costs by the number of units sold or expected to be sold. To illustrate: assume that a manufacturer of toys had a total cost for a given period amounting to $250,000 (for a single line within the firm's total product mix). Of this sum, $100,000 was allocated to fixed costs and variable costs absorbed $150,000. Fixed costs do not change with output; variable costs on the other hand, do vary in some relation to the number of units produced. For the sake of simplicity, assume that fixed costs include the costs of the plant and machinery and that variable costs include the cost of raw materials and direct labor. Assume further that 25,000 units of the toy were sold during this period. The average cost per unit was thus $10 ($250,000 total cost divided by 25,000 units sold). The next step is to determine the amount of profit that would appear "reasonable" and, if 15 percent was deemed so, then taking 15 percent of $10, or $1.50, and adding it to the $10 cost would result in a price of $11.50. The $11.50 price is supposed to cover all costs (including manufacturing and marketing costs) and generate a profit of $1.50 per unit. Another important point in regard to average cost pricing is that individual prices may be above or below the company's average, depending on given market conditions, the specific price policies of other sellers, the presence or absence of competing products, or the decision maker's estimate of the rate of sale of a particular product at various prices.[10]

Average cost pricing can be summarized as a method whereby an attempt is made to forecast costs and then to choose a price that at a given volume will generate sufficient sales revenue to cover all costs and provide a predetermined margin of profit.

Target Rate of Return Pricing.   Target rate of return pricing is another form of average cost pricing by which the decision maker attempts to receive some percentage of, or total dollar return on, investment, which is the capital required to support manufacturing and marketing activity. For example, assume a luggage manufacturer sold 5,000 underseat air travel bags last year, and that the firm expects to sell the same number again this year. Suppose that fixed costs allocated to the line are $50,000; variable costs per unit are $12.00; the total investment in assets required to manufacture, market, and support this line is $150,000; and a 20 percent return on investment (ROI) is desired. To get the dollar return on investment:

---

[9] Donald V. Harper, *Price, Policy and Procedure* (New York: Harcourt, Brace and World, 1966), pp. 247–249.
[10] See Robert J. Dolan, "The Extent of Suboptimality of Myopic Pricing Rules," *Marketing in the 1980s: Changes and Challenges,* 1980 Educators Conference Proceedings, Series No. 46, Chicago, IL., pp. 273–277.

$$\begin{array}{r} \$150,000 \quad \text{investment} \\ \times \quad\quad 0.20 \quad \text{return on investment} \\ \hline \$\ 80,000 \quad \text{return on investment} \end{array}$$

Total fixed costs plus target rate of return on investment:

$$\begin{array}{r} \$\ 50,000 \\ + \quad 30,000 \\ \hline \$\ 80,000 \end{array}$$

Target rate of return per unit:

$80,000 \div 5,000$ units sold $= \$16.00$

Therefore, price to reseller that will generate 20 percent return on investment will be:

$$\begin{array}{r} \$12.00 \quad \text{variable cost per unit} \\ + \quad 16.00 \\ \hline \$28.00 \quad \text{per unit} \end{array}$$

Shortcomings of Average Cost Pricing.   The shortcomings of average cost pricing apply with equal strength to the target rate of return model just described. Both rely on average cost determinations, which in turn have two critical requirements:[11] (1) to forecast sales with reasonable accuracy, and (2) to allocate costs among the various products in the company's assortment. During periods of erratic economic activity or when a product is new, forecasting sales can be a difficult task. Because average costs are a function of a particular sales level, any sales level that deviates widely from what is anticipated can throw pricing accuracy completely out of kilter. If actual sales do not vary too much from the previous period, average cost pricing methods will produce reasonably good results. If sales are much lower than expected, there probably will be losses. Conversely, if actual sales are much higher than anticipated, the company will reap large windfall profits.

There is a large amount of circular reasoning involved in average cost pricing. For instance, the decision maker must forecast sales to determine prices. Yet, intuitively, one knows that the level of sales actually achieved will depend on the level of prices set. There is no guarantee of good results with average cost methods of pricing, because sales volume may fluctuate either way.

Average Cost Pricing and Markup Policies

A knowledge of average cost pricing methods greatly aids in understanding retail markup policies. The typical retail decision maker, using average cost pricing methods, determines the retail selling price for each item in the store's

---

[11] See David R. Kamerschen, "The Return of Target Pricing," *Journal of Business,* April 1975, pp. 242–252.

100%

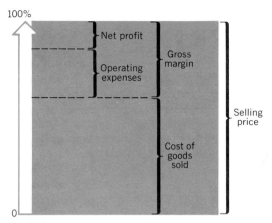

Figure 15-5 The components of retail selling price.

assortment mix by adding some markup (either in dollars or percentage) to the cost of the item. Thus, retail selling price is cost + markup, where cost is defined as acquisition cost of the merchandise, and markup is the amount added to cost in order to cover expenses and generate some "reasonable" or "target" profit. These relationships are shown in Figure 15-5. The figure shows exactly what has been shown before, though in slightly different fashion: namely, that sales − cost of goods sold = gross margin; and gross margin − expenses = profits. Figure 15-5 has simply combined or summed these elements so that net profit + operating expenses + cost of goods sold = selling price.

Average cost pricing is a method of determining prices by adding an average margin or markup to average costs. One of the interesting issues that arises in price determination is whether the decision maker should always add the same standard or uniform percentage margin to merchandise costs in order to determine the retail selling price. Practice varies among sellers in regard to this question. For instance, it was long standard practice in department stores to have a uniform gross margin of 40 percent on all merchandise. Furniture retailers set prices for all items by doubling the cost and adding 10 percent. Jewelry stores followed similar uniform percentage or gross margin practices.[12] However, because of two factors that are probably related, this practice is gradually being abandoned. One is the greater understanding of the concept of price elasticity, and the other is the aggressive use of this concept by certain retailing institutions, foremost of which is the discount store. This practice of applying uniform set markups to cost almost automatically left some types of retailers extremely vulnerable to the new competition from discount and other low margin operators who were more carefully examining such factors as cost, demand, and elasticity.

[12] For a fuller treatment see Rom J. Markin, *Retailing Management* (New York: Macmillan, 1977), especially chapter 15, pp. 351–368.

All these detergents give you great cleaning. There's one important difference...

This one costs less.

We've lowered the price on Arm & Hammer Laundry Detergent. That means a clean, fresh laundry now costs you less—every time. And when it comes to cleaning, you can rely on Arm & Hammer Laundry Detergent. It's the only laundry detergent that gives you Arm & Hammer quality—with Arm & Hammer value.

The Meaning of Markup.   Markup without question is a critical concept in retail pricing and it is important that the term be used correctly. Markup in dollars is the difference between original retail value and the cost of the merchandise. The markup percentage is the markup in dollars divided by the original retail price of the merchandise.

It is important to understand the relationship between markup and the retail price and the cost of the merchandise. This relationship can be shown by formula as follows:

$$markup = retail - cost$$

Or, solving for retail:

$$retail = cost + markup$$

Or, solving for cost:

$$cost = retail - markup$$

Often a manager desires to compute the markup percentage on either the retail price or the cost price of the merchandise. To illustrate, assume that an item selling for $10.00 carries a $4.00 markup. The markup on retail equals:

$$\frac{\$ \ markup}{retail \ price} = \frac{\$ \ 4.00}{\$10.00} = 40\%$$

The markup on cost equals:

Table 15-1 Equivalent Markups

Markup Percent on Selling Price	Markup Percent on Cost	Markup Percent on Selling Price	Markup Percent on Cost
20.0	25.0	34.0	51.5
21.0	26.6	35.0	53.9
22.0	28.2	35.5	55.0
22.5	29.0	36.0	56.3
23.0	29.9	37.0	58.8
23.1	30.0	37.5	60.0
24.0	31.6	38.0	61.3
25.0	33.3	39.0	64.0
26.0	35.0	39.5	65.5
27.0	37.0	40.0	66.7
27.3	37.5	41.0	70.0
28.0	39.0	42.0	72.4
28.5	40.0	42.8	75.0
29.0	40.9	44.4	80.0
30.0	42.9	46.1	85.0
31.0	45.0	47.5	90.0
32.0	47.1	48.7	95.0
33.3	50.0	50.0	100.0

$$\frac{\$ \text{ markup}}{\text{cost}} = \frac{\$4.00}{\$6.00} = 66\frac{2}{3}\%$$

How was the cost determined? By using the formula above, namely, cost = retail − markup. Therefore, retail = $10.00, and markup = $4.00, so the cost of the merchandise is $10.00 − $4.00, or $6.00.

Table 15-1 is a table of equivalent markups. By using similar though somewhat more detailed tables, buyers, department managers, and others concerned with pricing decisions can readily compare markup percentages on retail with markup percentage on cost, and vice versa. The standard procedure for using markup tables is first to determine the desired markup percentage on retail, then in the parallel column to find the markup percentage on cost. By multiplying the markup percentage on cost by the actual cost price, the actual retail selling price of the item can be determined.

In summary, an understanding of the various markup concepts is absolutely fundamental in retail price decision making. It should be thought of as a valuable retail tool—as a control and planning device and an important part of the retail firm's strategic planning activity.

Price Determination and Breakeven Point Analysis

In an earlier chapter, we looked at a simplified model of a marketing firm in the following form:

$$\text{sales revenue} - \text{cost of goods sold} = \text{gross margin}$$
$$\text{gross margin} - \text{expenses} = \text{profit}$$

This concept is introduced once again because it reveals a great deal about the financial workings of a company, especially the role of sales revenue and its relationship to pricing.

You will notice that sales revenue eventually must cover or exceed three relevant items shown in the model: (1) cost of goods sold or the purchase price paid to suppliers of raw materials, fabricating parts acquired for the manufacturing process, or goods acquired for purpose of resale; (2) all the firm's expenses, including expenses of administering the enterprise, advertising, depreciation, and so forth; and (3) profit, the amount left over after subtracting all expenses from sales revenue. A heavy burden then rests on sales revenue because from it must flow the funds to cover the costs of the firm's operation. Consequently, the term "breakeven" begins to take on a very significant meaning. The marketing firm is supposed to cover all of its costs for each operating period. When it does just cover its costs, the system is said to break even, and in terms of the previous statement, such a result would be viewed as follows:

$$\text{sales revenue} = \text{total costs}$$

When sales revenue is greater than total costs, it is shown as:

$$\text{sales revenue} > \text{total costs}$$

The result or difference is profit. When sales revenue is less than total costs, it is shown as:

$$\text{sales revenue} < \text{total costs}$$

The result or difference is loss. The breakeven point is that point or stage in a firm's operation where sales revenue just equals total costs.

Elements in the Breakeven Point Analysis

Breakeven point analysis is a management tool that underscores the relationship among several decision variables: namely, price, costs, and volume of sales.

Sales Volume.   We have already discussed the critical importance of sales volume in the firm's operation. Sales volume is a function of prices charged and quantity sold. Much of the marketing firm's critical planning hinges around its sales budget which in turn is based upon the forecast of sales volume.

Costs.   There are several kinds of costs in most marketing organizations, but for simplicity's sake, we shall treat costs as if there were only two major kinds—fixed and variable.

Fixed costs are the costs of being in business. In this sense they are sunk or historical costs, and their real significance is that fixed costs, for a given level or range of operations, are fixed or constant at that level. Fixed costs, therefore, do not vary with the number of units produced. Even if there is no production, fixed costs continue. Insurance payments, the decay of plant and equipment, and security guards' salaries are all fixed costs.

Variable costs vary with the number of units produced and to simplify the breakeven analysis, we assume that variable costs fluctuate directly with the number of units produced. For example, if for every unit sold the variable costs are $10.00, then two units sold would mean a variable cost of $20.00, three units $30.00, and so on. As production increases, more materials must be purchased, more labor hired, more fuel and electricity consumed, and so on. For example, the more records and tapes produced and sold by RCA, the more technicians it must hire and plastics and energy it must consume. The more salvation rendered at the local church, the more sheet music, robes, and light bulbs it must buy. Such costs are variable costs rising or falling with the firm's level of output.

Contribution. The concept of contribution is critical to breakeven point analysis. Once fixed and variable costs are understood, the concept of contribution should be relatively easy to grasp. Suppose a marketer who manufacturs and sells T-shirts has a selling price to retailers of $7.00. If the marketer's variable costs (consisting of cost of goods sold) equal $3.50 and selling and other direct expenses are $1.50 for a total variable cost of $5.00, then the contribution to profit and overhead per unit equals $2.00. This figure, which was obtained by subtracting variable costs from sales revenue, can be shown as

$$SR - VC = \text{unit contribution}$$

The contribution is an amount that when totaled from all sales must eventually be used to pay off fixed costs.

To simplify the illustration further, assume that our marketer only sells this one item and has total fixed costs of $10,000 per year. Every shirt sold for $7.00 returns (after paying the variable cost of $5.00 per unit) $2.00 as contribution. Obviously, when enough shirts are sold, the manufacturer will eventually have sufficient money to pay the fixed costs of $10,000; when he sells exactly 5,001 shirts he will have made a profit of $2.00. Do you understand why?

The Graphic Approach to Breakeven Analysis

Using the same example we can show graphically the essential elements of breakeven point analysis. Figure 15-6 shows that the breakeven point is 5,000 units of sales, or $35,000. Recalling that $7.00 is the selling price, $7.00 × 5,000 = $35,000. Observe that the fixed cost of $10,000 does not vary with the number of units sold. Observe further that beyond the breakeven point, profits are earned; and that to the left of the breakdown point, that is, before it is reached, losses are incurred. The level of sales can have a profound effect on profits or losses, given the relationship between fixed and variable costs.

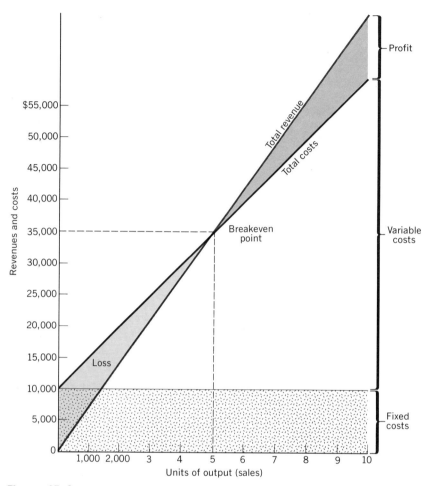

Figure 15-6 A graphic approach to breakeven analysis.

The fixed cost element of a firm's operation means that as more and more units are sold, the fixed costs can be increasingly spread over this larger output, a condition known as operating leverage.

The Arithmetic Approach to Breakeven Analysis

The graphic approach to breakeven analysis has the virtue of enabling one to visualize the relationships among the breakeven variables. Breakeven points can be computed much more readily by using simple arithmetic. To demonstrate the concept of operating leverage, consider again the previous illustration, where,

$$
\begin{aligned}
\text{selling price} &= \$7.00 \\
\text{variable cost} &= \$5.00 \\
\text{contribution} &= \$2.00 \\
\text{fixed costs} &= \$10{,}000
\end{aligned}
$$

In symbolic form,

$$
\begin{aligned}
\text{selling price} &= SP \\
\text{variable cost} &= VC \\
\text{contribution} &= C \\
\text{fixed costs} &= FC \\
\text{breakeven point} &= BP
\end{aligned}
$$

therefore,

$$
BP = \frac{FC}{SP - VC} \text{ or } \frac{FC}{C}
$$

From the example,

$$
\frac{\$10,000}{\$7.00 - \$5.00} \text{ or } \frac{\$10,000}{\$ 2.00} = 5,000 \text{ units, or}
$$

$$
BP = \$7.00 \times 5,000 \text{ units} = \$35,000
$$

Table 15-2 continues the illustration with some further modifications.

Table 15-2   Breakeven Table for Marketer of T-Shirts at Various Sales Levels*

	Level A	Level B	Level C
Revenue from sales	$21,000	$35,000	$49,000
Total variable costs	15,000	25,000	35,000
Total fixed costs	10,000	10,000	10,000
Profit or loss	4,000 loss	0	4,000 profit

*Given: Selling price, $7.00
Variable cost per unit, $5.00
Total fixed costs, $10,000

Table 15-2 shows that it is critical for a marketer to generate sales beyond the breakeven point. While there are a number of factors that affect the breakeven point, the most important is pricing. Under certain conditions a given marketer may enjoy a temporary monopoly condition. For example, the shirt we've been discussing may be a popular T-shirt or tank top with a unique picture or caption about a hit movie or a well-known rock group. A seller may be the only one to have the shirt at a particular time in a particular place. In such a situation, the seller may set a price higher than would be possible with more rigorous competition. An increase in selling price enables a marketer to reach the breakeven point much more rapidly. What would be the breakeven point if the price were $8.00 instead of $7.00?

Limitations to the Use of Breakeven Point Analysis

Breakeven point analysis is a simple yet valuable tool for marketing decision making and it has special usefulness for price decisions. However, its simplicity, at least the simplicity of the underlying assumptions regarding costs, is to some degree its undoing. It is unrealistic to assume that fixed costs remain the same at all levels of production and sales output. If sales volume falls enough, management is likely to react with drastic cuts in fixed cost, perhaps by reducing the number of marketing executives or slashing the advertising budget. On the other side of the coin, high levels of sales are likely to push the firm beyond a given scale of operations onto a higher plane of fixed costs. To continue using a given fixed cost figure for all levels of sales would be naive and unrealistic.

Elasticity

Elasticity is an economic concept which, when understood and measured, can be a valuable tool for price decision making. Earlier it was stated that the price decision maker is faced with considerable uncertainty regarding (1) the nature of demand for the company's product; (2) the competitive environment; and (3) competitors' reactions to the price decisions. The decision maker with some knowledge of elasticity will be less uncertain about the nature of demand, and should also be able to make better pricing decisions.

The concept of elasticity relates the percentage change in demand, or quantity of a commodity sold, to a percentage change in the commodity's price. Several relevant measures of elasticity can be drawn. For instance, a price elasticity of 1, or unitary elasticity, means that sales rise or fall by the same percentage as price falls or rises. Price elasticity greater than 1, or elastic demand, means that sales rise or fall by a greater percentage than price falls or rises. A price elasticity of less than 1—that is, inelastic demand—means that sales rise or fall by a smaller percentage than price falls or rises. Elasticity concepts affect sales revenue. When price elasticity equals 1, revenue remains the same; price elasticity greater than 1 means that sales or receipts increase with a decrease in price; and if price elasticity is less than 1, receipts fall when price does. All this is summarized in Table 15-3.

To the price decision maker, the concept of elasticity can be valuable in answering the question, "When is a price decision right?" Or looked at another way, if demand is the upper bound to pricing and cost the lower bound, elasticity can point out an unsatisfactory price decision, at least from the standpoint of maximizing sales revenues if not profits. From the standpoint of maximizing revenues, a given price is too high if demand is elastic at the price and too low if demand is inelastic.

Table 15-3 Relationships Between Prices and Sales Revenues

	(Given Different States of Elasticity)		
	Inelastic Demand (Less than 1)	Unitary Elasticity (Equal to 1)	Elastic Demand (Greater than 1)
Price increases	Revenues rise	Revenues constant	Revenues fall
Price decreases	Revenues fall	Revenues constant	Revenues rise

It is no simple matter for the price decision maker to estimate accurately the price elasticity of demand for the products in the total assortment mix. Price elasticity will vary with the magnitude of the price change, and it will vary considerably over time. The techniques for measuring price elasticity are beyond the scope of this treatment.[13] However, a general knowledge of elasticity concepts is needed in price decision making. The important generalization or decision rule for the price decision maker is that price elasticity of demand changes over the product's life cycle, in accordance with the extent of competition, over the selling season, and in relationship to the markup that is added to cost. It is an advantage in determining selling price to know what the elasticity of demand for a given product will be.

Elasticity is also an important determinant of market segmentation, the strategy based on the idea that the market for a particular product is composed of customers with different needs and wants. The crucial criterion for determining the desirability of segmenting a market on any basis is whether or not the different submarkets have different elasticities with respect to price and promotional policies of a firm.

Before proceeding, can you answer these questions:
1. What is meant by "administered pricing"?
2. Two administered pricing models are (1) cost plus pricing and (2) target rate of return pricing. Explain these two models.
3. What is meant by the elasticity of demand?

Price: **What You See Is Not Necessarily What You Pay**

Price, we have learned, is an amount of money paid by a buyer to a seller for a product or service. Price is the money value of a product or service as agreed upon in a market transaction. What we have is a kind of price equation, where

$$money = bundle\ of\ expectations$$

Included in the bundle of expectations may be a physical good or service plus other attributes such as delivery, installation, return privileges, and after-sale servicing.

Money is not just the list price either, because it is not always the final price. From the list price a series of discounts may be deducted and these affect the terms of trade and alter the price equation.

Either side of the price equation can therefore be altered and when it is, the price equation is affected. The list price is often altered in the price equation. Two factors are mainly responsible for altering the list price: *discounts* and *datings*.

---

[13] For a more detailed treatment of measuring price elasticity, see Douglas J. Dalrymple and Leonard J. Parsons, *Marketing Management,* 2nd ed. (New York: Wiley, 1980), pp. 369–375.

Discounts. Discounts are deductions from the billed invoice price that are granted under certain conditions. The most frequent forms of legal deductions are trade, quantity, and cash discounts.

Trade discounts are reductions from the list price given to all buyers in a certain class or category. They are sometimes referred to as "functional discounts," the logic being that they are given to cover a trade member's cost of performing a task in the distribution channel. Manufacturers, therefore, are likely to give retailers one discount, and wholesalers another. For example, a manufacturer with a list price of $14.50 for a woman's tailored shirt selling to either retailers, wholesalers, or both might grant them trade discounts of 30 percent and 20 percent. A wholesaler's purchase cost would be $14.50, less 30 percent ($4.35) less 20 percent ($2.03), or $14.50 − ($4.35 + $2.03), or $8.12. A retailer who purchased this item direct from the manufacturer would pay $14.50 less 30 percent, or $10.15. The 20 percent margin granted the wholesaler is an acknowledgement of his channel or functional contribution.

Quantity discounts are deductions from the billed or list price based upon the amount purchased. There are economies of scale or savings which accrue to a seller when large quantities are sold. Quantity discounts are limited to the actual savings that the large purchase makes possible. Although discounts have often taken the form of free goods, this form of discounting is subject to the same provisions of the Robinson Patman Act as an outright price concession.

Cash discounts are deductions from the list price granted by a seller to a reseller for the prompt payment of the net amount of the billed invoice. Typically, when talking about "cash discounts," business people mean a procedure applicable to marketers and resellers but not necessarily to ultimate consumers. Cash discounts can be taken by any buyer who wishes to pay the invoice on or before the stipulated discount period. Cash discounts are an important source of "other income" for many merchants. For example, a buyer may be offered terms of 2/10, N 30, which means a 2 percent discount can be deducted from the list price of the invoice total if the bill is paid within ten days after the date of the invoice, and the net amount is due thirty days after date of the invoice. A buyer who fails to take the discount is missing the opportunity to earn 36 percent on his or her money in terms of an equivalent annual rate of interest.[14]

Datings. Datings refer to the time period within which payment is required in order to obtain cash discounts (if offered) and the time at which payment for the goods eventually falls due. Many considerations affect a seller's attitudes toward datings. Competitive conditions are the most important factor, and it is the buyer's usual responsibility to negotiate for favorable dating provisions as part of buying behavior. Business conditions, the nature of the goods, the way they are marketed, the physical distance between buyer and seller, and trans-

---

[14] This conclusion is reached this way: There are 360 days in the business year. The buyer earns 2 percent for paying 20 days earlier. There are 18 such 20-day periods in a year, thus 2% × 18 = 36%, the equivalent annual rate of interest.

portation facilities available will all affect the kind of dating provisions provided as well as the negotiations that surround the other pricing and purchasing provisions.

The most popular dating provision is known as **ordinary dating.** This means that the credit period is based upon the date of the invoice, which usually coincides with the date the merchandise is shipped. For example, if the terms are 2/10, N 30, and the invoice date is April 14, the buyer may deduct 2 percent from the amount of the invoice if payment is remitted on or before April 24. If the buyer chooses not to take advantage of the discount, the full amount is due May 14.

Many other dating periods are often used. **Advanced dating** is used to induce a buyer to place early orders. It is a way, again, of affecting the true price of goods without affecting the money price or list price. **Extra dating** is a way of deferring the date on which credit terms begin to apply. It can take several forms. For example, **ROG** (receipt of goods) **dating** is used to give more reasonable treatment to buyers whose businesses are located a great distance from suppliers' shipping points. In these instances, credit terms apply from the date the goods are received rather than from the date of the invoice. **EOM** (end of the month) **dating** provides that credit terms date from the end of the month in which goods were purchased rather than from the date of the invoice; it is another popular dating and pricing provision.

It is obvious that **discounts** and **datings** are really extensions of a firm's pricing behavior. Such activities are a means of affecting the price equation. Giving the buyer "more" is enlarging the bundle of expectations being purchased by altering or manipulating the true money value without altering the list price of the merchandise.

Summary

Price is an important part of every firm's marketing strategy. It plays many roles in our economic system, but is primarily the mechanism that allocates scarce resources among alternative uses. Price decisions are perhaps the most complex and intricate decisions confronting the marketing manager. When they are made wisely, pricing practice becomes a powerful tool for assuring the success of the marketing program. When pricing decisions go awry, the firm loses volume and profits, and even suffers a diminished company image. Pricing affects the product image, is tied closely to promotional activity, and has a significant bearing upon the behavior of a firm's competitors. Price is known by many names: fees, rents, premiums, honorariums, bribes, assessments, and so on. Whatever it is called, however, price and pricing activities are usually responsible for most of the profit differences among similar firms.

Most marketers use cost oriented pricing approaches rather than demand oriented models. The economist sets price in an ideal way, where marginal cost equals marginal revenue. However, it requires that the decision makers know the precise shape and slope of their demand curves and have good information pertaining to their marginal costs of producing and selling. Since decision makers usually do not have this information and have difficulty obtaining it, they cannot rely too heavily on marginal cost-demand oriented pricing models.

Marketing prices are usually administered prices, that is, prices are not determined by the impersonal market forces of supply and demand. Instead, the price decision maker has some discretion in choosing the price that will be placed on the commodity or service. Most administered pricing models are either cost-plus or target rate of return models. Both require forecasting sales and standard costs and adding a margin to cover costs and return a profit.

Pricing decisions can be aided by using breakeven point analysis and by understanding the concept of price elasticity of demand. Price is not a clear-cut term. Instead of talking solely of price, it may be more realistic to talk of a price equation. The price equation acknowledges that there are two dimensions to each transaction and that price is what one pays to receive a bundle of expectations. When the bundle or package of expectations is changed, the true money value of price may also change. Consequently, datings, discounts, and other inducements that may be offered shade or affect the actual price paid.

Review Questions

1. How is price determined by the forces of supply and demand?
2. Define the concept of price. What is meant by "the role of price in marketing strategy"? Why does price "have many names"?
3. What is meant by "price competition"? How does price competition differ from nonprice competition?
4. Some pricing models are called normative pricing models. Explain. Most economic models are normative models. Why?
5. What is the economic model most relevant to real world marketing pricing? Why? What other economic model might have great relevance to some real world marketing-pricing behavior?
6. What is meant by the upper and lower bounds to a decision maker's pricing behavior? Explain.
7. Explain and define (1) average cost pricing and (2) target rate of return pricing.
8. A firm plans to market a new kind of pop-yogurt that will appeal to teenagers as a snack food. They have fixed costs of $10,000.00 and variable costs of 10 cents per unit, and are planning a selling price to the dealer of 25 cents per unit. What would be their breakeven point at this price?
9. If the company in question 8 wanted to estimate the demand for this new product, how might they proceed?
10. What is meant by the price equation? How do such things as delivery, installations, return goods privileges, discounts, and datings affect the price equation?

Case 15-1

Laker's Skytrain Air Service

Freddie Laker is the scrappy president of Britain-based Laker Airways. In 1971, Laker proposed what he called Skytrain "shuttle" flights between New York and London at rock bottom prices. After six years of transatlantic negotiations and government red tape on both sides, in mid-1977 the Carter administration approved Laker's plans and Skytrain service was ready for boarding.

Mr. Laker is considered an aggressive, hard-nosed businessman. He also appears to have taken Marketing 300, or its equivalent. In any event, his competitors fear that the combination of the two may result in a bargain for travelers to London and lots of money for Freddie Laker.

Laker airways won approval by the Civil Aeronautics Board for his proposal to provide low-fare Skytrain service between New York and London. His plan is based upon a simple idea known as "full plane economics." This concept is based upon the following simple reasoning: if he keeps his operating costs to a minimum and flies large planes, Laker may be able to fill all the seats by offering customers fares significantly lower than the cartel set rates, and still make more money than the regularly scheduled carriers which fly half-empty aircraft. This, presumably, should make both the customers—many of whom cannot now afford to fly—and Mr. Laker happy.

Consequently, his Skytrain shuttle is a bare bones, one-class operation. Travelers cannot purchase tickets more than six hours in advance. There is no extensive network of ticket offices and computer reservation systems. It is strictly first come, first served. When the available seats of each flight are sold—345 during the peak summer season and 189 during the rest of the year—that will be it. The only meals provided will be paid for when the traveler buys the ticket. And all of it must be paid for in cash;

no credit cards will be accepted. Laker plans to carry no cargo and have no mail operations—just people.

Under the license issued to him by the British government, the number of people he can carry is limited. He is restricted to eleven flights a week during the peak travel season, and one flight a day, with half the plane roped off, during the rest of the year.

The price for the flight will be $270 round trip, or $135 each way. The current coach fare between New York and London is $387 one way during the peak summer season and $323 one way the rest of the year. The lowest fare generally available from the scheduled airlines across the Atlantic and back is about $440, if the passenger is able and willing to make reservations and pay for the ticket forty-five days in advance of the flight and can stay twenty-two to forty-five days.

Laker has always contended that there are a number of market segments among air travelers and that his Skytrain will not appeal to all of them. He believes that many who can afford it will want to continue to fly the scheduled carriers. Families and others, he feels, who want to be assured of their seats and who can plan their vacations more than a month ahead of time will want to take advantage of charter flights, which offer significant savings over the scheduled fares. Expense account business executives who fly overseas will disdain to fly the Laker Skytrain because they prefer the first-class luxury accommodations of the scheduled lines. Laker's flights, he contends, are for the "little people," the "forgotten man" and the "forgotten woman"—for the travelers who may not otherwise be able to go to Europe.

Laker estimates that he will carry 111,337 eastbound passengers and 113,169 westbound the first year, thus filling 87.5 percent of the available seats. The other carriers argued before the Civil Aeronautics Board that Laker's proposal could not possibly make money. Laker, however, estimates that he will make $4 million a year.

Laker has a reputation as an efficient low-cost operator who is out to make a profit. Laker's enterprises have made consistent profits during the past thirty years he has been in business. Prior to the introduction of Skytrain, Laker was engaged in extensive air charter operations. His flights have carried about 1 million passengers a year—400,000 between England and North America (half to Canada and half to the United States), and 600,000 to European cities.

Questions

1. Appraise and evaluate Laker's marketing strategy.

2. What is the principal element in Laker's marketing mix? How does Laker perceive the importance of price in relationship to his other marketing activities?

3. Illustrate the use of the price equation with Laker's Skytrain and with the full service approach of the regularly scheduled airlines.

4. Is Laker's Skytrain pricing program a demand oriented or a cost oriented approach? Explain. Do you believe Laker is aware of the concept of price elasticity of demand? Explain.

5. If Laker fills 87.5 percent of the available Skytrain seats the first year of his operation, he forecasts profits of $4 million. Based on the concepts of breakeven analysis, what will happen if Laker should fill only 65 percent of the available seats? Why? What will happen if his flights are filled to capacity?

Case 15-2

The Maui Potato Chip Company

The Maui Potato Chip Company is facing an unusual dilemma—too much business and too much popularity. People are throwing their money at Dewey Kobayashi, owner of the Maui Potato Chip Company of Kahului, Maui, Hawaii. Kobayashi, 48, a stocky Mr. Five-by-Five, balding and brown-eyed, not only boasts a six-month order backlog, but he simply cannot keep abreast of the various financial offers cascading down on him.

The Wall Street Journal published a feature article about Kobayashi and his Maui Potato Chip Company and ever since then, he's gotten phone calls, letters, and telegrams offering all kinds of money. Everyone urges him to expand his business, and most who write or call are anxious to supply him cash for a piece of the

action. Many urge him to go national or international with his product; others urge him to franchise outlets of his business. The reason for all these offers is that Dewey Kobayashi makes excellent potato chips. Connoisseurs of potato chips insist they are the tastiest, crunchiest, most flavorful, eatable, satisfying potato chips in the world.

Kobayashi sells every pound he can bag, mostly to supermarkets, grocers, and hotels on the picturesque Hawaiian island. He has no surplus.

"I just can't fill the demand," he says as he holds up a sheaf of mail orders. "I just don't have time, and I don't have the personnel. Every day I just fill a few mail orders, mostly to people I think need them the most." Tourists from all over Maui flock to Kobayashi's factory to stock up on his "Kitch'n Cook'd" potato chips, which sell for $1.08 per package.

Maui Potato Chips are sliced from Burbank russet potatoes grown in the Tule Lake area of Northern California, where so many Japanese were interned during World War II. These potatoes contain a lot of sugar. After they have been thoroughly cleaned, they are sliced fairly thick. There is nothing uniform about the size of the chips. They are fried in Wesson Oil. There is, however, a secret process used for salting and drying that Kobayashi is not about to disclose. The firm right now is doing a gross annual volume of about $300,000, with a net profit of roughly 10 percent. The first year of his operation in 1957, sales were $25,000. In 1971 the firm moved to its present factory, which has 9,000 square feet. The building cost $87,000. Kobayashi currently has eleven employees and he himself works a twelve-hour day.

Kobayashi is somewhat uncertain as to what to do and how to proceed, even under such favorable conditions. To take advantage of his market opportunity—already other firms are marketing what they call "Maui-like potato chips"—Kobayashi needs to expand and for that he needs capital. He definitely does not want to lose control of his operation by taking on any partners or even other investors.

One of his associates has urged him to consider his product a premium product and to price and merchandise it accordingly. This would mean raising the price to, say, $1.79 or even $1.99 per package. Thus the added revenue could be used for expansion and the increased price would act as a brake on the soaring demand.

Questions

1. Do you believe Maui Potato Chips could be priced and merchandised as a premium product? What kind of price strategy or policy does a premium product call for?
2. To what other uses might the additional revenue from the increased price be put?
3. How much additional revenue would a price of $1.79 per bag as opposed to the $1.08 per bag price bring in? How much additional profit?

Chapter 16

Pricing: Policies and Practices

Too many people are under the impression that marketing activities inevitably yield large profits and that a given price for a commodity almost always contains both high dollar and high percentage profit. In most firms, this is rarely true. It is true that business managers hope that prices will cover operating costs and generate a profit, but the actual amount of profit is usually surprisingly small.

To demonstrate the impact of pricing and markup decisions on profitability throughout a marketing channel, consider the following. The Precision Instrument Company of Dallas, Texas, produces and sells a hand-held calculator. The calculator is sold to distributing companies, or wholesalers, who in turn sell to retail outlets, especially student book stores on college campuses. Suppose you purchase one of the four-function calculators from your student book store. The cost and pricing figures that transpire throughout the entire marketing channel might look something like this:

Step 1. The Student Book Shop selling price to you, the consumer, is $12.95.

markup on selling price	= 40%, or $5.18
retail price − markup	= cost
$12.95 − $5.18	= $7.77
profit (8%) + expenses (32%)	= markup (40%)
$1.04 + $4.14	= $5.18

Thus, given a $12.95 selling price, a markup of 40 percent yields a dollar markup of $5.18, of which 8 percent, or $1.04, is profit and 32 percent, or $4.14, is operating expenses.

Step 2. The student Book Shop bought the calculator from Tri-State Distributing Company.

The Student Book Shop's purchase price	= $7.77
Tri-State Distributing Company's selling price	= $7.77
Tri-State Distributing's markup on selling price	= 20%, or $1.55
price − markup	= distributor's cost
$7.77 − $1.55	= $6.22
profit (8%) + expenses (12%)	= markup (20%)
$0.62 + $0.93	= $1.55

In this transaction, the Tri-State Distributing Company received a price of $7.77 for the hand-held, four-function calculator. With a markup of 20 percent, after covering operating expenses of 12 percent, or $.93 per unit, Tri-State made a profit of $0.62, or 8 percent of selling price. When seen as a return on total investment, an 8 percent profit on sales could be a much larger (or smaller) return.

Step 3. Tri-State Distributing Company purchased the calculator from Precision Instruments Manufacturing Company.

Tri-State Distributing Company's purchase price = $6.22

Precision Instrument's selling price = $6.22

Precision Instrument's markup per unit = manufacturing cost (45%) + marketing cost (40%) + profit (15%) = selling price = $2.80 + $2.49 + $0.93 = $6.22

Step 3 shows that Precision Instruments made a profit of $0.93, or 15 percent, on a selling price of $6.22 after covering all costs of manufacturing and marketing. It is clear from this illustration that no member of the channel is making a huge profit. In each instance the selling price must cover (1) the acquisition cost of the goods, (2) the operating expenses, and (3) some amount of profit. An additional observation would appear warranted. This product was sold by three sellers—the manufacturer, the wholesaler, and the retailer; yet only $2.59 in profit was earned by all three. Notice that the profit figures are

retailer	$1.04
wholesale distributor	0.62
manufacturer	0.93
	$2.59

or as a percentage of final retail selling price,

$$\frac{\$2.59}{\$12.95} = 20\% \text{ profit}$$

Profits by most businesses—retailers, wholesalers, and manufacturers—are usually not excessive; selling price must cover a great many expenses before profits actually occur.[1] Determining the ideal price that will cover these expenses and generate profits requires an understanding of both cost oriented and demand oriented pricing approaches. Pricing decisions must also be tied to the firm's objectives and reflect a wide range of possible pricing objectives, all of which are the focus of this chapter. Pricing is a difficult part of determining a marketing strategy, demanding the application of both the art and science of price decision making.

Pricing Objectives and Price Determination

Pricing objectives are comprehensive goals that define the role of price in a company's long-range plans and overall corporate strategy. Therefore pricing policies, and specific pricing behavior in particular, are not the result of a series of mechanical acts, as one might infer from the opening illustrations.

[1] To learn more about the myth of "fat profits." see Gilbert Burck, "The Myths and Realities of Corporate Pricing,"*Fortune Magazine*, April 1972, pp. 85–89 and 125–126.

Markups are not just applied to costs to arrive at "a price." In nearly every price decision demand is measured when possible and considered, competitive behavior is anticipated, reseller needs and practices are evaluated, the importance of the specific product in the product line is analyzed, and overall company goals and objectives are reviewed. Managers pay special attention to the novel or nonrecurring decisions that affect many new-product introductions.

Pricing Objectives and Company Objectives

Like other operating objectives, pricing objectives stem from the company's overall corporate goals and aims. There are about as many objectives of organizations as there are organizations themselves but basically they can be distilled down to a number of goals common to many companies. Most firms aim to survive, make money and avoid losses, serve customer needs, gain community acceptance by fulfilling social responsibilities, win recognition and create favorable images for their products, minimize the risk of lawsuits and government intervention in the company's affairs. Such objectives become a kind of value system that guides the company and its officers in all operating matters including pricing.

A firm's pricing problems and opportunities mirror its overall objectives. When a firm is explicit and forthright about defining its corporate purposes, the price decision maker can then specifically evaluate the obstacles and opportunities it faces in the pricing situation. The objectives of profitability and growth, while important, constitute but a small part of the stated pricing objectives. Pricing is often undertaken to enhance the image of the firm and its offerings, build traffic, discourage entrants, stabilize the market, or maintain price leadership arrangements.

Not Meeting Your Objectives? Maybe Something's Wrong. The real value of pricing goals and objectives is that they are important benchmarks or guidelines for evaluating performance. For example, with clear-cut pricing objectives, the firm can assess its performance at the end of an operating period. If objectives are not being met, there may be weaknesses in the firm's pricing policies and practices. By comparing actual pricing performance with planned performance based upon objectives, a firm may readily identify some of the pricing problems it is facing. Among them may be the following:

1. Prices have declined.
2. Prices are too high in comparison with competitors' prices.
3. Price is too low, especially in some markets.
4. Company prices are perceived as exploitative and the company's image suffers.
5. The firm places excessive financial burdens on its resellers such as limiting or refusing trade credit, or permitting no return goods privileges.
6. Price differentials among items in the price line are objectionable and unjustifiable.
7. A company's price changes too frequently.
8. The firm's price downgrades both the product and the company.

9. A company's price destabilizes the market, which has become steady after great difficulty.
10. The company offers too many price variations and thus confuses its customers.
11. Prices are perceived by customers as higher than they really are.
12. The firm's policies attract customers who are only price conscious and therefore have no loyalty to firms whose strategy underscores product quality, dependability of service, or other nonprice attributes.[2]

It is obvious that a firm's price policies and behavior do not affect just current sales but have far-reaching implications for the enterprise's long-run market success as well. The list of pricing difficulties also suggests that the company should monitor its operations closely and if such problems occur, the price decision maker needs to reevaluate the firm's pricing behavior and possibly change some of its pricing practices.

Pricing is a Critical Management Function

Pricing is a controllable variable in every firm's marketing strategy. Indeed, it is often one of the easiest to control and the one that can most readily be changed. It may take weeks, months, or years to change the product. Its channel of distribution may be well established by tradition and practice. Advertising and sales promotion may take a long time to change. But price can be changed quickly. If a competitor lowers a price, you can retaliate at once. If sales are lagging and you believe your prices are too high, you can lower them immediately. Or if the product is designed and its marketing strategy approved by the venture team, last-minute assessment of demand and competition may suggest a higher price than that which was planned. Adopting the higher price is a simple matter.

Price is a critical part of every marketing strategy because nearly every buyer is sensitive to it. Many buyers are more responsive to price than they are to other sales or promotional inducements. As one wag eloquently stated, "There's no brand loyalty that 2 cents off won't overcome." A small price reduction or a price slightly lower than the competition's may give a greater boost to sales than increased expenditures on advertising, intensified personal selling, generous credit terms, or other inducements.

Determining the Right Price

There is seldom a sure way of setting the best price to charge under all circumstances. The situation often determines the price and since many firms sell in many different situations, they may have several different prices. However, it is useful to explore the two extremes in the pricing problem: "When is a price too low?" and "When is it too high?"

A price is too low (1) when the customer would pay more and when the

[2] Based upon Alfred R. Oxenfeldt, "A Decision Making Structure for Price Decisions," *Journal of Marketing* **37** (January 1973), pp. 48–53.

higher price would gain the firm a greater net return and (2) when the price does not cover at least the variable costs of producing and marketing the product in the short run. When too little can be sold because of the price, it is too high. The high price thus prevents the firm from gaining the greatest net return profitwise, increasing its market share to the fullest, penetrating new markets, or creating the most favorable image for its products. Prices are too high when a buyer's resistance is unusually stiff and cannot be attributed to his or her perceptions of the products, to service, distribution, or other aspects of the marketing program.

The right price falls between the two extremes and, once again, management must be familiar with and aware of the underlying demand forces and cost structures so that these two extremes can be avoided and the right prices charged for the company's products.

The Multistage Approach to Pricing

The pricing decision itself emerges out of a series of subdecisions all of which are related to pricing but that must be considered in a kind of stair-step fashion before the actual adoption of the price. In short, the price decision like those governing product planning and development, promotion, or channels, is not a single step but a series of analyses and resulting decisions on a sequence of subproblems. As each one is made, the uncertainty (which arises from lack of knowledge) is systematically reduced so that the final price decision can be made with greater assurance.

Nor are pricing decisions of a single type. Obviously, some are more critical than others. Pricing the pioneer product that has few if any substitutes, and thus few if any competitors, confronts the price decision maker with a special challenge.[3] But in many ways so does pricing the well-known and stable product with a known demand factor, scores of competitors, and a considerable number of acceptable substitutes. Uncertainty marks both of these extreme situations as well as the many possibilities between. For nearly all pricing decisions there exists a series of steplike procedures which tend, when used, to organize and systematize the process and hence produce better results.[4] Figure 16-1 shows the basic elements in a sequential, or **multistage, pricing process.**

As Figure 16-1 demonstrates, pricing decisions are always made as a part of the larger marketing strategy. If you compare Figure 16-1 with Figure 3-1 in chapter 3, you will observe that pricing decisions emerge out of and are an integral part of the firm's overall marketing strategy and planning and that pricing, as is the case with all marketing effort, begins with market opportunity analysis. As you can see, the first four steps are essentially the same in both figures. Pricing is a part of strategic market planning and as such fits neatly into the strategic planning diagram introduced in chapter 3.

---

[3] See Joel Dean, "Pricing Policies for New Products,"*Harvard Business Review*, November–December 1976, pp. 141–153.

[4] Based upon Alfred R. Oxenfeldt, "Multi-Stage Approach to Pricing,"*Harvard Business Review*, July–August 1960, pp. 125–133.

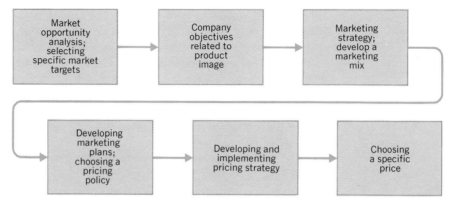

Figure 16-1 Multistage pricing process.

It should be recognized that no one step-by-step approach could possibly be applicable to all pricing decisions. The great diversity in pricing problems and situations would rule this out. Nor can any single approach ever guarantee that the decision maker will reach the best, or for that matter even a satisfactory, price. Every decision must be tailored to the existing circumstances—the product, the competition, the market, and the situation. As a consequence, experience, trial and error, good management, and quite often good luck all contribute to the quality of the price decision making process.

In order to understand the multistage approach to pricing, suppose we examine briefly each of the six stages in the process.

Step 1—Selecting Specific Market Targets.   Marketing targets are chosen after carefully assessing marketing opportunities. Based on this assessment and on a knowledge of company strengths and weaknesses, the firm commits its energies to specific marketing targets. To some extent the commitment imposes a set of broad constraints on the firm's pricing decisions: namely, the types of customers, or market segments it will seek. For example, the builder who decides to cater to the low-income single-family residence market will of necessity keep prices of the homes low. Or when Sears decides to include an early warning smoke alarm system in its merchandise line, company executives, who know their market, know that the item must meet certain price constraints. It must be low enough to penetrate the middle income market segment and high enough to merit the Sears image.

Step 2—Relating Company Objectives to Product Image.   Successful marketing increasingly depends upon creating favorable product images. Some products project an image of high intrinsic quality, others project low- or medium-quality images. Companies invariably seem to turn out products that are consistent with their own objectives. The firm's selection of its company and product image is usually dictated by the kind of customers it is trying to attract. Design, promotion, the channels of distribution all contribute to a product's image, but nothing may affect that image more than does the product's price.[5]

Step 3—Pricing and the Product Mix.

This step of the multistage approach to pricing calls for choosing a combination of marketing devices that will create and reinforce the desired company and product image while achieving maximum sales for the planned level of dollar outlays. All elements of the marketing mix are essential to the product's overall success but the role assigned to each must be planned with great care. For example, the marketing mix decision at this stage may call for at least tentative answers to these questions:

1. Will the product be advertised?
2. How heavily will it be advertised?
3. Are salespeople essential to the success of the product?
4. How much will be spent for its development and refinement?
5. Will the item complement our existing product line?
6. What physical distribution services are necessary to market the product?
7. How much will price appeal be emphasized?

Once these and similar questions are answered, the role of price becomes clearer and the decision maker is now better able to consider some specific pricing policies for the product.

Step 4—Select a Pricing Policy.

For example, questions such as these come up in nearly every company's pricing situation.

1. Should we meet competitors' price reductions?
2. If market demands rise because of industry shortages and our firm has ample supplies, should we raise prices?
3. Should our firm strive to stabilize market prices for its products?
4. Will our company attempt to price below, above, or at prevailing market rates?
5. Will we use price as a form of promotional activity?[6]

Pricing policies are broad guidelines that allow the firm to approach its pricing decisions consistently. However, when market opportunity and overall corporate objectives change over time, policies must be adjusted accordingly. Broadly speaking, price policies enable the firm to set upper and lower limits to its pricing decision, which means that determining price policies brings the firm one step closer to determining specific prices for its products.

---

[5] For example, see Kent B. Monroe, "Buyers' Subjective Perception of Price," *Journal of Marketing Research,* February 1973, pp. 70–80. Also, see Daniel A. Nimer, "Pricing the Profitable Sale Has a Lot To Do with Perception," *Sales Management,* May 19, 1975, pp. 13–14.

[6] For more related to this issue, see David A Goodman and Kevin W. Moody, "Determining Optimum Price Promotion Quantities," *Journal of Marketing* **34** (October 1970), pp. 31–39.

Step 5—Determine a Price Strategy.   Closely related to policy is strategy, a comprehensive plan of action. Policies are formulated to deal with broad general issues of a recurrent and more or less standard nature. Strategy permits the firm to react and accommodate to the changing conditions of the market place. For instance, markets are frequently beset with new and unanticipated developments such as:

1. A new, price-cutting competitor suddenly emerges.
2. Through a cease-and-desist order the Justice Department compels your firm to stop selling to a certain class of buyers at a special reduced price.
3. An economic recession has slowed down the demand for your product.
4. A new product falls drastically short of management's expectations about its market penetration.

Situations like these require special attention and possible adjustments in one's pricing procedures; they may even call for short-term adjustments in pricing policies. As long as such acute conditions endure, pricing strategy would suggest a careful day-by-day monitoring and assessment of price policies and practices. When the special situation has abated, the firm can relax its vigilance over its pricing activities.

Step 6—Setting a Specific Price.   At this point the price decision maker should find that much of the uncertainty surrounding the overall price decision has been eliminated. With each progressive step the decision maker's knowledge about the relevant factors affecting the price decision has been increased by careful study and analysis. Having arrived at this final stage, the executive will find that the price that can actually be charged is bounded by many factors, including cost and demand. However, in most market situations, the price maker will discover that fairly wide discretion is still possible in setting the final price for the product.

The Merits of a Multistage Pricing Process

The hallmark of good management decision making is analysis, the breaking down of a complex problem into a series of less complex subproblems. The multistage approach to pricing breaks the pricing decision into six relatively manageable pieces that can be analyzed separately and then put together again to arrive at a well-considered decision. Careful analysis minimizes the risk of impairing or destroying important elements of the firm's corporate and product images. Such a multistage approach to pricing also makes it possible to delegate authority and responsibility for decision making in this area to a number of individuals within the organization. Finally, this approach tends to minimize an inclination which may arise in some firms to take a more mechanical or formula approach to price determination. This multistage process, rather than emphasizing just cost or demand factors, looks carefully at intangible but equally important considerations, such as customer perception of the marketer and of the things he sells.

The Total Scope of Pricing

Pricing is a comprehensive management activity. To do it right, the price decision maker must consider many highly relevant internal and external factors. The internal factors include many of the activities just discussed under the multistage process of price determination: pricing objectives, the role of price in the marketing program, product characteristics and image, costs of production and marketing, and the firm's organization for pricing. These are, within the context of marketing strategy, controllable pricing variables. They are controllable in that the firm can determine their nature, assess their direct impact on the pricing decision, and if necessary modify them. By contrast, there are a host of variables which are largely uncontrollable and these include such factors as legal considerations, the nature of competition, the kinds and characteristics of buyers, price elasticity of demand, and others.[7] These are uncontrollable because they are largely beyond the direct control or influence of the firm. The price decision, as it is constrained or affected by both controllable and uncontrollable variables, is shown in Figure 16-2.

Every price decision maker must take into account both the controllable and uncontrollable variables when developing price policies and procedures. The entire range of pricing problems which confronts the firm such as transfer pricing (applied when one department in a company sells its product to another department in the same company), single versus multiple product pricing ($1.00 each versus three for $2.89), discounting, the selection of dealer margins, setting price policies, and developing pricing strategy generally must be made against the backdrop of the external environment within which the firm operates.

It is no easy task to solve this problem logically and systematically, but a multistage approach, as we have seen, can be helpful. As in other marketing endeavors, judgment and experience are also advantages. However, sheer guessing or pricing "by hunch and by golly" is not likely to lead to sound pricing policies or prices that propel the firm foward its pricing objectives of profits, sales volume, or unit volume.

Pricing *is* to some degree an art and not a science, and judgment is an important part of the pricing process; but for better than average success, it must be informed judgment, not gut-level intuition and hunch.

Before proceeding, can you answer these questions:
1. What is the relationship between pricing and company objectives?
2. Why is pricing a critical management function?
3. What is meant by a multistage approach to pricing? What are the merits of such an approach?

---

[7] For a more extended treatment, see Donald V. Harper, *Price Policies and Procedure* (New York: Harcourt, Brace and World, 1966), pp. 292–296.

Figure 16-2 Internal and external variables affecting pricing.

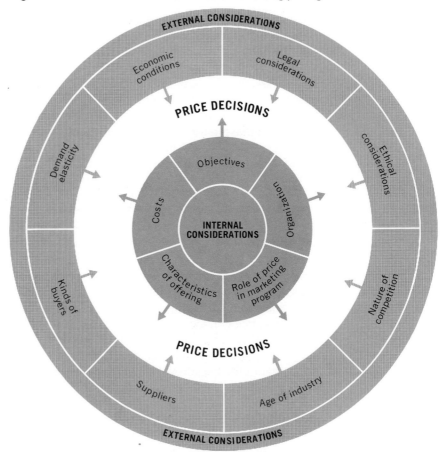

Source: Donald V. Harper, *Price Policies and Procedure* (New York: Harcourt, Brace and World, 1966), p. 293.

Alternative Pricing Policies in the Marketing Mix

There are many pricing policies that most firms might follow. For example, firms may adopt "high price and high quality" as their marketing policy; they may seek large volume at a low price; they may decide to keep prices below those charged by most other firms; they may elect to charge the same prices as other sellers; or they may try to attract the overprivileged market segment by charging substantially more than other firms. Each of these policies, and there are many others that we will explore, represents a general policy into which specific prices fit.

Many marketing firms do not explicitly state their pricing objectives or even what policies they will use to attain them; yet all have such policies even if they are only implicit and subjectively understood. Hence, in loose terminology a price policy means all those changes in price, or deliberate lack of changes in price, management decrees in pursuing its corporate objectives.

Drawing by Sauers; © 1974 The New Yorker Magazine, Inc.

The marketing firm's price policies determine and shape the firm's specific pricing decisions. For this reason, it is necessary to analyze and understand a whole range of pricing policies, in order to understand fully the firm's actual pricing decisions.

Pricing and Competition

The pricing policies of any specific firm are likely to be influenced by the pricing policies and behavior of its competitors. Most firms must reckon with their competition and modify their own pricing behavior in light of that of the other firms in the particular market. There are several pricing policy positions that any firm can adopt in relation to its competition. In some instances, a given firm may decide to follow the policy of *pricing at the market*. That is, it develops a systematized approach to pricing and its decision rule for pricing might be, loosely: What is our principal competition charging at this time? We will match their price.

Such a price policy has obvious disadvantages. First of all, it really means that the follower firm is abandoning its management perogative of decision making, choosing from among alternative courses of action. The price leader (barometric firm) may not be setting prices that are optimum or near optimum for the price follower. Yet many firms frequently practice price followership (pricing at the market).

A firm choosing not to price at the market has two remaining options: pricing *below the market* or pricing *above the market*. A specific firm may adopt either of these two alternatives as a blanket measure, each for good reasons.[8]

Pricing Below the Market.   Firms wishing to build a strong consumer franchise may want to underscore their low prices, which are ready means of gaining market share, increasing sales volume, or kindling customer awareness. Such a pricing policy is a consistent and meaningful part of many firms' profit goals. Supermarkets as well as department stores are good examples of firms whose pricing policies often reflect competitive considerations. In larger communities with many different stores, the diversity of the demand for food, clothing, and general merchandise items will generate a diversity in the quality of the product assortments and hence, in the price policies among stores. Some retailers—whether supermarkets, department stores, or general merchandisers—will attempt to be the price leaders and price below the market. Some will price with the majority of their competitors; and some will stress factors other than price, and price above the market. Manufacturer-marketers, largely for the same reason—diversity of demand—also follow the practice of pricing above, at, or below the market.

Penetration Prices.   **Penetration prices** are really "impact" prices. They are prices that are set deliberately low so that the product will penetrate the market and make an impact on customer awareness and response. Texas Instrument's low prices for its hand-held "student-model" calculators are an example of penetration prices. Penetration prices often result when a company relaxes an earlier, exclusive pricing policy to reach a broader market. in addition to the hand-held calculators, penetration prices are now evident in such commodities as CB radios and LED digital watches. Penetration prices are sometimes subtle, moving down in very small increments; others may be sprung on the market with great suddenness and catch other competitors unaware.

Many products are rescued from premature market decline by lowering the price enough to reach new markets. There are some important conditions that may signal a need for aggressive pricing for market penetration. As an example, pricing to gain new markets may deserve careful consideration when:

1. Sales respond vigorously to reduction in price.
2. Substantial savings in production costs are achieved as the result of ever-larger volumes of sales.
3. There is a perceived desire on the part of many consumers to possess the product in question.
4. There is a strong threat of potential competition.

[8] For an excellent discussion of these two pricing alternatives, see Robert A. Lynn, *Price, Policies and Marketing Management* (Homewood, IL: Irwin, 1967), pp. 131–145. Much of this section is built upon this treatment.

Keep-Out Prices.   A **keep-out price** is a preemptive price. Purposely designed to discourage potential market entrants or deter firms already in the market, a keep-out price is a signal to combat. It is, in effect, a challenge. "Here is my low price," it says, "I dare you to match it or go below it because if you do, I may go still lower and drive your product to the wall." Some keep-out prices may be well below the actual costs of production and marketing. Keep-out pricing is practical only for large firms with ample resources or for firms with unusual technological capabilities who may not wish to share a market with potential competitors. Such pricing is a high-risk venture, however, because some firm or firms may take up the challenge and instead of suffering short-term losses, the keep-out aggressors may fail to reach their objectives of market penetration or dominance and be forced to withdraw from the battle.

Promotional Prices.   A price is promotional when it is such a strong element in a product's total image that it becomes a natural part of the firm's advertising and selling. In an economy characterized by constantly and rapidly rising prices, **promotional prices** have become scarce.

There are still some promotional prices, however; Rexall continues its Rexall Sales and 2-for-1 promotions. Old Milwaukee beer is a promotional brand produced by Schlitz that enables them to promote and compete pricewise with other nonpremium beers. Sears has its low-priced Guardsman tires, which it uses to compete with the "third line" tires of other manufacturers and resellers. Gillette still uses promotional prices to introduce new products and to expand its market penetration for existing products.

Penetration prices, keep-out prices, and promotional prices are all policies that try to undersell competition. Price cutting can be a vicious form of competition. It often occurs when demand is sluggish, there are many competitors, and supplies of goods are ample. Price competition has abated some in recent years, the victim of shortages and inflation. A vanishing part of marketing Americana may be the gasoline price war, the milk price war, the dumping of agricultural products in overseas markets—examples of using price to clear the market of surplus products. There may soon be no surplus products!

Pricing Above the Market

When a firm chooses to price above the market, it is saying in effect that price, while important, is less so than other considerations. A price above the market conveys a strong message to buyers and consumers. It says, our quality may warrant this higher price. Or, because of this product's uniqueness, fine design, superior technology, and exclusiveness, or our superior distribution services, you will have to pay more if you want to buy.

Skimming Prices.   In setting prices above the market, one of the most common policies, especially for new products, is to set a figure that will "skim the cream." This means setting a high price for the buyers eager to purchase the new item and charging what the initial traffic will bear. **Skimming prices** are used for a variety of new products—children's toys, drugs, appliances, and clothing. Consumers who are innovators and early adopters often have markedly different demand preferences than do the middle majority adopters or the laggards. They are almost always willing to pay a premium price for what is new because it offers them the unique satisfaction of being an early or exclu-

Pricing strategy aimed at a specific market target.

If the price doesn't shock you, it could mean you're either very rich or very serious about cooking.

The Farberware Advantage™ Collection is designed expressly for the person who approaches cooking as an art, rather than a chore. The person who will take advantage of its extraordinary capabilities.

Food has never been treated with this much respect.

With this collection, Farberware has succeeded in creating the perfect environment for food to be cooked in.

Throughout each piece is a core of aluminum three layers thick. This is the reason heat is distributed more quickly and evenly than in ordinary cookware.

To give you the ultimate in strength and beauty, the aluminum core is surrounded by two layers of special high-grade stainless steel. This five layer construction is why there's no cookware in the world that can measure up to the Farberware Advantage Collection.

Consider the attention to detail. The stainless steel covers are designed to create a self-basting, flavor-retaining environment. The graceful rims of this cookware have been gently rounded so they pour without dripping and are easier to clean. And the handles are made like the ones that adorn the finest cutlery. They're crafted of specially-treated, hard American birch. And they're placed at just the right height and angle to allow maximum stability and comfort in handling.

Since you've got to start at the bottom to make it to the top, all the bottoms are gently roughed so they'll lie securely on the cooking surface.

A collection of American masterpieces.

The collection consists of over 20 pieces of the best conceived and executed cookware ever made.

It's also expensive. (By necessity, not choice.) Prices range from $36 to $120.

We suggest you think of this cookware as an investment. One where you'll be continually rewarded.

Farberware® 1500 Bassett Avenue, Bronx, New York 10461. Subsidiary of Kidde, Inc.

The Farberware Advantage Collection.

sive user of the latest thing. A skimming price policy skims off, or attracts, people at the top of the demand schedule for the new item.

Thus, the high "cream skimming" figure may give the firm a chance to recoup the heavy costs of developing and marketing a new product and to make adequate profits out of which further advertising, promotion, and distribution might be financed.

Being first with a new product often carries an opportunity to reap higher profits through skimming pricing tactics. However, it is generally assumed that competition will eventually force prices down. How high can the initial price be? How high the price can be set and how long the seller can enjoy a virtual monopoly will depend upon the nature of the product, the speed with which competition reacts, and whether the product's uniqueness is protected by patent or secret technology.

One virtue of price skimming is that it gives the seller a period to establish an aura of exclusiveness for a product. Developing and projecting this image may justify more extensive advertising than could otherwise be defended with the volume of sales at the skimming price. The marketer's objective at this stage is to build a longing for the expensive new product in the customer's mind. Later, when the price is lowered, a more thorough market penetration can be achieved.

Premium Prices. **Premium prices**, prices higher than the market average, usually suggest something about the quality of the product.[9] Thus, establishing premium prices is often a way of communicating to consumers that product quality warrants a higher price. For example, Curtis Mathes promotes its television as the highest-priced receiver in America because it is the finest quality and the company is the only television manufacturer in the country to offer a full four-year warranty on all parts including the picture tube.

The new Porsche 924 is deliberately advertised as "a high-priced automobile but worth it because of its distinctive styling, unusual engineering and incomparable roadability." Budweiser, the so-called king of beers, has a premium price, as does Michelob. Green Giant's Niblets Corn and Sara Lee pastries are all premium price products whose marketers justify their higher prices on the basis of the products' superiority. However, price is just one means of projecting an image of excellence. Advertising invariably helps to build such an image. Channels of distribution and the entire marketing program all need to be coordinated to promote and sustain the quality image, which in large measure, is the justification for the higher premium price.

Umbrella Pricing. Pricing policies are both offensive and defensive in nature. **Umbrella pricing** is basically a defensive strategy, primarily against government intervention and reaction. In umbrella pricing a dominant firm holds its price higher than necessary in order to protect and defend a number of

---

[9] See Alfred R. Oxenfeldt, "Developing a Favorable Price Quality Image," *Journal of Retailing*, Winter 1974–75, pp. 8–14.

smaller competitors. The larger, more efficient firm foregoes both volume and profit to hoist a protective "umbrella" over the weaker firms in the form of a higher price. General Motors allegedly keeps the prices of all its models higher than necessary (demand and costs would justify the company's charging lower prices) because if it were to charge lower prices, the company fears it would destroy competition and invite rigorous antitrust reaction from the government. U.S. Steel has hoisted a price umbrella for the steel industry. The Jello Division of General Foods is said to have held its prices higher than it needs to so as not to endanger the survival of other firms in the gelatin dessert market. Umbrella pricing is a luxury that can be indulged in only by well-known, profitable firms who already have sizable market shares. It is an unusual, even unique form of pricing in what is usually described as a competitive environment. It raises an interesting question. What is the impact of umbrella pricing on the overall welfare of society and the consumer?

Other Pricing Policies and Practices

In addition to pricing policies that guide the firm to set price at, below, or above the market, there are a number of other pricing policies and practices we need to explore briefly. Often firms do not choose deliberately to set prices at, above, or below the market for their entire price structure. Instead, there is usually much variation among the prices charged for different products within their entire assortment.

Percentage Markups Versus Dollar Contribution Margin.   Price decision makers often must decide which one of three policies to adopt: standard markup, variable markup, or a pricing policy that strives for a dollar contribution margin. Retailers especially are prone to adopt pricing policies based upon a stated markup percentage. Some marketers, again including many retailers, adopt variable markup policies. In other words, the markup percentage used to determine price is varied from product to product depending on demand and cost factors. Other marketers have abandoned the concept of percentage markups altogether. Their contention is that in pricing goods, markups should be based on dollars, not percentages. If dollars are considered, the percentages will look after themselves.

Pricing policies built upon the concept of dollar markups are known as **contribution pricing**. This implies that what is sought is profit, and profits are dollars, not percentages. It assumes further that the prices set will maximize not necessarily net profits, but dollars of contribution to overhead and profits. The department store characteristically has used percentage markup pricing. Recently it has modified its approach, especially in light of the success of the discount store and other low margin sellers and now looks increasingly to markup dollars instead of only percentages.[10]

[10] See Rom J. Markin, *Retailing Management,* 2nd ed. (New York: Macmillan, 1977), pp. 378–379.

Negotiated Prices Versus One-Price Policy.   Many marketing firms profess to have a one-price policy. A one-price policy means all buyers, buying similar quantities and operating on the same plane of distribution (that is, either as ultimate consumers, retailers, or wholesalers) are offered the product on the same basis. If discounts for cash are offered, they are offered to all buyers on the same basis. If trade discounts are available, they too are equally available to all. A one-price policy is a nondiscriminating price for all buyers. In retailing there is much talk about a one-price policy but there are notable exceptions. Trade-in allowances and other concessions can shave the price so that two buyers purchasing a $379.00 food freezer may actually pay different prices. Buyer A gets a $100.00 trade-in allowance for a freezer with a resale value of only $50.00. Buyer B has no trade-in and is not psychologically equipped to haggle over price, so she pays the full $379.00.

Many manufacturers profess to have one-price policies but in actuality they have a standard list price, but buyers with sufficient buying skills and buying power are often able to bargain down considerably from the list price.

In retail merchandising, most convenience and shopping goods items are subject to one-price policies. Yet the prices of many large consumer durables such as appliances, automobiles, furniture, and houses all are basically negotiated. Bargaining skill has a large bearing on the price the consumer pays. To a great extent, the average consumer is ill-equipped to dicker over prices. It is embarrassing and anxiety arousing. Consumers have little basis for knowing what the bargaining limits are and even in cases like automobiles, where bargaining is expected and justified, a large number of consumers pay the full or new sticker price because of their aversion to negotiation.

In large measure, a one-price system is more efficient than a negotiated one. The one-price system streamlines and facilitates the buying-selling transaction. These policies save time and much administrative effort.

Odd-Versus Even-Dollar Pricing.   Both manufacturers and resellers often set price in odd rather than even dollars. Retailers are especially prone to use odd numbers for price endings. Their original aim was twofold. Undoubtedly the practice was partially based upon the idea that odd prices led the customer to believe that he or she was getting more for less, a real bargain. However, the merchant's original interest in odd prices was not all customer oriented. The firm's owner-manager also wanted to force clerks back to the cash register to ring up every sale in order to make change, thus foreclosing on the possibility that a clerk might make an even-dollar sale and pocket the money from the transaction.

Odd pricing is a form of *psychological pricing*. It has been observed in some pricing experiments that a change in price has little effect over certain ranges of demand. Thus, the average revenue curve is viewed as a step-down curve with critical points located at prices that are psychologically significant to buyers.

Odd prices are commonplace among most retail firms. It has been shown that prices ending in 9 are more frequent than those ending in other numbers. One researcher points out that 64 percent of retail prices for processed meat

Figure 16-3 Assumed demand curve for odd-number pricing.

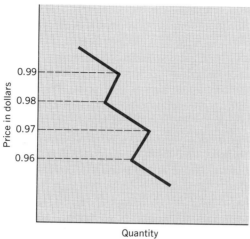

end in the digit 9 while 69 cents is a much more common price than 70 or 80 cents.[11]

Figure 16-3 shows the type of demand curve implicitly assumed by the seller who uses the odd-number rule to set prices.

Obviously, the decision maker *believes* that sales are larger when the price ends in an odd number than when it ends in the next lower number. You will observe that the quantity demanded is believed to be greater at $0.99 than at $0.98 and greater at $0.97 than at $0.96.

It should be pointed out that no conclusive evidence exists to support the contention that an odd-price policy actually results in larger sales.[12] Much experimentation is clearly called for to determine whether the popularity of odd numbers, and especially the "9" fixation, really stems from magic numbers that promote more sales or if they are only "sticky" prices that hinder more optimal pricing decisions and better profits.

Price Lining.   Another common price policy among many sellers, both manufacturers and resellers, is that of **price lining.** This practice consists of offering merchandise in a limited number of price lines, for example, women's street dresses at $44.95 to $59.95 and $72.95 to $89.95. The price lines supposedly are based upon differences in workmanship, materials, and design, all of which are cost considerations, and upon consumer expectations, which are a demand consideration. In short, price lines are based upon both cost and

[11] Dik Warren Twedt, "Does the '9' fixation in Retail Pricing Really Promote Sales?" *Journal of Marketing* **29** (October 1965), pp. 54–55. Also see Jan Stopel, "Fair or Psychological Pricing," *Journal of Marketing Research,* **9,** no. 1 (February 1972), pp. 109–110.

[12] This issue is explored in detail by Zarrel V. Lambert, "Perceived Prices as Related to Odd and Even Price Endings," *Journal of Retailing,* **51,** no. 3 (Fall 1975), pp. 3–22.

demand. Most marketers practice price lining to some degree. It is closely allied to product or merchandise assortment planning and is a natural spin-off of product differentiation and market segmentation. The automobile companies "price line" to a certain extent with their various models and with different combinations of accessories. Tire manufacturers and sellers engage in price lining by having low, medium, and high-price products.

Price lining is supposed to simplify the customer's decision process by the convenient grouping of the total merchandise assortment.[13] Two additional advantages frequently mentioned for price lining are that it simplifies the pricing structure and eliminates the need for frequent pricing decisions after the establishment of the original price lines. During periods of relatively stable prices, price lining is a fairly safe and effective policy for the marketing firm to follow. However, in periods of constantly rising prices like those experienced recently, price lining presents considerable difficulties to managers.

There remain just two additional pricing policies for us to examine: leader pricing and unit pricing.

Leader Pricing. In an attempt to increase profits for the firm as a whole or to convey an impression of overall low prices, some marketers follow a practice known as **leader pricing.** Leader pricing is defined as knowingly and willingly marking a part of the stock or an item at a price that will not yield the greatest dollar profit on these particular items. Items that are selected for special price emphasis are called *leaders.* In loss leader pricing goods are marked for sale with a price that does not cover costs. Many states consider loss leader pricing an unfair method of competition and prohibit it by unfair sales practices acts.

The term "loss leader" is a tricky one. In most instances, intelligent price setters hope to increase their total profits by the careful selection and use of price leaders. Given the prices of other products, a change in the price of the loss leader can produce larger sales of all products.

The use of price leaders, or "specials," as a promotional device appears to create less disturbance among competitors than do general price cuts. Leader prices usually are set on items with high frequency and rapid turnover or for which buyers are thought to be unusually price sensitive. The general characteristics of a good price leader are as follows:

1. The item is well known, widely used, and appeals to many customers.
2. It is priced low enough so that many people can buy it.
3. It is not already so low in price that a reduction will not arouse further interest.
4. It is not usually bought by consumers in large quantities and stored.
5. The item enjoys a high price elasticity of demand.

Unit Pricing. Unit pricing is hardly a means of determining price at all. Instead it involves indicating the cost per ounce or some other standard meas-

---

[13] See Kent B. Monroe, "Buyers' Subjective Perceptions of Price," *Journal of Marketing Research,* **10,** no. 1 (February 1973), pp. 70–80.

ure on the shelf ticket or on the actual product itself. Unit pricing is an attempt by the retail store (the supermarket has been the main institution to adopt the practice widely) to eliminate much of the confusion that arises from various package sizes. The commodity is priced as a total package, but the price per ounce is also given so that customers can decide for themselves which package size offers the best value. In some states unit pricing is required by law; in others, many retailers have voluntarily implemented the practice.[14]

Situational Factors and Price Decision Making

The decision maker, in determining price policies and setting actual prices, must always consider the nature of the pricing situation. For example, some customers may be located at great distances from the market while others are nearby. Thus, transportation costs become a significant factor in the distant supplier's ability to compete with more local ones and this has a special bearing on pricing behavior. In other instances, buyers purchase only after establishing careful specifications for the product; the buying firm then selects a supplier or product only on the basis of rigorous competitive bidding. In yet other situations a firm may find its pricing policies and its actual pricing behavior seriously constrained by government. A price concession may be challenged, a price set too low may be ruled to be injurious to competition and contrary to the public welfare. In this section, we shall examine two situational factors—competitive bidding and the government as referee—and we shall explain the impact of these two factors on pricing behavior and policy.

Competitive Bidding

The pricing procedure in which a buyer asks two or more competing suppliers to submit bids on a proposed purchase or contract is called **competitive bidding.** The buyer then makes the purchase from the supplier who offers the lowest bid price. The price must also be judged by how well the supplier meets the product specifications and the buyer's requirements concerning delivery time, quality of the product, service and maintenance, and other specified factors.

Competitive bidding is used extensively for many industrial products and is required by law when dealing with government buyers at nearly all levels. One of the United States astronauts who traveled to the moon was asked how he felt riding all those miles in the space capsule. He replied that he felt pretty good until he remembered that the space capsule was assembled out of parts and components all supplied by the lowest competitive bidder.

Competitive Bidding Strategy.   In competitive bidding[15] the strategy is aimed at submitting a bid that will help your firm attain its objective—profita-

The space shuttle— every part supplied by the lowest bidder.

[14] For more about unit pricing see Robert E. Wilkes, "Consumer Usage of Base Price Information," *Journal of Retailing* **48,** no. 4 (Winter 1972–1973), pp. 72–85.

[15] Much of the original work on the idea of competitive bidding was done by Laurence Friedman. See "A Competitive Bidding Strategy." *Operations Research*, February 1956. Also, Franz Edelman, "Art and Science of Competitive Bidding," *Harvard Business Review*, July–August 1965.

ble sales. But first your company has to beat competitive bids. To aid the seller in such situations, bidding strategies have been developed. The essence of these strategies is a set of guidelines that will permit the firm to determine the price that is the heart of the bid. Typically, the objective of a competitive bidder is to maximize the firm's immediate profits. These are defined as the difference between the bid and the costs of fulfilling the contract if it is won.

Competitive Bidding Model.   Consider this example. Suppose the costs of fulfilling a contract for a given bid are $40,000 and that a bid of $80,000 has a 30 percent chance of being accepted, while a bid of $60,000 has a 70 percent chance. Which of the two would be submitted? The following model can help the company determine its probable return with each alternative:

> Profit yielded by $80,000 contract:
> $$\$80,000 \ - \ \$40,000 \ = \ \$40,000 \text{ profit}$$
> Probability of $40,000 return: 0.30
> Therefore, expected profit is:
> $$0.30 \cdot (\$40,000) \ = \ \$12,000 \text{ expected profit}$$
> Profit yielded by $60,000 contract:
> $$\$60,000 \ - \ \$40,000 \ = \ \$20,000 \text{ profit}$$
> Probability of $20,000 return: 0.70
> Therefore, expected profit is:
> $$0.70 \cdot (\$20,000) \ = \ \$14,000 \text{ expected profit}$$

Because the $60,000 bid has the larger expected profit, it is the one that should be submitted, based upon competitive bidding strategy and expected profit. At each bid (level of price) there is some given probability of being awarded the contract if the bid is made. The essence or "kicker" to competitive bidding strategy is that if the decision maker is able to calculate the probability of the company's winning the contract for a certain bid, he or she can then estimate the expected profit.

A difficulty with the competitive bidding model is that many firms do not know clearly what their costs of fulfilling a contract will be. For these reasons, bidding models are not a pricing cure-all for competitive bidding problems. However, in the hands of the practiced professional bidder who possesses good cost information, such models can be a real help to a company in competing for a contract.

The Government as Referee

Government at many levels is a close observer of firms' pricing policies and behaviors. The general feeling persists that these, perhaps more than any other element in the marketing mix, have a great bearing on society's welfare. Price decision makers are often criticized regardless of whether their prices are low, high, or meet the market. If a firm prices low to gain market share and penetration, its behavior may be called *predatory*. When prices are set high and designed to skim the cream for a new product for which there is ample demand, such pricing policies may be called *exploitative*. Finally, if a firm prices at the market and meets all other competitors' prices, its behavior is frequently labeled *collusive*. From the standpoint of public policy and government regulation, it appears that pricing behavior is virtually a "no win" strategy for the firm—"damned if you do and damned if you don't." This isn't quite true, of course, but government is a frequent third party and a vocal and powerful referee in pricing behavior. It is important to know and play by the rules of the game, most of which are found in the many regulations that surround pricing policies and behavior. Those who break the rules must pay the penalties, which are sometimes simply admonitions or warnings, sometimes fines or assessments for damages, and for a player who frequently violates the rules, a stretch in the penalty box—jail!

To play the game, it is important to know the rules. The rules and regulations are extensive and complex but the major ones relate to the following issues.[16]

Price Collusion.   It is generally held to be unlawful for competitors to agree to charge identical prices. Both the Sherman and Clayton Acts prohibit this. Yet the government has something of a split personality about this because it does condone price fixing agreements in regulated industries such as transportation and milk marketing. Also, the government often has a difficult time proving collusion because similar or identical prices can result without any outright agreement. Very competitive markets often lead to closely similar costs of operation, and customer awareness of alternatives can tend to equalize prices throughout a given market. Sometimes similar or even identical prices result when a number of smaller firms follow the price leadership of a large barometric firm like General Motors, U.S. Steel, or the Aluminum Company of America.

Price Discrimination.   As you read earlier it is unlawful under the provisions of the Robinson Patman Act to sell a product of like grade and quality to different consumers for different prices. The specific prohibition states that such behavior is illegal "where the effect of such discrimination may be to substantially lessen competition or may tend to create a monopoly..." In selling commodities to similar buyers at different prices, the price differentials must be justified by cost, or as an attempt to meet the equally low price of another competitor.

Price Deception.   It is against the law to set prices that are deceptive and misleading. Such practices are regulated by the Automobile Information Disclosure Act, unit pricing statutes of many states, and the Truth in Lending Act. The Federal Trade Commission has even published a set of guidelines, *Guides against Deceptive Pricing,* so that the decision maker can be aware of and understand such practices.[17]

---

[16] For a more extended treatment, see Marshall C. Howard, *Legal Aspects of Marketing* (New York: McGraw-Hill, 1964), especially chapters 2 and 3.

[17] See John R. Nevin, Shelby Hunt, and Robert Ruekert, "The Impact of Fair Practice Laws on a Franchise Channel of Distribution," MSU *Business Topics* **28,** no. 3 (Summer 1980), pp. 27–38.

Predatory Pricing.   Competitors are always quick to label a rival's pricing policies as predatory, especially if the latter's prices are lower and help the rival firm to capture a larger share of the market. Predatory pricing often occurs when there are ample supplies of goods and demand is relatively weak. Predatory pricing, it is alleged, destroys not so much competition as competitors. At the national level, predatory pricing is regulated by the Sherman and Clayton Acts. The states usually control such pricing by Unfair Sales Practices Acts, which declare that prices ordinarily shall not be below acquisition costs plus some percentage margin, usually 6 percent at the retail level. Predatory pricing may infect international marketing as suppliers of each country price their products to penetrate and gain market shares in other markets. Many United States firms are bitterly complaining that Japanese firms are practicing predatory pricing in such lines as color television and footwear. The domestic firms usually tie such charges to corresponding demands for higher trade tariffs.

Exploitative Pricing. Exploitative pricing is a frequent charge when firms such as drug companies charge steep prices for new medicines or when sellers, during periods of rapidly rising prices, take price increases that seem both unreasonable and unjustified. During the mid-1970s the President's Council on Wages and Prices was established to monitor price increases and see whether they were economically justified. The United States has not had all-out wage and price controls since the 1940s and World War II. The nation's cultural and social commitment to the market enterprise system, however, sometimes wavers and there are those, especially the Democrats, who advocate a more vigorous role by the government in monitoring price behavior. In times of severe shortages or rapid inflation, many voices clamor for all-out price controls. It is a classic and perennial argument and you should know the issues and ask yourself what position you would take if push comes to shove.

As you can see, pricing policy and behavior is an area in which the price decision maker must know the legal as well as the social and economic implications of his or her behavior. Most large firms have competent legal staffs to assist them in this. Smaller firms are well advised to know the legal implications of these pricing behaviors and, when uncertain, to call in outside legal experts for advice.

Before proceeding, can you answer these questions:
1. What is the difference from the standpoint of the firm between percentage markup and dollar contribution margins?
2. What are the advantages of price lining? List one major disadvantage.
3. List and discuss three situational factors that affect price decision making.

Setting Price in a Dynamic Environment

One of the situational factors of greatest consequence to the price decision maker is the state of the economy or environment in which the business operates. Needless to say, the United States economy is dynamic. It changes rapidly, is often in tension and turmoil, and moves intermittently from one new state of equilibrium to another.

In the current market, the most prevalent condition, the one likely to persist for some time, is inflation. The constantly rising price level is caused in part by the economics of scarcity heightened by a psychology of fear—"If I don't buy it now, I'll have to pay more for it later." In such a climate, as costs soar and competition sharpens, pricing must be fast and flexible. This often means getting more and better pricing information, using it more effectively, and gaining as much control over the pricing situation as possible. To meet this need, many companies are setting up streamlined pricing committees or pricing czars who consult with and advise salespeople and other company members on pricing matters. Their task is to monitor and assess the price on every order before the sale closes. Another tactic often resorted to by price decision makers during periods of rapidly rising prices is the unbundling of services. Such services as deliveries, price marking, shopping bags, and gift wrapping are no longer offered with the ticketed price but are charged for on the basis of the user pay principle. This unbundling of services and charging separately for them means greater revenues for the firm but lower prices for the user-buyer who is willing to forego them. In an inflation economy it is extremely important that profits be monitored carefully. Rising prices may set loose a flood of increased sales volume, but rising costs can easily erode the firm's profit base. Setting prices to ensure or to maintain profits under inflationary conditions generally calls for raising prices. Raising prices often includes reducing or eliminating discounts, pricing products only at the time of shipment, providing escalator clauses in price lists, adding surcharges (extra fees) which permit a seller to pass on the appropriate cost adjustment and, most of all, as these tactics suggest, maintaining pricing flexibility.[18]

Eliminating Uncertainty and Avoiding Risk.   What it all comes down to is the bugaboo of uncertainty. "What's going to happen and on the basis of what might happen, how shall the firm decide on its price policy and behavior?" In other words, pricing policy and behavior must minimize, if not avoid, risk and assure the firm of survival, perhaps even of prosperity, during periods of great upheaval and uncertainty. Under such conditions price policies must be **risk aversive,** and based upon clearly defined price objectives which stem from a carefully analyzed pricing and cost environment, as well as well-organized and timely information. The price decision maker must also be committed to act positively and opportunely in creating pricing policy. The following policies reflect such a posture.[19]

- Balance price policies on a major product with policy on related items. For example, by raising prices on replacement parts service and complementary products, it may be possible to hold the price line for the firm's major items.
- Use a varying price policy, if legally possible, to orient demand toward those products that the firm wishes to promote and to ensure market penetration with new accounts where the firm may wish to gain a foothold.
- Use discounts and promotional allowances creatively to stimulate demand for products that do not require resources in short supply. Use the quantity discount structure sparingly or, unless it is uniquely justified, eliminate it entirely.
- If buyers fail to pay invoices on time, invoke a penalty charge of 1 or 2 percent. This reminds them that prompt payment is essential to lower their costs and maintain your company's cash flow and profits.

[18] For a contrast between U.S. pricing and European approaches, see John U. Farley, James M. Hulbert, and David Weinstein, "Price Setting and Volume Planning by Two European Industrial Companies: A Study and Comparison of Decision Processes," *Journal of Marketing* **44**, no.1 (Winter 1980), pp. 46–54.
[19] Based upon Joseph P. Guiltinan, "Risk Aversive Pricing Policies: Problems and Alternatives," *Journal of Marketing* **40** (January 1976), pp. 10–15.

- Conduct periodic audits of the cost structure of all the firm's products, both major and minor. Look for cost savings and the opportunity to reap economies through joint operating cost. Watch also for hidden costs, making sure all costs are covered. Try to anticipate what costs may be rising most rapidly in the near future—labor, materials, or energy. Be alert for ways of reducing these costs through substitution or elimination.
- Exploit the product's life cycle. New products may command special higher prices. Older ones that have reached the maturity saturation stage of the cycle may warrant price reduction or other special promotional activities to stimulate sales.
- Finally, the firm should employ new sales force incentives to meet production, cash flow, and profit margin incentives, which may place less reliance on price as a means of generating sales revenue.

In short, to eliminate at least some of the uncertainty surrounding the firm's price decision making, price policies and behavior should be developed to meet clearly defined price objectives which incorporate research on the probable effects of price changes. Such price policies need not be solely defensive but can, instead, be both positive and opportune. They can gain the firm the most desirable reward pricing brings, the greatest possible dollar net return.

Summary

Pricing is a critical management function. In many ways the firm's pricing policies and behavior constitute an important part of its crucial marketing program and strategy. Pricing policies must be coordinated with and flow out of the firm's overall marketing and company objectives. The firm's pricing policies convey much about the company to competitors as well as consumers.

The objectives of pricing are numerous but basically pricing is designed to bring the firm the greatest dollar net return over time. There is much that impedes the price decision maker from setting this ideal price. The greatest impediment to good price decision making is uncertainty. One of the ways both to avoid and cope with this uncertainty is to employ a multistage approach to pricing. This approach is helpful because it enables the decision maker to approach the pricing problem through a process of creeping commitment. By making a series of smaller, sequential decisions, the manager winds up with a decision that is the result of a number of approximations or refinements that have eliminated successive amounts of uncertainty. The multistage process consists of six steps: (1) selecting market targets, (2) choosing product and corporate images, (3) determining a marketing mix, (4) selecting pricing policy, (5) determining a pricing strategy, and (6) arriving at a specific price.

A wide variety of pricing policies, from high price to low, were explored and discussed. Other pricing policies were also evaluated as to their competitive advantages and their impact on the firm's operation.

Situational factors were shown to have a great bearing on the firm's pricing policies and behavior. Situational factors have led to such practices as competitive bidding, geographic price structures, and the increasing role of government as a pricing referee.

Price determination under the most ideal conditions is fraught with much uncertainty. In a dynamic environment it must be both fast paced and flexible. Such price determination involves the use of many risk aversive pricing policies.

Review Questions

1. What is the relationship between company objectives and pricing objectives?
2. Explain the term "administered pricing." Do many firms practice this kind of pricing? Does administered pricing suggest cost or demand oriented pricing?
3. List and discuss some of the pricing problems that firms face in the everyday conduct of their affairs.
4. Why is pricing such a critical management function?
5. What is meant by a multistage approach to price determination?
6. There are both internal and external variables that affect pricing. The external variables are largely uncontrollable. Why? Why are the internal variables more manageable?
7. What is the impact of competition on a firm's price policies and behavior?
8. The United States is characterized as having a one-price policy. Do you agree? Why or why not?
9. Discuss the government's position on (1) predatory, (2) collusive, and (3) exploitative pricing.
10. Discuss the implications of inflation on price policy and behavior. List and discuss some risk aversive policies that might be employed during such periods.

Case 16-1

General Motors Corporation Pricing Policy and Practices

General Motors' approach to pricing begins with the concept of standard volume and then, in order to arrive at a profit factor, introduces the notion that prices should reflect a preselected rate of return on invested capital. The exact manner in which the planned rate of return on capital is chosen is not generally known; but since the rate is on the high side, it undoubtedly reflects the corporation's dominant position in the industry, the confidence placed in its personnel by top executives, its effectiveness in product research and innovations, and the likelihood of a continuing strong demand for motor vehicles.

In each of the General Motors' operating units, costs based upon standard volume are computed, and to this is added an amount needed to secure the desired rate of return on investment. Costs of labor and raw materials and selling costs, including dealer margins, are all included because the object is to establish the announced retail price. All of the costs are anticipated ones that will prevail through the model year. Estimating forward costs is especially important in the automobile industry since new prices are announced when new models are introduced. Changes are made only with great reluctance from that time forward and only if needed to meet strong competition or a serious downturn in demand. The prices so computed are preliminary judgments suggested by long-run considerations. These preliminary judgments are hedges against uncertainties, and they are the coordinating link between policy and administrative procedure. The preliminary judgment prices are modified by shorter-run considerations, principally by the need to meet competitive prices and by the level and trend of national income.

It is recognized that the demand for automobiles largely depends on the level and probable change in national income. Therefore, the company must attempt to predict any changes in these areas for the purpose of modifying preliminary prices. As the purchase of automobiles can be deferred, demand in the past has dropped proportionately with decreases in the level of personal income. Thus, economic conditions and consumer expectations largely set the level of demand; the level of demand, in turn, determines the volume of automobiles that should be manufactured; and this volume will largely determine the level of costs, prices, and profits.

Yet price itself also affects the number of cars sold. Basing unit cost on standard volume keeps the price down because it includes unabsorbed overhead, or burden. The prices suggested by GM's basic formula may be decreased even further if those responsible for price determination think that a reduction will affect demand favorably. Also, since competitors may believe that there is a greater measure of price elasticity than actually exists, or that through price reduction, they can increase their share of the market, the price level of automobiles may go substantially below that suggested by the return-on-investment approach.

All of the General Motors operating units go through this pricing procedure and then submit their tentative prices to the appropriate group in the corporation's home office. There the prices are again scrutinized with the objective of presenting a coherent General Motors price structure. By comparing suggested prices from all the divisions by makes and models, out-of-line prices can be discovered and changed as seems desirable. Because of certain conclusions about likely changes in national income, the entire level of suggested prices may be raised or lowered.

The objectives of GM's pricing policy have been summarized as follows:

At $6993, Chevy Malibu is America's lowest-priced 6-passenger V6 sedan.*

Malibu Sport Sedan

GM

But you'd never know by looking at it.

When you consider the fact that some people are paying that much and more for smaller cars these days, you begin to understand what a value Malibu is.

Just look at it.

Handsome son-of-a-gun. Nice clean lines. A touch of class. Could pass for a lot more money. And it holds six.

Malibu not only looks more expensive than it is, it *feels* more expensive than it is. It has a nice solid feel on the road and a comfortable ride. Full Coil suspension, a front stabilizer bar, rubber body mounts and a strong full-perimeter frame all contribute.

Included in the $6993* are power steering, power brakes, radial tires, V6 engine. Even whitewall tires and full wheel covers.

The mileage? Pretty darn good for a car with so much room. The EPA highway estimate is 28. The EPA estimated MPG is [20]. (Use estimated MPG for comparisons. Your mileage may differ depending on speed, distance, weather. Actual highway mileage lower. Highway estimate higher in California. Chevrolets are equipped with GM-built engines produced by various divisions. See your dealer for details.)

Chevy Malibu Sport Sedan.

A lot for a little, in an age of a little for a lot.

Chevrolet

*Based on a comparison of Manufacturers' Suggested Retail Prices, including dealer preparation. $6993 includes: optional full wheel covers, whitewall tires, deluxe body side moldings, and wheel opening moldings. Tax, license and destination charges additional. Level of standard equipment varies. Optional automatic transmission required in California.

Setting prices is not a matter of cost accounting alone...Moreover a price policy cannot be entirely determined by the level of demand...In setting prices in a particular year, General Motors has therefore turned to a policy which has been formulated in the long-run interests of its workers and stockholders, as the management has been able to appraise these interests. In poor years this policy results in prices held at levels set by long-term considerations, even though such prices can contribute little, if anything, to profits in such years. In good years, there has been no attempt to charge, even temporarily all that the traffic would bear. Instead, weight has again been given, not to the opportunity of the moment, but to long-term factors which affect the demand for labor, the provision of plant and equipment, and the requirements that profits be earned for the stockholders over a period of years.

In light of this background, General Motors Corporation announced on June 16, 1980 that prices on 1981 model cars and trucks may rise as much as 3 percent. That would mean an average $250 to $350 increase for a new car. GM is the nation's largest auto maker and the traditional pricing leader for the industry. GM announcements come in the form of "price protection" letters that are mailed directly to all GM dealers. The letters do not represent official prices for 1981 models. Final increases are announced in late summer, when the new models go into production. The manufacturer promises the dealer to absorb anything above 3 percent. Usually, however, the "price protection" letters have provided a very close approximation of the actual increases.

In 1976, GM announced 6 percent price protection, then raised car prices by that amount—or $338 for the average fully equipped car including options—but less taxes and shipping charges. The increase included $269 in the base price and $69 for options.

In 1981 price increases will convert into more than $250 for the base vehicle and $70 for options. GM's typically equipped 1980 car with options carried an average suggested retail price of around $7,600 although the dealer's actual selling price averaged below $7,200.

Questions

1. Review and evaluate the General Motors Corporation approach to price decision making. What is the principal orientation of GM to determining the price of its automobiles?

2. In your estimation, does GM use a multistage approach to pricing? What other factors might General Motors consider if it wished to expand the use of the multistage approach? How does GM attempt to cope with the uncertainties of price decision making? Would GM be better able to cope with the problems of rapidly rising prices in an inflation-ridden economy than say one of GM's suppliers? How and why?

3. How do you believe the Ford Motor Company and the Chrysler Corporation determine the prices for their automobiles? Would their procedure differ significantly from the General Motors Corporation approach? How and why?

Case 16-2

Arrow Microwave Ovens

The microwave oven business could hardly be more robust. It is benefiting from skyrocketing energy costs, improved features in the newer ovens offered for sale, and declining concerns about safety.

"We can't come close to making enough of them," beams George C. Foerstner, president and chief executive officer of Amana Refrigeration, Inc., a subsidiary of Raytheon Company, which splits slightly more than 50 percent of the market with Litton Industries. "We could have sold 30 percent more microwave ovens last year if we only had them."

The boom in microwave sales is running directly counter to depressed sales elsewhere in the appliance industry. Last year sales of gas ranges dropped 17 percent and electric range sales plunged 31 percent, but microwave ovens recorded a 28 percent increase in 1980 on top of a 64 percent jump the year before. In 1980, appliance manufacturers, for the first time ever, did a bigger volume in microwave ovens ($370 million) than they did in gas stoves ($356 million).

Industry representatives believe that consumer purchases of microwave ovens will outstrip combined electric and gas range sales in dollar volume by 1985. Almost all the competitors in the industry are expanding to capitalize on the burgeoning market. Amana this year will spend a record $6 million to expand its microwave production capacity more than 50 percent. Litton completed a major expansion program last fall that lifted its daily microwave oven production from 800 units to 2,000 and is already planning to add 40 percent more capacity that will go on stream in another year.

Arrow microwave ovens are built by Hardwick Stoves, Inc., a 109-year-old firm that traditionally manufactures and distributes a line of gas ranges. Arrow is a relatively new entrant into the microwave field and its ovens have achieved limited market success because of low consumer awareness. The Hardwick Company itself was never a household word, and Hardwick has spent little or nothing on consumer advertising; instead it has promoted, in a limited way, its microwave oven line to dealers.

Arrow proposes to seek market penetration through more aggressive price competition—an approach no other firms have yet attempted. Microwave ovens are very nearly uniformly priced among most of the well-known manufacturers and prices range at retail from a high of $600 for the more elaborate "programmable models" to about $260 for a basic, stripped-down oven. Most manufacturers have a range of about five or six models covering the price and feature spectrum. Dealers are generally allowed about a 36 percent markup by the manufacturer-distributor. Markups are, of course, somewhat higher on the more expensive models but conversely are lower (only about 25 percent) on the stripped-down lower-priced models.

Arrow plans a dual or twofold pricing strategy, which it perceives as the heart of its marketing program: (1) to undersell most competitors by 10 to 15 percent across the board on all models and (2) to grant a discount structure to retail dealers that will assure them of markups in the 40 to 45 percent range on all models.

Questions

1. Appraise and evaluate Arrow's proposal.
2. How will this strategy be perceived by (a) consumers, (b) retail dealers, (c) the major microwave manufacturers?
3. What effect will Arrow's strategy have, if any, on the equilibrium, or pricing structure, of the industry?

Chapter 17

The Marketing of Services

Did you ever consider that you can shop for and purchase services all day long, yet at the end of the day you have no really tangible "products" to put in your shopping cart and load in your car? Neither do you have anything to bring home, put away, or otherwise add to your stocks or inventory of physical products. Such is the nature of services. Consider, if you will, some of the purchases that you, as a member of a typical family, may have made. You may have visited your dentist, had a tooth filled and your teeth cleaned. You may have visited a medical doctor for a routine checkup or to inquire about a specific illness. You may have seen a movie or a play; visited a roller rink or a fitness center where you swam and played racquetball; you may have visited a travel agency where you scheduled a flight for your forthcoming school vacation; you may have visited a bank and arranged a loan, or perhaps you saw a real estate agent who specialized in property management, about looking for a new apartment. As you continued your shopping excursion, you may have visited with an insurance salesperson located in one of the units of America's largest retail merchant—"Where America Shops—For Value," to see if he or she could offer you a better deal on your automotive insurance. Perhaps your shopping excursion was an extended one and you stayed overnight in the city in a hotel or motel. All of these activities involve spending money for services rather than for tangible goods.

The Service Revolution

The growing importance of services as a marketable commodity has been recognized for some time.[1] Nearly $600 billion will be spent by ultimate consumers for services this year—for rent, medical checkups, tuition, yoga lessons, treatment at alcohol abuse centers, for rides on ski lifts and, for that matter, for room service, note-taking services, and even computer dating agencies. Back just a few short decades ago, about a third of the average family's budget was spent on services, but in 1980, the proportion exceeded 45 percent. The rise in spending for services has been sharp and steady, rising more rapidly than outlays for both durable and nondurable goods.

Table 17-1 shows personal consumption expenditures for selected years beginning with 1960 and projected to 1985. These expenditures are broken down into purchases for durable goods, nondurable goods, and services. As can be seen from the table, the percentage of expenditures for services has risen from around 40 percent in 1960 to an estimated nearly 48 percent by the year 1985. Naturally, the growth of service expenditures has come at the expense of both durable and nondurable categories.[2] This supports the conten-

[1] One of the early scholars to recognize this emerging development was William J. Regan. See his "Economic Growth and Services," *Journal of Business,* no. 36 (April 1963), pp. 200–209. Also, "The Service Revolution," *Journal of Marketing* **27,** no. 3, (July 1963), pp. 57–62.

[2] For more related to the general outlook for continued growth in consumer related service industries, see Fabian Linden, "Service Please!," *Across the Board,* The Conference Board (April 1978), pp. 42–45. Also, by the same author, "The Business of Consumer Services," *The Conference Board Record* (April 1975), pp. 13–17 and "The Consumer Market in 1980: Services," *The Conference Board Record* (May 1972), pp. 50–52.

Table 17-1 Personal Consumption Expenditures

Year	Total	Durable Goods	Nondurable Goods	Services
1960	325.9 (100%)	43.1 (13.2%)	151.1 (46.3%)	130.7 (40.1%)
1965	430.2 (100%)	62.8 (14.6%)	188.6 (43.8%)	178.7 (41.5%)
1970	618.8 (100%)	84.9 (13.7%)	264.7 (42.7%)	269.1 (43.4%)
1975	973.2 (100%)	131.7 (13.5%)	409.1 (42.0%)	432.4 (44.4%)
1980	1249.9 (100%)	162.4 (12.9%)	521.2 (41.6%)	566.2 (45.2%)
1985	1677.7 (100%)	201.3 (11.9%)	676.2 (40.3%)	800.1 (47.6%)

*Totals are in billions of dollars.

Source: United States Department of Commerce. Data for 1980 and 1985 are estimated.

tion that as societies become more sophisticated they tend to shift, to some extent, from the consumption of goods to the increased consumption of services.

Business Buyers, Too, Consume Services. Business buyers or industrial users spend a large portion of their resources on services as well. Business and industrial buyers seek an array of services from accounting, legal, engineering, public relations, advertising, research, and other firms that specialize in providing various forms of technical and managerial assistance. Business firms must buy environmental impact statements, insurance to cover risks, financial advice, specialized educational services such as management development programs for planning education, transportation services to ship products, and a wide variety of other services necessitated by the growing competitive environment and the increased need for greater specialization. In many respects, that is exactly what service marketers in all fields offer—greater specialization, more skill or expertise at a cost equal to or lower than the cost at which the purchaser could perform the service.

Our focus in this chapter will be on the marketing of services to ultimate consumers. Therefore, the expenditures of business and industrial buyers for services are not reflected in the expenditure data of the tables and figures in this chapter.

Services Are Also Important in the Nonprofit Sector. Not-for-profit organizations also deal extensively in the marketing of services. Hospitals, colleges, and universities, mental health clinics, municipal transit systems, churches, and government agencies at all levels are all being asked to deliver larger amounts of user benefits or amenities—in short, more services to service demanding users. And such organizations must therefore learn more about the characteristics of service-dominant goods and how to market these goods more effectively, increase their product assortments, better assess the needs of the market, hold down costs, and generate sufficient revenues.

Consumer Services Are Our Interest. In spite of the growing importance of services and service marketing of business and industrial marketers and the dominant sale of services in many nonprofit organizations, our concern in this chapter is with consumer services. Our task is to look at some of the factors responsible for the growth of services, to examine the basic characteristics that distinguish services from tangible products, and to explore the special considerations necessary in marketing services.

Why the Growth in the Service Sector?

The growth of consumer services is the result of many related forces. These would include such factors as:

1. Growing affluence
2. The impact of technology
3. Changing consumer lifestyles

Each of these factors will be discussed briefly in terms of its impact on the growing clamor for more consumer services.

Growing Affluence. As we learned throughout the earlier chapters, we are growing richer. In accordance with the laws of consumption—one of which states that as income increases, the percentage spent for sundries increases rapidly—consumers are opting to spend a larger proportion for services as opposed to physical goods. This is consistent too with the well-known Clark-Fisher hypothesis which suggests that economically, societies move through a succession of stages of economic development.[3] Low-level societies emphasize such things as hunting, fishing, agriculture, and forestry. Emerging societies then turn to manufacturing of what are called transportable or physical goods. Third-level societies emphasize marketing, transport, finance, communication and professional, and personal and governmental activities. Because these are mostly services, a third-level economy should experience a rising share of expenditures in the service sector. We are, as was stated in chapter 2, in an era known as the Post-Industrial Society, that is, one in which the production and marketing of services is more important than the production and marketing of goods.

As consumers' income increases, a point is often reached where the satisfaction of acquiring increased services, for example, more travel, recreation, better health care, and increased education, surpasses the satisfaction of owning another car, more clothing, or a bigger stereo.

The Impact of Technology. Technology is largely responsible for producing more goods, but more goods often foster the need for more services. Televisions require maintenance and repair. New satellite technology and cable transmission systems create such service offerings as home-box-office or subscription television. Better telephones and communication systems enhance the satisfaction of more long-distance telephone communication. New,

---

[3] Colin Clark, *The Conditions of Economic Progress*, 3rd ed. (London: Macmillan, 1957), p. 491.

low-cost, clean, and efficient fast food franchises make eating out more simple and equally more attractive. The new fuel-efficient automatic transmissions of many automobiles, electronic ignitions, and changing emission controls make automobiles more sophisticated. While some may require less maintenance, nonetheless the ability of the average owner to do his or her own maintenance and repairs declines.

Changing Consumer Lifestyles.   Changing consumer lifestyles have been documented in numerous other places throughout the text. The important point is that most Americans no longer live the simple life. Our jobs, our environment, our personal lives are complex. Americans are busy, involved, on the run, and on the move. Time, next to money, is our most precious commodity. And for some, time is more precious than money.[4]

Few of us can cut our own hair or someone else's. We can't even cut our own grass, wash our car, clean our house, let alone repair our own appliances, manage our finances, prepare our income tax, or cure our personal ailments. Because so many of us are specialists, we need specialists to assist us in our affairs. Women are increasingly employed, as are many teenagers. Thus, our need for expert assistance, in both our private and business lives, most likely will continue to increase in the future.

In a Market System, Demand Creates Its Own Supply

The growing consumer demand for more services has brought forth an accelerated effort on the part of marketers to satisfy these consumer needs and to broaden their own customer base and add to revenues and profitability.

Many firms are now altering considerably their goods and service mix to take advantage of the changing consumer expenditure mix which was shown in Table 17-1 and which is shown more graphically in Figure 17-1. The rapid increase in consumer expenditures is expected to continue largely unabated throughout the 1980s. Even in periods of mild recession, consumer expenditures for services tend to fall off less rapidly than expenditures for durable and nondurable goods. Of course, you would understand that durable goods are the most postponable purchases and therefore are most likely to fall off rapidly during periods of economic decline.

Therefore, to meet the rising demand for an enlarged package of consumer services during the 1980s, marketers are increasingly expanding their offerings of a wide variety of nontraditional services, some of which are now being marketed on a routine basis.

What Is Nontraditional Often Becomes Routine

Many retailers today offer such services as driver training classes, travel services, exotic restaurants, day-care centers, dental and eye clinics, income tax help, shopper advisory services, and self-improvement lessons in everything from belly-dancing and yoga to backgammon, golf, or ski lessons.

[4] Staffan Burenstam Linder, *The Harried Leisure Class* (1970).

Figure 17-1 The allocation of consumer expenditures.

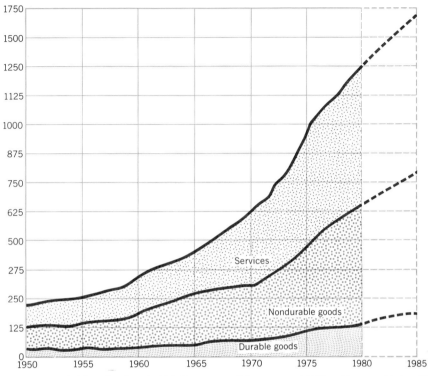

Source: Compiled from data from the U.S. Department of Commerce and *Guide to Consumer Markets,* The Conference Board.

One estimate places the proportion of general department store revenues from services at 20 percent by 1990, up from slightly less than 10 percent in 1980.[5]

One well-known company that has led the drive to a larger service marketing commitment is Sears, which now offers more than 40 different nonmerchandise "products" ranging from driver education for traffic violators to a mobile car service that will perform auto tune-ups at customers' homes. The company, for some time now, has offered such services as insurance policies, car rental, home improvement consultation, and housecleaning. More recently, Sears has begun installing pay television cables. Sears services the pay-TV patrons and adds the $20 monthly fee to the customer's charge account.

Some new service offerings are truly in the nontraditional category. Rich's store in Atlanta offers customers cooking classes in the store's gourmet kitchen, which is equipped with 18 ovens and space for 36 students. In Boston, Bloomingdale's promoted a three-month course called "The Future of Humanity." Some 225 persons signed up for the $40 program, which attracted noted

[5] "Retailers Shake a Staid Old Image," *U.S. News and World Report,* October 23, 1978, pp. 83–88. See also, "The Bonanza in Service Industries—Bound to Grow Even Bigger," *U.S. News and World Report,* February 16, 1976, pp. 54–55.

anthropologists and economists. The J.C. Penney Company in many areas of the country offers a ski school for both novice and intermediate skiers.

A major service innovation on the horizon is in-the-home retailing, using closed-circuit television hookups between stores and homes. One such system already in operation is Qube. Qube is a Warner Communications cable network that is connected to some 30,000 homes in Columbus, Ohio. The system allows instant two-way sales communications between retailers and consumers.

The Family's Service Dollar—Where the Money Goes. Figure 17-2 shows, with the use of a convenient bar graph, where the family's service dollar is spent.

Slightly less than half of the consumer service budget is related to the home—rent (or homeowner payments), utilities, and other household operations. Such expenditures have been growing rapidly in recent years, reflecting, in part, a substantial growth in the nation's household count, which has been expanding at a faster rate than the nation's total population.

The remaining part of the service budget goes for an extensive array of items; for example, medical care, personal business (such as brokerage charges, accountant, and legal fees), visits to the hair stylist, and bets on horses. Such service expenditures as medical care, recreation, education, and foreign travel are all likely to receive increases in consumer expenditures in the years ahead.

Characterizing the Nature of Services

Most of us have an intuitive notion as to what services are—but do we? Services are something other than physical products, right? The answer is neither yes, nor no, but maybe. We visit a retail store and purchase a TV set but we expect some service—maybe the extension of credit, delivery, an attractive department in which to shop, and a knowledgeable salesperson to assist us

Figure 17-2 The family's service dollar—total expenditures for services in 1980.

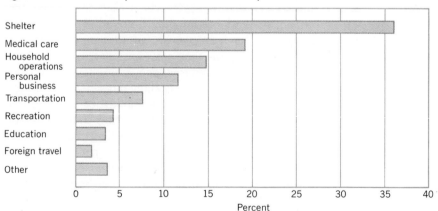

Source: Estimated from data compiled from U.S. Department of Commerce Statistics and *The Conference Board.*

with our choice. These are services in one sense of the word. The real problem is how we make a distinction between products and services. In one sense we can't. Remember our discussion of products in chapters 8 and 9. The total product concept says that the "product" is the sum total of its perceived attributes. Products are bundles of expectations and satisfactions sought by the buyer.

Thus, from the standpoint of the total product concept, product-related services are part of the product. The real problem, if there is one, is that most of the statistical data gathered about services is ambiguous. The data, for example, shown in this chapter is mostly for intangible "products" or, hence, services. Most of us have a fairly good notion of the meaning of the term "goods."

These are tangible economic products that are capable of being touched, seen, and may or may not be smelled, tasted, or heard. "Services" are generally considered to be everything else.

Services are "Products" Too.   One way to think about services is to consider services as an "act" and "goods" as things.[6] Goods as products are therefore objects, articles, devices, or something material. Services as "products" are deeds, a performance, or an effort. When goods are purchased, the buyer incurs an expense. Maybe you're wondering now why such a fuss is being made about all this. If you are, it's a good point and deserves a considered answer which is, namely, that precision of terms is necessary for precision in analysis and planning, and hence, decision making. A really clear-cut demarcation between products or "goods" and "services" permits describing the similarities and differences that exist in the marketing of products and services.

Marketed Services.   Therefore, for greater precision in our discussion of services we will consider services to be a "product" involving a market transaction where the object of the exchange is not the transfer of ownership of a tangible commodity.

One of the advantages of such definition is that it permits recognizing three broad, yet mutually exclusive areas of services within each of which a more complete list might be expanded. For example: [7]

1. Rented goods services. The right to rent or lease a product.
2. Owned goods services. The custom repair, creation, or improvement of a product.
3. Nongoods services. Nongoods have no physical or tangible product attributes but consist of acts or deeds provided by others.

Such a definition and classification scheme does more to tell you what services are not than it does to instruct you about the essential characteristics of a service, but we are on our way to a better understanding.

What Satisfactions Do Buyers Seek?   Another measure for distinguishing between a good or a service is to examine the attributes of each and seek to discover which of the major attributes contributes most to the buyer's satisfaction. Does the satisfaction or value for the buyer stem largely from the physical characteristics of the product, or from its intangible attributes arising from the nature of the experience or performance?

When this standard is applied there are few pure products and few pure services. Most products or goods, whether they are consumer or industrial, have attributes consisting of supporting services that add to their value or

---

[6] See John M. Rathmell, "What is Meant by Services?", *Journal of Marketing* **30** (October 1966), pp. 32–36.

[7] These ideas parallel but are not identical to those of Robert C. Judd. See "The Case for Redefining Services," *Journal of Marketing* **28** (January 1964), pp. 58–59.

The marketing of services.

satisfaction. On the other hand, most products as services often require supporting goods in order to be more useful and to create greater satisfaction.

The Goods-Services Continuum.   Most products lie along a goods-services continuum with goods whose attributes are most clearly tangible dominant at one end and goods whose attributes are most clearly intangible dominant at the other. Such a goods-services or tangible dominant versus intangible dominant continuum is shown in Figure 17-3.

The "either-or" terms such as goods versus services do not adequately describe the nature of marketed products. As mentioned earlier, the total product concept suggests that "products" are in reality combinations of relatively discrete elements or attributes which are linked together in molecular-like wholes. As shown in Figure 17-3, these elements or attributes may be either tangible or intangible but the whole will take on one or the other dominance.

The Molecular Model.   A molecular model provides an opportunity for analyzing more precisely the nature of a product entity in terms of both its tangible and intangible features or characteristics.[8] The model would suggest that if "products" have multiple elements or attributes, a deliberate or inadvertent

[8] Based upon G. Lynn Shostack, "Breaking Free from Product Marketing," *Journal of Marketing* (April, 1977), pp. 73–80.

Marketing the intangible product using the tangible image.

change in a single element may rather dramatically alter the nature of the product.[9]

Figure 17-4 is a simplified comparison which demonstrates the usefulness of the notion of a molecular model of product entities.

[9] This would suggest a scientific analogy. By the simple switching of FE_3O_2 to FE_2O_3, we create a new substance. Remember the little limerick we first learned in high school chemistry. "Little Willie was a scientist, Little Willie is no more. For what he thought was H_2O was H_2SO_4!"

Figure 17-3 A goods-service continuum.

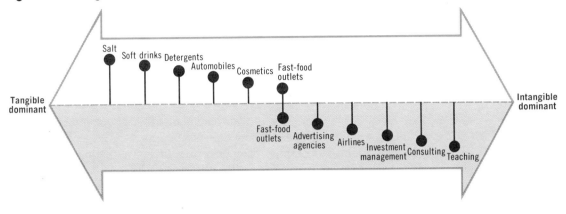

Source: G. Lynn Shostack, "Breaking Free From Product Marketing," *Journal of Marketing* (April 1977), p. 77.

In Figure 17-4, automobiles and airline travel are broken down into their major attributes. As can be seen, these two "products" have different nuclei and they also differ in dominance. Airline travel is decidedly intangible dominant; that is, it does not yield a physical ownership of a tangible good. Most of the other attributes of the "product" airline travel are intangible as well.

In many aspects, airline travel and automobiles are quite opposite in their attributes. A car is a physical possession that yields a service benefit. Airline

Figure 17-4 The molecular model of product entities.

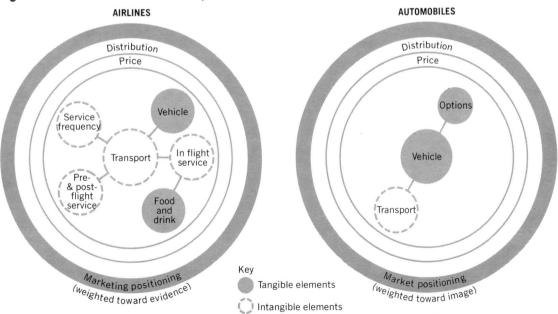

Source: G. Lynn Shostack, "Breaking Free from Product Marketing," *Journal of Marketing* (April, 1977), p. 76.

travel, on the other hand, cannot be physically possessed. The benefits of airline travel can only be experienced. The inherent benefit of a car is service. So too is the inherent benefit of airline travel.

What's the Point?   The point of our effort to make these distinctions and to get a better grasp of what services are and how they differ from more tangible dominant products is this: services are a special kind of product, they require a special understanding, and they require special and unique marketing efforts by marketers. Furthermore, the growth potential of the service market constitutes an already large and expanding market opportunity. Yet, as is ever true in a market-oriented economy, competition is forcing traditional service industries to increasingly emphasize marketing in order to compete more effectively.

Before proceeding, can you answer these questions:
1. Of total consumer expenditures, which are increasing more rapidly, those for services or those for nondurable goods?
2. What are the main factors that account for the growth of the service marketing industries?
3. What are services? How do services differ from other products?

How Product and Service Marketing Differ

Services usually manifest some distinctive characteristics that create both special marketing challenges and opportunities. The nature of these characteristics often results in marketing programs that are uniquely different from those found in the marketing of products. One study reported that service dominant firms often are less marketing-oriented and that service firms generally are less likely to:

1. Have marketing mix activities carried out in the marketing department
2. Perform analyses of their market opportunity
3. Handle their advertising internally rather than use outside agencies
4. Have an overall sales or marketing plan
5. Develop and implement a sales training program
6. Use marketing research firms and marketing consultants
7. Spend as much on marketing when expressed as a percentage of gross sales[10]

Such findings would suggest that service companies might well consider becoming more marketing-oriented. They could perhaps profit from a reevaluation of their more limited marketing activities to determine if they could

---

[10] William R. George and Hiram C. Barksdale, "Marketing Activities in the Service Industries," *Journal of Marketing* **38,** no. 4 (October 1974), pp. 65–70.

benefit from further integration and coordination of their marketing efforts. Service companies today are increasingly analyzing their marketing expenditures and attempting to assess whether their marketing programs are receiving adequate managerial and financial support.

The Marketing Program Is Geared to the Nature of the Product

Much of our preceding discussion has suggested that service products are varied and even more complex. Several characteristics of services also have special implications for marketing and complicate, in some instances, the creation of more effective marketing programs.

Intangibility.   Services, as pointed out, are intangible dominant in their major attributes. Services often are not physical in the sense of objects. This characteristic of services means that marketers must market service benefits. Firms marketing services sell such attributes as skill, professionalism, and competence. Insurance firms sell protection, retirement, freedom from worry, college education, and hospitalization and health benefits. Yet some firms find marketing intangibles difficult and meet with considerable customer resistance. Hence, the Prudential Insurance Company suggests to its customers that, instead of intangibles they cannot see, feel or touch, what they are really buying is "a piece of the rock," that is, something which is symbolically strong, permanent, enduring, physical, and tangible.

Inseparability.   In many instances, services cannot be separated from the person who markets them. We sign up for a particular course in marketing but we often sign up for the course from a particular person. We want our income tax returns completed, but we want them done by a certain C.P.A. We don't buy just hairstyles or facials or weight reduction; we want the services of those who create those unique satisfactions. Services of many varieties are therefore created and marketed simultaneously. This inseparability creates marketing complications in terms of promotion, "product" development, and even channels of distribution which, in the case of most services, means that direct sale is the only possible distribution channel. Such a characteristic as inseparability also suggests that the scale of the firm is restricted in size. A skillful performer or creator of services cannot clone himself in order to extend the scope of his operation. Yet others can sometimes be trained and through franchising and other arrangements, service offerings can be extended to wider market targets. Fred Astaire dance studios are a common example.

Perishability.   Services are perishable and they cannot be stored. A man's haircut will last at most several weeks and you cannot buy additional haircuts to take with you to the Canadian woods to last you over your summer vacation. Perishability is a distinguishing feature of many services, including such intangible service products as airline seats, unused hydroelectric power, or even a rock concert. Compounding the problem of perishability is the fact that demand for services is likely to fluctuate widely. There is little demand for ski lifts in July and August. Demand for electric power is greatest in the northern latitudes in winter for heating, but greatest in the southern latitudes in summer for cooling and air conditioning. Public transit systems are busiest between the hours of 7:00 to 8:30 A.M. and from 4:30 to 6:00 P.M. During other periods

Marketing the tangible product with the use of the intangible image.

Real quality has a way of creating its own image.

Images can be fleeting. A shadow. A rippling picture in a pond. Or they can be as lasting as a lifetime. A lifetime of hard work.

As a maker of home appliances, Whirlpool Corporation believes that a lasting quality image is simply the reflection of the people who build and stand behind the product. Special people. Motivated by pride of concept. Of craftsmanship. Of their ability to make things that last.

This is why we take pride in stocking parts for as many years as we do. Why we main-tain a toll-free Cool-Line® service number* you can call 24 hours a day. And why we have a nationwide organization of authorized Tech-Care® service companies that are as close to you as your phone book.

You see, at Whirlpool we believe every appliance we build should create its own image of quality. And do it for one person — you.

It's our way of saying this is more than just an appliance. This is our way of life.

Whirlpool Home Appliances

of the day, city buses are virtually empty. Yet it is difficult to shift the demand from one period to another. Telephone circuits are almost always overloaded on holidays such as Thanksgiving, Christmas, and Mother's Day. These factors create marketing challenges to find ways, through such marketing efforts as pricing, product planning, and promotion, to even out production capacity, to level demand, and to stimulate demand in off-season or low-peak periods of need. Because services provide benefits that are short-lived, they cannot be produced ahead of time and stored for periods of greater demand. Forecasting the demand for services over an extended period is likely to be fraught with difficulties. Failure to forecast such demand adequately will likely mean imbalances in capacity in relation to customer demand.

Heterogeneity.   Mass production of tangible dominant goods usually means standardization through specialization and division of labor or, put more simply, homogeneous products. One Mounds candy bar is pretty much like another. One Datsun 210X is like any other Datsun 210X similarly equipped. However, it is difficult to standardize intangible service dominant products. Service offerings are truly unique. No two "products" are ever exactly alike. An airline trip from Seattle to San Francisco, even in the same carrier, will not be the same two times in a row. Having your car tuned up by a mechanic is one "product" with a given level of satisfaction at one time, but a different "product" at another time because the attributes or benefits are likely to vary from period to period. The problems suggest that the service company should pay special attention to the way in which "products" are planned, the firm's "product" assortment mix, and pricing and promotion of the "product." In short, it should do everything feasible to ensure consistent and high-quality performance.

Improving Productivity in Marketing Services

While consumer expenditures for services have been increasing at a rather rapid clip, these expenditures do tend to somewhat overstate the case. To no small extent, the rise in the importance of services is accounted for by the rising rate of inflation. Until recently, the price of services rose almost half again as fast as prices for tangible dominant products. The reason is rather obvious: increases in wage rates are more easily offset by productivity gains in manufacturing than in the service trades.

Even after adjusting for inflation, consumer outlays for services have been growing at an annual rate of nearly 4.2 percent over the past 15 years, or faster than total consumer outlays.

Service Industries Have Generally Low Productivity.   One of the more formidable problems of the service industries is how to increase productivity. Productivity is the ratio of output to units of input and if you will recall the special characteristics of services outlined on the previous pages, you will more readily understand why service industries have trouble getting similar gains in productivity as those who produce and market tangible products.

Service industries are labor-intensive industries. This means that to increase output you need larger and larger amounts of labor. Tangible-dominant goods production is most often capital-intensive. This means that in order to increase output, you need more capital in the form of more and better machine technology. It is generally easier to lower per-unit cost of output in capital-intensive industries than in labor-intensive industries.

Wages in the service industries have been going up at least as fast as in the goods-producing industries. This means that low productivity service industries find themselves saddled with permanently rising costs. But unlike industries with rising productivity levels, service industries cannot offset rising pay per worker with rising output per worker. Because service industries account for more than 55 percent of U.S. employment and must pass on all or at least most of their cost increases as price increases, their lower productivity performance is one of the nation's major contributing factors to increased inflationary tendencies.

The Reasons for Low Productivity. There are at least two major reasons for the low levels of productivity in the service industries. These are (1) the small size of most service establishments and (2) the difficulty of using machine technology and other labor-saving devices.

Most service establishments are small and employ a relatively small number of people. Service workers, given the nature of the intangible-dominant product they produce, are generalists, not specialists. Hence, there is little opportunity in the smaller firms to develop much specialization or practice any division of labor.

Neither do service firms characteristically lend themselves to mechanization. This means that labor costs often make up the largest single element of the service product's total price. In services it's difficult to increase output with machines. You need to add more people to generate an increased output. Machines can't cut, wash, and style hair. Neither can machines fill teeth, or make bank loans, or teach classes...or can they?

Service Productivity Can Be Improved. Too frequently, marketers of service have thought of their businesses as being people-intensive and the rest of the economy as capital-intensive. Some would argue that this is a needless and phony distinction.[11] Their argument is that there is no such thing as service industries. There are only industries whose service components are greater or less than those of other industries. In keeping with our goods-services continuum, everybody to some degree is in service.

Much of the problem of the so-called service industries is that they think of services in an old-fashioned, archaic, preindustrial manner. What is needed to increase productivity in the service industries is to apply the kind of technocratic, engineering, and systems orientation which in other fields has replaced

[11] Theodore Levitt, "Production Line Approach to Service," *Harvard Business Review* (September–October 1972), pp. 41–52.

the high cost and low productivity of the artisan, with the low cost, high productivity of the goods-dominant manufacturer-marketer. Service markets, in short, must cease thinking about services in terms of personal ministration and attendance, cease focusing on ways to improve personal performance, and concentrate instead on finding entirely new ways of performing present tasks, or even of changing the tasks themselves. Service industries today are increasingly looking at their problems differently. They are asking what kinds of tools, new or old, and what kinds of skills, processes, organizational rearrangements, incentives, controls, and audits might be implemented to greatly improve their productivity. In short, they are more systems and technology oriented.

The Systems Approach to Service Marketing. The systems approach to service marketing is the principal way by which technology, engineering, and management science is being implemented into service industries in order to raise productivity, lower risk, increase output, and increase customer satisfaction. The systems approach is largely responsible for our higher productivity levels in manufacturing. It consists of looking at a task as a whole, devising new ways of performing each operation, creating new methods and "systems" that eliminate wasted effort and are better coordinated to related processes, and considering the cost of the total operation, not just the cost of each individual performance. The systems approach considers new layouts, better engineering, and coordinated efforts at each stage of the work process. A McDonald's fast service restaurant is a classic example of the systems approach which produces technocratic hamburgers and utilizes french fried automation. In short, McDonald's is an example of a basic service organization that, through better engineering and systems design, produces and markets a high-quality set of products at a low price and with marvelous efficiency and productivity.

The supermarket, where we all shop so frequently and take so much for granted, is another example of the systems approach in action. It represents the epitome of merchandising efficiency in terms of merchandise display, customer selection of items, merchandise handling, and storage and movement, all at a cost lower than its earlier counterpart—the clerk-service convenience grocery store. Productivity increases in the supermarket were made possible by a systems approach to merchandising, customer convenience, and the physical handling of goods.

There are lots of other ways in which the systems approach has been brought to the service industries. Some of them we take for granted, not realizing the revolutionary impact they have had on our lives and businesses. Several of these are worth mentioning because it will help to point out possibilities that might exist to increase productivity in other areas of the service industries.[12]

---

[12] I have chosen to call these activities "the systems approach." I am indebted to Theodore Levitt for these ideas which he refers to as the "industrialization of service." See his article, "The Industrialization of Service," *Harvard Business Review* (September–October 1976), pp. 63–74. Many of the examples used in this section are from this work.

Application of the Systems Approach to Service Activities.

The systems approach to service activities can be applied in three ways: through hard, soft and hybrid technologies.

Hard Technology. Hard technologies or systems are usually the most obvious. Such systems substitute machinery, tools, and other engineering devices for labor-intensive performance of service work. Thus:

1. The consumer credit card and bank balancing checking machine replaces a time-consuming manual check for each purchase.
2. Airport x-ray surveillance equipment replaces a personal body search and a usually embarrassing personal search of luggage.
3. The automatic car wash and hot wax process replaces the personal-manual effort of individuals washing and waxing by hand.
4. Automatic coin receivers at bridges, subway entrances, toll roads, and buses replace human collectors.

Soft Technologies. Soft technologies are the substitution of newly designed, preplanned systems for individual operators. These systems involve some modification of the technology employed but their basic characteristic is the system itself, where special hardware and routines are designed to produce optimal results. In short, "the system is the solution." For example:

1. Fast food restaurants such as McDonald's, Arby's, Wendy's, Pizza Hut, or Kentucky Fried Chicken. Rational systems of division of labor and specialization are rigorously followed to generate high quality, to control costs, to produce speed and efficiency, and to assure cleanliness and low prices.
2. Cafeterias, restaurant salad bars, open tool rooms in factories, and open-stack libraries that enable people to serve themselves quickly and efficiently.
3. Prepackaged vacation tours which eliminate the need for time-consuming and costly personal selling, extensive tailoring of the product to diverse kinds of customers, and extensive price haggling.
4. Fully systematized, almost production-line, yet personalized income tax preparation service on a walk-in basis. The pioneer and perfector of this service has been H & R Block which performs such services at low cost, and with the professional accountant's standard of accuracy and guarantees.

Hybrid Technologies. Hybrid technologies are those that combine hardware with carefully engineered systems to bring greater efficiency, order, and speed to the service process. Such technologies are demonstrated in the following examples:

1. Computer-oriented over the road truck routing and scheduling. By careful programming for types and grades of roads, location of stops, congestion of roads, toll road costs, and mixing point access, the system optimizes truck utilization and minimizes user cost. The soaring cost of energy makes such systems even more desirable. These systems were developed by Cummins Engine.

2. Preorder shipment of perishables at long distances. The system was developed by Sunkist to send trainloads of lemons from California east even before orders were placed. The system uses weather forecasting services for intermediate routing and drop-offs in time to reach cities where expected high temperatures will raise the consumption of lemonade and Tom Collinses.

3. Limited service, fast, low-priced repair facilities such as automotive diagnostic centers, muffler, and transmission shops. Pioneered by Midas, such systems feature high volume, specialization, and special purpose tools and machines which collectively produce fast and guaranteed results.

Thus, the systems approach to the development of services and to service-dominant product marketing, once we think about and understand it, can transform how we behave, what we do, and how we approach this expanding area of marketing activity. Such a systems procedure is as much a frame of mind, a set of attitudes, or outlook as it is hardware, engineering, or management science. But it can bring novel solutions to worrisome old problems. The systems approach can bring to the increasingly dominated service economies of the future the same kinds of quantum advances in productivity and living standards as the newly created goods-dominant factory economies brought to our world in the past.

Developing Effective Strategy for Service Marketing

Intangible dominant products or services require, in many instances, some special consideration in terms of marketing strategy. Recall that strategy is a major comprehensive plan of action. In service marketing enterprises, managers need to think creatively and the key to creative thinking lies in strategic planning. Many managers of service businesses are aware that strategic management of service businesses, which includes the total process of selecting and implementing a marketing plan, is different from that of more tangible product dominant firms. Much of the strategic planning process is similar for service businesses as that for tangible goods dominant businesses, but there are some unique differences. Thus service marketers require different marketing strategies from those employed by product marketers.[13] The unique aspects of services which give direction to service marketing strategy development and implementation are: (1) the intangible dominant nature of services which makes a consumer's choice of competitive offerings more difficult than is encountered in product purchasing; (2) the cohesion and inseparableness of the producer and the service, which tend to localize service marketing and permit the consumer a more restricted choice of alternatives; and (3) the perishability of services, which prevents storage and adds to the risks and uncertainties of service marketing.

---

[13] Richard M. Bessom and Donald W. Jackson, Jr. "Service Retailing: A Strategic Marketing Approach," *Journal of Retailing* **51**, no. 2 (Summer 1975), pp. 75–84.

A Marketing Orientation Is Required. Service firms need to think more consistently in marketing terms and the marketing concept, with all that it entails, is perhaps even more applicable for service marketers than it is for product marketers. The service firm must be customer-oriented and must develop a competitive marketing strategy. The service firm's strategy formulation, like that of the product-oriented firm, consists of two steps: (1) identifying target markets and their needs and (2) developing a marketing mix that satisfies the unique needs of these target markets.

Analysis Precedes Planning. Developing a marketing strategy is a very special kind of market planning and market planning is usually preceded by market analysis. Before proceeding to develop a strategic plan for a service business, managers should ask themselves at least six questions, the answers to which will have a solid impact on the overall strategic plan that emerges. The questions are fairly common but the answers for service businesses are often unique.[14]

[14] See Dan R.E. Thomas, "Strategy is Different in Service Businesses," *Harvard Business Review* (July-August 1978), pp. 158–165.

1. Do we fully understand the specific type of service business we are in? Although service dominant businesses are different from goods dominant businesses, the nature of the difference depends a great deal on the specific type of service business.

2. Who are our customers, how can we identify them, and what benefits are they seeking? As you can see, questions 1 and 2 are interrelated and must, to some extent, be raised and answered simultaneously.

3. How can we penetrate the market and how can we defend our business from competitors? Every firm must consider how it can best enter a market, whether through price, promotion, quality of effort, or some combination of these, and the firm must consider how it can build and protect a strong competitive position.

4. How can we acquire a comparative advantage and achieve more cost efficient operations? Most successful firms attempt to be different, to offer something unique through their marketing program. Also because of the labor-intensive nature of the service business, the firm must explore ways to implement the systems approach into its operation in order to gain economies of scale through division of labor and specialization.

5. What efforts will be used to develop and test new product-service offerings? Every firm depends on its ability to renew its customer franchise in the marketplace. The service-oriented firm must pay careful attention to its "product planning and development" processes because of the difficulty of developing defendable competitive positions and in order to have a balanced assortment of "goods" to meet expected customer demand.

6. What role should we assign to planning and research? Service organizations are discovering that planning and research are as critical to them as they are to product marketers.

When answers to these critical questions are provided, the service marketing firm is ready to begin its development of its strategic marketing plan.

Strategy Must Consider the Whole Range of Marketing Activities

Developing a strategic plan for a service business necessitates that the firm consider the whole range of marketing activities.[15] The marketing manager of the service firm should view planning as a process, not a project. Planning is deciding in advance what needs to be done. It is concerned with deciding on where we want to go and figuring out how we are going to get there. Research is a tool and a facilitator of the planning process, allowing the firm to monitor change and its environment. The customer's needs are the central focus of the firm's marketing efforts. Research is conducted to uncover these needs; planning is done to respond to these needs.

[15] Richard B. Stall, "Marketing in a Service Industry," *Atlanta Economic Review* (May-June 1978), pp. 15–18.

Analyzing Market Opportunity

As in product marketing, one of the first steps in analyzing market opportunity is to identify target markets and to determine the needs of customers and their bases for choosing among the many alternatives offered. Consumers usually have complex and sophisticated reasons for choosing a particular service supplier. Service expenditures are often quite discretionary and can easily be postponed. Customers of intangible dominant products often opt to forego purchasing and elect to perform the service for themselves. Services constitute an important element of the "do-it-yourself markets."

Buyers of services are, in effect, purchasing the capability of the seller. Therefore the buyer can be expected to evaluate the performance, behavior, and characteristics of the manager of the service firm or its representatives. It is important that service firms understand and identify the various reasons for consumer choice. Service marketers must determine what specific needs can be satisfied by the type of service offered and which attributes of the service offering are considered most important by consumers. Quite obviously, service marketers must also search for and identify needs that are not presently being satisfied.

Applying Market Segmentation Strategies

Because service needs in the marketplace are heterogeneous and because different consumers may perceive the same service quite differently, the marketer may wish to segment the total market into smaller target markets that are characterized by more homogeneous needs. Health spas and exercise centers will appeal to some users on the basis of improved health and the chances of enhanced well-being and longevity. Others may be attracted because of the improved appearance of a youthful, slimmer figure.

Marketing has virtually reached a stage in its development where it is inseparable from market segmentation.[16] It is an easy matter to say that segmentation offers many benefits to service marketers; however, it is not so easy to find good segmentation variables. Marketers in service oriented businesses are still working to identify key underlying variables which are good discriminators between classes of people having different response characteristics to either products or services.

Service marketers must be reminded that no firm can expect to appeal to all customers. The process of attracting one segment may act to repel another. A service marketer that is aimed simultaneously at more than one segment will not often be able to maximize its appeal to any single segment. Such efforts run the risk of creating an image that is not recognizable by any of the segments. If heavy users, because of their important market potential, are the most attractive and promising market segment, then management must create and implement its offerings for the heavy user segment and not dilute its efforts by trying to satisfy lighter use segments.

[16] See William R. Sevinyard, "Market Segmentation in Retail Service Industries: A Multiattribute Approach," *Journal of Retailing* **53**, no. 1 (Spring 1977), pp. 27–34 and pp. 92–93.

Service Offerings Must Be Favorably Positioned

Positioning is an equally important part of strategy considerations for service oriented products. Recall that positioning is concerned with the efforts of the firm to develop a clear image of its "products" in the minds of customers and then to communicate this image to buyers in comparison with their notions or images of other products.

Positioning offers some special problems for marketers in connection with services because by their very nature services are often intangible and their characteristics are usually more subjective than objective. Figure 17-5 graphically illustrates the nature of the positioning task with tangible dominant products (goods) and intangible dominant products (services). What Figure 17-5 conveys is that tangible dominant products like cosmetics, automobiles, motorcycles, and even clothing are often given intangible images, that is, beauty and allure (cosmetics), status and power (automobiles), fun and adventure (motorcycles), and dash, sex appeal, poise, and confidence (clothing). Products that have large elements of both tangible dominant and intangible dominant characteristics are given images that consist of both tangible evidence and intangible image characteristics. In the case of products that are largely intangible dominant, such as airline travel, insurance, banking services, diet and reducing salons, hair styling, and much of the hospitality industry (such as hotel, motel, restaurant, and tourism businesses), the task is to take an abstract entity such as an insurance policy, a flight from Dallas to Los Angeles, or a checking and savings account and create a more *concrete* image for these products. It is for such reasons that Prudential Insurance talks about "a piece of the rock," and Merrill Lynch associates itself with a bull and its corresponding bullishness. Such symbols are concrete ways to clearly identify firms in the minds of customers and they are useful for improving the marketing strategies of intangible dominant service organizations.

Figure 17-5 Principle of market positioning emphasis.

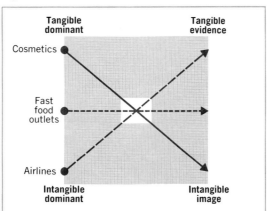

Source: "Breaking Free from Product Marketing," *Journal of Marketing*, April, 1977.

Before proceeding, can you answer these questions:
1. List and describe three ways by which product and service marketing differ.
2. What are the main reasons why service marketers have generally low productivity?
3. How does the systems approach lend itself to increasing productivity in service oriented firms?

Services Still Require a Marketing Mix

The essence of every marketing strategy is still the marketing mix. And in service marketing, the marketing mix, like that for tangible dominant products, consists of product planning and development, channel of distribution policies, pricing, and promotional activities. In many ways, the development of an optimal marketing mix strategy for service marketers will be similar to that of more tangible product marketers. However, there are some cautions. For example, there are profound differences in many instances between service and goods marketing. The best posture for the marketing manager to assume is: the more intangible dominant elements in a given market offering, the more the marketing strategy and the marketing mix are likely to diverge from the strategy and mix for tangible dominant products. In the following several pages we will examine some of the characteristics of the marketing mix in conjunction with the special nature of service marketing.

Drawing by Wm. Hamilton; © 1981 The New Yorker Magazine, Inc.

"I want more than a slogan—I want an aphorism!"

Product Development. Services are products; even though intangible, they are things. And service marketers must always remember that consumers do not buy products, they buy attributes that are converted into benefits. Like other consumer "goods," services are either convenience, shopping, or specialty goods with all that implies. Consumer services such as haircuts, shoe repair, dry cleaning, and clothing alterations are usually purchased on a convenience basis. Insurance, banking, airline travel, and automotive repair often involve comparison shopping or at least phoning around to compare prices, what's included in the total package, terms, and other attributes. Legal services, medical care, hair styling, or brokerage services are more likely to be specialty services and for these customers may be willing to go to considerable lengths to acquire the special attributes or benefits they deem essential to full and complete satisfaction.

Many services are custom-designed products. Recall that services are intangible and heterogeneous and cannot easily be separated from their producer. This has several implications for product planning and development. First of all, many new "products" are asked for from the field. For example, a client may request from IBM a special new program for processing accounts receivable or another client may ask IBM to design a special system utilizing point-of-sale cash register computers for facilitating both financial and merchandising decisions within the firm. In such instances, the client becomes an integral part of the design process itself.

Recall also that intangible dominant products like services cannot be stored, nor can they be transported. But the service marketer nonetheless has a product development and a merchandising task, which is to maintain a balanced assortment of goods to meet expected customer demand. To accomplish this many service marketers implement a policy of chasing demand, that is, attempting to supply an output that is balanced to demand at any point in time.[17] This usually means attempting to increase capacity for very short periods by using standby low-price help. Other service marketers are more likely to consider a level output strategy whereby, regardless of the short-run demand considerations, capacity is maintained at what was determined as the short-run forecasted optimum.

Service marketers often use the "chase" strategy in situations where unskilled workers perform jobs with little or no discretion, for low pay in a relatively unattractive environment. Service marketers use the level strategy most often where more highly skilled people perform jobs for high pay, with some or a lot of discretion in a relatively pleasant environment.

Thinking of service as an integral part of what is marketed can result in alteration of the product itself, sometimes with dramatic results. For example, new services are often an improved method of delivering an existing service.[18]

[17] See W. Earl Sasser, "Match Supply and Demand in Service Industries," *Harvard Business Review* (November–December 1976), pp. 133–140.
[18] John M. Rathmell, *Marketing in the Service Sector* (Cambridge, MA: Winthrop Publishers, 1974), p. 61.

There are some other related aspects of product planning and development in connection with marketing intangible dominant services which are likely to differ significantly from marketing more tangible dominant products. For example, it is rather difficult to brand services. Because of their intangible nature, packaging and "product" labeling decisions are difficult, which means that service marketers are limited in their use of the package to promote service offerings. Finally, the intangible nature of the product largely prohibits sampling as a means of introducing a new service to a target market.

Channels of Distribution.   Channels of distribution for intangible dominant products such as services are, as we learned from studying the characteristics of services, necessarily short. There are few, if any, wholesalers of services. Instead, channels of distribution for services are direct and short, that is, from manufacturer-marketer direct to ultimate consumers. However, though the channel is short, there are arising a number of marketing intermediaries whose task is to make the exchange process between manufacturer-marketer and consumer work more smoothly.[19]

The retailer who extends a bank's credit to its customers is an intermediary in the distribution of credit. Thus, when retailers become a part of a credit card plan they, in effect, become an intermediary in the channel of distribution for credit.

The vending machines located in airports for air travel accident insurance have found their way into other areas. Travel accident insurance is now available in many hotel chains. Group insurance plans written through employers, labor unions, and professional associations have also become extremely successful. In instances such as these, the insurance industry has used intermediaries to distribute their service.

Organizations that provide space for walk-up coin operated pay telephones or other vending devices serve as intermediaries for telephone communication or the distribution of other products.

In the examples just cited, means of distribution were used that consisted of distinct organizational entities between the producer of a service and the user for the purpose of making the service more readily available. In the more normal or traditional sense of a channel of distribution, these intermediaries would not be thought of as part of the channel. In a service oriented "product," however, it may be more fitting to consider that any extra-corporate entity between the producer of a service and prospective users which is utilized to make the service available and/or more convenient is a marketing intermediary for that service. Thus, service marketers should perhaps take a fresh look at the channels of distribution for services as distinct from the channels concept employed for goods.

It should be quite apparent that the most important marketing intermediary for services is the retailer. The manufacturer-marketer for most consumer serv-

[19] James H. Donnelly, Jr., "Marketing Intermediaries in Channels of Distribution for Services," *Journal of Marketing* **40** (January 1976), pp. 55–70.

ices is a retailer, one who by definition markets to ultimate consumers. In service retailing the sale must be made before production and consumption take place. Therefore, the notion that all customer contact employees are engaged in personal selling is much more real for the service firm than for the conventional goods firms.[20] Much of the thrust of consumerism is directed at the service oriented retailer and to be dissatisfied with the "product" is to be immediately dissatisfied with the retail seller of that product. One of the major customer complaints of services is the often impersonal, lackadaisical attitudes of service retailers toward their customers. Workers in retailing organizations whose principal products are services are both factory workers and salespersons. Therefore it is important because of the close and immediate interface between retailers and customers that the successful service company must first sell the job to employees before it can sell its services to customers.

Pricing.   Price policies for service marketers tend to parallel those used throughout the general field of marketing. Most service marketers follow competitive price policies, pricing their service either at the market or slightly below. Pricing above the market is generally employed by larger service firms or by all firms who wish to use price as a means of rationing the supply of their service offerings. This would suggest that the market for services, much like the market for tangible dominant products, may actually consist of three or four separate segments which are price-sensitive and responsive.

Flexible pricing seems much more prevalent in the marketing of services than in the marketing of goods. Some service marketers either do not have a written price list or do not follow it in making price quotations. Instead, prices are more arbitrarily determined in terms of eliminating peak demand or to increase demand during slack periods. In service marketing, neither is it unusual for the firm to charge different prices to different customers for essentially the same bundle of services. On the other hand, many firms attempt scrupulously to maintain a uniform price policy.

In quoting prices, some firms try mainly to meet competition, some firms attempt to use tables of standard costs, and a few even attempt to bargain with customers.[21] Apparently, in most cases, prices are quoted with certain flexible guidelines in mind. Most service marketers appear to have a definite profit margin in mind when quoting prices.

The pricing goals of service marketers vary, but typically the pricing goal of most is to maximize profits for each sale—not necessarily the wisest pricing practice. Other pricing goals of service marketers are to (1) attract new business and (2) increase sales volume. Typically, service marketers are most likely to view the market for their efforts as price-inelastic and for that reason pricing is often more demand-oriented than cost-oriented.

[20] William R. George, "The Retailing of Services—A Challenging Future," *Journal of Retailing* **53,** no. 3 (Fall 1977), pp. 85–97. See also Duane L. Davis, Joseph P. Guiltinan, and Wesley H. Jones, "Service Characteristics, Consumer Search, and the Classification of Retail Services," *Journal of Retailing* **55,** no. 3 (Fall 1979), pp. 3–23.

[21] Martin R. Schlissel, "Pricing in a Service Industry," *MSU Business Topics* (Spring 1977), pp. 37–48.

One method frequently employed by service marketers to shift demand from peak periods to nonpeak ones is to use a differential pricing scheme. This might also increase primary demand for the nonpeak periods. Examples of such pricing tactics include matinee prices for movies, happy hours at bars, family nights at the ball park, weekend and night rates for long distance calls, peak load pricing by utility companies, and two for one coupons at restaurants on midweek days or evenings.

Service marketers are not often well versed in the intricacies of sophisticated price decision making. To improve their competitive positions and their ultimate profitability, price decision makers in service marketing ventures would be well advised to consider the following:

1. Set annual total profit and sales volume goals.
2. Target a definite profit margin when quoting prices for each job.
3. Determine and understand their own cost structure.
4. Review and update their price schedules regularly.
5. Work to secure higher rather than lower average prices.
6. Strive for greater pricing flexibility.

In summary, pricing in service-oriented enterprises is casually demand-oriented with many sellers charging what the traffic will bear. This pricing method is still, in a sense, a kind of cost-plus pricing because costs become the primary bases for price determination. Marketing in general is not a great strength of service-oriented firms and pricing in particular may be their weakest and least developed marketing skill. Of all service firms, the smallest appear to be the poorest marketers and the medium to large firms appear to be the best.

Promotion.   Promotion is an important part of the marketing mix for many service marketers. The key to successful promotion, whether it be advertising or personal selling, is "benefitizing" the product. It is very important to define the "product" in terms of what the consumer wants and not in terms of what the marketer makes and sells. McDonald's doesn't promote just hamburgers; instead, "they do it all for you," which means a meal or a snack in clean, comfortable surroundings, in which the buyer is reassured of speed and efficiency of service, cheerfulness, and predictable consistency. Banks don't sell money, they promote the full range of their services such as better parking facilities, night depositories, Saturday service, conversion of overdrafts into loans, an open line of credit for emergency purposes, cash machines, and multiple locations. Thus, again we are to be reminded that products are not something people buy, but a tool they seek and use—a tool to solve their problems or to achieve their intentions.

Intangible dominant products such as services offer a challenge to the promotion manager. To successfully promote such services, they are often personalized, as in the case of Allstate Insurance's "You're in good hands with Allstate," or in the case of Western Savings and Loan Banks using a well-known and recognized figure such as John Wayne (before his death) to act as company spokesperson in their advertising campaign. Seattle First Bank utilizes a historical figure, Dexter Horton, the founder of Seattle First, as their spokesperson. Personalizing the service around a tangible person is one way of concretizing the fuzzy, intangible nature of service firms and their products.

To successfully promote services, they must be made to have a favorable positive image constructed to project attributes of the service such as safe and dependable (Safeco Insurance), long-lasting dependability and friendly and courteous service (Mutual of Omaha), science and technology oriented (Rockwell International) and fair, honest, and responsible (Mobil Oil Company).

Promoting the service marketer's image is a bit like "selling the sizzle and not the steak." Hence, insurance companies sometimes can make an intangible product even more intangible by promoting such things as "variable annuity premiums" or "careful estate portfolio analysis." Such appeals are too fuzzy and too abstract. By contrast, the phone company promotes "togetherness" with their slogan "Reach out and touch someone," or "extending your sales force into a new territory by telephone personal selling." Banks show couples with new homes or enjoying themselves on vacation. These and similar themes are ways service marketers promote benefits that are concrete and more comprehensible to service buyers.

In no product is personal selling more important than in service marketing. Recall again that in the case of services, the producer and the marketer are virtually inseparable. Sellers are often expected to be knowledgeable professionals who can give needed advice and counseling.

In some service lines, telephone solicitation and even direct mail are playing an increasingly important role. Thus certain forms of life, casualty, and hospitalization insurance were created especially to be sold via mail, newspapers, or television, using follow-up promotional efforts by direct response telephone solicitation.

Sales promotion in the traditional sense of sampling, demonstrations, and point-of-purchase display are severely limited because of the characteristics of the intangible dominant service product. But service firms do on occasion use premiums and contests. Market-oriented publicity is also used extensively for such service-oriented products as entertainment and sporting events. No astute service marketer would overlook the opportunity to positively affect public opinion through its news releases, or its staged activities designed in part to alter public perceptions or otherwise modify behavior.

The Future of Service Marketing

As we entered the decade of the 1980s, over 70 percent of the civilian labor force was employed in service marketing organizations, with the remaining nearly 30 percent employed in the production and marketing of goods. Services were also accounting for slightly more than 45 percent of personal consumption expenditures, the largest component in that category of expenditures.

The future for service marketing looks even brighter. By 1990, services will likely account for 50 percent of total general merchandise sales, up from less than 25 percent in 1975. Hence, in terms of dollar volume, number employed, and overall expanding market opportunity, much of the marketing "action" during the 1980s will be in the area of service marketing. This expanding market opportunity will, of course, reflect swelling consumer demand for services as we move further and further into the era of the Post-Industrial Society. This era promises the continuation and even acceleration of trends already underway. For example:[22]

1. A growth in product complexity and a decline in consumer ability to evaluate products.
2. A tendency for households to reduce their participation in such traditional household tasks as food preparation.
3. An increase in the value of time and an increase in the disutility of hours spent in shopping.
4. The growth of new technologies that may permit economic provision of new informational and purchasing services.

Such trends in American life support the contention that consumers are increasingly desirous of using the services of buyer-helping businesses who absorb much of the mental and physical work inherent in consumer purchasing. More and more consumers are purchasing the services of evaluators and appraisers, diagnosticians and recommenders, service locating agencies, product finding agencies, and package suppliers. Buyers are paying service organizations for advice on homemaking, decorating, financial and insurance management, fashions, cooking, recreation and travel, athletic techniques and equipment, health care, and legal assistance.

The Marketing of Professional Services. The future of service marketing will surely see a more pronounced tendency toward the increased use of marketing in a wide range of professional service organizations. Service marketers such as physicians, lawyers, and accountants are beginning to overcome their disdain for commercialism, are reconsidering the provisions of their codes of ethics, and are no longer simply equating marketing with selling.[23]

Professional firms, not unlike other business firms, have three major objectives: adequate demand, continued growth, and profitable operation. To attain these multiple objectives, many of the more traditional professional service-oriented practitioners such as doctors, dentists, lawyers, and accountants are embracing and practicing professional marketing.[24]

Professional marketing is a way of facilitating the exchange process between professional practitioners and their clients within a framework that is consistent with the profession's stated ethical and professional framework. The major attributes of professional marketing are:

1. Determining long-range marketing objectives and developing comprehensive marketing strategies.

[22] From Stanley C. Hollander, "Buyer Helping Businesses...and Some Not-So-Helpful Ones," *MSU Business Topics* (Summer 1974), pp. 52–68.
[23] Paul N. Bloom and Stephen E. Loeb, "If Public Accountants Are Allowed to Advertise," *MSU Business Topics* (Summer 1977), pp. 57–64.
[24] Philip Kotler and Richard A. Conner, Jr., "Marketing Professional Services," *Journal of Marketing* (January 1977), pp. 71–76.

2. Working to become more effective at marketing and personal selling.
3. Delegating and assigning formal responsibility to one or more people in the organization to manage and fully implement the marketing program.
4. Using those marketing practices and concepts which are consistent with the industry's professional code of ethics and which do not therefore cheapen or bring disrepute to the profession.

The real issue facing professional firms is not whether to engage in marketing—undoubtedly they all are. The question is how they can do it more effectively in markets that are becoming more competitive and where the desire for more and better service is growing.

Meeting the Challenge of Service Marketing. Marketing firms that are service oriented and wish to grow and prosper must be increasingly marketing oriented in the future and be aware of the changes that are taking place in service marketing. Their future success and well-being will largely be a function of their understanding and reaction to these propositions.

1. Market opportunities for growth and expansion today and tomorrow are greater in the area of services than in the area of goods.
2. Mass production, industrial design, and systems engineering previously used only in manufacturing are being increasingly implemented and adapted to service businesses.
3. The use of mass production and systems engineering in service industries increases productivity but leads to the increased depersonalization of service marketing.
4. The whole range of strategic marketing activities such as market planning, segmentation, and positioning, are relevant for service marketing and such efforts will tend to satisfy the growing demand for diversity in service market offerings.

Summary

Services are a growing sector of consumers' personal consumption expenditures. In 1980, service expenditures accounted for slightly more than 45 percent of personal consumption expenditures while durable goods accounted for nearly 13 percent and nondurable goods accounted for nearly 42 percent. Business firms also purchase large amounts of intangible or service dominant products. Services are products, but they are essentially intangible dominant products as opposed to physical goods, which are tangible dominant products. The growth of consumer services is the result primarily of (1) growing affluence, (2) the impact of technology, and (3) changing consumer lifestyles. Most products contain elements that are both tangible and intangible, hence goods exist on a kind of continuum from tangible dominant to intangible dominant. The important point is that consumers are increasingly purchasing more and more services. Services are products in the sense that consumers are buying bundles of expectations and, therefore, service marketers must also "benefitize" their service offerings. There are both similarities and differences between "goods" and "service" marketing. Usually, the more the product is intangible dominant, the more its marketing effort will differ from traditional goods marketing. Many service marketers are working to increase their productivity by developing and implementing mass production techniques, better design, and systems engineering approaches to their operation. Service marketers find it equally important to develop effective marketing strategies that are based upon careful market planning, market segmentation, and market positioning. The essence of the service marketers' strategy is, however, still the marketing mix. The future of service marketing appears promising, with many professionals such as doctors, dentists, lawyers, and accountants embracing marketing as a better way of aligning their organizations with the growing demand for professional services.

Review Questions

1. How are services defined? How do you distinguish between services and goods?
2. What factors largely account for the growing role and importance of services in personal consumption expenditures?
3. How have marketers responded to consumers' increased demands for services?
4. In what ways do "product" and "service" marketing differ?
5. List and discuss several of the more distinguishing characteristics of intangible dominant products such as services.
6. It is sometimes suggested that service markets have lower productivity than "goods" markets. What is productivity and to what extent is this assumption true?
7. Why is a marketing orientation for services industries deemed desirable?
8. What in your estimation would be the main difficulty in using a segmentation approach in a service-oriented enterprise?
9. In market positioning, the service marketer must frequently take an intangible dominant product and make it more tangible. How is this accomplished and how is it related to the positioning task?
10. Of all the elements in the service marketers' marketing mix, the one that is most likely to differ from all the others is channels. Why? Discuss.

Case 17-1

Tantrific Sun

The tanning industry used to be associated solely with the hides of animals, like cows. However, in recent years the tanning of human hides has become big business, and the nation's latest franchising fad. Spurred by people's desire to look healthy, affluent, well-traveled, and possessed of other attributes usually associated with a good tan, most major cities now have become home to the so-called tanning salons.

The business end of a tanning salon is the tanning booth. Generally speaking, it is a small booth, lined with special fluorescent lights that give off the midrange ultraviolet light which is thought to be best for tanning. The booths are almost always attached to private dresssing rooms where customers can take off as much or as little as they want before donning the mandatory eye protection and entering the booth.

Before you enter the booth, a technician trained in the use of the equipment will ask the patron some questions about his or her skin and then determine a program of exposure which will promote a tan instead of a burn. Most begin at somewhere between 30 seconds and two minutes for the first session, depending on the fairness of the skin. A minute in the tanning booth equals an hour in the sun.

Once exposure time is established, a timer outside the booth, controlled only by the salon operator, is set. Closing the door activates the timer, which cuts off automatically once you have reached the prescribed limit.

Customers are advised to come in once a day for the first ten sessions to get a noticeable base tan. However, 90 percent of the customers come in every day for the first 20 days to get a dark tan, then once or twice a week to maintain their tan.

Tantrific Sun Salons bring the "winter" tan into the price range of almost anyone. The going rate is usually $35 for 20 sessions. Some salons even offer annual memberships, with unlimited visits for $150.

Because many people want to come in either during their lunch hour or after work, the salons have accommodating hours, generally opening in mid or late morning and closing late in the evening.

The prime reason that people come to the facilities, managers say, is vanity. People want to look good. A lot of people also want to look good and affluent, which is what a winter tan suggests.

A number of salons have a very high percentage of male clients, and in many, men outnumber women.

Questions

1. What reasons might you suggest to explain the growth of a service such as Tantrific Sun Salons?
2. What satisfactions do the buyers of such services as Tantrific Sun Salons seek?
3. How is the marketing program for a service like Tantrific geared to the nature of the product?
4. Briefly discuss the merits of the pricing policies of Tantrific Sun Salons.

Case 17-2

McDonald's Corporation

The McDonald's Corporation is, by most accounts, one of the great marketing successes of the era, capitalizing as no other single company has on the "eating-out" trend. The company's revenues are nearly $2 billion, which places it high on the list of big companies.

The company's annual report for the year ending 1978 listed these highlights:

In its 14th year as a publicly held company, McDonald's Corporation achieved its 14th consecutive year of record growth. Net income and net income per share each increased 19 percent. Systemwide sales were up 22 percent and revenues rose 19 percent.

Net income for the year ending December 31, 1978 was $162,669,000, an increase of $25,973,000 over the 1977 total of $136,696,000. Net income per share was $4.00, 63¢ more than the previous year's figure of $3.37. Systemwide sales—sales by all franchised, company-owned and affiliated restaurants—totaled $4,575,000,000, an increase of $837,000,000 over the 1977 sales of $3,738,000,000.

Revenues for the past year totaled $1,671,891,000 or $265,743,000 more than the $1,406,148,000 achieved in 1977.

Return on average assets for 1978 was 20.9 percent and return on average equity, 22.6

percent. Sales volumes for McDonald's restaurants open 13 months or more averaged $942,000 in 1978, a growth of 9.5 percent over 1977.

At year end 1978, the McDonald's worldwide system included 5,185 restaurants, 514 more than at the close of 1977. Among the year's new restaurants was the first McDonald's in Belgium. Of the total restaurants, 4,465 are located in the United States and 720 in 24 other countries and territories. Sixty-nine percent of the McDonald's restaurants— or 3,573—are operated by independent franchises. In the United States 74 percent of the restaurants are franchised. The company celebrated the opening of the 5,000th restaurant in the system in October, 1978.

The developer and mentor of the McDonald's concept and one of the pioneers of the modern franchising system is Ray Kroc, the chairman of the board of McDonald's. Kroc, who had been a successful salesperson of malted milk machines, approached the owners of a San Bernadino, California restaurant, Richard and Maurice McDonald, with a proposal to sell franchises for their "fast food" concept. Hence, the modern McDonald's was born. It was based upon the notion that families were changing. There was the middle-class move to the suburbs and the dramatic increase in numbers of children. Most of these families had several things in common—they all owned automobiles, they traveled extensively, enjoyed a more common lifestyle, and made frequent trips to shopping centers. In addition, there was the growing trend to affluence by the middle-class and an increase in their discretionary income.

Ray Kroc saw these trends and envisioned a series of restaurants that would provide uniform quality, assurance of cleanliness, and affordable prices. He built his restaurant concepts around what he calls the QSC & V factors. QSC & V stand for Quality, Service, Cleanliness, and Value.

His restaurants were also unique in that they incorporated a new sense of service. Service to Kroc meant not just products in the total tangi-ble dominant sense, but in the sense of McDonald's slogan, "We do it all for you." This theme was built on the firm's basics (Quality, Service, Cleanliness, and Value) and on the proposition that McDonald's offers people more than just good food. McDonald's communication to its customers attempts to create the awareness and understanding that a visit to McDonald's is an experience that is the sum total of the food, folks, and fun found there.

What is the secret of McDonald's success? Sound financing and careful site selection are important. But most critical is the carefully controlled execution of each outlet's major function—the rapid delivery of a uniform, high-quality mix of prepared foods in an environment of cleanliness, order, and cheerful courtesy. The systematic substitution of equipment for people, combined with the carefully planned use and implementation of technology, enables McDonald's to attract and hold patronage. Raw hamburger patties are carefully prepacked and premeasured. Storage, preparation space, and related facilities are expressly designed for, and limited to, the predetermined mix of products. McDonald's food processing is similar to an automobile assembly line—the essence of which is order and standardization.

Nothing can go wrong—the employer never soils his hands, the floor remains clean, dry, and safe, and food quality is controlled. Best of all, the customer gets visibly generous portions with great speed, the employer remains efficient and cheerful, and the general impression is one of extravagant good service.

Questions

1. Is McDonald's a service business? In what sense? Explain.
2. What factors have contributed to McDonald's growing success?
3. On the goods-service continuum shown in chapter 17, where would you place the McDonald's Corporation?
4. Service industries generally have low productivity. Is this characteristic of McDonald's? Why or why not?

Chapter 18

Multinational Marketing

The world is shrinking. What may have once seemed foreign and strange now often seems natural and ours. A recent ad for Volkswagen read, "I don't want a foreign car, I want a Volkswagen." We Americans have adopted tacos, pizza, and coffee. We wear shoes made in Taiwan, shirts made in India, jeans and other slacks made in Mexico. We watch television sets made in Japan; our stereo sound systems also come from Japan, as do many of our automobiles, motorcycles, and bicycles. We ski on equipment imported from Italy and Germany. Truly, we are in the beginnings of an era of global marketing. However, it isn't all a one-way street. American products, ingenuity, and technology have swept around the world. American enterprise no longer considers our country a self-contained marketing Mecca. The market for many firms today, American and otherwise, is worldwide in perspective and scope.

Some economic systems, that of the United States for example, are mainly self-sustaining. Yet the growing scarcity in this country's domestic energy

Drawing by Wm. Hamilton; © 1975 The New Yorker Magazine, Inc.

"Hey! 'Made in U.S.A.'!"

sources has put an urgent emphasis on *multinational marketing* into our outlook. The United States is such a large and diverse economy that there tends to be at least one domestic firm producing almost any type of product that its people, firms, and governments may wish to buy. Moreover, the overall level of consumer spending in the American economy is so great that many firms can sell large amounts of their product. This permits them to use the most modern technologies and to take advantage of economies of scale. Costs per unit of output are thus kept at rock-bottom levels, making it difficult for foreign firms to compete. However, the difficult is seldom impossible and foreign firms are increasingly able to compete in the United States. When they do, the American consumer usually benefits by having a broader assortment of merchandise from which to choose and by paying lower prices brought about by the expanded competition. Some products that Americans love to consume are available only because they are produced abroad. South American bananas and coffee, Japanese and German automobiles, Danish furniture, even Russian caviar are commonplace in the American market.

Some economies less fortunate than the United States, like Britain and Japan, do not have enough natural resources to produce and market all the goods their people require. Yet their citizens can live comfortably. Consider the Netherlands. This tiny resourceless but resourceful nation has modern and efficient firms because a few large businesses concentrate on producing more of a few types of products than the Dutch people themselves can buy. The surplus is marketed abroad, and the money earned buys foreign-made goods the Dutch cannot produce themselves. The Dutch supply themselves by producing and marketing for others. This is the value of international or multinational marketing: it permits countries to concentrate on what each does best and, by so doing, lowers prices in all markets, thus contributing to the overall social welfare.

The American economic system is a powerful one but we are by no means self-sufficient. Indeed, we are becoming increasingly dependent on international marketing. For example, a substantial portion of all agricultural, pharmaceutical, and aircraft marketing by United States firms occurs in response to demand and purchases by foreign buyers.

Usually, the wider its base of natural resources, the larger its population, the higher its level of customer spending then the more self-sufficient an economy can be. Such economic systems are required to sell less abroad to operate their firms efficiently. Correspondingly, they do not need to buy as much abroad in order to have the many goods and services wanted by their people, businesses, and governments.

In this chapter we will examine some of the main elements in multinational marketing, especially the multinational corporations. We will consider how and why this form of marketing has increased so greatly in the last two decades and discuss the effect of demand from developing countries and less developed countries. We will also answer such questions as (1) Why does a company decide to go multinational? (2) How does a firm develop its strategies for multinational marketing? (3) What organizational structures are used for pen-

"OUR NEW MODEL MUST BE ROOMIER, FASTER,
AND HAVE AN EASIER NAME FOR AMERICANS
TO WRITE ON THEIR ORDER BLANKS."

etrating markets abroad? A glance at the way multinational marketing is changing will round out our discussion.

Multinational Marketing and World Trade

The importance of multinational marketing is reflected increasingly in the figures and statistics of world trade. For example, Figure 18-1 charts United States foreign trade from 1960 to 1980. The data shows that in those years the United States generally marketed more goods abroad than it, in turn, received from foreign marketers. Although our persistent and heedless demand for more oil than we produce reversed this pattern in the mid-to-late 1970s, trade with other countries continues to be a significant part of the American economy.

Foreign trade in 1980 amounted to about 10 percent of the total United States GNP. Our products and services marketed abroad were spread among different countries and regions of the world so that no country or region bought more than 1 or 2 percent of the goods marketed by American firms. Figure 18-2 shows what nations we do most of our international marketing with. In looking at Figure 18-2 you will observe that the United States markets 21 percent of its exports to Canada but that Canada in turn sends 23 percent of its exports to the United States.

Figure 18-1 United States foreign trade 1960–1980.

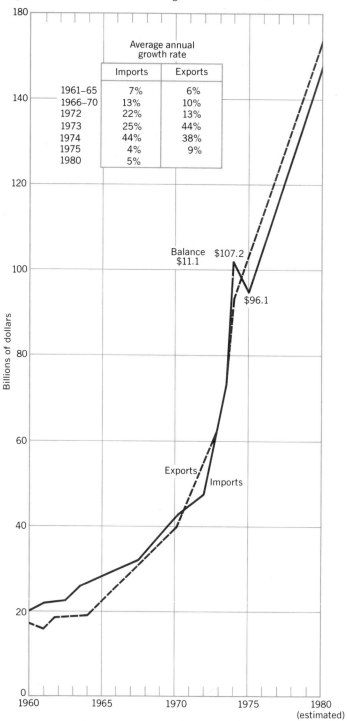

Source: Compiled from U.S. Department of Commerce data.

Figure 18-2 United States trading partners, 1980.

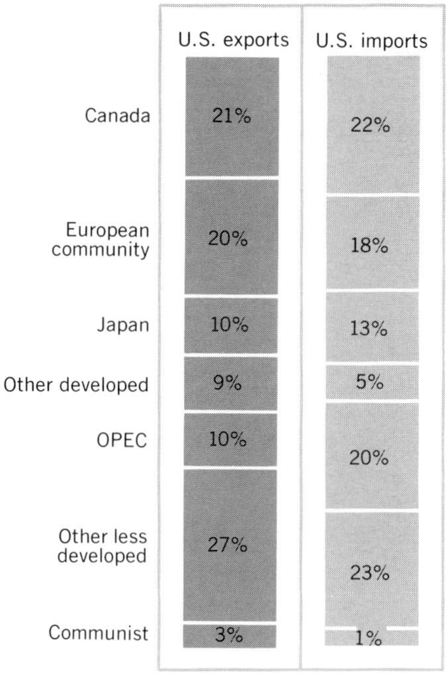

	U.S. exports	U.S. imports
Canada	21%	22%
European community	20%	18%
Japan	10%	13%
Other developed	9%	5%
OPEC	10%	20%
Other less developed	27%	23%
Communist	3%	1%

Source: Compiled from U.S. Department of Commerce data.

At the other extreme, the United States sells only 3 percent of its exported products and services to Communist nations while they in turn market only 1 percent of their exports to the United States. Also it is interesting to note that the more sophisticated and industrialized countries do business primarily with each other, not with the less developed countries.

Features of the Global Market

Multinational marketers see the world as one enormous market. Not a single homogeneous one necessarily but as a total market consisting of many diverse market segments. One of the simplest and most direct ways of sectioning the world market is to rank the countries by their gross national product per capita. By doing this, the world can be divided up into three separate segments: industrialized countries (ICs), developing countries (DCs), and less developed countries (LDCs).

The ICs, DCs, and LDCs have average GNPs per capita of about $3,700, $1,500, and $160, respectively. The GNPs for countries in each of these groups have grown at annual rates of 4.5 percent (ICs), 7.2 percent (DCs), and 4.8 percent (LDCs) over the past ten years.[1] The rapid population growth,

[1] John A. Weber, "Worldwide Strategies for Market Segmentation." *Columbia Journal of World Business* 9, no. 14 (Winter 1974), pp. 31–37.

Figure 18-3 GNP per capita—by major regions.

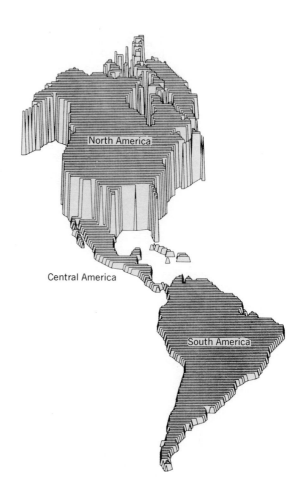

especially in the LDCs and the DCs, has stymied the GNP per capita growth in these countries. With less fertile populations, their economic growth and hence their value as markets would be even more enhanced.

Given the tremendous concentration of world income in relatively few industrialized countries, it is not surprising that the greatest opportunities for multinational marketing can be found in the ICs and DCs. However, the world is now experiencing a shift in the distribution of total world income, with more of it moving toward these developing countries. Figure 18-3 shows GNP per capita by regions of the world. Notice that the height of each region is proportional to its per capita income. The really potent markets are those of North America (especially the United States and Canada), Japan, Oceania, Europe, and the Union of Soviet Socialist Republics.

The DCs should be of particular interest to multinational marketers because such countries have 19 percent of the world's population and account for nearly one-third of its income. The Middle East, South America and Central America are important because of their high growth rate of income and their increasing industrialization.

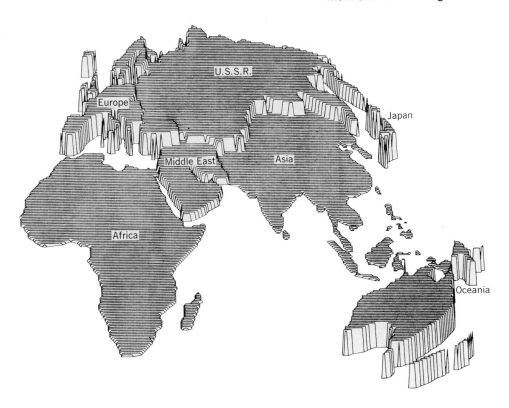

The height of each region is proportional
to per capita income.

Region or country	GNP per capita (US$)	GNP (US$000 millions)	Population (millions)
North America	6,130	1,425	233
Japan	3,630	393	108
Oceania	3,400	71	21
Europe, excluding USSR	2,990	1,516	507
USSR	2,030	506	250
Middle East	1,080	82	76
South America	840	170	203
Central America*	800	79	99
Africa	290	114	392
Asia, excluding Japan	200	399	1,947

Note: Due to rounding, the amounts in this table may not equal the
amounts or aggregates of the figures appearing in the regional tables.
*Including Mexico.

Source: World Bank Atlas

Figure 18–3   (continued)

The LDCs also deserve the attention of the multinational marketer since approximately two-thirds of the world's people live in this segment. Because LDCs account for less than 15 percent of the world's income at present, they have not yet excited the imagination of the multinational marketing executive. In time they will because the greatest markets of the future will be found among these nations. During the past few years, the growth in GNP of many countries has been impressive. In the 1960s, no fewer than twelve LDCs began to show meaningful economic growth. In Korea, the Republic of China, and Thailand the per capita income is now climbing at 4.5 percent per year. Similar growth rates can be found in Iran, Saudi Arabia, Zambia, and the Ivory Coast. Several Latin American countries with chronically depressed growth rates experienced expansions of 3.5 percent annually while Brazil has been enjoying a yearly rate of 6.7 percent. During the 1970s and early 1980s, growth rates for many of the LDCs will reach 5 percent or more annually, by 1985 perhaps only 5 percent of the world's population will still live in preindustrial, nondeveloping countries. Many are predicting a new international economic order aiming at a world economy in which the developing nations of Asia, Latin America, and Africa will come to play a more dynamic role than they currently do. This new economic structure will strive to accommodate the needs and demands of the developing countries and will seek to reconcile interdependence with self-reliance as well as free world trade with organized marketing activities.[2]

The Multinational Marketing Corporation

Multinational marketing takes many forms. Its basic embodiment does not begin simply with domestic organizations operating in foreign countries. Rather it is a truly multinational organization whose outlook focuses around a common corporate strategy evolved at a common nerve center and based upon a flow of information from all its extensions. In effect then, the contemporary embodiment of multinational marketing is the multinational corporation, abbreviated MNC.

It is almost easier to list the characteristics of the multinational corporation than to define it. Broadly, the multinational corporation is one that: (a) operates in many countries; (b) carries out some research, development and manufacturing in those countries; (c) has multinational stock ownership, and (d) has multinational management.

The term multinational was virtually unknown twenty years ago. Despite its newness it aptly describes the pharmaceutical company that integrates eleven drug-manufacturing plants, seven intermediate plants (which process raw materials but do not produce finished products), and four research laboratories, and markets their output in eighty different countries. The term also fits well the automobile company that integrates plants in Germany, Britain, Mexico, and Canada for marketing in the United States or the commercial bank that

[2] Anari van Dam, "Marketing in the New International Economic Order," *Journal of Marketing,* January 1977, pp. 19–23.

integrates banking resources in eight countries to raise money in a ninth country to finance a development and provide financial and marketing services in a tenth. With multinational corporations natural boundaries are no longer significant. The multinational corporation does business in many countries but even more significant is the company's outlook—its belief in a common world market—uniform to a great extent in its demands, in its visions, and in its values.

MNCs Are Big and Growing

Multinational corporations are large and they are growing. The foreign output of MNCs headquartered in the United States is five times the value of American exports. These MNCs employed, in 1980, thirty times as many workers as emigrated to the United States in the previous year. More than 20 percent of all reported American corporate profits comes from foreign subsidiaries and 25 cents out of every American corporate investment dollar is made abroad. Little more than a decade ago, less than 10 cents of every United States corporate investment dollar went abroad and the overseas operations produced fewer goods and services than the country exported. The multinational corporation today employs most of the Americans working outside the country and is responsible for much of American imports and exports.

The present growth rate of the world's 200 or so large multinational corporations (most of which are American) is two or three times that of the individual advanced nations. These businesses produce and market more goods and services than do most countries. If the trend continues, and it probably will, by the turn of the century, a few hundred large multinationals will be responsible for more than half the world's output.

To gain some further perspective, consider the case of General Motors. In 1979, General Motors affiliates marketed goods and services valued at approximately $40 billion, much of it abroad. Only a small handful of countries sold more than this. Ireland marketed goods valued at only one-fifth of GM sales. Some of the major multinational corporations of the world are shown in Table 18-1.

Table 18-1 suggests that multinational corporations market more than just goods or services. In the expanded view of marketing, the World Health Organization, the Roman Catholic Church, the Red Cross, and even the United States Army are important multinational organizations that play important roles in social marketing as well as in economics, health, defense, and general welfare.

A listing of large multinational corporations reads like a *Who's Who* of American marketing enterprise. In addition to those in Table 18-1, IBM, General Electric, Caterpillar Tractor, F.W. Woolworth, Sears Roebuck, Eastman Kodak, Union Carbide, Procter and Gamble, Singer Sewing Machine, Dow Chemical, International Harvester, Colgate-Palmolive, and National Cash Register are all deeply involved in international marketing activities and possess most of the characteristics of the MNC.

Table 18-1 A Cross Section of Major Multinational Corporations

American Corporations	Non-American Corporations	Nonprofit Organizations
General Motors	Shell Oil (Netherlands)	Roman Catholic Church (Italy)
Mobil Oil	Unilever (UK)	
ITT	Siemans Electric (Ger.)	Red Cross (Swiss)
Gulf and Western	Braun-Boveri (Swiss)	United States Army (US)
Ford Motors	Toyota (Japan)	
Pan Am	Lloyds Bank (UK)	
American Express		
Bank of America		
First National Bank		

There Are Many Multinational Corporations

The definition of multinational corporations is crudely imprecise, making it difficult to say how many companies could be considered multinationals. The Office of Foreign Direct Investment lists over 3,500 United States companies, although certainly not all of them would qualify as MNCs under the criteria established earlier. *Fortune's* list of the 500 largest American corporations and the 200 largest foreign corporations includes the most important MNCs.[3] Based upon *Fortune* data, in 1980, over ninety companies out of *Fortune's* 500 had 25 percent or more of their assets, earnings, employment, or production overseas, while 225 companies had 10 percent or more. It is much more difficult to generalize about foreign-based MNCs (those not considered primarily American corporations). Most foreign corporations, especially the European ones, are reluctant to make data available so the picture of foreign MNCs is much less complete. However, based upon sketchy but fairly solid data, the picture of the European MNCs abroad is that they too are large and growing.[4]

The Complete Picture on MNCs

It is easy to characterize the multinational corporate organization as (1) new, (2) big, and (3) American. Such a perspective is not only warped; it is wrong.

[3] *Fortune*, June 1980, p. 56.
[4] For contrast, see "Japanese Multinationals: Covering The World With Investments," *Business Week*, June 16, 1980, pp. 92–99.

McDonalds goes abroad.

Not All New. The roots of the multinational corporation go deep in time. Most major scientific and technical inventions of the nineteenth century led immediately to the formation of multinational corporations. Such inventions meant sales and marketing activities in overseas markets. During the early twentieth century, the big swing to multinationals was continually spear-headed by the chemical and pharmaceutical companies and by the auto mak-ers, especially Fiat and Ford. The way having been paved with these early developments, the years after World War II, especially the 1950s, saw explo-sive growth and development of the MNC.

Not All Big. Not all multinational companies are enormous. Big business is not the sole proprietor of the multinational corporation. The truth is the MNC comes in as many sizes and varieties as domestic companies do. There is a real question as to whether the concentration of economic power is necessarily greater in the multinational sector than it is within any national economy.

To some extent, the smaller firm as an MNC may even have some organi-zational and operating advantages when marketing on a global multinational scale, the most important being flexibility. The small-to-smaller MNCs may actually be growing faster and they may do better financially overall than their larger counterparts. They simply fail to make the headlines and *Fortune's* list of 500.

Not All American. Much of the real "push" behind the growth and devel-opment of the multinational corporation in the 1950s stemmed from the initiative and leadership of United States companies. There are many complex reasons for this. Many were political but most were economic. Even with the growing specter of the Common Market, the governments of Europe were opposed to letting their businesses become European businesses. Mergers and joint ventures across national boundaries by European enterprises were frowned upon. It was therefore up to the Americans and the British (the exception to the European model) to take advantage of the rapidly developing market opportunities.

Americans are often surprised to learn that many products they think they are buying from "good old American firms" are really marketed by businesses operated in the United States by foreign owned multinational organizations. Among such businesses are the following:

Bantam Books	Viceroy Cigarettes
Capitol Records	Kiwi Shoe Polish
Stouffer Foods	Rainier Ale
Ronson Lighters	Lipton Tea
Magnavox Televisions	Baskin-Robbins Ice Cream
Saks Fifth Avenue Stores	Libby, McNeill and Libby Foods
Clorox Bleach	Orchid Paper Napkins
Gimbel's Department Store	Lea and Perrins Steak Sauce

Surprising, isn't it?

Why Multinational Marketing?

Why do firms decide to engage in multinational marketing activities and then invest millions of dollars to do so? The answer is almost too simple. The fundamental forces impelling firms to seek multinational marketing opportunities and to invest abroad are the quest for profit and the fear that they will lose their present or prospective market position to foreign competitors. Such decisions are extensions of the corporation's strategic marketing planning. And all the variables that affect domestic strategic marketing planning—customers, costs, competition, political, and legal pressures—hold sway with equal force, if not greater complexity, in strategic planning for worldwide marketing. Among the many reasons companies seek multinational marketing opportunities are the need for more customers, the pressure to lower costs, competition, environmental problems, and political and financial incentives. Let us examine each of these.

Customers: The Basis of Demand. Certain industries almost by nature are international and to be engaged in them requires a multinational outlook. Extractive industries like petroleum, and plantation industries like rubber are obvious examples. The sources of the materials they process are primarily located abroad and exploiting them requires international operations relating to production, finance, and marketing.

For example, Shell Oil established firms in Indonesia to develop and refine oil to be marketed all over the world. United Fruit established banana plantations and related packing operations in Honduras so that they could tap the United States and other world markets for fresh fruits. Anaconda developed copper mines in Bolivia to secure copper and other raw materials to be marketed to firms around the world who use copper for such products as communications equipment, space technology, automobiles, home and industrial wiring and energy transmission. The existence of foreign customers who cannot be served as easily or cheaply by imports into their countries is perhaps the single most important reason that domestic organizations become multinational.

The decision to go multinational is overwhelmingly based upon market opportunity balanced by political risk. (The political risk relates to such factors as the stability of the foreign government and its attitudes toward direct investment by alien firms.) The market opportunity is usually viewed from either a defensive or offensive position.[5]

Many executives give defensive reasons for going multinational. A *defensive* strategy is followed when the primary motivation is to hold on to a foreign market opportunity that can no longer be exploited by direct exports from the United States. Companies reflect an *offensive* strategy when they seek a multinational market in a country in order to tap present and anticipated market opportunity more effectively than is possible through direct exports or other arrangements.

Lowering the Costs of Doing Business. Many firms are also persuaded to go multinational with the hope of lowering their overall cost of production or marketing.

Many of the electronic products so popular in the United States today—radios, televisions, stereos, CB receivers and transmitters, and digital watches—are increasingly assembled and produced abroad. For some of these, components are trucked into Mexico for assembly, then returned to the United States for sale or for marketing overseas. Some electronic products are completely produced and assembled in Taiwan, Japan, or Hong Kong. Both procedures are frequently used by American firms to lower costs of production and the final sales price of the items. In 1980 electronics assemblers were paid an hourly rate of $8.90 in the United States, 90 cents in Mexico, and 35 cents in Taiwan. Such cost differences have driven the once-booming American shoe industry to Italy and the production of television sets and other electronic products to Japan and other Asian countries. Is this bad? Well, maybe it is if you are a garment worker in New York, a skilled shoe cutter out of work in North Carolina, or a television assembler in Bloomington, Indiana. But overall, such shifts lead to lower prices worldwide and also tend to create new markets. They increase the world's standard of living significantly and even redistribute some of the world's wealth.

What about the unemployed American workers? More than likely they find jobs making other products. The statistics, at least, show that the American

[5] See Franklin R. Root. "U.S. Business Abroad and the Political Risks," *MSU Business Topics*, Winter 1968, pp. 73–80.

corporations with rapidly expanding overseas operations have also been among the fastest growing and highest paying employers in the United States. Increasing foreign production also usually means that more highly skilled workers and specialized products are needed at home to keep the economy humming.

Meeting and Coping With Competition.   Competition is another significant reason for going multinational. Imports from firms operating abroad can compete with those at home if they are not controlled by the same organization. One way of ensuring that foreign marketers do not compete is to own the foreign marketer. And the most practical way to keep a potential competitor from establishing itself in another country is to be the first one to establish it.

General Motors is the classic example of how a firm can minimize competition by buying up its competitors. Those General Motors didn't buy, Ford and Chrysler did, with the exception, however, of several European and Japanese small-car producers that the American auto makers believed nobody wanted to buy.

Environmental and Ecological Pressures.   Many industries are increasingly considered undesirable because of environmental and ecological pressures. United States communities no longer want steel mills, pulp and paper mills, or cement plants in their midst. American citizens live in an economy so productive that the people can spurn the products and jobs contributed by industries that also contribute dirty water, foul air, noise, clutter, and congestion. Companies producing and marketing such products can either fight the increasing regulation, bear the cost of cleaning up their operations and the environment, or switch to less restricted sites. Many would rather switch than fight. Such industries are perceived as desirable by less affluent economies whose people are eager for more jobs and output and so more willing to endure pollution and other social costs.

Workers in advanced nations of the world want a clean, tidy, status-laden work environment. They want to be engineers, teachers, and executives rather than coal miners, farm workers, and factory hands. Such attitudes compel Germany and Switzerland to hire "guest workers" who are Italian and Turkish, while the United States permits nearly 7 million Mexican aliens to pick crops and work as laborers in many of the industries along our southern border.

Political and Financial Incentives.   There are other reasons why domestic firms expand into multinational marketing organizations. *Tax incentives* are often crucial in such behavior. Different countries tax multinational organizations at different rates. By carefully manipulating profits and losses within these different countries, a corporation can often lower its overall rate of taxes. Some multinationals are able to avoid all taxes but typically pay at least token taxes to avoid being noticed. Other multinationals are simply good corporate citizens wherever they are located, paying their fair share of taxes and shouldering other social responsibilities as well.

Occasionally a *political incentive* is offered that will guarantee a foreign firm certain rights and dispensations if it will establish production and marketing facilities in a given country. Sometimes a foreign government will provide financial guarantees and insurance to persuade a corporation to set up factories and marketing networks in an economically unstable or potentially revolutionary economy. It is the responsiblity of marketers to operate a profitable business whether at home or overseas. Such political incentives and guarantees entail a transfer of risk to the host country or government, an arrangement in which everybody gains.

The *exchange rate* can be a powerful financial incentive to motivate firms to engage in multinational marketing activities. Say steel costs $200 per ton in the United States and 700 francs in France. Which country has the lower price for a foreign buyer? The answer depends upon the *exchange rate,* the rate at which one nation's money is exchanged for another. Using the same example, the trade is made between dollars and francs. If it takes 4 francs to get one dollar, the rate is 4 to 1. Regardless of what price firms set for their products, it is the exchange rate that determines whether their prices are lower or higher than those of firms in other countries' markets. Suppose that something sells for 3,500 marks in Germany and $1,000 in the United States. If the exchange rate between francs and dollars is 4 to 1, and between francs and marks is 1 for 1, French buyers will buy in Germany because they would have to give up only 3,500 francs to get enough marks to buy the German-made product. In contrast, they would have to give up 4,000 francs to get enough dollars to buy the identical American-made product. The conditions are reversed if the exchange rate between francs and marks remained 1 for 1, while that of francs for dollars was 3 for 1. Then the French would find the American-made products less expensive, requiring only 3,000 francs to get enough dollars in contrast to the 3,500 francs needed to get enough marks to buy in Germany.[6] The exchange rate alone is not a sufficient reason to engage in international marketing, because the differences in prices between commodities produced in different countries will be due primarily to long-run cost factors, not to exchange factors. However, short-run differences in exchange rates can induce companies to operate all over the globe, especially when commodities are involved.

For all these reasons international marketing operations have been changing rapidly in recent years. Germany, which for many years had an undervalued currency and whose foreign marketing operations benefited from a favorable exchange rate, has seen its favorable balance of trade with the United States virtually reversed. The revalued yen has also slightly curtailed Japan's explosive growth and expansion in multinational marketing operations. Yet, Germany, Japan, the United States, and scores of other countries are still pursuing multinational marketing opportunities with vigor. Multinational corporations have discussed marketing trade with the Socialist Bloc countries.[7] Even the

[6] To learn more about exchange rates, see John Lindauer, *Economics: A Modern View* (Philadelphia: W. B. Saunders, 1977) pp. 710–711. The examples in this section are based in part upon this work.

[7] See G. Peter Lauter and Paul M. Dickie, "Multinational Corporations in Eastern European Socialist Economies," *Journal of Marketing* **39** (October 1975), pp. 40–46; also J. Hart Walters, Jr., "Marketing in Poland in the 1970s: Significant Progress," *Journal of Marketing* **39** (October 1975), pp. 47–51.

People's Republic of China, one of the staunchest, most self-denying advocates of Marxist self-sufficiency, has become more interested in participating in global marketing opportunities.

Before proceeding, can you answer these questions:
1. What is the importance of multinational marketing?
2. What is multinational marketing? How does it differ from domestic marketing?
3. List and discuss in detail three reasons why firms seek multinational marketing opportunities.

Developing International Marketing Strategies

As we know from previous chapters, marketing strategy is a dynamic or changing comprehensive plan of action. The development and implementation of effective marketing strategy, domestic or international, is the essence of sound managerial planning and control processes. The fact that a firm is engaged in multinational marketing operations does not necessarily mean that its strategy is more complex than that of a firm operating solely within its own national borders.

The nature of the firm's marketing strategy may hinge on the extent of its involvement in multinational marketing. The situation is not too different from that of a domestic marketer. Consider a domestic firm that is primarily a marketer of consumer goods and only incidentally concerned with industrial mar-

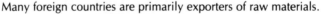

Many foreign countries are primarily exporters of raw materials.

Figure 18-4 Levels of involvement in multinational marketing.

Source: Based upon Vern Terpsted, *International Marketing* (Hinsdale, IL: Dryden Press, 1972), pp. 11–14.

kets. Such a commitment will affect that firm's marketing strategy. If it remains almost solely focused on consumer goods, its strategy will reflect that attitude. If on the other hand, the firm increases its commitment to industrial markets without relaxing service to its consumer segment, its strategy will need to be modified. In other words, the extent of a firm's involvement with its various markets will necessarily have great impact on the development and implementation of its marketing strategy. Figure 18-4 shows several levels of involvement or commitment that a firm may embrace in multinational marketing operations. As Figure 18-4 indicates, the marketing strategy is hardly affected while the commitment to foreign markets is low. However, as overseas market opportunities begin to loom larger in the firm's outlook, its strategy must begin to incorporate this broader scope, The marketing mix in all its ramifications will then reflect this multinational or global market perspective.

The expanding emphasis on world trading relationships, their growing complexity, and the increasing commitment of many firms to multinational marketing operations have created a need for a conceptual framework on which to base the firms' practices and programs. This framework is the multinational marketing strategy.

Marketing Concepts Are Universals

There are similarities and differences in all markets whether domestic or foreign, but the concepts of marketing are, with few exceptions, universal.[8] Such basic concepts as the product life cycle, average cost pricing, market segmentation, and product positioning are as applicable in London, England, as they are in New London, Connecticut.

The multinational marketing company functions in clusters of national market environments and opportunities, as shown in Figure 18-5. The number of clusters shown in the figure is arbitrary. The actual number in a real setting

[8] See Warren J. Keegan, "A Conceptual Framework for Multinational Marketing," *Columbia Journal of World Business* **8**, no. 6 (November–December 1972), pp. 67–76.

Figure 18-5 The company in a world of clusters of national market environments.

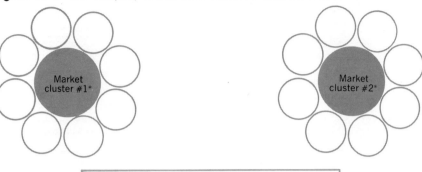

THE COMPANY	
Products	**Marketing skills** • Identifying global opportunities and threats • Product development • Advertising and promotion • Distribution • Pricing • Research
Resources • Manpower • Financial • Physical	**Other skills** • Production • Research • Logistic • Managerial • Financial

*Note: The number of market clusters shown here is arbitrary. In any specific situation, the number of clusters used for operating and analytical purposes will depend upon the characteristics of the markets and the operating strategy of the company.

Source: Warren J. Keegan, "A Conceptual Framework for Multinational Marketing," *Columbia Journal of World Business* **8**, no. 6 (November–December 1972), p. 68.

will depend upon the market's characteristics and the company's operating strategy. Viewing a company in this type of setting is in reality an extension of the market segmentation concept because the objective in forming clusters is to maximize both the similarity of specific characteristics of markets within each cluster and the differences in these features between clusters. These characteristics include such factors as location, income levels, market size, channel structure, culture, and communication. The essence of marketing strategy as reflected by Figure 18-5 is that each company must identify the attributes that are crucial to its own market success and weigh them appropriately.

Major Problems in the Development of Strategy.   There are at least three major dimensions of multinational marketing which affect the basic development of market strategy. The first of these is environment. A multinational marketer must cope with many national environments. A firm's success will in large measure depend on the way it responds to the different cultures, economic and political systems and conditions, and patterns of consumption within which it pursues its goals. In some instances, it will even face hostility to what is considered foreign intrusion.

The second major problem in developing multinational marketing strategies is related to the crossing of national borders. Crossing these boundaries requires passing through national restrictions such as tariffs and quotas and it usually means some loss of control over the total marketing effort. Laws regulating safety or health vary from one country to the next. Pricing, product development, and promotional activities will be subject to different laws in various countries. All these differences in regulation, attitudes, and controls must be considered as boundary constraints which will shape marketing plans and strategies.

Finally, the third major aspect of multinational operations which will affect strategy arises because the company sells its products simultaneously in many markets. A multinational firm must have both keener and wider management vision than the domestic firm. Instead of just one or two, a number of market opportunities must be continually monitored and evaluated. Each "market" must be organized, managed, and controlled, and the whole multiple, polyglot operation coordinated.

Obviously, without a conceptual framework in the form of a multinational marketing strategy, the conduct of affairs of the multinational firm would be difficult if not impossible.

Look carefully at Figures 18-6 and 18-7 because they both show how the assessment of each national market environment and opportunity becomes the basis for the development and implementation of all the firm's strategic planning, its structure, and its operational planning. Finally, they show how the firm should control its marketing program.

Most Markets are Different.   The market comparison method of assessing and evaluating national markets for the purpose of developing multinational marketing strategy usually leads to the conclusion that while there are some gross similarities, most national markets are different. Being so, they call for differences in market planning.

Such differences further complicate the process of developing multinational marketing strategies, but they do not necessarily make it an impossible mission.

Figure 18-6 Dimensions of a national market environment: absolute and compared with other nations.

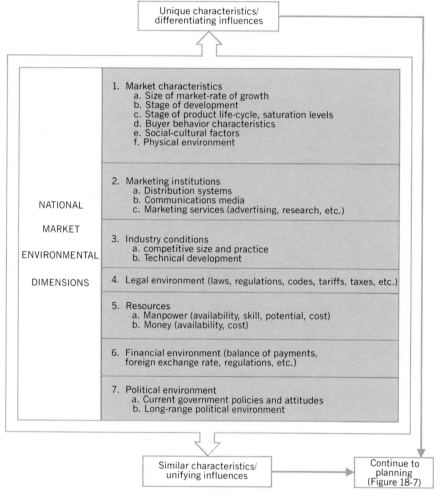

Source: Warren J. Keegan, "A Conceptual Framework for Multinational Marketing," *Columbia Journal of World Business* **8**, no. 6 (November–December 1972), p. 71.

The Cultural Imperative.   The most striking difference between a national at-home market and one located in another country is in culture. The impact of culture is sometimes obvious: the Watusi diet of curdled cow's milk, the Kurdish manner of dress, the Eskimos' communal attitudes toward ownership of goods. Sometimes the impact of culture is less obvious, but when ignored it can bring disaster to a marketing program.[9]

Customs, language, the concepts of time, space, and even color have profound implications for multinational marketing. For example, Maxwell House,

[9] See Guy J. Manaster and Robert Havighurst, *Cross-National Research: Social Psychological Methods and Problems* (New York: Houghton Mifflin, 1972), pp. 157–176.

Figure 18-7 The multinational market management process.

ENVIRONMENTAL ANALYSIS OF NATIONAL MARKETS	KEY QUESTIONS FOR ANALYSIS, PLANNING AND CONTROL OF GLOBAL MARKETING Environmental analysis 1. What are the unique characteristics (see Figure 18-6 for characteristics) of each national market? What characteristics does each market have in common with other national markets? 2. Can we cluster national markets for operating and/or planning purposes? What dimensions of markets should we use to cluster markets?
STRATEGIC PLANNING	Strategic planning 3. Who should be involved in marketing decisions? 4. What are our major assumptions about target markets? Are they valid? 5. What needs are satisfied by our products in target markets? 6. What customer benefits are provided by our product in target markets? 7. What are the conditions under which our products are used in the target markets? 8. How large is the ability to buy our products in target markets? 9. What are our major strengths and weaknesses relative to existing and potential competition in target markets? 10. Should we extend, adapt, or invent products, prices, advertising, and promotion programs for target markets? 11. What is the balance-of-payments and currency situation in targer markets? Will we be able to remit earnings? Is the political climate acceptable? 12. What are our objectives given the alternatives open to us and our assessment of opportunity, risk, and company capability?
STRUCTURE	Structure 13. How do we structure our organization to optimally achieve our objectives, given our skills and resources? What is the responsibility of each organizational level?
OPERATIONAL PLANNING	Operational planning 14. Given our objectives, structure, and our assessment of the market environment, how do we implement effective operational marketing plans? What products will we market, at what prices, through what channels, with what communications, in which markets and market clusters?
CONTROLLING THE MARKETING PROGRAM	Controlling the market program 15. How do we measure and monitor plan performance? What steps should be taken to ensure that marketing objectives are met?

Source: Warren J. Keegan, "A Conceptual Framework for Multinational Marketing," *Columbia Journal of World Business* **8**, no. 6 (November–December 1972), p. 75.

billed as the great American coffee, spent a potful to find out that Germans have little respect for American coffee. Procter and Gamble found that Crest's fluoride appeal meant little or nothing to the English public.[10]

Foreign markets invariably have their unique national character—their own style of life based upon centuries of customs, habits, language, and values.[11]

[10] For more on this theme see David Ricks, Marilyn Y.C. Fu, and Jeffrey S. Arpan. *International Business Blunders* (Columbus, Ohio: Grid Publishing Co., 1974), especially chapter 2.

[11] S. Watson Dunn, "Effect of National Identity on Multinational Promotional Strategy in Europe," *Journal of Marketing* **40**, no. 4, (October 1976), pp. 50–57.

Japan has become both consumption and marketing oriented.

This national identity has a significant impact on the development and implementation of multinational marketing strategies.

Despite their apparent Americanization, the Japanese, one of America's principal trading partners, have a very distinctive national character which affects negotiations with United States executives. The Japanese possess much greater emotional sensitivity than do most Americans; while they hide them, their feelings about a person are important in business dealings. The Japanese are more group oriented, less individualistic and selfish than most Americans. They often are embarrassed to say no but they will, shyly and discreetly. They place great value on friendship and a continuing relationship, so once associations are begun the stage is set for a solid on-going relationship.[12]

The Market Comparison Method and Marketing Strategy

Marketing strategy always begins with an assessment and evaluation of market opportunities matched to the firm's capabilities. As the firm moves from one opportunity to another, whether domestic, regional or worldwide, the firm's strategy for each new market is based largely on the market's difference from or similarity to existing markets. The greater the difference in the new market opportunity, the greater the change and accommodation in market strategy. Or conversely, the more similar the markets, the less change required in strategy planning and operations. Figure 18-6 shows the major dimensions of a

---

[12] See Howard F. VanLandt, "How to Negotiate in Japan," *Harvard Business Review* (November–December, 1970), pp. 45–56.

national market environment. When these dimensions are compared with other national (but foreign) markets the unique and differentiating components of each can then be determined and incorporated into the multinational strategy.

The task of the multinational marketer is to recognize both similarities and differences. By doing so, the marketing firm can respond to the unique characteristics of each market and still effectively transfer its know-how to develop effective comprehensive marketing strategies and programs. The analysis in Figure 18-6 is then continued and used as the basis for the development of multinational marketing management processes which entails, as shown in Figure 18-7, all the elements of strategic planning.

All this suggests that "the people are alike" theory is a dangerous oversimplification that has wrecked the programs of many multinational marketers. The notion of the world as one big market has been greatly overrated. The equalizing effect of affluence and the establishment of international standards of consumption are important in generating new multinational marketing opportunities but customers everywhere still search for differences through consumption. Standardized marketing strategies may be of less value in the future because tailor-made strategies designed for each unique market are frequently more effective.

The Frustrations of Overseas Market Research.   Truly successful marketing programs everywhere, domestic or multinational, are based upon sound and careful planning. As we learned earlier, this usually translates into "marketing research." However, marketing research in many foreign countries is several steps behind the sophisticated studies, surveys, panels, and data banks utilized at home by American marketing firms. In comparison with the United States, marketing research, even in the more advanced or developed foreign countries, leaves much to be desired.

For example, simple demographic data that we take for granted is not available in many countries. Such standard information as age, income, occupation, number of dependents, and size of household may or may not be available. If it is, it may be out-of-date or incorrect because of unreliable collection and tabulation methods.

Telephone surveys may be completely out of the question in many countries because (1) only a small percentage of the population may have telephones, (2) it may take forty-five minutes to an hour to reach the party being called, and (3) the person called, being unfamiliar with such a use of the telephone, may be unwilling to talk fully with the caller or may even hang up. In many countries, a part of the national character is suspicion of strangers and distrust of both business and government. Hence, all inquiries, whether face-to-face, by mail, or on the telephone are met with either quiet or hostile resistance. "It's none of your business" is often the prevailing attitude.

In spite of the limited use of formal or sophisticated marketing research, there are still three principal methods of obtaining information in multinational markets:

• Collect and further analyze existing data.

- Utilize the knowledge of informed persons in the host country.
- Send your own experts to the foreign country for personal "hands on" observation and systematic research efforts.

Facts and knowledge about foreign market opportunities are beginning to build up. The more successful multinational marketers are excellent planners and they develop, as best they can, "fact books" for each country, specific rules for preparing both yearly and longer-term plans and stipulations. The methodology of planning is one concept that seems to have near-universal applicability and this may foster a better climate for sophisticated market research efforts in multinational markets.

The Ingredients of Strategy Are Still the Marketing Mix

The marketing strategy in any setting, foreign or domestic, is still based essentially on the four controllable variables of the marketing mix—product, promotion, pricing, and channels of distribution. Because of the overwhelming complexity of multinational marketing opportunities, the great disparity among countries and cultures, and variations in the degree of commitment by companies to multinational operations, it is both difficult and dangerous to overgeneralize as to how the different variables in the marketing mix will be affected by the particular market opportunity. The important point is that the marketing mix and the strategy that ultimately evolves will be largely determined by the nature of the host country.

Product. Inadequate product planning may be the major deterrent to growth and profitability for many multinational marketers. Keegan has identified five strategies for adapting a product and the communication relating to it to a foreign market.[13] In strategy one, the multinational firm markets the same product and communicates the same message in all markets. Pepsi Cola, Coca-Cola and, to some extent, Seven-Up have all used this basic approach. Strategy two suggests that the firm market the same product but communicate differently about it. For example, bicycles are used mainly for recreation in the United States but serve as basic transportation in most other markets of the world. So a Japanese marketer would sell the same bicycle in both the United States and Indonesia, but the advertising and promotion would vary in accordance with the way bicycles are used in the two different markets. In strategy three, the product is adapted or modified but the communication extended is basically the same. Many products are adapted to meet local needs—agricultural products to match soil and climate, soaps and detergents to meet water conditions or to match the nature of local washing machines. Yet the basic appeal of such products is largely standardized. Strategy four recommends a real adaptation. That is, both product and communication are modified to meet host country needs and considerations. And finally, strategy five suggests

[13] Warren J. Keegan, "Multinational Product Planning: Strategic Alternatives," *Journal of Marketing* **33** (January 1969), pp. 58–62.

that new products be specifically developed to capitalize on a special foreign market opportunity. This may even mean "inventing backward." This was the case when a leading manufacturer of mechanical washing machines was asked to apply its know-how not to produce a better automatic machine but to develop a better manual washer. The result was an inexpensive ($10) hand-powered, plastic washer that had the same tumbling action of the modern automatic machine.

Like all elements of the marketing mix, the product must be matched to the market. Primitive markets may call for primitive products. Yet there is a rising tide of affluence throughout much of the world. In some foreign markets, product planning and development is already being guided by segmentation,[14] positioning,[15] and the product life cycle.[16]

Promotion. The promotional task is essentially the same in domestic as well as foreign markets: namely, to communicate information and persuasive appeals effectively. However, specific promotional messages and media strategy must, more often than not, be changed from country to country. In multinational promotion, communicators must define market segments as precisely as possible and study their audience's cultural backgrounds and behavioral predispositions in detail before beginning a promotional effort.

The factors that influence promotional strategy such as copy, appeals, media, the use of symbols, and even whether to use standardized promotional campaigns from one market to another will depend upon the following factors:

1. *The type of product.* Some products may possess universal selling points; some may not. Razor blades, ballpoint pens, automobile tires, and electric irons may be promoted in a more standardized way than cosmetics, pharmaceuticals, clothing, major appliances, and luxury items. Some products are promoted on the basis of their physical characteristics; others, as we have learned, on their symbolic significance.

2. *The homogeneity or heterogeneity of markets.* When aggregate characteristics like national income, education, and occupation are alike, individual consumer characteristics like needs, attitudes, and customs may be alike. Thus, the marketer may use the same selling points.

3. *The characteristics and availability of media.* If some media are available in one country but not in another, certain messages and materials may not be usable.

4. *The type of advertising agency service available.* If some markets offer only poor agency service, a marketer may be forced to rely on centralized control of promotion, with necessary uniformities in messages and media

[14] Cunningham, Moore, and Cunningham, "The Sao Paulo Experience."
[15] David R. McIntyre, "Multinational Positioning Strategy," *Columbia Journal of World Business* **10,** no. 3, (Fall 1975).
[16] Jose de la Torre, "Produce Life Cycle as a Determinant of Global Marketing Strategies," *Atlanta Economic Review,* September–October 1975, pp. 9–14.

strategy. However, the number of United States multinational advertising agencies is growing.[17]

5. *Government and legal restrictions.* Some governments prohibit certain types of messages; others tax advertising or art work. Also, there are legal and ethical constraints in many countries which prohibit mentioning a competitor's product or which limit the claims that can be made for the company's own products. Yet, in other countries there are virtually no prohibitions whatsoever on promotional activities.

People satisfy their needs in different ways. So, just as it is important to provide physical variations in products to meet the demands of diverse market segments, it is also important to tailor promotional efforts to each segment of a foreign market.

Pricing. Pricing decisions are made in multinational markets in much the same way as in domestic markets. Demand is always an important determinant of a firm's pricing policies, but actual prices in foreign markets are most often based upon cost plus or administered models.

In fact, lower labor costs abroad are often given as the reason for foreign investment (building plants and marketing facilities) abroad because they are seen, from the standpoint of average cost pricing, as being a means of lowering the final price of the goods. While this may be true for labor intensive industries, it does not always hold when considering the relative productivity (output per worker hour) of workers from various areas. Many foreign firms (especially from France, England, and Germany) are increasingly locating manufacturing and marketing facilities in the United States because while their own labor costs have risen (they are still slightly lower than in the United States) the productivity of their labor force does not nearly equal that of workers in the United States.

The Japanese are alleged to be practicing a "dumping" policy in pricing the television receivers they sell in the United States. Dumping was a term originally used to describe sales abroad at prices below those charged in the domestic economy. The term now includes pricing products that are unsalable at home below their average costs of production for sale abroad. Sometimes, though not always, these are products not wanted by local customers, or left over when models change, or banned for health or safety reasons.

Worldwide inflation continues to be a nagging problem of multinational marketers in their price decision making. In periods of rapidly rising price levels, prices established today may be inadequate to cover costs in tomorrow's market place.

Channels of Distribution. Many Western-based multinational marketers operating in the less developed countries find they must significantly alter their thinking about channels of distribution. In many instances, warehousing and

---

[17] Arnold K. Weinstein, "The International Expansion of U.S. Multinational Advertising Agencies," *MSU Business Topics,* Summer 1974, pp. 29–35.

storage facilities are nonexistent and facilities for physical distribution, so vital in such markets, must be built from nothing to efficiency.

Physical distribution systems are improving rapidly in many more developed countries, notably in the Netherlands, Great Britain, West Germany, Switzerland, and Scandinavia, where centralized warehouse facilities for food distribution similar to those in the United States have been developed. However, France and Italy are still hampered by primitive food distribution systems.

There is little standardization of channels of distribution among various countries. Most multinational marketers are forced to choose different channels of distribution for each nation they decide to penetrate and develop as a market.[18] Distributors may be the dominant channel in one area, while agents and brokers are more extensively used in another. American marketers abroad are often frustrated with the chain of channels available to them and the poor service, if any, provided by intermediaries. In addition, their small size and independent nature make channel management difficult and control virtually impossible.

Though the diversity found among foreign market opportunities makes it difficult to generalize, we can identify three main channels of distribution for international marketing.

- Representatives of foreign firms
- Resident buyers within a host country who work for foreign firms or governments
- Intermediaries such as export commission houses, export merchants, agents, brokers, and export managers

Obviously, multinational channel decisions are difficult to manage because of the variety in channel structure from one country to another—and because of the great differences even within countries. However, certain patterns of change associated with market development provide the multinational marketer who recognizes them the opportunity to innovate and thus gain a further competitive advantage in the markets.[19]

Before proceeding, can you answer these questions:
1. How and why has multinational marketing increased so greatly during the last two decades?
2. What problems are likely to arise in attempting to use marketing research in some foreign country?
3. On the basis of what you have read thus far, do you believe a multinational organization should standardize its marketing strategy?

[18] Warren J. Keegan, *Multinational Marketing Management* (Englewood Cliffs, NJ: Prentice-Hall, 1974) especially Chapter 9, "Channel Decisions, " pp. 294–349.
[19] See James M. Hulbert, William K. Brand, and Raimar Richers, "Marketing Planning, the Multinational Subsidiary: Practices and Problems," *Journal of Marketing* **44**, (Summer 1980), pp. 7–15.

Organizational Arrangements for Penetrating International Markets

When a firm seeks to market its products abroad, it can, at the extreme, choose between two divergent strategies.[20]

- Initially, the firm can enter a few of the most promising markets. After its presence is established and its product's potential proved, it penetrates new and presumably less profitable markets.
- The firm may choose to enter simultaneously as many potential markets as possible. The initial broad-scale penetration is then followed by a period of consolidation during which the less profitable markets are abandoned.

Marketers intuitively find the first strategy superior and actually seem to use it more widely because it requires a lower investment in marketing and permits the firm to test its products and concentrate on markets with the highest expected return. Most firms become multinational through this kind of creeping commitment (see Figure 18-4) rather than in one fell swoop.

Although some firms "go international" almost by accident, most do so with great deliberation. Once the decision is made to penetrate multinational markets, the next decision is how to do it. The company has several major options including exporting, joint ventures, direct investment, and others.

Exporting. Many companies become involved in multinational marketing by selling some of their products to foreign markets. Many United States firms have entered this way by selling to Canadian and Mexican buyers or to buyers in Western countries such as the United Kingdom who share a similar language and culture and are receptive to American goods. This is simply exporting. The company makes no investment in overseas production plants and generally extends both its product and promotional efforts unchanged to these markets. For some export markets, however, as we mentioned above, many elements of the firm's marketing mix—including product design, price, promotional effort, and channels—must be modified.

There are many types of export arrangements. Several of these are shown in Figure 18-8.

You will notice from the figure that a number of different channels of distribution are actually possible within this exporting framework. As a company's foreign operations expand, it passes through different stages of export development in which an increasing proportion of exports go to foreign sales and manufacturing affiliates for resale rather than to customers or agents. Three basic stages of exporting can be defined.

Stage 1: Exports to customers and agents
Stage 2: Exports to customers, agents, and sales subsidiaries
Stage 3: Exports to foreign manufacturing affiliates

[20] See Hirsch and Baruch Lev: "Foreign Marketing Strategies—A Note," *Management International Review* **13** (1976), pp. 81–88.

Figure 18-8

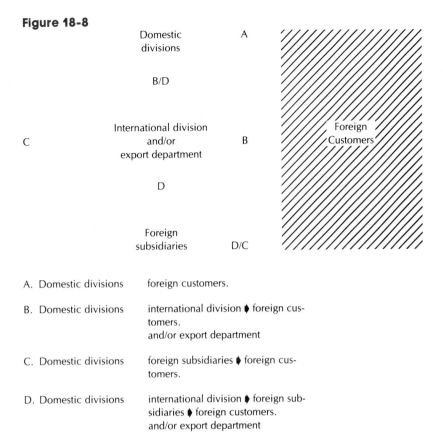

A. Domestic divisions   foreign customers.

B. Domestic divisions   international division ◗ foreign customers.
         and/or export department

C. Domestic divisions   foreign subsidiaries ◗ foreign customers.

D. Domestic divisions   international division ◗ foreign subsidiaries ◗ foreign customers.
         and/or export department

Source: Cedric L. Suzman. "The Changing Nature of Export Management," Atlanta *Economic Review,* September-October 1975, p. 20.

Joint Ventures.   Exporting, especially when it reaches stage 3, is likely to lead to the establishment of some **joint venture** with companies in a foreign market. Such arrangements mean a sharing of risks (and profits) and they may be based upon manufacturing or marketing efforts, or even both. That is, the development of manufacturing and/or marketing facilities in the foreign country will be jointly undertaken. Such joint ventures involve either licensing, contracting, or joint ownership.

Licensing.   Licensing is much like franchising in that the company provides the licensee the right to use a manufacturing process, a patent, a management system, trademarks, or logos in exchange for a fee or royalty. McDonald's is now licensing, or franchising, many firms to operate its type of restaurant in foreign countries. At the same time McDonald's is buying out many of these foreign operations in order to get better control over them. Companies such as Westinghouse, General Electric, and Continental Can license foreign firms throughout the world to use their processes, know-how, and patented technology. These companies feel that such arrangements are relatively riskless and tend to generate sizable incremental revenues with little or no additional investment.

Contracting.   Many firms who wish to acquire production and marketing facilities in foreign countries do so by *contract*. A United States manufacturer, for example, may pay a foreign manufacturer to make so many units of its product. The American firm may then either market the product itself or contract further, say with a foreign sales agent, to market the product within the foreign country. Contracting may work still another way. A United States firm may contract to market the products of foreign manufacturers. This means that the American firm is marketing its services rather than physical products that it has produced.

Joint Ownership.   In joint ownership, local and foreign investors share ownership and control of the multinational firm. There has been much discussion concerning joint ownership arrangements between United States and foreign auto makers, particularly between Chrysler on the one hand and both Japanese and German organizations on the other. To date, the discussions have not actually led to such arrangements. However, Mitsubishi, the giant Japanese multinational, has entered into joint ownership arrangements with two large fast food chains, Kentucky Fried Chicken and Shakey's Pizza Parlors. Joint ownership is a useful device for sharing risks, raising capital, and solving other managerial problems.

Direct Investment.   Increasingly, many multinational firms are looking to direct investment as a means of penetrating and, more importantly, expanding foreign markets. Direct investment means ownership of production and marketing operations in other countries rather than exporting or licensing. Direct investment is the ultimate in managing multinational operations. All aspects of planning and control—the development of all strategic options—now fall within the authority of the owning company. Risks are increased, but so too are rewards and profits. By 1985, United States firms will likely have invested $200 billion abroad, compared with $50 billion invested here by foreign firms.
   Local businesses generally welcome multinationals no matter whether they are establishing a new firm or merely buying one already in operation. There are many reasons, chief among them the following: (1) the multinationals inevitably buy their supplies and other product inputs locally. (2) Any increase they bring in local wages means more customers for firms in the area. (3) The owners of the local firms may themselves hope to sell out to the multinational for a relatively high price.

The Changing Nature of Multinational Marketing

Because it reflects the new reality of an emerging world economy, the multinational organization is perhaps the major economic instrument today. It is furthermore an important and effective tool for optimizing the earth's shrinking resources, resources that will likely be even scarcer in the future. But, because the multinational marketing organization reflects a new reality rather than the simple extension of yesterday's old business, it requires new structures, new methods of operation, and better methods of adaptation. To accomplish these objectives and to deliver on its promises, the multinational firm must be aware that its market mission and the environment in which it must be carried out are changing dramatically. These changes in their simplest explanation are as follows.[20]

1. *From global expansion to coverage.* Many multinational marketers have moved from the stage of global expansion to global coverage. Their emphasis consequently changes from choice of new markets, entry patterns, and speed of development to a concern for maintaining their established market positions.

2. *Increasing product decay.* Related to the achievement of global coverage will be a shift from an emphasis on product lines that are new to a market to emphasis on the pursuit of profits in markets where the products are no longer innovations. Product life cycles will show long but gradual decays, forcing management to concentrate on meeting competition in individual markets.

3. *Decline in home-base orientation.* Many multinational marketers will become true citizens of the world. Firms will lose much of their national identity. Decentralization and diffusion of identity is well underway for many multinational marketers.

4. *Multinational customers.* Multinational firms capable of developing global strategies for marketing and production are also capable of developing global purchasing strategies. More and more, multinational suppliers selling to intermediate buyers need to organize to cope with customers using their worldwide buying strength.

5. *Increasing political pressures.* There is increasing evidence that governments are concerned about controlling multinational firms. In Argentina over half the sales revenues of the country's fifty largest corporations go to multinational firms. In Chile more than 160 companies belong to multinational organizations. These multinationals provide a majority of the output in almost all of Chile's industries; almost all of the twenty-five largest multinationals operate as either monopolists or oligopolists. Multinationals can play havoc with local economies. It is estimated that each major Sears shopping center established in Central or South America causes the closure of 2,000 small shops. An economy benefits from such changes if the unemployed workers and other resources can be put to work producing additional goods and services. Nonetheless, many governments will increase their restraints on such organizations.

6. *Need for increasing social responsibilities.* Multinational corporations need to lose their image as "foreign exploiters" and become socially responsible world citizens. Many have already done so; others are in the process. The

---

[21] Based in part upon the work of Kenneth Simmonds, "Managing the Multinationals: Seven Forces for Change," *Atlanta Economic Review,* September–October 1975, pp. 5–8.

need and desire for trade have made capitalists of nearly all nations, but capitalists need not be rapists. The capitalist creed worldwide is rapidly embracing a value system which encompasses a growing social responsibility. Business people the world over recognize that carrying on trade, production, and marketing in all environments is a privilege not a right, and that the privilege must be honored with clear awareness of its political, economic, and social consequences.

Summary

The world is shrinking, and we are in an era of global or multinational marketing. Marketers and nations have discovered that the free international exchanges of goods and services yield benefits to all and that multinational marketing activity stands as a basic stimulus to economic growth. The United States economic system is an enviable one but we are by no means self-sufficient; indeed, we are becoming increasingly dependent on international marketing.

Foreign trade in 1975 amounted to 83 percent of the total United States GNP. Foreign markets, like domestic markets, vary in quality. International markets are evaluated much like domestic ones—demand created by population, income, and propensity to buy is the primary determinant.

Multinational marketing does not involve marketing principles different from those used in domestic marketing. The basic difference between domestic and multinational marketing is that consideration of the host country culture is critical. Multinational marketing deserves special emphasis because of its growing importance and because of the high risk and uncertainty in penetrating and operating within an alien culture. The contemporary embodiment of multinational marketing is the multinational corporation. Basically the multinational corporation is a company that attempts to operate on an international scale as though there were no national boundaries, and on the basis of a common strategy directed from a corporate center. Firms become multinational marketers for many reasons. Most often the firm wants to tap market opportunities wherever they are. Some firms want to lower their costs of doing business. Others seek to meet and cope with competition. Still others go multinational for environmental, ecological, political, or financial reasons.

Like their domestic counterparts, multinational marketers must develop and implement a marketing strategy. The essence of this task for the MNC is to decide upon the extent to which the marketing mix—product, pricing, promotion, and channels—should be adapted and tailored to individual foreign markets.

Review Questions

1. What is multinational marketing? What is a multinational organization?

2. Discuss the importance of multinational marketing. Does the average consumer in the United States benefit from such marketing? How and why?

3. Multinational marketing facilitates world trade. Is this important? The text states, "Where demand is, marketers follow." Explain.

4. Some believe that multinational corporations are mostly big and mostly American. Is this true? Explain.

5. List and discuss four reasons why firms seek multinational marketing opportunities.

6. What is meant by "the exchange rate"? When the United States lowers the value of its dollars in relation to German marks, what effect does this have on trade between the two countries?

7. Describe some of the changes that are taking place in multinational marketing. How will these changes impact upon such firms' marketing strategies?

8. Are marketing concepts universal? If so, couldn't a firm easily standardize its marketing strategy and use it worldwide without modification? Explain.

9. List and discuss some of the frustrations associated with overseas marketing research.

10. Discuss very briefly some of the problems associated with each of the variables of the marketing mix—product, price, promotion, and channels—likely to arise in overseas marketing.

Case 18-1

"Pepski" Cola

Pepsi Cola's newest market is in the Soviet Union. Since 1974, "Pepski," as it is called in Russia, has been bubbling out of a new plant in the Black Sea port city of Novorossisk. Sales reached 50 million bottles in 1976 and they are expected to increase about 20 percent a year for the next several years. Pepsi's venture in Russia has set a new pattern for future such arrangements in the vast awakening market for Western consumer goods in Russia.

Pepsi's entrance into the Russian market began with the 1959 Moscow trade fair, at which then Vice President Richard Nixon had his celebrated "kitchen debate" with Soviet Premier Nikita Khrushchev. Donald M. Kendall, who was head of Pepsi's international operations at the time, persuaded Nixon to steer Khrushchev to the Pepsi kiosk, where the Soviet premier drank eight bottles of Pepsi. This was the beginning of the Russian "Pepski Generation." Twelve years later, after Kendall had become Pepsi Company chairman and as detente became a reality, a workable but peculiar international marketing arrangement was made.

The Russians, always concerned about trade balances, wanted a straight barter arrangement. PepsiCo agreed to furnish the Russians with the essentials for making Pepsi, including bottling equipment from West Germany, over a five-year period. The Russians would make their own bottles and handle all distribution. In return for Pepsi's contribution, Pepsi got the rights to sell Russian wine and vodka in the United States. What this amounts to is this; the more Soviet wine and vodka Pepsi can market in the United States, the more Pepsi concentrate and bottling equipment the Russians get in return.

Pepsi's main Russian import is Stolichnaya vodka, distributed by the company's Monsieur Henri subsidiary. It is a high-price, high-quality product that sells for $7.99 a fifth—which is

more than American-made Smirnoff, the best selling brand. Another Russian product that is part of the deal is a champagne called Nazdorovya, which is a product supposedly of vineyards planted in 1870 on the estate of Czar Alexander II.

In 1976, Stolichnaya sales in the United States totaled 115,000 cases, 70 percent of the imported vodka market, but only a small share of the total vodka market. Pepsi officials are looking for improvement in Stolichnaya's sales but are still pleased with the arrangement. The company gets a generous return on its cola concentrate and the arrangement has also cleared the way for Pepsi's entry into other Eastern European communistic countries.

The Novorossisk plant mainly supplies the sunny Black Sea area but other plants are being developed in the Crimea, Moscow, Leningrad, and Tallin. Pepsi is promoted as a health-giving tonic—an ideal way to "quench the thirst, invigorate the body, and raise the tone." One of the major marketing problems related to Pepsi in the Soviet Union has to do with the low rate of bottle returns. Despite a 12-cent deposit included in the 54-cent price per bottle, souvenir-minded Russian consumers have been failing to return two of every five bottles sold.

Questions

1. Why do you suppose PepsiCo was anxious to have Pepsi marketed in the Soviet Union?

2. Are there consequences of Pepsi's Russian market penetration which go beyond the economic goals of making money?

3. In spite of PepsiCo's obvious pleasure over the arrangement with the Soviet Union, what disadvantages or drawbacks could occur, especially as they relate to overall marketing strategy?

Case 18-2

Japanese Export Fever

Although Tokyo disavows a resurrection of its "export or die" philosophy, Japan's leading companies are poised for a powerful export drive and the United States is a prime target. As the Japanese witness the beginnings of a saturation point for consumer products in their own home market and realize the importance of maintain-ing high levels of output and productivity, many Japanese trade experts predict considerable aggresiveness to push the products of many Japanese manufacturing giants overseas with a vengeance.

Yet the Tokyo ministry of International Trade does fear that a too aggressive export policy by

the Japanese could kindle a protectionist backlash in the United States—a market that absorbs fully 26 percent of Japan's $103 billion in exports in 1980. Japanese products that are flooding U.S. markets consist of electronics, office copiers, air conditioners, semiconductors, and, of course, automobiles.

American TV manufacturers have long been upset by the flood of Japanese TV sets on the U.S. market. American labor unions have agreed that 70,000 jobs have been lost to Japanese imports, which amount to over three million TV sets or about 40 percent of the domestic market.

United States government investigators are looking into charges that Japanese manufacturers have been making illegal kickbacks to United States importers as a way of getting around federal "antidumping" regulations and selling TV sets in this country at bargain basement prices.

The kickbacks are alleged to work this way: if a Japanese manufacturer sells a TV set in the United States for a price lower than it charges for the same set in Japan, that constitutes "dumping" under international trade rules and subjects the manufacturer to a penalty tariff. So the Japanese manufacturer quotes the American importer an official price equal to the Japanese price, then makes under the table payments which in effect are illegal rebates. This allows the importer to offer the set at prices that undersell American-made TVs by $100 or more. In some instances the illegal payments are disguised as rebates or "credits" for advertising or shipping. United States industry figures assert that the practice has been going on for years and that several large Japanese makers are involved. A senior official at the United States Embassy in Tokyo stated that eighty-six United States importers, basically distributors and retailers, including some well-known U.S. chain stores, were probably involved.

In May 1977, the Carter administration presumably worked out an arrangement with Japanese makers to limit their exports, but the picture had not materially improved by late 1980.

Slacker sales at home and the yen's decline enhances the relative competitiveness of the Japanese exports. In the early 1980s, exports are expected to account for as much as 50 percent of the annual growth in the Japanese economy. Yet, in the United States the economy is somewhat depressed and there are likely to be continuing problems associated with inflation, slow economic growth, and nagging unemployment.

Questions

1. Why do Japanese TV manufacturers wish to "dump" their products in the United States?

2. Why don't U.S. TV manufacturers turn the tables on the Japanese companies and begin dumping American TV sets in Japan?

3. If the kickbacks that permit the Japanese practice of dumping were all eliminated, what impact should this have in helping to preserve the American TV manufacturing industry?

4. Will U.S. consumers benefit from the elimination of the Japanese kickbacks and the dumping of Japanese TV sets onto the United States market?

5. Would American marketing benefit from higher tariffs and import restrictions, which would protect American jobs and purchasing power?

Chapter 19

Marketing in the Future: Problems and Prospects

The Time: 1990
The Place: Troy, Michigan, a suburb of Detroit
The Characters: The American Consumer as represented by Curt and Sally
                   Lewis*

Following the talk of sacrifice and the urgency to trim consumption patterns and lifestyles which emerged out of the decade of the 1970s and 1980s, consumption, and to some extent life styles, have been markedly altered. Yet in 1990, the American core culture remains basically intact; personal incomes have risen, and so has the consumption of durables, nondurables, and services. Many families are still two-car families, most still live in the suburbs, and the life styles of most Americans as represented by Curt and Sally Lewis still reflect strong overtones of materialism and the urge to consume. The "good life" not only continues, but in some respects it may even be better.

Curt and Sally Lewis, like most middle-income Americans, were faced with a new challenge if not fear. They were told that the energy crisis, which had developed in the early 1980s and the American consumer's response to it, should be viewed as "the moral equivalent of war." The Lewises braced themselves to "use less and pay more." Their gas and electric bills had tripled from 1980 to 1990 and gasoline had gone up almost as much.

Nevertheless, they did manage to cope and their life went on. Today Curt works as a data processor in one of Detroit's major automobile companies, and Sally is a part-time practical nurse. Between them they earn $45,000 a year—enough for the mortgage payment on their house, the upkeep on their two cars, an occasional holiday, braces for Melinda's teeth, and frequent doctor bills for young Jeff, who is either clumsy or accident-prone. They even save a little money on occasion.

However, direct energy costs for their home and transportation take a larger and larger share of their income, while more costly industrial energy has driven up the prices of almost everything they consume. Their home heating bills, even after the new insulation was installed, are high. They now heat much of their hot water with solar energy but the cost of this installation was well over $1,000 and Curt estimates that the system will not pay for itself for seven or eight years. The family sold its eighteen-foot inboard-outboard water-ski boat in 1984 and replaced it with a twenty-foot sailboat with an auxiliary motor with a small galley but no bunks. They trailer their boat with the larger of the two cars—a small, six-cylinder station wagon which burns a mixture of gasoline and methyl alcohol and gets twenty-seven miles per gallon on the highway. The car cost Curt and Sally $15,900 but it is virtually pollution free, is low in maintenance, and therefore much cheaper to operate than the ones they previously owned. Curt uses the car during the week to carpool with several of his neighbors and fellow workers to their jobs—about ten miles from Troy.

---

* This scenario is fictional but based upon projections that are both factual and conjectural.

Sally has a small gas-sipping Japanese auto that gets nearly fifty miles a gallon even in city traffic. Nonetheless, she drives frugally because a gallon of gasoline is now $2.90. Sometimes, for occasional food shopping expeditions, Sally even pedals her three-wheel bicycle to the neighborhood grocery store when she purchases fill-in items. For major shopping trips she uses the larger car on weekends to travel to the regional discount supermarket. There she buys staple items in large quantities—sometimes several weeks' supply—in order to cut down on her shopping trips. In many mid-sized to larger cities efficient new systems of rapid public transportation have been developed, causing a resurgence of retailing in the central business districts. Scores of large regional shopping centers have closed because they drew their customers from as far away as forty to fifty minutes' driving time and were too dependent on automobile traffic for their success.

Curt, Sally, and the two children are a close-knit family and they do many things together. They bicycle frequently on the miles of new bike trails that have recently been developed. The children, instead of being driven, ride their bicycles to school; teachers encourage this practice as part of the school's emphasis on physical fitness. Eating out is still fun whether it is for burgers or pizza. However, a large number of the fast food franchise operators have gone out of business because of out-of-the-way locations and their dependence on the automobile. Many others have relocated, and not too surprisingly, many firms, especially MacDonald's, have pioneered the use of solar energy and reconversion (the reuse of heat generated in frying burgers and french fries to produce electricity for heating and cooling their buildings).

So there have been many changes as a result of the energy shortages. Some were profound and some subtle. But whether they are aware of it or not, the Lewises have been affected by the shortages all along. Because of them, Curt and Sally are paying more for just about everything they buy. Not surprisingly, energy-intensive goods, from polyester suits to plastic garbage cans, have gone up the most. Cosmetics, many foods, entertainment devices such as television, radios, and stereos, and plastic for records and tapes have soared in price. For that matter, prices for almost all products and even many services have gone up. Dwindling energy added to the inflation of the early 1980s. The increased cost of energy compelled local governments to raise taxes and the Lewises, like all other Americans, have been forced to pay for the added cost of all public services, from heating schools to running garbage trucks.

However, in the final analysis, the Lewises aren't too unhappy. They still have a feeling of optimism and rising expectations. The United States standard of living remains the highest in the world by most standards. And Curt and Sally are pleased with the cleaner environment. The air is cleaner and there seem to be fewer colds. The streets are clean and, downtown, legs are king in the cities of 1990, where people either walk or bike everywhere far into the night. The crime rate has dropped so the parks are full, and there is mutual protection in crowds. There is new hope as new energy sources are being introduced. Many firms now specialize in marketing solar and geothermal devices for the home, and the solar cell and battery is being viewed as the next possibility for powering small cars. Homes are smaller but much more efficient and perhaps even more comfortable. American marketers by and large are more socially responsible, some as a result of their own initiative, but more of them as a result of rising consumer awareness and insistence mobilized through government and legislative action. Consumerism still agitates forcefully for better business practices and increased social responsibility. All in all, the Lewises in 1990 are not so different from their predecessors in 1980. Like the French proverb, things have changed in order that they can remain the same: Earth abides! The Lewises' world is still largely one of increased abundance, affluence, and an improved quality of life. Marketing, in large part, has helped to create these conditions.

In this chapter we will examine some of the marketing developments that have maintained this comfortable, hopeful world despite shortages, crowding, inflation, and inconvenience. We will consider first the marketing opportunities and implications of the national energy program and the new marketing era it may well inaugurate. The social responsibilities of business and social marketing in the decade ahead will be our next concern. Developing these societal aspects of marketing, the discussion will then focus on business ethics and how they are changing, criticism of business, and government regulation. Next we will trace the emergence and achievements of the consumer movement, a growing force linking marketers to social problems. Finally, we will examine marketing strategies that will enable firms to thrive in the challenging years just ahead.

National Energy Program

For many years, Americans have been told, warned, and threatened about the looming energy shortage. Fossil fuels, and especially oil are running out in the United States and world shortages forced OPEC (Oil Producing Exporting Countries) to raise the price of their crude to $30.00 per barrel. This drastic increase caused a serious problem with the United States balance of payments. America's use of energy was increasing rapidly at a time when its supplies were dwindling and when prices for imported oil were rising rapidly. To continue using oil as America's principal energy source would mean persistently rising prices, growing dependence on foreign suppliers, decreases in our standard of living and quality of life, and threats to our actual existence.

Even in 1980, however, the American public was not fully convinced that the energy "crunch" was genuine. Some believed that the shortage was contrived by the large oil companies who wished simply to raise prices and hence reap large windfall profits.

The Goals and Objectives of the Program

The principal objective of the National Energy program is to curtail energy use primarily through conservation and the redirection of energy utilization. Its

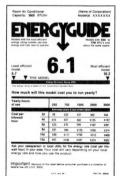

Figure 19-1 Energy demand. Total U.S. consumption from all sources in quadrillions of BTU's.

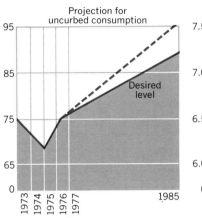

Figure 19-2 Gasoline consumption. U.S. demand in millions of barrels a day.

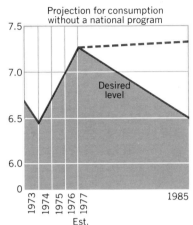

Figure 19-3 Oil imports. U.S. consumption in millions of barrels a day.

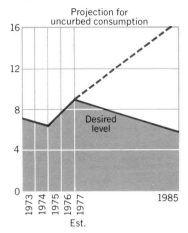

NOTE: Auto mileage standards in present law will hold down usage.

Source: Time, May 2, 1977, p. 18.

goals are quite specific.[1] The three main ones are: (1) to cut growth in United States demand for energy to less than 2 percent a year by 1985, from the nearly 3 percent it was otherwise expected to reach and the 6 percent it was in 1977; (2) to reduce gasoline consumption 10 percent under 1977's expected level of 7.2 million barrels a day by 1985; and (3) to reduce imports of foreign oil to 6 million barrels a day in eight years (they averaged 7.2 million barrels a day in 1977 and government administrators estimated that such imports could grow to 16 million barrels daily by 1985 if nothing were done). Data for energy demand, gasoline consumption, and oil imports are shown in Figures 19-1, 19-2, and 19-3.

Why the Furor over Energy.   So we are using too much energy. What if the United States supplies are dwindling. We can always import more oil, right? Wrong! World oil reserves are finite and if America keeps gulping energy at its current rate, it could spell disaster for our economic and even our social system. Energy is one of the major costs of production and production is what determines economic growth. As energy costs rise, the prices of goods and services also rise. As consumers pay more for goods whose price reflects the higher cost of energy, the total package of goods consumers can purchase will shrink. Hence, as consumers purchase less, standards of living will shrink, and the quality of life as we know it may actually decline. The growth of GNP is in one sense a measure of the United States standard of living. When we are

[1] Thomas C. Lowinger, "U.S. Energy Policy: A Critical Assessment," *MSU Business Topics* **28** (Winter 1980), no. 1, pp. 13–22.

forced to pay unnecessarily high prices for energy, the real growth in GNP is slowed down. To maintain our economic growth at high levels so that our consumption levels and standard of living do not deteriorate, government and industry planners have embraced the National Energy Program.

A New Marketing Era

What sounds like an energy program is in many ways a new marketing era. A national campaign to conserve energy will generate both winners and losers as far as marketing firms are concerned. Americans are being asked to sacrifice, though not a lot. People are already beginning to make small but significant changes in their life styles—remodeling the older house instead of building, insulating existing homes, turning down thermostats, shifting to smaller cars, buying more energy-efficient appliances, and walking and bicycling more. Over time the bundle of goods and services marketed will change. Some firms and products will be skipped over by energy-conscious, socially aware consumers, but new firms and new products will arise to meet their needs.

Marketing firms will be called upon to broaden the scope of their social responsibilities. Marketing itself will continue to expand its scope and function and the broadened concept of marketing will become even more relevant during the 1980s. The extended concept of marketing, you will remember from chapter 1, aims at generating customer satisfaction and long-run public welfare as the keys to meeting organizational goals and responsibilities. Marketing will play an important role in "selling" the National Energy Program. Already we are seeing posters and buttons reminding us to save energy, turn down the thermostats, and use less hot water. Marketing has the capacity to create awareness and develop interest that can not only increase sales for a firm but can also advance overall consumer and public welfare.

Marketing strategies always reflect the surroundings from which they spring. The energy-starved environment of the 1980s will likely beget a growing clamor for increased social responsibility on the part of business. Besides demanding more consumer rights, the socially conscious citizen of the 1980s will keep a close watch on the environment, energy utilization, and the fairness of business practices. In short, a continuing and robust consumerism will be an important backdrop for future marketing strategies.

The Social Responsibilities of Business

In the new era of marketing, business will devote more attention to what is loosely called their social responsibilities. We hear much about such obligations these days, but viewpoints differ as to what constitutes the firm's social responsibilities. Scholars like Milton Friedman, Eugene Rostow, and Theodore Levitt argue that the responsibility of business is to pursue and earn profits.[2] By

[2] Milton Friedman, "The Social Responsibility of Business Is to Increase Its Profits," *New York Times Magazine* **13,** September 1970, pp. 32–33; Theodore Levitt, "The Dangers of Social Responsibility," *Harvard Business Review,* September-October 1958, pp. 44–50; Eugene Rostow in *The Corporation in Modern Society,* ed. Edward S. Mason (Cambridge, MA: Harvard University Press), 1959, p. 63.

You can count on Sears for satisfaction

Satisfaction guaranteed or your money back is a promise Sears has lived by for half a century. Other things you can still count on at Sears: fair prices, good workmanship, wide selection, competent service.

You pay good money at Sears. In return, Sears believes that you should be completely satisfied with everything you buy.

You must be satisfied with performance, quality of workmanship, fit, styling—even *color*. Suppose you buy a blue sweater through the catalog and the blue strikes you as different, however slightly, from the blue on the printed page.

Says Sears catalog: "In such a case, as with everything we sell, we guarantee your satisfaction or your money back."

Sears goes to extraordinary lengths to make certain that you will be satisfied. For instance:

1. *Men and women from Sears spend thousands of hours a year at factories that make Sears products.*

These men and women are called buyers, but they do a lot more than place orders. They study the needs and desires of Sears customers—and work personally with manufacturers to make certain that Sears products perform as expected.

2. *The Sears Laboratory tests over 10,000 products a year.*

Sears maintains one of the world's largest private laboratories for testing consumer goods. It tests for strength, durability, handling, and performance.

3. *Sears employs engineers to help manufacturers improve their efficiency.*

This is one of many steps Sears takes to help hold down costs. Others include an almost fanatically efficient distribution system.

Example: Refrigerator door handles are left off refrigerators for shipment to Sears stores. With door handles tucked neatly into cartons instead of sticking out, each carton can be a little smaller, Sears can get more refrigerators on each truck—and the shipping cost for each refrigerator goes down a few cents.

Dozens of small efficiencies like this explain why Sears regular prices are so reasonable, and Sears sale prices such terrific bargains.

So it's first to Sears for millions of shoppers —more than shop at any other store. These millions have found again and again that they are likely to spot exactly what they're looking for at Sears, to pay a fair price for it—and to be completely satisfied with it once they get it home.

its doing so, society benefits and people's material needs are met. However, this older, more traditional view is rapidly being replaced by a newer one resting on the assumption that business belongs to the people. Advocates of this doctrine argue that business in effect has a franchise granted to it by society and the franchise (which is a privilege, not a right) will be continued only as long as society is satisfied with the way it is handled. Business is viewed from this standpoint as a socio-economic institution rather than a strictly economic one, and as such the business firm has obligations to many recognized constituencies.

Today's, and increasingly tomorrow's, socially responsible business firm will recognize its duty to respond to the needs and desires of stockholders, employees, suppliers, consumers, and the general public, and not just to one or two of these groups at the expense of the others.

What Are the Firm's Social Responsibilities?

For the past several years there has been a trend, with a growing momentum, toward a broader set of goals and objectives for business. The essence of the trend is that the concept of marketing must be expanded to include a number of societal aspects. The concept of **social marketing** has thus emerged, the notion that the effects of marketers' activities on our national life must contribute toward the well-being of society generally, not just a few individual consumers. The impact and scope of societal marketing can be summarized like this:

- *Satisfaction of human needs.* The central issue is *human* needs, not those met solely by products and services but those of humans living in a delicate societal and ecological setting. Social marketing is thus charged with the obligation to advocate clean air, pure water, and adequate housing, and to promote conservation and meaningful life styles.
- *Expansion to social fields.* Marketing, in a social as well as economic context, is seen as a set of institutions and practices that can be used to further all the goals of society. Its techniques can assist in achieving socially desirable goals such as population control, improved racial tolerance, and increased support of education. They can create public awareness and mobilize action on any range of social issues.
- *Consideration of societal impact.* A new standard of marketing and general business performance is created: business must assess not only the profitability of its actions, but also, the overall effect those actions have on society:[3]

Social marketing is not necessarily the same thing as social responsibility. For example, promoting the United Crusade is a social marketing program but not necessarily a social responsibility issue. Eliminating stereotypes of women in advertising, however, is a social responsibility issue but not a social marketing program.

Social marketing is the natural outgrowth and extension of the marketing firm's assuming more social responsibilities, and the growth of social marketing as reflected in the increasing social responsibility of business has become an established trend. It is more than a fad. It is a genuine new response by businesses—a response to new needs based upon new market realities. Not all organizations, of course, practice social marketing nor do all of them behave in a socially responsible way. But one recent comprehensive study of the actions and attitudes of ninety-six major corporations revealed the following highlights:

- Corporations involved in what they consider social responsibility activities are interested in publicizing these activities.
- Specific professional positions have begun to appear in organizations as a job specialty in this area.
- Those holding such positions are better educated and older than the general run of executive. They are usually from communication areas such as public relations or marketing.

[3] Andrew Takas, "Societal Marketing: A Businessman's Perspective," *Journal of Marketing* **38** (October 1974), p. 2. See also George A. Steiner, "An Overview of the Changing Business Environment and Its Impact on Business," *Business Environment/Public Policy,* 1979 Conference Papers, Lee E. Preston, ed., American Assembly of Collegiate Schools of Business, 1980, pp. 3–18.

- The usual activities of this group may be described as voluntary, such as making contributions to education and the arts.
- The most usual efforts of these major corporations are related to ecology and to minority hiring and training.
- Company size (measured by sales volume) is related positively to social responsibility efforts.
- The great majority of those engaged in these activities view them as effective, even though "hard" standards of evaluation seem to be lacking.
- Larger firms tend to justify these activities to shareholders, who do not appear to object to them.
- These firms all say they intend to continue and even expand their efforts in social marketing and in exercising social responsibilities.[4]

The highlights of the study indicate that social marketing may well be the reigning business philosophy during the decade of the 1980s.

Making Money or Doing Good

Does social marketing mean that firms are no longer eager to make money and that they are only interested in "doing good"? Has marketing become a kind of religion? A new "Protestant ethic"? Not really. The focus of marketers has traditionally been and will continue to be, on sales and profits. Business people at all levels throughout an organization are under continual pressure to produce results. Without profit, a business organization can achieve no social objectives. However, given the changes likely in the next decade, a marketing revolution is inevitable. Marketing, while still seeking profits, will be guided by other considerations and will be subject to many new legal, administrative, and ethical restrictions.

Social marketing will recognize tightening global limitations. Marketers will have to take seriously the fact that when any input anywhere falls short, we all will have less. They must not ignore the new axiom that when the price of anything goes up in the world, we all will pay more. Nor can they forget that waste and a "throwaway culture" have no place in a world striving to cleanse its environment and conserve its resources.

In evaluating the opportunities for new products and services in the past, marketing people have focused on the question: Can it be sold? During the present decade they will pay increasing attention to the questions: Should it be sold? Is it worth its cost to society? In the future, marketing must struggle with the problem of meeting the goals of society as well as those of individuals and of helping to supply the demand for more public goods and services.

The rising tide of consumerism and the growing belief of a whole new generation that there is more to life than materialism—simply owning more and more things—will create even more pressure for increased social responsibility and lay more emphasis on social marketing. Demand for greater auto-

[4] Robert Parket and Henry Eilbert, "Social Responsibility: The Underlying Factors," *Business Horizons,* August 1975, p. 5.

mobile safety, more livable cities, more restrained use of resources (especially energy), cleaner air and water, and stricter strip-mining legislation all show that the mass of consumers increasingly want something that business so far has not given them in any great degree. Social marketing tomorrow may promote mass transportation instead of automobiles, literacy instead of lanolin, birth control instead of snowmobiles, and schools instead of hair sprays.[5]

Demands like these will increasingly force marketers to recognize that traditional marketing is myopic and outmoded. Only increased business social responsibility and social marketing will be in tune with tomorrow's reality.

Social Responsibilities and Business Ethics

Marketers' social responsibilities flow out of their conception of business ethics.[6] Ethics is the study of right and wrong. The conduct of most business people today is highly ethical, but there are always exceptions. There are false or misleading advertisements; over-priced, shoddy merchandise; bribes to win lucrative contracts; polluting industries and products that harm our health. There are, in short, greedy rapacious marketers just as there are the benevolent and the socially responsible. In some quarters, it is charged that business and industry are warped with greed, exploitative of their employees, and devious in their methods. The charges go on and on, with the fingers of alleged guilt being pointed, it seems, at all organizations with more than a handful of employees. There is no question that some less-than-honorable practices do occur, but these are rare and, for the most part, the world of business is highly ethical.

A Critic's View of Business

Without glossing over business ethics and behavior, however, let's look at some of the abuses of business through the eyes of the critic.[7]

Monopoly Capitalism.   In the radical view of business huge monopolistic corporations dominate the economy. These corporations control technological innovations, manipulate prices, generate unending consumer wants while expanding to an international scale. The primary objective of business managers is to be accomplished profit gatherers. These heartless firms, say the radicals, are able to shift risk and social costs to the consumer, the taxpayer, and others less powerful. Such corporations mouth the doctrine of social responsibility but adeptly practice private greed. Most of all, such firms make huge profits but impose on society a large part of the costs of the pollution and environmental damage they cause.

[5] Andrew Takas, "Societal Marketing," pp. 2–7.
[6] Robert H. Bock, "Modern Values and Social Responsibility," *MSU Business Topics* **28,** no. 2 (Spring 1980), pp. 5–18.
[7] Campbell R. McConnell, "The Economics of Dissent," *MSU Business Topics*, Autumn 1975, pp. 27–40.

Domination of the State.   The radical view is that business firms have come to dominate the state. Rather than controlling corporate power for the good of society, the public sector has become the handmaiden of the corporate giants. Consequently, the regulatory commissions set up to control monopolies in the public interest are ineffective because they are controlled by the corporate monopolies they are supposed to regulate. Most regulation was enacted to protect the consumer from abuse, but much of today's regulatory machinery does little more than shelter producers from the normal consequences of competition.

Need for Expansion and Greed.   Critics of marketing and of the large corporation argue that the need for new markets to absorb expanding production is the source of one of the grossest features of business—expansion and greed, the desire for ever-expanding profits through sales exploitation. Greater output leads to expanded profits and capital accumulation but in order to realize profits on the newly accumulated capital, even greater sales of output are required. This, the critics claim, means that firms can never truly be socially responsible. The firm's own greed and need for expansion wipe out social responsibility.

Alienation and Moral Bankruptcy of People.   Critics of the American enterprise system and big business argue that capitalism is a major source of alienation. That is, the large bureaucratic organization allows individuals less and less control over their destinies, and the masses of people are more and more remote from the decision processes shaping the character and quality of their lives. The corporation promotes only materialism and the consumption of goods, which are increasingly trivial and meaningless.

The Production of Waste.   Finally, the severe critics of business ethics and practices argue that the pursuit of profits and the desire to accumulate lead to more and more production simply for its own sake. The economy markets incredible quantities of television sets, cosmetics, and alcoholic beverages while at the same time many families are without adequate housing, medical care, or diet. The fact that some $45 billion is "squandered" each year on advertising is seen as ample evidence that the production of many consumer goods fails to fulfill the true needs of many consumers. At a time when the country spends $100 billion per year on military hardware, the maintenance of overseas military bases, and space exploration, such areas as urban decay, mass transit, and social services are woefully ignored.

The critics are unrelenting. But what do you think? How would you defend marketing if these charges were being leveled at you by an acquaintance who had embraced such ideas?

Neither the issues nor the arguments are simple. Is a manufacturer of skateboards being ethical if the product is injuring children? Or should Procter and Gamble be criticized for showing a woman in a housewife's role if that is the best way to communicate to its major target audience? Are companies who

592 Marketing in the Future: Problems and Prospects

market cigarettes ethical when strong statistical evidence links lung cancer to smoking? Finally, should Ford or General Motors be expected to produce an emission-free automobile even if it has to sell for $50,000? Often it is not a question of simple ethics. Marketers generally want to do the "right thing" because they are long-run profit maximizers. Their decisions usually reflect not just an interest in immediate sales but longer-run considerations that motivate them to take socially responsible action. However, as their awareness is expanded, their point of view regarding ethics and social responsibility changes. There are few ethical absolutes, almost no objective standards for determining what is, and is not, ethical.

The Ethics of Business Are Changing

Business ethics and the resulting business practices are always in something of a state of change. Are the criticisms of marketing valid? Yes and no. Yes, they are valid on the basis of the behavior of a limited, shrinking number of firms. No, they are not valid as universal generalizations about business ethics and behavior. Many of the critics' observations and their subsequent deductions about business are based upon faulty perception. One or two corrupt businesses do not mean business as a whole is corrupt and without responsible ethics. Many critics of business substitute rhetoric for reasoning and fail to acknowledge the solid social contributions of thousands of business organizations. Over thirty years ago, Peter Drucker declared that the emergence of big business was the most important recent event in the history of the Western world.[8] The institution of business—modern marketing, if you will—has given Americans the highest standard of living in the world while improving the lives of people in many other countries. We owe much of our freedom, our unlimited choices, wealth, leisure, art, literature, and the quality of our lives to marketing and the efficiencies of the large organization. The battle is not one of the self-interest of the corporation pitted against that of the public. Corporations in growing numbers are recognizing that the public interest and their own are one. Many of America's problems are not solely related to business. They are the problems of society, of differing ideologies, large-scale technology, and swelling populations trying to make do with inadequate food supplies and dwindling resources. Marketing is not so much a part of the problem as it is a part of the solution.

Specific Changes in Business Ethics.   In a major study of business ethics, a number of questions were put to 1,227 Harvard Business Review readers concerning business ethics. The results of the survey are too numerous and detailed to quote here. However, one significant finding was that most respondents' firms had overcome the traditional ideological barriers to the concept of social responsibility and had embraced its practice as a legitimate and

---

[8] As cited in James R. Krum, "Perspectives on the Consequences of Big Business," *MSU Business Topics,* Summer 1975, pp. 60–68.

achievable goal for business.[9] The study also found that public disclosure and concern over unethical business behavior were the most potent forces for raising ethical standards.

The study found that the basic factors which have lead to the raising of ethical standards were such things as: (1) public disclosure, publicity, medical coverage, and better communications; (2) increased public concern, public awareness, consciousness, and scrutiny; (3) government regulation, legislation, and federal court action.

The study also was able to identify the groups to whom executives feel the greatest responsibility. Clearly, their first duty was directed toward customers while stockholders and employees were second and third. The study revealed that for most business managers, maximizing profits ranked third in their priority ranking of objectives, confirming the observation that today's executives no longer perceive it as their major responsibility. The two areas of greatest importance to managers in this survey were: (1) being an efficient user of energy and natural resources and (2) assessing the potential environmental effects flowing from the company's technological advances.

These findings demonstrate the desire of business people to define their responsibility in those areas where externalities rise directly from their operations. In such areas the marketing manager and other executives can see clearly the benefits they will gain by their "socially responsible actions," either in reduced costs or averted government regulation.

What Is the Response to Corporate Irresponsibility?

The business firm is not immune to its own wrongdoing. When irresponsible, as they sometimes are, corporations provoke the wrath of consumers, fueling ardent and militant consumerism that in turn leads to increasing crackdowns and regulation by government.

Since 1960 the United States Congress has enacted over ninety significant laws regulating almost all phases of business activity.[10] In addition, federal agencies have issued thousands of rules, procedural requirements, and interpretations. Some indication of the scope and direction of federal legislation affecting business can be observed from the list shown in Table 19-1 of sixty of the significant bills enacted by Congress since 1960. Increasingly regulation today is focused on pollution, consumerism, minority employment, employment of women, safety, and job satisfaction. These issues are often summed up by the phrase "a better quality of life." While we all want a better environment, consumer protection and product information, fairness in employment, and safe and healthful workplaces, many serious questions can be raised about the impact of specific regulations on society and the economy. We may well ask if there has been adequate research into whether the proposed regulation

[9] Steven N. Brenner and Earl A. Molander, "Is the Ethics of Business Changing?" *Harvard Business Review,* January-February 1977, pp. 57–71.
[10] Alfred L. Seelye, "Societal Change and Business-Government Relationships," *MSU Business Topics,* Autumn 1975, pp. 5–12.

*". . . and please grant me and the rest of the board
the grace not to abuse deregulation."*

Drawing by Donald Reilly; © 1981 The New Yorker Magazine, Inc.

will lead to the best solution. Here again, marketing through the use of marketing research can perform a social service.[11] We should also ask if the proposed regulation provides sufficient time for the required implementation and whether its costs exceed its actual benefits.

Both business and government need to work more closely to increase consumer well-being and promote the general welfare. The roles of both partners in such an arrangement have been described as follows: The role of government is to weigh the goals and values of society, fix priorities and trade-off relationships, lay down the rules, and motivate private enterprise. The role of business is to act vigorously within the framework established by government to satisfy the demands of the public which are expressed in markets.

Guided by this framework, business is becoming increasingly more socially responsible. Consumers, government, and society in general demand no less. More and more companies are undertaking socially responsible activities and reporting them to their customers and stockholders as well as to the general public.

A Marketing Reorientation.   Social responsibility has led to an increased emphasis upon social marketing, which has caused something of a marketing reorientation. Today, and in the marketing world of tomorrow, effective marketing means more than the satisfaction of consumer expectations concerning product performance or benefits. Truly effective marketing means an ever more precise interpretation of consumer needs within the framework of the consumer's increased social and environmental consciousness.

[11] Robert F. Dyer and Terrance A. Shimp, "Enhancing the Role of Marketing Research in Public Policy Decision Making," *Journal of Marketing,* January 1977, pp. 63–67.

Table 19-1 Significant Legislation Since 1960 Charts the Changing Course of Business-Government Relationships

Civil Rights Act of 1960	Child Protection and Toy Safety Act of 1969
Federal Hazardous Substances Labeling Act of 1960	Federal Coal Mine Health and Safety Act of 1969
Fair Labor Standards Amendments of 1961, 1966, and 1974	Natural Environmental Policy Act of 1969
Federal Water Pollution Control Act Amendments of 1961	Tax Reform Act of 1969
Oil Pollution Act of 1961 and Amendments of 1973	Investment Company Amendments of 1969
Food and Agriculture Act of 1962	Bank Holding Act Amendments of 1970
Air Pollution Control Act of 1962	Bank Records and Foreign Transactions Act of 1970
Antitrust Civil Process Act of 1962	Economic Stabilization Act of 1970 and Amendments of 1971 and 1973
Drug Amendments of 1962	Environmental Quality Improvement Act of 1970
Clean Air Act of 1963 and Amendments of 1966 and 1970	Fair Credit Reporting Act of 1970
Equal Pay Act of 1963	Noise Pollution and Abatement Act of 1970
Civil Rights Act of 1963	Occupational Safety and Health Act of 1970
Food Stamp Act of 1964	Securities Investor Protection Act of 1970
Automotive Products Trade Act of 1965	Water and Environmental Quality Improvement Act of 1970
Federal Cigarette Labeling and Advertising Act of 1965	Export Administration Finance Act of 1971
Water Quality Act of 1965	Consumer Product Safety Act of 1972
Clean Water Restoration Act of 1966	Equal Employment Opportunity Act of 1972
Fair Packaging and Labeling Act of 1966	Federal Environmental Pesticide Control Act of 1972
Federal Coal Mine Safety Act Amendments of 1966	Noise Control Act of 1972
Financial Institutions Supervisory Act of 1966	Agriculture and Consumers Protection Act of 1973
Oil Pollution of the Sea Act of 1966	Emergency Petroleum Allocation Act of 1973
Age Discrimination in Employment Act of 1967	Highway Safety Act of 1973
Air Quality Act of 1967	Water Resources Development Act of 1974
Agricultural Fair Practices Act of 1968	FTC Improvements Act of 1975
Consumer Credit Protection Act of 1968	Hart-Scott-Rodino Act 1976
Natural Gas Pipeline Safety Act of 1968	
Radiation Control for Health and Safety Act of 1968	
Cigarette Smoking Act of 1969	

Social consciousness arises from three forces: (1) the firm's own increasing sensitivity to its social responsibilities, (2) growing public pressure arising from society's expectations of business conduct as expressed by opinion shapers, and (3) more formal government regulatory pressures stemming from legal prescriptions for ethical conduct.

Figure 19-4 An integrated hierarchy of business purpose.

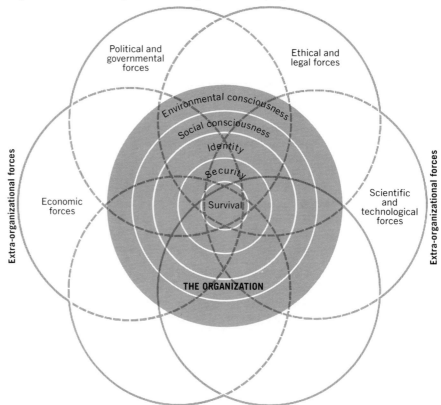

Source: W. Thomas Anderson, Jr., Louis K. Sharpe, and Robert J. Boewaat, "The Environmental Role for Marketing," *MSU Business Topics,* Summer 1972, p. 70.

Environmental consciousness on the part of business organizations is a natural response to an increasingly complex technology that imposes a social cost on all of society, business, and consumers alike. Figure 19-4 is a sketch of the integrated hierarchy of business purposes within the framework of economic, social, political, and technological forces operating today. In the past, business has most frequently interpreted its role as one of reacting to shifts in consumer demand. However, businesses of the future must cope not only with such core problems as survival, security, and identity but also with a growing social and environmental consciousness. Besides satisfying wants that can be met by conventional production and distribution, the new consumer of the 1980s will seek to fulfill aesthetic needs of a higher order.

Perhaps people may not even consider themselves as "consumers" in the future. The term may fall out of fashion because it connotes to some "greed," "waste," and "irresponsibility." People will see themselves increasingly as something beyond consumers—perhaps as persons creating their own life styles by using the services of marketers. In such a context marketers will be selling not individual products that can be viewed as symbols but a life style and quality of life which will be pieces of a larger symbol.

Before proceeding, can you answer these questions:
1. How will the coming period of energy shortages affect marketing?
2. What is the relationship between business ethics and social responsibilities?
3. What have been two principal reactions to corporate irresponsibility?

A Growing Interest in Consumerism

The marketer of the future will confront a growing and continuing surge of consumerism. Consumers not only will expect but will demand fairer treatment in the marketplace. Consumers of the future will be more affluent, better educated, and probably more aware. This increased awareness will reflect itself in an insistence that they be treated fairly. When they are not, their response will likely be either individual or group reaction to seek redress.

When consumers feel that they have been unfairly treated, or "ripped off," by corner-cutting or deceptive or fraudulent practices, they undergo a psychological phenomenon known as the **frustration-aggression syndrome.** When a consumer does not receive the satisfaction expected from a purchase, or feels a marketer is acting unethically, he or she gets angry. This anger is a form of frustration which, when not alleviated, is converted into aggressive behavior, often directed toward a marketer. When consumers' expectations about marketers' performance are poorly fulfilled, they are apt to react militantly and this aggressiveness itself has satisfying and reinforcing qualities.

The History, Meaning, and Development of Consumerism

Consumerism has been defined or described in various ways, among them the following:

- Consumerism expresses itself in efforts to bring pressure on business firms as well as government to correct business conduct thought unethical.[12]
- The most common understanding of consumerism is in reference to the widening range of activities of government, business, and independent organizations which are designed to protect individuals from practices (of both business and government) that infringe upon their rights as consumers.[13]

---

[12] David W. Cravens and Gerald E. Mills, "Consumerism: A Perspective for Business," *Business Horizons,* August 1970, p. 21.
[13] George S. Day and David Aaker, "A Guide to Consumerism," *Journal of Marketing* **34** (July 1970), p. 13.

- The organized efforts of consumers seeking redress, restitution, and remedy for dissatisfactions they have accumulated in the acquisition of their standard of living.[14]

Regardless of which definition is embraced, the underlying theme is evident. Consumerism is related to several major issues: consumer choice, information, protection, and representation; all of these areas embody the consumers' organized effort to promote their interests.[15]

Consumerism grew markedly during the past two decades and it still takes its creed and manifesto from the so-called consumers' bill of rights. These rights include:

1. The right to safety: to be protected against the marketing of goods hazardous to health or life.
2. The right to be informed: to be protected against fraudulent, deceitful, or grossly misleading information, advertising, labeling, or other practices, and to be given the facts needed to make an informed choice.
3. The right to choose: to be assured, wherever possible, access to a variety of products and services at competitive prices; and in those industries in which competition is not workable and government regulation is substituted, to be assured of satisfactory quality and service at a fair price.
4. The right to be heard: to be assured that consumer interests will receive full and sympathetic consideration in the formulation of government policy, and fair and expeditious treatment in its administrative tribunals.

To promote the fuller realization of these consumer rights, consumers have organized, and now voice their grievances.

Emergence of Consumerism.   Consumerism in a free society is the natural outgrowth of many factors: consumer unrest from rising price levels, exposés by the American press and the general literature of unhealthful and fraudulent business practices, and a paternalistic government with a growing concern for the consumer's welfare. In short, for many years consumers have been sensitized to expect more than they were getting.

What the Movement Has Achieved

Consumerism as an organized, on-going social and economic protest has succeeded in raising business's level of social responsiveness and in generating more interest in social marketing. It is perhaps fair to say that though its success rate is certainly well below 100 percent, the movement has advanced the cause of consumer rights by insisting on safer goods, providing more information, and adding to the fund of alternatives from which consumers can

---

[14] Richard H. Buskirk and James T. Rothe, "Consumerism: An Interpretation," *Journal of Marketing* **34** (October 1970), p. 62.
[15] See Donald W. Hendon, "Toward a Theory of Consumerism: *Business Horizons*, August 1975, pp. 16–24.

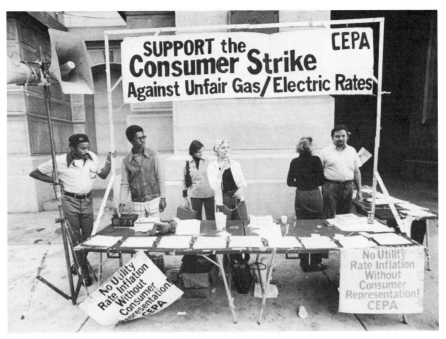

An example of the consumer movement.

choose. Finally, the movement has been a powerful force for instilling new sensitivity into business and government, impressing them with the consumers' right to be heard.

Consumerism has won these gains through the combined efforts of consumer groups, government, and business.

Consumer Groups.   Consumer groups have been the vocal vanguard of the consumer movement. Although attempts to organize a national consumer movement have met with mixed success, local, regional, and statewide organizations now flourish. Today there are consumer organizations in most major cities and counties of the country. In many instances, state and local organizations have been successful in obtaining legislation on very specific issues. These local and regional efforts are usually dependent on parttime, nonprofessional, volunteer staffs, thus compounding the difficulty of maintaining continuing programs. However, such groups have proved useful in providing the needed support for state and local representatives who are sympathetic to consumer problems.

Business.   The response of business to consumerism's demands has not always been positive. Business reactions have run the entire gamut from (1) "Deny everything," (2) "Pass the buck," (3) "Discredit the critics," (4) "Hire a public relations firm," (5) "Defang the legislation," and (6) "Launch a fact-finding committee," through (7) "Actually do something."

The response of individual firms is varied, but in general there has been an increasing tendency for business firms, especially the more socially responsible ones, to listen better. Other efforts have included providing more and better information, toning down the rhetoric of sales and advertising programs, improving product warranties and guarantees, the adoption of unit pricing, abandoning trading stamps, recalling defective products, deleting hazardous products, improving packages and packaging materials, promoting recycling, and discontinuing price specials intended as bait advertising. Some firms have actually reorganized so that consumers are at the center of the corporate universe. They have established separate divisions for consumer affairs concentrating on consumer complaints, better product design, and information.

Some firms are acknowledging the validity of the aroused consumer by implementing simple but effective systems of two-way communication. In one such plan, RCA Whirlpool installed a "cool line" telephone service by which consumers can dial the firm direct to register their complaints about its products and service or the practices of its dealers.

Government. Government at all levels has been particularly responsive to the consumer movement. The states are often champions of consumer oriented actions and causes. Most states now have consumer fraud bureaus in their attorney general's offices and many have consumer councils as well as consumer protection offices. Consumers' expectations regarding government's role in the consumer movement are rising, and government appears to be responding readily. Among the many laws relating to consumer affairs that have been passed in recent years are the Fair Credit Reporting Act of 1970, the Consumer Product Safety Act of 1972, the Motor Vehicle Information and Cost Saving Act, and the Transportation Safety Act of 1974.

Impending legislation would establish a permanent consumer protection agency within the White House as well as a consumer protection division within the Justice Department; would beef up the 1966 Fair Packaging and Labeling Act; and would set up a federal body to develop standards of quality, size and form, and definitions of identity. These would be designated as United States "official standards" and would have standing in international markets.

It appears likely that the coming years will see federal, state, and local governments adopt much additional consumer legislation. Business groups will launch more consumer education services. Consumer associations will lobby more aggressively and we can expect more pressure on federal agencies to enforce existing laws with greater vigor.

Consumerism: An Expanded Meaning

The final challenge of consumerism for business and marketers is to end hunger and malnutrition; alleviate pollution of the air, water, and soil; educate and train the disadvantaged; to eliminate these and other social wrongs rather than solving strictly industrial problems. Today, consumerism is the philosophy, indeed the battle cry, of the socially conscious consumer. The movement is

Table 19-2 Contrast Between Economic and Social Orientation

Economic Man	Social Man
Production	Distribution
Quantity	Quality
Goods and services	People
Money values	Human values
Work and discipline	Self-realization
Competition	Cooperation
Laissez-faire	Involvement
Inflation	Unemployment

turning more of its attention to the quality of the physical environment and the impact of marketing practices and technology on the ecology. The movement will not likely abate.

Consumerism will not only remain a force with which marketers must contend in the future but will broaden its concern to include atomic energy, ecology, medicine, chemistry, conservation, economics, manufacturing, and all those promotion and selling activities that come under the term *marketing*. Our marketing systems and the business philosophy underlying them are clearly undergoing drastic change. Marketers' interest in consumers must reflect the new ethic of consumerism and must be concerned with both humanism and ecology. We are faced with the prospect of a consumer oriented economy in which the individual is regarded as having a natural inclination toward excellence and self-improvement as well as wanting improvement of the overall environment.[16]

Marketers: Economic or Social Man?

Much of the marketers' dilemma can be traced to the conflict between economic and social man—a confrontation that stems from marketers' concern with earning a living on the one hand and living with their fellows on the other, in short, the paradox of "making a living" versus "making a life." Those who are primarily economically oriented see life differently from the more socially oriented. Even those with a more balanced view are likely to be torn by conflicting beliefs.

It is easy to overdraw a generalization, including the contrast between economic and social values and concerns, but Table 19-2 gives a fairly adequate shorthand definition.

As can be seen, marketers are often too deeply steeped in the economic values to appreciate the social values as reflected in increased social responsibilities, consumerism, and social marketing. But the times are changing. Marketers are, and must be, more sensitive to the needs of society as voiced

[16] Hiram C. Barksdale and William D. Perreault, Jr., "Can Consumers Be Satisfied?" *MSU Business Topics*, **28**, no. 2 (Spring 1980), pp. 19–30.

Tomorrow's consumers—will they be different?

by the social person in a consumer oriented economy. Marketers are beginning to make the boundary between the public and private sectors less rigid. Social marketing can enable all of us to reap the rewards of sociocommercial enterprise; it will be the framework for the marketing strategies of the 1980s.

Marketing in The Future

Marketing decision making has always required an orientation both to the present and the future. The former is necessary for stability and continuity, the latter for change and adaptability. However, while both are essential, today's environment requires much heavier reliance on a long-range perspective than formerly.

Marketing in the 1990s will emerge out of the environmental conditions of the 1980s. Among the many dynamic forces shaping the decade will be advancing technology, resource shortages, rapid inflation, wide swings in the business cycle, and changing social values, most of which have been chronicled throughout this text.[17] Consider again, however, how some of these conditions will mold and shape marketing strategy during the next decade.[18]

[17] For a look at the environment of the future, see Jon G. Udell, Gene R. Laczniak, and Robert F. Lusch, "The Business Environment of 1985," *Business Horizons,* June 1976.
[18] Based upon Burt Navus, "The Future-Oriented Corporation," *Business Horizons,* February 1975, pp. 5–12.

Values in Transition. Such fundamental values as the role of the family, the quality of life, the work ethic, the social responsibilities of business are being significantly reinterpreted. If the values of the future are to be considerably different from those of the present, then it seems reasonable to assume that today's market preferences will be poor indicators of tomorrow's demand for goods and services.

Increasing Complexities. In the future things will be even more complicated than they are today. The current energy crisis is an accurate foretaste of the intricate interrelationship of political, economic, and technological factors in the years ahead and the enormous significance this complexity holds for marketing decision making.

The Acceleration of Change. The environment of the future will not be static. Rapid changes and the acceleration of technological advances virtually assure shorter product life cycles and quicker reaction times. At the same time the costs and lead time needed to develop new marketing programs and alter existing ones are increasing, so there is more at stake in these critical decisions.

More Consumerism Will Breed More Social Responsibility. As we learn more about the fragile ecosystems in which we live and our vulnerability to shortages of resources, marketers will strive to preserve resources and recycle wastes. At the same time they will be much more concerned with the interdependence of international marketing. This deeper understanding alone will trigger major changes within the marketing oriented firm in the next decade.

Marketers Must Be Future Oriented

Marketing firms must, in light of these environmental changes, become more future oriented without ignoring decisions that must be made in the present. What will be the nature of such organizations? They will each have their separate and identifiable character but certain general operating principles will be evident.

First, future oriented marketers will take responsibility for *creating* their own future whenever possible, while *adapting* to uncontrollable change when necessary through a continuous process of future research, long-range planning, and objectives setting. The probable long-range consequences of all decision making will guide strategic marketing planning.

Second, foresighted marketing firms will operate on the assumption that the future is the most important resource available to any organization and that like any other resource it must be managed carefully.

Third and finally, the marketer who looks to the future places a high value on anticipation of change and the systematic design of marketing operations to meet it as opposed to merely reacting to change that has already occurred. Marketers must squarely face the fact that decisions taken today do constrain and influence the future and that there is no way to avoid such decisions. However, farsighted managers will also lengthen their time horizons and broaden their search for opportunities.

The Coming Changes in Marketing Strategy.   The future is nearly upon us. The year 1985 is not so far away. Therefore, marketing strategy in the 1990s should not really be so hard to predict. Marketing success in the 1980s and the 1990s will still be attained by having the right product linked with the right promotion at the right price in the right place. Customer orientation, still the essence of the marketing concept and the underpinning of the marketing strategy, will be based upon three fundamental ideas.

- The satisfaction of consumer wants is the social and economic justification for a company's existence; providing this satisfaction is also the means to attaining customer patronage and earning a profit.
- Profits are a major incentive for being in business and a prerequisite for remaining in business.
- The profitable satisfaction of customer wants requires the integration and coordination of all business activities.[19]

The marketing concept will be increasingly applied to *serving the public,* not just *servicing consumers.* This means a greater potential for the use of marketing concepts and strategy by nonprofit institutions as well as by marketing professionals who are interested in expanding their public service role. Potential areas of application would include urban public transportation; government enterprises such as the United States Postal Service, the Tennessee Valley Authority, and the Bonneville Power Authority; universities, churches, and birth control and health care services. In the future, nonbusiness institutions will serve the public more effectively by using marketing know-how.[20]

The Consumer. The consumer of the future will likely be tougher, more volatile, more affluent, have a wider range of individual tastes and preferences, and will probably be more unpredictable. In the future the poor will be richer and the rich a little poorer; the blacks will think whiter and the whites blacker; the blue and white collars will intermingle and the whole population will grow slightly more homogeneous. Yet consumers will want to break from the homogenized masses to be individualistic in their personal life styles and therefore in their purchases.

Family spending will probably follow a pattern of "conspicuous conservation" dictated by economic necessity while changing American life styles. Four basic factors will determine spending in the future: saving energy, alterations in economic and demographic patterns, new technologies, and shifting values. The need to save fuel in particular may change people's perceptions of what constitutes a good life. Energy demanding products and activities may be expensive, and if the ethic gains acceptance, unpopular. Inflation will diminish purchasing power in many households, forcing people to change their consumption patterns whether they wish to or not. Consumers faced with the necessity to spend less because they have less may come to look on the decrease as desirable because it saves energy.

Consumer values will change in the future. Outward-directed consumers, those who buy to impress others and set national consumption patterns, will be replaced in part by the inward-directed, those who buy to satisfy inner needs and create highly fragmented markets. Such inward-directed consumers are likely to embrace the conservation ethic.

---

[19] From Robert F. Lusch, Jon G. Udell, and Gene Laczniak, "The Future of Marketing Strategy," *Business Horizons,* December 1976, pp. 65–74. This article forms the basis of much of this section.
[20] David W. Cravens, "Marketing Decisions in the Decade Ahead," *Atlanta Economic Review* **24** (September–October 1974), pp. 4–8.

There will continue to be a sharp rise in the number of two-earner families, with a big chunk of the extra money they spend—about 40 percent—going for transportation. American families will spend considerably more for transportation than they will for food.

Consumers generally will be older in the late 1980s and early 1990s but the older consumer will still strive and spend to stay youthful. The key shift in the age mix of the population will be the advance of post-World War II babies toward middle age. By 1985, Americans between the ages of 35 and 39 will number 17.2 million, a jump of 48 percent over 1975. This group will comprise 7.3 percent of the population instead of the 5.4 percent they made up ten years earlier. By 1985, there will be fewer Americans in their late 40s and early 50s. Also reduced will be the hordes of teenagers who, during the 1970s, set so much of the style in consumer markets.

Product Strategy.   Great attention will be devoted to product strategy in the next decade. Like today, it will be concerned with the ways products and services are designed, improved, and eventually abandoned. Technical research, development, and testing of new products, combined with customer oriented marketing research, already important aspects of product strategy, will be even more critical. Conspicuous conservation will generate demand for many new products like electric automobiles, motor bikes, heat pumps, high performance insulation, and electronic devices for controlling household temperature, cooking, and lighting. We can also expect innovations such as video phones and shopping by computer-assisted cable television, both of which will substitute communications for transportation.

Style, design, and packaging of new products will likely be more utilitarian and slightly less pleasing to the eye. Furthermore, to conserve resources, product lines may be somewhat narrowed and throwaway products and planned product obsolescence will be grossly out-of-step with the new consumer ethic and the consumer's perception of the social responsibilities of the marketing firm.

Because of the increasing technological emphasis on product, both *presale* and *postsale* service may be increasingly considered integral parts of the "total product concept."

Promotional Strategy.   Truth in advertising and in all aspects of promotional effort will be an absolute must in the economic environment of the future. The emphasis in promotion may well shift from stimulating demand to getting the greatest possible benefits from the product, making it last, and curbing the consumer's ardor for more and more possessions. Consumer pressures will force companies to reevaluate the form and content of the promotional warranties they offer to induce buyers to choose their product.

The shortage economy of the 1980s may witness a decline per dollar of sales in the actual outlays for all promotional efforts. Yet product branding and promotional expenditures for market penetration and product positioning will continue to be the focus of many marketing firms' promotional efforts. Personal selling will become slightly more important while the development of sales managers will be a major activity for industrial marketers. In addition, markets are likely to be more specialized and segmented in the future, requiring more specialized forms of promotion.

Pricing Strategy.   Prices will be higher in the 1980s and 1990s for nearly all merchandise and service categories primarily because of the economy's inflationary tendency, which will mean a rising cost of doing business. Because price levels in the future, like those at present, will be determined largely on the basis of average cost pricing policies, these increased costs will push general price levels higher. There will be a tendency for most firms to price their products competitively but the major firms will continue to charge what the traffic will bear. However, a militant consumerism and the business community's increasing acceptance of social responsibility will curb unconscionable price increases and windfall profits. All firms will feel the need, however, to maximize their returns on their investment. To a great extent, the achievement of such a goal is the consumers' and public's assurance that the firm is utilizing its resources efficiently and effectively and fulfilling its social franchise. Both federal and state governments will set more pricing and profit guidelines for business firms, leading to some retraction in free market forces and additional government regulations.

Distribution Strategy.   Distribution strategy will be critically important in the future, more so perhaps than any other element in the marketing mix, because it accounts for so much of the price of products and because marketers have spent less on research and improvement in this area than they have on the other elements. Increased fuel and energy costs will justify a great deal of innovation in distribution and will force more attention on getting the product to customers with the best possible service and least transportation cost. Warehousing and inventory control will be heavily emphasized. Furthermore, managers will be much more careful in determining basic channels of distribution to be used in marketing products and services and more critical in selecting individual establishments for distributing goods. For many products in high demand and short supply, selective distribution will be much more widely utilized. And, there will be a pronounced tendency for more channel captaincy by the larger, better-known manufacturer-marketer because these firms will play a dominant role in developing and assisting the other members of the marketing channel.

Strategic Remarketing.   Marketing strategy in the future will reflect what is now being called strategic remarketing.[21] The marketer must consistently reexamine market needs and opportunities in both the long and short run. Then, as a part of strategy, the marketer must redetermine the best markets to be in,

---

[21] Philip Kotler and V. Balachandran, "Strategic Remarketing: The Preferred Response to Shortages and Inflation," *Sloan Management Review*, Fall 1975, pp. 1–17.

customers to serve, and competitors to compete with, so as to maximize the company's long-run profitability. The marketer must develop and implement plans for a transition to the future market position he or she wants to occupy. The crux of strategic remarketing is that it does not spell out specifically what the marketer should do with prices, products, advertising, and distribution. Instead, it calls for quick adjustment, ready accommodation, and suppleness to permit the changes in the marketing mix demanded by the current situation.

Before proceeding, can you answer these questions:
1. What is consumerism? List and discuss what has come to be called "the consumer's bill of rights."
2. Describe several of the main features of the marketing environment of the future.
3. What is meant by "strategic remarketing"?

The Innovative Marketer

For the past three decades the Western nations and Japan have been evolving toward a postindustrial society. We will have reached it when technological advancements and economic developments have made the task of producing and distributing the necessities of life trivially easy. However, we have not yet attained full postindustrial development, nor are we likely to in anything approaching the near term. Figure 19-5 shows us something of our progress, however: what we have done in the past, the problems we face in the present, and the prospects for the future.

In advancing from the present to the future, marketers will have to deal with the problems of transition to a postindustrial society. To reach the future and to help create the postindustrial society, they will have to be innovative in their thinking. Marketers must develop and implement innovative strategies. Innovation is not usually a technical term; it is more often an economic and social one. It generally refers to a change in social or economic behavior, the way people do things. It can take place within or outside of an organization. The measure of an organization's innovativeness is its impact on the environment. This means that innovation in a business enterprise must always be market focused.

Like any other marketing strategy, an innovative strategy starts out with the question "What is our business and what should it be?"[22] However, the underlying assumption of an innovative strategy is that whatever exists—product lines and services, present markets, present technologies, present distribution channels—is aging. Entropy, or the statistical tendency for things to run down

---

[22] See Peter F. Drucker, *Management: Tasks, Responsibilities and Practices* (New York: Harper and Row, 1974), especially chapter 61. Remember that our earlier discussion, in chapter 1, also began with that central question.

Figure 19-5   The great transition

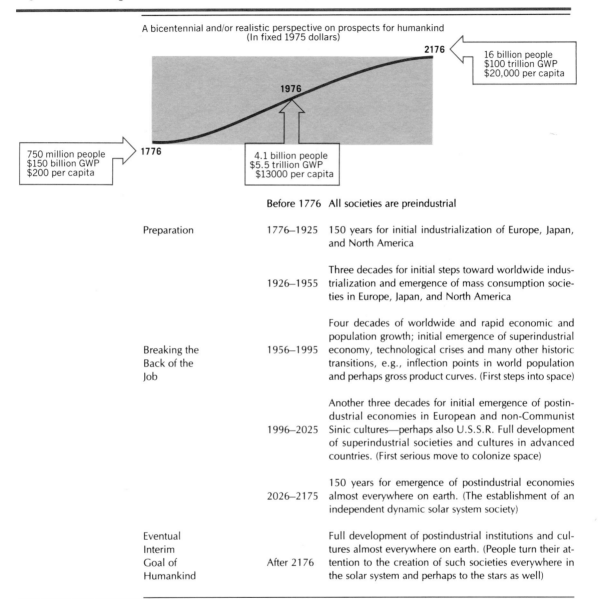

A bicentennial and/or realistic perspective on prospects for humankind
(In fixed 1975 dollars)

2176 — 16 billion people / $100 trillion GWP / $20,000 per capita

1976 — 4.1 billion people / $5.5 trillion GWP / $13000 per capita

1776 — 750 million people / $150 billion GWP / $200 per capita

	Before 1776	All societies are preindustrial
Preparation	1776–1925	150 years for initial industrialization of Europe, Japan, and North America
	1926–1955	Three decades for initial steps toward worldwide industrialization and emergence of mass consumption societies in Europe, Japan, and North America
Breaking the Back of the Job	1956–1995	Four decades of worldwide and rapid economic and population growth; initial emergence of superindustrial economy, technological crises and many other historic transitions, e.g., inflection points in world population and perhaps gross product curves. (First steps into space)
	1996–2025	Another three decades for initial emergence of postindustrial economies in European and non-Communist Sinic cultures—perhaps also U.S.S.R. Full development of superindustrial societies and cultures in advanced countries. (First serious move to colonize space)
	2026–2175	150 years for emergence of postindustrial economies almost everywhere on earth. (The establishment of an independent dynamic solar system society)
Eventual Interim Goal of Humankind	After 2176	Full development of postindustrial institutions and cultures almost everywhere on earth. (People turn their attention to the creation of such societies everywhere in the solar system and perhaps to the stars as well)

Source: Herman Kahn, William Brown, and Leon Martel. *The Next 200 Years* (New York: Morrow, 1976), p. 6.

and wear out, faces the firm, its products, and its markets. The watchword then for the innovative marketer is "New and Different"; that of the noninnovative firm may be "Better and More." The basis of an innovative strategy is systematic discarding of the old, the dying, the obsolete. Systematic abandonment of yesterday alone can free the firm's resources for work on the new. In the innovative organization, the first and most important job of management is to convert half-baked, wild ideas into concrete innovative reality. Obviously there will be much of this to do in coming years.

The marketer who promotes change, who builds bridges between the present and the future, who meets crisis with new solutions, and resists stagnation is the major hope for our future. That such organizations are possible there can be no denying. We have had some in the past, there are some today, and some will emerge in the future. But the task looming ahead is how to promote innovative enterprises more widely and on a larger scale.[23] How can we make them more productive for society, the economy, and the individual alike? There is every indication that the period ahead will be an innovative one, a time of rapid change in consumption, technology, institutions and values, business ethics, and consumer attitudes. Thus, the innovative marketer has the potential for becoming a paramount institution—a social-innovative force for the last decades of the twentieth century. How about it? Will you help? Will you be a part of the problem or part of the solution?

Summary

The coming period of intensifying energy shortages will have a strong impact on marketing in the 1980s. Our consumption patterns will change; nearly everything we buy or want to buy will be more scarce and will consequently cost more money. Our attitudes and values about consuming and marketing practices will probably change. All of this is likely to bring about a new marketing era.

Marketing in the new era will reflect the environment of which it is a part. It will play an increasingly important role in "selling" energy programs, reminding us to turn down thermostats, use less hot water, to conserve more and waste less of everything. Social marketing will mature as a discipline to induce awareness, awaken interest and attention, and to provoke action in the interest, not just of increased sales for a firm, but also of society's and the consumer's welfare.

During the 1980s there will be a renewed interest in social responsibility as practiced by the marketing oriented enterprise and a continuing and even more militant surge of consumerism. Businesses will be expected to satisfy a wide range of human needs, expand their resources to social fields, and consider the social impact of their programs when evaluating them. Social responsibility will be more widely embraced as a corporate philosophy because of the business community's growing awareness of business ethics and because of pressures from concerned, militant consumers—consumerism. The growing trend toward business regulation by government will also encourage greater social responsibility.

---

[23] Reginald H. Jones, "Managing in the 1980's," An Executive Speech Reprint, General Electric Company, Presented at the Wharton School, University of Pennsylvania, Philadelphia, PA, February, 4, 1980.

Marketing in 1985 will still be the dynamic, exciting activity it is today. The marketing strategy of 1985 will still focus on consumer needs and wants, and the firm will respond with its own unique version of the marketing mix. Innovative marketers will help us to cope with and accommodate to the many changes stirring in the environment of that period. Innovative marketing is the bridge between the present and the future, a future that will see the emergence of a real postindustrial society.

Review Questions

1. How will marketing be affected by a serious energy shortage? Give some specific examples.
2. What is meant by "the social responsibilities of business"? Do marketers have responsibilities other than making money?
3. What are business ethics? How do they affect the concept of social responsibility?
4. What are externalities? What changes are likely to occur in the future concerning business's creation of adverse externalities?
5. Packages that litter and cannot be recycled create adverse externalities. Explain.
6. What have been two major responses to business irresponsibilities?
7. Consumerism, social responsibility, and government regulation all have led to a marketing reorientation. Explain and assess the implications of this reorientation.
8. What is the difference between a marketer as an economic man and as a social man.
9. What is meant by social marketing?
10. What is strategic remarketing? Is it important to the innovative marketer?

Case 19-1

The Trident Company

The Trident Company was founded in 1946, after World War II. It began as a small firm that produced hand tools which were sold directly to large mail order firms and other large retailers. The firm's product line was gradually expanded throughout the years to include three major lines: (1) electrical or battery powered hand tools such as drills, saws, planes, routers, and so on; (2) hand-held electrical or battery powered home appliances such as mixers and blenders; and (3) a line of home equipment accessories such as bathroom and kitchen exhaust fans, sump pumps, and automatic garage door openers. Trident had ceased selling its products through mail order firms because such companies wished to place their own distribution labels on these products and because they bought almost strictly on a "price for quality" basis. That is, the mail order firms stipulated the price they wished to sell the product for at retail and the quality level desired. A company like Trident then had to produce such a product and try desperately to come in with one that met the buyer's specifications and still permitted the manufacturer to make a profit. Trident managers disliked this squeeze and in the mid-1950s, therefore, the company began selling through wholesalers and large retailers, their own branded products in each of the three lines. The company has had considerable market success; sales in 1980 amounted to nearly $75 million and generated profits of $3.75 million.

In late 1981, prior to the beginning of the company's annual review of operations which always precedes the corporate planning session for the following year, the vice president and director of corporate market planning made the following statement at a meeting of the executive committee for corporate planning and development:

The continuing energy crisis may likely have a serious impact on our operation. Strict guidelines will be laid down to produce highly efficient irons, hair dryers, refrigerators, electric ranges, and the like. In the long run, thriftier appliances will help consumers to offset, at least in part, rising energy costs. Stringent efficiency standards will also be mandated for factory equipment. On the whole, this program is indeed comprehensive, and its thrust is in the right direction. However, I don't really see that it should affect our company for some time to come.

Questions

1. If you were the chief executive officer of Trident, how would you respond to the statement of the vice president and director of corporate market planning?
2. Suppose you were the vice president and director of corporate market planning and the chief executive officer responded to your statement as follows:

Well, I believe that our company had better begin preparing for the new era of energy shortages now, and I would like you to develop for us a comprehensive plan as to how we can best do it. What will the national energy program mean to our firm in terms of the following: product development, new market opportunities, promotion strategy, distribution policies, and pricing.

Prepare a two-or three-page report that responds to the directive of the chief executive officer.

Case 19-2

Gulf and Western Industries

Gulf and Western Industries is one of the world's largest conglomerates. Its sales approach $3.5 billion. The company, however, is currently under three separate governmental investigations. The SEC (Securities and Exchange Commission) is looking into, among other things, the adequacy of the company's public disclosure in connection with Gulf and Western's securities, the company's pension fund, and its dealings in the shares of an auto parts subsidiary that had some stock traded on the over-the-counter exchange. The New York State Senate Committee on Crime and Correction is examining the possibility that organized crime may be linked to the operations of Madison Square Garden Corporation, another Gulf and Western affiliate. One middle-level employee describes the current atmosphere at G&W as "paranoid." Management was startled when a routine registration statement filed lately by Associates First Capital Corporation, a financial-services subsidiary of Gulf and Western, was rejected by the SEC because of incomplete disclosure. Stockholders have suffered even more anguish because of the drop in the company's stock; it has sagged by more than 20 percent in 1977, leaving the conglomerate in the humiliating position of selling for less than $14 a share, or $8 a share below book value.

Gulf and Western's problems were begun, in part, by a lawyer named Joel Dolkart. He was Gulf and Western's general counsel for almost twenty years and a close friend and associate of G&W's chairman and chief executive officer, Charles Bluhdorn. In 1974 Dolkart was indicted on 89 counts for stealing $2.5 million through fraudulent checks from law firms representing Gulf and Western. Dolkart pleaded guilty to one count of forgery in 1975, and was sentenced to a jail term of up to three years. Because he "cooperated" with the SEC and the

district attorney, Dolkart received several stays in the execution of his sentence. But even though he gave the SEC sealed testimony on G&W's transactions that was called "reliable and objective," New York State Supreme Court Justice James Leff ordered that Dolkart begin serving his time in July 1977. In an angry mood the judge declared, "The real danger is the cynicism that is engendered when, at the level at which this kind of fraud takes place, the general public believes that ultimately there isn't any effective sanction which will punish or which will be feared by these corporate thieves."

If the legal probes were not giving G&W managers enough headaches, there were problems with several subsidiary companies ranging from Paramount Pictures in Hollywood to New Jersey Zinc, Inc. While operating revenues for the first three quarters of fiscal year 1977 were up 7.2 percent, net income was down 11 percent because of depressed prices for sugar and paper, products of two big G&W divisions. The company's enormous long-term debt of $1.1 billion must be serviced, at high cost. A large investment portfolio that includes stakes in such companies as Simmons (mattresses and bedding products), Wurlitzer (juke boxes), Amfac (sugar, processed foods, hotels), Esquire (magazines), and a Japanese maker of coin operated machines has added little to G&W's successes or fortunes.

Charles Bluhdorn, the company's chairman of the board, has often characterized Gulf and Western by saying, "We are not a conventional company, and we are never going to be a conventional company."

Questions

1. When companies like Gulf and Western have such legal difficulties, what impact does this have on

a. Consumerism and the consumer movement?

b. Those who feel that government ought to impose stricter regulations on business enterprise?

2. Do you agree with the judge's statement that in such situations, "The real danger is the cynicism that is engendered when, at the level at which this kind of fraud takes place, the general public believes that ultimately there isn't any effective sanction which will punish or which will be feared by these corporate thieves."

3. Does the case of G&W substantiate the criticisms of big business discussed in the text?

4. Suppose you have been asked to give a presentation before a consumer advocate group on "The Relevance of Social Responsibility" and after making your presentation a member of the audience suggests that the payment of bribes by firms like Lockheed and questionable practices such as those of Gulf and Western make the concepts of social responsibility, business ethics, and social marketing just so many "buzz words, empty phrases and concepts to cover up the true nature of business, which is rapacious greed." How would you respond?

Appendix

Careers in Marketing: How to Market Yourself

Introduction

For every student the time eventually comes when we must leave the sanctuary of the college or university campus and go forth in the world—sometimes called the real world—to market our skills and abilities. At this time we begin a personal journey toward fulfilling the goals and ambitions forged during our years of preparatory work. Toward the end of this preparatory period, we come face to face with the problem of getting our first major, career oriented job.

Getting a job, especially the right job, is a challenging task requiring considerable marketing skill. You are, after all, marketing a product—yourself—and you will have to do a lot of persuasive communicating to convince a prospective employer that you have what they need. Marketing, you remember, facilitates transactions and a transaction occurs when things of value are exchanged, in this case your abilities for the employer's money.

As an astute marketer yourself now, sit down and analyze the situation, your own and that of the market, and ask yourself "How can I best develop a plan for marketing myself?" This appendix is a set of suggestions to enable you to do just that, to guide your thinking and direct you to some sources of information and ideas which, it is hoped, will assist you in your task.

Planning Your Future

The secret to attaining goals is to plan well in advance. This is the essential principle in your own professional preparation and development, in evaluating your personal market opportunity, and in seeking a job. Planning, however, must be paired with flexibility, because the world is changing. Don't plan for a career that may be nonexistent when you're ready to launch yourself as a "new-product offering." You should start doing some thinking now about what the future business world will be like, because that's where your career lies. It isn't easy to predict the future, but sometimes it can be glimpsed in the present.

Trends That Will Affect Your Future

There are several trends, all of which are quite clear, that will affect your future and the employment and career opportunities you should be considering now. Let's discuss some of these briefly.

Energy Shortages.

Chapter 19 detailed the seriousness of the growing energy shortages in our own economy and worldwide. These shortages will create shock waves in many enterprises and the traditional ways of doing things will change. Many jobs will be eliminated, practices we have taken for granted will be abandoned, and whole industries may even disappear. Yet, problems are opportunities in disguise. Industries, products, and marketing institutions undreamed of today will surely emerge, creating new employment and career opportunities. You will need to monitor and assess the coming changes in energy usage and development carefully because the energy options chosen will affect your future employment and, consequently, your employment choices. The energy shortage may accelerate a trend toward reurbanization—people moving out of the suburbs back to the central city. More homes in the future may be apartments in multistoried buildings located close to major transportation terminals such as bus lines, commuter trains, or even airlines. Cities may become more attractive; retail stores may favor the downtown central business district they once fled over the outlying controlled shopping center. Many of the drive-in facilities so numerous in the 1970s—banks, dry cleaners, laundries, restaurants, and so on, may relocate to take advantage of increased foot traffic downtown.

Leisure, Technology, and Materialism.

Technology has greatly reduced the amount of labor required to produce a given level of output and has resulted in an extremely high standard of living for many throughout the world. We stand on the threshold of the Post Industrial Society, a period which will stress services over tangible goods, the importance of leisure and the aesthetic life, and which may signal some downturn in the striving for success as measured by the possession of material goods. Employment opportunities in such fields as recreation, tourism, hobbies and crafts, and restaurant and hospitality industries will surely grow as working hours shrink and vacations and leisure time expand.

Longer Life Expectancy.

One of the marvels of medical science is that it keeps us alive longer. It is a clear fact that Americans are living not only longer, but healthier lives as well. When older persons are healthier, they are also more active and this activity, when supported by increased financial strength from private pensions and Social Security, means more market or consuming power. The proportion of persons 60 years of age or older in the total population is increasing and in the near future, our society may, at last, lose its youth orientation. This will create far-reaching merchandising and marketing changes—new products, new channels, and new promotional themes will accommodate the many senior citizens of our culture. You should also plan to compete with older workers for the job you may want. There is an increasing trend against early retirement and therefore you will probably have to work and compete with older workers on an equal basis.

Women's Rights.

In every field of endeavor there are growing opportunities for women, who will keep pressing for even more career equality in the years ahead. One out of every two households today has a working wife. This means greater family income, more purchasing power, and a changing package of goods and services in many households—more cars, more leisure products, second homes, ready-to-eat meals, more travel, and more dining out. It spells greater opportunity for women and perhaps more competition for men. As we become a more egalitarian culture in sex and race, the nature of marketing practices as well as employment opportunities will shift.

Smaller Families and Changing Life Style.

If current birth rates continue, families in the 1980s and beyond will become smaller, with corresponding changes in life styles. Families of no more than two children will be common and couples with one child or none will not be unusual. Many family decision makers, husbands and wives, have simply opted for smaller families in order to improve their standards of living. More couples in the future will choose life styles which do not include formal marriage contracts. This will alter our conventional notion of the family life style altogether. All these changes will result in shifting marketing practices. Builders will put up smaller houses; apartments, and multiple-family dwellings may be featured over single-family residences. Food marketers and processors will package in smaller units; and toy manufacturers may diversify, produce fewer units of products, or build more quality and expensive units. Childless couples may have fewer pets, and this may impact negatively on pet food manufacturers' sales and product assortments.

Other Trends.

It is impossible to catalog and discuss all the trends that might affect your employment future. Yet there are others that should at least be acknowledged, if only to alert you to future possibilities such developments may hold. First, remember that the world is becoming smaller. You may wish to begin thinking in terms of global or international marketing employment opportunities. Tensions throughout the world are hopefully lessening and as this occurs wars may be replaced with a more wholesome form of international competition—trade. The Eastern Bloc countries, the Eurocommunists, and even the truculent Red Chinese are showing increasing signs of wanting to exchange goods, technology, and even ideas. As we become more international in our outlook and as trade flourishes, the United States will find itself more vulnerable to imports and some of our basic industries may decline seriously. This could occur in steel, television and radio, textiles, footwear, and even automobiles.

Career Possibilities: What They Are and Where to Find Them

Training in marketing and knowledge of its processes equip one to pursue a career in a number of marketing related fields. Even during times of severe economic downturn—sometimes especially during such times—marketing skills are critically needed and oftentimes during such periods the marketing trades flourish. In business the saying goes that nothing really happens until somebody markets something. To get an economy or a particular business moving, marketing activity is frequently accelerated. More people are hired, new products to stimulate sluggish buyers are launched calling for more promotional effort and more personal selling and marketing services in general are expanded.

Marketing careers abound in nonprofit organizations as well. So in pursuing a career in marketing or in a marketing related venture, you can choose from innumerable specific occupations to be found in a number of industry opportunities. Appendix Table 1 will give you some idea of the scope of the opportunities.

It is virtually impossible to list and describe all the jobs one might consider in this large field. However, as a marketer you could examine the following general areas.

Product Management.

Product management is concerned with planning, organizing, and controlling a number of given products. Many firms consider each product or product group as a separately identifiable part of their business. In such firms product management is an important midlevel management position. People at this level deal with all aspects of the company's business. Product management is an integral part of many consumer goods as well as industrial goods companies.

Marketing Research.

Marketing research consists of the collection and analysis of data from both primary and secondary sources. The market researcher plans market studies, consumer surveys, and the implementation of research projects. Appendix Exhibit 1 is a detailed description of marketing research work. The exhibit is a good example of the kind of information available in the *Occupational Outlook Handbook*, a publica-

Appendix Table 1 Marketing Career Paths

These Occupations

May be Undertaken in These
Industry Opportunities

Occupations	Industry Opportunities
— Marketing planning and sales analysis	— Manufacturing Consumer Industrial
— Product management	
— New-product development	— Government Local, regional
— Marketing research	State National
— Advertising	International
— Public relations	
	— Retailing
— Sales management	
— General merchandising and promotion	— Service trades Banking and finance Stock and commodity marketing Management consulting
— Personal selling	
— Physical distribution and channel management	Real estate
— Marketing systems analysis	— Nonprofit organizations

Exhibit 1 Marketing Research Workers

Nature of the Work

Businesses require a great deal of information to make sound decisions on how to market their products. Marketing research workers provide much of this information by analyzing data on products and sales, making surveys, and conducting interviews. They prepare sales forecasts and make recommendations on product design and advertising.

Most marketing research starts with the collection of facts from sources such as company records, published materials, and experts on the subject under investigation. For example, marketing research workers making sales forecasts may begin by studying the growth of sales volume in several different cities. This growth may then be traced to increases in population, size of the company's sales force, or amount of money spent on advertising. Other marketing research workers may study changes in the quantity of company goods on store shelves or make door-to-door surveys to obtain information on company products.

Marketing research workers are often concerned with customers' opinions and tastes. For example, to help decide on the design and price of a new line of television sets, marketing research workers may survey consumers to find out what styles and price ranges are most popular. This type of survey usually is supervised by marketing researchers who specialize in consumer goods; that is, merchandise sold to the general public. They may be helped by statisticians who select a group (or sample) to be interviewed and "motivational research" specialists who phrase questions to produce reliable information. Once the investigation is underway, the marketing research worker may supervise the interviewers as well as direct the office workers who tabulate and analyze the information collected.

Marketing surveys on products used by business and industrial firms may be conducted somewhat differently from consumer goods surveys. Marketing researchers often conduct the interviews themselves to gather opinions of the product. They also may speak to company officials about new uses for it. They must therefore have specialized knowledge of both marketing techniques and the industrial uses of the product.

Places of Employment

Most jobs for marketing research workers are found in manufacturing companies, advertising agencies, and independent research organizations. Large numbers are employed by stores, radio and television firms, and newspapers; others work for university research centers and government agencies. Marketing research organizations range in size from one-person enterprises to firms with a hundred employees or more.

New York City has the largest number of marketing research workers. Many major advertising agencies, independent marketing organizations, and central offices of large manufacturers are located there. The second largest concentration is in Chicago. However, marketing research workers are employed in many other cities as well—wherever there are central offices of large manufacturing and sales organizations.

Training, Other Qualifications, and Advancement

Although a bachelor's degree is required for marketing research trainees, graduate training is necessary for many specialized positions and for advancement to higher level positions. Many graduates qualify for jobs through previous experience in other types of research, while employers may hire university teachers of marketing or statistics to head new marketing research departments.

College courses considered to be valuable preparation for work in marketing research are statistics, English composition, speech, psychology, and economics. Some marketing research positions require skill in specialized areas, such as engineering, or substantial sales experience and a thorough knowledge of the company's products. Knowledge of data processing is helpful because of the growing use of computers in sales forecasting, distribution, and cost analysis.

Trainees usually start as research assistants or junior analysts. At first, they may do considerable clerical work, such as copying data from published sources, editing and coding questionnaires, and tabulating survey returns. They also learn to conduct interviews and write reports on survey findings. As they gain experience, assistants and junior analysts may assume responsibility for specific marketing research projects, or advance to supervisory positions. An exceptionally able worker may become marketing research director or vice president for marketing and sales.

Either alone or as part of a team, marketing research workers must be resourceful as they analyze problems and apply various techniques to their solution. As advisers to management, they should be able to write clear reports informing company officials of their findings.

Employment Outlook

Opportunities should be best for applicants with graduate training in marketing research or statistics. The growing complexity of marketing research techniques also will expand opportunities in this field for psychologists, economists, and other social scientists.

Marketing research employment rises as new products and services are developed requiring information to identify potential buyers. The demand for new products and services will grow most quickly when business activity and personal incomes are rapidly expanding. In periods of slow economic growth, however, the demand for marketing services may be reduced and limit the hiring of research workers.

Over the long run, our growing population and the increased variety of goods and services that businesses and individuals will require is expected to stimulate a high level of marketing activity. As a result, employment of marketing research workers is expected to grow much faster than the average for other occupations through the mid-1980s.

The competition among manufacturers of both consumer and industrial products will make it increasingly important to appraise marketing situations. As techniques improve and more statistical data accumulate, company officials are likely to turn more often to marketing research workers for information and advice.

Earnings and Working Conditions

Starting salaries for marketing research trainees were about $16,000 a year in 1980* according to the limited information available. Persons with master's degrees in business administration and related fields usually started with somewhat higher salaries.

Experienced workers such as senior analysts received salaries over $25,000 a year. Earnings were highest, however, for workers in management positions of great responsibility. Vice presidents of marketing research earn well over $45,000 a year.

Marketing research workers usually work in modern, centrally located offices. Some, especially those employed by independent research firms, do a considerable amount of traveling in connection with their work. Also, they may frequently work under pressure and for long hours to meet deadlines.

*Updated by the author and based upon latest available data.

Sources of Additional Information

Additional information on careers in marketing research is available from:
American Marketing Association, 222 South
Riverside Plaza, Chicago, Ill. 60606.

Source: Occupational Outlook Handbook, 1976–1977, U.S. Department of Labor, Washington, DC, pp. 141–143.

tion of the U.S. Department of Labor. This is an important reference resource and you may wish to consult it for information pertaining to other marketing career opportunities.

Advertising.

Advertising is one of the glamour areas within marketing. The work combines planning, fact gathering and creativity. New recruits begin as trainees but advance rapidly to other areas such as design and creativity, copy writing, or sales. Account executive is a high-paying, mid-management position. Of course, you may find advertising work with an agency; a corporation of any size; the media; a management consulting firm; or with a marketing research department or research agency.

Marketing Systems Analysis.

Marketing systems analysis is primarily staff work undertaken to assist managers in designing and implementing better marketing systems. Training in operations research, computer applications, and general systems analysis is required. Marketing systems analysts undertake demand measurement, sales analysis and forecasting, solving field sales problems, and market territory analysis. Employment opportunities exist primarily with larger marketing firms and in management consulting.

International Marketing.

There are countless career opportunities in international marketing. However, these usually go to more experienced persons who have held one or several marketing positions in the company's domestic headquarters. Entry level jobs usually are staff related positions in research, planning, or coordination.

Industrial Marketing.

Industrial marketers often have technical backgrounds in engineering, chemistry or other physical sciences. Many positions, though not all, in this field require technical selling specialists who are familiar with complex product and process applications.

Retailing Management.

Retailing offers a number of career opportunities in sales, merchandising, or store operations. Entry level positions are usually in sales but retailing uses many different talents and skills so jobs may be had in promotion, interior design and display, store management, controllership, and physical distribution.

"Up The Organization"

To give you an idea of specific career paths or avenues available in different marketing situations, let us examine three prominent areas: general marketing, retailing, and advertising.

General Marketing

The Salesperson.

Most entry level positions beyond the training program in marketing are in field selling. A field salesperson is assigned a territory and is responsible for selling a given level of output there. Work consists of both selling and nonselling responsibilities and usually involves considerable travel.

Sales Management.

Sales management is concerned with planning, organizing, motivating, and controlling the work of a number of field sales persons. The lowest sales management positions are at the regional level, the next may be at the divisional level. The exceptionally capable individual can hope to become general sales manager over the entire national organization.

The Product Manager.

The product manager, sometimes called the brand manager, has sole responsibility for managing a particular product or product line, including planning and development, pricing, promotion, and channel selection. Each product or product group is looked upon as a separate business and treated as a profit center. The product manager is expected to assume full responsibility for his or her business.

The Brand Manager.

The brand manager's position is nearly identical to that of the product manager's and such persons have the full range of responsibilities as do product managers.

The V.P. or Director of Marketing.

The vice president or director of marketing is the chief marketing executive in an organization. This person is responsible for the design and implementation as well as the final control of all marketing operations. All other marketing personnel and executives are ultimately responsible to and report to the chief marketing executive.

Other Marketing Positions.

There are other marketing executive positions, but these are staff, as opposed to line, positions. People holding line positions have direct responsibility and authority in the line organization. Staff people assist and facilitate the work of the line persons. There are several high-level staff positions worth noting.

The Director of Marketing Research.

This person determines the marketing research needs of the organization in conjunction with line officers in marketing. The research director plans and implements various stages of the marketing research project, formulating the problem; generating the research design; directing the data gathering and the analysis and interpretation of results.

The Director of Advertising.

The director of advertising, or advertising manager, plans and controls the promotion of the company's products and services. This person is responsible for formulating advertising policy, selecting agencies, evaluating creative promotional ideas, and coordinating advertising and promotion with the other elements in the firm's total marketing mix. The director of advertising is responsible for formulating the advertising budget and for making the most effective use of it.

The Director of Public Relations.

The director or manager of public relations directs and controls all the activities required to project and maintain a favorable image for the total organization. Such activities include sending out press releases; holding press conferences; arranging for new-product exhibition; and working with government agencies, consumer groups, and legislative bodies.

Retailing

The typical entry level position in retailing is as a trainee in the firm's initial management training program. The management training program is designed to prepare the individual for immediate executive responsibilities in the firm's merchandising operations, or control division. The career path for retailing management usually consists of the following positions:

Assistant Department Manager.

Initial placement as an assistant department manager exposes the trainee to basic management techniques and responsibilities. At this level trainees acquire their first experience in managing people, time, and merchandise. It is the trainee's first deep involvement in directing some aspect of business.

Assistant Buyer.

As an assistant buyer you will work in a buying office. Here you will learn the skills and techniques of a buyer, knowing what and how to buy: merchandise planning and presentation, how to coordinate many separate businesses into one total business, and learning how to work with and through other people. The position requires that one learn merchandise classification philosophy and how to apply it. You also learn how to run a business and manage it with other people's money.

Department Manager.

The department manager oversees the operation of an entire department, which usually consists of several merchandise classifications. The department manager has major independent responsibilities, being in charge of the operation and maintenance of the unit—scheduling work activities, staffing, arranging, and presenting merchandise so as to achieve maximum sales impact while at the same time managing the expenses of running the department.

Buyer.

The buyer is the person who really decides the store's merchandise assortments. This executive's major task is to have a balanced assortment of goods to meet expected customer demands. Buyers therefore plan merchandise assortments, schedule and plan all seasonal sales events, and are often responsible for millions of dollars of sales volume and heavy expenses. Buyers travel to domestic and foreign markets seeking goods, and negotiating with vendors the terms of sale surrounding their purchases.

Other Retailing Management Positions.

Beyond buyers there are branch divisional managers, branch store managers, and divisional merchandise managers. These are all high-level executive positions with demanding, challenging responsibilities. The pay is high, commensurate with the risk and responsibility the positions carry.

Advertising

Most large advertising agencies today have training programs with career paths somewhat similar to those in both general marketing and retailing. The beginner undergoes six months to one year of intensive training in a number of the agency's departments such as sales, creative design, and operations.

Assistant Account Executive.

The assistant account executive, the first step in the advertising career path, is primarily a marketing specialist in sales. The responsibilities of this position include working with clients to learn their needs and

to develop a package or campaign that will enable them to attain their advertising and promotional objectives.

The Account Executive.

The account executive supervises and helps to train assistant account executives. The primary responsibility of this individual is as the major contact between the agency and the client. The account executive must know and understand the needs of each client and develop a promotional package which satisfies their needs. The package must arouse sufficient customer awareness of the firm's products and services and generate levels of sales response that will satisfy the profit constraints of the firm.

Manager or Director of Accounts.

The manager or director of accounts supervises and coordinates the work of a number of account executives. This person makes sure that clients are satisfied with the quality of advertising and promotional work undertaken by the agency and assigns accounts to account executives whose interests and skills match clients' needs.

Media Planners.

Media planners initiate all media planning; supervise all media purchases; participate with media management in programming network relations, and in the evaluation and negotiation of network schedules. The media planner acts as a kind of "media account executive." Media planners, or directors of media as they are sometimes called, are responsible for two functions: the planning of clients' expenditures for media exposure and the scheduling and execution of media events which means actually running the print ads and placing the commercials.

Other Advertising Positions.

There are numerous other management positions within the advertising agency, the large marketing oriented firm, and in management consulting firms. Within the agency one may move up to the management of a regional office and eventually reach the management ranks at the corporate level. Appendix Figure 1 shows a typical advertising agency organization chart. It can give you an idea of the many

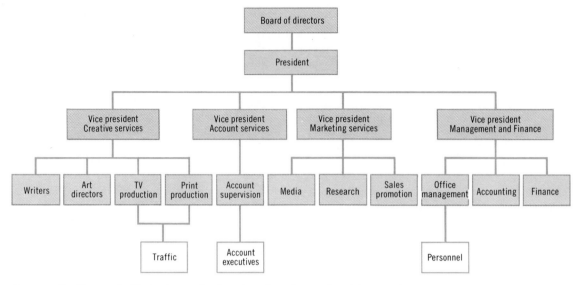

Appendix Figure 1 Typical organization chart for a large advertising agency.

different talents and jobs found in the advertising field.

Looking for More Information

In considering career opportunities it is important to look before you leap. The Department of Labor is a good source of information about the job market because they make frequent estimates of the employment outlook. A recent study is presented in Appendix Table 2. It shows expected growth rates of employment in major job classifications to 1985. This includes new jobs resulting from economic growth and replacements for persons who have left the labor force.

As the table shows, there will be more than 60 million job openings during the period, almost two-thirds of them in white collar jobs. Of these, 17 million are clerical jobs, 3.8 million are sales jobs, 5.9 million are for managers and administrators, and 12 million are in professional-technical occupations.

From what you know about marketing, however, you should remember that these job openings represent environmental opportunities. They are not necessarily market opportunities for you. Whether or not they are a market opportunity for you depends on your comparative advantage, that is, what special skills, abilities, attributes, and motivation you bring

to a specific job classification or industry. These factors will determine your particular success in getting a job and advancing through the ranks to develop your own career path.

However it is good to know as much as you can about general employment opportunities as well as to explore particular job openings in specific industries or trade groups. Statistics about employment opportunities, industry trends, and regional differences can show you how these factors may affect your job prospects and career chances. However, you will also want to know something specific about the jobs you are investigating—expected earnings, working conditions, rate of advancement, and career paths. Of course, you should learn as much as you can about each specific company you may wish to consider. One place to start looking for such information is the Labor Department's *Occupational Outlook Handbook* cited earlier; a comprehensive survey of job opportunities. Check your local library for the latest edition. For each job it reports on (1) the nature of employment, (2) the places of employment, (3) training and other qualifications needed, (4) the rate of advancement, (5) the employment outlook, (6) earnings and working conditions, and (7) additional information sources. For example, you can always get additional information concerning career opportunities in marketing, retailing, or advertising by writing such groups as: the American Marketing

Appendix Table 2 Projected Requirements and Job Openings for Major Occupational Groups 1972–1985

Occupational Group	1972 Employ- ment	Projected 1985 Require- ments	Percent Change	Openings, 1972–85		
				Total	Growth	Replace- ment
Total	81,703	101,500	24.2	61,200	19,800	41,400
White-collar workers	39,092	53,700	37.3	38,800	14,600	24,200
Professional and technical workers	11,459	17,000	48.8	12,000	5,600	6,400
Managers and administrators	8,032	10,500	30.1	5,900	2,400	3,500
Salesworkers	5,354	6,500	21.3	3,800	1,100	2,700
Clerical workers	14,247	19,700	38.2	17,000	5,400	11,600
Blue-collar workers	28,576	32,800	14.7	13,800	4,200	9,600
Craft and kindred workers	10,810	13,000	20.2	5,300	2,200	3,100
Operatives	13,549	15,300	13.1	7,200	1,800	5,500
Nonfarm laborers	4,217	4,500	5.9	1,300	200	1,000
Service workers	10,966	13,400	22.2	8,500	2,400	6,100
Private household workers	1,437	1,100	− 26.1	700	− 400	
			29.0	7,800	2,800	5,000
Farm workers	3,069	1,600	− 47.1	100	− 1,400	1,500

Note : Detail may not add to totals because of rounding,

Source: Occupational Management and Training Needs, rev. 1974 Bulletin 1824 U. S. Department of Labor, Bureau of Labor Statistics, 1974, p. 14.

Association, the National Retail Merchants Association, or the National Council of Advertisers. An extended list of sources of additional information can be found at the conclusion of this appendix.

Matching Your Skills to Career Possibilities

Your working life will account for nearly fifty years, or two-thirds, of your total existence. The job you choose or that chooses you will markedly affect your career and life chances. It will either contribute to your happiness and well-being or seem like a long sentence to be served. Try to avoid the latter; you can, but you will have to exercise you own marketing and management skills. You will have to plan your career and carry out your plan.

In getting a job and laying out a career; the astute person does a lot of introspection, sometimes called soul searching. This means knowing yourself: what you want from life, what you want from a job, where and how far in the organization you wish to go, and most important, knowing the price in commitment and dedication you are willing to pay to reach your career goals. It is a good idea to develop a career

value checklist. Write down all the things you value in a career—money, security, advancement, location, nature of work, time and commitment required, need for recognition, desire for privacy, flexible work hours and any others you may think of — and then assign each of these values a priority in light of your own ambitions.

What Are Your Skills?

You must also remember that every good marketer knows the attributes of his or her product. In this case, you are the product; you must assess your skills and attributes and then convert them into benefits for a prospective employer. You must, in effect, sell yourself and this means that on your personal resumé and in interviews it is better to use convincing examples than merely to make claims. When you say, "I get along with people," no one is particularly impressed. But when you say, "I was president of my class," or "I was secretary-treasurer of the student chapter of the marketing club," it clearly demonstrates that you do get along well with people and that you have true leadership capability.

Don't Become Immune to What You Know

Once you're actively marketing yourself, don't ignore or forget all the good solid marketing knowledge you already possess. Marketing, remember, is "finding a need and then filling it." You will need, as has been suggested, to know your market and to know yourself. Now is the time for you to do some strategic marketing planning: look at the market opportunities, compare and relate these to your own short- and long-run objectives, both career and personal, examine the various segments of the job market, think of how you can effectively differentiate your own product (yourself) in relation to market needs, and then position yourself in such a way as to create maximum buyer (employer) appeal.

Merchandise Your Three Skill Groups

What you really have to market are three groups of skills. First of all, most employers will be interested in you initially for your *technical skills,* the ability to perform adequately at an entry level position, say to sell or replenish stock or assist someone else. However, if you're hired, it will probably not be because the employer is interested only in your immediate contribution through your technical skills. What they really are going to be interested in is the contribution you will make later, a year or five years after you have been with the firm. This will depend upon two other groups of skills, your *social* and *conceptual skills.* Social skills are related to your ability to get along with others: to achieve results while at the same time securing other people's cooperation. In short, to interact meaningfully and positively with others. Without minimum social skills, you won't reach even the first rung on the career ladder. Con-

ceptual skills pertain to your ability to see the organization as a whole: to understand the functioning and the interrelationship among the various parts of the organization. Conceptual skills give you a macroscopic, or "big picture," view of the organization, enabling you to pinpoint the relevant and ignore the trivial. The importance of your social and conceptual skills can be seen in Appendix Figure 2.

As your career path carries you up the organizational hierarchy; you will be valued less for your specific technical abilities and more for your social and conceptual ones.

As you can see from Appendix Figure 2, bottom management people are valued and retained for their technical and social skills, but to progress up the organization and become a top manager, you must demonstrate high social and conceptual skills.

Anticipate the Market's Needs

Every good marketer attempts to anticipate the market's needs. Can you afford to be an exception? Because most of you reading this will soon be college seniors and seeking employment through college recruiters, you should ask yourself, "What do recruiters look for in college graduates?" Do you know? Well, of course, recruiters for individual companies all have somewhat different criteria for judging applicants, but there are some attitudes they definitely prefer and some guideposts you should observe.

Preferred Attitudes.

Characteristics that earn mildly positive ratings for applicants are assertiveness, intelligence, independence, and inquisitiveness. Applicants make a strong positive impression if they are composed, cordial,

Appendix Figure 2 A manager's three skill groups.

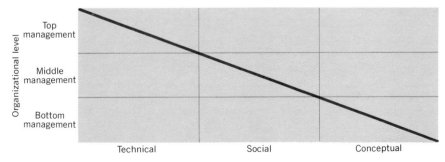

cooperative, enthusiastic, and sincere. Negative ratings go to applicants who appear nervous, defensive, quiet, skeptical, and shy. Interviews are given high positive ratings if the interviewer considers the atmosphere to be relaxed, balanced and professional. The ratings will be mildly positive if the interview is casual, negative if it is tense or dominated by either party.

Your speech tells a stranger much about you. A voice pitched too high hints at immaturity, and slurred speech may indicate that you have difficulty communicating. So remember, speak naturally but add some deep tones. Be wary of speech larded with jargon. Interviewers prefer plain spoken English. Also, be sure to maintain eye contact with the interviewer and watch your overall body language—awkward gestures that signal nervousness, aggressiveness, or other feelings of inadequacy.

Make a Good Appearance.

In marketing terms, you should pay careful attention to the way you package your product. Male applicants make a mildly positive impression in sport coat and slacks, but they make a better impression in a suit. Shorter and neatly trimmed hair and beards also make a more favorable impression. In the case of female applicants, jeans, shorts, sandals, and the absence of bras draw ratings from mildly to strongly negative.

Both your behavior and your appearance will affect your "product" image. The image you project and the impression you make may determine whether or not you get the job and, if you do, how far in the organization you will go. Outward changes can create inner effects; poise and self-confidence are enhanced by suitable dress and grooming. You should stand out while at the same time fit in. All these things should help you to better market your product—yourself.

Market Penetration: The Résumé and the Interview

Knowing the market and how to get a job will be just another academic exercise unless you really follow through and land one. Inevitably there comes a time when you must lay "theory" aside and apply what you know in order to get some practical results. Getting a job is as practical an exercise in marketing as anything you may ever do; it is absolutely imperative

that you be able to market yourself.

Fortunately; many of you will attempt to launch yourselves in a kind of venture team setting. Helping you in this introduction, will likely be a job placement or a career placement center on your campus. This group will give you much support: help you to better understand the market, guide you in preparing your résumé, and arrange interviews with prospective employers. The placement bureau cannot, however, get you a job—they cannot market your product for you. Only you, in the final analysis, can do that.

The Résumé

The most important piece of promotional literature you will want to develop for marketing yourself is a résumé. The résumé is a biographical summary of your education, experience, activities, interests, career goals, and other relevant information that promotes you truthfully, but that, like any piece of promotional literature, also creates awareness, interest, desire, and conviction in the potential purchaser—the employer. A résumé can be a big headache to prepare, but if done conscientiously and creatively it can greatly boost your chances of getting an interview and ultimately "closing the sale." People who are ordinarily articulate can become positively mute when it comes time to write a résumé, and the result often resembles nothing so much as an obituary. The obituary résumé is simply a dry chronological listing of schooling and employment. Such a presentation doesn't promote, and it doesn't promote because it isn't creative. Creative résumés emphasize an applicant's attributes and convert them into benefits: "industriousness," "high energy levels," "trainable," "commitment and dedication," "achievement and results oriented," "flexible and resilient," "quick to catch on," "self-starting and requiring minimum supervision," "eager to learn and willing to assume greater responsibility." These are benefits that a prospective employer seeks and that can differentiate you from other candidates for the position.

To the extent you know the product—yourself—you will write better résumés. Your campus placement office can show you several styles and formats for preparing a personal résumé. Appendix Exhibit 2 is a campus interview form. From such forms usually emerge the formal résumé, or personal data sheet, one of which is shown as Appendix Exhibit 3. But remember, you are not writing an obituary. Use your imagination and creativity within the bounds of good taste and use a clear writing style to promote your best attributes. Your résumé should contain and elaborate on at least these basic items:

1. *Work experience.* Most employers are impressed by work experience regardless of the level or the nature of the work. Having held a job reflects initiative, industry, a degree of self-reliance, and maturity employers perceive as desirable traits likely to carry over into subsequent work situations. Work experience, especially in selling or any area involving personal interaction and the development of your social skills, is likely to be highly valued. What a person does in the future will probably be affected by what he or she has done in the past. Employers know this and use it as a guide in selecting and evaluating job candidates. The persons you have worked for during summer vacations or at other times also become excellent references when you begin seeking more permanent career oriented employment. Be sure to name them (with their permission) on your résumé as individuals who can and will vouch for your competence, reliability, and good character. (See below for more on references.)

2. *Extracurricular activities.* In your job search extracurricular activities play much the same role as does your work experience. To a great extent they are indicative of your life style, the things you like to do, and are largely a reflection of your personality traits. Extracurricular activities indicate that you are an extroverted, social, and people oriented person; that you enjoy the give and take of social interaction; that you can be both a follower and a leader; a group or a team member and at the same time an individual. Extracurricular activities are important cues to an employer—signals that alert them to traits or attributes about you as someone who can make an important contribution to their operation. Be sure to list all honors, sports involvement, student government activities, summer camp, special travel, special training, leadership experiences, and any other evidence of your overall good citizenship.

3. *References.* Your references are important and of course, some will be more important than others. Try to obtain references who will write favorably about you because they know your good traits, but are not overly biased because of close family ties or friendship. Employers give great weight to the positive, praise-oriented, unbiased reference. A sports coach, a club counselor, a teacher, a former employer are all good possible references. Be sure to secure the permission of your references before using their names and be sure that they are familiar with all your recent achievements as well as your career goals. It is sometimes advisable to work up a preliminary data sheet to give to your references which describes your attributes, career goals, work experiences, and the like. An informed person will undoubtedly give you a better reference because he or she will be more aware of your skills and ambitions.

4. *Grades.* You will remember that grading is an important marketing function. Grades convey a great deal of information about product quality. You will not need to list all the courses you have taken and the grade you received in each, but you might indicate something about your overall academic achievement, such as 3.2 on a 4.0 basis. You might also indicate the trend of your grades, such as 2.8 during the first two years of college and 3.4 during the last two. Another approach is to differentiate your grades between courses in your major and courses outside it, such as 2.9 in supporting courses; 3.4 in courses within the major. Different employers will place different weights on the role of grades. Extremely low grades will, of course, be a serious handicap, but average grades combined with other positive attributes will usually get you serious consideration by many prospective employers.

The Interview

The interview is perhaps the most critical activity in the entire job seeking-employment sequence. The best way to prepare oneself for it mentally is to think of it as a personal selling opportunity. Perhaps it would be wise to reread chapter 14 of the text to remind yourself that an effective personal selling encounter calls for careful planning and attention to the personal selling process.

It is important to:

1. *Get ready: Anticipate the interviewing situation.* This means finding out about your customer, the employer—the company, their products and services, their problems, the nature and trend of their current operations.

2. *The approach.* Use your common sense. Don't

come on too strong nor be too shy. The best approach is to be natural, relaxed, poised, confident, and responsive. Manage the situation because that's what good selling really is. Be courteous, ask intelligent questions, show genuine interest but don't try to dominate the interview.

3. *The presentation.* Selling is persuasive communication, so don't be overly reluctant to sell and persuade. But avoid the hard sell! Point out your attributes, tell why you think you want to work for the company and what you would bring to the job. Good sellers are also good listeners, so be attentive and don't get caught mentally rehearsing your response to a comment while you should be genuinely listening. Selling is a transactional process. Your performance will be affected by the behavior of the interviewer, and his in turn, by yours. What each is ultimately concerned with is an effective and satisfactory exchange process. If the exchange doesn't go well it doesn't always mean the interview was a failure. You may have learned something about the company which changed your mind altogether. Maybe the company did likewise, so look a little further.

4. *Closing the interview.* Closing the interview is not quite like closing the sale. Seldom, if ever, will the recruiter tell you at the end of the interview that you are hired or even that the company will want to make you an offer. Neither would you necessarily want to accept if such were the case. In closing the interview, it is important to end on a positive note. Make sure you get all your questions answered and then thank the interviewer. As you leave, the interviewer will probably signal something about the firm's next move—a possible follow-up interview, a forthcoming letter stating their intentions, or maybe a hint about a possible visit to one of their plants, offices, or stores. If nothing is indicated, don't be too frustrated. You may get a positive response in a few weeks.

5. *The follow-up.* After the interview if you are genuinely excited about the prospect of working for the company, write them a letter and thank them for the interview, but use the letter as an extension of the personal selling effort. You might indicate that after the interview you were even more intrigued by the company and spent some time in your library learning about it. Or, write and request more information—maybe a copy of the

company sales letter to its field sales force, or a copy of the company's magazine or annual report. You might mention that you would like a second interview. If you were especially nervous during the first interview, say so and ask for another opportunity to present your skills and interest. Companies are strongly impressed with persistence but don't confuse persistence with overt aggression. You're not a hard sell salesperson with your foot in the door.

The Personal Audit: Don't Forget the Control Process

It is essential to remember that control is the other side of the planning process. If you have trouble marketing yourself, there may be a problem with your market plan. You might try submitting yourself to a personal audit. A personal audit is simply a systematic, critical, objective review and appraisal of You: of your basic objectives and behaviors and the assumptions that underlie them as well as of the methods you use to reach your objectives. There are several things to avoid in your personal audit, especially if you are having little luck in landing a job. First, the problem does not lie necessarily in the nature of "the system." You can never determine with any precision why a given applicant was or was not hired. If you have difficulty don't be too quick to blame either yourself or your method of operating. But do reappraise both in a positive and meaningful way. Second, don't downgrade yourself if you fail to connect. A big myth among job seekers is that the job goes to the most qualified applicant. If we get the job, we like to believe that. If we don't, we still often believe it. It is not necessarily the case. The process by which people find work is at best imperfect. The job may go to the person who is most articulate, who prepares the best résumé or who performs best in the interview. But this candidate may not be the best qualified. The point to remember is to play up your strengths while at the same time eliminating your weaknesses by practice, experience, or increasing your motivation. Third and finally, avoid tunnel vision or marketing myopia. In other words, don't define your talent too narrowly or restrict your outlook too severely concerning the job or industry you want to work in. It is important to know what you want and what you can do, but think big, not small. The job you might be best at could be one you haven't even

Employer _____ _____ 40 G 6/77

Before any on-campus interviews, this form must be _typed_ and turned in to Room 203, Admin. Annex

(Photocopies are acceptable)

CAMPUS INTERVIEW FORM for GENERAL PLACEMENT	Washington State University Career Services and Placement Center Pullman, WA 99164 (509) 335-2546

PERSONAL DATA

NAME _____

| Last | First | Middle |

| | Month | Day | Year |

Date of Birth   /   /   /

COLLEGE ADDRESS _____

| Street | City | State/Zip |

Social Security Number /   /   /

PERMANENT ADDRESS _____

| Street | City | State/Zip |

College Phone (include area code)   Permanent Phone (include area code)

Can you provide proof of U.S. citizenship, or an alien registration number if hired?   ☐ Yes   ☐ No
Are you restricted by visa from employment in the U.S.?   ☐ Yes   ☐ No

COLLEGE INFORMATION

DEGREE _____ MAJOR _____ MINOR OR OPTION _____ GRAD. DATE____|____

Names and Locations of Colleges Attended	Dates from/to		Degree	Major	Minor	GPA Data (A=4.0) Major GPA	Accum. GPA
Washington State University Pullman, WA							

Name of Academic Advisor and/or Major Advisor _____

College Honors, Professional Societies, and Activities (list positions held) _____

EMPLOYMENT INFORMATION

TYPE OF WORK DESIRED:

1st Choice _____ 2nd Choice _____ 3rd Choice _____

Geographic Preferences (if any) _____

SIGNIFICANT WORK EXPERIENCE

List most recent first—names and locations of Employers	Description—Job Title or Major Duties	Hours per week	Dates from/to

U.S. MILITARY

Veteran ☐ Yes ☐ No   Branch of Service _____

Dates: From _____ To _____ Discharge Rank _____

GENERAL

_____ I do have a placement file with letters of evaluation available from this office.

_____ I do not have a file established at the Career Services and Placement Center.

Other information (Community Activities, Hobbies, Interests, Languages, etc.) _____

DATE_____   SIGNATURE _____

Appendix Exhibit 3

PERSONAL RÉSUMÉ OF
CONNIE STARK

Permanent Address	Current Address
1205 E. 2300 N.	Box 285 Graduate Center
Logan, UT 84321	Pullman, WA 99163
801/752-9166	509/335-6474

JOB OBJECTIVE

To obtain a management position where my background in Finance and Marketing will be developed, ultimately leading to higher levels of responsibility.

EDUCATION

1979
to
1981
Candidate for the degree of *Master of Business Administration*, June 1981, Washington State University. Concentrating in Finance with strong preparation in Management Accounting and Quantitative Methods. 100% self-supporting.

1976
to
1979
Received B.S. degree, Utah State University, June, 1977. Majored in *Marketing* with minor in *Economics*. Also courses in Computer Science, Management, Finance and Accounting. 3.81 G.P.A. business courses; 100% self-supporting: completed bachelor's degree in three years while working 30 hours per week.

EXPERIENCE

Sept. 1979
to
present
Teaching Assistant, Washington State University. Duties include library research, grading papers and tests, and occasional lecturing to undergraduate classes.

March, 1975
to
Aug. 1979
Shift Supervisor, High Rise Food Service, Logan, Utah. Supervised up to twenty part-time employees involved in cafeteria operation. Responsible for opening and closing of food service, training new employees.

INTERESTS

Enjoy skiing, photography, chess, and softball; speak some German and Dutch.

REFERENCES

Placement file with letters of recommendation available from Career Services and Placement Center, Washington State University, Pullman, Washington 99164. 509/335-2536

---

yet considered. Keep alert and cast a wide net. There are many wonderful and exciting ways to make a living, but remember too—you also have to make a life. So make, and have, a happy one.

A Closing Note

There is much to learn about careers in marketing and how to market yourself. The information provided in this appendix should at least be an important starting point for you. Yet, it is really hardly more than the tip of the iceberg. To guide you further, two lists of sources of additional information are given below, one fairly extensive and the other quite brief. The longer list is by no means exhaustive. The lists cover the two main topics in this appendix. The first will enable you to learn more about careers in marketing and marketing related fields. The second lists books about the task of marketing yourself; how to find employment opportunities, work up résumés, conduct yourself during an interview, and so on. Both these kinds of information should be useful.

Sources of Additional Information

Trade and Professional Association Materials

Administrative Research Associates, Inc., Irvine Town Center, Box 4211, Irvine, CA 92664, (Choosing Your Career, $1.00).

Advertising Education Publications, 3429 Fifty-fifth Street, Lubbock, TX 79413

Advertising Research Foundation, 3 East 54th Street, New York, NY 10022.

Alpha Kappa Psi, 3706 Washington Boulevard, Indianapolis, IN 46206 (Careers in Business, 10 cents; Planning Your Career, 10 cents).

American Association of Advertising Agencies, 200 Park Avenue, New York, NY 10017 (Advertising: A Guide to Careers in Advertising, 50 cents).

American Bankers Association, 1120 Connecticut Avenue, Washington, DC 20036.

American Collegiate Retailing Association, Rochester Institute of Technology, c/o Dean Raymond F. Von Deken; College of Business, One Lomb Memorial Drive, Rochester, NY 14623 (Careers in Retailing, free).

American Management Association, 135 West 50th Street, New York, NY 10020 (Your Career in Management, 50 cents).

American Marketing Association, 222 South Riverside Plaza, Suite 606, Chicago, IL 60606 (Careers in Marketing).

American Psychological Association, 1200 Seventeenth Street NW, Washington, DC 20036 (Careers in Psychology, free).

American Statistical Association, 806 Fifteenth Street NW, Washington, DC 20005 (Careers in Statistics, free).

Association of Industrial Advertisers, 41 East 42nd Street, New York, NY 10017.

Association of National Advertisers, 155 East 44th Street, New York, NY 10017.

Bank Marketing Association, 309 West Washington Street, Chicago, IL 60606.

Business and Professional Women's Foundation, 2012 Massachusetts Avenue, NW, Washington, DC 20003 (Women in Management, 50 cents).

Chemical Marketing Research Association, 100 Church Street, New York, NY 10007.

Chronicle Guidance Publication, Inc., Moravia, NY 13118.

Industrial Marketing Associates, 516 Pleasant Street, St. Joseph, MI 49085.

Institute of Life Insurance, 277 Park Avenue, New York, NY 10017 (A Life Career, free).

Life Insurance Marketing and Research Association, 170 Sigourney Street, Hartford, CT 06105 (The Life Insurance Career, 30 cents).

Market Research Association, P.O. Box 145, Grand Central Station, New York, NY 10017.

National Association of Bank Women, 111 East Wacker Drive, Chicago, IL 60601 (*Careers for Women in Banking,* free).

National Association of Broadcasters, 1771 "N" Street, NW, Washington, DC 20036 (*Careers in Television,* free; *Careers in Radio,* free).

National Association of Business Economists, 888 Seventeenth Street, NW, Washington, DC 20006, Suite 208 (*Business Economics Careers,* 25 cents).

National Association of Purchasing Management, 11 Park Place, New York, NY 10007 (*Purchasing as a Career,* 50 cents; *Your Career in Purchasing Management,* free).

National Association of Wholesalers, 1725 "K" Street, NW, Washington, DC 20006 (*Career Opportunities in Wholesaling,* free).

National Automobile Dealers Association, 2000 "K" Street, NW, Washington, DC 20006 (*Your Career in Retail Car and Truck Business,* free).

National Food Brokers Association, NFBA Building, 1916 "M" Street, NW, Washington, DC 20036 (*Job Previews,* free).

Sales and Marketing Executives-International, 380 Lexington Avenue, New York, NY 10017 (*Opportunities in Selling,* free).

Sales Promotion Executives Association, 2130 Delancey Street, Philadelphia, PA 19103.

Savings Institutions Marketing Society of America, 111 East Wacker Drive, Chicago, IL 60601.

U.S. Government Sources

Department of Health, Education and Welfare, Office of Education, Washington, DC 20202.

Department of Labor, Bureau of Labor Statistics, Washington, DC 20212. (Occupational Outlook Series, free).

Department of Labor, Bureau of Labor Statistics, New York office, 1515 Broadway, New York, NY 10036.

Department of Labor, Employment Standards Administration, Washington, DC 20210.

Department of Health, Education, and Welfare, Manpower Administration, Washington, DC 20402.

Books on How to Get a Job

Burdette E. Bostwick, *How to Find Just the Job You're Looking For* (New York: John Wiley and Sons, 1976).

Richard Bolles, *What Color Is Your Parachute?* (Berkeley, CA: Ten Speed Press, 1972).

Norman File and Bernard Hauraya, *Job! How to Beat the Establishment and Get That Job.* (Los Angeles, CA: Apple One Publishing Company, 1971).

Harry C. Groome, Jr., *This Is Advertising: The Ayer Book on What Advertising Is All About, Who Does What, and How to Get a Job in It* (Philadelphia, PA. Ayer Press, 1975).

Richard K. Irish, *Go Hire Yourself an Employer* (New York: Anchor Press/Doubleday, 1973).

Tom Jackson and Davidyn Mayleas, *The Hidden Job Market* (New York: Quadrangle/The New York Times Book Company, 1976).

Robert Jameson. *The Professional Job Changing System* (Verona, NJ: Performance Dynamics, 1976).

Martha Douglas, *Go For It! How to Get Your First Job* (San Francisco: Chronicle Books, 1979).

Leonard Corwen, *Job Hunter's Handbook* (New York: Arco Publishing Co. Inc., 1976).

Richard N. Bolles, *The Three Boxes of Life and How to Get out of Them* (introduction to life/work planning) (Berkeley, CA: Ten Speed Press, 1978).

James M. Boros and J. Robert Parkinson, *How to Get a Fast Start in Today's Job Market* (Englewood Cliffs, NJ: Prentice-Hall, Inc., 1980).

Key Concepts and Terms

ABC analysis. A technique for classifying total inventory assortments into three categories: (A) low-value items. (B) medium-value items, and (C) high-value items for planning and control purposes.

Administered marketing networks. Channel systems in which the members remain semiautonomous, but their efforts are directed by a channel captain.

Advertising. Any paid form of nonpersonal presentation and promotion of ideas, goods, and services by an identified sponsor.

Advertising sales response curve. The plotted relationship between advertising expenditures on the horizontal axis, and the results in sales volume as shown on the vertical axis. The usual presumption is that the relationship is positive, that is, sales increase with advertising expenditures.

Affirmative disclosure. A procedure used by the Federal Trade Commission which stipulates that if an advertisement is considered insufficient by the commission, it may require a company to disclose in its advertising some of the limitations of its product or service so that the consumer can judge the product's negative as well as its positive attributes.

Attitudes. Special kind of cognition or bit of knowledge. Attitudes are learned and relatively enduring predispositions to respond in specific ways to specific stimuli. Attitudes have three components: (1) knowledge, (2) affect, and (3) action tendency.

Average cost pricing. A cost oriented pricing system whereby a reasonable or standard markup is added to the cost per unit in order to determine the selling price.

Boutique merchandising. A shop-within-a-shop merchandising theme. Its essence is individuality. Atmosphere is critical in boutiques, which emphasize cluster selling: showing customers how to complement different items of purchase.

Business ethics. The study of what is morally right and wrong in business conduct.

Business-industrial markets. Those individuals and organizations who buy goods and services for use in the production of further goods or services. Business-industrial goods are sold to organizations such as food growers, transportation firms, public utilities, construction companies, extractive firms, and non-profit enterprises.

Buyer behavior. Human actions in the consumption role. The acts of individuals and organizations directly involved in obtaining and using goods and services. Includes the decision processes that precede and influence these acts.

Brand. A name word, mark, term, symbol, or device, or a combination of these, used to identify the goods or services of one seller or group of sellers and to differentiate them from those of competitors.

Broker. Specialist in the contactual function of marketing. Acts principally as go-between bringing buyer and seller together. Is seldom a permanent representative of either buyer or seller. Does not take title to nor possession of the goods being traded. Does not store, handle, or process the merchandise, and offers no financial services to buyers or sellers.

Channel captain. A leader, usually a manufacturer, wholesaler, or retailer, who either guides, directs, or demands that channel member behavior conform to certain acceptable standards.

Channel of distribution. The firms or agencies through which the seller, who is often though not always the manufacturer, markets products to the ultimate consumer. The path taken, as evidenced by title or ownership, by goods in moving from producer to consumer.

Cognition. Knowing. Is concerned with the mental processes by which people come to know: thinking; reasoning; memory; information processing, storage, and retrieval.

Commodity approach. The study of marketing focused upon commodities, that is, the goods, ideas, and services marketed. Commodity characteristics are studied and these characteristics are seen as largely shaping marketing processes and channels.

Communication. A process by which senders and receivers exchange ideas in the form of messages over a channel for the purpose of creating a commonness of understanding between them.

Company demand. The total projected volume of sales expected under given environmental conditions for a specific company.

Competition. See Monopolistic competition, Nonprice competition, Price competition, Pure competition.

Competitive bidding. A situation where a buyer asks two or more competing suppliers to submit bids on a proposed purchase or contract. The buyer then makes the purchase from the supplier who offers the lowest price.

Concept statement. A simple two- or three- paragraph description of the product idea and all the benefits it will supposedly provide.

Conspicuous conservation. The practice of scaling down consumption by obviously purchasing and consuming nonpolluting goods that use less energy and whose consumption is likely to be less detrimental to the overall social welfare.

Consumer decision processes. A series of related, somewhat sequential activities in buyer behavior. Consists of problem recognition; search for alternatives: evaluation and assessment of options; decision to buy, postpone, or search further; and postdecision evaluation.

Consumerism. The attempts of individuals and groups to seek redress of their grievances by militant behavior toward marketers or those who influence marketing practices. The collective and organized effort of all those working to promote the objectives of consumerism is called "the consumer movement."

Consumer markets. The goods and services sold to this segment are purchased by ultimate consumers, who buy for their personal use.

Consumer panel. A preselected group of respondents who regularly report on their buying and consumption behavior to a marketing firm, a broadcast network, or a newspaper or magazine.

Contractual marketing systems. Distribution systems in which autonomous firms on different levels of the network coordinate and balance their efforts on a contractual basis.

Contribution. A term used in breakeven point analysis. It is Sales Revenue minus Variable Operating Expenses, or Dollar Price per Unit minus Variable Operating Costs per Unit.

Contribution pricing. Pricing built upon the concept of dollar rather than percentage markups. It implies that what is sought is profit, and profits are dollars, not percentages. Prices are set that maximize not necessarily net profits, but dollars of contribution to overhead and profits.

Control. The follow-up to planning whereby management compares actual with planned performance. Consists of (1) setting standards, (2) comparing results, (3) taking corrective action where needed.

Convenience goods. Goods bought frequently and having a high replacement rate. Consumers will spend only a minimum of effort and shopping time for these purchases. They are items of low unit value such as milk, snacks, newspapers.

Cooperative advertising. A means of sharing the cost of advertising. A degree of financial cooperation among the firms or persons sponsoring the ad is assumed. Usually the cooperation involves a manufacturer with other sponsors such as retailers or wholesalers, but may be between a wholesaler and retailer.

Corrective advertising. An attempt to correct inaccurate information that has been communicated by advertisers. For a stated period of time, the firm may be compelled by the FTC to spend a percentage of the advertising budget allotted to the misrepresented product for messages designed to correct prior questionable claims.

Correlation analysis. See Statistical demand analysis.

Cost-plus pricing. A method of determining price whereby a margin is added to a basic cost figure. The margin is intended to cover the firm's operating costs and to provide for a given level of profit.

Cost trade-offs. A concept that states that while some physical distribution costs may decrease, others may actually increase. For example, reducing the costs of storage may increase the costs of inventory management or transportation.

Cultural assimilation. The sharing by the major segments of United States society of a common core of cultural values.

Culture. A set of procedures, most of which have been worked out by trial and error, for solving the problems of collective living. Culture is our nonbiological heritage—our system of laws, customs, norms, and institutions.

Datings. Sometimes called the dating period. Refers to the time periods within which payment is required to obtain cash discounts (if offered) and the time at which payment for the goods actually falls due.

Demarketing. In a shortage era, the shift in emphasis from stimulating buyer demand to managing demand, and possibly urging buyers to consume less.

Demography. The study of population and its characteristics: size, age, sex, location, income, occupation, stages in the life cycle.

Derived demand. The demand of business-industrial and government markets as an outgrowth of the needs of final users, consumers. Demand for business-industrial goods and goods purchased by government arises from the demand for consumer products and services.

Developing countries. Countries who are rapidly adopting technology and are making great strides in their overall economic development. They rank somewhat below the industrialized countries in economic development with average GNPs per capita of about $1,500.

Diffusion process. The pattern in which innovations or new products spread through a population. The sequence is: minor acceptance of the innovation by early adopters, speeding up through the early majority and late majority categories, and tapering off as it moves through the final category, referred to as laggards.

Direct investment. Ownership of production and marketing operations in other countries rather than exporting or licensing. Entails all aspects of planning and control; responsibility for development of all strategic options now falls to the owning company.

Distribution center. A special kind of market related warehouse facility emphasizing the rapid movement of merchandise rather than storage. Stresses turnover and a lower cost of carrying, storing, and handling merchandise.

Distribution warehouse. Storage facility that serves as a place to assemble and then distribute products. Sometimes called distribution center.

Distributor brand. See Reseller brand.

Dumping. The practice of making sales abroad at prices below those charged in the domestic economy. The term has lately come to mean pricing products that are unsalable at home below their average costs of production for sale abroad.

Durable goods. Tangible products which have an extended period of use. Automobiles, boats, and major household appliances fall in this category.

Economics. The allocation of scarce resources to alternative uses. Sometimes referred to as the science of rationing.

Elasticity. A concept that relates the percentage of change in demand or quantity of a commodity sold, to a percentage change in price. A price elasticity of 1 means that sales rise (or fall) by the same percentage as price falls (or rises).

Entropy. The statistical tendency for things to run down and wear out.

Environmental opportunity. A situation where there is demand for goods and services that has not yet been matched by sufficient supply. A market opportunity is a special kind of environmental opportunity.

Evoked set. Refers to the few brands that the consumer considers in his or her purchase choice.

Exchange rate. The rate at which one nation's money is exchanged for another's.

Exclusive distribution. The ultimate in selective distribution. Under exclusive distribution, a manufacturing firm chooses one or two distributors or outlets for its product and excludes all others.

Expected profit. The profit that can be expected from a bid, given the probability that the bid will be accepted and the contract awarded.

Exporting. A way of reaching a foreign or multinational market without investing in overseas production plants. The firm generally extends both its product and promotional efforts unchanged to these markets.

Extensive distribution. A marketing strategy for convenience goods which calls for maximum exposure of the product to sales possibilities, or saturation of the market opportunity.

Extensive market opportunities. Often undertaken when there appears to be a limit, or unusual barriers, to further growth through intensive and integrative opportunities. Extensive opportunities generally lie outside of the company's traditional lines of endeavor.

Externality. The costs and benefits that accrue to others as a result of a market transaction between two parties. Externalities can be negative or positive.

Family brand. A brand name that is used for several products made or distributed by the same firm, such as Johnson & Johnson or A & P's Ann Page.

Federal Trade Commission Act (1914). An act designed to regulate trade and promote competition. Established a commission to oversee the more technical and complicated issues in antitrust endeavors. Listed specific methods of unfair competition.

Form utility. The result of combining raw materials, processes, machines, and labor in such a way as to change the structure or composition of goods and thus enhance their ability to satisfy wants or needs.

Franchising. The granting in return for the sale of products or services or for a stipulated fee, of supporting and facilitating services by a supplier or reseller, especially a retailer. The supplier is called a franchisor and the retailer or buyer is called a franchisee. The contractual agreement between them is called a franchise. For a franchise fee, the customer (franchisee) may use a supplier's (franchisor's) name and receive assistance in location, merchandising, or other matters in return for the purchase for resale of the supplier's (franchisor's) product.

Freight forwarder. Specialized transportation intermediary who works with all kinds of transportation carriers. Assembles small shipments, usually full boxcars or full trucks. The forwarder then ships the consolidated shipments by common carrier to destination area. There they are broken down again into smaller shipments and routed to the specific destination. Freight forwarders earn their fee by charging shippers an amount between the full and the less-than-carload rate.

Frustration-aggression syndrome. A psychological term that describes the relationship between frustration arising from unresolved conflict and the tendency of that frustration, if unresolved, to lead to aggressive behavior.

Full service wholesaler. A merchant middleman who offers a wide and nearly complete array of marketing services such as broad assortments, credit, delivery, advice, and return goods privileges.

Functional approach. The study of marketing focused upon the functions or activities necessary in managing the demand structure for goods, ideas, and services and in facilitating the exchange process.

Generic product. See Total product concept.

Government markets. The units of local, state, and federal government who purchase goods and services in order to carry out their various programs.

Gross margin. The difference between sales revenue and cost of goods sold, shown as sales minus cost of goods. Cost of goods sold is beginning inventory plus purchases minus ending inventory.

Horizontal competition. Competition between middlemen of the same type; for example, discount store versus discount store or department store versus department store.

Hierarchy of effects. A series of stages or a progression of activities which consumers move through in the persuasion process. Beginning with awareness, the hierarchy proceeds in ascending order through knowledge, liking, preference, conviction, and purchase.

Industrial distributors. The full service wholesalers' counterparts in the industrial marketing area. Stock the products they sell and perform a broad variety of marketing functions.

Industrialized countries. The most technologically advanced nations with the highest average GNPs per capita. The average GNP per capita for these countries is about $3,700.

Inflation. A rapidly rising price level generally caused by too many buyers (excessive demand) for too few goods or services (insufficient supply).

Initial markup. Maintained markup plus reductions divided by sales plus reductions.

Innovative marketer. Those marketers who utilize novel or innovative strategies to get from the present to the future. Innovative marketers accept the fact that whatever exists—product lines, services, technologies, distribution strategies—is aging.

Innovators. The first adopters of new ideas or products. They are risk-takers, young, well educated, and often with higher than average incomes. They tend to hold new values and are frequently opinion leaders.

Institutional advertising. Advertising that makes no direct bid for action. Instead of promoting specific products, it stresses the firm's overall quality, social responsibility, and established reputation.

Institutional approach. The study of marketing focused upon marketing institutions, that is, (1) the firms or agencies that perform marketing functions and participate in exchange processes with consumers or other firms or agencies, and (2) firms or agencies that attempt to manage the demand structure for goods, ideas, and services.

Integrative market opportunities. Opportunities where the firm seeks new growth by moving to a different plane or level of distribution or productive services. This can be the result of backward, forward, or horizontal integration.

Intensive market opportunities. Efforts to achieve greater market penetration (such as sales or market share) by more aggressive activities directed to the firm's already-tapped market opportunities.

Intercorporate stockholding. A situation whereby one company owns a large share of stock in another firm so that the second firm's policies and destinies are largely controlled by the first.

Interlocking directorates. A situation in which the boards of directors of companies have a number of overlapping members. For example, at one time several of the directors of General Motors were also on the board of Du Pont.

Inventory management. That set of activities—planning and controlling—concerned with having a balanced assortment of merchandise for sale to meet expected customer demand.

Joint venture. A means of tapping a foreign or multinational marketing opportunity by sharing the risks and profits of developing either manufacturing or marketing facilities, or both, in the foreign market. Such arrangements involve either licensing, contracting, or joint ownership.

Keep-out price. A preemptive price. A price purposely designed by a firm already in the market to discourage potential market entrants. It is set low to challenge market entrants to a price war.

Laggards. The last category of adopters. The group is made up of low-income older people, less educated and not really well integrated into the social structure of the community.

Laissez faire. The notion that whatever business firms do will be in harmony with the needs of society. The concept advocates totally free enterprise whereby the activities of firms are completely unregulated.

Leader pricing. The practice of deliberately marking a part of the stock or an item at a price that will not yield the greatest dollar profit return on these particular items.

Learning. The process by which an activity originates or is changed through reacting to an encountered situation. It is the product of cognitive activities. Consumers learn by reasoning, modeling, association, conditioning, and shaping.

Less developed countries. Countries who are most backward in economic development and have the most primitive economic base. They are not technologically oriented, have low economic performance, and an average GNP per capita of about $160.

Life cycle. The characteristic patterns of behavior, expenditures, and life style manifested as a person or family moves from one age period to another. The family life cycle is usually depicted as having six stages: (1) the bachelor stage; (2) newly married couple; (3) the full nest, young couples with dependent children; (4) the full nest, older couples with dependent children; (5) the empty nest, older couples with no children at home; (6) the solitary survivor, older single people.

Life style. The characteristic mode of living of a particular consumer or segment of consumers. Determined in part by economic or demographic characteristics—age, income, occupation, education level—and in part by activities, interests, and opinions.

Limited function wholesalers. Merchant wholesalers, many of whom operate in the food industry, who own the goods in which they trade but who perform fewer functions than full service wholesalers.

Logistics. The process of managing all activities required to move raw materials, parts, and finished inventory strategically from vendors, between enterprise facilities, and to customers.

Logo. A picture or symbol which is the trademark or other figure frequently associated with an enterprise. Logos are sometimes referred to as logotypes, trademarks or trade names embodied in distinctive lettering or design. Most famous example is Coca-Cola.

Maintained markup. The gross margin minus cash discounts earned plus alteration costs.

Manufacturer's agent. A functional middleman who acts as a salesperson in a defined territory. May represent a number of noncompeting clients or manufacturers in the assigned territory. Has limited control or authority over the marketing or sales program for the products sold.

Manufacturer's branch office. Office from which salespersons solicit orders by telephone and personal contact. The major distinction between a manufacturer's sales office and a manufacturer's branch office is that the sales office has no inventory while the branch office does. Delivery is therefore quicker from the branch office and a higher level of marketing support can be provided.

Manufacturer's brand. A brand owned and controlled by a firm whose primary commitment is producing or manufacturing.

Manufacturer's sales office. An office from which salespersons solicit orders by telephone and personal contacts. Such offices carry no inventory and thus have no warehousing or storage facilities.

Market. A set of forces that facilitate an exchange process. Also sometimes considered as a place where the forces of supply and demand meet and operate. A market implies a set of conditions—buyers with money and the inclination to spend—that affect the exchange process, thus determining prices and other terms of exchange.

Marketing concept. A business operating philosophy that states that the purpose of every business is to create satisfied customers. The philosophy holds that all the firm's decisions and planning should be evaluated according to their impact on the customer's well-being.

Market demand. Some theoretical upper limit of sales for the entire industry of which the firm is only a part.

Marketing. In the traditional sense and as defined by the American Marketing Association: the performance of business activities that directs the flow of goods and services from producer to consumer or user. In the more modern and acceptable view: the set of activities by which the demand structure for goods, ideas, and services is managed in order to facilitate the exchange process satisfactorily.

Marketing environment. The legal, social, political, competitive, and economic framework within which the firm operates.

Marketing functions. The activities and combination of efforts necessary to effectuate exchange. Include buying, selling, transporting, storing, standardization, grading, risk-taking, and market information. Sometimes listed as contactual, merchandising, pricing, promotion, and physical distribution.

Marketing information system. A structured complex of persons, procedures, and machines (computers) interacting to generate an orderly flow of relevant information from both inside and outside the firm to help marketing managers make decisions.

Marketing institutions. Those firms or agencies that perform marketing functions. Marketing institutions emerge as a result of specialization and division of labor in the performance of a set of marketing functions.

Marketing mix. The set of controllable variables that the firm can use to influence the buyer's response. The elements in the marketing mix include price, promotion, product, and distribution.

Marketing research. The systematic gathering, recording, and analyzing of data about problems relating to the marketing of goods and services.

Marketing strategy. A major comprehensive plan of action; an overall company program based upon selecting a particular target market(s) and planning in detail for satisfying the target(s) through the unique and careful blending of the marketing mix.

Marketing structure. The various components, including the persons, establishments, companies, or other agencies important in the marketing process. The organization, size, and relationship of marketing institutions in relation to one another.

Market opportunity. A unique or specific market situation that permits a given company to match its capabilities with particular market requirements in which that firm enjoys a competitive advantage.

Market oriented public relations. Public relations efforts directed to the firm's market related publics: customers and resellers. In market related public relations, the firm concentrates heavily on activities that increase its chances of making sales.

Market penetration. The process of tapping or moving into a market opportunity with a market strategy designed to generate sales and to achieve a given share of the market.

Market positioning. Determining the market segment(s) toward which major marketing effort will be directed on behalf of a product, service or idea, and deciding on the appeals to be used in promoting the item to those segments. Market positioning creates a strong image for the company and its products and communicates this image vividly to the customer.

Market segmentation. The division of the total market for a product, service, or idea into relatively homogeneous demand segments according to age, occupation, income, and geographic location; or according to behavioral criteria such as brand loyalty, degree of usage, and so forth.

Market share. The proportion of a given market held by each of the firms competing in it. If there are ten firms competing for a given market and each has $\frac{1}{10}$ of the market, each firm's share would then be 10 percent.

Merchant wholesaler. A marketing intermediary who takes title to or owns the goods in which he deals.

Monopolistic competition. A market structure characterized by a relatively large number of sellers; but unlike the situation in pure competition, the monopolistic competitor sells a differentiated product and has some ability to differentiate his marketing mix. See also Oligopoly, Pure competition, Monopoly.

Monopoly. A market or competitive situation in which there is a single seller of a product for which there are no reasonably close or acceptable substitutes. The seller, a monopolist, constitutes the entire industry for that commodity. See also Oligopoly, Pure competition, Monopolistic competition.

Motivation. A whole series of factors that help to explain behavior. Motivation in this sense is concerned with the reasons that impel people to undertake certain actions. In older theories of psychology the term often referred to inner causes of behavior.

Multinational corporation. A corporation that (1) operates in many countries; (2) carries out some research, development, and manufacturing in these countries; (3) has multinational stock ownership; and (4) has multinational management.

Multinational marketing. Marketing from a worldwide perspective. A marketing outlook focused around a common corporate strategy and the capability of having that strategy, while centrally guided, globally applied.

Multistage pricing. The concept of pricing as an exercise in sequential decision making under conditions of uncertainty. Final price decision emerges out of a series of subdecisions all related to pricing but which must be considered in sequence before actual price decisions can be made.

Needs-wants hierarchy. A ranking of needs-wants ranging from lower, or basic needs to higher, more complex ones. Maslow contended that the order consisted of physiological needs, safety needs, social needs, need for esteem, and need for self-actualization.

Net profit. The residual, or what's left after subtracting operating expenses from gross margin.

New products. Products (goods, services, ideas, and bundles of benefits) that are basically different from those already in the market place.

New-product committees. Groups of top executives from marketing, engineering, finance, and other company areas who plan and control the new-product planning and development process. See also Venture team.

Nondurable goods. Tangible products which have a short period of use. As a matter of fact, they are considered to be consumed at the very moment of purchase. Food, clothing, gasoline, fuel oil are all nondurable goods.

Nonprice competition. An attempt to manipulate total revenue by manipulating nonprice variables such as product assortments, quality and design, promotion or personal selling, and channels of distribution.

Nonstore retailing. Merchandising directly to the ultimate consumer without the intermediary store facility. Consists of such activities as telephone and in-the-home selling as well as mail order, catalog, and vending machine selling.

Oligopoly. A market structure with only a few sellers. The action of one is likely to affect the others noticeably. If an oligopolist lowers the price, rivals are likely to retaliate with comparable price cuts. However, if an oligopolist raises prices above the level of the competition, the competition will probably not raise their prices. Therefore, the demand curve has a "kink" at the level of the going market price. See also Monopoly, Pure competition, Monopolistic competition.

Optimal product mix. The combination of products in each firm's total assortment which best satisfies its target customers and best maximizes its long-run profit or other objectives.

Packaging. The practice of enclosing products in containers for purposes of both protection and promotion.

Penetration prices. Really "impact" prices. Prices set deliberately low so that the product will make an impact on customer awareness, generate a response, and so penetrate the market.

Perception. The process by which information is extracted from the environment and used for the purpose of problem solving—to make sense out of our experience. To perceive is to see, hear, touch, taste, smell, or otherwise sense some thing, event, or relationship and to organize, interpret, and give meaning to the experience.

Personal consumption expenditures. That amount of personal income spent by consumers for goods and services. Sometimes the total of personal consumption expenditures is referred to as personal outlays. Personal outlays subtracted from disposable income equals personal savings.

Phantom freight. A situation that sometimes arises under geographic pricing structures such as basing point systems. If a firm is using a basing point that is further from the buyer than the place from which the goods are actually shipped and freight is charged from the basing point rather than the actual shipping point, the buyer is charged for freight costs which were not actually incurred.

Physical distribution. A broad range of activities concerned with the efficient movement of finished products from the end of the production line to the consumer. Includes transportation, materials handling, storage, and inventory management.

Planned product obsolescence. The designing, engineering, producing, and marketing of products with a deliberate attempt to make them obsolete or less useful before their real usefulness has been exhausted.

Postindustrial society. An economic and social period when people grow less interested in the quantity of their possessions and more interested in the quality of their lives.

Premium prices. Prices set higher than the market average in order to let buyers know that the products involved are of premium quality.

Price. The mechanism for translating into money the value of a product to a customer at a point in time. Pricing involves setting terms like the time of payment; the currency used, which can be critical when currency rates are changing; and the discounts offered, if any. See also Keep-out prices, Leader prices, Multistage pricing, Penetration prices, Promotional prices, Risk aversive prices, and Skimming prices.

Price competition. An attempt by a firm to manipulate total revenue, and thus profit opportunity, by manipulating the price variable.

Price discrimination. The practice of charging different prices to different buyers even though such differences are not attributable to differences in quantities bought, the nature of the buyers, or the costs of servicing the buyers.

Price elasticity of demand. See Elasticity.

Price lining. The pricing policy and practice often employed by retailers, in which merchandise is offered in a limited number of price categories, for example, women's street dresses at $44.95 to $59.95 and $72.95 to $89.95.

Pricing policy. A set of predetermined guides to action designed to assist price makers in reaching their pricing goals.

Primary data. Original data gathered for the specific project underway. It is collected by or specifically for the user in such a way that the conditions and assumptions under which it is collected are known and understood by the user.

Product. A bundle of expectations; the right to own or use a bundle of need satisfactions; all those things offered to a market including physical objects, services, amenities, and satisfactions not only from the physical product or services offered, but also from personalities, ideas, and organizations.

Product concept. See Concept statement.

Product differentiation. The creation and introduction of differential features, quality, style or image into a firm's products as a basis for commanding a premium price or inducing a strong preference for the firm's offering.

Product life cycle. The various stages in the market existence of a product. The product life cycle suggests that products do not last forever. They are originated, developed, launched, and then presumably move through periods of (1) introduction, (2) growth, (3) maturity, and (4) decline.

Product line. A group of products closely related either because they satisfy a class of needs, are used together, are sold to the same customer groups, marketed through the same outlets, or fall within given price ranges.

Product manager. The person charged with the major responsibility for determining the objectives and generating the marketing strategy for a given product or product line.

Product mix. The aggregate (total number) of products offered for sale by a firm or business unit.

Product mix strategy. The firm's comprehensive plan of action designed to lead to an optimal product mix.

Product planning and development. The originating, evaluating, and development of new-product ideas that can be profitably sold in the market place.

Product planning and development process. A systematic, coordinated, and managed procedure for creating new products. It involves searching for new-product ideas, screening these ideas, analysis of their costs and benefits, development and testing, test marketing, introduction, and evaluation.

Promotion. Broadly, the coordinated efforts initiated by the seller to establish channels of information and persuasion to foster the sale of goods or services, or the acceptance of ideas or points of view.

Promotional prices. Prices which are so strong an element in a product's total image that they become an integral part of the firm's advertising and selling. Five-cent cigars and 10-cent candy bars are examples, unfortunately swept away by inflation.

Promotional quadrangle. A concept stating that in communication related to marketing, the promotional effort must reflect four factors: (1) the product, (2) the potential buyer, (3) the seller, and (4) the distribution channel.

Promotion blend. The mix of promotional activities whereby all the promotional elements are used effectively and each is assigned adequate weight in the total effort.

Psychographics. A technique which seeks to describe the behavioral characteristics of consumers that may affect their response to products, packaging, advertising, and public relations efforts. Focuses upon person-centered factors by analyzing the role of personality in consumption behavior. Also focuses upon situation-centered factors affecting buyer behavior by emphasizing the importance of life style in consumption.

Publicity. Nonpersonal stimulation of demand for a product, service, or business unit by commercially significant news about it in a publication or favorable presentation of it on radio, television, or stage that is not paid for by the product or service's sponsor.

Public relations. A programmed or planned effort by management to shape and affect the attitudes and behavior of the public. An attempt to earn the understanding and goodwill of the firm's customers, employees, resellers, the government, and the general public.

Public warehouse. A warehouse owned and operated by a warehouse specialist who sells storage space and other warehousing services for a fee to different users.

Pure competition. A market structure in which there are many buyers and sellers, none of whom is large enough to affect price appreciably, either by heavy selling or heavy buying. The products sold are homogeneous and the market is characterized by a high degree of knowledge, mobility of resources, and quick adjustment of supply to demand. See also Monopoly, Oligopoly, Monopolistic competition.

Quantity discounts. Deductions from the billed or list price based upon the amount purchased.

Rationalizations. A psychological process in which socially acceptable reasons for behavior are offered instead of what may be the real reasons. It is a person's unique verbal account of his or her behavior.

Research design. A kind of blueprint for a market research study that gives in written form a clear statement of the hypothesis to be tested, and details the objectives of the study and the method of gathering the information.

Reseller brand. A brand owned and controlled by an organization whose primary commitment is distribution or marketing.

Risk aversive pricing. An approach to pricing during periods of rapid change and uncertainty whereby every effort is made to eliminate the risks of price decisions by passing these risks from the seller to the buyer.

Robinson Patman Act (1936). An act stipulating that it is unlawful for a seller to discriminate in price between different purchasers of commodities of like grade and quantity if such discrimination substantially lessens competition.

Sales forecast. The expected or planned level of sales based upon a given marketing strategy.

Sales management. The activity of directing the personal selling effort. It consists of recruiting, selecting, training, and maintaining an effective selling force and coordinating the personal selling effort with the firm's overall marketing program.

Sales promotion. Marketing activities *other than* personal selling, advertising, and publicity that stimulate consumer purchasing and enhance dealer effectiveness. Refers to such special devices as coupons, premiums, push money, dealer contests, and salesperson prizes.

Sales territory. A bounded geographical area within which salespeople have the responsibility of generating sales and performing their other regular selling duties.

Scientific method. An approach toward solving problems (1) that is based upon careful and accurate classification of facts and observation of their relationships and sequence; and (2) that seeks the discovery of scientific laws through observation, the formulation of hypotheses, testing the hypotheses, and, through creative imagination, drawing of inferences and conclusions from them.

Secondary data. Information that is already existing usually in published form. It was not collected directly by, nor specifically for, the user. It is often gathered under conditions that are neither well known nor understood by the user.

Selective distribution. A marketing strategy that seeks a selected number of outlets for distributing a product; only the more preferred outlets are chosen.

Self-image. A person's own conceptualization of himself or herself. The self-image is a bundle of cognitions, attitudes and beliefs about ourselves which, in turn, affects our perceptions of ourselves as unique individuals.

Selling agent. Specialist in performing marketing services for manufacturers. Generally works under a continuing contractual arrangement with a manufacturer, selling the entire output and assuming responsibility for the total marketing program for their principals.

Selling, high-level. Creative selling. It involves arousing demand for new products, or new brands or models of products or influencing changes in patronage from one source of supply to another. Requires more persuasive initiative and more knowledge on the part of the salesperson than low-level selling.

Selling, low-level. Characterizes much of retail selling and route selling, which is essentially delivery. Requires little special knowledge and limited, if any, special training. Is basically order taking.

Selling, personal. An oral presentation in a conversation with one or more prospective purchasers for the purpose of making sales.

Services. Nontangible products. They are activities, benefits, satisfactions, and behaviors which are purchased. The category includes housing, transportation, household repair, hair styling, and entertainment, among many others.

Sherman Antitrust Act (1890). The first law to establish a statutory public policy toward restraint of trade and monopoly in interstate and foreign commerce. Prior to its passage, such situations were governed only by the provisions of the common law.

Shopping goods. Goods bought only after a certain amount of comparison shopping, during which the consumer evaluates alternatives for style, suitability, quality, and price. Many items of clothing, furniture, hardware, and major appliances, are normally considered shopping goods.

Situation management. An approach to personal selling that views the interactive nature of the selling situation as part of a persuasive communication process. Each potential customer is seen as unique, with unique problems and needs.

Skimming prices. Prices set to capture buyers eager to purchase a new product. Skims off, or attracts, those people who are at the top of the demand schedule for the new item, charging what this traffic will bear.

Social class. Unique groups of persons who have similar social-economic positions and consequently, similar political, economic, and purchase-consumption interests. Is usually determined by such factors as occupation, source of income, residential area, and type of dwelling.

Social-cultural system. (1) A body of traditions, customs, folkways, values, beliefs, and institutions that affect the firm's behavior. (2) A set of rules, regulations, roles, customs, and traditions which guide and affect the behavior of all members of society. (3) A set of solutions to societal problems acquired and shared by groups.

Socialization. The process by which people influence one another through interaction of thought, feelings, and behavior. Through this interaction society teaches us to value particular actions. Such reinforcement leads to repeating those actions. Sometimes called social learning.

Social marketing. A broadened concept of marketing whereby social objectives are achieved through a planned strategy utilizing marketing or marketing-like techniques.

Social responsibility. The broadened awareness of business persons and firms that self-gain is less important than concern for the larger social welfare.

Specialty goods. Goods that consumers perceive to be unique and for which they exhibit unusual shopping-buying behavior. A special purchasing effort is put forth to acquire these goods, for which the consumer has particular brand or product loyalties. Specialty goods are important to the life styles and self-images of their purchasers. Photographic equipment, high-priced luxury autos, high-fidelty sound equipment, and men's and women's high-fashion clothing are standard examples.

Staffing. A sales management activity concerned with determining sales force size. Aims at a balanced number of salespeople to service explicit customer demand at a level of service consistent with buyer needs and the expense and profit constraints of the firm.

Statistical demand analysis. Also called correlation analysis. Rests on the assumption that a dependent variable like sales is related to an independent variable like income. The relationship is thus expressed as a simple linear equation such as $y = a + bx$ where y represents the dependent variable, sales; x the independent variable, income; a represents a constant; and b, the slope of the line. Values of a and b are estimated and by substituting values for x, one can solve for y.

Storage warehouse. A fixed facility where products are stored for relatively long periods. Contains stocks of goods that are in excess of the inventory needed for normal replacement.

Strategic marketing planning. The process of assessing market opportunities. It consists of anticipating and evaluating market developments and deciding how best to approach the emerging situations.

Strategic remarketing. A new approach to marketing in which marketers consistently reexamine needs and opportunities in both the long and short run. As a part of strategy, each marketer must then redetermine the best markets to be in, customers to serve, and competition to stand against for long-run profitability.

Strategy. A long-range, comprehensive plan of action. It is the combination of major decisions the firm must make in order to survive profitably.

Structural pluralism. The retention by major groups or subcultures of a strong sense of group identity that means embracing some values that are counter to those of the mainstream culture.

Suboptimization. Describes conditions which are less than ideal or maximal. For example, an inventory manager may hold inventories low to reduce total inventory costs, but the result may be frequent stock-outs, back orders, increased order processing, special production runs, and special shipments. Such a condition is then suboptimal.

Substantiation. An FTC requirement that advertisers submit, on demand by the commission, data to back up advertising claims concerning a product's safety, performance, quality, or price comparability.

Survey. The organized gathering of information or opinions from a select number of people (called a sample) drawn from a larger group (called a universe) for the purpose of drawing generalizations about the whole population.

Synergism. The actions of separate entities that, when combined, produce a result greater than the sum of their efforts taken individually.

Systems approach. The study of marketing focused upon the dynamic interdependence and interaction between marketers and consumers. This approach studies marketing inputs, processes, and output. It is concerned with the linkages that exist between all parties both directly and indirectly facilitating marketing transactions.

Target rate of return pricing. Another form of average cost pricing with which the decision maker attempts to receive some percentage of, or total dollar return on, his investment, which is the capital required to service or support a level of manufacturing and marketing.

Test marketing. A procedure for testing new or modified products under actual market conditions. A city or area considered reasonably typical of the total market is chosen and the product is then marketed there. Test results are used to determine whether the product should be introduced on a wider scale, removed, or modified further.

Thematic merchandising. A retail marketing program based on a theme such as leisure, youth, travel, hobbies, sports, education, wealth, or luxury.

Time series analysis. A set of observations on the same variable such that the observations are ordered in time. The data of the series is regarded as being composed of four elements: a secular trend (T), a seasonal variation (S), a cyclical movement (C), and an irregular variation (I). The most common practice is to assume that these elements are bound together in a multiplicative system expressed by the formula $O = TSCI$.

Total cost approach. The measure of all expenditures required to accomplish a firm's physical distribution mission. The total cost approach implies that it is less important to minimize the cost of any one element than to minimize the cost of all elements of the physical distribution system.

Total product concept. Sometimes referred to as the generic product. The concept that consumers do not buy products just for their utilitarian value, but buy total bundles of expectations. Consumers buy benefits that are derived from the total product's attributes.

Trade audit. A method of gathering market information whereby a survey is made to measure the stocks and flows in distribution channels, at both wholesale and retail levels. Often used to measure the volume of store traffic in particular items.

Trade discounts. Reductions from the list price given to all buyers in a certain class or category. They are sometimes referred to as functional discounts, the logic being that they are given to cover a channel member's cost of performing his part in the distribution effort.

Trademark. A legal term. It refers to a brand or brand mark that has been given protection under the law, either by the common law provision of prior usage or by registration with the United States Patent Office.

Transloading. Allows a shipper to speed delivery of separate parts of a carload shipment to multiple destinations.

Tying and exclusive agreements. An arrangement whereby a seller forces a buyer to agree to sell no products competing with those of the seller and to sell that particular seller's products only.

Umbrella pricing. A situation in which a dominant firm holds its price higher than necessary in order to protect a number of smaller competitors.

Uniform commercial code. A large set of laws and regulations designed to structure and guide commercial activities. A specific regulation stipulates that all products sold carry an implied warranty of merchantability and fitness.

Venture team. Organizational arrangements based upon a systems approach to creative problem solving which utilize highly trained specialists from different disciplines. Such teams are sometimes used to manage the new-product planning and development process, especially for unique, large-scale undertakings or for those which require cooperation between two or more companies.

Vertical marketing systems. Professionally managed networks that are predesigned and engineered to achieve operating economies and maximum impact by providing total integrated marketing effort throughout the distribution network.

Warranty. A guarantee to a buyer that the manufacturer or reseller will replace a defective product or refund its purchase price during a specified period of time if certain benefits of the product and/or sale conditions are not met. A warranty is an obligation assumed by a seller.

Wheel of retailing. A theory which purports to explain the growth and development of retailing institutions. In this theory, the wheel is always revolving and moving forward. The cycle begins with an innovation. Its originators enter the market as low-status, low-margin, low-price operators. Gradually they acquire more elaborate facilities and trade up. This trading up raises margins and prices, leading to vulnerability in the next revolution of the wheel—the next low-price, low-margin innovator.

Wholesalers. Marketing middlemen who buy goods for resale to manufacturers, other wholesalers or retailers, or to industrial middlemen. Wholesalers do not, by definition, sell to ultimate consumers.

Credit List

Chapter 1

Page 6: Used with permission of the copyright owner, Bristol Myers Company © 1981.
Page 8: New York Public Library.
Page 14: © Donald Dietz/Stock, Boston.
Page 15: Sidney Harris.
Page 19: Owen Franken/Stock, Boston.
Page 30: Tim Carlson/Stock, Boston.

Chapter 2

Page 33: Peter Menzel/Stock, Boston.
Page 39: Nancy Kaye/Leo de Wys.
Page 44: Arthur Grace/Sygma.
Page 61: Courtesy American Motors.

Chapter 3

Page 79: Yan/Rapho-Photo Researchers.

Chapter 4

Page 86: Steven M. Stone/The Picture Cube.
Page 91: Courtesy Coca-Cola Company.
Page 99: U.S. Army Recruiting Command.
Page 118: © Johnson & Johnson 1980.
Page 122: Courtesy Toyota.
Page 125: © 1981 Lorinda Morris.

Chapter 5

Page 128: Anders L. Zorn, Carnegie Institute.
Page 133: Owen Franken/Stock, Boston.
Page 144: © Jim Berry 1977 by NEA, Inc.
Page 151: Rick Smolan/Stock, Boston.
Page 152: Arthur Grace/Stock, Boston.
Page 157: By permission of Johnson Products Co.

Chapter 6

Page 171: Cary Wolinsky/Stock, Boston.
Page 177: Tyrone Hall/Stock, Boston.
Page 181: © 1980 The O.M. Scott & Sons Company.
Page 183: (top) Alan Mercer/Stock, Boston (bottom) Gerber Products Company.

Chapter 7

Page 196: Robert De Gast/Rapho-Photo Researchers.
Page 199: Sidney Harris.
Page 200: © 1981 Jockey International Inc.
Page 207: Owen Franken/Stock, Boston.
Page 220: Courtesy Weber Grills.
Page 222: Courtesy Sears, Roebuck & Company.

Chapter 8

Page 232: Courtesy Striderite.
Page 233: © Ralston Purina Company 1981.
Page 234: Casio, Inc.
Page 249: Courtesy The Cherry Company, Ltd.

Chapter 9

Page 256: © 1981, the Procter & Gamble Company.
Page 267: Reprinted by permission from Consumer Reports.
Page 269: (top) Del Monte Corporation (center) Star Market Company (bottom) Jewel Companies, Inc. © 1977.
Page 274: © 1980 Revlon, Inc./Grey Advertising, Inc.
Page 276: Reprinted with permission from Advertising Age. Copyright by Crain Communications, Inc.
Page 283: © Peter Menzel/Stock, Boston.

Chapter 10

Page 298: © Richard Kalvar/Magnum.
Page 314: IGA, Inc.

Chapter 11

Page 322: Arthur Grace/Stock, Boston.
Page 332: (top) Tim Caplson/Stock, Boston.
   (bottom) Homart Development Company.
Page 336: Courtesy Century 21.
Page 345: Courtesy Macys.
Page 350: Courtesy K-Mart Enterprises.

Chapter 12

Page 353: J. P. Laffont/Sygma.
Page 356: (top) Peter Southwick/Stock, Boston
   (bottom) Cary Wolinsky/Stock, Boston.
Page 377: J. P. Laffont/Sygma.
Page 379: Dick Hanley/Photo Researchers.

Chapter 13

Page 392: © 1979 The Advertising Council, Inc.
Page 395: Courtesy E. F. Hutton Company.
Page 398: © 1980 The Hearst Corporation.
Page 407: Illustration by Eugene Payne, compliments
   of Spring Mills, Inc.
Page 409: Reprinted with permission of Triangle
   Publications, Inc.
Page 411: Knudsen Corporation.
Page 413: The Borden Chemical Company.

Chapter 14

Page 419: Con Edison.
Page 424: McGraw Hill Magazines.
Page 436: (left) General Foods (right) © 1981
   Triangle Publications, Inc.
Page 443: American Motors Corporation.

Chapter 15

Page 447: © Barbara Alper/Stock, Boston.
Page 457: Daniel S. Brody/Stock, Boston.
Page 462: Courtesy Arm & Hammer.

Chapter 16

Page 481: Jan Lukas/Rapho-Photo Researchers.
Page 490: Courtesy Farberware.
Page 496: NASA
Page 499: Mary Stuart Lang.
Page 505: Courtesy General Motors Corporation.

Chapter 17

Page 515: Hyatt Hotels.
Page 517: Swoger/New York Health & Racquet Club.
Page 518: Prudential Insurance Company.
Page 522: Whirlpool Corporation.
Page 528: H & R Block, Inc.
Page 542: © Barbara Alper/Stock, Boston.

Chapter 18

Page 547: Sidney Harris.
Page 555: © 1979 Peter Menzel/Stock, Boston.
Page 560: Bernard Pierre Wolff/Photo Researchers.
Page 566: J. R. Holland/Stock, Boston.
Page 578: Pepsico, Inc.
Page 579: J. Daune/Sygma.

Chapter 19

Page 584: U.S. Department of Energy.
Page 587: © Sears, Roebuck and Co. 1981.
Page 599: Peter Menzel/Stock, Boston.
Page 602: © James R. Holland/Stock, Boston.
Page 604: Courtesy American Library Association.

Author Index

Subject Index

as persuasive communication, 384–386
  coercion *vs.*, 386
  consumer receptiveness to, 384–385
  persuasive process, 385–386
planning campaign, 419
product life cycle and, 247, 390
promotional blend, 417–418
by public relations, *see* Public relations
by sales promotion, *see* Sales promotion
by service industries, 536–537
see also Promotional strategy
Promotional prices, 489
Promotional strategy, 24, 34, 389–390
  in future, 607–608
  for gaining marketing share, 82
  promotional quadrangle, 389–390
  "push" and "pull," 418
Prudential Insurance Company, 521, 531
Psychographics, 174, 180–185, 190
  explanation of, 181–182
  life style classifications, 184–185
  psychographic profiles, 182–185
  see also Demographics
Psychological needs, 175
"Psychological" prices, 168, 493
Psychology Today, 122
Public assistance programs, 52
Publicity, *see* Public relations
Public relations, 383, 384, 438–440, 537
  market oriented, 438–439
  in promotional blend, 417, 418
  reasons for, 438, 439
"Pull" and "push" promotional strategies, 418
Purchasing, 10
Pure competition model, 452–453
Purina, 231
Puritan cooking oil, 233
"Push" and "pull" promotional strategies, 418

Quaker Oats, 266
Quantity discounts, 470
Qube, 514

Rabbit, Volkswagen, 111
Rack jobber, 314–315, 325

Radio, 236
  advertising, 393, 394, 398–399, 400
Raid, 189
Railroads, 71, 371, 372, 373, 374–375
Rain Barrel fabric softener, 271
Random sample, 207
Raw materials, 134, 231
Raytheon Company, 507
RCA, 465
R.C.A. Whirlpool, 270, 293, 522, 600
R.C. Cola, 71, 94
Reach of advertising, 400
Reader's Digest, 122, 382, 394
Realistic hair straightener, 156
Recall of defective product, 263–264
Receipt of goods (ROG) dating, 471
Record industry, 34
Recreational activities, 13, 18
Red Cross, 9, 553
Reference groups and buyer behavior, 172
  leaders, 172, 206
Refund offers, 437
Regulations by government, *see* Government, regulation of business by
Regulatory agencies, 52, 593
  consumers and, 50
  see also specific agencies
Reinhardt, Phil, 86–87
Renault, 36
Rent, 448
Repairs, 257, 278, 280–281
Replacement rate, 300, 301
Repositioning, 117–119, 124, 125
Resale price maintenance, 49–50
Research, marketing, *see* Marketing research
Research and development, 54. *See also* Discoveries; Marketing research; Product planning and development
Research design for marketing research, 203–205
Resellers brands, *see* Distributor brands
Response functions, 101
Retail cooperatives, 309
Retailing and retailers, 10, 11, 228, 290, 291, 292, 293, 321, 328
  case studies, 349–351

in distribution channel, 328–347
  as captain in vertical channels, 307–308
  changing nature of, 333–334, 344
  classification of retail stores, 330, 331
  current scene, 329–330
  diversity in, 334
  franchising, 296, 317, 334–337, 338
  full service wholesaler and, 324
  growth and development of, 329
  nonstore retailing, 334, 337–343
  objectives in channel management, 305–306
  shopping center, 330–333
  thematic merchandising, 333, 334, 343–344
  theories of institutional change, 334–337
  in-the-home, 339–340, 514, 606
  markup and pricing by, 461–463
  profit margins of, 318–320
  service oriented, 534–535
  value of marketing services of, 318–320
Retainers, 448
Return on investment, 459–460, 504, 607
Revlon, 156, 189, 274
Rexall, 489
Rich's, 513
Road and Track, 122
Roberts, Oral, 194
Robinson-Patman Act, 46, 48–49, 470, 498
Rockwell International, 537
ROG (receipt of goods) dating, 471
Rolling Stone, 101
Rondo, 91
Roosevelt, Theodore, 45
Royal Crown Bottling Company, 94
Royal Crown Cola, 71, 94

Saccharine, 23
Sackheim, Judd, 221–222
Safeco Insurance, 537
Safety, 590, 598
  of new products, 240–241
  recall of defective product, 263–264
Safety needs, 175
Safety stocks, 365, 366, 367